T0336783

Assessing the Role of Mobile Technologies and Distance Learning in Higher Education

Patricia Ordóñez de Pablos
University of Oviedo, Spain

Robert D. Tennyson
University of Minnesota, USA

Miltiadis D. Lytras
American College of Greece, Greece

A volume in the Advances in Mobile and Distance
Learning (AMDL) Book Series

Information Science
REFERENCE
An Imprint of IGI Global

Managing Director:	Lindsay Johnston
Managing Editor:	Austin DeMarco
Director of Intellectual Property & Contracts:	Jan Travers
Acquisitions Editor:	Kayla Wolfe
Production Editor:	Christina Henning
Development Editor:	Hayley Kang
Typesetter:	Cody Page
Cover Design:	Jason Mull

Published in the United States of America by
Information Science Reference (an imprint of IGI Global)
701 E. Chocolate Avenue
Hershey PA, USA 17033
Tel: 717-533-8845
Fax: 717-533-8661
E-mail: cust@igi-global.com
Web site: http://www.igi-global.com

Library of Congress Cataloging-in-Publication Data

CIP Data

ISBN: 978-1-4666-7316-8
eISBN: 978-1-4666-7317-5
Print & Perpetual:978-1-4666-7319-9

This book is published in the IGI Global book series Advances in Mobile and Distance Learning (AMDL) (ISSN: 2327-1892; eISSN: 2327-1906)

British Cataloguing in Publication Data
A Cataloguing in Publication record for this book is available from the British Library.

Advances in Mobile and Distance Learning (AMDL) Book Series

Patricia Ordóñez de Pablos
Universidad de Oviedo, Spain

ISSN: 2327-1892
EISSN: 2327-1906

MISSION

Private and public institutions have made great strides in the fields of mobile and distance learning in recent years, providing greater learning opportunities outside of a traditional classroom setting. While the online learning revolution has allowed for greater learning opportunities, it has also presented numerous challenges for students and educators alike. As research advances, online educational settings can continue to develop and advance the technologies available for learners of all ages.

The **Advances in Mobile and Distance Learning** (AMDL) Book Series publishes research encompassing a variety of topics related to all facets of mobile and distance learning. This series aims to be an essential resource for the timeliest research to help advance the development of new educational technologies and pedagogy for use in online classrooms.

COVERAGE

- E-Books
- Snack Learning
- Pedagogy and Design Methodology
- Technology Platforms and System Development
- Accreditation
- Course Design
- Tablets and Education
- Economics of Distance and M-Learning
- Mobile Learning
- Lifelong Learning

IGI Global is currently accepting manuscripts for publication within this series. To submit a proposal for a volume in this series, please contact our Acquisition Editors at Acquisitions@igi-global.com or visit: http://www.igi-global.com/publish/.

Titles in this Series

For a list of additional titles in this series, please visit: www.igi-global.com

Critical Examinations of Distance Education Transformation across Disciplines
Abigail G. Scheg (Elizabeth City State University, USA)
Information Science Reference • copyright 2015 • 333pp • H/C (ISBN: 9781466665552) • US $185.00 (our price)

Promoting Active Learning through the Integration of Mobile and Ubiquitous Technologies
Jared Keengwe (University of North Dakota, USA)
Information Science Reference • copyright 2015 • 331pp • H/C (ISBN: 9781466663435) • US $195.00 (our price)

Artificial Intelligence Applications in Distance Education
Utku Kose (Usak University, Turkey) and Durmus Koc (Usak University, Turkey)
Information Science Reference • copyright 2015 • 329pp • H/C (ISBN: 9781466662766) • US $195.00 (our price)

Handbook of Research on Emerging Priorities and Trends in Distance Education Communication, Pedagogy, and Technology
T. Volkan Yuzer (Anadolu University, Turkey) and Gulsun Eby (Anadolu University, Turkey)
Information Science Reference • copyright 2014 • 480pp • H/C (ISBN: 9781466651623) • US $315.00 (our price)

Practical Applications and Experiences in K-20 Blended Learning Environments
Lydia Kyei-Blankson (Illinois State University, USA) and Esther Ntuli (Idaho State University, USA)
Information Science Reference • copyright 2014 • 519pp • H/C (ISBN: 9781466649125) • US $175.00 (our price)

Cases on Professional Distance Education Degree Programs and Practices Successes, Challenges, and Issues
Kirk P.H. Sullivan (Umeå University, Sweden) Peter E. Czigler (Örebro University, Sweden) and Jenny M. Sullivan Hellgren (Umeå University, Sweden)
Information Science Reference • copyright 2014 • 315pp • H/C (ISBN: 9781466644861) • US $175.00 (our price)

Mobile Pedagogy and Perspectives on Teaching and Learning
Douglas McConatha (West Chester University, USA) Christian Penny (West Chester University of Pennsylvania, USA) Jordan Schugar (West Chester University, USA) and David Bolton (West Chester University, USA)
Information Science Reference • copyright 2014 • 335pp • H/C (ISBN: 9781466643338) • US $175.00 (our price)

Outlooks and Opportunities in Blended and Distance Learning
B. Tynan (University of Southern Queensland, Australia) J. Willems (Monash University, Australia) and R. James (University of New England, Australia)
Information Science Reference • copyright 2013 • 513pp • H/C (ISBN: 9781466642058) • US $175.00 (our price)

www.igi-global.com

701 E. Chocolate Ave., Hershey, PA 17033
Order online at www.igi-global.com or call 717-533-8845 x100
To place a standing order for titles released in this series, contact: cust@igi-global.com
Mon-Fri 8:00 am - 5:00 pm (est) or fax 24 hours a day 717-533-8661

Editorial Advisory Board

Table of Contents

Preface xiii

Chapter 1
Distance Learning in Architecture/Planning Education: A Case Study in the Faculty of
Architecture at Selcuk University 1
    H. Filiz Alkan Meshur, Selcuk University, Turkey
    Havva Alkan Bala, Selcuk University, Turkey

Chapter 2
A Comparative Study of Business and Engineering Students' Attitude to Mobile Technologies in
Distance Learning 29
    Andreas Ahrens, Hochschule Wismar, Germany
    Jeļena Zaščerinska, Centre for Education and Innovation Research, Latvia

Chapter 3
Using iPads in University Mathematics Classes: What Do the Students Think? 60
    Rim Gouia, American University of Sharjah, UAE
    Cindy Gunn, American University of Sharjah, UAE
    Diana Audi, American University of Sharjah, UAE

Chapter 4
Leveraging Asynchronous Online Instruction to Develop Elementary School Mathematics
Teacher-Leaders 78
    Drew Polly, University of North Carolina at Charlotte, USA

Chapter 5
Evaluation of Mobile Learning Project at the UAE University: College of Engineering Case
Study 100
    Mousa. I. Hussein, UAE University, UAE

Chapter 6
Challenges and Opportunities for Virtual Universities in the 21st Century 131
    Luísa Margarida Cagica Carvalho, Universidade Aberta, Portugal & CEFAGE, University
        of Évora, Portugal

Chapter 7
Promoting Interaction in an Asynchronous E-Learning Environment 154
    Maria Pavlis Korres, University of Alcalá, Spain

Chapter 8
M-Learning in the Middle East: The Case of Bahrain..176
    Evangelia Marinakou, Royal University for Women, Bahrain
    Charalampos Giousmpasoglou, Bahrain Polytechnic, Bahrain

Chapter 9
Mobile Education Mitigating the Heavy Magnitude of Illiteracy in India 200
    Kshama Pandey, Dayalbagh Educational Institute, India

Chapter 10
The Role of Internet Technology in Higher Education: A Complex Responsive Systems
Paradigm 228
    Robert J. Blomme, Nyenrode Business Universiteit, The Netherlands

Chapter 11
Internet Technology and its Application in Competence Development of Highly Educated Staff:
The Role of Transfer 249
    Robert J. Blomme, Nyenrode Business Universiteit, The Netherlands

Chapter 12
Google Educational Apps as a Collaborative Learning Tool among Computer Science Learners 272
    Vasileios Paliktzoglou, University of Eastern Finland, Finland
    Tasos Stylianou, Technological Educational Institute of Central Macedonia, Greece
    Jarkko Suhonen, University of Eastern Finland

Chapter 13
Factors Influencing Behavior of Selecting Touch Screen Mobile Phones 297
    Muhammad Khalique, Universiti Malaysia Sarawak, Malaysia
    Senorita Lokie Tunggau, Universiti Malaysia Sarawak, Malaysia

Chapter 14
Mobile Wireless Technologies Application in Education 311
    Maryam Haghshenas, MAGFA Company, Iran
    Abouzar Sadeghzadeh, University of Bradford, UK
    Roghayeh Shahbazi, Alzahra University, Tehran–Iran
    Mojtaba Nassiriyar, University of Tehran–Iran

Compilation of References 333

About the Contributors 369

Index 375

Detailed Table of Contents

Preface xiii

Chapter 1

Distance Learning in Architecture/Planning Education: A Case Study in the Faculty of
Architecture at Selcuk University 1
  H. Filiz Alkan Meshur, Selcuk University, Turkey
  Havva Alkan Bala, Selcuk University, Turkey

This chapter introduces asynchronous learning, which is rapidly becoming a key element of institutional teaching and learning strategies with many academic departments seizing the opportunity to use new technologies to enhance their educational provision. It argues that design education has not been well served by asynchronous learning tools despite their many advantages. Educators are reluctant to use these tools due to the preconception of the unique nature of the studio-based learning of design. The purpose of this chapter is to provide an alternative media supporting the traditional studio for architectural/planning education that comprises digital pedagogy. Furthermore, the authors hope to bring about a better understanding of the reasons why asynchronous learning has been implemented by schools of architecture, how educators incorporated asynchronous learning into their curriculum, what advantages might be achieved, what kind of difficulties schools might encounter, and how they could be overcome in the case studies in architectural schools in Turkey.

Chapter 2

A Comparative Study of Business and Engineering Students' Attitude to Mobile Technologies in
Distance Learning 29
  Andreas Ahrens, Hochschule Wismar, Germany
  Jeļena Zaščerinska, Centre for Education and Innovation Research, Latvia

Mobile technologies are widely employed in distance learning in higher education to provide students with an opportunity to learn regardless of time and place in order to obtain a higher education degree. However, little attention has been paid to a comparative study of business and engineering students' attitudes toward mobile technologies. The aim of the chapter is to compare business and engineering students' attitudes toward mobile technologies in distance learning, underpinning elaboration of a hypothesis. The meanings of the key concepts of distance learning, blended learning, and attitude are studied. Moreover, the study demonstrates how the key concepts are related to the idea of mobile technologies and shows how the steps of the process are related: students' attitudes toward mobile technologies in distance learning→ empirical study within multicultural environments → conclusions. The results of the present research show that both business and engineering students' attitudes toward mobile technologies are positive.

Chapter 3

Using iPads in University Mathematics Classes: What Do the Students Think? 60

Rim Gouia, American University of Sharjah, UAE

Cindy Gunn, American University of Sharjah, UAE

Diana Audi, American University of Sharjah, UAE

This chapter reports on two studies carried out with first-year undergraduate students in Mathematics classes. The first study investigates regular use of iPads over the course of one semester. Overall, the students reported positive impressions regarding the use of iPads in their Mathematics classes. However, only 47% stated that they would join an iPad class in future semesters. The second study is a qualitative follow-up to the first to find out why the majority said they would not join an iPad class in the future. The students in the two studies could see both the value and the drawbacks that the use of iPads in their Mathematics classes would provide. The findings suggest that as supplement to instruction the use of iPads has the potential to enhance the learning process, but classes delivered using iPads only would not meet the educational requirements or expectations of the study's participants.

Chapter 4

Leveraging Asynchronous Online Instruction to Develop Elementary School Mathematics
Teacher-Leaders 78

Drew Polly, University of North Carolina at Charlotte, USA

This chapter describes how the author leveraged asynchronous online instruction to develop elementary school teacher-leaders' knowledge of elementary school mathematics content and pedagogies in a graduate program in the United States. This chapter provides the theoretical framework of learner-centered professional development and explains how the six courses in the program embody the framework and support teachers' development of knowledge and skills related to mathematics teaching and learning. This chapter also shares the findings of a study that evaluated teacher-leaders performance on five student-learning outcomes in the program as well as feedback on course evaluations and end-of-program surveys. Data analysis indicated that every teacher-leader demonstrated proficiency on each student-learning outcome. Implications for the design of asynchronous online programs are also shared.

Chapter 5

Evaluation of Mobile Learning Project at the UAE University: College of Engineering Case
Study 100

Mousa. I. Hussein, UAE University, UAE

The relentless expansion of information technology in educational institutions is widely acknowledged. There is substantial evidence that technology enhances student learning and educational outcomes. Many colleges and universities have adapted technology in their education system. The college of Engineering at the United Arab Emirates University launched its IT-based active learning (Laptop) project at the first semester of the academic year 2002-2003. After several years of implementation, the college is reviewing its course development technology strategy and is asking a very important question, "Did our investment in technology result in enhanced learning outcomes and promote the new, learner-centered pedagogy, or did it have little impact on learning?" The work presented in this chapter highlights the main outcomes and conclusions of a survey study, which was developed to answer the raised question. Many lessons have been learned about the benefits and difficulties in being a laptop college. These lessons are documented in this chapter.

Chapter 6

Challenges and Opportunities for Virtual Universities in the 21ˢᵗ Century 131

    Luísa Margarida Cagica Carvalho, Universidade Aberta, Portugal & CEFAGE, University
        of Évora, Portugal

This chapter aims to provide a theoretical approach concerning challenges and opportunities to virtual universities in 21st century. Virtual universities have an important role in capturing different audiences to the e-learning programs, such as long life learning, executive programs, etc. Additionally, the virtual model allows a more efficient internationalization of the education and improves the attraction of the students from several countries. Nevertheless, the virtual universities front some problems and challenges on the global education market and could be important to identify and present some good practices followed by virtual universities around the world. This chapter presents some remarks about virtual universities, the advantages and challenges fronted, and the case of the Portuguese virtual university, Open University of Lisbon, as a complement to the theoretical approach.

Chapter 7

Promoting Interaction in an Asynchronous E-Learning Environment 154

    Maria Pavlis Korres, University of Alcalá, Spain

Interaction is at the heart of the online learning experience. Theorists consider interaction a defining characteristic of education and regard it as vitally important in the design of e-learning courses. Interaction is a significant component in promoting learners' positive attitudes towards online education and affects their educational performance. This chapter examines the various ways an e-learning environment can promote interaction among participants by using the appropriate communication tools. It presents the results of a pilot e-learning course, confirming that different types of interaction can be promoted at a high level in an online environment and will contribute effectively to the achievement of the learning objectives.

Chapter 8

M-Learning in the Middle East: The Case of Bahrain...176

    Evangelia Marinakou, Royal University for Women, Bahrain
    Charalampos Giousmpasoglou, Bahrain Polytechnic, Bahrain

The introduction of e-learning in higher education has brought radical changes in the way undergraduate and postgraduate programmes are designed and delivered. University students now have access to their courses anytime, anywhere, which makes e-learning and m-learning popular and fashionable among university students globally. Nevertheless, instructors are now challenged, as they have to adopt new pedagogies in learning and teaching. This chapter explores the adoption of m-learning at universities in the Kingdom of Bahrain, as well as the relevant current developments and challenges related to the major stakeholders (educators and students) in higher education. It mainly investigates the educators' views and perceptions of m-learning, as well as its future potential in higher education. Most of the educators use m-learning tools to some limited extent, and there is still opportunity to reach full integration with curriculum and the blended learning approach. Further, it is proposed that professional development should be provided to instructors to enable them to use the available new technologies in an appropriate and effective way.

Chapter 9

Mobile Education Mitigating the Heavy Magnitude of Illiteracy in India 200

Kshama Pandey, Dayalbagh Educational Institute, India

This chapter introduces the concept of mobile learning as a means of portable learning. Through the use of mobile technology, citizens of the world will be able to access learning materials and information from anywhere and at any time. Learners will not have to wait for a certain time to learn or go to a certain place to learn. It presents the evolution of classroom learning to mobile learning. There has been made an effort to explore current perspectives of mobile learning. Approaches of m-learning suggest implication of mobile devices in the classroom. Pedagogical methods and instructional approaches of m-learning have also been explored in this chapter. Further, the authors make an attempt to give rational of mobile learning through various theories of m-learning. It suggests opportunities of mobile learning in the Indian scenario. Mobile learning can effectively support a wide range of activities for learners of all ages.

Chapter 10

The Role of Internet Technology in Higher Education: A Complex Responsive Systems
Paradigm 228

Robert J. Blomme, Nyenrode Business Universiteit, The Netherlands

This chapter introduces the perspective of complex responsive systems for organizational and individual learning. It also discusses how these systems may profit from the use of Internet Technology. Using Herbert Mead's perspective on interactions and learning, the authors discuss the theory of complex responsive systems as learning systems. They also elaborate on the implications of this perspective for the use of Internet Technology as a driver for individual and organizational learning.

Chapter 11

Internet Technology and its Application in Competence Development of Highly Educated Staff:
The Role of Transfer 249

Robert J. Blomme, Nyenrode Business Universiteit, The Netherlands

This chapter discusses how Internet technology can be used as a distant learning means for individual competence development of highly educated staff. By formulating clear perspectives on competencies, competence development, and transfer, it is argued that Internet technology can only partly be used as a means for competence development. Furthermore, hopes are expressed that by understanding the assumptions underlying competencies, competence development, and transfer, researchers and practitioners find themselves invited to develop varied and effective ways to apply Internet technology in highly educated staff learning processes.

Chapter 12

Google Educational Apps as a Collaborative Learning Tool among Computer Science Learners 272

Vasileios Paliktzoglou, University of Eastern Finland, Finland
Tasos Stylianou, Technological Educational Institute of Central Macedonia, Greece
Jarkko Suhonen, University of Eastern Finland

The purpose of this chapter is to investigate students' engagement using Google Educational Applications as educational social media tools to support teamwork. The participants of the study were a cohort of Computer Science students enrolled in the State-of-Art Technologies in Education (SOAT) online course at the University of Eastern Finland. The data was collected through pre- and post-Google Educational Collaborative Applications experience questionnaires and an interview. Based on the findings, it is evident that social media, and more specifically Google Educational Applications, can support social-constructivist models of pedagogy and that Google Educational Applications (as social media tools) have the potential to play an important role in the future of learning environments. The chapter provides experimental evidence that the use of Google Educational Applications can increase student engagement, and thus, Google Educational Applications can be used as an educational tool to support teamwork.

Chapter 13
Factors Influencing Behavior of Selecting Touch Screen Mobile Phones 297
Muhammad Khalique, Universiti Malaysia Sarawak, Malaysia
Senorita Lokie Tunggau, Universiti Malaysia Sarawak, Malaysia

The main aim of this chapter is to examine the influence of factors affecting the behavioural intention of customers. In this chapter, perceived ease of use, perceived usefulness, and social influence are considered as predictors while behavioral intention is employed as dependent variable. A total of 260 participants were involved in this study. The participants were selected through non-probability sampling technique, namely Snow Ball. In order to achieve the objective of this study, three research hypotheses were constructed. The proposed hypotheses were tested by using multiple regression analysis. The findings demonstrate that three hypotheses are supported. The findings show that three factors are playing a significant role in developing the behavioral intention. This study will be a millstone for the potential researchers.

Chapter 14
Mobile Wireless Technologies Application in Education 311
Maryam Haghshenas, MAGFA Company, Iran
Abouzar Sadeghzadeh, University of Bradford, UK
Roghayeh Shahbazi, Alzahra University, Tehran–Iran
Mojtaba Nassiriyar, University of Tehran–Iran

This chapter brings the reader's attention to understanding how technologies are aiding education with a focus on mobile technologies. In the early sections of this chapter, mobile technologies are explained briefly along with their significance to education. Implications for all involved in the education process using these technologies are then discussed. A pedagogical framework for mobile learning is then introduced along with standard theories commonly used, such as the transactional distance theory. Technological limitations and considerations are discussed to highlight future measures when designing these technologies specifically for educational purposes. Examples of mobile technology implementations in current education stages are then presented, such as mobile technology uses in higher education along with technologies used for early learners. Finally, the main objective of this chapter is presented to discuss the future of mobile technologies thoroughly, including assumptions of how these technologies will be part of everyday life for future learners.

Compilation of References 333

About the Contributors 369

Index 375

Preface

KNOWLEDGE, IT, AND UNIVERSITIES: KEY FACTORS FOR COMPETING IN A GLOBALISED ECONOMY

INTRODUCTION

In its Commission Work Program 2013, the European Commission (2012) states that:

Education and training systems are not keeping up with changing labour market needs – resulting in short-ages in key areas like science, mathematics and e-skills. Higher education is not sufficiently connected to research and innovation activities and is slow to build capacity in areas like ICT – which both reflects and contributes to a lack of internationalization. Life-long learning is still developing, and public policy and business practices do not reflect the need for older workers to extend their working careers. (p. 7)

The European Commission has funded a number of successful R&D projects focused on mobile learning. Additionally, several EU countries (e.g., Denmark, The Netherlands, and UK) have supported the used of mobile learning in schools and universities.

KNOWLEDGE, NEW LABOUR MARKET, AND UNIVERSITIES

A key debate is why do some companies gain a long-term competitive advantage and others do not. The resources and capacities theory states that it is the heterogeneity of resources within the companies and their imperfect mobility, which helps to explain the sustained differences in the profitability observed. Intangible resources, such as knowledge, present these characteristics (Crook, Ketchen, Combs, & Todd, 2008; Helfat, Finkelstein, Mitchell, Peteraf, Singh, Teece, & Winter, 2009; King, 2007; Lockett, Thompson, & Morgenstern, 2009; Newbert, 2008; Peteraf & Barney, 2003).

Literature states that resources and capacities are heterogeneous among firms, that is, resources that nourish the production process of an industry are distributed among the firms that form it in a hetero-geneous way. Resources heterogeneity inside one industry is explained in this theory context by the lack of higher resources. In addition, they must be durable in order to enable a long-term competitive advantage. If they depreciate rapidly, the incomes generated will be squandered shortly (Barney, 1991;

Peteraf, 1993). Moreover, there must be limits to the ex-post competence so that rival firms cannot easily substitute or imitate critical resources (Grant, 1991). On the one hand, the absence of substitute products diminishes the importance of competitive pressures. On the other hand, several factors called "isolating mechanisms" avoid, limit, or delay the capacity of copying critical resources and thus protect firms from imitation and keep their incomes flow. Some examples of these isolating mechanisms can be causal ambiguity, the time-understanding diseconomies, efficiency of large-scale resources, interconnections or interrelations between resources´ stocks or resources´ erosion (Dierickx & Cool, 1989a, 1989b; Lippman & Rumelt, 1982).

Finally, the possession of resources that competing companies cannot imitate or substitute is not a sufficient condition to achieve a sustainable competitive advantage. Therefore, the existence of limits to mobility becomes necessary. The resources immobility presents two levels: perfect or imperfect immobility. Perfect immobility means that these resources cannot be marketed, as in the case of idiosyncratic resources that lack an alternative use out of the firm. However, imperfectly immobile resources are marketable although their value inside the firm that uses them at that moment is higher than the value they would have in another firm.

Knowledge within companies, organisations, and nations are intangible resources. These resources constitute their knowledge-based resources, which, despite contributing towards the creation of value within the company, are not reflected in its economic-financial statements. For example, the value to a Spanish company of a business relationship with a strategic partner in Myanmar or the knowledge of an employee with working experience in Tajikistan.

A typology of knowledge-based resources (intellectual capital) differentiates between human capital, relational capital, and structural capital. The essential components of *human capital* are the skills and knowledge of the company's employees. The scope of human capital is internal and resides in the mind of the employee, which makes it difficult to codify. *Relational capital* refers to the flows of knowledge between individuals within a network and, therefore, includes the knowledge present in the relationships established with the environment, both internal and external. The first group would contain the relationships between company employees, managers, and shareholders. The second group would consist of the relationships developed by the company with customers, suppliers, competitors, public administrations, and other interest groups. Finally, *structural capital* represents the knowledge that remains behind in the company when the employees have finished their working day, in other words it is that knowledge that does not depend on certain individuals or specific relationships but belongs to the company (for example, organisational routines, strategies, and organisational culture) (Ordóñez de Pablos, 2012).

Managers must know what knowledge types exist in their companies and organisations and where each of these is located. To ensure this, it is necessary to measure the existing intellectual capital within companies, draw up organisational knowledge maps, and compile intellectual capital reports.

The European Commission makes special mention of the strategic role played by the knowledge triangle—education, research, and innovation—in regional economic and social development. Universities and research centres are an essential pillar of the knowledge society.

According to OECD (2008), tertiary education policy is increasingly important on national agendas as it is a major driver of economic competitiveness in an increasingly knowledge-driven global economy. Countries must raise higher-level employment skills to sustain a globally competitive research base and to improve knowledge dissemination in societies.

Education contributes both to social and economic development through four major missions:

- The formation of human capital (primarily through teaching);
- The building of knowledge bases (primarily through research and knowledge development);
- The dissemination and use of knowledge (primarily through interactions with knowledge users); and
- The maintenance of knowledge (inter-generational storage and transmission of knowledge).

The "Education and Training" chapter of the European Commission states that:

...open and flexible learning is about fully exploring the potential of ICT to improve education and training systems, aligning them with the current digital world. ICT tools, Open Educational Resources, and open practices allow for an increase in the effectiveness of education, allowing for more personalised learning, a better learning experience, and an improved use of resources. Such measures also promote equity by increasing the availability of knowledge. Ultimately, opening up education may lead to a situation where all individuals may learn anytime, anywhere, with the support of anyone, using any device. (European Commission, 2014)

The European Commission (2008) describes nine possible actions for responding to the challenges and obstacles facing universities today, in a context of modernisation and international crisis, and for achieving the objectives of the Lisbon Agenda, identified by the European Commission in its Communication of 2006, "Delivering on the Modernization Agenda for Universities: Education, Research, and Innovation." These reforms can be grouped into three principal areas: curricular reform, university governance, and research and innovation. These nine actions are the following:

1. Break down the barriers around universities in Europe
2. Ensure real autonomy and accountability for universities
3. Provide incentives for agreements with the universities
4. Provide the right mix of skills and competencies for the labour market
5. Reduce the funding gap and make funding work more effectively in education and research
6. Enhance interdisciplinarity and transdisciplinarity
7. Activate knowledge through interaction with society
8. Reward excellence
9. Make the European higher education area and the European research area more visible and attractive in the world

In the knowledge economy and society, there are four basic interdependent elements: 1) the production of new knowledge, 2) the transmission of knowledge through education and training, 3) the dissemination of knowledge via new information and communications technologies, and lastly, 4) the use of knowledge through new services or industrial processes. In all these actions, the universities and research centres are key players with respect to achieving success.

Universities perform their activity within a globalised competitive environment and compete with each other to attract and retain the best possible human capital whilst at the same time competing for funding. They also face the risk of losing knowledge, for example, when a researcher with a solid international career decides to leave and go to another university because the remunerative conditions or career development opportunities do not fulfil expectations (Blackman & Kennedy, 2009).

The evolution of information technologies, mobile devices, and social media, as well as the needs of students, workers, and academics has experienced rapid changes in the past several years. This complex and dynamic reality requires new forms of delivery of learning content to students, the building of special learning environments, and new teaching methodologies for academics. Old teaching practices (from the building of teaching materials to the evaluation processes and tutorial services) need to be adapted to provide customized and context-adapted learning opportunities. There are drivers, barriers, and success factors within distance and mobile learning devices and systems that need to be explored and tested, such as widespread availability and/or the lack of policy support.

CONTENTS OF THE BOOK

The purpose of this book is to analyze the role and challenges of distance and mobile learning in higher education today. The book will focus on real experiences of higher education institutions and academics implementing distance and mobile education courses.

The book presents a collection of 14 chapters that addresses different key topics from distance learning, education challenges, and mobile learning to life-long learning, role of faculty, virtual universities. Now, we will briefly describe the contents of each chapter.

Chapter 1 ("Distance Learning in Architecture/Planning Education: A Case Study in the Faculty of Architecture at Selcuk University," by H.Filiz Alkan Meshur and Havva Alkan Bala) states that creating alternative learning environments within present architectural education systems results in significant added value to a student's education. Architectural problems solved in an international context are more in-depth and layered than the conventional process. They also state that all the opportunities that modern education technology offers should be effectively used in order to provide higher quality education services to a larger and wider range of students. Turkish students could reach the SAIT's planning and architectural accumulation by using ICT.

Chapter 2 ("A Comparative Study of Business and Engineering Students' Attitude to Mobile Technologies in Distance Learning," by Andreas Ahrens and Jeļena Zaščerinska) discusses the findings of an empirical study that shows that both business and engineering students' attitude to mobile technologies in distance learning within the institutionalized blended educational process of higher education is positive. Students' positive attitude to mobile technologies in distance learning is considered as a favorable opportunity for the increase of the level of students' knowledge and skills, as well as competence, in general.

Chapter 3 ("Using iPads in University Mathematics Classes: What Do the Students Think?" by Rim Gouia, Cindy Gunn, and Diana Audi) reports on two studies carried out with undergraduate students in first-year Mathematics classes. The first study investigates regular use of iPads over the course of one semester and compares the students' performance in a traditional classroom and the iPad classroom. Overall, the students reported positive impressions regarding the use of iPads in their Mathematics classes. However, only 47% stated that they would join an iPad class in future semesters. The second study is a qualitative follow-up to the first to gather more information on why the majority of the students said they would not join an iPad class in the future. This chapter further argues that although the use of technology has become the expected norm in higher education it is important to understand the students' views on the use of technology, in the case of this chapter, iPads, before introducing any new technology in class. The students in the two studies could see both the value and the drawbacks that the use of iPads in their Mathematics classes would provide. The findings suggest that as supplement to instruction the use of iPads have the potential to enhance the learning process but classes delivered using iPads only would not meet the educational requirements or expectations of the study's participants.

Chapter 4 ("Leveraging Asynchronous Online Instruction to Develop Elementary School Mathematics Teacher-Leaders," by Drew Polly) provides the theoretical framework of learner-centered professional development and explains how the six courses in the program embody the framework and support teachers' development of knowledge and skills related to mathematics teaching and learning. The author, Drew Polly, shares the findings of a study that evaluated teacher-leaders performance on five student-learning outcomes in the program as well as feedback on course evaluations and end-of-program surveys. Data analysis indicated that every teacher-leader demonstrated proficiency on each student-learning outcome. Implications for the design of asynchronous online programs are also shared.

Chapter 5 ("Evaluation of Mobile Learning Project at the UAE University: College of Engineering Case Study," by Mousa. I. Hussein) states that results from faculty and students' surveys identified that IT-based learning and laptops are valuable tools in the education process and are convinced that they contributed significantly to the improvement of the learning process. However, the effective implementation of learning technologies in general and laptops in particular requires a preliminary framework of infrastructure and faculty development for blended learning. To enhance teaching with laptops and to improve student outcomes, it is indispensable to take a close look at existing course curricula and pedagogical strategies to create a meaningful teaching and learning environment. The author believes that the use of laptop in the classroom is discipline and course specific. Faculty needs to find ways to implement different technologies (not necessarily laptop) to assist students to better understand difficult concepts more easily, to expand classroom discussion and to better integrate classroom theory with laboratory experimentation.

Chapter 6 ("Challenges and Opportunities for Virtual Universities in the 21st century," by Luísa Margarida Cagica Carvalho) addresses the importance of virtual universities, the advantages and challenges on the global education market in 21st century, and also presents the case of the Portuguese virtual university, Open University of Lisbon, as a complement to the theoretical approach.

Chapter 7 ("Promoting Interaction in an Asynchronous E-Learning Environment," by Maria Pavlis Korres) analyzes the various ways an e-learning environment can promote interaction among participants by using the appropriate communication tools and presents the results of a pilot e-learning course, confirming that different types of interaction can be promoted at a high level in an online environment.

Chapter 8 ("M-Learning in the Middle East: The Case of Bahrain," by Evangelia Marinakou and Charalampos Giousmpasoglou) studies the adoption of m-learning at universities in the Kingdom of Bahrain, as well as the relevant current developments and challenges related to the major stakeholders (educators and students) in higher education. It mainly investigates the educators' views and perceptions of m-learning, as well as its future potential in higher education. Most of the educators use m-learning tools to some limited extent, and there is still opportunity to reach full integration with curriculum and the blended learning approach. Further, it is proposed that professional development should be provided to instructors to enable them to use the available new technologies in an appropriate and effective way.

Chapter 9 ("Mobile Education Mitigating the Heavy Magnitude of Illiteracy in India," by Kshama Pandey and K. C. Vashishtha) states that advances in technology during the past decade have created a worldwide boom in the sale of this kind of technology, permitting private individuals to enjoy personal, mobile wireless connectivity. The widespread ownership of mobile technology in the form of mobile phones, especially among young people, has created opportunities and challenges for educators.

Chapter 10 ("The Role of Internet Technology in Higher Education: A Complex Responsive Systems Paradigm," by Robert J. Blomme) shows that learning can be facilitated when Internet Technology is used to increase the quality of interaction between organizational members, leading to the Social Act. As is widely agreed upon, modern Internet Technology can be used to set up information portals, e-learning possibilities, and social media tools. In view of the perspective on organizational learning reported in this chapter, the added value of Internet Technology likely lies in the use of social media and interactive portals which promote responses and interactions and which facilitate the speedy delivery of feedback. Finally, the authors concludes that Internet Technology may particularly contribute to learning when organizations are viewed as complex responsive systems. With the help of the insights developed through Mead's and Stacey's approaches, learning processes can be stimulated even better when people interact directly and when social acts are possible. Since the social act remains the major condition for learning and knowledge development, a final word of caution is needed here: effective face-to-face interaction can only partially be replaced by Internet Technology.

Chapter 11 ("Internet Technology and its Application in Competence Development of Highly Educated Staff: The Role of Transfer," by Robert J. Blomme) discusses how Internet Technology can only partly be used as a means for competence development and aims to understand the assumptions underlying competencies, competence development, and transfer.

Chapter 12 ("Google Educational Apps as a Collaborative Learning Tool among Computer Science Learners," by Vasileios Paliktzoglou, Tasos Stylianou, and Jarkko Suhonen) describes a study to examine the reception of the students towards Google Educational Applications as used to support teamwork. The data was collected through pre- and post-Google Educational Collaborative Applications experience questionnaires and an interview. The authors conclude that social media, and more specifically Google Educational Applications, can support social-constructivist models of pedagogy and that Google Educational Applications (as social media tools) have the potential to play an important role in the future of learning environments. The study provides experimental evidence that the use of Google Educational Applications can increase student engagement, and thus, Google Educational Applications can be used as an educational tool to support teamwork.

Chapter 13 ("Factors Influencing Behavior of Selecting Touch Screen Mobile Phones," by Muhammad Khalique and Senorita Lokie Tunggau) analyze the influence of factors affecting on the behaviour intention of customers. The authors used perceived ease of use, perceived usefulness, and social influence as predictors, while behavioral intention was employed as dependent variable. A total of 260 participants were involved in this study. The participants were selected through non-probability sampling technique, namely Snow ball. The results of the empirical research suggest that students would only adopt touch screen mobile phones if they find their usefulness, thus the adoption rate of touch screen mobile phones will increase if the young generation finds that there are more practical benefits, compared to using traditional phones. The rational is possibly because of the fact that touch screen mobile phone are based on a new technology, contributing to the unique characteristic of touch screen mobile phones. Finally, social influence has a significant relationship with behaviour intention. The result shows that students would only adopt touch screen mobile phones if they find their usefulness, thus the adoption rate of touch screen mobile phones will increase if the young generation finds that there are more practical benefits, compared to using traditional phones. The rationale is possibly because of the fact that touch screen mobile phone are based on a new technology, contributing to the unique characteristic of touch screen mobile phones. Finally, social influence has a significant relationship with behaviour intention.

The last chapter of the book, Chapter 14 ("Mobile Wireless Technologies Application in Education" by Maryam Haghshenas, Abouzar Sadeghzadeh, Roghayeh Shahbazi, and Mojtaba Nassiriyar), examines examples of mobile technology implementations in current education stages are then presented, such as mobile technology uses in higher education along with technologies used for early learners.

This collection of 14 chapters aims to provide comprehensive coverage and understanding of the learning processes, its complexities and challenges in the context of higher education, and the role of information technologies for mobile and distance learning. The chapters bring together researchers in the field of technology and higher education, both theoretical and practical contributions, to help readers in the development and dissemination of new approaches to both mobile and distance learning.

Patricia Ordóñez de Pablos
University of Oviedo, Spain

Robert D. Tennyson
University of Minnesota, USA

Miltiadis D. Lytras
American College of Greece, Greece

REFERENCES

Barney, J. B. (1991). Firm resources and sustained competitive advantage. *Journal of Management, 17*(1), 99–120. doi:10.1177/014920639101700108

Blackman, D., & Kennedy, M. (2009). Knowledge management and effective university governance. *Journal of Knowledge Management, 13*(6), 547–563. doi:10.1108/13673270910997187

Crook, R. T., Ketchen, D. J. Jr, Combs, J. G., & Todd, S. Y. (2008). Strategic resources and performance: A meta-analysis. *Strategic Management Journal, 29*(11), 1141–1154. doi:10.1002/smj.703

Dierickx, I., & Cool, K. (1989a). Assets stock accumulation and sustainability of competitive advantage. *Management Science, 35*(12), 1504–1511. doi:10.1287/mnsc.35.12.1504

Dierickx, I., & Cool, K. (1989b). Assets stock accumulation and sustainability of competitive advantage [Reply]. *Management Science, 35*(12), 1512–1513.

European Commission. (2008). *Report from the commission to the council on the council resolution of 23 November 2007 on modernising universities for Europe's competitiveness in a global knowledge economy.* Brussels, Belgium: Author.

European Commission. (2012). *Communication from the commission to the European parliament, the council, the European economic and social committee and the committee of the regions.* Retrieved from http://ec.europa.eu/atwork/pdf/cwp2013_en.pdf

European Commission. (2014). *Opening up education through new technologies.* Retrieved from http://ec.europa.eu/education/policy/strategic-framework/education-technology_en.htm

Grant, R. (1991). A resource-based theory of competitive advantage: Implications for strategy formulation. *California Management Journal, 33*(3), 114–135. doi:10.2307/41166664

Helfat, C. E., Finkelstein, S., Mitchell, W., Peteraf, M., Singh, H., Teece, D., & Winter, S. G. (2009). *Dynamic capabilities: Understanding strategic change in organizations.* London: Wiley-Blackwell.

King, A. W. (2007). Disentangling interfirm and intrafirm causal ambiguity: A conceptual model of causal ambiguity and sustainable competitive advantage. *Academy of Management Review, 32*(1), 156–178. doi:10.5465/AMR.2007.23464002

Lippman, S., & Rumelt, R. P. (1982). Uncertain imitability: An analysis of interfirm differences in efficiency under competition. *The Bell Journal of Economics, 13*(2), 418–438. doi:10.2307/3003464

Lockett, A., Thompson, S., & Morgenstern, U. (2009). The development of the resource-based view of the firm: A critical appraisal. *International Journal of Management Reviews, 11*(1), 9–28. doi:10.1111/j.1468-2370.2008.00252.x

Newbert, S. L. (2008). Value, rareness, competitive advantage, and performance: A conceptual-level empirical investigation of the resource-based view of the firm. *Strategic Management Journal, 29*(7), 745–768. doi:10.1002/smj.686

OECD. (2008). *Skills beyond school: Executive summary.* Retrieved from http://www.oecd.org/edu/skills-beyond-school/41303688.pdf

Ordóñez de Pablos, P. (2012). Knowledge in universities and research centres: Proposed indicators for measuring relational capital. In *Knowledge management and drivers of innovation in services industry* (pp. 7–14). Hershey, PA: IGI Global.

Peteraf, M. A. (1993). The cornerstone of competitive advantage: A resource based-view. *Strategic Management Journal, 14*(3), 179–191. doi:10.1002/smj.4250140303

Peteraf, M. A., & Barney, J. B. (2003). Unravelling the resource-based tangle. *Managerial and Decision Economics, 24*(4), 309–323. doi:10.1002/mde.1126

Chapter 1
Distance Learning in Architecture/ Planning Education:
A Case Study in the Faculty of Architecture at Selcuk University

H. Filiz Alkan Meshur
Selcuk University, Turkey

Havva Alkan Bala
Selcuk University, Turkey

ABSTRACT

This chapter introduces asynchronous learning, which is rapidly becoming a key element of institutional teaching and learning strategies with many academic departments seizing the opportunity to use new technologies to enhance their educational provision. It argues that design education has not been well served by asynchronous learning tools despite their many advantages. Educators are reluctant to use these tools due to the preconception of the unique nature of the studio-based learning of design. The purpose of this chapter is to provide an alternative media supporting the traditional studio for architectural/planning education that comprises digital pedagogy. Furthermore, the authors hope to bring about a better understanding of the reasons why asynchronous learning has been implemented by schools of architecture, how educators incorporated asynchronous learning into their curriculum, what advantages might be achieved, what kind of difficulties schools might encounter, and how they could be overcome in the case studies in architectural schools in Turkey.

INTRODUCTION

Today, technology is perceived as an effective and indispensable element of life and has become the most distinctive characteristics of modern culture. The improvements in information and communication technologies (ICTs) offer new opportunities in business world, in education and in every field of

DOI: 10.4018/978-1-4666-7316-8.ch001

life. Using ICTs in architecture/planning education are very important. Because, architecture/planning has been evolved into a multidisciplinary and international business by means of the development of the internet. Participants in architecture/planning profession are from all parts of the world and come together to complete designs, either in person to person contact or via the internet (Bala & Arat, 2013). The purpose of this chapter is to provide an alternative media supporting the traditional studio for architectural/planning education that comprises digital pedagogy issue.

In scientific literature, different terminology is used as distance learning, distance education, dlearning or D-Learning. In general, distance learning provides delivering education and teacher to students who are not physically present in traditional setting such as a classroom, atelier, studio, meeting hall or conference hall. Distant learning is performed in two ways as synchronous and asynchronous learning according to the application method.

This chapter is about a specific teaching/learning methodology which includes synchronous, asynchronous and traditional approaches supporting each other in design studio. SAIT Polytechnic Architectural Technologies and Selcuk University carried out a project using the potential of information technologies. Students from Canada and Turkey cooperated to solve the design problem of sustainable housing in Canadian's East Village. The project has involved both planning and architectural scale. The outputs of this study are:

- A better understanding of the reasons of distance education,
- Why synchronous/ asynchronous learning has been implemented by faculty of architecture,
- How educators incorporated asynchronous learning into their curriculum,
- What advantages might be achieved,
- What kind of difficulties schools might encounter and

- How they could be overcome in the case studies in architectural/planning education.

THE CONCEPT AND HISTORICAL DEVELOPMENT OF DISTANCE LEARNING

Man's desire to communicate with somebody far away is older than desire to educate somebody who is far away. Human beings can neither put on wings and fly nor can move too far distances like smoke. However, they build gigantic vehicles that go faster and reach farther than cranes and smoke, together with sending his/her voice to other end of the world in a matter of seconds. Second step of human being which fulfilled this, is educating of the human beings; knowledge reaches human being, no matter where he/she is. Information and communication technologies submit for human use, those which were merely dream of yesterday. Acquaint us with new teaching and learning procedures which have more functions and with more content compared to those procedures which already known (Alkan & Bala, 1998).

The literatures and studies related to distance learning expanded considerably in the last years. Studies researched different aspects of distance learning from its technologies, methods, and pedagogy to perceptions, opinions and attitudes of students and academicians toward distance learning (Buselic, 2012). Some authors defined distance education according to both communication and technology.

"Distance education implies that the majority of educational communication between (among) teacher and student(s) occurs non-contiguously (at different times and at separate places-separating the instructor-tutor from the learner). It must involve two-way communication between (among) teacher and student(s) for the purpose of facilitating and supporting the educational process. It uses technology to mediate the necessary two-way communication" (Garrison & Shale, 1987).

"Telecommunications-based distance education approaches are an extension beyond the limits of correspondence study. The teaching-learning experience for both instructor and student(s) occurs simultaneously-it is contiguous (same time) in time. When an audio and/or video communication link is employed, the opportunity for live teacher-student exchanges in real time is possible, thereby permitting immediate response to student inquiries and comments. Much like a traditional classroom setting, students can seek on–the-spot clarification from the speaker" (Barker et al., 1989).

"It is clear from the research literature that distance education works (Hanson et al., 1997; Simonson, 2002). Why it works and how it works are important concepts to understand, however. The following conclusions about instruction delivered to distant learners are directly related to effectiveness: Training in effective instructional strategies is critical for teachers of distant learners. Distance education courses should be carefully designed and developed before instruction begins. Visualization of ideas and concepts is critical when designing instruction to be delivered to distant learners. Adequate support systems must be in place to provide the distant learner with access to resources and services. Interaction between the instructor and students and among students must be possible and encouraged. Assessment should be designed to relate to the specific learning outcomes of the instructional experiences. In summary, distance education can be as effective as any other category of instruction. Learning occurs and knowledge is retained. Students report that they have learned and that they feel their distance learning experiences are as successful as more traditional education. The keys to successful distance education are in the design, development, and delivery of instruction, and are not related to geography or time" (Simonson et al., 2011).

The Characteristics of Distance Education

Typical features of distance education are ranked as follows: (Toker, 2008).

- **Personalization:** Traditional education is organized according to the general level of groups. However, ideal education system should be prepared taking into account the personal characteristics of each student. Here are, distance education is an effective way in order to achieve this understanding.

- **Customization:** Distance learning system can be trained students taking from the class moves to a position. Students will be educated individually in these circumstances. In this system, individual learning takes place institutional learning.

- **Industrialization:** Like the establishment of related industries in order to meet the growing needs of any product of a large audience, opening of distance education institutions has become inevitable in order to respond the increasing demand for training quickly and effectively.

- **Education for Non-Traditional Students:** Distance education is an expected choice for people who are unable to participate the course hours/time in their academic institution (full-time employees, officers and soldiers-different city/country dwellers). In addition, this education system is the only option for people with disabilities, bed ridden and criminals.

- **Movement Capability:** Nowadays, in addition to two-way video conferencing systems, computers and mobile phones have been used significantly. Many people have increased access to the computer. Distance education system has also provided freedom of movement during training to people with the possibility of wireless communication

- **Fast Feedback:** Today, thanks to distance learning students are able to send their homework through e-mail any time of the day and anywhere in the world. Also, they are able to receive the assessment results of this study by the same way over the WEB.
- **It is Cheaper Compared to Other Educational Systems:** Distance education is one of the most inexpensive ones in the education system except in the case of a very high level of investment for infrastructure, payment for per student is high than traditional education or the number of students who meet the cost of investment, cannot be found.
- **Technology and Education:** Virtual classrooms can connect with each other by using satellite, compressed video coding or full bandwidth. And in this way, people can be trained with face to face even in remote locations.
- **Education for Taxpayer:** Elementary, high school and university-level education of individuals are provided with National Education Budget. The state is created this budget with taxes collected from employees. Nowadays professional life requires constant renewal and lifelong education. Hence, distance education is indispensable for these people who can continue the work. In this way, the source will always be able to find for the national education budget.

Distance education can be used instead due to lack of teaching staff in higher education courses. It can also be used instead of the lessons performed in the crowded amplifier. Instead of unskilled labour, course will be given by experts on the subject and these experts prepared lectures which are available on the internet. So, when training is desired, these courses can be used by internet. Distance education can be used for the continuing education, professional advancement, obtaining

better career. And also, it can be used for learning evolving and changing information which is available for vocational success or this education system can be used for training people who both working and learning at the same time. In short, web-based distance learning in the internet environment can be used in every area of education. The most common and efficient training can be carried out within the scope of continuing education. Continuing education of the people that they have a certain level of maturity with their requests and needs will be better able to analyze. This is a fundamental condition of the active learning (Burma, 2008).

The Important Considerations in Distance Education

Universities which will give distance education services should done some arrangements in their instructional structure in addition to the technical equipment. Solem et al., (2006) highlighted that three obstacles should be overcome by providing international distance education services. The first of these obstacles, the inter-university collaboration, partner, professional editing programs is required. Second, international students will encounter some technical and practical problems in the future courses. These obstacles should be eliminated and found solutions to the problems. The accreditation, quality assurance and certification of the program are the third obstacle. In order to overcome these three obstacles, from 2003 until today, HERODOT network (http://www.herodot.net) used in geography education brings together lecturers of the geography education departments in more than hundred universities of Europe. Concerned educators come together in this network and they cooperate and discuss about the required quality in distance education, certification and accreditation (Toker, 2008).

Başaran and Tulu (2002) stated that during the development of web-based educational application should be considered the following issues (Türkoğlu, 2003):

- In accordance with the best opportunities, the determination of the strategic objectives (the questions like what, when, where) should be determined in order to provide services to users.
- Decision-making method should be improved, the choice of the parameters should be determined; the process should be improved for stakeholder participation and institutionalization of the selection of course and program.
- Online course to be given should be eligibility for online, the absence in the program, have the traditional records. Also, these courses should have financial resources for the development. A faculty member should be assigned and the topics of course contents have an interesting structure for the target audience.
- Online courses to be offered should be developed according to the principles of program development. Also, these courses should be evaluated by experts.
- Graphic design and style should ensure the integrity and consistency.
- Courses should have cover, course content, information, study materials, additional courses, discussion groups, student lists/notes, assignments/exercises and frequently asked questions page.
- The consequences of the developed academic programs should be evaluated carefully and also, acceptance and approval of the campus should be made.

The History of Distance Education in the World

Distance education and distance learning terms are often used interchangeably. Descriptions of these terms are made alike. Distance education provides rarity opportunities for people to work but distance education is not concerned with conditions or professional obligations of persons. Hence, firstly distance education was used synonymous with the word "correspondence course". Later, distance education was used with television education. But the real growth of the distance education has been through the video, teleconferencing, e-mail and communication technologies, including the internet. Distance education is a convenient education system for adults and university students who are living remote places. Additionally, distance education, can be used effectively in providing university education such as developing countries like Turkey and countries without adequate number of universities and having more students (Balaban, 2012).

Firstly, distance education began with the correspondence course and it has come to the present day. Mail sent to students with lecture notes formed the basis of distance education. Correspondence learning has provided training for cultural development, professional training in almost every branch of science. The correspondence course (letter learning) can be considered the beginning of distance education. This type of teaching method was carried out by the competent authority or institution through the mail ("Uzaktan Eğitim", n.d.).

Distance education studies can be traced back more than 200 years old. For example, in 1728, advertisements of shorthand courses by letter was found in Boston Newspaper. In the 1890s the campus of the University of Queensland in Australia has carried out an educational program. A similar program was conducted at Columbia University in the 1920s. Radio has been used as a distance education training tool by many schools in the 1930s. In the America, especially paper-based communication environment has been used for military purposes distance education in the 1950s. When it comes to today thanks to technological advances, floppy disks, videotapes, CD-ROM, satellite broadcasts, video conferenc-

Table 1. The history of distance education in the world

1728 The first study of distance education began with "Shorthand Courses" in the Boston papers.
1833 "Absentee Composition Courses" were given to women in Swedish University.
1892 The first "Absentee Education Department" opened at the University of Chicago.
1898 Hermands, one of the world's leading institutions, was established in Sweden. Language education was given in these institutions.
1906 Correspondence Primary School began in the United States.
1919 The first educative radio station was founded in the United States.
1920 176 radio station units were established for educational purposes in the United States.
1923 High School Education began with letters in the United States.
1932-1937 In the United States, educational television broadcasts began in the university of IOWA.
1939 France led to the education of students with distance education during the war years.
1960 "British Open University" was opened in the United Kingdom.

ing and the internet have an important place in the distance education implications. Especially, correspondence learning courses was organized for people with disabilities and bed ridden people. Also, special programs were arranged for parents of blind and deaf people. Businesses, associations and armed forces are institutions that have benefited extensively from correspondence education ("Uzaktan Eğitimde Eğitimcinin", n.d.). The history of distance education can be ordered in the following (Karakaya, 2005) shown in Table 1.

The History of Distance Education in Turkey

The technologies used in distance education aims to minimize the limitations of distance education and also rise to level of training. At the same time, this must be used in the absence of formal education. But such an understanding about distance education is not the case in Turkey. Initially, distance education seems to have shed light on all educational problems as a knowledge transfer. But it can be clearly seen that it is not true when look at the functioning. Universities performed with distance education have the potential to very crowded students. The control of students and knowledge transfer are quite difficult. It can be

clearly seen that distance learning is not a teaching way given in this way. So distance education is not a system that thousands of students of an instructor have fallen. Students interact and know each other of their classmates, teachers during the distance education courses. This is not a teaching system that teachers following the students about the process of a system. Also, they do not offer feedback and correction to the students. Although distance education is low cost, effective use of technology, to appeal to more students, it cannot be said that distance education improve the quality of education. With distance education has become a way of an education system not maintaining a healthy that teacher-student and student-student interaction. All of them are located within the distance education qualifications but they are not in continuous processing (Demirkan & Silahtaroğlu, 2010).

In Turkey, firstly distance education was discussed at a meeting dealt with the problem of education in 1927. However, this idea could not be implemented. Discussions on the subject were continued until 1950. The history of distance education can be ordered in the way shown in Table 2.

Firstly, Ministry of Education (M.E.B), Vocational and Technical Education Organization take steps to distance education to teach some technical

Table 2. The history of distance education in Turkey

1927 Distance education was discussed Mustafa Necati-The minister of National Education-
1956 Distance education started to be used in Ankara University Faculty of Law, Research Institutes of Banking and Commercial.
1961 Correspondence Course Centre was established in The minister of National Education.
1975 YAY-KUR training implemented distance education applications.
1978 Open University was decided to establish.
1981 Anadolu University Faculty was opened. With TRT cooperation, Anadolu University started to give training by television.
1992 Open Education High school was opened.
1996 IDEA package education implementation started in METU by using the internet.

issues with letter in 1960. Also, "Absentee Education Centre" was carried up by Statistics-Release Directorate. Correspondence course studies have been implemented with the approval of the two ministries in 1974. With these approvals, a massive distance education opportunity has appeared for particularly various areas and levels of formal and non-formal education (Demirkan & Silahtaroğlu, 2010).

Anadolu University Open Education Faculty begun to training students with the written material and TRT channel. This situation has led to a little more development of distance education. Nowadays, it is evident that televisions are not enough for this type of education. TV is replacing its place to more advanced technology. With increased demand, the need for renewal has increased and by entering in search for new technological developments were closely followed (Karakaya, 2005).

It was the beginning of drastic changes in the sense of distance education that the computers into our lives. It is a reality that visual and auditory terms of computer technology are more motivating. However, there are many factors that will distract students used computers. Some applications of computer technology have been facilitated to traditional teaching with its qualifications. Anymore, people can see each other and discussing course with new Technologies. They can be able to learn by asking. Starting with a limited letter of distance education have brought the location where the video conferencing ap-

plications. There is a no longer limited facility of computer and internet technology (Demirkan & Silahtaroglu, 2010).

Firstly, distance education took place legally into the Turkish education system in the university structure Act of 2547 (1981). This distance education system in Turkey is a phenomenon of great importance in the future. As an extension of this, in 1982 the Faculty of Open-education in Anadolu University was established with 2809 law. This faculty was mandated to conduct distance education as a centre for the country level (Özer, 1989).

METU (Middle East Technical University) are carried out distance learning activities from 1998. Still ongoing METU-Online project is an important part of these studies that appeal to the widest audience. Middle East Technical University, Informatics Institute began METU-Online application into the 1998–1999 academic years. METU has offered an interactive training service by this project. Graduate and undergraduate courses were presented to nearly 4000 students into the various universities' faculties. This application covers a web-based software system and aims to active learning. A part of this application was performed by completely from the internet and a portion of the course was done in the classroom with face to face interaction. Some courses are prepared lessons on the internet was used as a support in the classroom. All courses might be given entirely over the internet to the participants in special student status who were not in the university. Each course has involved equation, animations, graphics, discussion lists and multi-media online lecture notes. Also, these courses consist of interactive management tools prepared for both students and instructors. Another study in METU is the project of the training of trainers. This Project is an Informatics Certificate Program given to fifty faculty members from various universities in Turkey. The program was launched in February 1999; include six courses (240 hours total). Its duration is eight months. At the beginning of the program, participants were attending the course at METU for two weeks. Then, they followed lectures from their own universities. This project is different from the METU-Online project, the number of students is quite less, whereas almost all the students from different cities could follow the course. The results obtained from the findings of the measurement and the evaluation relating to the effectiveness indicated that student involvement and motivation was high in the courses given in the internet environment. This achievement level of students was equal or high according to the traditional classroom environment lectures (Başaran & Tulu, 1999).

DISTANCE EDUCATION TECHNOLOGIES

Distance learning is regarded by many as an alternative to traditional learning systems. However, the realization and utilization of the opportunities and benefits offered by technology in distance learning can lead to more effective results if it is used as a complement to traditional education. The four basic elements of distant education are; the separate locations of the academic representative the student for most of the education process, the use of education media which brings together the educator and the student conveys the content of the lesson, the effectiveness of the educational organization including the opportunity for the evaluation of the student, and the existence of bilateral communication between the academic member/representative and the student (Keegan, 1986). Distance learning presents some difficulties for individuals. In this process, success can only be achieved if people are capable of increased self-discipline in studying. In addition, distance learning may hinder the social integration of people. The construction of the course content must be comprehensive, and that can involve a long and costly process. There needs to be an appropriate information and technology infrastructure in order for asynchronous learning to reach the mass of the population. Individuals need to have an interest in e-learning, as well as a sufficient level of personal income. This problem can be solved through the public support of cheap and reliable access. In addition, changing traditional learning habits may take time (Yıldırım & Öner, 2005; "Türkiye Bilişim Derneği", 2003).

The difference between this type of education and traditional education is that here the student is at the centre of education. Teaching and learning in a distant learning network is fundamentally different than face to face education. Distant learning (comprises distance learning, synchronous, asynchronous, virtual design etc.) can create an alternative and be as successful as face-to-face education (Alkan & Bala, 1998). Also, it provides an effective communication between the educators and the students through the use of the correct methods and technologies.

Distance learning may be perceived as an approach that can significantly meet the need for academic member openings and improve the quality of education in universities with insufficient academic staff. It should not be considered as an education technique to entirely replace face to face dialogue between the student and academic staff. Possible problems that can be encountered in the process should be realized and met. Figure 1 shows the basic characteristics of the traditional education system and the distant education system.

As we mentioned in introduction chapter distant learning is performed in two ways as syn-

Figure 1. A comparison of the traditional education system with asynchronous learning

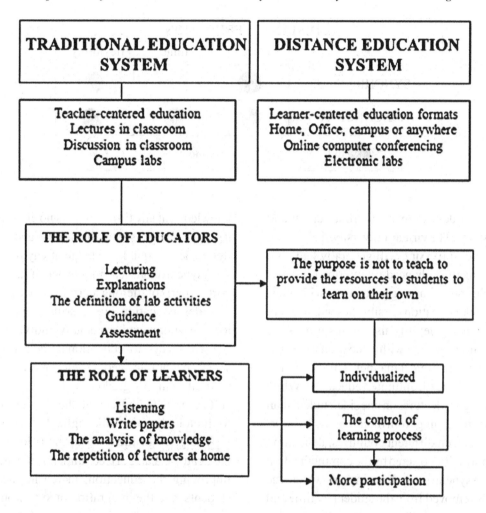

chronous and asynchronous learning according to the application method.

Synchronous/ Asynchronous Learning

Synchronous and asynchronous learning has common properties namely both are distant education methods. On the other hand, there is nuance using the place, time and relations (Figure 2).

In synchronous distant learning, the student is in mutual communication with the teacher in the education process. Synchronous distant learning can be exemplified by lessons that can simul-taneously be watched through jointly prepared reports, using audio and video materials, or with an environment where ideas can be exchanged through any means of communication.

Asynchronous learning is a student-centred teaching method that using online technology which is e-mail, electronic mailing list, conference system, online discussion board and blocks. Previously, voice tapes, telephone, teleconference, radio, television, tele-courses, microwave broadcasts, video and satellite broadcasting have been used to convey the programs to students. Currently, internet systems including computer assisted education and computer managed educa-

Figure 2. The difference and similarities of synchronous and asynchronous

DISTANCE EDUCATION			
	place	time	flexibility
SYNCHRONOUS	●	◐	◑
ASNCHRONOUS	●	●	●
● independent ◐ dependent			

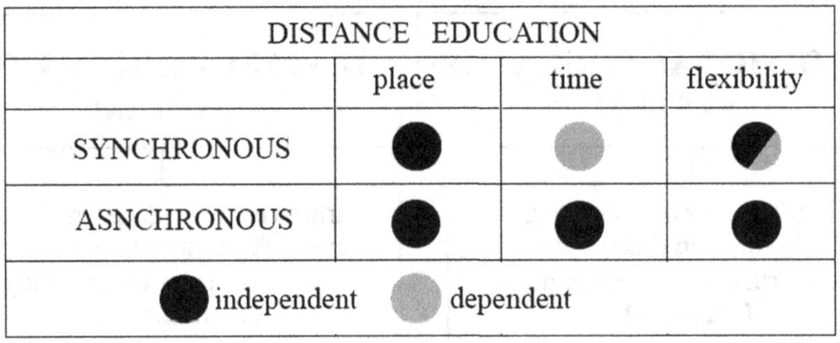

tion enable the development of virtual centres and virtual systems. The virtual-university, developing from the tele-university, will generally be based on printed media enhanced by multimedia.

Asynchronous learning procedures with interaction provide education possibilities independent from place and time; it is also makes it possible to educate more people with education of higher quality in an economical manner. This education type opens the door to unlimited education. While the educator gives lectures on one side, students can participate in learning from their homes, in different places or even different countries, depending on the opportunities offered by the communication pathway. Asynchronous learning, in which the educator is removed from the student by time and place, uses several delivery systems that involve computer-mediated technologies. By contrast with education where the subject is learnt in the classroom, in asynchronous learning the student can learn subjects and get in touch with the educator independently of time and place. Individuals can receive education through e-learning without going to school and wasting their time on travel. People who live in places distant from schools can receive an education without leaving their homes due to reasons of work, health or family. It also provides giving education circumstance to the people who are disabled.

In asynchronous distant learning, the educator conveys knowledge through communication pathways and the student can then access the knowledge at any time. There is no effective sharing. Knowledge is available for use and student is free to access that knowledge at any time.

Asynchronous learning is one of the most important parts of lifelong learning and it potentially provides education and learning opportunities for everybody and especially individuals with limited access to educational facilities due to social, economic, geographic or other reasons. Currently, simply graduating from a school is not sufficient for an individual - he/she feels the need for lifelong learning (İnceoğlu, 2002) (Figure 3).

The goals of the asynchronous learning system can be categorized under three headings, improving the education, increasing access for students, and the integration of synchronous and asynchronous education systems (Table 3).

The advantages and problems related with the process of the asynchronous education system can be seen in Table 4.

Virtual Architectural/Planning Design Studio (VADS)

In scientific literature, different terminology is used as part of distance education "virtual design studio", "online studio", "tele-collaborative design", "web-based design", "cyber-studio", "distance education" and some definition as IRDE (International Reciprocal Distance Education), ODLE (Online Design Learning Environment), OLE (Online Learning Environment), REAL

Figure 3. The components of asynchronous learning

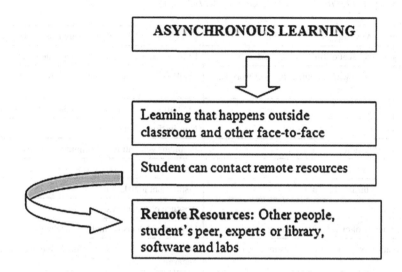

Table 3. The goals of the asynchronous learning system

To Improve Education
Compatible, flexible and personal education
More rapid and accurate distribution of study materials with the help of multimedia
Giving an opportunity for students to communicate with their advisors and other students through the use of electronic facilities
Developing learning opportunities independent of time and space
Providing more participatory, interactive, motivational and creative opportunities to the student
Developing student computer skills and helping them to succeed in their working lives
Compliance with the new forms of 21st century education through multidimensional education
Equal Access to Higher Education
Including new student groups by going beyond traditional geographical limits
Creating student support services
Providing effective interaction between the student and their educators
Giving courses and seminars to students aimed to demonstrate the usage of the system
To Integrate Traditional Education System and Asynchronous Learning
Autonomous learning
Less-populated classrooms
Integrated technological education environment

(Rich Environment for Active Learning), and WYSIWIS (What You See Is What I See) to describe this situation (Bala & Arat, 2013). Schön defines VADS as an organization within the frame-work of the concept "knowing in action". Similar to Schön, Boyer and Mitgang define VADS as an arrangement that combines theory with practice. The activities of the VADS typically involve in-

Table 4. Advantages of asynchronous learning and problems regarding the process (*Yıldırım & Öner, 2005; "Türkiye Bilişim Derneği", 2003; Çavaş &Huyugüzel (2001)

Advantages	Problems related with the process
Education opportunity independent of time and space *	Limited reach of e-Learning implementations*
Individuals' receiving education without hindering their work and education processes*	Insufficiency of quality and standardization*
Rapid and effective learning*	Limitations in communication due to high number of students
Continuity in education	Non-institutionalization*
Increasing efficiency in education	Problems generating by technological systems and equipment
Education opportunities for more people*	Deficiencies in internet infrastructure*
Education opportunities for disabled people	Insufficient legislation*
Equal opportunities in education	Absence of incentives*
Solution for the insufficiency of qualified staff members	Uninformed decision making mechanisms*
Contribution to the solution of financial problems in education*	Ambiguous individual tendencies and preferences regarding e-learning*
Decreased transportation and other education costs *	Lack of motivation in students unable to develop their study skills
Solving space problems in faculties	Difficulties in the conduct of practice-oriented lessons
Opportunity for educators to be in touch with many students simultaneously	Possible problems to be faced with the removal of face-to-face communication
Being student oriented and giving opportunities to students to improve their creativity, talents and skills, as opposed to the traditional education which is teacher oriented	Not solving problems encountered in learning process simultaneously
Increasing the qualities of developing rural universities by realizing their participation in courses and programs conducted at other universities through asynchronous learning	Difficulty in controlling students
Increasing the competition between universities in quality education	Impossibility of reviewing the lesson
Increasing international cooperation and participation with the use of asynchronous learning programs in universities	Difficulties in following lessons for students with insufficient skills in the use of communication and information technologies

dividual design proposals, group works, formal criticism and/or informal interactions.

The first virtual distance studios, where students collaborated over the internet with students in other physically remote studios, such studios have to rely on web-based databases to store shared design information. In scientific literature virtual design studio as a part of architectural education is analyzed as below generally; 1-Building a base for digital future, 2-Using digital tools while designing, 3-Digital visualization and Digital practices, 4-Digital thinking and "computer-aided architectural design", 5-Methods of network communication (Bala & Arat 2013). According to Munoz and

friends (2009) at present, little empirical research has been conducted on the value of Web 2.0 in education (Crook & Harrison, 2008). Research has begun to examine social network sites, but few studies have specifically addressed its role in pedagogy for notable exceptions see (Crook & Harrison, 2008; Hewitt & Forte, 2006; Mathews, 2006; Mazer et al., 2007; Selwyn, 2007; Towner & VanHom, 2007). The VADS with network communication has started since 1988 and the first important educational experience has occurred with British Columbia, Canada (UBC) and Harvard (Cambridge) in 1992 named "Distance Collaboration" (Charnigo & Barnett-Ellis, 2007).

After that Project a lot of different institutes and architectural schools had done similar projects.

When we look at VADS with network background in Turkey; Istanbul Technical University (ITU) is the pioneer with Çağdaş and her friends making collaboration with Sydney University in 2000. According to Duru (2006), in this project Net-Meeting and Active Worlds was used efficiently. In ITU during years other academic staffs organized similar studio as paperless medium like Cocoon, PG.W [kutu], Cyber museum atelier and collaboration with Zurih University organized by Erdem and Pak (2006). Other department of architecture at different institutes like Anadolu University in Eskisehir followed ITU. In 2007 at Anadolu University E-Design studio has been organized by Tokman and friends with architecture and interior design students (http://v3.arkitera. com). Yıldırım at Gazi University, Tong at Yıldız Technical University is same of the researchers/ educators who are dealing with VADS in Turkey.

The concept of "virtual architectural design studio" (VADS) symbolizes; (Bennett & Broadfoot, 2003; Çağdaş, 2005; Çağdaş & Tong, 2005; Çağdaş et al., 2000; Mayer & Smoff, 2000);

- Studying in web connection at digital media free from space or time limitation,
- Sharing all documents, knowledge, opinion, critics with other actors,

- Studying at digital circumstance and present at computer format rather than paper unlike traditional VADS and
- Possibility to share and to transfer all design process and documentation with the other easily and effectively and fast.

The success and efficiency of VADS may change with factors like time, geography, cultural and technological distance, tools, and digital infrastructure and design itself. The internet and web have resulted in new methods of working both in practice and education. The web technology provides students, educators and researches opportunities to get new cyber media (Malins et al., 2003). Students from different universities have made design experiment by using collaborative environment founded by computer and VADS has been tried to be improved with different tools. Virtual design applications may be expanded from simple action like file transfer with e-mail to get partner in virtual world for solving design problem in cooperation (Malins et al., 2003). Many universities and IT companies have developed packages online learning environment like Virtual U, WebCT, Blackboard, Learning Space and Active Worlds (Chen & You, 2003). Active Worlds is improved as an immersive design approach. There are avatars that can behave very similar to human being considering communication and visual perception (Figure 4).

Figure 4. Active worlds ("Activeworlds Offers", n.d.)

Digital Pedagogy in Architectural Education Supported by Facebook

Tutors and students may use the same social network tools that students around the world are familiar with: Microsoft Windows Messenger, Net Meeting, SKYPE and Facebook as not informal but formal educational media. Most of the time students can adopt themselves technology and all over the world they are in general the member of social media like Facebook. On the other hand, tutors found that social media informal, not enough serious and not useful. Teachers who engage with a technological medium are more likely to value that technological tool in their teaching (Russell et al., 2003; Bala & Arat 2013).

It is important for teacher educators to introduce students to social networks. It is explained below to get benefit for architectural education in Facebook sense. The is some Practice Policies below:

1. First, an instructor should create an additional Facebook profile for professional use only. This profile should be entirely separate to their social/personal profile, where privacy settings need to be implemented.
2. Then, instructors can simply list the web link to their Facebook profile in their course syllabus. In addition, instructors can simply display their Facebook profile during class, inviting students to look at their profile.
3. A separate page can be created specifically for a course. Students can virtually find other classmates through this page, learn about their classmates, communicate with their classmates and professor, and post/discuss relevant class information.
4. Discussions that traditionally have taken place on web course boards can also occur on Facebook discussion boards. Instant messaging functions are also available online. Instructors can post information and websites on their profile and group page for students to download and use for class.
5. It is also recommended that instructors mention that they will not be viewing their students' profiles and encourage students to designate them on their "limited profile" list
6. Lastly, if using the site as a course tool, it is suggested that instructors websites, and videos on Facebook, and, using Google Documents, link students to study guides, power points, assignments, and tutorials. Instructors can contact students via Facebook by sending messages, posting comments on "the wall" or chatting with students during virtual office hours. By increasing student involvement through communication and community, instructors can tailor their courses towards a variety of learning styles (Bala & Arat, 2013).

Hamann and Wilson (2003) found that students who participated in a web-enhanced class outperformed those students in a traditional lecture format. This suggests that Internet based learning modules actively engage students in a manner unique from the traditional class lecture. Facebook increases both teacher-student and student-student interaction in the form of web-based communication. Facebook helps instructors connect with their students about assignments, upcoming events, useful links, and samples of work outside of the classroom. Concerns related to privacy and anxiety in interacting with professors in this environment (Hewitt & Forte, 2006). Using Facebook in the studio may be very simple and modest idea that can be pragmatic. It may be very small difference however it created big differences pedagogical issue (Figure 5).

In traditional studio circumstance paper and sketch, technical drawings, images, mock-ups are the common items of the architectural education. Jury members from outside the faculty or contribution of other academic staff at the same institute, formal relations, and the knowledge flow from tutor to student are the basic relations in the space time axes in linearity (Figure 6).

Figure 5. Traditional studio circumstance and ADS supported by network communication (Bala & Arat 2013)

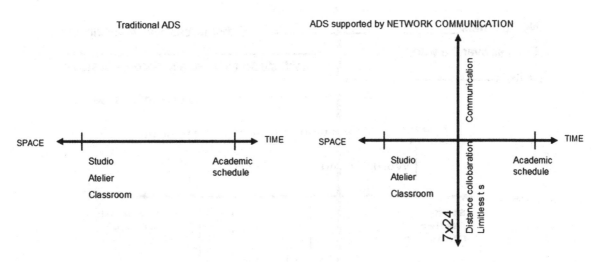

Figure 6. Traditional studio items and relations (Bala & Arat 2013)

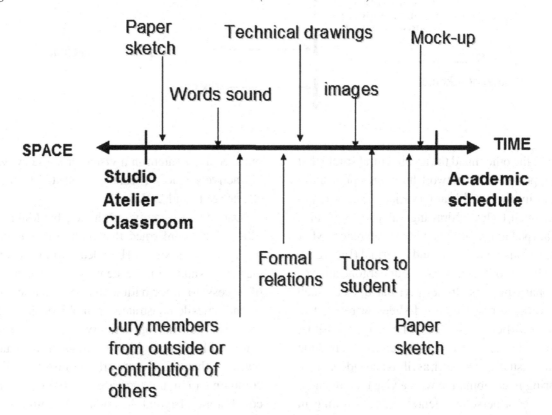

Figure 7. Traditional studio circumstance supported by social network (Bala & Arat 2013)

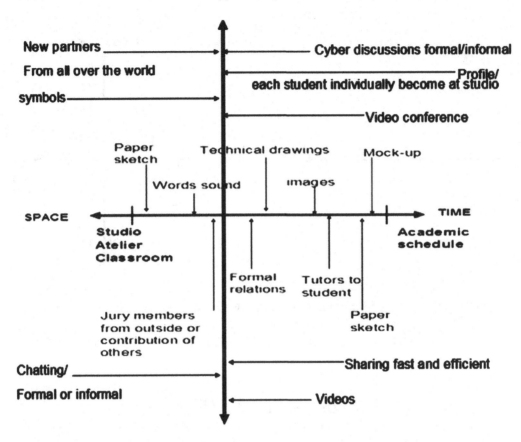

On the other hand the architectural studio that is supported social network has more opportunity regarding tools and relation variety. Except for paper, sketch, technical drawings, images, mock-ups, digital pedagogy provides video conference, cyber discussions both formal and informal (Figure 7).

The use of technology has undergone an evolutionary process. Initially visual devices such as overhead projectors and slides were used to explain difficult material as concretely as possible. Visual devices were later extended to include audio-visual devices such as films and videos since hearing in combination with a visual component enhances a person's attention span resulting in better retention of the content. In the following phase the focus shifted to communication. Technology, such as computers, is utilized to promote interactive teaching and learning. Learners do not only receive content in a visual or auditory way but actively react to what is presented to them (Bester & Brand, 2013).

Data from a study conducted by Mayisela (2013) have confirmed that mobile technology has a potential to support blended learning beyond classrooms and computer centres. The framework of access to information and communication technologies demonstrated that mobile technology increased students' opportunity to access courseware and Facebook. Also, findings of this study revealed that social networks improved online communication and increased participation and collaboration beyond the computer centre.

"Teachers' responses to the questions indicated that there was a definite need for a model for the implementation of group work in the IT class. Not only were teachers uninformed, but they did not seem to appreciate the dynamics of group work and the contribution that group work could make to effective learning and teaching in the IT class. Without informed teachers there will be no effective group work. Learners should be able to work effectively with other members in order to prepare learners to function effectively in a group context within the work environment. It is therefore of the utmost importance that teachers be trained in effective handling of group work in the IT class" (Mentz & Goosen, 2007).

According to Mizban & Roberts (2008), a number of schools of architecture have explored e-learning in their educational programmes. Early attempts to integrate computer science in architecture took place in the 1950s, although computers in teaching within schools of architecture became more familiar in the 1970s and 80s, with the advent of low cost hardware and commercial CAD software. Schools of architecture also generated their own rudimentary software to assist with design development although this was not widely integrated into teaching. The advent of advanced communication technologies in the 1990s including the development of the World Wide Web has provided more recent opportunities to establish new ways for students to work, collaborating with students locally and globally. Many of the innovations have been conducted by enthusiasts interested in seeing the potential for the technology. What appears to be missing is any form of evaluation of the pedagogic benefits of introducing e-learning in architecture (Mizban & Roberts, 2008).

The case study which is explained in the following section is also used Facebook effectively.

CASE STUDY: DEPARTMENT OF ARCHITECTURE AT SELCUK UNIVERSITY

In the 2010-2011 Spring Semester, SAIT Polytechnic Architectural Technologies and Selcuk University Department of Architecture carried out a project in international cooperation as common studio. The case study mentioned in that study has been discussed in the aspect of pedagogical implication for "international cooperation" with Marc Bussier who is the tutor of this studio, teaching at SAIT (Bala & Bussier, 2012). Students from Calgary and Konya worked together to solve the design problem of sustainable housing in Calgary`s East Village. This studio was based on two main concepts: experience architectural design in an international context and address issues of sustainability with students from another country.

Selcuk University (SU), as the biggest university in Turkey by virtue of numbers, has already applied to European University Association Institutional Review Program, with an innovative view and understanding, to attain international quality standards to improve its education (Self Evaluation Report, 2005). SU offers architectural education since 1970s in Konya, which is located in Central Anatolia with its long historical and cultural background as the part of Engineering and Architecture Faculty and in 2012 the faculty is separated from Engineers and continue education independent as the Faculty of Architecture. Department of Architecture at SU regarding digital pedagogy has two different approaches. One is rejecting to let the students to use computer in the beginning namely from first to third semester. The second approach is "the earlier, the better". The first group claiming that "ironically less time is provided to old skills like freehand drawing/sketching because more time goes to learning a variety of digital skills". The atelier we carried out is one of the design studio in the Faculty of Architecture at Selcuk University, is in the second group and it opens to experimental educational approach.

The project has involved both planning and architectural scale. Calgary Land Municipal Corporation (CMLC) prepared an Area Redevelopment Plan (ARP) for the East Village. The ARP is sustainable master plan having shade and

Figure 8. The cooperation and collaboration between Selcuk (Turkey) and SAIT (Canada) in the context of sustainability

Figure 9. The using of synchronous-asynchronous learning technologies in virtual design studio (VAD)

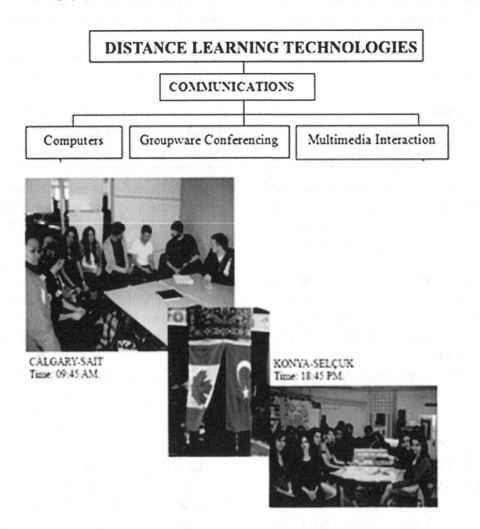

shadow analysis for each building block, ratio of commercial to residential, desired density targets as well as more general social, economical and cultural design inputs according to sustainable building criteria (Bala & Bussier, 2012). The Studio was carried out in the virtual environment for a two month period (Figure 9).

In this studio teaching/learning experience has started with asynchronous and then when one Canadian student has been paired with a Turkish student by the tutors, they started to communicate asynchronous using SKYPE and Facebook. At the end of the semester Canadian students came to Turkey and made the juries face to face namely we used the traditional learning methods in the studio. Briefly, in this case study adding distance education to the traditional teaching method has created more improved educational climate.

Studio tutors carried out the regular studio program in their own countries with the shared design project, common presentations and requirements as well as monitor the interaction in the shared

virtual environment. Canadian students sent short movies, detailed photographs and information about the project site, Cad drawings, and land by-law information and of course discussions about how people live day to day in Calgary despite the time zone difference of nine hours between two countries. The first step of this collaboration was to introduce the Canadian and Turkish students to one another. We used the same social network tools that students around the world are familiar with: SKYPE and Facebook (Figure 10, 11, 12).

After rather formal introductions on SKYPE with students and tutors, the students from both countries then connected with each other on FACEBOOK. They immediately started to exchange information about their favourite buildings, favourite architects, relevant architectural articles, interesting YouTube videos and personal information (Figure 13).

The East Village was the first settlement within what is now Calgary. Calgary Land Municipal Corporation (CMLC) prepared an Area Redevel-

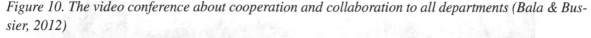

Figure 10. The video conference about cooperation and collaboration to all departments (Bala & Bussier, 2012)

Figure 11. The meetings of CDADA at Skype (Bala & Bussier, 2012)

Figure 12. The meetings of CDADA at Skype

opment Plan (ARP) for the East Village. Each lot has different building regulation rules according to the master plan. The ARP contains defined shade and shadow analysis for each building block, ratio of commercial to residential, desired density targets as well as more general social, economic and cultural design inputs according to sustain-able building criteria. Students had to study the existing Area Redevelopment Plan in order to fully understand the requirements for their building lots. Tutors provided additional necessary documents and information for the Project. The East Village was the first settlement within what is now Calgary. Calgary Land Municipal Corporation (CMLC)

Figure 13. Communication at Facebook for the course (Bala & Bussier, 2012)

prepared an Area Redevelopment Plan (ARP) for the East Village. The web technology provides Turkish students and educators opportunities to get new cyber media (Figure 14, 15).

While construction that type of architectural studio circumstance some challenges occurred which is below (Bala & Bussier, 2012).

- Starting and finishing the design using the data in virtual platform can reduce the quality of design and the efficiency of time management.
- It is challenging for students to try to understand a site on the other side of the world which they have never seen or do not know the culture of only by means of digital communication.
- Using the videos, design parameters specified in the master plan, photographs and analyses of their student partners as mentors may cause uncertainties from time to time.

- Starting the international studio under institutes' different academic calendars can pose certain challenges with regards to deadlines and delivery of critical information at key periods.

Despite the fact that we faced some challenges, we had got several advantages creating that studio work; the advantages can be account as below:

1. It is possible to create motivating alternative educational experiences in conventional architectural educational environments. Such initiatives are not a mainstay of most institutes but rather the fruition of certain individuals in each institute who have the wherewithal and passion to see this through. This requires the will of the participating institutes to allow this to happen, and the willingness of instructors to persevere.
2. Alternative teaching methods and methodologies force everyone (institutes, instruc-

Figure 14. Studying in web connection at digital media provides all necessary information about the Calgary site using links

tors, students) outside of their comfort zones. Creativity is usually the result of this. ICT on design learning and practice as changing from command and control to coordination of communication.

3. Students of architecture leave the studio with a wider vision of being a "citizen of the world" and "creating a design by universal values" which they were not previously aware of.

4. The awareness for the similar architectural design problems in the essence of different cultures, different religions, different climates and different geographies was raised.

The more they got to know each other through their work, the more they realized that they have a lot in common. We began this process with preconceptions of how different we are.

5. This cooperation has provided the students and instructors of both countries with an opportunity to start setting up an international network with their colleagues. It is quite possible that this network will serve them both in their educational life and after graduation. It also gives students access to what other institutes provide on the subject of architecture instead of merely getting what their own institution provides.

Figure 15. Corporation owned by city of Calgary ("East village", n.d.)

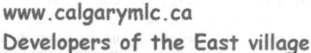

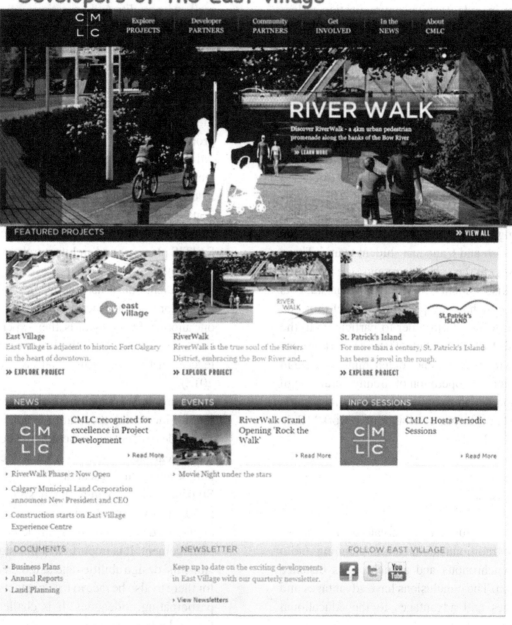

6. The synergy created by such an intense experience will continue long after the study is complete.

7. Creating alternative learning environments within present architectural education systems results in significant added value to a student's education. Architectural problems

solved in an international context are more in-depth and layered than the conventional process.

8. The features of collaboration in design education include effective communication, reflection, appropriate tools, and the effective use of artifacts. Information and communication technologies present online applications for collaboration design that offer educators the possibility to change design pedagogy.

What was the final result of the student projects? "Turkish design concepts in the second phase of the studio were examined and discussed online with Canadian students and scaled project drawings and models were developed. The following are the project analyses created by two Turkish and Canadian student teams. These projects were then shared amongst the Canadian and Turkish students. In May, Canadian students who by now had completed their final projects, travelled to Konya in order to participate in the jury with Turkish students. There are certain conclusions to the experience of teaching/learning in international cooperation of architectural design education which may be generalized as a guide or template for future collaborative work" (Bala & Bussier 2012).

CONCLUSION

This study focused on to create an alternative media to traditional architectural/planning studio using synchronous and asynchronous distance education. The conclusions have advantages and challenges and advantages to the educational outputs as follows:

1. ICT on design learning can create alternative teaching methods. Using ICT forces everyone (institutes, instructors, students) to improve themselves. It can be stated that education policies will not answer the needs of today's society or its individual requirements. As a result of these basic factors, swift changes are on the table concerning the concept and content of education, as well as its quality and operation.

2. Creating alternative learning environments within present architectural education systems results in significant added value to a student's education. Architectural problems solved in an international context are more in-depth and layered than the conventional process.

3. All the opportunities that modern education technology offers should be effectively used in order to provide higher quality education services to a larger and wider range of students. Turkish students could reach the SAIT'S planning and architectural accumulation by using ICT.

4. The students have had the chance to both learn from one another as well as to teach one another. In other words, they experience the state of being both the learner and the teacher at the same time (Bala & Bussier 2012).

5. Asynchronous education is an important tool for increasing the quality of education; it provides students with the skills to increase their creativity, curiosity, knowledge, and ability to conduct research.

6. Starting and finishing the design using the data in virtual platform can reduce the quality of design and the efficiency of time management. It is important at this stage of students' design abilities and language skills for there to also be face to face contacts with participating colleagues. It is challenging for students to try to understand a site on the other side of the world which they have never seen or do not know the culture of only by means of digital communication. Using the videos, design parameters specified in the master plan, photographs and analyses of their student partners as mentors may

cause uncertainties from time to time (Bala & Bussier 2012).

7. When asynchronous learning is developed for architectural education, location problems are solved in faculties, educators can contact more students at the same time and rural universities which are developing are encouraged by using asynchronous learning.

Consequently, changes in the concepts of the social and the individual drive forward the requirement for innovation in education. Education processes gain a new dimension with lifelong/continuous learning, with synchronous and asynchronous education. In line with this, asynchronous education constitutes a dimension of the new education technology. The integration of this educational method with the traditional education system is an important factor that must be taken into consideration for the realization of greater quality teaching and learning in universities.

REFERENCES

Activeworlds offers a comprehensive platform. (n.d.). Retrieved July 13, 2012 from http://www.activeworld.com

Alkan, F., & Bala Alkan, H. (1998). Asynchronous learning in planning and architecture education. In *Proceedings of Forum II, Architectural Education for the 3RD Millennium*, (pp. 555-560). Gazimagusa, North Cyprus: Academic Press.

Bala Alkan, H., & Arat, Y. (2013). Digital pedagogy using social network tools in architectural education. *AWERProcedia Information Technology & Computer Science*, *3*, 160–166.

Bala Alkan, H., & Bussiere, M. (2012). Pedagogical implication for international cooperation in architectural design studio. *AE-Lusafona Architectural & Education Journal*, *6*(7), 9–27.

Balaban, M. E. (2012). Dünyada ve Türkiye'de uzaktan eğitim ve bir proje önerisi. *Bilgiye Erişim ve Paylaşım Projesi: Uzaktan Eğitim.*

Barker., et al. (1989). Interactive distance learning technologies for rural and small schools: A resource guide. ERIC Mini-Review. New Mexico State University, ERIC Clearinghouse for Rural Education and Small Schools.

Başaran, S., & Tulu, B. (1999). Bilişim çağında asenkron eğitim ağlarının konumu. In Proceedings of 5nci. Ankara: İnternet Konferansı Tebliğleri. Retrieved from inet-tr.org.tr/inetconf5/oneri/asekron.doc

Bennett, R., & Broadfoot, O. (2003). Design studios: Online? In *Proceedings of Apple University Consortium Academic and Developers Conference,* (pp. 9-21). Wollongong: Apple University Consortium Academic and Developers. Retrieved from http://auc.uow.edu.au/conf/conf03/papers/AUC_DV2003_Broadfoot.pdf

Bester, G., & Brand, L. (2013). The effect of technology on learner attention and achievement in the classroom. *South African Journal of Education*, *33*(2), 1–15.

Boyer, E. L., & Mitgang, L. D. (1996). *Building community: A new future for architecture education and practice*. Princeton, NJ: The Carnegie Foundation for the Advancement of Teaching.

Burma, Z.A. (2008). AB'ye geçiş sürecinde meslek elemanlarının uzaktan öğretim ile eğitimi. *Bilişim Teknolojileri Dergisi, 1*(2).

Buselic, M. (2012). *Distance Learning-concepts and contributions*. Oeconomica Jadertina.

Çağdaş, G. (2005). Enformasyon teknolojilerindeki evrimsel sürecin mimari tasarım eğitimine Yansımaları. *Stüdyo Tasarım Kuram Elestiri Dergisi, 2* (4-5). Retrieved from http://www.studyomim.itu.edu.tr/sayi2/enformasyon_tek_evrimsel_sur_2-6.pdf

Çağdaş, G., Kavaklı Thorne, M., Özsoy, A., Altaş, N. E. & Tong, H. (2000). Virtual design studio VDS 2000 as a virtual construction site: Digital media is design media, not a drawing tool. *International Journal of Design Computing*.

Çağdaş, G., & Tong, H. (2005). Global bir tasarım stüdyosuna doğru. *Stüdyo Tasarım Kuram Elestiri Dergisi, 3*(4-5). Retrieved from http://www.studyomim.itu.edu.tr/sayi3/global_bir_tasarim_studyosuna_dogru.pdf

Çavaş, B., & Huyugüzel, P. (2001). *Web destekli eğitim: Teletop yaklaşımı*. Retrieved February 18, 2003, from http://www.bilisimsurasi.org.tr/cg/egitim/kutuphane/WebDestekliEgitim.doc

Çetiner, M., Gencel, Ç., & Erten, M. (2009). *İnternete dayalı uzaktan eğitim ve çoklu ortam uygulamaları*. Retrieved from http://inet-tr.org.tr

Charnigo, L., & Barnett-Ellis, P. (2007). Checking out facebook.com: The impact of a digital trend on academic libraries. *Information Technology and Libraries, 26*, 23–34.

Chen, W., & You, M. (2003). A framework for the development of online design learning environment. In *Proceedings of 6th Asian Design Conference*. Retrieved from http://www.idemployee.id.tue.nl/g.w.m.rauterberg/conferences/CD_doNotOpen/ADC/final_paper/584.pdf

Crook, C., & Harrison, C. (2008). *Web 2.0 technologies for learning at key stages 3 and 4: Summary report*. Retrieved from http://schools.becta.org.uk/upload-dir/downloads/page_documents/research/ web2_ks34_summary.pdf

Demirkıran, V., & Silahtaroğlu, G. (2010). *Uzaktan eğitim; Ne zaman, nasıl?* Retrieved from http://uzaktanegitim.istanbul.edu.tr/index.php/component/content/article/187.html

Duru, S. (2006). *Sanal mimari tasarım stüdyosunda pedagojik yaklaşımlar*. İstanbul: İstanbul Teknik Üniversitesi, Fen Bilimleri Enstitüsü, Yüksek Lisans Tezi.

East Village. (n.d.). Retrieved March 12, 2011 from http://www.evexperience.com/

Hamann, K., & Wilson, B. M. (2003). Beyond search engines: Enhancing active learning using the internet. *Politics & Policy, 31*(3), 533–553. doi:10.1111/j.1747-1346.2003.tb00161.x

Hanson, D., Maushak, N., Schlosser, C., Anderson, M., & Sorensen, M. (1997). *Distance education:Review of the literature* (2nd ed.). Washington, DC: Association for Educational Communications and Technology.

Hewitt, A., & Forte, A. (2006). Crossing boundaries: Identity management and student/faculty relationships on the facebook. In *Proceedings of Computer Supported Cooperative Work Conference*. Banff, Canada: IEEE.

İnceoğlu, M. (2002). Mobil öğretime hazır mıyız? In *Proceedings of Anadolu Üniversitesi*. Eskişehir: Açık ve Uzaktan Eğitim Sempozyumu.

Karakaya, M. (2005). *Uzaktan eğitim*. Ankara: Ankara Üniversitesi, Eğitim Bilimleri Enstitüsü, Eğitim Bilimleri Anabilim Dalı, Eğitim Yönetimi ve Teftişi Yüksek Lisans Programı, Eğitim Reformu Dersi.

Keegan, D. (1986). *The foundations of distance education*. London: Croom Helm.

Maher, M. L., & Simoff, S. J. (2000). Collaboratively designing within the design. Collaborative design. In *Proceedings of Codesigning*, (pp. 391-400). London: Springer-Verlag. Retrieved from http://www.acmc.uq.edu.au/pdfs/Collaborative_designing_within_the_Design.pdf

Malins, J., Gray, C., Pirie, I., Cordiner, S., & Mckillop, C. (2003). The virtual design studio: Developing new tools for learning, practice and research in design. In Proceedings of Techne. Barcelona, Spain: Design Wisdom European Academy of Design. Retrieved from http://www.ub.es/5ead/PDF/10/Malins.pdf

Mathews, B. S. (2006). Do you facebook? Networking with students online. *College & Research Libraries News*, *37*, 306–307.

Mayisela, T. (2013). The potential use of mobile technology: Enhancing accessibility and communication in a blended learning course. *South African Journal of Education*, *33*(1), 1–18.

Mazer, J. P., Murphy, R. E., & Simonds, C. J. (2007). I'll see you on 'Facebook': The effects of computer-mediated teacher self-disclosure on student motivation, affective learning, and classroom climate. *Communication Education*, *56*(1), 1–17. doi:10.1080/03634520601009710

Mentz, E., & Goosen, L. (2007). Are groups working in the information technology class? *South African Journal of Education*, *27*(2), 329–343.

Mizban, N., & Roberts, A. (2008). A Review of experiences of the implementation of e-learning in architectural design education. *CEBE Working Papers*.

Munoz, C. L., & Towner, T. (2009). Opening facebook: How to use facebook in the college classroom. In *Proceedings of Society for Information Technology and Teacher Education Conference*. Charleston, SC: Academic Press.

Özer, B. (1989). *Türkiye'de uzaktan eğitim: Anadolu Üniversitesi Açıköğretim Fakültesi'nin uygulamaları*. Retrieved from www.emu.edu.tr/.../1989.Türkiye'de%20uzaktan.pdf

Russell, M., Bebell, D., O'Dwyer, L., & O'Connor, K. (2003). Examining teaching technology use: Implications for preservice and inservice teacher preparation. *Journal of Teacher Education*, *54*(4), 297–310. doi:10.1177/0022487103255985

Schön, D. A. (1987). *Educating the reflective practitioner*. San Francisco: Jossey-Bass Inc.

Self Evaluation Report. (2005). *Self evaluation report*. European University Association Institutional Review Program, Selcuk University Accreditation Committee, Konya.

Selwyn, N. (2007). "Screw blackboard...do it on Facebook!": An investigation of students' educational use of Facebook. In *Proceedings of Poke 1.0-Facebook Social Research Symposium*. University of London.

Simonson, M. (2002). In case you are asked: The effectiveness of distance education. *Quarterly Review of Distance Education*, *3*(4).

Simonson, M., Smaldino, S., Albright, M., & Zvacek, S. (2011). Teaching and learning at distance foundations of distance education (4th ed.). Academic Press.

Solem, M., Chalmers, L., Dibiase, D., Donert, K., & Hardwick, S. (2006). Internationalizing Professional Development in Geography through Distance Education. *Journal of Geography in Higher Education*, *30*(1), 147–160. doi:10.1080/03098260500499808

Toker Gökçe, A. (2008). Küreselleşme Sürecinde Uzaktan Eğitim. *D.Ü. Ziya Gökalp Eğitim Fakültesi Dergisi*, *11*, 1–12.

Towner, T., & VanHorn, A. (2007). Facebook: Classroom tool for a classroom community? In *Proceedings of the Annual Meeting of the Midwest Political Science Association*. Chicago, IL: Academic Press.

Türkiye Bilişim Derneği. (2003). Retrieved April 21, 2014, from www.tbd.org.tr

Türkoğlu, R. (2003). İnternet Tabanlı Uzaktan Eğitim Programı Geliştirme Süreçleri. *The Turkish Online Journal of Educational Technology, 2*(3).

Ünkap, Ö. (2006). *Sanal mimarlik stüdyosu uygulamalari üzerine bir değerlendirme.* İstanbul: İstanbul Teknik Üniversitesi, Fen Bilimleri Enstitüsü, Yüksek Lisans Tezi.

Uzaktan eğitim. (n.d.). Retrieved April 21, 2014 from http://www.uluslararasiegitim.com/uzak/default.asp

Uzaktan eğitimde eğitimcinin rolü ve sorumlulukları. (n.d.). Retrieved April 21, 2014 from http://www.ceng.metu.edu.tr/~e1448737/ceit321/proje/week1_reading_1.php

Yıldırım, U., & Öner, Ş. (2005). Bilgi toplumu sürecinde yerel yönetimlerde eğitim-bilişim teknolojisinden yararlanma: Türkiye'de e-belediye uygulamaları. *The Turkish Online Journal of Educational Technology, 3*(1). Retrieved April 18, from http://www.tojet.net/articles/318.pdf

KEY TERMS AND DEFINITIONS

Architectural/Planning Education: Architectural/Planning education provides people professional skills of design cities and buildings.

Asynchronous Learning: Asynchronous learning is a student-centered teaching method that using online technology which is e-mail, electronic mailing list, conference system, online discussion board and blocks.

Distance Learning: A learning/teaching system which students are educated using a variety of communication tools without coming face to face, being free from place and time.

Selcuk University: Selcuk University, as the biggest university in Turkey by virtue of numbers is settled in Konya.

Virtual Architectural Design Studio: Virtual Architectural Design Studio is a student-centered teaching method that studying in web connection at digital media free from space or time limitation, sharing all documents, knowledge, opinion, critics with other actors.

Chapter 2

A Comparative Study of Business and Engineering Students' Attitude to Mobile Technologies in Distance Learning

Andreas Ahrens
Hochschule Wismar, Germany

Jeļena Zaščerinska
Centre for Education and Innovation Research, Latvia

ABSTRACT

Mobile technologies are widely employed in distance learning in higher education to provide students with an opportunity to learn regardless of time and place in order to obtain a higher education degree. However, little attention has been paid to a comparative study of business and engineering students' attitudes toward mobile technologies. The aim of the chapter is to compare business and engineering students' attitudes toward mobile technologies in distance learning, underpinning elaboration of a hypothesis. The meanings of the key concepts of distance learning, blended learning, and attitude are studied. Moreover, the study demonstrates how the key concepts are related to the idea of mobile technologies and shows how the steps of the process are related: students' attitudes toward mobile technologies in distance learning → empirical study within multicultural environments → conclusions. The results of the present research show that both business and engineering students' attitudes toward mobile technologies are positive.

DOI: 10.4018/978-1-4666-7316-8.ch002

INTRODUCTION

Many universities throughout the world have already adopted or are planning to adopt mobile technologies in many of their courses as a better way to connect students with the subjects they are studying (Ferreira, Klein, Freitas & Schlemmer, 2013). Particularly, mobile technologies in distance learning of higher education have already become an indispensable tool in both university staff and students' daily life. Mobile technologies are widely employed in distance learning of higher education to provide students with an opportunity to learn regardless of time and place in order to obtain a higher education degree. In distance learning, mobile technologies allow students to access content anywhere/anytime to immerse himself/herself into that content (alone or interacting with educators or colleagues via web communication forms) and to interact with that content in ways that were not previously possible (via touch and voice recognition technologies, for instance) (Ferreira et al., 2013). Therein, mobile technologies and distance learning are closely inter-related as depicted in Figure 1.

Evaluation of the educator/student acceptance and adoption of mobile technologies has been carried out (Ferreira et al., 2013). Against this background, students' attitude to mobile technologies in distance learning plays a two-fold role within the institutionalized blended educational process of higher education as shown in Figure 2.

- On the one hand, students' attitude to mobile technologies influences students' distance learning, and,
- On the other hand, students' attitude to distance learning shapes students' application of mobile technologies.

Figure 1. The relationship between distance learning and mobile technologies

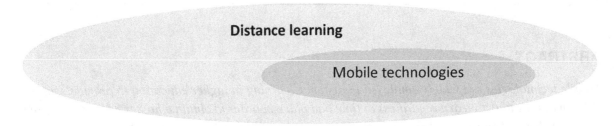

Figure 2. The relationship between students' attitude, mobile technologies and distance learning

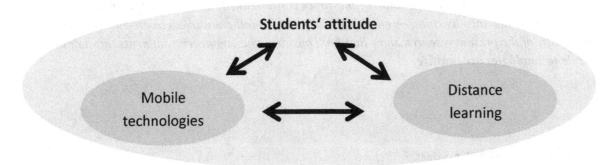

Figure 3. The relationship between lifelong education, higher education and distance learning

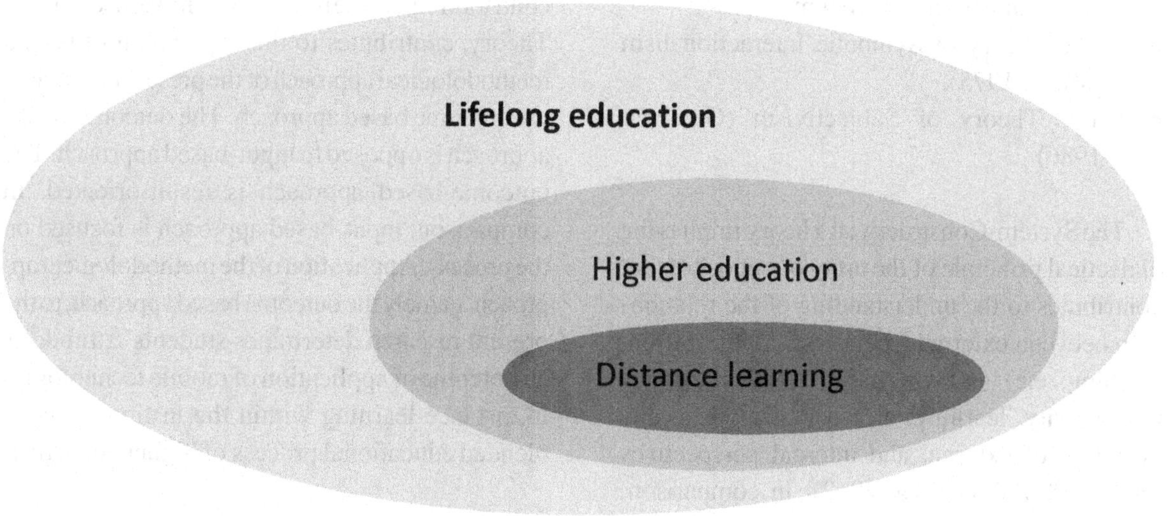

Thus, application of mobile technologies in distance learning is driven by students' attitude to mobile technologies in distance learning.

However, little attention has been paid to a comparative study of business and engineering students' attitude to mobile technologies in distance learning within the institutionalized blended educational process of higher education.

The aim of the paper is to compare business and engineering students' attitude to mobile technologies in distance learning within the institutionalized blended educational process of higher education underpinning elaboration of a hypothesis. The meaning of the key concepts of *distance learning, blended learning* and *attitude* is studied. Moreover, the study demonstrates how the key concepts are related to the idea of *mobile technologies* and shows how the steps of the process are related: students' attitude to mobile technologies in distance learning within the institutionalized blended educational process of higher education → empirical study within multicultural environments → conclusions.

In the present contribution, distance learning is considered as part of higher education, and higher education as part of lifelong education as demonstrated in Figure 3.

Efforts of modern research on lifelong education reveal that higher education in general and distance learning in particular is currently generated by the transition from opportunity to choose towards qualities and purposes in the context of higher education globalization and internationalization (Bassus & Zaščerinska, 2012). This shift changes the nature of higher education as well as distance learning. For the advancement of higher education as well as distance learning, social nature of change has become dominant (Bassus & Zaščerinska, 2012). Social nature of change in higher education as well as distance learning is mediated via the System-Constructivist Theory. The System-Constructivist Theory is introduced as the New or Social Constructivism Pedagogical Theory. The System-Constructivist Theory serves as the basis of the methodological background of the present contribution. The System-Constructivist Theory is formed by:

- Parsons's System Theory (Parsons, 1976) on any activity as a system,

- Luhmann's Theory (Luhmann, 1988) on communication as a system,
- The Theory of Symbolic Interactionalism (Mead, 1973),
- The Theory of Subjectivism (Groeben, 1986).

The System-Constructivist Theory implies the dialectical principle of the unity of opposites that contributes to the understanding of the relationship between external (social, social interaction, teaching, etc) and internal (individual, cognitive activity, learning, etc) perspectives as the synthesis of external and internal perspectives (Bassus & Zaščerinska, 2012). In comparison, the Constructivism Theory focuses on learning and, consequently, the internal perspective, the Social Constructivist theory – on teaching and, consequently, external perspective as well as on the balance between teaching and learning and, consequently, the balance between the external and internal perspectives (Bassus & Zaščerinska, 2012).

The System-Constructivist Theory and, consequently, the System-Constructivist Approach to learning introduced by Reich (Reich, 2005) emphasizes that human being's point of view depends on the subjective aspect:

- Everyone has his/her own system of external and internal perspectives (Ahrens & Zaščerinska, 2010) that is a complex open system (Rudzinska, 2008), and
- Experience plays the central role in the knowledge construction process (Maslo, 2007).

Therein, the subjective aspect of human being's point of view is applicable to the present research on this comparative study of business and engineering students' attitude to mobile technologies in distance learning within the institutionalized blended educational process of higher education.

The methodological background of the present contribution, namely the System-Constructivist Theory, contributes to the application of such a methodological approach of the present research as the outcome based approach. The outcome-based approach is opposed to input-based approach. The outcome-based approach is result-oriented. In comparison, input-based approach is focused on the process. Application of the methodological approach, namely the outcome based approach, to the present research determines students' attitude as an outcome of application of mobile technologies in distance learning within the institutionalized blended educational process of higher education.

The novel contribution of this paper is the definition of attitude and attitude's indicators and constructs newly identified by the contributions' authors as well as the educational model of application of mobile technologies in distance learning within the institutionalized blended educational process of higher education. The educational model of application of mobile technologies in distance learning within the institutionalized blended educational process of higher education represents the inter-connections between distance learning as part of blended learning and mobile technologies as a means of distance learning.

Our target population to generalize the educational model of students' attitude to mobile technologies in distance learning within the blended educational process of higher education is students in formal higher education.

The remaining part of this paper is organized as follows: the next section introduces theoretical framework on students' attitude to mobile technologies in distance learning within the institutionalized blended educational process of higher education. The associated results of an empirical study will be presented in the following section. Finally, some concluding remarks are provided followed by a short outlook on interesting topics for further work.

THEORETICAL FRAMEWORK

The present part of the contribution demonstrates the definitions of:

- Attitude,
- Mobile technologies,
- Distance learning, and
- The institutionalized blended educational process of higher education.

As the outcome based approach is used as the methodological approach in the present contribution, the present research is result-oriented. Therein, the present research identifies *outcome* on the pedagogical discourse as the direct results of the instructional programme, planned in terms of student/learner growth in all areas (Vlăsceanu, Grünberg & Pârlea, 2004). Outcome includes learning outcome as demonstarted in Figure 4.

Furthermore, in many publications the terms *outcome*, *result* and *output* are used synonymously as shown in Figure 5.

The synonymous use of the terms *outcome*, *result* and *output* determines three criteria of learning results (Huber, 2004) as depicted in Figure 6.

Learning outcome is defined as direct results of learning, planned in terms of student growth in all areas. Criteria of learning outcome are determined as students' learning achievements, social competence and individual development.

The present contribution focuses on students' social competence as a criterion of students' learning outcome. It should be noted that the notion of social competence has been constantly changed and accompanied by a change in the originally used terms such as social competencies, communicative competence, etc (Zaščerinska, 2013). Despite the changes in the notion of social competence and its terms, social competence remains the overall concept as shown in Figure 7.

Thus, in the further text of the present contribution, the term *competence* is used. Students' attitude is part of competence as competence includes knowledge, skills and attitudes (European Commission, 2004) as shown in Figure 8.

The elements of competence, namely knowledge, skills and attitude, are inter-related. Students' negative attitude fails to promote the increase in the level of students' knowledge and skills as well as competence, in general. In contrast, students' positive attitude ensures the enrichment of the level of students' knowledge and skills as well as competence, in general.

As students' attitude is an outcome of application of mobile technologies in distance learning within the institutionalized blended educational process of higher education, application of mo-

Figure 4. The relationship between outcome and learning outcome

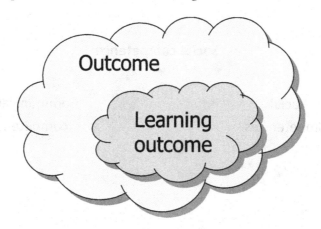

Figure 5. The relationship between outcome, result and output

Figure 6. Three criteria of learning results

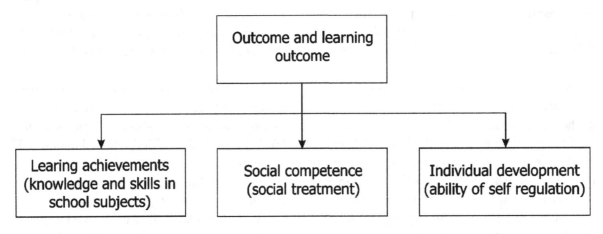

Figure 7. Inter-relationships between terms of social competence

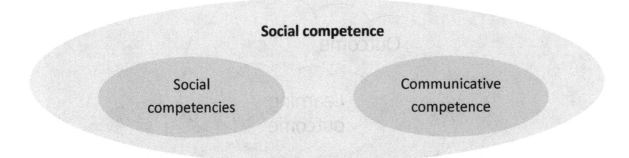

Figure 8. Elements of competence

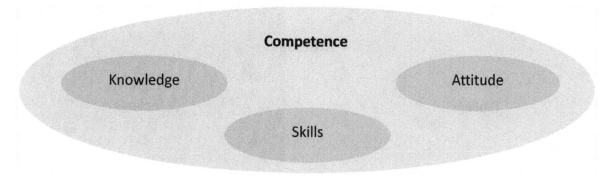

bile technologies in distance learning within the institutionalized blended educational process in higher education is able to enrich students' digital competence. Students' digital competence is of great importance as it serves as

- One of eight key competences outlined by the European Commission for lifelong learning (European Commission, 2004), and
- A condition, factor and evaluation criterion of application of mobile technologies in distance learning (Surikova, 2007).

Hence, students' attitude serves not only as an outcome but also as a criterion of application of mobile technologies in distance learning within the institutionalized blended educational process of higher education. It should be noted that criteria serve to structure, assess and evaluate while indicators determine developmental dynamics (Lasmanis, 2003; Špona & Čehlova, 2004), and constructs differentiate a variable which is not directly observable. Criteria, indicators and constructs are identified via analysis of (Špona & Čehlova, 2004).

- Definition of the research object,
- Structure of the research object, and
- Factors.

Attitude has been defined by a number of researchers. Palmer and Holt define attitude as an individual's positive or negative feelings about performing the target behavior (Palmer & Holt, 2009). This implies that learners' positive or negative feelings about their use of mobile technologies in distance learning would directly influence their behavior to use mobile technologies in distance learning. Consequently, attitude comprises positive as well as negative feelings as shown in Figure 9.

Another definition of attitude that is of the interest of the contribution's authors is attitude identified as a combination of evaluative judgements about a phenomenon (Crites, Fabrigar & Petty, 1994).

Analysis of these definitions of attitude by the contribution's authors and complementing the attitude definition formulated by Crites, Fabrigar and Petty (Crites et al., 1994) with the word *individual* leads to such a newly determined definition of student's attitude as an individual combination of evaluative judgements about a phenomenon. As well as, in comparison to attitude's positive or negative feelings determined by Palmer and Holt (Palmer & Holt, 2009), the contribution's authors differentiate attitude into positive, neutral or negative as illustrated in Figure 10.

Understanding students' attitudes towards mobile technologies in distance learning can help to determine the extent to which students utilize

Figure 9. Feelings of attitude

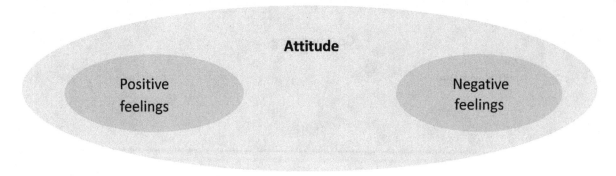

Figure 10. Differentiation of attitude

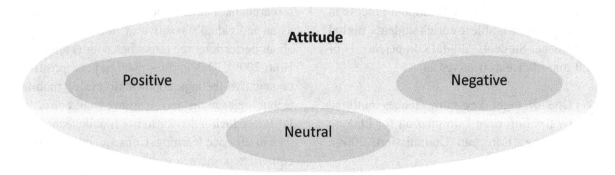

Table 1. Attitude as a criterion of application of mobile technologies in distance learning and levels of attitude

Criterion	Levels		
	Level 1	Level 2	Level 3
	Low	Optimal	High
	1	2	3
Students' attitude to mobile technologies in distance learning	Negative	Neutral	Positive

Figure 11. Components of motivation

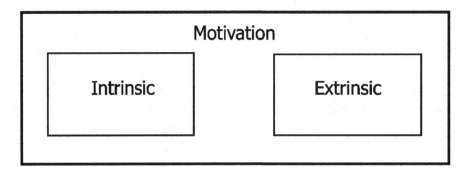

mobile technologies in distance learning (Ong & Lai, 2006).

Attitude differentiation is considered as levels of attitude shown in Table 1.

A positive attitude is associated with the evidence of motivated behaviour, while a negative change is linked to a less motivated behavior (Berg, 2005; Movahedzadeh, 2011).

It should be noted that motivation comprises (Harmer, 2001) as shown in Figure 11:

- Extrinsic motivation caused by a number of outside factors, and
- Intrinsic motivation that comes from the individual and is especially important for encouraging.

Intrinsic motivation is formed by internal factors of three groups (Pintrich, 1994) as demonstrated in Figure 12.

Expectancy components include (Pintrich, 1994):

- Control beliefs,
- Attributions,
- Learned helplessness, and
- Self-efficacy.

Value components comprise (Pintrich, 1994):

- Intrinsic/extrinsic goals,

- Task value, and
- Personal interest.

Affective components involve (Pintrich, 1994):

- Test anxiety,
- Self-worth, and
- Other emotions (pride, shame).

For the attitude change from negative to positive, such methods are proposed to motivate students extrinsically as:

- Educators' adapting teaching styles (Movahedzadeh, 2011) to the students' needs,
- Showing students the relevance of the learning topics to their everyday lives (Movahedzadeh, 2011),
- Creation of learning environment that helps motivate students not only to participate in distance learning but also wish to learn and enjoy learning (Movahedzadeh, 2011),
- Asking students to consider the preconceptions about subject-related topics that they bring to distance learning (Etkina & Mestre, 2004).

Figure 12. Components of internal factors that form intrinsic motivation

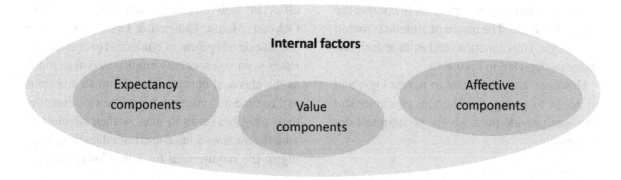

Figure 13. Domains of attitude

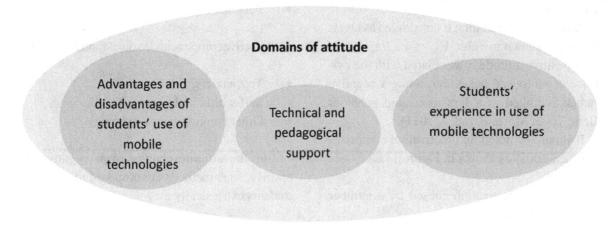

Figure 14. The relationship between attitude and emotions

For the measurement of students' attitude, three domains are identified (Al-Musawi, Al-Bustan & Al-Mezel, 2013) as shown in Figure 13.

For the determination of indicators and constructs of students' attitude to mobile technologies in distance learning within the institutionalized blended educational process of higher education, the contribution's authors propose to analyse the nature of attitude. The nature of attitude is rooted in emotions. Thus, emotions and attitude are interrelated as depicted in Figure 14.

However, emotions refer to psychology, and attitude – to pedagogy. Therein, psychological processes provide the basis for pedagogical developments.

Emotions defined as nerve impulses ensure this faster reaction to a problem situation as emotions encourage for acting by use of an immediate plan of action (Kriumane, 2013). The main thing is that emotional processes and states have their own special positive development in man (Leont'ev, 1978). Therein, it is widely believed that men and women differ in their emotional responding (McRae, Ochsner, Mauss, Gabrieli & Gross, 2008). The positive development of emotional processes and states must be especially emphasized in as much as the classical conceptions of human emotions as "rudiments" coming from Darwin, consider their transformation in man as their involution, which generates a false ideal of education, leading to the requirement to "subordinate feelings

Figure 15. Elements of experience in pedagogy

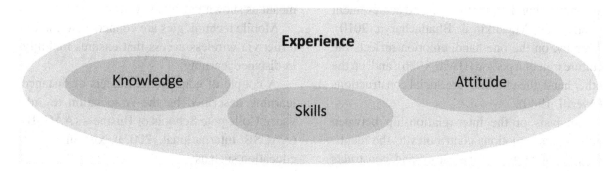

Table 2. Attitude's indicators and constructs

Criterion	Indicators	Constructs
Students' evaluative judgements on mobile technologies in distance learning	Verbal expression	A word, sentence, etc
	Non-verbal expression	Face expression, body language, mimicry, etc
	Cultural expression	Cultural habits

to cold reason" (Leont'ev, 1978). Consequently, the relationship between human emotions and age has to be further analysed. Emotions are not only feelings, but also other elements, such as expressions in the face or the voice, physiological changes, and changes in action tendencies or action readiness (De Vierville, 2002). Emotions fulfill the functions of internal signals, internal in the sense that they do not appear directly as psychic reflection of objective activity itself (Leont'ev, 1978). The special feature of emotions identified by Leont'ev (Leont'ev, 1978) is that they reflect relationships between motives (needs) and success, or the possibility of success, of realizing the action of the subject that responds to particular motives. Therein, emotions do not reflect those relationships but reveal a direct sensory reflection of emotions, about experiencing (Leont'ev, 1978). In pedagogy, experience includes knowledge, skills and attitude (Zaščerinska, 2013) as shown in Figure 15.

Consequently, the terms *experience* and *competence* are used synonymously in pedagogy in

general and in the present contribution in particular. Further on, emotions are relevant to the social activity and not to individual actions or operations that realize it (Leont'ev, 1978). As a result emotions are not subordinated to activity but appear to be its result and the "mechanism" of its movement (Leont'ev, 1978). For the cultural dimension of the process of application of mobile technologies in distance learning within the institutionalized blended educational process in higher education, it is important that the experience and expression of emotions is dependent on learned convictions or rules and, to the extent that cultures differ in the way they talk about and conceptualize emotions, how they are experienced and expressed will differ in different cultures as well (Cornelius, 1996). Consequently, taking into consideration the discipline culture, as emotional practitioners, students can make the process of application of mobile technologies in distance learning within the institutionalized blended educational process in higher education exciting or dull (Hargreaves, 2000). Moreover, students' interactions can be crucial in developing students' academic self-concept and enhancing their motivation and achievement (Komarraju, Musulkin & Bhattacharya, 2010). Thereby, on the one hand, emotion reflects the culture trait of a person (Harré, 1986), and, on the other hand, the emotions are social constructions (Averill, 1980).

Analysis of the inter-relationship between attitude and emotions contributes to the identification of attitude's indicators and constructs presented in Table 2.

Such constructs of verbal expression as a word or sentence may express a positive or negative meaning. For example, "excellent" is considered as a construct that demonstrates a positive attitude, "moderate" – neutral, and "bad" - negative.

Regarding non-verbal expression, smiling face means positive attitude, a neutral voice tone – neutral attitude, crossing one's arms – negative attitude.

Such constructs of cultural expression as applauding demonstrates positive attitude, listening without a comment – neutral, and turning one's back to a colleague – negative.

In distance learning within the institutionalized blended educational process of higher education, students' attitude is mediated via application of mobile technologies. By mobile technologies, smart phones, laptops, tablet personal computers, ultra compact computers, hybrid devices, etc. are meant as shown in Figure 16.

Mobile technologies are connected to the Internet via wireless access that ensures mobility in distance learning.

A couple of educational models of distance learning described by the Association to Advance Collegiate Schools of Business (AACSB) (AACSB International, 2007) exist in higher education such as:

- Distance learning means any learning system where teaching behaviors are separated from learning behaviors. The learner works alone, guided by study material arranged by the instructor in a location apart from students. Students have the opportunity to communicate with an instructor with the aid of a range of media (such as text, telephone, audio, video, computing and Internet technology, etc).
- Distance learning may be combined with various forms of face-to-face meetings.
- Remote access to learning materials, databases and libraries, electronic communication, computer-connected workgroups, archived lectures, and other features of distance learning increasingly are used in campus-based instruction.

Figure 16. Elements of mobile technologies

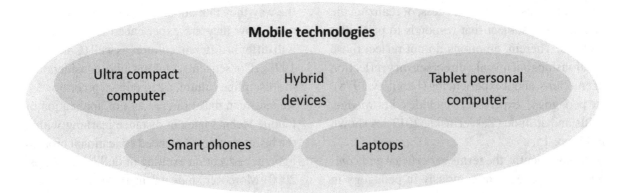

Figure 17. The relationship between higher education, institutionalized educational process and distance learning

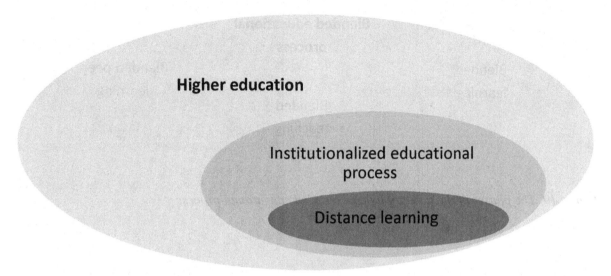

Analysis of these educational models of distance learning reveals that despite that fact that all the students' focus is put on distance learning, distance learning is not activated till teaching is provided. Thereby, distance learning is part of the institutionalized educational process in higher education as demonstrated in Figure 17.

Further on, analysis of these educational models of distance learning allows concluding that distance learning is inter-connected with teaching as well as blended teaching (archived lectures, databases, libraries, etc.). Moreover, the relationship between teaching and distance learning, in other words, the educational process of higher education have been transformed into the institutionalized blended educational process (Zaščerinska & Ahrens, 2013) that demands on the re-design of educational models of distance learning in higher education.

In the present research, educational process, training, instruction and educational act are employed synonymously. Consequently, educational process, training, instruction and educational act in formal higher education are considered as the institutionalized processes. Therein, by formal higher education, an organized higher education model (university, institution, college, academy, summer school, etc), systematic, structured and administered according to a given set of laws and norms is meant. Thereby, the institutionalized educational process has to be relevant to the university's (institution, college, academy, summer school, etc) requirements such as lecture or seminar framework. Thus, the institutionalized educational process is organized, systematized, structured and administered within formal higher education according to a given set of laws and norms. The institutionalized blended educational process includes blended teaching, blended peer-learning and blended learning as depicted in Figure 18.

The institutionalized blended educational process proceeds as demonstrated in Figure 19.

- From blended teaching in Phase 1.
- Through blended peer-learning in Phase 2.
- To blended learning in Phase 3.

Figure 18. Elements of the institutionalized blended educational process

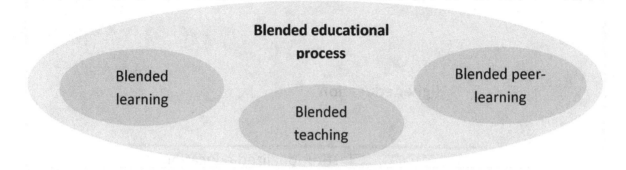

Figure 19. The phases of the institutionalized blended educational process

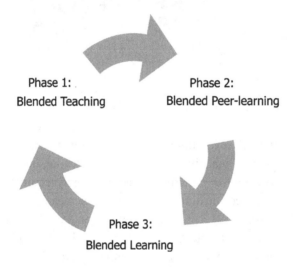

Blended teaching means a purposefully organized joint process of educator's sharing experience (knowledge, skills and attitudes) with students (Ahrens, Zaščerinska & Andreeva, 2013) via use of mobile technologies. Blended peer-learning is the sub-phase between blended teaching and blended learning in the institutionalized blended educational process. Blended peer-learning is aimed at students' interacting with each other via mobile technologies to learn something new. Therein, the blended teaching phase of the implementation of the institutionalized blended educational process is aimed at promoting students' motivation and their readiness to implement joint process. The blended peer-learning and blended learning phases of the implementation of the institutionalized blended educational process increase the level of difficulty in contents, students' autonomy, type of the institutionalized blended educational process, etc. Further on, each phase of the implementation of the institutionalized blended educational process is differentiated into two sub-levels as illustrated in Table 3, thereby providing opportunities for the development of students' competence (Maslo, 2006).

These phases and sub-phases of the implementation of the institutionalized blended educational process and corresponding six levels of students' competence determine the essence and sequence of the implementation of the institutionalized

Table 3. Levels of implementation of the institutionalized blended educational process

Phase of the Institutionalized Blended Educational Process	Sub-Phase of the Institutionalized Blended Educational Process	Level of Student's Competence
Phase 1 Blended Teaching	Sub-Phase 1 - Beginning of Phase 1	Level 1 - very low
	Sub-Phase 2 - End of Phase 1	Level 2 - low
Phase 2 Blended Peer-Learning	Sub-Phase 1 - Beginning of Phase 2	Level 3 - critical
	Sub-Phase 2 - End of Phase 2	Level 4 - average
Phase 3 Blended Learning	Sub-Phase 1 - Beginning of Phase 3	Level 5 - optimal
	Sub-Phase 2 - End of Phase 3	Level 6 - high

blended educational process. The implementation of the institutionalized blended educational process is described as following:

Phase 1 *Blended Teaching* is aimed at a safe environment for all the students. In order to provide a safe environment, the essence of constructive social interaction and its organizational regulations are considered by both the educator and students. The present phase of the institutionalized blended educational process is organized in a frontal way involving the students to participate. Blended teaching process is under educator's guidance.

- Educator makes previous experience rational. The institutionalized blended teaching process includes choice of forms and use of resources that motivates the students.
- Peers do not participate in guidance of the institutionalized blended educational process. This phase of the institutionalized blended educational process is carried out qualitatively only with the help of the educator. Dependence on the educator is observed. The students study alongside but not together.
- Students create the system of the aim and objectives, search for a variety of information source and obtain techniques of information compiling. Students fulfil the present phase of the institutionalized blended educational process qualitatively only with

the educator's help. Dependence on the educator is observed, not dependent on peers.

Phase 2 *Blended Peer-learning* is designed for the students' analysis of an open academic problem situation and their search for a solution. The same educational materials can be prepared for all of the group students. But these educational materials are different whereas learning styles and opportunities are different. This phase of the institutionalized blended educational process involves the students to act in peers.

- Educator functions as a resource and moderator. Educator delegates his/her duties to the students.
- Peers regulate each other: it is typical for students to regulate each other. The students study together, study from others and teach others. The present phase of the institutionalized blended educational process is under peer's guidance. Forms and methods of the institutionalized blended educational process are exchanged.
- The students fullfil the present phase of the institutionalized blended educational process qualitatively with the peers' help. Partial independence is observed. The relevant process is performed jointly with other students and with shared responsibility. It is typical for students to regulate each other.

Phase 3 *Blended Learning* emphasizes the students' self-regulation with use of assessment of the process and self-evaluation of the results.

- Educator functions as a consultant and an assistant. Educator delegates his/her duties to the students.
- Peers have consultative and advisory functions.
- Students' self-regulation is typical. The students learn independently. The students fulfil the present phase of the institutionalized blended educational process qualitatively on their own, and their independence is observed. The participants' self-regulation on the basis of the process assessment and the result of self-evaluation is used. The relevant activity is performed with a high sense of responsibility. Self-regulation is typical, and a student does not depend on peers.

The advantages of the blended educational process and, consequently, the institutionalized blended educational process are identified as follows:

- Widening opportunities for each student in order to construct the experience in social interaction and cognitive activity, and

- Promoting opportunities for self-realization.

Many researchers define blended learning as a combination of face-to-face (traditional classroom) and online instruction (Grgurovic, 2011; Qiu & Chen, 2011). Some authors suggest that blended learning proceeds in the educational act of two main phases (Porumb, Orza, Vlaicu, Porumb & Hoza, 2011) as shown in Figure 20:

- Regular teaching in Phase 1 and
- Internet-based learning in Phase 2.

However, learning is learning, and instruction (teaching, training) is instruction. Hence, learning is neither teaching or instruction, or training. This differentiation between blended instruction and blended learning is highly significant as blended instruction (teaching, training) does not provide positive results in the improvement of students' individual experience and, consequently, competence (knowledge, skills and attitudes) till blended learning is engaged (Ahrens et al, 2013). Blended (hybrid) learning is one of the approaches that is utilized to help students for meaningful learning via information and communication technologies (Gecer & Dag, 2012). In the present research, the process of blended learning proceeds as a cycle. The cycle of the process of blended learning of three phases is proposed, namely preparation in

Figure 20. The educational act of blended learning

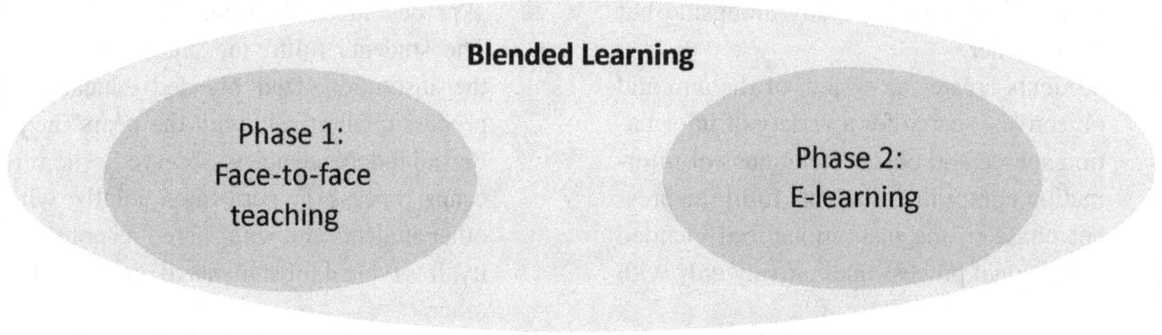

44

Figure 21. The cycle of the process of blended learning

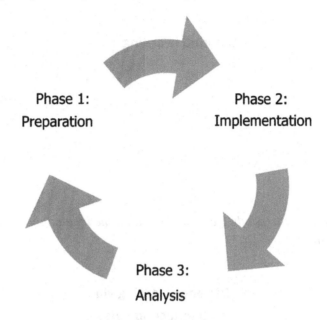

Phase 1:
Preparation

Phase 2:
Implementation

Phase 3:
Analysis

Phase 1, implementation in Phase 2 and analysis in Phase 3 as demonstrated in Figure 21.

Phase 1 *Preparation* is aimed at planning the implementation of blended learning, choosing forms of information compilation and using resources for the implementation of blended learning. Phase 2 *Implementation* is focused on analysis of an open problem situation and search for a solution. Phase 3 *Analysis* includes evaluation of the blended learning results and elaboration of further perspectives.

Blended learning is differentiated into learning and distance learning as depicted in Figure 22.

Moreover, the terms "distance learning" and "e-learning' are used synonymously in the present contribution. Distance learning is defined as a purposefully organized or spontaneous process of students' improvement of his/her individual experience and, consequently, competence (knowledge, skills and attitudes) based on cognition via use of mobile technologies. Hence, distance learning differs from learning by use of mobile technologies in the process of cognition. As higher education is centred on research, and research is a kind learning, distance learning in higher education

via use of mobile technologies as demonstrated in Figure 23 focuses on use of:

- University e-Libraries,
- Patent databases such as European Patent Office (EPO), US Patent and Trademark Office (PTO),
- Bibliographic databases such as SciVerse Scopus (SCOPUS), Thomson Reuters, Education Resources Information Center (ERIC),
- Research communities' networks such as www.researchgate.com, www.ResearcherID.com, etc.

University e-Libraries provide access to eResources such as electronic resources, i.e., online journals, indexes, databases, and books that is restricted by licenses with vendors to university's students, faculty, and staff. A particular university's students, faculty, and staff have off-campus access that is only ensured to these licensed eResources.

Patent database enables users to search the full text of multiple international patent collections.

Figure 22. The relationship between blended learning, learning and distance learning

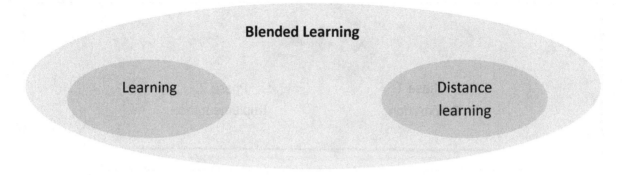

Figure 23. Distance learning via mobile technologies within the institutionalized blended educational process in higher education

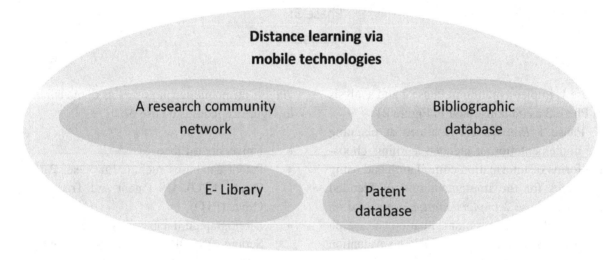

Users can search published applications, granted patents and utility models mostly from 1985 to the present time. The data available includes full text patents, English machine translations and full document images. These collections are periodically updated to include additional years of coverage.

A bibliographic database is a database of bibliographic records, an organized digital collection of references to published literature, including journal and newspaper articles, conference proceedings, reports, government and legal publications, patents, books, etc. In contrast to library catalogue entries, a large proportion of the bibliographic records in bibliographic databases describe articles, conference papers, etc., rather than complete monographs, and they generally contain very rich subject descriptions in the form of keywords, subject classification terms, or abstracts (Feather & Sturges, 2003). A bibliographic database may be general in scope or cover a specific academic discipline. A significant number of bibliographic databases are still proprietary, available by licensing agreement from vendors, or directly from the indexing and abstracting services that create them (Reitz, 2004). Many bibliographic databases evolve into digital libraries, providing the full-text of the indexed contents. Others converge with non-bibliographic scholarly databases to create more complete disciplinary search engine systems, such as Chemical Abstracts or Entrez.

Research community networks in the present contribution mean use of web-based tools to discover and use research and scholarly information about people and resources (Clinical and Translational Science Award, 2012). Research community networking tools serve as knowledge management systems for the research enterprise. Research community networking tools connect institution-level/enterprise systems, national research networks, publicly available research data (e.g., grants and publications), and restricted/proprietary data by harvesting information from disparate sources into compiled expertise profiles for faculty, investigators, scholars, clinicians, community partners, and facilities. Research community networks are designed for such target groups as (Barnett & Jardines, 2012):

- Investigators
  - To discover potential collaborators,
  - More rapidly and competitively to form teams,
  - To identify targeted grant opportunities and
  - To create digital vitae,
- Administrators
  - To work with better data for institutional business intelligence,
  - To better assess performance for annual reviews,
  - To recruit new faculty and attract students,
- Researchers
  - To study networks of science teams to improve research effectiveness.

Research community networks (Barnett & Jardines, 2012) include four technology components such as:

- A controlled vocabulary (eg., the VIVO Ontology) for data interoperability,
- An architecture for data integration and sharing (Linked Open Data),
- Applications for collaboration, funding, business intelligence, or administration, and
- Rich faculty profile data of publications, grants, classes, affiliations, interests, etc.

Further on, repositories of profile data need to talk to institutional systems like faculty directories (Barnett & Jardines, 2012).

Research community networks' tools facilitate the development of new collaborations and team science to address new or existing research challenges through the rapid discovery and recommendation of researchers, expertise, and resources (Carey, 2011; Fazel-Zarandi, Devlin, Huang & Contractor, 2011).

Research community networks' tools differ from search engines such as Google in that they access information in databases and other data not limited to web pages. They also differ from social networking systems such as LinkedIn or Facebook in that they represent a compendium of data ingested from authoritative and verifiable sources rather than predominantly individually asserted information, making research community networks' tools more reliable (Gewin, 2010). Yet, research community networks' tools have sufficient flexibility to allow for profile editing. Research community networks' tools also provide resources to bolster human connector systems: they can make non-intuitive matches, they do not depend on serendipity, and they do not have a propensity to return only to previously identified collaborations/collaborators (Contractor & Monge, 2002). Research community networks' tools also generally have associated analytical capabilities that enable evaluation of collaboration and cross-disciplinary research/scholarly activity, especially over time.

Importantly, data harvested into robust research community networks' tools is accessible for broad repurposing, especially if available as linked open data (RDF triples). Thus, research community networks' tools enhance research support activities by providing:

- Data for customized,
- Up-to-date web pages,
- CV/biosketch generation, and
- Data tables for grant proposals.

A short description of a research community network such as *ResearchGate* gives a short overview of functions of a research community network: ResearchGate is a social networking site for scientists and researchers to share papers, ask and answer questions, and find collaborators (Lin, 2012). The site has been described as a mashup of "Facebook, Twitter and LinkedIn" that includes "profile pages, comments, groups, job listings, and 'like' and 'follow' buttons" (Lin, 2012). Members are encouraged to share raw data and failed experiment results as well as successes, in order to avoid repeating their peers' scientific research mistakes (Dolan, 2012). Microsoft co-founder Bill Gates is among the company's investors (Levy, 2013). ResearchGate announced in 2013 that the site had two million members.

Research community networks demonstrate such opportunities as (Barnett & Jardines, 2012):

- Support to innovative team building approaches,
- Provision of richer data for comparative institutional studies, and
- Potential for national networks of collaborative research.

Research community networks reveal the existence of such threats as (Barnett & Jardines, 2012):

- Some desired data are private (eg., award amounts) or restricted (eg., FERPA),

- Negotiation between research and administrative efforts is required, and
- Efforts threaten established networks of research influence.

For the success of research community networks, such issues are to be considered as (Barnett & Jardines, 2012):

- Leveraging existing institutional efforts for research networking and annual faculty review,
- Understanding institutional culture and policy for faculty information sharing,
- Making the technology investments to develop the required new capabilities, and
- Identifying sources of available high quality profile data (institutional, corporate, federal, Linked Open Data cloud),
- Use of existing research or administrative initiatives and workflows that manage profile data,
- Overcome of institutional cultures that may not prevent data use for research networking, and
- Bringing together (typically) multiple initiatives that manage faculty profile data in a sustainable institutional strategy.

EMPIRICAL STUDY

The present part of the contribution demonstrates:

- The design of the empirical research,
- Survey results, and
- Findings of the comparative study.

The design of the present empirical research comprised the purpose and question, sample and methodology of the present empirical study as demonstrated in Figure 24.

The question of the empirical study was as follows: are there any similarities and differences

Figure 24. Elements of the design of the present empirical research

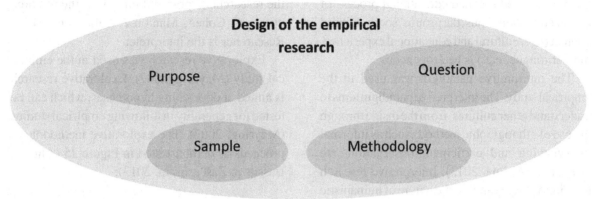

between business and engineering students' attitude to mobile technologies in distance learning?

The purpose of the empirical study was to compare business and engineering students' attitude to mobile technologies in distance learning underpinning elaboration of a hypothesis.

The present empirical study involved:

- 13 second-year bachelor part-time students of the *Business Management* programme of the Northern Business School, Neumuenster, Germany, in January 2014, and
- 23 engineering students of Baltic Summer School *Technical Informatics and Information Technology* held at Vilnius Gediminas Technical University, Vilnius, Lithuania, July 20 - August 4, 2013.

It should be noted that the *Business Management* part-time programme of the Northern Business School, Neumuenster, Germany, as well as Baltic Summer School *Technical Informatics and Information Technology* held at Vilnius Gediminas Technical University, Vilnius, Lithuania, are organised as formal higher education institutions, thereby they are based on the institutionalized blended educational process of higher education.

The respondents of 13 second-year bachelor part-time students of the *Business Management* programme of the Northern Business School, Neumuenster, Germany, in January 2014 included seven male and six female students. The age of students ranged between 20 and 50. All the students obtained working experience in different fields of business. Although the students studied in the same group, they represented different cultures, namely, German, Polish and Russian.

The respondents of 23 engineering students of Baltic Summer School *Technical Informatics and Information Technology* held at Vilnius Gediminas Technical University, Vilnius, Lithuania, July 20 - August 4, 2013 involved four female and 19 males. The age of the respondents differentiated from 22 to 35. All 23 students had got Bachelor Degree in different fields of engineering and computing. Working experience of the students was different, too. The students represented the cultures of Lithuania, Russia, Poland, Pakistan, France, Estonia, Serbia, Czech Republic, Finland, Ireland, Germany, Mexico, Georgia and Ethiopia.

Therefore, the sample is multicultural as the respondents with different cultural backgrounds and diverse educational approaches were chosen. Students' different cultural and educational experience emphasized the significance of each student's contribution to the analysis of their attitude to mobile technologies in distance learning within the institutionalized blended educational process of higher education. Thus, the groups' socio-cultural context (age, cultural and educational experience, mother tongue, etc.) is heterogeneous.

The interpretive paradigm was used in the empirical study. The interpretive paradigm aims to understand other cultures, from the inside through the use of ethnographic methods such as informal interviewing and participant observation, etc (Taylor & Medina, 2013). Interpretive research paradigm corresponds to the nature of humanistic pedagogy (Luka, 2008). The interpretive paradigm creates an environment for the development of any individual and helps them to develop their potential (Luka, 2008). The core of this paradigm is human experience, people's mutual everyday interaction that tends to understand the subjectivity of human experience (Luka, 2008). The paradigm is aimed at understanding people's activity, how a certain activity is exposed in a certain environment, time, conditions, i.e., how it is exposed in a certain socio-cultural context (Luka, 2008). Thus, the interpretive paradigm is oriented towards one's conscious activity, and it is future-oriented (Luka,

2008). Interpretive paradigm is characterized by the researcher's practical interest in the research question (Cohen, Manion & Morrison, 2003). Researcher is the interpreter.

Explorative research was used in the empirical study (Mayring, 2007). Explorative research is aimed at developing hypotheses, which can be tested for generality in following empirical studies (Mayring, 2007). The explorative methodology proceeds as demonstrated in Figure 25 (Ahrens, Bassus & Zaščerinska, 2013):

- From exploration in Phase 1.
- Through analysis in Phase 2.
- To hypothesis development in Phase 3.

Phase 1 *Exploration* is aimed at data collection. Phase 2 *Analysis* focuses on data processing, analysis and data interpretation. Phase 3 *Hypothesis Development* ensures analysis of results of the empirical study and elaboration of conclusions and hypotheses for further research.

In order to analyse the students' feedback regarding their attitude to mobile technologies in distance learning within the institutionalized

Figure 25. Methodology of the explorative research

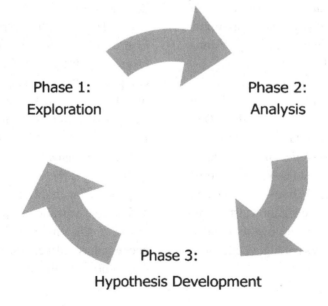

Table 4. Indicator and levels of students' attitude to mobile technologies in distance learning

Indicator	Levels				
	Level 1	Level 2	Level 3	Level 4	Level 5
	Very Low	Low	Average	Optimal	High
	1	2	3	4	5
Verbal expression	Strongly disagree Very negative	Disagree Negative	Neither disagree nor agree Neither negative nor positive	Agree Positive	Strongly agree Very positive

blended educational process of higher education, the informal structured interviews were based on the following question: Do you use mobile technologies in distance learning? Only verbal expression of business and engineering students' attitude to mobile technologies in distance learning was taken into consideration. The evaluation scale of five levels for the question was given, namely, strongly disagree "1", disagree "2", neither disagree nor agree „3", agree "4", and strongly agree "5". The evaluation scale was transformed into the level system as illustrated in Table 4.

The business students' results of the question (students' attitude to mobile technologies in distance learning) used in the informal structured interviews are demonstrated in Figure 26 where:

- The vertical numbers show five levels to measure students' attitude to mobile technologies in distance learning, and
- The horizontal numbers present the code number of the business student who participated in the survey.

The business students' results of the question (students' attitude to mobile technologies in distance learning) reveal that:

- One business student's evaluation of his/her attitude to mobile technologies in distance learning refers to the low level,
- Two business students' evaluation of their attitude to mobile technologies in distance learning refers to the optimal level,

- 10 business students' evaluation of their attitude to mobile technologies in distance learning refers to the high level.

In comparison, the engineering students' results of the question (students' attitude to mobile technologies in distance learning) in the informal structured interviews are shown in Figure 27.

The engineering students' results of the question (students' attitude to mobile technologies in distance learning) reveal that:

- One engineering student's evaluation of his/her attitude to mobile technologies in distance learning refers to the low level,
- Three engineering students' evaluation of their attitude to mobile technologies in distance learning refers to the average level,
- Three engineering students' evaluation of their attitude to mobile technologies in distance learning refers to the optimal level,
- 16 engineering students' evaluation of their attitude to mobile technologies in distance learning refers to the high level.

The comparison of the results of the question (students' attitude to mobile technologies in distance learning) shows that the majority of both business and engineering students' evaluate their attitude to mobile technologies in distance learning to be of the high level.

The data were processed applying *Excel* software.

Figure 26. The business students' results of the question (students' attitude to mobile technologies in distance learning)

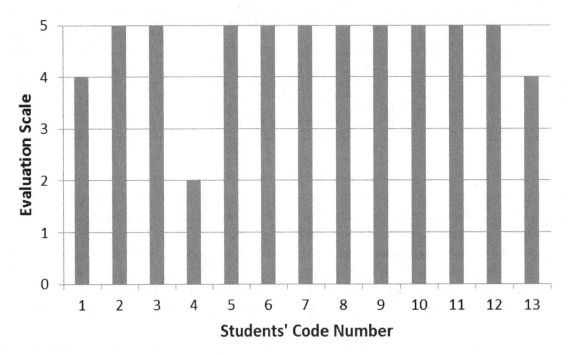

Figure 27. The engineering students' results of the question (students' attitude to mobile technologies in distance learning)

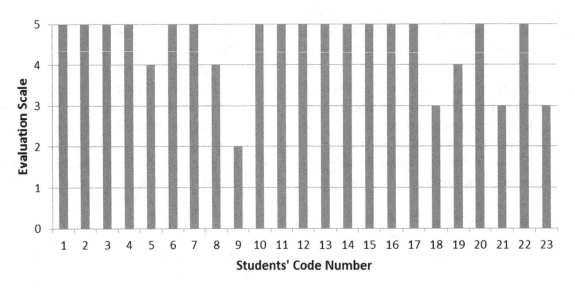

Table 5. Frequency of the students' answers

Question	Levels	Students' Group	Number of Answers	Percentage
Do you use mobile technologies in distance learning?	Very Low	business	0	0%
		engineering	0	0%
	Low	business	1	8%
		engineering	1	4%
	Average	business	0	0%
		engineering	3	13%
	Optimal	business	2	15%
		engineering	3	13%
	High	business	10	77%
		engineering	16	70%

Frequencies of the business and engineering students' answers were determined in order to reveal students' attitude to mobile technologies in distance learning as shown in Table 5.

The comparison of the frequencies of business and engineering students' answers to the question (students' attitude to mobile technologies in distance learning) shows that the majority of both business and engineering students evaluate their attitude to mobile technologies in distance evaluates learning to be of the high level (77% and 70% respectively).

Further on, the mean results determine the high level of both business and engineering students' attitude to mobile technologies in distance learning (4.6 and 4.5 respectively) as shown in Table 6.

The findings of the empirical study allow concluding that both business and engineering students demonstrated the high level of attitude to mobile technologies in distance learning (4.6 and 4.5 respectively). The summarizing content analysis (Mayring, 2004) of the data reveals that both business and engineering students' attitude to mobile technologies in distance learning within the institutionalized blended educational process of higher education is homogeneous.

Table 6. Mean results

Question	Levels	Students' Group	Number of Answers	Percentage
Do you use mobile technologies in distance learning?	Very Low	business	0	Business students 4.6
		engineering	0	
	Low	business	1	
		engineering	1	
	Average	business	0	
		engineering	3	Engineering students 4.5
	Optimal	business	2	
		engineering	3	
	High	business	10	
		engineering	16	

CONCLUSION

The theoretical findings on the inter-relationship between students' attitude, mobile technologies and distance learning within the institutionalized blended educational process of higher education in the present research allow determining such outcome and criterion of use of mobile technologies in distance learning within the institutionalized blended educational process of higher education as students' attitude.

The findings of the present empirical study allow drawing conclusions that both business and engineering students' attitude to mobile technologies in distance learning within the institutionalized blended educational process of higher education is positive. Students' positive attitude to mobile technologies in distance learning is considered as a favourable opportunity for the increase of the level of students' knowledge and skills as well as competence, in general.

Further on, validity and reliability of the research results have been provided by involving other researchers into several stages of the conducted research. External validity has been revealed by international co-operation as following:

- Working out the present contribution in co-operation with international colleagues and
- Assessment of the present research by international colleagues on the basis of co-operation between universities,
- Participation in workshops given by the international colleagues,
- Presentations of the research at international conferences and
- Use of individual consultations given by the Western researchers.

Therein, the researchers' positive external evaluation of the research of the present contribution validates the findings of the present research.

The following hypothesis has been formulated: students' positive attitude to mobile technologies in distance learning within the institutionalized blended educational process of higher education promotes the increase of the level of students' knowledge and skills as well as competence in general if:

- A favourable blended educational (blended teaching, blended peer-learning and blended learning) environment focused on use of mobile technologies in distance learning is organized within the institutionalized blended educational process of higher education,
- Students are externally motivated to use mobile technologies in distance learning within the institutionalized blended educational process of higher education by
  - Asking students to consider the preconceptions about subject-related topics that they bring to the distance learning (Etkina & Mestre, 2004),
  - Educators' adapting teaching styles (Movahedzadeh, 2011) to the student while use of mobile technologies in distance learning within the institutionalized blended educational process of higher education,
  - Showing students the relevance of the learning topics to their everyday lives (Movahedzadeh, 2011),
- Students as well as educators are provided with technical support in use of mobile technologies in distance learning within the institutionalized blended educational process of higher education,
- Educators are ensured training courses focused on use of mobile technologies in distance learning within the institutionalized blended educational process of higher education.

The present research has limitations. The interconnections between students' attitude, emotions, mobile technologies, distance learning and the institutionalized blended educational process of higher education have been set. Another limitation is the empirical study conducted by involving only the business and engineering students. Therein, the results of the study cannot be representative for the whole area. Nevertheless, the results of the research, namely an outcome, indicators, constructs and levels of students' attitude to mobile technologies in distance learning within the institutionalized blended educational process of higher education, may be used as a basis of analysis of students' attitude to mobile technologies in distance learning in other institutions. If the results of other institutions had been available for analysis, different results could have been attained. There is a possibility to continue the study.

Further research tends to analyse students' attitude to mobile technologies in distance learning within the institutionalized blended educational process in higher education on the basis of the methodological background different from the methodological background of the present contribution, namely the System-Constructivist Theory introduced as the New or Social Constructivism Pedagogical Theory. Further on, application of another methodological approach different from the methodological approach of the present contribution, namely the outcome based approach, to the analysis of students' attitude to mobile technologies in distance learning within the institutionalized blended educational process in higher education is proposed. Future research intends to re-shape applications of mobile technologies in distance learning within the institutionalized blended educational process in higher education. Students' extrinsic motivation on a positive attitude to mobile technologies in distance learning has to be further investigated. The relationship between human emotions and age has to be further analysed, too. An educational model that comprises five phases of the institutionalized blended educational

process in higher education to be implemented for the improvement of students' distance learning via mobile technologies is of great research interest:

- Blended teaching,
- Blended teaching with the elements of blended peer-learning,
- Blended peer-learning,
- Blended peer-learning with the elements of blended learning, and
- Blended learning.

Teaching methods of use of mobile technologies in distance learning that increase students' positive attitude to mobile technologies in distance learning are of great interest for a scientific discussion. Efficiency of use of mobile technologies in distance learning within the institutionalized blended educational process of higher education could be analysed in future. The search for relevant methods, tools and techniques for evaluation of students' attitude to mobile technologies in distance learning is proposed. Further research tends to implement empirical studies in other students' groups. Further empirical studies could be focused on the analysis of other indicators of attitude, namely, non-verbal and cultural expression. Constructs of students' attitude to mobile technologies in distance learning are to be further polished. A comparative study of students' groups of other university's programmes is to be proposed. Particularly, a study of student teachers' attitude to use of mobile technologies in distance learning is to be ensured as teachers have a two-fold role:

- In society, teachers are the agents of change and,
- In education and training, teachers are the key actors for the development of learners' use of mobile technologies in distance learning.

A comparative research as well as studies of other countries could be carried out, too.

REFERENCES

Ahrens, A., Bassus, O., & Zaščerinska, J. (2013). Engineering Students' Direct Experience in Entrepreneurship. In *Proceedings of 6th ICEBE International Conference on Engineeirng and Business Education Innovation, Entrepreneurship and Sustainability*, (pp. 93-100). Wismar, Germany: University of Wismar.

Ahrens, A., & Zaščerinska, J. (2010). Social Dimension of Web 2.0 in Student Teacher Professional Development. In *Proceedings of Association for Teacher Education in Europe Spring Conference 2010: Teacher of the 21st Century: Quality Education for Quality Teaching,* (pp. 179-186). Riga, Latvia: University of Latvia.

Ahrens, A., Zaščerinska, J., & Andreeva, N. (2013). Engineering Students' Blended Learning in Higher Education. In *Proceedings of International Scientifical Conference Society, Integration, Education of Rezekne Higher Education Institution Faculty of Education and Design Personality Socialization Research Institute in collaboration with Department of Civil Engineering and Architecture*, (vol. 1, pp. 34-44). Rēzekne, Latvia: Rēzeknes Augstskolas Izdevniecība 2013.

Al-Musawi, N., Al-Bustan, A. A., & Al-Mezel, S. M. (2013). Developing a Scale to Measure Attitudes of University Students towards E-learning. In *Proceedings of Association for Teacher Education in Europe (ATEE) Winter Conference "Learning & Teaching with Media & Technology"* (pp. 13-20). Brussels: Association for Teacher Education in Europe (ATEE).

Association to Advance Collegiate Schools of Business (AACSB) International. (2007). *Quality Issues in Distance Learning*. Tampa, FL: The Association to Advance Collegiate Schools of Business. Retrieved from http://www.aacsb.edu/publications/whitepapers/quality-issues-distance-learning.pdf

Averill, J. R. (1980). A constructivist view of emotion. *Emotion: Theory, Research and Experience, 1*, 305-339.

Barnett, W., & Jardines, J. (2012). *Technology now: Research Networking*. Washington, DC: The Clinical and Translational Science Award (CTSA) Research Networking Affinity Group. Retrieved from https://www.aamc.org/download/278098/data/technologynowresearchnetworking.pdf

Bassus, O., & Zaščerinska, J. (2012). *Innovation and Higher Education*. Berlin: Mensch & Buch.

Berg, A. (2005). Factors related to observed attitude change toward learning chemistry among university students. *Chemistry Education Research and Practice, 6*(1), 1–18. doi:10.1039/b4rp90001d

Carey, J. (2011). Faculty of 1000 and VIVO: Invisible colleges and team science. *Issues in Science and Technology Librarianship, 65*.

Clinical and Translational Science Award (CTSA) Research Networking Affinity Group. (2012). *Clinical and Translational Science Award (CTSA) Research Networking Evaluation Guide*. Retrieved from https://www.ctsacentral.org/documents/CTSA-RN-Guide.pdf

Cohen, L., Manion, L., & Morrsion, K. (2003). *Research Methods in Education*. London: Routledge/Falmer Taylor & Francis Group.

Contractor, N. S., & Monge, P. R. (2002, November). Managing knowledge networks. *Management Communication Quarterly, 16*(2), 249–258. doi:10.1177/089331802237238

Cornelius, R. R. (1996). *The science of emotion: Research and tradition in the psychology of emotion*. New York: Prentice Hall.

Crites, S., Fabrigar, L. R., & Petty, R. E. (1994). Measuring the affective and cognitive properties of attitudes: Conceptual and methodological issues. *Personality and Social Psychology Bulletin, 20*(6), 619–634. doi:10.1177/0146167294206001

De Vierville, J. P. (1999). Emotion. *Electronic library of Waikato University*. Retrieved from http://72.14.253.104/search?q=cache:lqr5mSpe6MQJ: ww.accd.edu/spc/mitchell/powerpoint3d/emotion.ppt+definition+of+emotion&hl=zh-CN&ct=clnk&cd=6

Dolan, K. A. How Ijad Madisch Aims To Disrupt Science Research With A Social Network. *Forbes*. Retrieved from http://www.forbes.com/sites/kerryadolan/2012/07/19/how-ijad-madisch-aims-to-disrupt-science-research-with-a-social-network/

Etkina, E., & Mestre, J. P. (2004). *Implications of Learning Research for Teaching Science to Non-Science Majors*. Washington, DC: SENCER. Retrieved from http://www.sencer.net/Resources/pdfs/Backgrounders/ImplicationsofLearningResearchforTeachingScience.pdf

European Commission Directorate-General for Education and Culture. (2004). *Implementation of "Education and Training 2010" Work Programme: Working Group B "Key Competences" Key Competences for Lifelong Learning*. a European Reference Framework. Retrieved from http://europa.eu/legislation_summaries/education_training_youth/lifelong_learning/c11090_en.htm

Fazel-Zarandi, M., Devlin, H. J., Huang, Y., & Contractor, N. (2011). Expert recommendation based on social drivers, social network analysis, and semantic data representation. In *Proceedings of 2nd International Workshop on Information Heterogeneity and Fusion in Recommender Systems* (pp. 41-48). New York: Association for Computing Machinery. doi:10.1145/2039320.2039326

Feather, J., & Sturges, P. (Eds.). (2003). *International Encyclopedia of Information and Library Science* (2nd ed.). London: Routledge.

Ferreira, J. B., Klein, A. Z., Freitas, A., & Schlemmer, E. (2013). Mobile Learning: Definition, Uses and Challenges. In L. A. Wankel & P. Blessinger (Ed.), Increasing Student Engagement and Retention Using Mobile Applications: Smartphones, Skype and Texting Technologies (Cutting-edge Technologies in Higher Education, Volume 6) (pp. 47-82). Bingley, UK: Emerald Group Publishing Limited.

Gecer, A., & Dag, F. (2012). A Blended Learning Experience. *Educational Sciences: Theory and Practice*, *12*(1), 438–442.

Gewin, V. (2010, December 15). Collaboration: Social networking seeks critical mass. *Nature*, *468*(7326), 993–994. doi:10.1038/nj7326-993a

Grgurovic, M. (2011). Blended Learning in an ESL Class: A Case Study. *CALICO Journal*, *29*(1), 100–117. doi:10.11139/cj.29.1.100-117

Groeben, N. (1986). *Handeln, Tun, Verhalten als Einheiten einer verstehend-erklärenden Psychologie*. Tübingen: Francke.

Hargreaves, A. (1998). The emotional practice of teaching. *Teaching and Teacher Education*, *14*(8), 835–854. doi:10.1016/S0742-051X(98)00025-0

Harmer, J. (2001). *The Practice of English Language Teaching*. London: Longman.

Harré, R. (1986). *The social construction of emotion*. New York: Basil Blackwell.

Huber, G. (2004). *Cooperative learning*. Riga, Latvia: RaKa.

Komarraju, M., Musulkin, S., & Bhattacharya, G. (2010). Role of Student-Faculty Interactions in Developing College Students' Academic Self-Concept, Motivation, and Achievement. *Journal of College Student Development*, *51*(3), 332–342. doi:10.1353/csd.0.0137

Kriumane, L. (2013). *Mūzikas skolotāja emocionālās kompetences pilnveide augstskolas studiju procesā*. (Unpublished doctoral dissertation). University of Latvia, Riga, Latvia.

Lasmanis, A. (2003). *Māksla apstrādāt datus: pirmie soļi*. Riga, Latvia: "P&K". (in Latvian).

Leont'ev, A. N. (1978). *Activity, Consciousness, and Personality*. Prentice-Hall.

Levy, A. (2013). Bill Gates Joins $35 Million Funding in Startup ResearchGate. *Bloomberg*. Retrieved from http://www.bloomberg.com/news/2013-06-04/bill-gates-joins-35-million-investment-in-startup-researchgate.html

Lin, T. (2012). Cracking Open the Scientific Process. *The New York Times*. Retrieved from http://www.nytimes.com/2012/01/17/science/open-science-challenges-journal-tradition-with-web-collaboration.html?ref=thomaslin&_r=0

Luhmann, N. (1988). *Erkenntnis als Konstruktion*. Bern: Benteli.

Lūka, I. (2008). Development of Students' ESP Competence and Educator's Professional Activity in Tertiary Level Tourism Studies. In *Proceedings of ATEE Spring University Conference Teacher of the 21st Century: Quality Education for Quality Teaching* (pp. 689-697). Riga, Latvia: University of Latvia.

Maslo, E. (2007). Transformative Learning Space for Life-Long Foreign Languages Learning. In *Proceedings of International Nordic-Baltic Region Conference of FIPLV Innovations in Language Teaching and Learning in the Multicultural Context* (pp. 38-46). Rīga: SIA "Izglītības soļi".

Maslo, I. (2006). Kompetences jēdziena izpratnes daudzveidība un ar to saistītas problēmas Latvijas izglītības organizācijas sistēmas izveidē. In I. Maslo (Ed), *No zināšanām uz kompetentu darbību*, (pp. 46.-56). Riga, Latvia: Latvijas Universitātes Akadēmiskais apgāds. (in Latvian).

Mayring, P. (2004). Qualitative Content Analysis. In U. Flick, E. Von Kardoff, & I. Steinke (Eds.), *A Companion to Qualitative Research* (pp. 266–269). Glasgow, UK: SAGE.

Mayring, P. (2007). On Generalization in Qualitatively Oriented Research. *Forum Qualitative Sozialforschung / Forum: Qualitative. Social Research*, *8*(3), 1–8.

McRae, K., Ochsner, K. N., Mauss, I. B., Gabrieli, J. J. D., & Gross, J. J. (2008). Gender Differences in Emotion Regulation: An fMRI Study of Cognitive Reappraisal. *Group Processes & Intergroup Relations*, *11*(2), 143–162. doi:10.1177/1368430207088035

Mead, G. H. (1973). *Geist, Identitat, und Gesselschaft*. Frankfurt: A. M.

Movahedzadeh, F. (2011). Improving Students' Attitude Toward Science Through Blended Learning. *International Journal Science Education and Civic Engagement, 3*(2).

Ong, C. H., & Lai, J. Y. (2006). Gender differences in perceptions and relationships among dominants of elearning acceptance. *Computers in Human Behavior*, *22*(5), 816–829. doi:10.1016/j.chb.2004.03.006

Palmer, S. A., & Holt, D. M. (2009). Students' perceptions of the value of the elements of an online learning environment: Looking back in moving forward. *Interactive Learning Environments*, *18*(2), 135–151. doi:10.1080/09539960802364592

Parsons, T. (1976). *Theorie sozialer Systeme*. Opladen: Westdeutscher Verlag. doi:10.1007/978-3-322-83798-1

Pintrich, P. R. (1994). Student motivation in the college classroom. In K. W. Prichard & R. M. Sawyer (Eds.), *Handbook of college teaching theory and applications* (pp. 23–43). Westport, CT: Greenwood.

Porumb, S., Orza, B., Vlaicu, A., Porumb, C., & Hoza, I. (2011). Cloud Computing and its Application to Blended Learning in Engineering. In *Proceedings of Cloud Computing 2011: The Second International Conference on Cloud Computing, GRIDs, and Virtualization*. Red Hook, NJ: Curran Associates.

Qiu, M., & Chen, L. (2011). A Problem-based Learning Approach to Teaching an Advanced Software Engineering Course.In *Proceedings of 2nd International Workshop on Education Technology and Computer Science* (pp. 252-255). Los Alamitos, CA: The Printing House.

Reich, K. (2005). *Systemisch-konstruktivistische Pädagogik*. Beltz: Weinheim u.a.

Reitz, J. M. (2004). Bibliographic database. In *Dictionary for Library and Information Science*. Westport, CT: Libraries Unlimited.

Rudzinska, I. (2008). The Quality of Aim Setting and Achieved Results in English for Specific Purposes-Study Course in Lecturers and Students' Opinion. In *Proceedings of the ATEE Spring University Conference Teacher of the 21st Century: Quality Education for Quality Teaching* (pp. 366-373). Riga, Latvia: University of Latvia.

Špona, A., & Čehlova, Z. (2004). *Pētniecība pedagoģijā*. Riga, Latvia: RaKa. (in Latvian)

Surikova, S. (2007). *Organisation of Micro-group Activity for the Improvement of Pupils' Social Competence*. (Unpublished Dissertation). University of Latvia, Riga, Latvia.

Taylor, P. C., & Medina, M. N. D. (2013). Educational Research Paradigms: From Positivism to Multiparadigmatic. *The Journal of Meaning-Centered Education, 1*.

Vlăsceanu, L., Grünberg, L., & Pârlea, D. (2004). *Quality Assurance and Accreditation: A Glossary of Basic Terms and Definitions*. Bucharest: UNESCO.

Zaščerinska, J. (2013). *Development of Students' Communicative Competence within English for Academic Purposes Studies*. Berlin: Mensch & Buch.

Zaščerinska, J., & Ahrens, A. (2013). E-business Applications to Students' Blended Learning in Higher Education. In *Proceedings of the 4th International Conference on Data Communication Networking (DC NET 2013), 10th International Conference on e-Business (ICE-B 2013) and 4th International Conference on Optical Communication Systems (OPTICS 2013)*, (pp. 290-297). Lisboa, Portugal: SciTePress - Science and Technology Publications.

KEY TERMS AND DEFINITIONS

Attitude: A combination of evaluative judgments about a phenomenon (Crites, Fabrigar, Petty, 1994).

Blended (Hybrid) Learning: One of the approaches that is utilized to help students for meaningful learning via information and communication technologies (Gecer, Dag, 2004).

Blended Teaching: A purposefully organized joint process of educator's sharing experience (knowledge, skills and attitudes) with students (Ahrens, Zaščerinska, Andreeva, 2013) with use of mobile technologies.

Distance Learning: A purposefully organized or spontaneous process of students' improvement of his/her individual experience (knowledge, skills and attitudes) based on cognition with use of mobile technologies.

Institutionalized Educational Process: A process organized, systematized, structured and administered within formal higher education according to a given set of laws and norms.

Mobile Technologies: Smart phones, laptops, tablet personal computers, ultra compact computers, hybrid devices, etc.

Students' Attitude: A part of competence as competence includes knowledge, skills and attitudes.

Chapter 3
Using iPads in University Mathematics Classes:
What Do the Students Think?

Rim Gouia
American University of Sharjah, UAE

Cindy Gunn
American University of Sharjah, UAE

Diana Audi
American University of Sharjah, UAE

ABSTRACT

This chapter reports on two studies carried out with first-year undergraduate students in Mathematics classes. The first study investigates regular use of iPads over the course of one semester. Overall, the students reported positive impressions regarding the use of iPads in their Mathematics classes. However, only 47% stated that they would join an iPad class in future semesters. The second study is a qualitative follow-up to the first to find out why the majority said they would not join an iPad class in the future. The students in the two studies could see both the value and the drawbacks that the use of iPads in their Mathematics classes would provide. The findings suggest that as supplement to instruction the use of iPads has the potential to enhance the learning process, but classes delivered using iPads only would not meet the educational requirements or expectations of the study's participants.

INTRODUCTION

The move towards mobile learning has been on the rise world-wide in both K-12 and higher education since the beginning of the 21st Century (Motiwalla, 2007, Sharples, 2002). However, according to Wishart and Green (2010) the use of mobile devices in higher education has been on a smaller scale compared to K-12 institutions. In their investigation of iPads in higher education, Gawelek, Spataro and Komarny (2011) found that faculty and students who do use iPads do so for convenience, portability, communication, information gathering, note taking, reading, and interactive work. In another study in

DOI: 10.4018/978-1-4666-7316-8.ch003

2011, looking into mobile technologies and apps in higher education, Khaddage, Lattemann and Bray also found that the use of mobile devices in higher education is limited. This may quickly change as per the 2013 NMC Horizon Report which listed tablet use in classrooms in Higher Education as a key trend with a time to adoption being one year or less. As Salmon points out, "as we move forward, higher education will become increasingly mobile, resulting in students carrying their university in their pockets" (2012, para 1). Reasons for this include students' familiarity with technology and the wide, and reasonably priced, availability of smart phones and tablets. However, as Matias and Wolf point out, "mobile learning is not just about using or learning with a mobile device. The appeal of mobile learning is about learning across contexts such that the nature of the learning is mediated through the portable technology" (2013, p. 118).

Reasons for the growth in mobile learning include more than availability of devices; it also has to do with the changing student population and their expectations. As Fee (2009) notes, "today's young people have been using digital technology from a very early age: desktop and laptop computers, games consoles, mobile/cellular phones and other handheld devices, and all the connectivity of the internet" (p. 2).Some believe that this early and ongoing exposure to technology has created a new kind of environment for the current generation to grow and learn (Holmes & Gardner, 2006, Warschauer, 2003). White and Le Cornu (2011) proposed the term "digital residents" to describe, not only today's students, but anyone who:

...see [s]the Web as a place, perhaps like a park or a building in which there are clusters of friends and colleagues whom they can approach and with whom they can share information about their life and work. A proportion of their lives is actually lived out online where the distinction between online and off–line is increasingly blurred. Residents are happy to go online simply to spend time with others and they are likely to consider that they 'belong' to a community which is located in the virtual.

This notion of digital residents fits in with the characteristics of the Connected Learner. As Masie noted, "the 'e' in e-learning initially meant electronic. Now it means everyone and everywhere. It means effective and engaged experiences. It means experiential. Now we're talking about the connected learner" (2012). Learners can now connect to an ever-widening circle of mentors, peers, experiences and information sources. All these opportunities to connect in the virtual world bring people together who want to learn together to create mutually beneficial relationships. These relationships create communities which help to form pathways so that formal and informal learning are no longer separated to the same extent as they have been in the past (http://coopcatalyst.wordpress.com/2011/02/01/connected-teaching/).

Plekta (2007) notes that the expectations of the learning process have also changed for today's students and suggests that this generation, more than any other generation, "expects a personalized educational setting that meets their needs, provides immediate feedback, and enables them to move at their own rate" (p. 129). McGlynn (2008) agrees and lists the following characteristics of today's learners:

- Expect to be entertained,
- Expect a fun and interactive learning environment,
- Expect the teacher to take a proactive/active role,
- Expect to be engaged in the classroom,
- Expect 24/7 access,
- Expect immediate feedback (instant gratification),
- Expect a customized learning environment / expect info that is relevant to their lives,
- Expect to work in groups / enjoy collaborative learning,
- Expect a learner-centered / process driven classroom.

Appropriate use of technology is one way to meet the changing needs of today's students.

However, as Ally (2013, p. 12) points out, the bulk of the research into mobile learning "has looked at student satisfaction in using mobile technology, and these studies have reported that students like the flexibility of using the technology" (see also Oliver & Gorke, 2007, Wang, et. al., 2009, for example). In addition, Fabian and MacLean (2014) found in their review of university/college practices that amongst the attributed benefits of mobile learning in Further Education were the improvement of communication channels, updating students about course materials via SMS (Derwen College 2008) and other forms of alerts and updates through mobile devices. This process has proven to be useful in engaging students and has improved learner welfare and retention (Northampton College 2010; Yorkshire Coast College 2010).

Some of the benefits reported in the literature include the view that iPads are effective tools to bolster student participation during classroom by increasing collaboration and stimulating class discussion (Brown et al., 2012; George et al., 2013; Sheperd &Reeves, 2011; Thornburg et al., 2012). Results from a study done implementing all digital classes at Abilene Christian University (ACU) in Texas, USA, illustrate that iPads increase students' engagement and have a positive impact in an academic environment (Nilsson & Pareto, 2010). In Oklahoma State University, an iPad pilot program was conducted in five sections of two courses across two colleges to study how iPads affect student learning (Douglas, 2011). The collected data are uniformly positive and indicate that the iPad pilot was a very successful experience to a point that the university is considering the deployment of iPads for all students. In a case study at Kanda University of International Studies in Chiba Japan conducted to investigate the integration of iPads into an existing English language curriculum, the findings indicate that the value and appropriateness of iPads are best seen in collaborative situations. Western Illinois University had undertaken initiatives to implement the use of iPads in order to satisfy students' expectations for using technology in the classroom (Sheperd & Reeves, 2011). The program coordinator Dawn Sweet said "there is a mobile evolution taking place in society today, and we felt it was time to move toward a more mobile and personalized device in order to prepare our faculty for mobility within the classroom" (Sheperd & Reeves, 2011). Findings from the Western Illinois study showed that iPads enhanced the study skills of the students and promoted active learning.

As part of the move to more technology enhanced classrooms, many universities distributed iPads to all incoming freshmen students to integrate new technologies into the classroom and provide more innovative and engaging curriculum such as Illinois Institute of Technology in USA, George Fox University in USA, University of Adelaide in Australia (Cross, 2010), the University of Western Sydney in Australia (Tapscott, 2009), Penrhos College (Hetebry & Caporn, 2007). In the Gulf region, mobile learning is following the world-wide trend. In the UAE and Qatar the Governments have introduced iPad initiatives in the Federal Institutions of Higher Education as well as select Government High Schools (Barth, et. al., 2013, Gitsaki, et. al., 2013, Stein & Alsaleh, 2013). Some of the institutions have provided the students with iPads and others have required the students to buy their own.

As noted in the literature, there is a move towards mobile learning and the use of tablets and other mobile devices in education throughout the world, particularly iPads. Alyahya & Gall point out, "with more than 1.5 million iPads used specifically for education and more than 20,000 education applications built especially for iPads, the technology has the potential to fundamentally change learning and teaching (2012, p. 1266). Regarding the use of iPads in Mathematics classes there are numerous examples of use in K-12; however, in higher education, the discussion of use of iPads is mainly around teacher education programs preparing K-12 Math teachers (Bannon, et.al, 2013, Handal, et.al, 2012, Pelton and Pelton, 2013). The two studies reported in this chapter hope to shed some light on the students' view of iPads in university Mathematics class and offer some suggestions on the value of appropriate use of iPads to enhance the students' learning experience in Mathematics.

BACKGROUND TO BOTH STUDIES

Both studies took place at the American University of Sharjah (AUS) located in Sharjah, United Arab Emirates. AUS was founded in 1997 by His Highness Sheikh Dr. Sultan Bin Mohammad Al Qassimi, Member of the Supreme Council of the United Arab Emirates, Ruler of Sharjah and President of American University of Sharjah (AUS). It is an independent, non-profit coeducational institution offering both undergraduate and graduate degrees. In the 2012 – 2013 academic year, the time frame of the first study, there were 5,886 students enrolled, 54% male and 46% female representing 89 nationalities. In the 2013 – 2014 academic year, the time frame for the second study, there 6,046 students enrolled, 53% male and 47% female.

In order to improve the learning opportunities for their students, two Professors in the Mathematics Department at American University of Sharjah conducted a pilot study in 2012 into the use of iPads in introductory Math classes. They thought that the use of iPads would be welcomed by the students, would help to increase their interest in the subject and would help to improve their performance. However, their study with two classes yielded mixed results. Although 65% rated the overall iPad experience highly and 76% agreed that the use of the iPads helped them to better understand the material and the professors could track that the students' performance did improve, 47% indicated they would not join an iPad class. In the original study, no qualitative data was obtained so the Professors could not explain why the students said the students preferred a traditional class over an iPad class. In order to find out whether or not to expand the use of iPads in Mathematics classes, a follow up study to gather qualitative data was conducted. The rest of this chapter will first outline the original study, followed by second study, concluding with a discussion of the implications from both studies and the impact of the findings on the use of iPads in university mathematics classes.

STUDY ONE

Context and Participants

Two classes of undergraduate AUS students enrolled in MTH 001 "Pre-Calculus for engineers" participated in this study. Each class had 17 students enrolled for a total of 34 participants, 11 female and 23 male. The lead author taught both sections; one was taught in a traditional textbook, whiteboard, pencil and paper fashion while the second class was paperless and taught using iPads only. The trigonometry concepts covered in the class included trigonometric identities and solving trigonometric equations. These concepts are crucial for the Engineering students' future academic success which further supports the need to find the most suitable and effective method of instruction for them.

Methodology

The following research questions guided the first study:

1. Can iPads be leveraged to increase students' interest and learning?
2. What impact, if any, did the use of the iPads have on classroom interactivity?
3. How did the students feel about using iPads in the classroom?

4. Is there any difference in students' quiz grades in the iPad classroom compared to the traditional classroom?

5. If given a choice, would students rather join an iPad or a traditional class?

Data was collected by surveying the students who participated in the iPad classroom to get their feedbacks and opinions. In order to answer the fourth research question, quizzes were also given to the students of both sections at different parts of the lecture. The final quizzes results of the two sections were compared to explore the impact of integrating iPads into the learning process.

Classroom Delivery with iPads

Research shows that the iPad offers many possible applications that have a significant potential to support teaching (Shuler, 2012). The applications chosen for this study were:

- **Air Sketch:** Allows PDF documents or images to be annotated live and projected to the entire class.
- **Blackboard:** Designed to upload documents in any format, post announcements, upload media, course roaster, and possibly students' grades. The students can access this course material on their iPads without internet connection.
- **Drop Box:** Used to put files, documents, and photos in multiple remote computers simultaneously after class.
- **E-Text:** An application to access to the E-text version of the book for marking and other related notes.
- **Nearpod:** An interactive white board that synchronizes the use of iPads in the classroom. It combines presentation, collaboration, and real time assessment tools into one integrated solution.

- **Quick Office:** Developed to edit any word documents, excel worksheets, or power point presentations.

These applications aided in delivering the course content, conducting in class quizzes, referring to book materials and real time communication with the students. The instructor ensured that a set of applications were installed on students' iPads prior to the start of the class. The iPads were provided by AUS for the students to use in class. They could not take these iPads home with them. The students were also allowed to use their personal iPads if they had one.

Students logged onto the Nearpod session using their usernames and pins. This pin was provided by the instructor and once all students were logged in, the instructor had complete visibility of all the students participating in the class delivery. Of the many advantages of using iPads one was a fast way to take attendance and monitor students' active participation in the class discussions when needed. The instructor prepared the power point presentation before class which was saved in a PDF format and then uploaded on Nearpod. During the class delivery, the instructor inserted some slides to represent some quiz questions to monitor the students' progress and learning outcomes. The students were given 5 minutes to answer every quiz question during the class delivery. The quiz questions were designed to match the learning outcome of every subpart of the lecture. At the end of the lecture, the instructor saved the quiz data and added it to an excel file to monitor the students' performance in each class. Although this was not utilized during the research project, one more advantage of this class delivery was that absent students could still join the class even if they were not on campus. All that they needed was a wireless connection on their iPads allowing them to see the class lecture notes and also take the quizzes that the instructor conducted in class. The instructor also used Air Sketch as a white board to do further calculations and explanations away from the PowerPoint lecture notes as needed. All of the applications were used at various points throughout the semester, however, Nearpod and Air Sketch were the most widely used applications in this research.

Results

At the end of the semester, the participating students in the iPad class were asked to complete a short survey related to their learning and engagement with the iPads. The survey asked the students to rate, on a scale of 1 – 5, with 1 being lowest and 5 being highest how they felt about the overall iPad experience, their interest level in the content, the delivery of the class content, their understanding of the content, and their interaction in class. The students were also asked whether or not they would join an all iPad class again.

As shown in Figures 1 to 5 the majority of the students felt that the use of iPads in their Mathematics class was overall a rewarding experience

and beneficial for them to better understand the concepts. They also noted that the use of the iPad promoted better classroom interaction and engagement.

Students responding favorably to a teaching method does not necessarily equate to improved grades and performance on quizzes. The students of both sections were asked four quizzes questions at different parts of the lecture to help determine their progress in the course. The questions were the same in both sections to minimize the discrepancy in the findings, although we acknowledge that there are many other factors that need to be taken into consideration regarding students' performance on quizzes other than just the use of iPads in class. In section 1 the students solved the problems on paper and handed them in to the instructor for later evaluation. In section 2, the students used Nearpod to execute the quizzes and could immediately view the pie-chart centralizing the quiz performance. The types of questions given to the students varied, for example:

Figure 1. The overall iPad experience

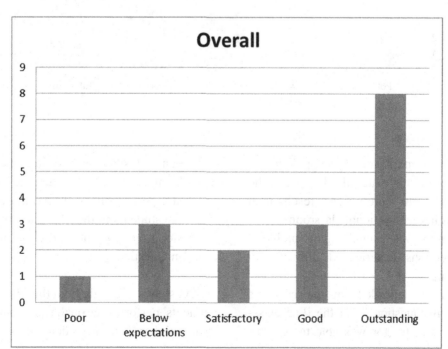

Figure 2. Students' interest level

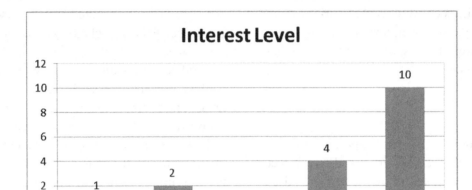

Figure 3. Students' reaction to content delivery using iPads

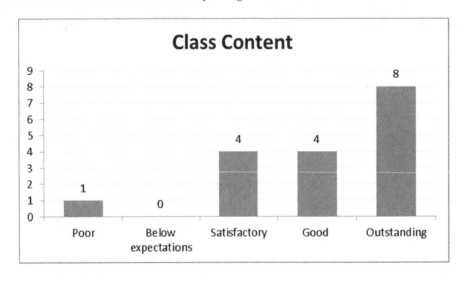

- Questions 1 and 2 were direct applications on the explained material. Students in the iPad classroom scored higher results than the ones in the traditional classroom.
- Question 3 was a challenging problem. Both sections experienced difficulty in answering.
- Question 4 depended on the concepts learned in Question 3. In the iPad classroom, the instructor was able to see students' answers in real time and direct the lecture content according to their needs and performances. Therefore, on average, the students in the iPad class better understood the concepts and got a higher score in Question 4.

As shown in Figure 6, in the iPad classroom, students' performance on the quizzes was consistently higher than the students in the traditional

Figure 4. Students' understanding of course content

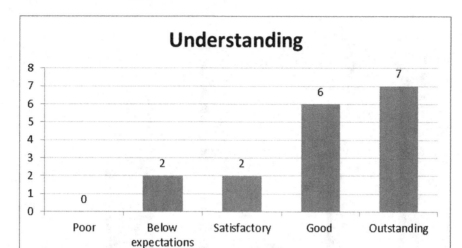

Figure 5. Students' interaction in class

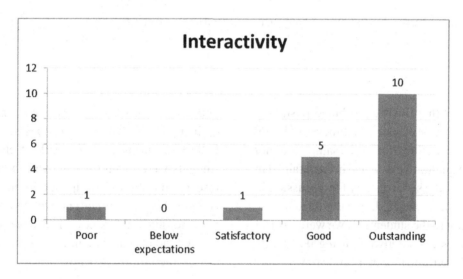

classroom for questions one and two. It is useful to note that question three proved to be difficult for both sections. However, in the iPad class, the instructor was able to give immediate feedback on question three and since answering question four correctly often depended on answering question three correctly, students in the iPad class were then able to perform better on questions four. Thus, the iPads potentially can provide a change in the performance of the students due to the availability of immediate feedback from the instructor to the students.

Overall, the results of the survey indicate that the students using iPads had a positive experience in their in introductory math class in all measures: understanding the class content, classroom interactivity, and interest level. However, in answer to the question whether or not they would join an iPad class in future semesters, only 47% of the students stated that they would. In fact, some students even

Figure 6. Performance results of the iPad class vs. the traditional class

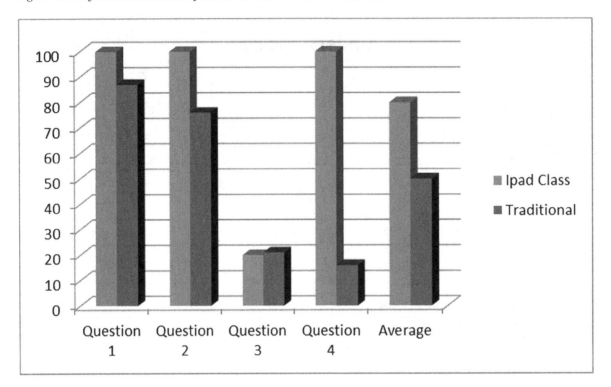

though agreed that iPads contributed positively to their learning, still stated that they would not join an iPad class. Since the initial sample was not large and no qualitative data had been obtained in the first study, the second study for discussion in this chapter was conducted. It was guided by one main question to the students: If we were to offer a Mathematics class delivered using iPads only would you be willing to join it? Why or why not?

STUDY TWO

Context and Participants

A total of 105 students from three classes participated in this study: 26 women and 79 men. The students were all enrolled in MTH 103 at American University of Sharjah. MTH 103 is an introductory mathematics course for Engineers that covers limit of functions, differentiation, ap-

plications of derivatives and theory of integration with applications. The survey was distributed in Fall 2013 during the 13th week of classes. The students were given time in class to answer the research question. Participation in the study was completely voluntary and anonymous and students were not given any kind of incentive or exposed to any kind of punishment for their involvement, or lack thereof, in the study.

Results

In response to the question, *If we were to offer a Mathematics class delivered using iPads only would you be willing to join it? Why or why not?*, 19% of the women said yes, they would join the class compared to 42% of the males who said they would join.

Figure 7. Reasons for joining an iPad class

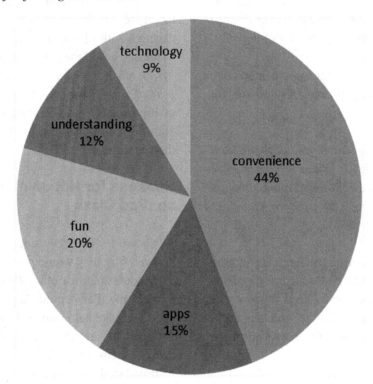

Reasons for Joining an iPad Class

As shown in Figure 7, coding of the qualitative data resulted in five main categories that students identified as reasons why they would join an iPad class.

Students discussed the convenience afforded by the use of the iPad mentioning that they are lightweight and allow them to access their course work anytime and anywhere. As one student commented[1]:

It is a easier way. We can have ebooks available all time, teacher can send notes instead of writing and copying everything from the board, I have tried this once and it is really beneficial. I think you should go for it.

Other students commented on the weight of Mathematics book in particular:

…calculus books are very heavy. ebooks would be a great help. It would be much easier to carry an iPad. I can carry the electronic version of the huge calculus book everywhere easily. I can create more neat and organized notes of iPads than I do in my copybook.

Students also commented on the usefulness of having access to advanced apps to enhance their understanding as noted in the following comments:

…regular books and notebooks are only used for taking notes while iPads have additional options and sources that support the ideas mentioned in class.

…we can have everything in one application which makes life much easier.

...*accessibility to videos and more organized information during studies. Unless a person doesn't own an iPad/tablet, this is the better option.*

Students commented on the fun and interactive aspects of using iPads in class. As one student noted:

...*in my opinion, iPads are more fun to use than books and copybooks. It makes the class more interesting and the student will pay more attention to the professor as there is less hard work involved (writing on the copybook).*

Along with considering the fun, entertaining aspect, students also noted that using the iPads would help them better understand the material as they could focus more in class and take notes more easily. These ideas are summed up in the two comments below:

Taking notes in class will be much easier and a student shouldn't worry about getting a new notebook every month or so.

It might be easier to instructor and the student to get the information...easier and faster.

The final reason students gave for taking an iPad class related to the use of the technology itself as illustrated in the following comments:

...*because these skills might be important therefore helpful in our careers in the future.*

Technology is a key role in our lives and education should advance with the technology.

I will be willing to join it to improve my skills in solving using tablets.

The five reasons given by the students, convenience, fun, helpful apps, enhanced understanding and the value of using technology support what is found in the literature on mobile learning and tablet use in higher education. For example, in their research with 144 university students, Fabian and MacLean asked the students on a scale of $1 - 4$, *"How much did you enjoy using the tablets as part of your learning activities?"* The majority of the students gave a rating of 3 or 4 and also commented on how the use of tablets enhanced their learning.

Reasons for Not Joining an iPad Class

As shown in figure 8, students noted three main reasons why they would not join an iPad class.

Students in favor of an iPad class commented on how the iPads could help them focus on the class and take better notes. Other students noted the opposite - that having an iPad in class would distract them and hinder their note taking as illustrated in the following two comments:

If iPads are used during class hours then there would be a lot of distractions. As we can tend to look into other things like Facebook, etc...rather than concentrating in the class.

...*could be major distractions (applications, web surfing, etc...). I personally believe that I understand the course more efficiently while writing my own notes using pen and paper rather than technology.*

Students were also concerned that an iPad class would result in diminished understanding of the material. Many students commented that they believe they need to write out by hand the formulas and mathematical concepts to truly understand them. The following two comments sum up many other students' points:

Math as a subject requires lots of practice and the actual writing helps it register better. Use of

Figure 8. Reasons for not joining an iPad class

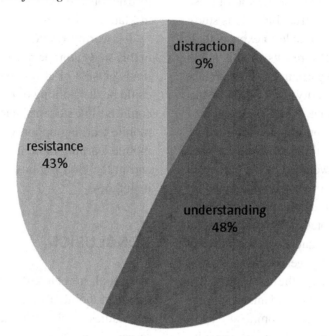

technology completely in classrooms, will hinder the process of understanding.

With iPads will be no challenge when doing questions, it is the easy way to allow students to just get the answer. Using a notebook and a pencil/pen is the best way to solve math.

The final reason for not joining an iPad class related to the students' resistance to change and their views that iPad use in the Mathematics class would not be convenient or efficient. For example, two students commented that:

I have never used this technology and I am comfortable with the way I am taking calculus.

I am used to writing on books and since calculus is a math subject we need to write many formulas and calculations.

The three main reasons for not taking an iPad class: decreased understanding, resistance to

change and distractions caused by having an iPad readily available are important concerns that need to be considered. As Matthew notes, "First year students attend face-to-face classes armed with an arsenal of internet enabled digital devices. The conundrum is that while these devices offer scope for enhancing opportunities for engagement in face-to-face learning, they may simultaneously distract students away from learning and compound isolation issues". Fabian and MacLean also found that some students were resistant to change. As they note, "In the open-ended questions, a student clarified that she was not keen on using touch screen interfaces and preferred to use a standard keyboard. These results highlight that the use of tablets or new technologies will not be an automatic hit with all students" (2012).

Discussion

Broad, Matthews, and Mc Donald (2004) note that teachers should not assume that just because students are familiar with technology that they are also familiar with appropriate technology use in education. This may be true, but as this study has illustrated students are able to express their learning preferences. The results of this study have brought to light the participants' mixed reactions to joining a University level Mathematics class taught entirely using iPads. The perceived advantages of fun and convenience afforded by the iPads, i.e., using e-textbooks to avoid carrying heavy textbooks, is outweighed by the perceived disadvantages related to reduced understanding of the material and distractions provided by the iPads. As one student noted, "With iPads will be no challenge when doing questions, it is the easy way to allow students to just get the answer. Using a notebook and a pencil/pen is the best way to solve math". Another student expressed mixed feelings about using the iPads in his/her comment, "I will be willing to join it to improve my skills in solving using technology but I prefer manual work so that I am able to understand what is being taught step by step and be able to apply it elsewhere". It is important to note that results pertain to the use of iPad use in Mathematics classes only. A larger scale research project looking at the use of iPads in different subjects would build on this initial research and add to the body of literature.

Another finding of interest is students' resistance to change. As noted earlier, many Government schools in the UAE and Qatar are now involved in the iPad initiative and other technological innovations and as a result the way information is delivered to students in K-12 schools is changing. However, for the students involved in this study the majority of them were educated in a more traditional fashion. As such, based on their comments it appears that they are comfortable and familiar with that mode of instruction. As a result, with a content heavy course such as Mathematics, many participants noted they are not willing to take the risk of trying to learn in a new or different manner. Although not the focus of this study, the some students noted, and the authors believe, that as a supplement to regular

instruction, the iPads may serve a useful purpose in Mathematics classes.

It is worthy to note that none of the participants in this study commented on the usefulness of the iPads outside of class time. One reason for this could be the wording of the question and another could be the students' lack of experience with mobile learning opportunities. As noted earlier, mobile learning in higher education world-wide and in the Gulf region is growing but is still in its infancy.

CONCLUSION

Wu, et. al, in their 2012 literature review of the trends in mobile learning point out that, "previous studies of mobile learning fall into two broad research directions: evaluating the effectiveness of mobile learning, and designing mobile learning systems" (p. 818). This small scale study investigated the effectiveness of iPad instruction from the students' perspective. According to McGlynn, the current generation of students are lauded to be the most tech-savvy and "socially connected of all generations" (2008, p. 19) and recommends using technology to leverage their interest in higher education. However, the findings have shown that the students involved could see the value that iPads could add to their learning, but they were also able to keep in mind and articulate the drawbacks. In other words, they did not assume that the use of iPads would be beneficial just because they are familiar with them and comfortable using technology. As O'Donnell and Sharp point out, "All the time and effort that lecturers put into creating suitable teaching resources for use with technology is wasted, unless students actively engage with and gain some benefits from using the material provided" (2012, p. 205). In the case of Mathematics classes at AUS, the time and effort to create an iPad only class would indeed be wasted given the high percentage of students who do not agree that using iPads as the main form of instruction would increase their learning opportunities. However, as the student population and their educational expectations change, so might their attitudes towards this issue. As Matthew points out, "It is imperative that we consider the use of current and emerging technologies in terms of the nature of our learners" (2012, p. 45), thus, regularly involving the students in any decisions about technology choices in the classroom is a step in the right direction to enhancing their learning opportunities.

REFERENCES

Ally, M. (2013). Mobile learning: From research to practice to Impact Education. *Learning and Teaching in Higher Education: Gulf Perspectives*, *10*(2), 9–22.

Alyahya, S., & Gall, J. E. (2012). iPads in Education: A Qualitative Study of Students' Attitudes and Experiences. In AmielT.WilsonB. (Eds.), *Proceedings of World Conference on Educational Multimedia, Hypermedia and Telecommunications 2012* (pp. 1266-1271). Chesapeake, VA: AACE.

Attard, C., & Northcote, M. (2011). Teaching with technology: mathematics on the move: Using mobile technologies to support student learning (Part 1). *Australian Primary Mathematics Classroom*, *16*(4), 29–31.

Bannon, S., Martin, G., & Nunes-Bufford, K. (2012). Integrating iPads Into Mathematics Education. In P. Resta (Ed.), *Proceedings of Society for Information Technology & Teacher Education International Conference 2012* (pp. 3519-3522). Chesapeake, VA: AACE.

Barth, K., Jones, V., Le Joly, K. & Alsaleh, K. (2013). *iPads in the Classroom: Teaching and learning innovations at Education City*. Paper presented at the Technology in Higher Education 2013 conference (THE2013). Doha, Qatar.

Broad, M., Matthews, M., & McDonald, A. (2004). Accounting education through an online-supported virtual learning environment. *Active Learning in Higher Education*, *5*(2), 135–151. doi:10.1177/1469787404043810

Brown, M., Castellano, J., Hughes, E., & Worth, A. (2012). Integration of iPads into a Japenese university English language curriculum. *The Jalt Call Journal*, *8*(3), 197-209.

Clark, W., & Luckin, R. (2013). *What the research says iPads in the classroom*. London Knowledge lab & The Institute of Education at the University of London. Retrieved from https://www.lkldev.ioe.ac.uk/lklinnovation/wp-content/uploads/2013/01/2013-iPads-in-the-Classroom-v2.pdf

Connelly, J., & Gregory, P. (2012). Instructor use of Tablet PCs in a college pre-calculus course: Implementation & assessment. *Mathematics Faculty Publications* (Paper 9). Sacred Heart University. Retrieved from http://digitalcommons.sacredheart.edu/math_fac/9?utm_source=digitalcommons.sacredheart.edu%2Fmath_fac%2F9&utm_medium=PDF&utm_campaign=PDFCoverPages

Cross, K. (2010, September 11). iPad replaces uni textbooks at University of Adelaide science faculty. *The Advertiser*. Retrieved from http://www.adelaidenow.com.au/technology/ipad-replaces-uni-textbooks-at-university-of-adelaide-science-faculty/story-fn5jhv6y-1225918213032)

Doiron, G. (2012). The digital divide and single-gender undergraduate education in the UAE. *Learning and Teaching in Higher Education: Gulf Perspectives*, *9*(2), 1–10.

Douglas, D. (2011, May 3). *iPad study released by Oklahoma State University*. Retrieved from https://news.okstate.edu/press-releases/929-ipad-study-released-by-oklahoma-state-university

Fabian, K., & MacLean, D. (2014). Keep taking the tablets? Assessing the use of tablet devices in learning and teaching activities in the Further Education sector. *Research in Learning Technology, 22*(0). doi:10.3402/rlt.v22.22648

Fee, K. (2009). *Delivering e-learning*. London: Kogan Page Limited.

Fister, K. R., & McCarthy, M. L. (2008). Mathematics instruction and the tablet PC. *International Journal of Mathematical Education in Science and Technology, 39*(3), 285–292. doi:10.1080/00207390701690303

Galligan, L., Loch, B., McDonald, C., & Taylor, J. (2010). The use of tablet and related technologies in mathematics teaching. *Australian Senior Mathematics Journal, 24*(1), 38–51.

Gawelek, M. A., Spataro, M., & Komarny, P. (2011). *Mobile perspectives: On iPads. Why mobile?* Retrieved from EDUCAUSE Learning Initiative website: http://www.educause.edu

Geist, E. (2011). The game changer: Using iPads in college teacher education classes. *College Student Journal, 45*(4), 758–768.

George, P., Dumenco, L., Doyle, R., & Dollase, R. (2013). Incorporating iPads into a preclinical curriculum: A pilot study. *Medical Teacher, 35*(3), 226–230. doi:10.3109/0142159X.2012.735384 PMID:23425119

Gitsaki, C., Robby, M., Priest, T., Hamdan, K., & Ben-Chabane, Y. (2013). A research agenda for the UAE iPad initiative. *Learning and Teaching in Higher Education: Gulf Perspectives, 10*(2), 23–41.

Gorgievski, N., Stroud, R., Truxaw, M., & DeFranco, T. (2005). Tablet PC: A preliminary report on a tool for teaching calculus. *The International Journal for Technology in Mathematics Education, 12*(3), 95–102.

Gupta, M. L. (2009). Using emerging technologies to promote student engagement and learning in agricultural mathematics. *The International Journal of Learning, 16*(10), 497–508.

Handal, B., Campbell, C., Cavanagh, M., Petocz, P., & Kelly, N. (2012). Integrating Technology, Pedagogy and Content in Mathematics Education. *Journal of Computers in Mathematics and Science Teaching, 31*(4), 387–413.

Hetebry, J., & Caporn, N. (2007). *Tablet PC's a tool for teaching-learning at Penrhos College*. Paper presented at IADIS. New York, NY.

NMC Horizon Report. (2013). Higher Education Edition. New Media Consortium.

Illinois Institute of Technology. (2011, April 14). *Illinois Institute of Technology confirms iPads for undergraduates each year*. Retrieved from http://www.iit.edu/departments/pr/mediaroom/article_viewer_db.php?articleID=434

Jelemenská, K., Cicák, P., & Dúcky, V. (2011). Interactive presentation towards students' engagement. International Conference on Education and Educational Psychology (ICEEPSY 2011). *Procedia: Social and Behavioral Sciences, 29*, 1645–1653. doi:10.1016/j.sbspro.2011.11.407

Khaddage, F., Lattemann, C., & Bray, E. (2011). Mobile apps integration for teaching and learning: Are teachers ready to re-blend? In M. Koehler & P. Mishra (Eds.), *Proceedings of Society for Information Technology & Teacher Education International Conference 2011* (pp. 2545-2552). Chesapeake, VA: AACE.

Looi, C., Seow, P., Zhang, B., So, H., Chen, W., & Wong, L. (2009). Leveraging mobile technology for sustainable seamless learning: A research agenda. *British Journal of Educational Technology, 41*(2), 154–169. doi:10.1111/j.1467-8535.2008.00912.x

Maisie, E, (2012). *Blueprint for Change in an Era of Rapid Reinvention.* Paper presented at Educause. Denver, CO.

Matias, A., & Wolf, D. F. (2013), Engaging Students in Online Courses Through the Use of Mobile Technology. In L. A. Wankel & P. Blessinger (Eds.), Increasing Student Engagement and Retention Using Mobile Applications: Smartphones, Skype and Texting Technologies (Cutting-edge Technologies in Higher Education, Volume 6) (pp. 115-142). Emerald Group Publishing Limited.

Matthew, A. (2012). Managing distraction and attention in diverse cohorts: 21st century challenges to law student engagement. *QUT Law & Justice Journal, 12*(1), 45–65.

McGinley, S. (2012). UAE colleges switch to iPad-only classrooms. *ITP.net.* Retrieved from http://www.itp.net/590333-uae-colleges-switch-to-ipad-only-classrooms#.Uim3wCIoH1w

McGlynn, A. P. (2008). Millenials in College: How do we motivate them? *Education Digest*, 20–22.

Motiwalla, L. (2007). Mobile learning: A framework and evaluation. *Computers & Education, 49*(3), 581–596. doi:10.1016/j.compedu.2005.10.011

Murray, O. T., & Olcese, N. R. (2011). Teaching and learning with iPads, ready or not? *TechTrends, 55*(6), 42–48. doi:10.1007/s11528-011-0540-6

Nilsson, A., & Pareto, L. (2010). The Complexity of integrating technology enhanced learning in special math education–A case study. Sustaining TEL: From Innovation to Learning and Practice. *Lecture Notes in Computer Science, 6383*, 638–643. doi:10.1007/978-3-642-16020-2_67

O'Donnell, E., & Sharp, M. (2012). Students' views of E-Learning: The impact of technology on learning in higher education in Ireland. In K. Moyle & G. Wijngaards (Eds.), *Student Reactions to Learning with Technologies: Perceptions and Outcomes.* Hershey, PA: Information Science Reference (an imprint of IGI Global). doi:10.4018/978-1-61350-177-1.ch010

Oliver, B., & Gorke, V. (2007). Australian undergraduates' use and ownership of emerging technologies: Implications and opportunities for creating engaging learning experiences for the Net Generation. *Australasian Journal of Educational Technology, 23*(2), 171–186.

Omar, M. (1992). Attitudes of college students towards computers: A comparative study in the United States and the Middle East. *Computers in Human Behavior, 8*(2-3), 249–257. doi:10.1016/0747-5632(92)90009-4

Pai, D. D., & Borba, G. S. (2012). The role of digital technologies for the innovation of the learning experience in the university classroom. *Strategic Design Research Journal, 5*(2), 59–69.

Pelton, T., & Pelton, F. L. (2013). 1:1 iPad Adoption – Preparing Middle School Teachers to Teach Math. In R. McBride & M. Searson (Eds.), *Proceedings of Society for Information Technology & Teacher Education International Conference 2013* (pp. 4837-4842). Chesapeake, VA: AACE.

Pletka, B. (2007). *Educating the net generation: How to engage students in the 21st century.* Santa Monica, CA: Santa Monica Press.

Rahal, T. (2010). Learning styles: Learning that empowers students? *Learning and Teaching in Higher Education, 7*(2), 33–51.

Romney, C. (2010). Tablet PCs in undergraduate mathematics. In *Proceedings of ASEE/IEEE Frontiers in Education Conference.* IEEE.

Romney, C. (2011). Tablet PC use in freshman mathematics promotes stem retention. In *Proceedings of ASEE/IEEE Frontiers in Education Conference*. IEEE.

Sharples, M., Corlett, D., & Westmancott, O. (2002). The design and implementation of a mobile learning resource. *Journal of Personal and Ubiquitous Computing, 6*(3), 220–234. doi:10.1007/s007790200021

Sheperd, I.J., & Reeves, B. (2011, March 1). *iPad or iFad - The reality of a paperless classroom.* Paper presented at the Abilene Christian University - Mobility Conference.

Shuler, C. (2012). *ILearnII: An analysis of the education category of the iTunes App Store.* New York: The Joan Ganz Cooney Center at Sesame Workshop.

Sneller, J. (2007). The Tablet PC Classroom: Erasing borders, stimulating activity, enhancing communication. In *Proceedings of 37th ASEE/IEEE Frontiers in Education Conference*. IEEE.

Stein, A., & Alsaleh, K. (2013). *Lesson learned: Supporting iPads at Education City.* Paper presented at the Technology in Higher Education 2013 conference (THE2013). Doha, Qatar.

Stickel, M. (2008). Effective use of Tablet PCs for engineering mathematics education. In *Proceedings of Frontiers in Education Conference*, (pp. S3J-7 – S3J-12). doi:10.1109/FIE.2008.4720564

Swan, M. (2012, September 24). HCT and UAE University students to learn using iPads. *The National.* Retrieved from http://www.thenational.ae/news/uae-news/education/hct-and-uae-university-students-to-learn-using-ipads

Tapscott, D. (2009). *Grown up digital: How the Net Generation is changing your world.* New York: McGraw-Hill.

Thornburg, E., Hung, B., & Jackson, J. (2012). *Learning with iPad: Does this technology help or hinder student understanding.* Paper presented at Joint Mathematics Meeting. Boston, MA.

Thornburg, E. J. (2012). *Using iPads in undergraduate mathematics: Master Teacher Program.* Center for Teaching Excellence.

Wang, M., Shen, R., Novak, D., & Pan, X. (2009). The impact of mobile learning on students' learning behaviours and performance: Report from a large blended classroom. *British Journal of Educational Technology, 40*(4), 673–695. doi:10.1111/j.1467-8535.2008.00846.x

Warschauer, M. (2003). Technological change and the future of CALL. In S. Fotos & C. M. Browne (Eds.), *New perspectives on call for second language classrooms* (pp. 15–26). Mahwah, NJ: Lawrence Erlbaum Associates.

White, D. S., & Le Cornu, A. (2011). Visitors and residents: A new typology for online engagement. *First Monday, 16*(9), 9–5. doi:10.5210/fm.v16i9.3171

Wise, J., Toto, R., & Lim, K. Y. (2006). Introducing Tablet PCs: Initial results from the classroom. In *Proceedings of the 36th Annual ASEE/IEEE Frontiers in Engineering Conference*, (pp. S3F-17 - S3F-20). IEEE. doi:10.1109/FIE.2006.322657

Wishart, J., & Green, D. (2010). *Identifying Emerging Issues in Mobile Learning in Higher and Further Education: A report to JISC.* University of Bristol.

Wu, W., Wu, Y. J., Chen, C., Kao, H., Lin, C., & Huang, S. (2012). Review of trends from mobile learning studies: A meta-analysis. *Computers & Education, 59*(2), 817–827. doi:10.1016/j.compedu.2012.03.016

KEY TERMS AND DEFINITIONS

iPads in Higher Education: The use of iPad apps and other features both inside and outside the classroom.

Mobile Devices in Contemporary Mathematics Education: The adoption of mobile technologies in mathematics education contexts.

Mobile Learning in Higher Education: The use of tablet devices and smart phones both inside and outside the classroom.

Students' Perceptions of Technology Use: The pros and cons of using technology from the students' point of view.

Technology for Teaching: Tools and materials used inside and outside of class time to enhance learning opportunities.

ENDNOTES

[1]   Students' comments have not been edited.

Chapter 4

Leveraging Asynchronous Online Instruction to Develop Elementary School Mathematics Teacher–Leaders

Drew Polly
University of North Carolina at Charlotte, USA

ABSTRACT

This chapter describes how the author leveraged asynchronous online instruction to develop elementary school teacher-leaders' knowledge of elementary school mathematics content and pedagogies in a graduate program in the United States. This chapter provides the theoretical framework of learner-centered professional development and explains how the six courses in the program embody the framework and support teachers' development of knowledge and skills related to mathematics teaching and learning. This chapter also shares the findings of a study that evaluated teacher-leaders performance on five student-learning outcomes in the program as well as feedback on course evaluations and end-of-program surveys. Data analysis indicated that every teacher-leader demonstrated proficiency on each student-learning outcome. Implications for the design of asynchronous online programs are also shared.

INTRODUCTION

The Need for More Elementary Mathematics Leaders

Internationally, there have been recommendations to develop and employ school-based personnel that have the knowledge and skills related to leading and supporting efforts related to mathematics teaching and learning (Bay-Williams, McGatha,

Kobett, & Wray, 2013; Polly, 2012; U.S. Department of Education [USDE], 2008). This need is especially prominent in elementary school settings (Ages 5-11), as teachers commonly are responsible for teaching multiple subjects and hence, do not have the opportunity to focus more deeply on only one or two subjects (Bay-Williams et al., 2013).

In some schools, resources have been provided to hire faculty members to hold mathematics-specific jobs and positions, such as mathematics

DOI: 10.4018/978-1-4666-7316-8.ch004

coach, mathematics facilitator, mathematics lead teacher, or curriculum specialist. In other cases, however, elementary mathematics leaders are full-time classroom teachers who take on additional roles of leading their colleagues by providing resources, leading planning meetings, and facilitating professional development (Polly, 2012). As the number of these mathematics-specific positions has increased, there has, in turn, been a need to delineate and specify the types of knowledge and skills that elementary mathematics leaders should have.

Seeing a need to specify the knowledge and skills related to leadership in elementary school mathematics, the Association for Mathematics Teacher Educators (AMTE) published a set of Standards specifying the needs for elementary school mathematics specialists (AMTE, 2013). These standards speak about specialists as school-based personnel who have knowledge about mathematics content, pedagogy, as well as how to support their colleagues who teach mathematics in their school (AMTE, 2013). This work follows the Report of the National Mathematics Research Panel (USDE, 2008) who called for more school-based mathematics leaders to support teachers. The authors of the National Math Panel wrote:

The panel identified at least three types of "math specialist teachers": the math coach (lead teacher), the full-time elementary mathematics teacher, and the pull-out program teacher. Math coaches are more common than the other two types, but there is considerable blurring across types and roles. Math coaches (sometimes called lead teachers) tend to act as resources for their colleagues and do not directly instruct students. They work at the state, district, and school levels, providing leadership and information to teachers and staff and often coordinating mathematics programs within a school, a district, or across districts (p. 43).

Regardless of the job title or specific job requirements, there is a need to provide specific types of support to faculty in elementary school settings to develop the skills and knowledge related to leading and supporting efforts related to mathematics teaching and learning.

North Carolina's Response to a Need for Elementary Mathematics Leaders

In a response to these calls and recommendations, a group of mathematics educators and mathematicians in North Carolina convened with other mathematics leaders from across the United States for a week-long conference. The purpose of this meeting was to study and explore the potential content of professional learning activities that would develop knowledge and skills related to the duties of elementary school mathematics leaders.

As a result of that meeting and extensive discussions about potential ways to design these learning experiences, a group of faculty from across the state convened in order to create a graduate program of six mathematics education courses focused on mathematics content and high-leverage teaching practices (pedagogies). Those individuals who complete all 6 courses successfully would earn an additional teaching license in Elementary School Mathematics. The program was designed for individuals that already had initial teaching credentials and teaching experience in elementary school classrooms. This working group originally included 13 faculty from 7 universities who synthesized the AMTE Standards and applied their expertise from the fields of mathematics education and mathematics to design the program. These faculty initially taught the courses in face-to-face settings to 2 different cohorts of teacher-leaders across the state. Through feedback from elementary school partners and North Carolina's university administration, the working group was advised to create online formats of the course in order to increase the opportunities and flexibility for teachers to participate in and complete the program.

To that end, the original working group collaborated in small groups to create possible online versions of the 6 courses. Most faculty members in the group worked towards online courses that would include synchronous meetings as well as asynchronous work and projects to complete over the duration of the semester. However, numerous teachers reported a need for even more flexibility and there was a great deal of curiosity about completing the program in a 100% asynchronous format. Seeing the need for this type of program, the first author further revised the courses to create asynchronous versions of each of the 6 courses. This chapter describes the theoretical framework and components of the asynchronous elementary school mathematics program.

Online Learning in Teacher Education

Overview

Online learning continues to provide new opportunities for individuals to participate in teacher education programs (HEFCE, 2011; Ko & Rosen, 2010; Polly, 2013). The flexibility offered by online programs and online courses allow people to seek initial teaching credentials or advanced degrees while also completing full-time jobs and other responsibilities in their lives (Tallent-Runnels et al., 2006). While the flexibility of online programs has been repeatedly noted in research, prior studies have noted that education courses have potential to be problematic in online environments due to the need for teachers to demonstrate effective teaching competencies in classroom settings in order to successfully meet the requirements of their program (Sobel, Sands, & Dunlap et al., 2009). Prior research shows that the student learning outcomes in online teacher education courses and programs are greatly enhanced

with the inclusion of rich, classroom-embedded activities (Polly, 2013).

As online teacher education courses and programs have become more popular, researchers have raised questions and called for an in-depth examination about the quality of work products in online courses compared to face-to-face courses (Dede, Ketelhut, Whitehouse, Breit, & McCloskey, 2009; O'Connor, 2011). Prior studies on online mathematics education courses in an initial teacher licensure program noted that teacher candidates' quality of work was not significantly different from those in face-to-face sections (Polly, 2012; Polly, 2013) and that teacher candidates' positively impacted elementary school students' mathematics achievement on curriculum-based assessments (Polly, 2014). While researching a science education course in an initial teacher licensure program, O'Connor (2011) noted that students completed quality work in their course, but struggled to effectively implement student-centered pedagogies when they video-recorded their classroom teaching projects. Based on these studies more research is needed to examine how to best scaffold and support teachers' and pre-service teachers' development of knowledge and skills in the context of online teacher education courses.

Components of Effective Online Courses

Research about online courses and online learning experiences has led to some noteworthy components of effective online courses (Ko & Rosen, 2010; Quality Matters, n.d.). Intensive, engaging activities with content have been cited as a significant factor in students' depth of learning and reflection (Dennen, 2007; McCrory, Putman, & Jansen, 2009). Further, the amount and level of interaction between course instructors and students is crucial for student success (Delfino & Persico, 2007; Hodges & Cohen, 2012). Further, Hodges and Cohen (2012) found that an instructor's speed of response, clarity of instructions, and instructors' availability were the primary concerns of students in an online course. Also, researchers have found that clear rubrics and examples of exemplar work products (Dyment, Downing, & Budd, 2013; Moallem, 2003) and opportunities to write reflections (Downing & Dyment, 2013) play a significant role in students' success.

In an online teacher education course, O'Connor (2011) noted that teachers need more extensive support to apply the pedagogies and skills taught in online teacher education courses. Polly (2013) found that teacher candidates seeking initial licensure were more likely to plan for and enact reform-based pedagogies when they were placed with a clinical internship teacher who either used or embraced those types of pedagogies. The asynchronous elementary school mathematics graduate program described in this chapter includes many of the components of online courses that are highlighted above.

THEORETICAL FRAMEWORK OF THE ELEMENTARY MATHEMATICS PROGRAM

Learner-Centered Professional Development

The work of revising the courses in the graduate program was grounded in the framework of learner-centered instruction and the notion of learner-centered professional development (LCPD) (NPEAT, 2000; Polly & Hannafin, 2010). LCPD is grounded in the American Psychological Associations' learner-centered principles (APA Work Group, 1997), which originate from a detailed synthesis of research on teaching, learning, learning theories, and cognition (Alexander & Murphy, 1998). LCPD reflects a synthesis of literature on learner-centered instruction as well as empirical studies on teacher learning. For the revision of these courses, LCPD provided an appropriate framework as each program participant

held a teaching license in elementary school and was participating in the graduate program as a form of professional development.

Programs that embody principles of LCPD are grounded in the ideas that opportunities for teacher learning should:

- Address student learning issues and provide teachers with strategies to address student learning deficiencies (Heck, Banilower, Weiss, Rosenberg, 2008);
- Actively engage teachers in the learning process including giving them ownership and choice of some activities (Garet et al., 2001);
- Simultaneously develop their knowledge and skills related to the content that they teach and research-based pedagogies (Heck et al., 2008; Garet, et al., 2001);
- Include collaborative activities with colleagues and more knowledgeable others who can support their work (Glazer & Hannafin, 2006);
- Include ongoing activities that occur over a sustained amount of time (Fishman, Marx, Best, & Tal, 2003; Orrill, 2001);
- Provide opportunities for teachers to reflect on student work samples or their own instructional practices (Cohen, 2005; Loucks-Horsley et al., 2009).

Table 1 shows the alignment between the components of LCPD and features of the program. Each component of LCPD is addressed in each of the 6 courses.

COMPONENTS OF THE PROGRAM

Program Goals

The faculty members who created this program wrote a proposal to the University of North Carolina General Administration for the degree

Table 1. Alignment of learner-centered professional development and program components Adapted from Polly, 2012

Learner-Centered Professional Development Components	Course Activities
Address student learning issues	Each course had classroom-based activities that teacher-leaders completed with students. They examined student work samples, students' learning, and created strategies for addressing student learning issues.
Provide teachers with ownership	Each course allowed teacher-leaders to select which mathematics Standards and which tasks to pose to elementary school students based on the students' needs and teachers' preference.
Promote collaboration	On discussion forums in the Learning Management System or a wiki, teacher-leaders participate in collaborative activities sharing strategies for solving cognitively-demanding mathematical tasks, discussing course readings and sharing teacher-leaders' experiences doing projects with students.
Provide ongoing support	Each of the 6 courses lasts a semester. Most teacher-leaders complete between 4 to 6 courses which lasts between 18 months and 2 years of ongoing learning experiences.
Develop knowledge of content and pedagogy	Each course included cognitively-demanding mathematical tasks for teacher-leaders to solve, analyze, and consider how to modify to implement with elementary school learners.
Support the reflection process	Each course included projects to complete with elementary school learners and their colleagues (other teachers).

program. In that proposal they stated that each course in the program will have specific features detailed below.

"All courses will:

- Include graduate level expectations & accountability that balance direct instruction with project-oriented teaching methods.
- Stress mathematical content needed to support the teaching of elementary mathematics, illustrating how a deeper understanding of subject matter can actually enhance problem solving, critical thinking, and other 21st century skills. Mathematical content strands include: number systems and operations; rational numbers and operations; spatial orientation and visualization; measurement and data analysis; fostering the development of algebraic reasoning including patterns structure, conjecture, generalizations and proof; and algebraic operations as generalized arithmetic. Courses will stress the mathematical connections and representations across content strands.

- Provide connections to practice and the NC Standard Course of Study with a focus on a thorough development of basic mathematical ideas and skills, with an emphasis on understanding the sequential nature of mathematics and the mathematical structures inherent in the content strands.
- Balance the needs of K-2 and 3-5 teachers with links to the mathematics content and skills students need to successfully learn middle grades mathematics.
- Enable 21st century professional learning communities for teachers that models the kinds of classroom learning that best promotes 21st century skills for students.
- Cultivate teachers' ability to identify students' particular learning styles, intelligences, strengths and weaknesses.
- Help teachers develop their abilities to use various strategies (such as formative assessments) to reach diverse students and to create environments that support differentiated teaching and learning.

Table 2. Overview of the six elementary education mathematics courses

	Mathematics Content Primary	Mathematics Content: Secondary	High-Leverage Teaching Practice
1	Number systems and operations	Number theory and rational numbers	Designing and selecting mathematical tasks
2	Geometry	Number sense in the early grades	Assessment
3	Algebraic reasoning	Number systems and operations	Discourse and questioning strategies
4	Rational numbers and operations	Measurement	Learning trajectories
5	Data analysis	Measurement	Classroom interactions
6	Mathematical modeling	Number sense and algebraic reasoning	Leadership and supporting mathematics teaching

- Encourage knowledge sharing among communities of practitioners, using face-to-face, virtual and blended communications.
- Support the use of technology to improve teaching and learning mathematics.

    Beyond these features that support improving the teaching and learning in an individual's classes the program of study includes coursework that helps teachers develop as school-based leaders:

- Collaborating with teachers through co-teaching, mentoring, and coaching;
- Identifying colleagues' individual professional development needs, and individualize staff development efforts to include both formal and job-embedded professional learning experiences; and
- Facilitating staff development in mathematics content, mathematics pedagogy, and assessment of student learning. (NC EMAoL Team, 2009, p. 2)"

The UNC General Administration approved the proposal for the Program of Study and the licensure.

COURSES

The Elementary Mathematics Add-on Licensure Program consists of 6 graduate courses, each consisting of 3 credit hours at the 8 universities in the state of North Carolina that offers this program. Each course has specific emphases on mathematics content and high-leverage teaching practices or pedagogies. These are detailed in Table 2. The primary mathematics content was intended to be approximately 80% of each course, while the secondary mathematics content was intended to be approximately 20% of each course.

Components of Each Course

At UNC Charlotte, each course is offered by the first author in an asynchronous online format. Each course consists of 9, 10, or 11 modules or sets of activities. These modules are provided through a website and each module takes between 2 to 4 hours to complete. Most modules include similar activities which are detailed below.

Cognitively-Demanding Mathematical Tasks

Using the framework of cognitively-demanding mathematical tasks (Henningsen & Stein, 1997; Table 3), teacher-leaders solved a variety of mathematical tasks that were categorized at the Doing Mathematics level during each of the course. The table below shows 2nd grade examples. In the courses, teacher-leaders completed tasks that ranged as young as Grade 2 content and as high

Table 3. Types of mathematical tasks

Cognitive Demand	Name of Task Type	Description	Example
High Cognitive Demand	Doing Mathematics	Students explore mathematical tasks that require them to choose an approach, complete the task, and explain their steps and decision-making.	There are 17 students in Mrs. Smith's class. There is one more student in Mrs. Thomas' class. How many students are in both classes? Write an explanation about how you solved the task.
	Procedures with Mathematical Connections	Students explore tasks that can be solved with an algorithm, but generate more than one representation for their answer.	What is 17 + 18? Show your answer using pictures and numbers.
Low Cognitive Demand	Procedures without Mathematical Connections	Students explore tasks that require only an algorithm and only one mathematical representation.	What is 17 + 18?
	Memorization	Students recall a fact that is expected to be known.	What is 7+8?

Table 4. Example of a doing mathematics task

Part One	A professional fisherman caught 550 bass during an 11-day tournament. Each day he caught five more fish than he did the day before. He caught 25 fish on day one. How many fish did the fisherman catch on each individual day? Write an equation to describe how you solved the problem.
Part Two	A professional fisherman caught salmon during a 11-day tournament. Each day he caught 5 more fish than he did the day before. He caught 25 fish on day one. How many fish did the fisherman catch on each individual day? Write an equation to describe how you solved the problem.
Reflection	How were your approaches for the two tasks similar? How were they different? How did you "model" or represent these tasks?

as Grade 7 content. The goal of the cognitively-demanding mathematical tasks was to simultaneously develop teachers' knowledge of mathematics content related to Grades K-5, but also expose them to mathematically rich tasks that could be adapted and used with elementary school students (Polly, McGee, & Martin, 2010).

An example of a task from Course 6 on Mathematical Modeling is below (Table 4). Teacher-leaders explore tasks similar to this in every module. Each course has a task discussion board, in which students discuss and share different ways for exploring this task. Teacher-leaders in are reminded consistently to use this discussion board to talk about their starting strategies but not provide answers to the task.

In the program's online environment, a PB Works wiki (www.pbworks.com) or a discussion forum was used in order to support teacher-leaders' exploration of these tasks. For each task teacher-leaders posted their entry point or approach to solving the mathematical tasks for each other to view. This structure allowed students to collaborate if they wanted to gain some insights and support from their colleagues. In many cases, teacher-leaders provided each other with feedback about their approaches and process of solving the tasks.

Analyzing Documents Related to Mathematics Standards

In the United States, the adoption of the Common Core State Standards for Mathematics ([CCSS-M], CCSSI, 2011) has led many teachers to consider how to modify what they teach and how they teach. In that spirit, modules in this program included opportunities for teacher-leaders to study various documents including the state's Common Core Unpacking Documents (http://www.ncpublic-schools.org/acre/standards/common-core-tools/) as well as the national Common Core Progressions Documents (http://ime.math.arizona.edu/progressions/). The Unpacking Documents were written separate for each grade level, so often modules had teacher-leaders intensively examine Standards in one grade or look at 2 or 3 different Unpacking documents to see how the Standards and examples vary across grade levels. In the case of the Progressions Documents, they were organized by content domain and emphasized the building and progression of Standards across grades. The Progressions Documents allowed teacher-leaders to see how one mathematics concept built across grade levels. In all cases teacher-leaders were charged with explicitly analyzing sets of Standards and connecting it to mathematical tasks that they had explored.

In the program's asynchronous online format, the Discussion Forum on the Learning Management System or a PB Works wiki provided a locaton for teacher-leaders to share their insights. These writing prompts aligned to the research on written reflections in online courses (Downing & Dyment, 2013), as teacher-leaders synthesized content from multiple documents and make connections between mathematics concepts.

Analyzing Classroom Vignettes

During the revision of this program into an asynchronous online format for the elementary school mathematics program, there was a need to provide opportunities for teacher-leaders to examine teachers' strategies. The amount of videos freely available is limited, but serve well as objects of inquiry for teacher-leaders to examine both teachers' instructional decisions as well as evidence of student understanding. Most of the videos used in the program came from the

Annenburg's Foundation Mathematics Library (Grades Kindergarten through Grade 4 - http://www.learner.org/resources/series32.html and Grades 5 through Grade 8- http://www.learner.org/resources/series33.html). Written responses and reflective prompts dealt specifically with the high-leverage teaching practices described in Table 2.

In the program's asynchronous online format, the Discussion Forum on the Learning Management System or a PB Works wiki provided a location for teacher-leaders to share their insights. These writing prompts aligned to the research on written reflections in online courses (Downing & Dyment, 2013), as teacher-leaders synthesized content from multiple documents and make connections between mathematics concepts.

Completing Classroom-Based Projects

The final component included in each course was a set of classroom-based activities focused on both the content and the high-leverage teaching practices. These activities were purposefully left open-ended so that teacher-leaders could adapt the activity to the classroom contexts that they had. Teacher-leaders ranged in the Grades that they taught from Kindergarten through Grade 6. Further, numerous teacher-leaders in the program were employed as building-level or district-level leaders. As a result, they had to find a classroom to complete these projects. Table 5 provides a summary of the major classroom-based project in each course. While these were typically the culminating project in the course, teacher-leaders posed tasks to students, analyzed student work, and reflected on the teaching and learning processes with classroom-based activities throughout each course.

These classroom projects provided teacher-leaders with opportunities to apply knowledge and skills that they were developing from other program activities into an elementary school class-

Table 5. Classroom-based projects in the program

	Mathematics Content	High-Leverage Teaching Practice	Classroom-based Projects
1	Number systems and operations	Designing and selecting mathematical tasks	Posing a series of mathematical tasks to students and analyzing student work samples using the Thinking Through a Lesson Protocol
2	Geometry	Assessment	Ongoing assessments of students' mathematical understanding
3	Algebraic reasoning	Discourse and questioning strategies	Analysis of opportunities to address algebraic reasoning in classrooms
4	Rational numbers and operations	Learning trajectories	Posing rational number tasks to students, and facilitating professional development to colleagues about a progression of rational number ideas in the Common Core Standards
5	Data analysis and measurement	Classroom interactions	Analysis of classroom interactions between themselves and students and how those interactions influence students' understanding
6	Mathematical modeling	Leadership and supporting mathematics teaching	Facilitating professional development to a group of teachers Mentoring another teacher through using an instructional intervention with a group of students

room and then reflect on their work and students' mathematical understanding. In the program's asynchronous online format, these projects were largely completed in a manner similar to an independent study. For each course, the instructor provided feedback on drafts and versions of the course. This idea of "chunking" the assignment into smaller components and providing feedback was designed to make teacher-leaders feel more comfortable taking on such large projects. Teacher-leaders frequently e-mailed the professor questions and drafts of these assignments in addition to the required drafts in order to get more feedback and ensure that they were on track to completing a successful project.

Summary of Program Activities

The framework of learner-centered professional development (NPEAT, 2000; Polly & Hannafin, 2011) provided guidelines for designing opportunities for teachers' to further develop their knowledge and skills. In this asynchronous elementary mathematics program designed to enhance teacher-leaders' mathematics content, pedagogical skills, and leadership skills, a variety of program activities embody LCPD and

work cohesively to support teacher-leaders. The classroom-based projects serve as culminating projects in each course where teacher-leaders apply knowledge and skills from the course to complete assignments that involve analyzing and reflecting on the teaching and learning of mathematics. This work is only made possible after teacher-leaders complete extensive experiences exploring cognitively-demanding mathematical tasks, analyzing Standards and other supporting documents, and analyzing classroom vignettes.

METHODS

Research Questions

In order to remain in compliance with the Southern Association of Colleges and Schools (SACS), student performance data is collected and analyzed each semester in order to monitor the outcomes of the program and to establish a process of continuous program improvement. For this chapter, the student performance data for the program were analyzed in order to answer the following research questions:

1. To what extent did teacher-leaders meet the program requirements on the specified student learning outcomes?
2. What did teacher-leaders report as the benefits of a 100% online graduate program in mathematics education?
3. What did teacher-leaders report as ways to improve a 100% online graduate program in mathematics education?

Participants

All participants were current teachers or school-based leaders who held a state teaching license in Elementary Education (Grades K-6; Ages 5-11). There were a total of 18 teacher-leaders who took at least one course in the program. Seven participants completed all 6 of the courses at the time of the study.

Data Sources and Analysis

For the first research question the primary data sources were the assignments completed by candidates during each course and the grades. Using a rubric (Appendix A) each assignment was graded and scored. The students' scores on each rubric were analyzed for frequency counts and percentages for each of the six courses. Students' assignments were broadly examined to look for themes about which tasks were chosen for the portfolio and which tasks best supported more deep reflections about the problem solving processes that teacher-leaders used.

The primary data sources for research questions two and three were from course evaluations and written anonymous surveys that teacher-leaders completed after completing all six courses in the entire program. The surveys were a simple form that had only two questions, "what were the benefits of the program?" and "what were some things that you would like to see improved?" This data from the evaluations and surveys were entered into an Excel spreadsheet. In the spreadsheet

each excerpt had its own row and was initially coded using an open coding process (Coffey & Atkinson, 1996). Each excerpt was coded and then each excerpt was sorted and organized by code. After excerpts had been sorted and grouped, each excerpt was rechecked to make sure that codes precisely matched the excerpt. Groups of codes were then analyzed holistically to identify themes which accurately represented the excerpts that had similar codes.

Findings

In this section we describe the primary themes that were identified during the data analysis process. Within each theme we provide quotes that best illustrate the themes that came from the data.

Research Question One: Student Learning Outcomes

The student learning outcomes in the program are major projects that are required for students to successfully complete during various courses in the program. Appendix A displays the rubrics for the assignments, which we will describe in further detail below.

Student Learning Outcome One: Portfolio of Mathematical Tasks

In each course students completed mathematical tasks that were aligned to mathematics concepts that they were studying. These tasks were multi-step and often required the teacher-leaders to come up with their own strategy of solving problems. After solving tasks teacher-leaders had to summarize the problem solving and also answer reflection questions which required them to synthesize their strategies and connections between mathematical concepts that were embedded in the task.

All ten students (100%) successfully completed the portfolio of mathematical tasks by scoring at the Proficient or Accomplished levels on each element of the rubric. On Element One, correct answers, each teacher-leader scored at the Accomplished level. On Element 2, explanation of processes, 9 out of 10 students (90%) scored Accomplished and 1 student (10%) scored at the Proficient level. The Proficient student did not provide a thorough explanation of their problem solving process on one of the task reflections in their portfolio. On Element 3, connection of mathematical concepts, 6 out of 10 students (60%) scored Accomplished and 4 students (40%) scored at the Proficient level. The portfolios that were proficient had one task (2 students) or two tasks (2 students) that did not include accurate connections between mathematics concepts.

Student Learning Outcome Two: Knowledge of Mathematics Pedagogical Content Knowledge

For student learning outcome two, teacher-leaders completed a major assignment that required them to design mathematical tasks for elementary school learners, consider questions prior to teaching the tasks, collect and analyze student work, and then reflect on the elementary school learners' performance. This assignment took place in the first course in the program and the instructor provided feedback on drafts of the assignment before it was graded. All 18 (100%) of the students who took this course and completed this project scored at the Accomplished level on each element of the rubric for the final version of the project. When teacher-leaders submitted drafts of these assignments they were not scored, but the instructor provided extensive feedback. Feedback was needed on the aspects of the project related to Element 3, analysis of student work and Element 4, reflection. Teacher-leaders struggled in their drafts providing recommendations for future tasks and activities based on the data as well as connecting those recommendations to the actual student work that they analyzed.

Student Learning Outcomes Three and Four: Designing an Educational Intervention and Making an Impact on Student Learning

Student learning outcomes 3 and 4 come from the Mentorship project that teacher-leaders complete in their final course. This project requires teacher-leaders to find a colleague to consult and support in an area related to mathematics teaching and learning. Teacher-leaders focus on a concept in which students are struggling to understand, and use data from their colleague to plan and help implement an educational intervention. On the rubric (Appendix A), each of the 10 teacher-leaders (100%) scored at the Accomplished level on Element 1, mentoring a colleague, and Element 3, the analysis of impact on student learning. On Element 2, 8 teacher-leaders (80%) scored Accomplished and 2 teacher-leaders (20%) scored at Proficient. The two Proficient projects did not adequately address diverse learners and developmentally appropriate strategies to support their mathematical understanding.

Student Learning Outcome Five: Data Analysis Project

Teacher-leaders completed the last student learning outcome during the Geometry/Formative Assessment course. The project requires teacher-leaders to collect data from elementary school students during individual interviews about students' understanding of number sense. Teacher-leaders collect data and then prescribe future instruction and activities based on the data that they collected and analyzed. All seven of the teacher-leaders (100%) scored at Proficient of Accomplished on the rubric for this student learning outcome. Six of the 7 (85.71%) teacher-leaders scored Proficient since the project did not include multiple options for future instruction. One of the 7 teacher-leaders (14.29%) included multiple options, which was scored at the Accomplished level on the rubric.

Summary of Research Question One about Student Learning Outcomes

Each of the teacher-leaders in the program scored at the Proficient or Accomplished levels on each rubric for the different student learning outcomes. Teacher-leaders' success on these outcomes provides evidence that these teacher-leaders were able to navigate the online format of the course and successfully demonstrate their understanding of the mathematics content, research-based pedagogies, and the leadership skills that were emphasized during the program's courses.

Research Question Two: Benefits of the Online Program

Data analysis related to question two led to a few key themes, which include: 1) the flexible nature of the courses, 2) the emphasis on classroom-based projects, and 3) the opportunity to receive support and feedback from colleagues and the instructor.

Flexible Format of the Courses

Each of the teacher-leaders noted that the flexible nature of the courses in the program was a strength that they valued. Each assignment was given either one week or two weeks before it was due, allowing the teacher-leaders to work at their own pace on assignments during times of the week that were most beneficial to them.

One teacher-leader commented about the flexible format of the courses: "I needed this kind of course format that we had in order to complete all of the work. With so many afterschool and evening meetings I would not have been able to participate in a class that had regularly scheduled meetings."

Another teacher-leader, also wrote about the flexible format of the course in one of her course evaluations.

It was very beneficial and helpful to have 1 to 2 weeks to work on our assignments and projects at

our own pace. As a full-time teacher, the amount of work for my day job ebbs and flows, so I needed to have a flexible format to complete the requirements for this additional license. Being able to do things whenever we wanted to before the deadline was very helpful.

The flexible course format was discussed as a positive by all students on surveys and course evaluations.

Emphasis on Classroom-Based Projects

Numerous teacher-leaders reported that they were very pleased with each courses' emphasis on classroom-based projects that they had to carry out in their classroom with their students. Since all program participants were current educators who were earning an advanced degree, the course content primarily included mathematical tasks to solve and projects to complete that required teacher-leaders to apply skills, knowledge, and information in their classroom, and then synthesize their experience with their understanding of mathematics concepts and pedagogies. A teacher-leader wrote the following on her survey about the classroom-based activities:

Each course was loaded with opportunities and activities to try different approaches out with our students in our classroom. This made the concepts and teaching strategies just come to life as we studied and learned about them in the different modules, and then tried them in our classrooms, and finally reflecting about our experiences built on what we were learning about the different concepts and strategies.

Many teacher-leaders reported on their end-of-semester course evaluations that the most powerful learning came when they applied their knowledge in a classroom setting. After completing the course that included Student Learning Outcomes 4 and 5, one participant commented:

The most learning came when I had taken the ideas from the online modules and put them to use in my class with my students. There were projects that required me to work with co-workers in my school to support student learning, design professional development workshops, and interview my students about their problem solving strategies. These activities were a great blend of the information we were learning about and the opportunity to learn more from our own experiences.

Teacher-leaders favorably and willingly completed the classroom-based activities in each course, and successfully connected their own experiences to the mathematical concepts and instructional pedagogies that they were studying.

The Opportunity for Support and Feedback

Teacher-leaders reported on course evaluations and surveys that the support and feedback that they received from instructors on assignments significantly contributed to their success. Major course projects, such as the Student Learning Outcomes, were completed over multiple weeks and involved sending a draft to the instructor to get feedback on various parts of the project. One teacher-leader commented:

On the TTLP Project (Student learning outcome two), I was a bit unsure at first about the kinds of mathematical tasks that I was supposed to plan for and find to give to my students. It made a huge difference and helped myself and my students to be able to get immediate feedback on my draft prior to posing the tasks and doing the project in my classroom.

Many evaluations and surveys included similar comments about feedback on various projects. Some projects, such as the TTLP Project, were mentioned more frequently than others, since it involved a comprehensive list of tasks, including designing tasks, planning a lesson, teaching lessons, collecting student work, and analyzing student work.

While feedback and support were also provided about the mathematical tasks that the teacher-leaders solved and about the analysis of readings and Standards documents, there were only two comments about feedback that was not focused on the course projects. One teacher leader commented,

I like the structure of support for the mathematical tasks and being able to go online and see how other people have started to explore and solve the tasks. However, I noticed that I just didn't use that support as much as I thought that I would.

While the support was there for tasks and the analysis of readings on the various discussion boards, this teacher-leader admittedly did not use that support resource frequently. Further, since there were only two comments in the entire data set about these types of supports, it could be interpreted that teacher-leaders did not value this type of feedback as much as they valued feedback on drafts and parts of the large course projects.

Summary of Findings from Research Question Two about Benefits of the Online Degree Program

In the course evaluations and the end-of-program survey, teacher-leaders reported that the primary benefits of the program were the flexible nature of the course, the emphasis on classroom-based projects, and the opportunity to receive support and feedback from colleagues and the instructor.

RESEARCH QUESTION THREE: AREAS TO IMPROVE THE ONLINE PROGRAM

The analysis of data related to question three focused on three primary themes: 1) just-in-time help and support, 2) collaboration and interaction, and 3) examples of assignments. These themes are described below with excerpts from the data set.

Just-in-Time Help and Support

One of the areas of possible improvement mentioned by teacher-leaders on the course evaluations and surveys was looking for ways to provide just-in-time help and support throughout the course. This comment was often associated with the mathematical tasks that were included in each module. One teacher-leader commented on a survey after completing the program,

There have been tasks during each of the courses that have been very rigorous and hard to figure out. While we have the discussion board where we all post about how we start the tasks, it would be nice to be able to have an immediate place to get hints or tips about how to start the tasks. I definitely spent over an hour on a few tasks just because I wasn't completely confident about how to get started.

While the task discussion board was there to provide support to teacher-leaders while they explored these mathematical tasks, participants wanted a faster way to get feedback than waiting for their colleagues to post ideas on the discussion board.

Collaboration and Interaction

Consistent with prior research about online teaching (Polly, 2013), teacher-leaders in this study provided feedback that there should be more exploration about ways to increase the amount of collaboration and interaction among colleagues. In the first course there is an assignment in which teacher-leaders work in groups of 2 or 3 to explore a task and analyze the ideas of place value in our number system. That project is the only current one that requires collaboration and interaction. Teacher-leaders have expressed the need for more of these types of projects.

One teacher leader mentioned, "The project in the first course where we collaborated in small groups was very beneficial to get the perspectives and the input of others. Also, since it was a large project, dividing the work load and sharing our ideas was very helpful too."

Another teacher leader commented on the evaluation form for the first course:

My favorite experience was the group project because we could collaborate with other students and share ideas. It was very challenging, so it was very helpful to be able to hear other people's thoughts and get help when we got stuck. I hope that we will have more opportunities like that in all of the courses.

While most sought more opportunities to interact and collaborate with each other, a few teacher-leaders commented that they enjoyed being able to do most projects independently on their own time. In fact, some comments seemed to be quite mixed about collaboration. After completing the program, one teacher-leader wrote,

We all signed up for a 100% online program and knew what we were getting into. The idea of collaborating is not a bad one, and in some cases collaborating and helping each other was made possible through the discussion boards or the group project that we had. However, with our busy schedules and different responsibilities, it was beneficial to be able to do most of the work independently and not have to collaborate with others on most assignments and projects.

While many students wanted more collaboration and opportunities for interaction, this feeling was not unanimous among all of the teacher-leaders in the program.

Examples of Projects and Assignments

The last frequently mentioned theme about ways to possibly improve the program was the inclusion of examples of projects and large assignments. For each project, teacher-leaders were provided with instructions and a rubric about how they were going to be graded. Since each course was an asynchronous online course, all questions about the assignments were handled over e-mail. On the course evaluations for the courses that had Student Learning Outcomes, some teacher-leaders requested more clarity on assignments, including examples of projects.

One teacher-leader wrote on the course evaluation for the course which contained the Data Analysis project (Student Learning Outcome five):

The data analysis project was a good application of everything that we had learned in this course and it was nice to connect the information to our classroom. But it was complicated and had many parts. It would have been nice to see an example of a great project so we could know the level of depth for our description of student work and the reflection about the next instructional steps.

Another teacher-leader added:

The rubric for the data analysis project did not give us as much details as I wanted. Examples of previous projects that earned A's would have been great to include so we would know how detailed we needed to be in our analysis of student work and our recommendations for future instruction.

While instructions and a rubric provided some information about the assignment, teacher-leaders reported a desire for more clarity and sample exemplars in order to improve their understanding about what was expected from them.

Summary of Research Question Three about Possible Program Improvements

The analysis of data from the course evaluations and surveys indicated that the teacher-participants desired more just-in-time help and support, more frequent opportunities for collaboration and interaction, and examples of exemplar projects to clarify the expectations on assignments. While these data sources showed overall positive feelings about the online experience, these suggestions could possibly improve the quality of the online asynchronous program.

DISCUSSION AND IMPLICATIONS

The implementation of this program and findings from this study indicate that teacher-leaders have been successful and demonstrated the expected student learning outcomes in each course. Through the Fall, 2013 semester, eight individuals completed the program and another ten individuals took courses in the program en route to a different advanced education degree. Below we provide implications and future directions based on the revision and the implementation of the 6 courses in the program.

Build Asynchronous Courses around Experiences not Content Delivery

Through the design of all six courses in this program the learner-centered professional development (LCPD) framework encouraged the design of course experiences that actively allowed teacher-leaders to develop their knowledge of content and pedagogy in areas that were specifically relevant to their careers in elementary schools. Further, the course activities that were classroom-based allowed teacher-leaders to examine concepts and pedagogies related to student learning and reflect on their learning experience.

In the case of this asynchronous online elementary mathematics program the teacher-leaders completing the courses already had base knowledge related to learning how to teach elementary school mathematics, but gained advanced skills in a graduate program. As a result of their prerequisite knowledge this program could focus intensively on having teacher-leaders complete experiences rather than participate in online lectures or engage in long presentations of information. As a result of this program's focus on providing rich professional learning experiences teacher-leaders completed a lot of classroom-based tasks. Further, they engaged with the content in multiple ways through the completion of mathematical tasks, examining documents related to Standards, analyzing vignettes, and completing activities with students. This comprehensive set of activities provided ample opportunities for teacher-leaders to deepen their knowledge and skills related to elementary school mathematics.

As program developers and course instructors look to build asynchronous online learning experiences, they should begin with a needs analysis and first determine what skills and knowledge students already have, in addition to establishing goals for the overall program as well as individual courses (Moallem, 2003). In the case of this program, the higher education faculty that composed the state-wide working group determined goals for the program and courses. When courses were moved from a face-to-face to an asynchronous online format, those goals were maintained; however, the way in which the goals were reached shifted slightly to include more experiences and activities instead of presentation of information.

Provide Adequate yet Flexible Opportunities for Collaboration and Communication

The teacher-leaders who enrolled in this program had very diverse backgrounds and goals for their program. Some teacher-leaders opted to participate in this program due to the 100% asynchronous format, and did not have any goals related to professional networking and collaboration. Other teacher-leaders participated and desired opportunities to collaborate with their fellow teacher-leaders in the program. Knowing the importance of collaboration and interaction in asynchronous online courses, the instructor established a few program components.

At a minimum, each teacher-leader posted responses to a discussion board or wiki for each module and responded to their colleagues. These responses were reflective questions about their analysis of Standards documents and classroom vignettes. By posting and responding to discussion boards and wikis, teacher-leaders were able to exchange their thoughts and opinions with each other and collaboratively form their thoughts about the materials they were examining. In addition to the discussion on course materials, the instructor also set up a discussion board for participants to share how they explored cognitively-demanding mathematical tasks. Since these tasks were complex, teacher-leaders were able to get hints from each other about ways to start each task.

Discussion boards are often one of the least favorite parts of online courses (Polly, 2012). However, course designers should look for writing prompts or writing activities that more intently address the modules and require students to synthesize and analyze content and ideas at higher levels of thinking. The mere summary of information is not worthwhile forms of communication, but the collaborative analysis of ideas provides potential to intrinsically motivate learners and builds off the foundational ideas of learner-centered instruction (Alexander & Murphy, 1998).

Open-Ended Activities Provide Flexibility and Relevance yet Need Structure

As detailed earlier, LCPD provides teachers with opportunities to take ownership of their learning activities and provides them with flexibility and some elements of choice. In this program, it was essential for teacher-leaders to have choice of the grade and to some degree the concepts that they chose for their classroom-based activities. For example, in the Number Systems and Operations course, when students were working on the relationship between multiplication and division, they had flexibility to work with students from Grade 3 through Grade 5 and could choose the size of numbers that they used for the activity based on students' ability levels. As teacher-leaders continued to work through this activity they each answered the same general reflection questions which focused on students' strategies used to solve the tasks, how students explained their reasoning, and what connections teacher-leaders could make between students' work and other course materials that they analyzed.

Future asynchronous online programs need to explore the option of flexible yet structured activities. The open-ended nature of this program's activities provided teacher leaders with ease in implementing classroom-based activities in settings that they were already working in. However, the structure and set reflection questions were needed to ensure that each teacher-leader was able to come back together and contribute to the class discussion on the discussion board about some central themes and ideas.

Future Directions for Research

There continues to be a need for future research studies to examine the impact of online courses and online programs on participants in these learning experiences. Prior to designing and conducting research studies there is a need for researchers and online instructors to establish and ground projects and studies in a theoretical landscape in order to establish empirical and theoretical rationale for the design of these online programs.

In this chapter the framework of learner-centered professional development (LCPD) was used to revise the six courses in the program and transform them from face-to-face versions into 100% asynchronous online course formats. Specifically, research about the impact of this program should examine the research questions that are detailed in Table 6. These questions are built off

Table 6. Possible research questions to examine

Guskey's Levels of Evaluation (Guskey, 2000)	Research Questions	Data Sources
1: Participants' reactions	What do teacher-leaders think about the various aspects of the courses/program?	Surveys Interviews
2: Participants' knowledge and skills	What knowledge do teacher-leaders gain during the courses/program?	Tests
3: Participants' use of knowledge and skills	To what extent and how do teacher-leaders enact their knowledge gained from the courses/program?	Projects Reflections Classroom observations
4: Impact on organization	What influence does the participation in the courses/program have on schools and school districts' decisions about mathematics teaching and learning?	Surveys Interviews
5: Student learning outcomes	What influence do the courses/program have on the learning of elementary school students?	Tests Student work samples

of Guskey's framework for examining the influence of professional development (Guskey, 2000).

As Table 6 indicates there are a variety of research questions that can be examined based on the multiple levels of Guskey's framework for evaluating the impact of professional development. Future research studies should include multiple data sources to examine some of the research questions detailed above.

REFERENCES

Alexander, P. A., & Murphy, P. K. (1998). The research base for APA's learner-centered psychological principles. In N. M. Lambert & B. L. McCombs (Eds.), *Issues in school reform: A sampler of psychological perspectives on learner-centered schools* (pp. 33–60). Washington, DC: American Psychological Association. doi:10.1037/10258-001

Association of Mathematics Teacher Educators (AMTE). (2013). *Standards for elementary mathematics specialists: A reference for teacher credentialing and degree programs.* Retrieved from: http://amte.net/sites/all/themes/amte/resources/EMS_Standards_AMTE2013.pdf

Bay-Williams, J. M., McGatha, M., Kobett, B. M., & Wray, J. A. (2013). *Mathematics coaching: Resources and tools for coaches and leaders, K-12.* Upper Saddle River, NJ: Pearson.

Cohen, S. (2005). *Teachers' professional development and the elementary mathematics classroom: Bringing understandings to light.* Mahwaw, NJ: Lawrence Erlbaum Associates, Inc.

Common Core State Standards Initiative. (2011). *Common Core State Standards in Mathematics.* Retrieved from: http://www.corestandards.org/Math

Dede, C., Ketelhut, D. J., Whitehouse, P., Breit, L., & McCloskey, R. M. (2009). A research agenda for online teacher professional development. *Journal of Teacher Education, 60*(1), 8–19. doi:10.1177/0022487108327554

Delfino, M., & Persico, D. (2007). Online or face-to-face? Experimenting with different techniques in teacher training. *Journal of Computer Assisted Learning, 23*(5), 351–365. doi:10.1111/j.1365-2729.2007.00220.x

Dennen, V. P. (2007). Presence and positioning of online instructor persona. *Journal of Research on Technology in Education, 40*(1), 95–108. doi:10.1080/15391523.2007.10782499

Downing, J. J., & Dyment, J. E. (2013). Teacher educators' readiness, preparation, and perceptions of preparing preservice teachers in a fully online environment: An exploratory study. *Teacher Educator, 48*(2), 96–109. doi:10.1080/08878730.2012.760023

Dyment, J. E., Downing, J. J., & Budd, Y. (2013). Framing teacher education engagement in an online environment. *Australian Journal of Teacher Education, 38*(1), 134–149. doi:10.14221/ajte.2013v38n1.6

Fishman, B. J., Marx, R. W., Best, S., & Tal, R. T. (2003). Linking teachers and student learning to improve professional development in systemic reform. *Teaching and Teacher Education, 19*(6), 643–658. doi:10.1016/S0742-051X(03)00059-3

Garet, M., Porter, A., Desimone, L., Briman, B., & Yoon, K. (2001). What makes professional development effective? Analysis of a national sample of teachers. *American Educational Research Journal, 38*(4), 915–945. doi:10.3102/00028312038004915

Glazer, E. M., & Hannafin, M. J. (2006). The collaborative apprenticeship model: Situated professional development within school settings. *Teaching and Teacher Education, 22*(2), 179–193. doi:10.1016/j.tate.2005.09.004

Guskey, T. R. (2000). *Evaluating professional development*. Thousand Oaks, CA: Corwin Press.

Heck, D. J., Banilower, E. R., Weiss, I. R., & Rosenberg, S. L. (2008). Studying the effects of professional development: The case of the NSF's local systemic change through teacher enhancement initiative. *Journal for Research in Mathematics Education, 39*(2), 113–152.

HEFCE. (2011). *Collaborate to compete: Seizing the opportunity of online learning for UK higher education*. Report to the Higher Education Funding Council for England (HEFCE) by the Online Learning Task Force. Retrieved from: http://www.hefce.ac.uk/pubs/year/2011/201101/

Henningsen, M., & Stein, M. K. (1997). Mathematical tasks, and student cognition: Classroom-based factors that support and inhibit high-level mathematical thinking and reasoning. *Journal for Research in Mathematics Education, 28*(5), 534–549. doi:10.2307/749690

Hodges, C. B., & Cowan, S. F. (2012). Preservice teachers' views of instructor presence in online courses. *Journal of Digital Learning in Teacher Education, 28*(4), 139–145. doi:10.1080/21532974.2012.10784694

Ko, S., & Rosen, T. (2010). *Teaching online: A practical guide*. New York: Routledge.

Loucks-Horsley, S., Love, N., Stiles, K. E., Mundry, S., & Hewson, P. W. (2009). *Designing professional development for teachers of science and mathematics* (3rd ed.). Thousand Oaks, CA: Corwin Press.

McCrory, R., Putnam, R., & Jansen, A. (2008). Interaction in Online Courses for Teacher Education: Subject Matter and Pedagogy. [Chesapeake, VA: SITE.]. *Journal of Technology and Teacher Education, 16*(2), 155–180.

Moallem, M. (2003). An interactive online course: A collaborative design model. *Educational Technology Research and Development, 51*(4), 85–103. doi:10.1007/BF02504545

National Partnership for Excellence and Accountability in Teaching (NPEAT). (2000). *Revisioning professional development: What learner-centered professional development looks like*. Oxford, OH: Author. Retrieved September 10, 2003, from http://www.nsdc.org/library/policy/npeat213.pdf

North Carolina Elementary Mathematics Add-on Licensure Team. (2009). *Elementary Mathematics Add-on*. License. Proposal to the UNC General Administration for Proposed Program of Study and Licensure Recognition.

O'Connor, E. A. (2011). The effect on learning, communication, and assessment when student-centered Youtubes of microteaching were used in an online teacher-education course. *Journal of Educational Technology Systems, 39*(2), 135–154. doi:10.2190/ET.39.2.d

Orrill, C. H. (2001). Building learner-centered classrooms: A professional development framework for supporting critical thinking. *Educational Technology Research and Development, 49*(1), 15–34. doi:10.1007/BF02504504

Polly, D. (2012). Designing and teaching in an online elementary mathematics methods course: Promises, barriers, and implications. In R. Hartshorne, T. Heafner, & T. Petty (Eds.), *Teacher education programs and online tools: Innovations in teacher preparation* (pp. 335–356). Hershey, PA: IGI Global; doi:10.4018/978-1-4666-1906-7.ch018

Polly, D. (2013). The influence of an online elementary mathematics pedagogy course on teacher candidates' performance. *Journal of Distance Education, 27*(2). Retrieved from http://www.jofde.ca/index.php/jde/article/view/854

Polly, D. (2014). Deepening pre-service teachers' knowledge of technology, pedagogy, and content (TPACK) in an elementary school mathematics methods course. *Journal of Computers in Mathematics and Science Teaching, 33*(2), 233–250.

Polly, D., & Hannafin, M. J. (2010). Reexamining technology's role in learner-centered professional development. *Educational Technology Research and Development, 58*(5), 71. doi:10.1007/s11423-009-9146-5

Polly, D., & Hannafin, M. J. (2011). Examining how learner-centered professional development influences teachers' espoused and enacted practices. *The Journal of Educational Research, 104*(2), 120–130. doi:10.1080/00220671003636737

Polly, D., McGee, J. R., & Martin, C. S. (2010). Employing technology-rich mathematical tasks to develop teachers' technological, pedagogical, and content knowledge (TPACK). *Journal of Computers in Mathematics and Science Teaching, 29*(4), 455–472.

Quality Matters. (n.d). *Higher Education Program: Rubric*. Retrieved from: https://www.qualitymatters.org/rubric

Sobel, D. M., Sands, D. I., Dunlap, J. C. (2009). Teaching intricate content online: It can be done and done well. *Action in Teacher Education, 30*(4).

Tallent-Runnels, M. K., Thomas, J. A., Lan, W. Y., Cooper, S., Ahern, T. C., Shaw, S. M., & Liu, X. (2006). Teaching courses online: A review of the research. *Review of Educational Research, 76*(1), 93–135. doi:10.3102/00346543076001093

U.S. Department of Education (USDE). (2008). *Foundations for Success: The Final Report of the National Mathematics Panel*. Retrieved from: http://www2.ed.gov/about/bdscomm/list/math-panel/report/final-report.pdf

Work, A. P. A. Group of the Board of Educational Affairs (1997). Learner-centered psychological principles: A framework for school reform and redesign. Washington, DC: Author.

KEY TERMS AND DEFINITIONS

Add-On License: An additional credential to a teacher's license in the United States.

Asynchronous: Online instruction where students complete assignments on their own time and no online course meetings occur.

Elementary School: School that educates learners from Grades Kindergarten through Grade 5 typically Ages 5 through 11.

Learning Outcomes: Predetermined goals for learners in a course, class, unit, or lesson.

Mathematical Tasks: Problems that students explore and/or solve.

Mathematics Education: The field related to the teaching and learning of mathematics.

Online Course: A course that is taken via the internet that either has online meetings (synchronous) or no online meetings (asynchronous).

Teacher-Leaders: School employees who teach students in a school and also have either informal or formal leadership responsibilities.

APPENDIX: RUBRICS FOR STUDENT LEARNING OUTCOMES

Table 7. Student Learning Outcome 1: Knowledge of mathematics content portfolio of mathematical tasks rubric

	Developing	Proficient	Accomplished
Element 1: Correct Answers	Three or more tasks in the portfolio do not have a correct answer.	All but one or two mathematical tasks in the portfolio has a correct answer.	Every mathematical task in the portfolio has a correct answer.
Element 2: Explanation of Processes	Three or more tasks in the portfolio do not have a thorough and accurate explanation of the processes.	Every mathematical task except one or two is accompanied by a thorough and accurate explanation of the processes.	Every mathematical task is accompanied by a thorough and accurate explanation of the processes.
Element 3: Explanation of the connection of mathematical concepts	Three or more tasks in the portfolio do not have a through and accurate explanation about how the mathematical concepts in the task connect to one another.	Every mathematical task except one or two is accompanied by a through and accurate explanation about how the mathematical concepts in the task connect to one another.	Every mathematical task is accompanied by a through and accurate explanation about how the mathematical concepts in the task connect to one another.

Table 8. Student Learning Outcome 2: Knowledge of mathematics pedagogical content knowledge thinking through a lesson plan protocol rubric

	Developing	Proficient	Accomplished
Element 1: Sequence of Mathematical Tasks	The TTLP lacks a sequence of cognitively-demanding tasks.	The TTLP includes a sequence of cognitively-demanding tasks focused on one mathematics concept.	The TTLP includes a sequence of cognitively-demanding tasks focused on one mathematics concept that addresses various levels of student development.
Element 2: Planned Pedagogies	The TTLP lacks appropriate pedagogies, including questions and manipulatives.	The TTLP includes appropriate pedagogies, including questions and manipulatives.	The TTLP includes a diverse range of pedagogies, including questions and manipulatives, intended to address various levels of student development.
Element 3: Analysis of Student Work	The TTLP lacks an in depth analysis of student work.	The TTLP includes an analysis of student work, including a summary of students' experiences with each of the tasks.	The TTLP includes an analysis of student work, including a summary of students' experiences with each of the tasks, and recommendations for future tasks.
Element 4: Reflection	The TTLP lacks a reflection that provides an analysis of the candidate's experiences and student learning.	The TTLP includes a reflection that provides an analysis of the candidate's experiences and student learning.	The TTLP includes a reflection that provides an analysis of the candidate's experiences and student learning, and implications for future instruction.

Table 9. Student Learning Outcome 3 and 4: Designing an Educational Intervention and Impact on Student Learning Mentorship Project Rubric

	Developing	Proficient	Accomplished
Element 1: Mentoring Colleague	The Mentorship project lacks evidence about how the candidate has mentored a colleague.	The Mentorship project includes evidence about how the candidate has mentored a colleague.	The Mentorship project includes evidence about how the candidate has mentored a colleague, including ways in which the mentorship has addressed colleagues' specific needs.
Element 2: Design of Intervention	The Mentorship project lacks evidence about how the intervention embodies research-based pedagogies.	The Mentorship project includes evidence about how the intervention embodies research-based pedagogies.	The Mentorship project lacks evidence about how the intervention embodies research-based pedagogies, including varied strategies for diverse students.
Element 3: Analysis of Impact	The Mentorship project lacks a thorough analysis of how the project impacted their colleague and students.	The Mentorship project includes a thorough analysis of how the project impacted their colleague and students.	The Mentorship project includes a thorough analysis of how the project impacted their colleague and students. There are implications for future mentorship activities.

Table 10. Student Learning Outcome 5: Knowledge of mathematics formative assessment strategies data analysis project rubric

	Developing	Proficient	Accomplished
Element 1: Analyzing Data	The Data Analysis Project lacks a thorough analysis of data from 3 students.	The Data Analysis Project includes a thorough analysis of data from 3 students, including an itemized analysis for each student.	The Data Analysis Project includes a thorough analysis of data from 3 students, including an itemized analysis for each student. The analysis includes qualitative descriptions of students' errors.
Element 2: Prescribing Future Instruction	The Data Analysis project lacks prescriptions for future instruction.	The Data Analysis project includes prescriptions for future instruction that are based on the data.	The Data Analysis project includes prescriptions for future instruction that are based on the data. These prescriptions include multiple options in case students have success or continue to struggle.

Chapter 5

Evaluation of Mobile Learning Project at the UAE University:
College of Engineering Case Study

Mousa. I. Hussein
UAE University, UAE

ABSTRACT

The relentless expansion of information technology in educational institutions is widely acknowledged. There is substantial evidence that technology enhances student learning and educational outcomes. Many colleges and universities have adapted technology in their education system. The college of Engineering at the United Arab Emirates University launched its IT-based active learning (Laptop) project at the first semester of the academic year 2002-2003. After several years of implementation, the college is reviewing its course development technology strategy and is asking a very important question, "Did our investment in technology result in enhanced learning outcomes and promote the new, learner-centered pedagogy, or did it have little impact on learning?" The work presented in this chapter highlights the main outcomes and conclusions of a survey study, which was developed to answer the raised question. Many lessons have been learned about the benefits and difficulties in being a laptop college. These lessons are documented in this chapter.

INTRODUCTION

According to Felder (1992), of all instructional methods, lecturing is the most common, the easiest, and the least effective. Unless the instructor is a real splendor, most students cannot stay focused throughout a lecture: after about 10 minutes their attention begins to drift, first for brief moments and then for longer intervals; they find it increasingly hard to catch up on what they missed while their minds were wandering. Various studies indicated that immediately after a lecture students recalled 70% of the information presented in the first ten minutes and only 20% of that from the last ten minutes, Hill, Reeves & Heidemeier (2000); Felder (1992) and Barr & Tagg (1995).

Nonetheless the challenges faced by today's university graduates are very diverse and stimulating. Imagination and ingenuity are required to convert recent advances into useful and effective

DOI: 10.4018/978-1-4666-7316-8.ch005

applications. Such advancements and changes, ultimately, form a challenging task for educators, Brophy, Norris, Nichols & Jansen (2003). Technology is a recognized part of the overall tools for supporting and enhancing teaching and learning. Many colleges and universities have responded by making technology more ubiquitous.

Throughout the world, Information Technology (IT) is generating a new revolution more significant and out-reaching than those of the past. The relentless expansion of information technology into society in general and educational institutions specifically is widely acknowledged. The use of information help to harness the vast array of resources available and stimulate the development of lifelong learning skills. The "stand and deliver" theory of education needs to be modified or replaced. Learners are required to have interpersonal skills that allow them to have visions of the larger picture and to work together in collaboration with others to reach solutions presented to them in daily working and living. Thus, the instructor will no longer be the universal fountain of knowledge and the student will no longer be graded on his or her ability to remember facts and relate them back to the teacher. Educational institutions will be *learner-based rather than-instructor based.*

In order to overcome the traditional lecture drawbacks, students must be actively involved in the various learning activities within class time. Active involvement in learning, instead of simply lecturing to students, leads to improved attendance, deeper questioning, higher grades, and greater lasting interest in the subject. Various institutions have come to realize that it is better to couple the shift towards active learning by utilizing the full potential of mobile computing and e-learning technologies to facilitate the transition, McGhee & Kozma (2001), McKenzie (2001) and Moody & Schmidt (2004). Moreover, the UAE University strategic plan has emphasized the need to shift from traditional lecture to student-centered active learning methods.

DEVELOPING UBIQUITOUS COMPUTING INFRASTRUCTUTRE AT UAEU

Like many universities all over the globe, the UAE University approach to meeting student computer needs has been one of placing computers and state-of-the-art technology in specialized classrooms, laboratories, the library, and in dormitories. Some students owned computers, which in some cases were not compatible with those in the campus facilities. Despite the continuous upgrade and expansion in IT services and facilities, there were still problems associated with the utilization of the current advanced computing/IT infrastructure such as:

- Students are tied to a limited physical space;
- Time/space limitation and utilization of computing labs due to its occupancy by lectures almost all day long throughout the week, this common type of utilization has limited the use of computers and technology;
- There were usually few empty seats in all classrooms each hour of the day. Computers were in classrooms but they were unavailable for student use during class hours; and
- Faculty also competed for access to the limited computer laboratory time.

These problems have limited the use of computers and technology as an education enabling tool for enhancing teaching and learning. There has been a growing need for student use of computers outside the classroom. In order to overcome the problems of traditional computing labs at UAE University and to take full advantage of the power of mobile (ubiquitous) computing, UAE University has initiated a study of implementing and integrating mobile technologies into the curriculum.

The "laptop program" and "laptop project" are the names given at UAE University to the largest e-learning project in the region that applies the concepts of ubiquitous computing. However, the primary objective of the project is to use the laptop and wireless network (ubiquitous computing) to promote active learning and student-centered learning environment. The laptop program is not only geared towards solving the problems of traditional computer labs, but it also aims at shifting from traditional lecture environment to active learning, student-centered learning environment. The laptop project at UAE University should be viewed as the climax of synchronized efforts, planning and projects that started since the early 1990's.

Background and History

UAE University has started to seriously address the issue of implementing IT in the educational environment since the early 1990's. It has started to aggressively develop and expand its IT infrastructure. Since the late 1990's, UAEU has focused on IT with a shift in strategy:

- Integration, rather than implementation, of IT into its curriculum;
- Expanding, upgrading and developing its network, hardware and software infrastructure;
- Enhancing learning and teaching as the primary objective;
- Integrating Video Conferencing Technology and Smart Classrooms into teaching and learning to open new venues for distance learning and the integration of IT in learning and teaching; and
- Linking all IT plans to UAEU strategic plan.

In addition to the infrastructure development and expansion, UAEU has launched various programs, seminars and workshops to assist and to support the ongoing development of the IT skills for faculty and staff such as:

- The program for IT in learning and teaching
- Innovative Teaching Fund
- The program for basic IT skills
- Staff Workshops
- Workshops and training courses for IT technical staff

Furthermore, studies to establish the Center for Technology in Learning and Teaching in order to assume a leading role in the implementation of UAEU's vision and plans to integrate IT into learning and teaching has been completed. Similar studies, such as enhancing the technical support has been completed to address the current and future needs of IT technical support whether in terms of quality and/or quantity. All studies are synchronized and coordinated within an overall IT plan that focuses on the integration of IT into learning and teaching and in light of UAEU's strategic plan.

Building the Mobile (Laptop) Environment

In order to overcome the existing problems (e.g. traditional lectures and traditional computing labs) and to successfully integrate IT into learning and teaching, a study of integrating the laptop into the curriculum has been conducted.

The study for the Laptop Project has been completed during the academic year 2001-2002. The implementation of the project started during the first semester 2002-2003. The main objective is to create a mobile computing environment (ubiquitous computing) where students and faculty can access the university computing environment ANYTIME, ANYWHERE. Furthermore, it aims at enhancing the learning and teaching processes to maintain its leading IT role in the region. The objective of the project has been to induce improvements in:

- Curriculum integration with IT
- Lifelong learning skills

- Asynchronous and synchronous communication skills
- Retention rate
- Student-centered, active learning skills
- Team building and cooperation skills

UAE University has devised a framework to continue developing its mobile computing environment. The framework consists of integrated and synchronized components/activities to facilitate successful implementation. Initial preparation of the components has been completed during the summer of 2002 that included classrooms preparations and remodeling, installing wireless networks in selected classrooms and open spaces, completing the laptop tender and preparing for delivery, and completing the preparation for unprecedented technical support operation . During the first semester 2002-2003 the laptop program has started in four colleges, for practical purposes: 1) College of information Technology; 2) College of Engineering; 3) College of Business and Economics; and 4) College of Food Systems. The following are some critical issues from the first year experience of implementation:

- An instructor who is currently using active learning activities in the classroom will have no difficulty in introducing the laptop into some of these activities. Using the laptop effectively for a small part of a class period is better than using it ineffectively all of the time. It is best if the introduction of the laptop is natural and not forced. An instructor who is currently teaching entirely in lecture mode will find it more difficult to introduce the laptop into the classroom.
- Instructors must first be convinced that mini-lectures together with active learning activities can be more effective than lecturing. It is rather difficult to convince most faculty to shift, especially the older generation. One approach that helps in disseminating the concept is to conduct seminars that focus on

successful case/experiences whether inside the institution or in other institutions.
- Not all courses are suitable for early implementation in the laptop projects. Only courses with clear and well defined objectives are suitable for early implementation. Courses that rely on tacit knowledge and learning by action, are suitable for early implementation. Courses with a heavy computational component and humanity courses like English composition and history are good fits for laptops (courses that rely on explicit knowledge).
- Set expectations to students. Students have to contribute in this experiment and they must be considered as part of a bold experiment. Communication with students prior to the start of the program is critical. Students need to be told why the university is starting this program and what the expected benefits are. Students need to understand that they will find many uses for the laptop outside of the classroom. They need to understand that laptop courses are under development and that there will be a learning period for both students and faculty. When experimenting with new learning activities students need to know that their opinions about the effectiveness of these activities will be considered. Students should be told to expect an increase in the amount of student-student collaboration in learning.

It is interesting to note that some of these questions were addressed when engineers shifted from the sliding ruler to the calculator. UAEU devised two venues for funding the course restructuring processes and activities: 1) innovative teaching fund; and 2) laptop course development fund. A supporting website for the laptop program helped provide faculty with required information for development. It should be noted that *No laptop courses are perfect from day one.* They will evolve over 2-3 semesters.

Course Management Software (Blackboard)

Critical to the success of the pedagogical issues mentioned above is the selection of a Course Management Software. UAE University along with the other federal Institutions has launched a study to select course management software. The UAE University has selected Blackboard as its official course management software for its technical capabilities and ease of use and its fast learning curve.

The decision to deploy Blackboard has proven to be successful for various reasons:

1. After the initial training for selected team of faculty members (20), the administration had to respond to an unprecedented demand and requests for training workshops from all colleges.
2. During the first year the Center for Technology in Teaching and Learning completed the training of more than 360 faculty members.
3. During the first year 350 courses (1176 sections) have been re-structured for online delivery on Blackboard with more than 10 million hits.

When an institution attempts to select course management software (CMS), it is critical to focus on the end user as much as the technical capabilities. If the CMS is loaded with options and complex tasks and tools, the majority of the faculty will not use it. If the CMS is equipped with sufficient capabilities and is easy to use, then the majority of the faculty will attempt to test it and then use it. The selection process for UAE University was rather difficult and tedious, however, the initial outcome as demonstrated above, indicates successful selection.

Technology and Support

From the first day of planning it was clear that in order to sustain the successful growth of the project it is eminent to devise a multifaceted technology plan that would provide the following.

1. **Standardize Hardware**
   a. Experiences from the other universities indicate that standardization of computer hardware and software has become a must. During the academic year 2001-2002 all academic units will have Windows 2000 as the standard operating system(OS) and MSOffice (Word, Excel, Power Point, Outlook, and IE) as the standard installed software
   b. The utilization of standardized OS and software will help developing hard disk images/ghosts for the laptops and thus, enhancing the technical support and crash recovery procedures from days and hours to minutes.
   c. UAEU has selected DELL laptops for the first year (renewable for three years) through a tender procedure. The technical specs for the laptop vary and reviewed every semester. Typically, almost all laptop programs are using either DELL or IBM. Both vendors are the only major vendors who provide special arrangements for this type of projects.
2. **Standard Laptop Configuration:** All laptops are configured at the factory according to pre-designed images developed by the technical staff at UAEU as follows:
   a. Disk Drive: Partition C: for OS and programs, D: for data and documents and E: for images of C:.
   b. Install University licensed software on the laptop, i.e. vendor loads image at factory

c. Configure laptop for University use (UAE University network identification and authentication).

This standard configuration has proven very successful and helped the support team to resolve unexpected problems. The average response time to recover the hard disk image did not exceed 10-15 minutes.

3. **Help Desk and Repair Operation:** A sudden increase of 2100 laptops during the first year of implementation represents a real challenge. This requires an innovative and serious preparation of various support activities, processes and procedures. Help desk are the first line of support and their primary function is to solve minor problems and sort the more complicated problems into one of the following channels:

a. On-campus hardware support by the vendor. This includes loan laptop if the repairs take more than 4 hours

b. Software support via UAE University IT support engineers

c. Faculty & Students orientation regarding technical aspects and help desk operations

Although, this structure is very important, however, defining the boundaries and responsibilities of both hardware and software support can prevent unnecessary problems, especially the boundaries and overlap between software and hardware support.

4. **Wireless Environment Needs**

a. 66 new/remodeled classroom in 3 campuses have been connected to the network via wireless access points in addition to selected public/open spaces.

b. UAE University started with Class A wireless network because it provides more bandwidth

c. Currently the wireless network is being upgraded to class G (provides more bandwidth and better performance) than class B or A

d. The wireless technology in the classroom must be identical (or at least fully compatible) with wireless network to avoid multiple wireless cards

e. Wireless network security is so immature at this point that only a few universities and businesses have implemented an Enterprise level plan. Starting the second semester 203-2004, UAE University will implement a security plan for the wireless network.

The wireless network is only as good as the underlying wired infrastructure. UAE University has upgraded its network to Gigabit network in all campuses with fiber optic backbone between campuses that provides up to 155 Mbps between the campuses. After 10 years of the initial development and launching, the new campus backbone network was enhanced to 10 gigabits per second (Gbps). This major infrastructure improvement enables faster data flow through the campus network. Increasing network speed facilitates data-intensive services for teaching, research and communications. Behind the scenes, hundreds of wired & wireless network equipment, servers connect computers to applications used daily, link to the Internet, and store files, email messages, and other data vital to the UAE University. Nonetheless the new wireless was enhanced to the speed of 54Mb.

Course Development Guidelines

In order to clarify the expected outcome for course development, it is rather critical to provide a standard form and guidelines for the restructuring and course development for the laptop program. The form and guidelines communicate the expectations and minimum requirements to all faculty members. The guidelines have been carefully developed to communicate the underlining concepts to the faculty members involved and help them to understand of what is required. The guidelines focus on various issues that can be summarized as follows:

Effective Integration of Content & Technology

The issue of integrating technology into the curriculum in order to shift from traditional teaching practices to a student-centered learning environment is the primary objective of the laptop project. Therefore, it is critical to highlight some of the critical issues for course development and restructuring:

- **Define & Revise:** Course objectives and Outcomes
- **Restructure:** course delivery and content according to appropriate technology (technology appropriate and suitable for the course and discipline)

Course Delivery and Restructuring (Studio Model)

- Effective Integration of Technology and Content:
  - ◦ Restructuring content;
  - ◦ Redesigning and Restructuring Delivery methods;
  - ◦ Integrating Delivery methods and content; and
  - ◦ Developing the interactive mobile work environment: Spatial and Virtual
- Lecture Replaced by (active learning methodology and approach):
  - ◦ Mini lectures;

- ◦ Collaborative & Cooperative learning experience;
- ◦ More hands-on experience; and
- ◦ Instructor as "Mentor" or "Facilitator"
- Technology
  - ◦ Select the appropriate technology for your course and discipline
  - ◦ Integrate technology into most of the class activities
  - ◦ Use technology to facilitate communication, collaboration and cooperation among students.
- *Develop* various types of faculty/students & student/student interaction and select appropriate technology for interaction (e.g., synchronous and asynchronous)
- *Design* collaborative activities among students (teamwork) and use suitable active learning methods such as engaged learning, problem-based learning, project-based learning, etc.
- *Assess* (assessment techniques for both course and students)

LAPTOP PROJECT TEN YEARS LATER

Many years have elapsed since the first implementation of the laptop project, and classes have been taught using laptops in a variety of ways depending on the subject matter. Currently all the College of Engineering courses are restructured to take advantage of the laptop and the wireless network as extra teaching and learning aids.

After several years of implementation and substantial investment, the college of engineering at UAE university decided to review its technology strategy by asking a very important question such as, "Did our investment in technology results in enhanced learning outcomes and promote the new, learner-centered pedagogy or did it have little impact on learning?"

METHODOLOGY

In order for the college to be able to address this question, two surveys are prepared. Thus the work presented in this chapter is the outcome of two surveys, one developed to cast students' opinion and the other survey was prepared to cast instructors' feedback and opinion about such experience. The surveys were then distributed to students and faculty members at the college, and several interviews were conducted with the faculty members to gauge their opinions. Many lessons have been learned about the benefits and difficulties in being a laptop college of engineering. These lessons are documented in this paper.

Student Survey

A fifty four (54) structured question survey (Appendix A) was developed by the college committee and distributed to all students who are enrolled in the college of engineering and using laptop in all classes taught by the college. This includes Engineering Requirement Unit (ERU), first year engineering students, and the Department of Architectural engineering, Civil and Environmental engineering, Chemical and Petroleum engineering, Electrical engineering, and Mechanical engineering. A total of 476 students participated in this survey.

The survey was designed to include personal questions regarding the student's academic department, number of Laptop courses registered in and number of years at UAE University. In addition, the survey included several questions about the student's use of Laptop both inside and outside the classroom and their perception of the usefulness of the laptop project. The 54 questions in the survey were grouped in five categories, covering the following topics:

- Learning Quality & Satisfaction (composed of 15 questions),

- Use of e-Learning Tools in learning and teaching (composed of 10 questions),
- Laptop and Online Usage (composed of 12 questions),
- Infrastructure and IT Services (composed of 17 questions),
- Comments and Suggestions.

Faculty Survey

Faculty survey was made of thirty three (33) structured questions and 9 interview questions (Appendix B). The survey was developed by the committee and distributed to all faculty members who are involved in Laptop teaching. A total of 51 faculty member participated in this survey. The 33 questions were grouped in the same categories as in the students' survey. The Comments and Suggestions category was made of 9 interview questions, covering the following topics:

- What are the strengths of the "laptop project developed courses" applied at UAEU?
- What are the current weaknesses of the "laptop project developed courses" applied at UAEU?
- How can UAEU enhance the "laptop project" to become more beneficial in learning and teaching?
- What threats can the "laptop project" pose to the quality and delivery of interactive teaching and learning?
- What percentage of adjustments did you introduce to your course and teaching style to adapt the new technology?
- If you can, please mention some examples.
- What problems have you encountered as an instructor as part of teaching a 'laptop course'?
- How do you define hands-on teaching?
- How do you define Interactive teaching?
- Do you have other Comments?

Table 1. Grading choices used in all surveys

Strongly Disagree - 1	Disagree - 2	Neutral - 3	Agree - 4	Strongly Agree - 5

SURVEY RESULTS AND ANALYSIS

Structured questions were given five choices starting with the least preference as *Strongly Disagree*, and ending with the highest preference as *Strongly Agree*, each preference is assigned numerical value as shown in Table 1.

For the purpose of analysis the five choices were combined into three categories of responses as negative response, neutral response, and positive response. Such that *Strongly Disagree* and *Disagree* were grouped together as negative responses, and *Strongly Agree* and *Agree* were grouped together as positive. Whereas neutral remained as the third choice. The detailed results of students' and faculty's surveys are given in appendices C and D respectively.

Students' Survey Results

The survey covered four main areas, these are, learning quality and satisfactions, the use of e-learning tools in learning and teaching, laptop and online usage, and infrastructure and IT services. The following is an analysis of the survey results.

Learning Quality and Satisfaction

This part of the survey was made of 15 questions. These questions can be grouped into three main categories; these were learning quality and students' added capabilities, class environment and interaction, and overall quality and satisfaction.

Students' learning quality and satisfaction is directly linked to the students' opinion as to whether having laptop has enhanced students' learning, students' capabilities of self-learning, communication skills, in/outside class interac-

tions and teamwork and class materials presentation. Students' perception and responses were significantly positive in all three categories; this is clearly illustrated in Figure 1.

Use of e-Learning Tools in Learning and Teaching

A total of ten (10) questions were developed in this part of the survey. The questions may be grouped into three categories, such as Laptop teaching activities, online teaching activities, and lecture delivery and class interaction.

Figure 2 shows that close to 60% of the students surveyed believed that laptop teaching activities and online teaching activities have enhanced students' understanding of the material, and enhanced students' capabilities of communication and interaction with colleagues and instructors. More the 50% believed that lecture delivery with laptop is far more informative than the traditional way.

Laptop and Online Usage

In this part the questions were categorized as, overall usage of laptop, software usage, Blackboard activities, and traditional teaching during class. As Figure 3 illustrates, students seemed be satisfied with *"Laptop online use"*, both in and out of the classrooms, such as using the course website (Blackboard) and internet, simulation software, students' interaction among themselves and with the course instructor, and online assessment. Nonetheless traditional way of teaching (White Board) is still highly used by instructors; close to 50% of students believe that instructors are still teaching using the traditional way, along with IT-based methods.

Figure 1. Student survey results on learning quality and satisfaction

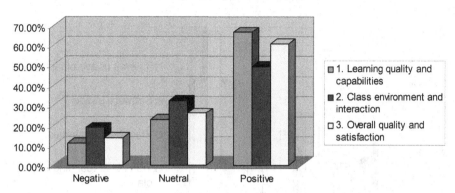

Figure 2. Student survey results on the use of e-Learning tools in learning and teaching

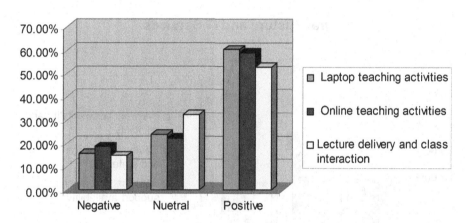

Infrastructure and IT Services

The questions here are grouped into three categories, Figure 4, these are network accessibility and reliability, classroom environment and suitability, and software and technical support availability.

As for the quality and satisfaction with *"Infrastructure and IT services"* about 50% of the students seemed to have no problem and they are satisfied with *network accessibility and reliability, classroom environment, and software and technical support*, however, some students showed concern about accessibility of server based software such as MATLAB and AUTOCAD, due to the number of licenses and lack of accessibility from hostels.

Faculties' Survey Results

The survey was designed to cover five areas, these are: Learning quality and satisfactions, the use of e-learning tools in learning and teaching, laptop and online usage, infrastructure and IT services, and nine interview questions. The interview questions were aimed to gauge the variety of views and perceptions that faculty members have about the laptop project applied at the college, as well as to

Figure 3. Student survey results on laptop and online usage

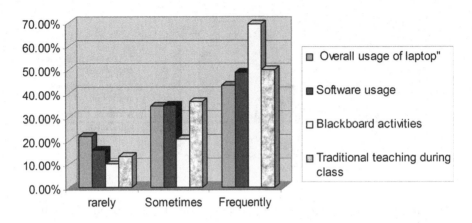

Figure 4. Student survey results on infrastructure and IT services

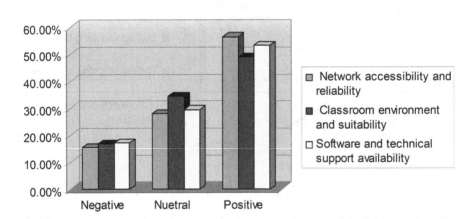

communicate any further difficulties or remarks that might be raised by the faculty members.

Learning Quality and Satisfaction

This part of the survey was made of 6 questions. These questions were related to the quality of teaching and learning using laptop. Such as:

- 2.7, 2.8 Laptops aid students to solve challenging problems that are needed to understand the material

- 2.9 Laptops aid instructors to present their materials more effectively
- 2.10 It is difficult/inconvenient to use my laptop during class
- 2.11 Students' attention is distracted due to the use of their laptops during lectures
- 2.12 Interactive teaching is directly linked to the laptop project
- 2.13 The improvements of interactive teaching using the laptop project are excellent overall

Figure 5. Faculty survey results on learning quality and satisfaction

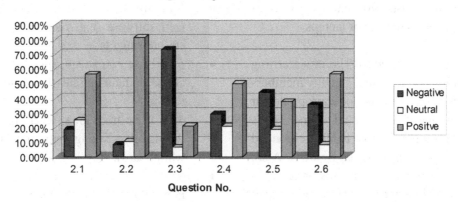

Figure 6. Faculty survey results on the use of e-learning tools in learning and teaching

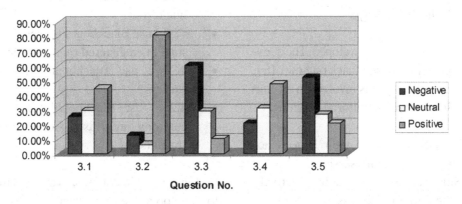

Analyzing faculty members feedback regarding the "*Learning quality and learning satisfaction*" as shown in Figure 5, the responses were 50%-80% positive in questions 2.1, 2.2, 2.3, 2.4 and 2.6. Question 2.5 which relate to direct link between interactive learning and the use of laptop the responses were 40% in the negative side and 30% positive. This reflects the awareness of faculty members on the importance of incorporating other active learning tools and methods side-by-side with the IT-based methods.

Use of e-Learning Tools in Learning and Teaching

Five (5) questions were developed in this part of the survey; they were related to the convenience of using laptop, and developing student–instructor interaction.

- 3.6, 3.7 Laptops are convenient for students to use during in-class exercises and exams
- 3.8 Laptops are convenient for students to use in homework assignments and term projects
- 3.9 Online (Blackboard) exams are appropriate for all course levels and types

- 3.10 The Blackboard system is the key towards IT-based active learning
- 3.11 Student-instructor interaction is directly linked to the use of laptops

In the questions related to "Use of e-learning tools in learning and teaching", faculty members believed that Blackboard is not appropriate for conducting online exams for all course levels and types (Question 3.3), close to 60% responded negatively to this questions, see figure 6. Also, question 3.5 which relates to the link of laptop to students' interactions received 50% negative responses. This, again, reflects the faculty members' awareness of the relative importance of other tools and methods of interactive learning.

Laptop and Online Usage

In this part 12 questions were developed. The questions are designed to get a feedback on how often the instructor gets the students involved in on-line activities during lecture and tutorial sessions.

- 4.13, 4.14 Students use their laptops actively during the lecture sessions.
- 4.15 Students use their laptops actively during the tutorial / lab sessions.

- 4.16 Students are required to use the Internet during class (<u>NOT</u> Blackboard).
- 4.17 Students use course specific/specialized software (e.g. modeling, simulation, etc.) during class.
- 4.18 I use course specific software during class to demonstrate the concepts being taught.
- 4.19 I use traditional teaching techniques during class along with the laptop (e.g. whiteboard).
- 4.20 I use Blackboard for posting PowerPoint presentations and lecture documents.
- 4.21 I use Blackboard for posting and receiving assignments.
- 4.22 I use Blackboard for conducting online tests.
- 4.23 I use Blackboard for sending emails to students registered on my class.
- 4.24 I use Blackboard for conducting surveys.
- 4.25 I use Blackboard for creating discussions and discussion groups among students.

Figure 7 illustrates survey's results related to "Laptop and online usage", responses related to using software packages in teaching, simula-

Figure 7. Faculty survey results on laptop and online usage

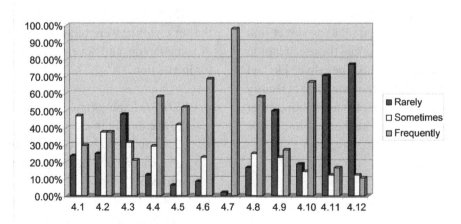

tion software, use of presentation software, use of Blackboard, and use of traditional teaching method (whiteboard), received 60%-100% positive responses in terms of frequent usage. While as questions related to the use of internet during class session and use of Blackboard for online testing, conducting surveys, and creating discussion groups the responses were 50-75% in the negative side.

Infrastructure and IT Services

This section is made of 10 questions related to the instructors' preparation on using Blackboard system and active learning, and casts instructors' satisfaction with infrastructure and IT services available at the college.

- 5.11, 5.12 Faculty members may need training for using the Blackboard system.
- 5.13 Faculty members may need training on interactive teaching methods.
- 5.14 Laptop-based classes usually start smoothly without much need for debugging problems (e.g. missing cable, defective lamp, data projector problems).
- 5.15 The Blackboard system is efficient and easy to access at all times.

- 5.16 Faculty members receive adequate support for the required software packages.
- 5.17 Faculty members receive adequate support for laptop problems.
- 5.18 I am able to use all software packages I need on my laptop (e.g licenses, cpu speed, RAM etc.).
- 5.19 The facilities at the College (e.g., data show projectors, screens, classrooms … etc) are adequate for the full implementation of the interactive teaching using the laptop project.
- 5.20 The College's technical infrastructure (e.g. network / wireless connections) is adequate for the full implementation of the use of wireless laptops.
- 5.21 The College's infrastructure and IT support services are excellent overall.

As for the "Infrastructure and IT services", close to 40% of the faculty members support the idea of conducting training sessions for faculty members on the use of Blackboard system, and more the 60% are in favor of attending training sessions on Interactive teaching methods. Close to 55% of the faculty are having problems with laptop classrooms, either data cable is not available, defected projectors lambs, or data projector

Figure 8. Faculty survey results on infrastructure and IT services

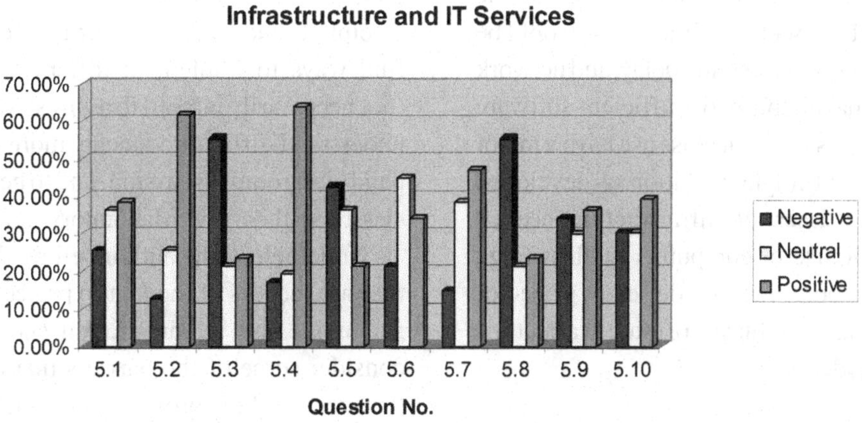

start up problems. Faculties' response for software packages support (College/University) was more that 40% negative.

Interview Survey by Faculty

The interview survey is introduced to give faculty members freedom to express their opinion and provide their feedback about the weaknesses and threats, strengths, and possible enhancements that laptop teaching might have on the education process. Most faculty showed concern that laptop courses, in general, may distract the student from exploring primary sources of learning (i.e., textbook or reference books) and others feel that laptop project sacrifices the students ability to conduct experiments and calculations by hand (and shortcut methods), and they fear that this will severely affect the quality of graduates.

Others showed concern about the development time assigned by the administration to faculty developing laptop courses. They feel that the time assigned, typically two weeks, for developing a laptop course is not sufficient to prepare a complete and adequate course. Also it was found that the short service durations and the high turnover of faculty members lead to the discontinuity of laptop course development.

Some faculty members showed concern regarding IT infrastructure, software support and classroom furniture and fixtures. Due to many laptop courses running at the same time and sharing the same network bandwidth, online exams would be difficult in terms of connection delay, and network congestion. Unavailability of sufficient software licenses for in class and out class use have a major effect on efficient implementation of developed laptop courses. Lack of infrastructure needed for comfortable use of computers in class (e.g., improper classroom lighting, deficient projector lamps, and unsuitable furniture) surely affect the delivery method.

However, most of the faculty members believe that the laptop is a valuable tool in the education process and the laptop project can be successful once the above stated difficulties are resolved. Nonetheless, it was highly recommended by faculty member to have training sessions for "Interactive learning", and "Blackboard".

CONCLUSION AND RECOMENDATIONS

The laptop project at the college of engineering has been in implementation for many years. It was designed to provide an innovative, high technology learning environment in the classroom and access to technology outside of the classroom. Results from faculty and students' surveys identified that IT-based learning and laptops are valuable tools in the education process and are convinced that they contributed significantly to the improvement of the learning process. However, the effective implementation of learning technologies in general and laptops in particular, requires a preliminary framework of infrastructure and faculty development for blended learning.

To enhance teaching with laptops and to improve student outcomes, it is indispensable to take a close look at existing course curricula and pedagogical strategies to create a meaningful teaching and learning environment. The author believe that the use of laptop in the classroom is discipline and course specific. Faculty need to find ways to implement different technologies (not necessarily laptop) to assist students to better understand difficult concepts more easily, to expand classroom discussion, and to better integrate classroom theory with laboratory experimentation.

Nonetheless, the author believe that for a continuous success of the laptop project, the college and university administration should seriously consider some of the barriers that might hinder the success of the project. University administration should find more rewarding incentives for instructors developing laptop courses, taking into consideration the high teaching load of instructors. Administration should look seriously at the high faculty turnover, since faculty employment continuity and stability is a crucial factor in the successful and effective implementation of the project, training sessions and workshops on the use of Blackboard and Interactive learning are a must. Support of computing resources and lecture rooms infrastructure, such as furniture, internet connectivity, power outlets and data-show equipment and cables, should continue.

REFERENCES

Barr, R., & Tagg, J. (1995). From Teaching to Learning: A New Paradigm for Under Graduate Education. *Change*, *27*(6), 12–26. doi:10.1080/0 0091383.1995.10544672

Brophy, S. P., Norris, P., Nichols, M., & Jansen, E. D. (2003). Development and Initial Experience with a Laptop-based Student Assessment System to Enhance Classroom Instruction. In *Proceedings of the 2003 American Society for Engineering Education*. ASEE. Retrieved from http://www.asee.org/

Felder, R. (1992). How About a Quick One? *Chem. Engr. Education*, *26*(1), 18–19.

Hill, J., Reeves, T., & Heidemeier, H. (2000). *Ubitquitous Computing for Teaching, Learning and Communicating: Trends, Issues and Recommendations, White Paper*. Department of Instructional Technology, College of Education, University of Georgia. Retrieved from http://lpsl.coe.uga.edu/Projects/AAlaptop/pdf/Ubiquitous-Computing.pdf

McGhee, R., & Kozma, R. (2001). *New teacher and student roles in the technology-supported classroom*. Paper presented at the Annual Meeting of the American Educational Research Association. Seattle, WA. Retrieved from http://www.cehd.umn.edu/carei/publications/documents/newrolestechnology.pdf

McKenzie, J. (2001). The Unwired Classroom: Wireless Computers Come of Age. *From Now On-The Educational Technology Journal*, 10(4).

Moody, L., & Schmidt, G. (2004). Going wireless: The emergence of wireless networks in education. *Journal of Computing Sciences in Colleges*, *19*(4), 151–158.

KEY TERMS AND DEFINITIONS

e-Learning: The use of electronic media and information and communication technologies in education.

Laptop Program, Laptop Project: Names given at UAE University to the largest e-learning project in the region that applies the concepts of ubiquitous computing.

Learning Quality & Satisfaction: Learning Satisfaction Surveys are commonly used in higher education institutions as feedback mechanisms to determine the level of delivery of education.

Mobile Learning: Modern ways to support learning process through mobile devices, such as handheld and tablet computers.

Survey: A survey is a data collection tool used to gather information about individuals, things, or service.

APPENDIX A

Table 2. Laptops in Learning and Teaching: Student Assessment Form. Your views and opinions in this new leading project are valuable and important. Please complete this form as accurately as possible. Your answers should be based on ALL laptop courses taken.

Section I: Personal Information					
1.4 Department	Arch. ☐	Civil ☐	Chem/Pet ☐	Elect. ☐	Mech. ☐
1.5 Number of Laptop courses taken	1 – 2 ☐	3 – 4 ☐	More than 4 ☐		
1.6 Number of Years at UAEU					
Section 2: Learning Quality & Satisfaction					
Please mark the appropriate answer with a tick (✓)	Strongly Disagree	Disagree	Neutral	Agree	Strongly Agree
2.16 Laptops make learning more enjoyable					
2.17 Laptops in class significantly enhances my learning					
2.18 Laptops significantly enhance my ability to learn on my own (self-learning)					
2.19 Laptops significantly enhance my communication skills (e.g. email, writing reports, presentations)					
2.20 Laptops enable higher quality interaction with my course instructors					
2.21 Laptops distract me from concentrating during class					
2.22 Laptops help me during tutorials and lab sessions					
2.23 Laptops significantly enhance the acquisition of skills that I will need in my future work					
2.24 Laptops greatly improve in-class teamwork compared to courses that do not use laptops in-class					
2.25 Laptops help me to solve problems that are needed to understand the material					
2.26 Laptops aid the instructors to present their materials more effectively					
2.27 The Laptop environment encourages me to participate in class discussions					
2.28 Laptops encourage student-student interaction and participation					
2.29 Course organization is better than non-laptop courses					
2.30 Improvements to interactive teaching using the laptops are excellent overall					
Section 3: Use of e-Learning Tools in Learning and Teaching					
Please mark the appropriate answer with a tick (✓)	Strongly Disagree	Disagree	Neutral	Agree	Strongly Agree
3.22 Laptops are convenient to use in class exercises and exams					
3.23 Laptops are convenient to use in homework assignments and term projects					
3.24 Online tests are good for all course levels and types					

continued on following page

Table 2. Continued

3.25 Information on Blackboard is organized in a clear way					
3.26 The e-learning software packages used in laptop courses are useful in learning and teaching					
3.27 The e-learning software packages used in laptop courses is easy to use and access at any time					
3.28 Instructors use methods of delivery in 'laptop classes' better than those used in traditional classes					
3.29 Student-student interaction is directly linked to the use of laptops					
3.30 Student-instructor interaction is directly linked to the use of laptops					
3.31 Instructors' use of various e-learning tools (software) enhances my learning experience overall					
Section 4: Laptop and Online Usage					
Please mark the appropriate answer with a tick (✓)	**Never**	**Rarely**	**Sometimes**	**Frequently**	**All the time**
4.38 I use my laptop actively during the lecture sessions					
4.39 I use my laptops actively during the tutorial / lab sessions					
4.40 I use the Internet (NOT Blackboard) during class when the instructor tells me					
4.41 I use course specific/specialized software (e.g. modeling, simulation, etc.) during class					
4.42 The instructor uses course specific software during class to demonstrate the concepts being taught					
4.43 The instructor uses traditional teaching techniques during class (e.g. whiteboard)					
4.44 I download course material from Blackboard (e.g. lectures notes, presentations)					
4.45 I use communication options in blackboard (e.g. discussion boards, email, announcements)					
4.46 I use Blackboard (or other software) for online tests / quizzes					
4.47 I use Blackboard for posting and seeing assignments					
4.48 I use Blackboard to check for Announcements					
4.49 I use different software packages for hands-on (practical) training during class time					
Section 5: Infrastructure and IT Services					
Please mark the appropriate answer with a tick (✓)	**Strongly Disagree**	**Disagree**	**Neutral**	**Agree**	**Strongly Agree**
5.39 My laptop is too heavy to carry with me					
5.40 There is sufficient wireless network coverage on campus					
5.41 There is sufficient wireless network coverage in the dorms (students' housing)					
5.42 There are convenient power outlets available on campus and classrooms					
5.43 Classrooms are convenient for laptop use (LCD Projector, Screens, Furniture, etc.)					

continued on following page

Table 2. Continued

5.44 Laptop-based classes usually start smoothly without much need for debugging problems (e.g. missing cable, defective lamp, data projector problems)					
5.45 The Blackboard system is efficient and easy to access at all times					
5.46 I do *not* use my laptop in class because the instructor does not ask me to					
5.47 The Network is subject to frequent problems					
5.48 I am able to use all the software packages I need on my laptop (e.g licenses, cpu speed, etc.)					
5.49 It is easy to access course-related material / information on the web on campus (classrooms)					
5.50 It is easy to access course-related material / information from the dorms (students' housing)					
5.51 It is easy to access the UAEU email system					
5.52 The laptops are subject to frequent problems					
5.53 I am able to use my laptop at anytime					
5.54 I am satisfied with the quality of the technical support by the University IT staff					
5.55 The College's technical infrastructure and IT support services are excellent overall					
Section 6: Comments and Suggestions					

APPENDIX B

Table 3. Laptops in Learning and Teaching: Faculty Assessment Form. Your views and opinions as a partner in this new leading project are valuable and important. Please complete this form as accurately as possible. Section 6 should be completed with a Laptop Survey committee member.

Section I: Personal Information and Level of Involvement in the Laptop Course Development Program					
1.11 Department	Arch. ☐	Civil ☐	Chem/Pet ☐	Elect. ☐	Mech. ☐
1.12 Years of using Laptop-Based Teaching at UAEU					
1.13 Number of Laptop Courses You Developed at UAEU					
1.14 Number of Laptop Courses You Taught at UAEU					
Section 2: Learning Quality & Satisfaction					
Please mark the appropriate answer with a tick (✓)	**Strongly Disagree**	**Disagree**	**Neutral**	**Agree**	**Strongly Agree**
2.20 Laptops aid students to solve challenging problems that are needed to understand the material					
2.21 Laptops aid instructors to present their materials more effectively					
2.22 It is difficult/inconvenient to use my laptop during class					
2.23 Students' attention is distracted due to the use of their laptops during lectures					
2.24 Interactive teaching is directly linked to the laptop project					
2.25 The improvements of interactive teaching using the laptop project are excellent overall					
Section 3: Use of e-Learning Tools in Learning and Teaching					
Please mark the appropriate answer with a tick (✓)	**Strongly Disagree**	**Disagree**	**Neutral**	**Agree**	**Strongly Agree**
3.37 Laptops are convenient for students to use during in-class exercises and exams					
3.38 Laptops are convenient for students to use in homework assignments and term projects					
3.39 Online (Blackboard) exams are appropriate for all course levels and types					
3.40 The Blackboard system is the key towards IT-based active learning					
3.41 Student-instructor interaction is directly linked to the use of laptops					
Section 4: Laptop and Online Usage					
Please mark the appropriate answer with a tick (✓)	**Never**	**Rarely**	**Sometimes**	**Frequently**	**All the time**
4.62 Students use their laptops actively during the lecture sessions					
4.63 Students use their laptops actively during the tutorial / lab sessions					
4.64 Students are required to use the Internet during class (NOT Blackboard)					
4.65 Students use course specific/specialized software (e.g. modeling, simulation, etc.) during class					

continued on following page

Table 3. Continued

	Strongly Disagree	Disagree	Neutral	Agree	Strongly Agree
4.66 I use course specific software during class to demonstrate the concepts being taught					
4.67 I use traditional teaching techniques during class along with the laptop (e.g. whiteboard)					
4.68 I use Blackboard for posting PowerPoint presentations and lecture documents					
4.69 I use Blackboard for posting and receiving assignments					
4.70 I use Blackboard for conducting online tests					
4.71 I use Blackboard for sending emails to students registered on my class					
4.72 I use Blackboard for conducting surveys					
4.73 I use Blackboard for creating discussions and discussion groups among students					
Section 5: Infrastructure and IT Services					
Please mark the appropriate answer with a tick (✓)	**Strongly Disagree**	**Disagree**	**Neutral**	**Agree**	**Strongly Agree**
5.66 Faculty members may need training for using the Blackboard system					
5.67 Faculty members may need training on interactive teaching methods					
5.68 Laptop-based classes usually start smoothly without much need for debugging problems (e.g. missing cable, defective lamp, data projector problems)					
5.69 The Blackboard system is efficient and easy to access at all times					
5.70 Faculty members receive adequate support for the required software packages					
5.71 Faculty members receive adequate support for laptop problems					
5.72 I am able to use all software packages I need on my laptop (e.g licenses, cpu speed, RAM, etc.)					
5.73 The facilities at the College (e.g., data show projectors, screens, classrooms … etc) are adequate for the full implementation of the interactive teaching using the laptop project					
5.74 The College's technical infrastructure (e.g. network / wireless connections) is adequate for the full implementation of the use of wireless laptops					
5.75 The College's infrastructure and IT support services are excellent overall					
Section 6: Comments and Suggestions *(Structured Interview – To be completed with Committee member)*					
6.10 What are the strengths of the "laptop project developed courses" applied at UAEU?					
6.11 What are the current weaknesses of the "laptop project developed courses" applied at UAEU?					

continued on following page

Table 3. Continued

6.12 How can UAEU enhance the "laptop project" to become more beneficial in learning and teaching?
6.13 What threats can the "laptop project" pose to the quality and delivery of interactive teaching and learning?
6.14 What percentage of adjustments did you introduce to your course and teaching style to adapt the new technology? If you can, please mention some examples.
6.15 What problems have you encountered as an instructor as part of teaching a 'laptop course'?
6.16 How do you define hands-on teaching?
6.17 How do you define Interactive teaching?
6.18 Do you have other Comments?

APPENDIX C

Table 4. Student Survey Results / Student Survey Section I: Personal Information*. Total number of student surveys carried out: 476

		Count	%
Department	Architectural	130	27.3%
	Civil	81	17.0%
	Chem/Pet	61	12.8%
	Electrical	141	29.6%
	Mechanical	63	13.2%
Number of Laptop Courses Taken	1	3	.6%
	1-2	61	13.1%
	3-4	136	29.3%
	More than 5	264	56.9%
Number of Years at UAEU	1	1	.2%
	2	2	.5%
	2	80	19.8%
	3	1	.2%
	3	139	34.3%
	4	1	.2%
	4	136	33.6%
	5	28	6.9%
	6	1	.2%
	6	14	3.5%
	7	1	.2%
	8	1	.2%

* These numbers include students from CRU intending to enroll in their indicated departments

Table 5. Student Survey Section 2: Learning Quality & Satisfaction

	Strongly Disagree - 1		Disagree - 2		Neutral - 3		Agree - 4		Strongly Agree - 5		
	Count	%	Count	%	Count	%	Count	%	Count	%	Mean
2.1 Laptops make learning more enjoyable	27	5.7%	30	6.3%	95	20.0%	190	40.0%	133	28.0%	3.78
2.2 Laptops in class significantly enhances my learning	15	3.2%	45	9.5%	135	28.4%	211	44.4%	69	14.5%	3.58
2.3 Laptops significantly enhance my ability to learn on my own (self-learning)	14	3.0%	38	8.1%	96	20.4%	202	43.0%	120	25.5%	3.80

continued on following page

Table 5. Continued

	Strongly Disagree - 1		Disagree - 2		Neutral - 3		Agree - 4		Strongly Agree - 5		
	Count	%	Count	%	Count	%	Count	%	Count	%	Mean
2.4 Laptops significantly enhance my communication skills (e.g. email, writing reports, presentations)	6	1.3%	19	4.0%	53	11.2%	182	38.5%	213	45.0%	4.22
2.5 Laptops enable higher quality interaction with my course instructors	14	3.0%	48	10.2%	135	28.6%	193	40.9%	82	17.4%	3.60
2.6 Laptops distract me from concentrating during class	20	4.3%	79	16.8%	181	38.5%	134	28.5%	56	11.9%	3.27
2.7 Laptops help me during tutorials and lab sessions	30	6.4%	53	11.3%	118	25.1%	179	38.1%	90	19.1%	3.52
2.8 Laptops significantly enhance the acquisition of skills that I will need in my future work	4	0.9%	27	5.7%	92	19.6%	188	40.0%	159	33.8%	4.00
2.9 Laptops greatly improve in-class teamwork compared to courses that do not use laptops in-class	21	4.4%	71	15.0%	147	31.1%	161	34.0%	73	15.4%	3.41
2.10 Laptops help me to solve problems that are needed to understand the material	21	4.4%	38	8.1%	148	31.4%	174	36.9%	91	19.3%	3.58
2.11 Laptops aid the instructors to present their materials more effectively	20	4.2%	61	13.0%	123	26.1%	170	36.1%	97	20.6%	3.56
2.12 The Laptop environment encourages me to participate in class discussions	28	5.9%	71	15.1%	178	37.8%	139	29.5%	55	11.7%	3.26
2.13 Laptops encourage student-student interaction and participation	16	3.4%	69	14.6%	154	32.6%	174	36.9%	59	12.5%	3.40
2.14 Course organization is better than non-laptop courses	29	6.2%	73	15.5%	141	29.9%	152	32.3%	76	16.1%	3.37
2.15 Improvements to interactive teaching using the laptops are excellent overall	16	3.4%	56	11.9%	150	31.8%	184	39.0%	66	14.0%	3.48

Table 6. Student Survey Section 3: Use of e-Learning Tools in learning and teaching

	Strongly Disagree -1		Disagree -2		Neutral - 3		Agree - 4		Strongly Agree - 5		
	Count	%	Count	%	Count	%	Count	%	Count	%	Mean
3.1 Laptops are convenient to use in class exercises and exams	38	8.1%	63	13.3%	120	25.4%	182	38.6%	69	14.6%	3.38
3.2 Laptops are convenient to use in homework assignments and term projects	12	2.5%	28	5.9%	86	18.2%	217	46.0%	129	27.3%	3.90
3.3 Online tests are good for all course levels and types	52	11.1%	86	18.3%	116	24.7%	145	30.9%	71	15.1%	3.21
3.4 Information on Blackboard is organized in a clear way	10	2.1%	27	5.8%	94	20.0%	196	41.8%	142	30.3%	3.92
3.5 The e-learning software packages used in laptop courses are useful in learning and teaching	26	5.6%	43	9.2%	119	25.4%	183	39.1%	97	20.7%	3.60
3.6 The e-learning software packages used in laptop courses is easy to use and access at any time	25	5.3%	60	12.8%	125	26.7%	158	33.7%	101	21.5%	3.53
3.7 Instructors use methods of delivery in 'laptop classes' better than those used in traditional classes	32	6.8%	59	12.5%	135	28.6%	171	36.2%	75	15.9%	3.42
3.8 Student-student interaction is directly linked to the use of laptops	22	4.7%	61	13.0%	156	33.1%	172	36.5%	60	12.7%	3.40
3.9 Student-instructor interaction is directly linked to the use of laptops	16	3.4%	43	9.1%	172	36.5%	180	38.2%	60	12.7%	3.48
3.10 Instructors' use of various e-learning tools (software) enhances my learning experience overall	9	1.9%	36	7.6%	151	32.1%	197	41.8%	78	16.6%	3.63

APPENDIX D

Table 7. Student Survey Section 4: Laptop and Online Usage

	Never - 1		Rarely - 2		Sometimes - 3		Frequently - 4		All the Time – 5		
	Count	%	Count	%	Count	%	Count	%	Count	%	Mean
4.1 I use my laptop actively during the lecture sessions	39	8.3%	66	14.0%	178	37.8%	127	27.0%	61	13.0%	3.22
4.2 I use my laptops actively during the tutorial / lab sessions	31	6.6%	70	14.9%	148	31.6%	149	31.8%	71	15.1%	3.34
4.3 I use the Internet (NOT Blackboard) during class when the instructor tells me	36	7.7%	50	10.6%	171	36.4%	131	27.9%	82	17.4%	3.37
4.4 I use course specific/ specialized software (e.g. modeling, simulation, etc.) during class	27	5.8%	51	10.9%	148	31.7%	149	31.9%	92	19.7%	3.49
4.5 The instructor uses course specific software during class to demonstrate the concepts being taught	10	2.2%	45	9.7%	173	37.2%	167	35.9%	70	15.1%	3.52
4.6 The instructor uses traditional teaching techniques during class (e.g. whiteboard)	19	4.0%	44	9.4%	171	36.4%	137	29.1%	99	21.1%	3.54
4.7 I download course material from Blackboard (e.g. lectures notes, presentations)	9	1.9%	16	3.4%	68	14.5%	100	21.4%	275	58.8%	4.32
4.8 I use communication options in blackboard (e.g. discussion boards, email, announcements)	22	4.7%	47	10.1%	115	24.7%	117	25.1%	165	35.4%	3.76
4.9 I use Blackboard (or other software) for online tests / quizzes	21	4.5%	58	12.3%	147	31.3%	130	27.7%	114	24.3%	3.55
4.10 I use Blackboard for posting and seeing assignments	10	2.1%	26	5.6%	81	17.3%	141	30.1%	210	44.9%	4.10
4.11 I use Blackboard to check for Announcements	11	2.3%	15	3.2%	71	15.1%	136	28.9%	238	50.5%	4.22
4.12 I use different software packages for hands-on (practical) training during class time	19	4.0%	62	13.2%	164	34.9%	153	32.6%	72	15.3%	3.42

Table 8. Student Survey Section 5: Infrastructure and IT Services

	Strongly Disagree - 1		Disagree - 2		Neutral - 3		Agree - 4		Strongly Agree - 5		Mean
	Count	%	Count	%	Count	%	Count	%	Count	%	
5.1 My laptop is too heavy to carry with me	17	3.7%	32	6.9%	92	19.9%	126	27.3%	195	42.2%	3.97
5.2 There is sufficient wireless network coverage on campus	31	6.8%	59	12.9%	104	22.7%	187	40.7%	78	17.0%	3.48
5.3 There is sufficient wireless network coverage in the dorms (students' housing)	59	13.0%	76	16.7%	139	30.5%	119	26.2%	62	13.6%	3.11
5.4 There are convenient power outlets available on campus and classrooms	33	7.2%	57	12.4%	147	31.9%	146	31.7%	78	16.9%	3.39
5.5 Classrooms are convenient for laptop use (LCD Projector, Screens, Furniture, etc.)	11	2.4%	41	8.9%	145	31.5%	181	39.3%	83	18.0%	3.62
5.6 Laptop-based classes usually start smoothly without much need for debugging problems (e.g. missing cable, defective lamp, data projector problems)	16	3.5%	74	16.1%	184	39.9%	146	31.7%	41	8.9%	3.26
5.7 The Blackboard system is efficient and easy to access at all times	10	2.2%	54	11.7%	113	24.6%	186	40.4%	97	21.1%	3.67
5.8 I do not use my laptop in class because the instructor does not ask me to	16	3.5%	75	16.2%	174	37.7%	138	29.9%	59	12.8%	3.32
5.9 The Network is subject to frequent problems	7	1.5%	39	8.5%	177	38.6%	173	37.8%	62	13.5%	3.53
5.10 I am able to use all the software packages I need on my laptop (e.g licenses, cpu speed, etc.)	22	4.8%	60	13.0%	140	30.4%	164	35.7%	74	16.1%	3.45
5.11 It is easy to access course-related material / information on the web on campus (classrooms)	7	1.5%	29	6.3%	131	28.4%	201	43.5%	94	20.3%	3.75
5.12 It is easy to access course-related material / information from the dorms (students' housing)	29	6.3%	72	15.7%	153	33.4%	134	29.3%	70	15.3%	3.31
5.13 It is easy to access the UAEU email system	7	1.5%	19	4.1%	83	18.0%	210	45.7%	141	30.7%	4.00
5.14 The laptops are subject to frequent problems	8	1.7%	46	10.0%	155	33.5%	163	35.3%	90	19.5%	3.61

continued on following page

Table 8. Continued

	Strongly Disagree - 1		Disagree - 2		Neutral - 3		Agree - 4		Strongly Agree - 5		
	Count	%	Count	%	Count	%	Count	%	Count	%	Mean
5.15 I am able to use my laptop at anytime	12	2.6%	40	8.7%	110	23.8%	166	35.9%	134	29.0%	3.80
5.16 I am satisfied with the quality of the technical support by the University IT staff	40	8.7%	64	13.9%	132	28.7%	166	36.1%	58	12.6%	3.30
5.17 The College's technical infrastructure and IT support services are excellent overall	27	5.9%	77	16.7%	145	31.5%	155	33.6%	57	12.4%	3.30

Table 9. Faculty Survey Results. Faculty Survey Section I: Personal Information and Level of Involvement. Total number of faculty surveys carried out: 51

		Count	%	Mean	Range
Department	Architectural	10	19.6%		
	Civil	6	11.8%		
	Chem/Pet	10	19.6%		
	Electrical	12	23.5%		
	Mechanical	13	25.5%		
Years of using Laptop-Based Teaching at UAEU				2	4
Number of Laptop Courses You Developed at UAEU				1	6
Number of Laptop Courses You Taught at UAEU				2	6

Table 10. Faculty Survey Section 2: Learning Quality & Satisfaction

	Strongly Disagree - 1		Disagree - 2		Neutral - 3		Agree - 4		Strongly Agree - 5		Mean
	Count	%	Count	%	Count	%	Count	%	Count	%	
2.1 Laptops aid students to solve challenging problems that are needed to understand the material	2	4.2%	7	14.6%	12	25.0%	23	47.9%	4	8.3%	3.42
2.2 Laptops aid instructors to present their materials more effectively	1	2.1%	3	6.3%	5	10.4%	19	39.6%	20	41.7%	4.13
2.3 It is difficult/ inconvenient to use my laptop during class	11	22.9%	24	50.0%	3	6.3%	10	20.8%	0	.0%	2.25
2.4 Students' attention is distracted due to the use of their laptops during lectures	3	6.3%	11	22.9%	10	20.8%	17	35.4%	7	14.6%	3.29
2.5 Interactive teaching is directly linked to the laptop project	9	18.8%	12	25.0%	9	18.8%	15	31.3%	3	6.3%	2.81
2.6 The improvements of interactive teaching using the laptop project are excellent overall	2	4.2%	15	31.3%	4	8.3%	21	43.8%	6	12.5%	3.29

Table 11. Faculty Survey Section 3: Use of e-Learning Tools in learning and teaching

	Strongly Disagree - 1		Disagree -2		Neutral - 3		Agree - 4		Strongly Agree - 5		Mean
	Count	%	Count	%	Count	%	Count	%	Count	%	
3.1 Laptops are convenient for students to use during in-class exercises and exams	0	.0%	12	25.5%	14	29.8%	17	36.2%	4	8.5%	3.28
3.2 Laptops are convenient for students to use in homework assignments and term projects	2	4.2%	4	8.3%	3	6.3%	22	45.8%	17	35.4%	4.00
3.3 Online (Blackboard) exams are appropriate for all course levels and types	12	25.0%	17	35.4%	14	29.2%	3	6.3%	2	4.2%	2.29
3.4 The Blackboard system is the key towards IT-based active learning	4	8.3%	6	12.5%	15	31.3%	19	39.6%	4	8.3%	3.27
3.5 Student-instructor interaction is directly linked to the use of laptops	11	22.9%	14	29.2%	13	27.1%	9	18.8%	1	2.1%	2.48

Table 12. Faculty Survey Section 4: Laptop and online usage

	Never - 1		Rarely - 2		Sometimes - 3		Frequently - 4		All the Time - 5		Mean
	Count	%	Count	%	Count	%	Count	%	Count	%	
4.1 Students use their laptops actively during the lecture sessions	2	4.3%	9	19.1%	22	46.8%	13	27.7%	1	2.1%	3.04
4.2 Students use their laptops actively during the tutorial / lab sessions	1	2.1%	11	22.9%	18	37.5%	17	35.4%	1	2.1%	3.13
4.3 Students are required to use the Internet during class (NOT Blackboard)	7	14.6%	16	33.3%	15	31.3%	10	20.8%	0	0.0%	2.58
4.4 Students use course specific/specialized software (e.g. modeling, simulation, etc.) during class	2	4.2%	4	8.3%	14	29.2%	24	50.0%	4	8.3%	3.50
4.5 I use course specific software during class to demonstrate the concepts being taught	1	2.1%	2	4.2%	20	41.7%	21	43.8%	4	8.3%	3.52
4.6 I use traditional teaching techniques during class along with the laptop (e.g. whiteboard)	0	0.0%	4	8.3%	11	22.9%	22	45.8%	11	22.9%	3.83
4.7 I use Blackboard for posting PowerPoint presentations and lecture documents	0	0.0%	1	2.1%	0	0.0%	6	12.5%	41	85.4%	4.81
4.8 I use Blackboard for posting and receiving assignments	5	10.4%	3	6.3%	12	25.0%	16	33.3%	12	25.0%	3.56
4.9 I use Blackboard for conducting online tests	13	27.1%	11	22.9%	11	22.9%	6	12.5%	7	14.6%	2.65
4.10 I use Blackboard for sending emails to students registered on my class	3	6.3%	6	12.5%	7	14.6%	12	25.0%	20	41.7%	3.83
4.11 I use Blackboard for conducting surveys	17	35.4%	17	35.4%	6	12.5%	7	14.6%	1	2.1%	2.13
4.12 I use Blackboard for creating discussions and discussion groups among students	23	47.9%	14	29.2%	6	12.5%	4	8.3%	1	2.1%	1.88

Table 13. Faculty Survey Section 5: Infrastructure and IT services

	Strongly Disagree - 1		Disagree - 2		Neutral - 3		Agree - 4		Strongly Agree - 5		
	Count	%	Count	%	Count	%	Count	%	Count	%	Mean
5.1 Faculty members may need training for using the Blackboard system	3	6.4%	9	19.1%	17	36.2%	14	29.8%	4	8.5%	3.15
5.2 Faculty members may need training on interactive teaching methods	0	0.0%	6	12.8%	12	25.5%	23	48.9%	6	12.8%	3.62
5.3 Laptop-based classes usually start smoothly without much need for debugging problems (e.g. missing cable, defective lamp, data projector problems)	9	19.1%	17	36.2%	10	21.3%	10	21.3%	1	2.1%	2.51
5.4 The Blackboard system is efficient and easy to access at all times	2	4.3%	6	12.8%	9	19.1%	22	46.8%	8	17.0%	3.60
5.5 Faculty members receive adequate support for the required software packages	5	10.6%	15	31.9%	17	36.2%	9	19.1%	1	2.1%	2.70
5.6 Faculty members receive adequate support for laptop problems	3	6.4%	7	14.9%	21	44.7%	15	31.9%	1	2.1%	3.09
5.7 I am able to use all software packages I need on my laptop (e.g licenses, cpu speed, RAM, etc.)	3	6.4%	4	8.5%	18	38.3%	17	36.2%	5	10.6%	3.36
5.8 The facilities at the College (e.g., data show projectors, screens, classrooms … etc) are adequate for the full implementation of the interactive teaching using the laptop project	5	10.6%	21	44.7%	10	21.3%	9	19.1%	2	4.3%	2.62
5.9 The College's technical infrastructure (e.g. network / wireless connections) is adequate for the full implementation of the use of wireless laptops	3	6.4%	13	27.7%	14	29.8%	13	27.7%	4	8.5%	3.04
5.10 The College's infrastructure and IT support services are excellent overall	2	4.3%	12	26.1%	14	30.4%	15	32.6%	3	6.5%	3.11

Chapter 6
Challenges and Opportunities for Virtual Universities in the 21ˢᵗ Century

Luísa Margarida Cagica Carvalho
Universidade Aberta, Portugal & CEFAGE, University of Évora, Portugal

ABSTRACT

This chapter aims to provide a theoretical approach concerning challenges and opportunities to virtual universities in 21ˢᵗ century. Virtual universities have an important role in capturing different audiences to the e-learning programs, such as long life learning, executive programs, etc. Additionally, the virtual model allows a more efficient internationalization of the education and improves the attraction of the students from several countries. Nevertheless, the virtual universities front some problems and challenges on the global education market and could be important to identify and present some good practices followed by virtual universities around the world. This chapter presents some remarks about virtual universities, the advantages and challenges fronted, and the case of the Portuguese virtual university, Open University of Lisbon, as a complement to the theoretical approach.

INTRODUCTION

The democratization of higher education and the emergence of the Information and Communication Technologies (ICT) represent a central argument for this change on boundaries (Guri-Rosenblit, 2001). ICT are implanted in economic and social structures of the several countries. ICT comes also as an important tool in education. Furthermore, ICT have encouraged higher education institutions to enter in the "distance education business" at various levels of experimentation and applica-

tion (Bates, 1995, 1999; Evans & Nation, 2000; Khan, 1997; Littleton & Light, 1999; Rumble, 1996; Selinger & Pearson, 1999; Trow, 1999). ICT contributed to change the status of distance education within the academic world. Traditionally distance teaching was regarded as operating on the margins of higher education systems (Guri-Rosenblit, 1999). See Table 1 with the concept of distance education.

Currently, millions of people, traditional students and working adults students, are studying

DOI: 10.4018/978-1-4666-7316-8.ch006

Table 1. Distance learning

Distance learning or distance education is a mode of delivering education and instruction on conditions which occur due to the limited traditional teaching-learning methods in a classroom where it is not possible to carry out in class activities and therefore the interaction and communication between the planners of educational activities and the practitioners and the students are provided from a specific centre via specially prepared teaching units and various means (Alkan, 1987: cited by Gurbuz, 2014).

Distance learning is the most modern education system, which is independent of time, and distance, enables individualized education opportunities, and is implemented via information technologies and especially via Internet (Baturay & Bay, 2009: cited by Gurbuz, 2014).

Source: Gurbuz, 2014, p.240

through distance teaching methods for a plethora of reasons and purposes (Guri-Rosenblit, 2001).

Nevertheless, are yet in development new and more efficient ways to operate and to carry out pedagogical and organizational innovation (Ossiannilsson, 2011). In the last decade, digital world becomes popular in all learning and educational activities and push the boundaries in daily life, in a global sustainable environment (Bates, 2010; Bonk, 2009; Conole, 2010; Ehlers & Pawlowski, 2006).

Other authors (Ehlers & Svhneckenberg, 2010; Johnson et al, 2011; O'Reilly & Batelle, 2009) argue that there is no longer a need for definition for e-learning due their role and implications on a huge number of fields.

Bonk (2009) provide a new inside to this topic with the concept of ubiquitous learning (u-learning). This perspective focused on the personalisation and in learners' rights and responsibilities.

Nowadays, several institutions offering distance teaching or using ICT, though there are differences influenced by different academic cultures dominant in various higher education systems (Rothblatt, 1997). These cultural differences influence the adoption of new traditions and teaching innovations (Guri-Rosenblit, 2001). Its possible to note important differences among different higher education systems in their attitudes towards distance education.

Furthermore, other studies suggest that more rigorous research is required in the field of state-level virtual universities (Xu & Morris, 2009). Some conclusions about this topic are based on opinions and in the individual case reports and not on rigorous research methods, and reveal limitations to understanding the concept of virtual university (Epper & Garn, 2003; Smith, 1998; Wolf & Johnstone, 1999) or the organizational models of virtual universities (Dutton & Loader, 2002; Farrell, 1999; Hanna, 2000), and created various frameworks to analyze policies and structures of virtual universities (Berge, 1998; Gellman-Danley & Fetzner, 1998; Rosevear, 1999).

This chapter are organized in the following sections: virtual universities (provide some remarks about the models of virtual universities); dimensions of e-learning (explore the e-learning methodologies, attending to the student behaviour and attitudes); technology and e-learning (consider the impact and relation of the technology with e-learning); instructional strategies (explain some instructional strategies to achieve learning objectives); virtual universities (virtual universities front some problems and challenges on the global education market in XXI century); quality challenge (quality is a challenge and a key factor fronted by virtual universities); the case of Open University – Portugal and some remarks and good practices.

VIRTUAL UNIVERSITIES: SOME KEY REMARKS

Accompanying global technological changes education changed tremendously over the last years. Technology, mainly Information Technology (IT) provides a huge flexibility and new ways, time and spaces to learn. The dynamic nature of IT create new environments to apprenticeship and have been enhanced during the financial limitations to the public financing mainly in the case of higher education. The virtual model, appear as an interesting model whose improve knowledge storing and sharing, and also broken the barrier of rigid organizational structure allowing adaption and flexibility (Shabha, 2000).

Additionally, virtual universities revolutionize the culture and environment of apprenticeship shared by students and teachers. Nowadays, virtual universities are becoming strongly networked and deep changes in the organization of education are occurring (Wang et al, 2009). In the fact, geographical isolation is no longer a factor for virtual universities. However, new challenges emerge in virtual learning environments, namely, the imperative to increase efficiency and quality. Shaba (2000) identified some repercussions associated to the creation and dissemination of knowledge fronted by virtual universities:

- Huge uncertainty and ambiguity about the new role and aims of university and uncertain about how incorporate technology;
- Inadequacy of the campus to technology, financial constraints and organizational limitations mainly in traditional universities;
- Higher diversity in the type of learning requirements and learners attributed to the multitude of teaching courses/programs offered by universities and also the multiplicity of entrants in fulltime, part time and work students.

Additionally, virtual universities reduce labor costs. This argument was the driver for the creation of most online programs (Forsyth et al, 2010). Nevertheless, this perspective have been gradually reject by the institutions and also by the higher education sector, for compelling reasons related to quality of student experience (Kirp,

2007; Laurillard, 2006). Rising costs, shrinking budgets, and an increasing requires for e-learning are causing educational institutions to re-examine the way education is delivered (Wagner et al, 2008).

Weller (2004), argue that cost-effective models of large-scale e-learning have reveal some difficulties in the implementation. The technological infrastructure and the implementation of e-learning courses can imply extraordinarily costly technology upgrades, for the reason that e-learning systems involve distinctive components, such as sufficient bandwidth, course management systems, and technology equipped laptops or computers for instructors (Wagner et al., 2008). These budgetary constraints could become a huge problem for many universities, and sometimes universities not integrated e-learning harmonized in different departments. This aspects could reduces the potential for cross-departmental efficiencies, and cause difficulties in the process for faculty, staff, and students, especially if they are involved with more than one department (Wagner et al., 2008). Other limitation identified is associated with the resistance from instructors. Several studies have revealed that there is no significant difference between the performances of students in the two methods (Huynh, et al 2003), various faculty members still consider that e-learning is inferior to the face-to-face instruction (Omar et al, 2010).

Literature about virtual universities presents two different perspectives sometimes contradictories, the traditional and the modern perspective. The traditional approach consider that learning must take place in fixed locations, with rigid timetables, due that in their perspective this model guarantee the quality and contributes to pass experiences easily memorized by the students. In the other hand, modern perspective, argue that technological changes modify radically the way of learning and also the university. The main arguments referred that learning and acquisition of knowledge not need to be developed in classrooms, since technology provide new ways to communicate and new forms of social organization, that able new spaces to learning using IT. In this context location becomes as an irrelevant variable to the learning process. Students can learn from their homes or work place. They also can arrange groups to work together and develop tasks with the support of the tutor from different places, cities or countries.

However some problems can be address to virtual universities. Some students could have limitations in access to computers and internet due financial constraints (O'Leary, 2000). And students that don't have a personal computer at home or in work place could stay in a disadvantage position. Other aspect is about the environment where student attend to the lesson and develop collaborative work. Sometimes, at their own home or in work place could be difficult separate tasks and roles and the external environment influences negatively the learning process. Frequently it's not easy to separate home involvement, family, leisure or work place demands from learning environment. Shaba (2000) refer that these problems could be over passed through the use of spaces and urban facilities, such as, libraries or other community infrastructures associated to education.

Remote working it was a discussed issue during the last years, frequently are used expressions that associate remote working with working tasks, such as teleworking, telecottage, remote working, hotdesking, and so on and so forth (Lovejoy, 1993; Lawrence, 1999). Remote learning assumes particular importance in the case of virtual schools. Though, remain some myths about virtual models of learning:

1. Virtual public school is the same as home school. These two concepts are different, virtual schools deliver public education providing adequate learning methodologies, certified that teachers deliver a rigorous curriculum and appropriated learning materials to virtual learning environment;

2. Virtual schools are linked only with technology. This association its not truth, in the fact virtual schools must provide a curriculum and other tools e.g. virtual classrooms. This approach implies full-time, certified, and qualified teachers, availability of technological resources, community activities, extra curricular activities and study visits for students;

3. Virtual learning is predominantly student's study alone or "teacher less". The efficacy of virtual schools depends directly from the teachers, its important to have certified teachers, trained in working with virtual classes and alert to students needs and learning styles. In several virtual schools teacher works directly with student and propose individual learning contracts, provide instruction, and grade assignments;

4. In virtual schools students spend all their time in front of the computer. In fact, students must use textbooks, pencils, interactive curricula and develop a set of tasks similar with they would do in traditional schools. Technology and computers are very important but are understanding as tools for teachers manage learning environment, to communicate, to deliver curricular materials, etc;

5. Virtual schools limit the quality of social interactions. Truly, students continue to socialize and interact with peers and virtual students are not so different in this perspective from the students in a traditional school. Many times, virtual students have higher flexibility to manage their tasks and have the possibility to become involved in outside extracurricular activities, volunteer, or other tasks and developing their personal talents.

DIMENSIONS OF ONLINE LEARNING

Some studies tried to analyse the best practices in asynchronous and synchronous online instruction in higher education (Sunal et al., 2003). However, recently researchers highlighted the importance of study student behaviour and attitudes concerning e-learning and referred some dimensions:

1. **Affect:** Respecting to the individual feelings, such as, euphoria, pleasure, depression, distaste, discontentment or hatred relatively to a particular behavior (Triandis, 1979). A positive affect towards technology allows gaining experience, knowledge and self-efficacy regarding technology. In opposite, a negative affect origin avoiding technology, thus not learning about them or developing perceived control (Arkkelin, 2003);

2. **Perception of Course:** Studies about e-learning students perceptions are mixed (Kum, 1999; Picciano, 2002). Some of them reveal uncomforted mainly due the constructivist pedagogical theory that put student on the center of the learning process and increase their responsibility in apprenticeship process. Lowell (2001) also refer that e-learning requires that students answer to frequent computer-based instruction demands which reduced student engagement in the course and led to a decline in student success. Students less familiarized with technology and with learning tools used could develop negative perceptions that could affect their outcome results;

3. **Perceived Learning Outcome:** Associated with learning results and connected with learning tools. According with Saadé et. al (2007) perceived learning outcome could be measured according with three items: (1) performance improvement; (2) grades benefit; and (3) meeting learning needs. Some studies reveal the importance of the instructor/professor/tutor in this process as a facilitator and moderator in online learning environment (Faigley, 1990; Feenberg, 1987; Krendl & Lieberman, 1988);

4. **Attitude:** Literature highlight the importance of student and tutor attitudes towards online learning (Sunal et al., 2003). And their impact on learning achievements (Marzano & Pickering, 1997);

5. **Intrinsic Motivation:** Motivational perspectives are also relevant to understand behavior (Davis, et al, 1992; Vallerand, 1997; Venkatesh, 1999). Intrinsic motivation applied by learning theories is also used as a construct to measure user perceptions of game/multimedia technologies (Venkatesh & Davis, 2000; Venkatesh, et al., 2002);

6. **Extrinsic Motivation:** Deci & Ryan (1985) consider that extrinsic motivation involves the behavior to achieve a specific reward such as a higher grade in the exams, an awards, a prizes etc.

Moreover, others studies refers several factors that influences the creation of a success e-learning model for higher education, and grouped this factors into four main aspects: human deliberation factor, instructional design factor, technology development factor, and social delivery factor (Soong et al, 2001; Oliver, 2001; Govindasamy, 2002; Vate-U-Lan, 2008).

Technology and E-Learning

Some professors use technology in the traditional classroom, however don't prefer teach online due the lack of personal interaction (Lyons, 2004). The same study also reveal that online instructors complained that answering emails and participating in discussion boards represent that online teaching implies spending more of their time than in a traditional class. And besides criticized the attitudes and behaviors of online students who do not consider deadlines seriously.

Tunison & Noonan (2001) confirmed that the development of e-learning may have a considerable impact on the students and teachers lives since it represents improvements and innovation in the classical models. In last years, the developments in e-learning and gradual emergence of more sophisticated learning technologies have a key impact in universities. It is clear that universities need to adapt to the impact of technology on learning. Communication technologies allow access without time or space constraints and provide new challenges to universities and to their courses organization (Jones & O'Shea, 2004).

Wagner et al. (2008) proposed an organization of the online courses (table 2). And argue that some courses are delivered synchronously and others asynchronously. Nevertheless, mainly courses available on the Internet are based on the asynchronous model (Greenagel, 2002). Asynchronous e-learning, frequently assisted by email and discussion board, supports work relations among learners and between teachers and learners, even when participants cannot be online at the same time (Omar et al, 2010). This possibility allows flexibly in e-learning (Hrastinski, 2008). The asynchronous e-learning permits that learners can log on to an e-learning environment every time and download documents or send messages to teachers or peers. At the same time, students may dispend more time improving their contributions, which therefore are commonly more thoughtful than those in synchronous communication (Hrastinski, 2008).

Moreover, e-learning promotes access to higher education to some students that in other case are not able to study due the geographic or time constraints (Kabassi & Virvou, 2004). And synchronous e-learning commonly supported by media, such as videoconferencing and chat, has the potential to support e-learners in the development of learning communities (Omar et al, 2010). It is important to note that learners and teachers experience synchronous e-learning as more social and less frustrating since they can ask and answer questions in real time (Omar et al, 2010). Synchronous sessions facilitate e-learners feel more involved and less isolated. Isolation can be overcome through more frequent contacts,

mostly synchronously, and by becoming aware of themselves as members of a community rather than as isolated individuals communicating with the computer (Haythornthwaite & Kazmer, 2002).

Instructional Strategies

Other crucial aspects in e-learning are the instructional strategies. It's possible to find several instructional strategies in e-learning environment:

1. Mentorship: One-on-One

This strategy implies a one-on-one learning relationship between a student and a tutor/professor in a certain topic or discipline. Mentorship in e-learning is reciprocal and collaborative learning relationship between a mentor and a student and join learning with the compelling human need for connection (Ekwensi et al., 2006; Wilson, 2006; Wisker et al, 2007) through email, instant messenger, conferencing or text messaging.

2. Small Group Work

Small group work is one of the most used e-learning strategy, because facilitating users to share knowledge. Group work increases learners' ability to better coordinate and manages their view and research (Ekwensi et al., 2006; Rana, 2005).

3. Projects

Projects can be allocated to an individual or to a group. Projects allow the study and research of specific topics and give to the students the possibility of experiencing the management of a project from the beginning to the end. Projects developed in-group are suitable to create a dynamic learning environment. When the tutor/professor receives the projects could maintain their results private or share the results with the class. In the last case class could present the feedback and contributes to the discussion and to the futures improvements in

Table 2. E-learning dimensions

Dimension	Attribute	Meaning	Example
Synchronicity	Asynchronous	Content delivery occurs at different time than receipt by student.	Lectured module delivered via Email.
	Synchronous	Content delivery occurs at the same time as receipt by student.	Lecture delivery via web cast.
Location	Same Place	Students use an application at the same physical location as other students and/or the instructor.	Using a Group Support System (GSS) to solve a problem in a classroom.
	Distributed	Students use an application at various physical locations, separate from other students and the instructor	Using GSS to solve a problem from distributed locations.
Independence	Individual	Students work independently from one another to complete learning tasks.	Students complete e-learning modules autonomously.
	Collaborative	Students work collaboratively with one another to complete learning tasks.	Students participate in discussion forums to share ideas.
Mode	Electronically Only	All content is delivered via technology. There is no face-to-face component.	An electronically enabled e-learning course.
	Blended	E-learning is used to supplement traditional classroom learning.	In class lectures are enhanced with hands-on computer exercises.

Source: Wagner et al, 2008

the project. According with Ekwensi et al. (2006) students learn with the collaboration and sharing of the opinions and different perspectives that could also support the discovery of a common solution. Thomas (2000) argues that projects engage students in a constructive research, which is a goal-directed process that includes inquiry, knowledge building, and resolution.

4. Cooperative and Collaborative Learning

Cooperative and collaborative learning is an instructional strategy that at the same time addresses academic and social skill learning by students and has been related as a highly successful strategy in the classroom. This strategy requires the interac-

tion between two or more students with different skill set levels.

Collaborative learning allows that students learn to work in a group environment and improve their communication and critical thinking skills (Omar et al, 2010). Some studies evidence that interaction between students contributes positively to learning (Laurillard, 1993; Ramsden, 1992). A research developed by So & Brush (2008) suggests that collaborative learning has a positive and prominent influence on students' learning satisfaction. Chia & Chiu (2011) argues that during collaborative problem solving, learners communicate with peers and accumulate learning experiences through discussion, negotiation, and information sharing. This interaction and collaboration simultaneously enhances learning for groups and for individuals.

5. Case Study

Case study favored the creation of an effective learning environment. In a first phase student's access to the case, know the problem and in the follow phases they provide conclusions and possible solutions to the problem. At the final, students could compare their results with results of actual decisions used to solve the problem in the study. Students could discuss the results and also present the results to the class by email or videoconference. Case study strategy allows active participation to achieve a community result better than that, which could be attained by individual effort (Rosenthal, 2002; Ertmer & Stepich, 2002; Waterman & Stanley, 2005).

6. Learning Contracts

Learning contracts involves an agreement between the learner and the instructor with details about learning strategies and objectives. The tutor/professor determine the objective however student have the responsibility of writing and carry out the content of the contract. The final contract could be negotiated between student and tutor/professor to guarantee a meaningful learning experience that meets the expectation of the professor/tutor (Ekwesi et al., 2006). This kind of strategy could be appropriated to solve or reduce the problem of dealing with wide differences within some group of learners (Omar et al, 2010). Generally, disciplines includes a tacit contract, i. e., professor provide in the first class syllabus and identify the expected outcomes.

7. Lecture

Lectures present a basis of subject knowledge on which other knowledge, such as declarative, procedural, and conditional knowledge can be built (Hardy, 2002). In the e-learning environment, lectures can assume different formats. A complete set of lecture notes can be presented as a web page or accessible as a PDF or as a Microsoft Word file that can be played directly from the source or offered to the learner as a download (Omar et al, 2010). Lectures may also be recorded and presented in a Podcast format, as a PowerPoint presentation, or as a flash file. Lectures could includes graphics, animation, sound, etc., the lecture can be prepared into a multimedia presentation or presented in streaming video, in an effort to motivate the learner and appeal to different styles of learning. Clark & Pitt (2001) propose that no lecture should exceed twenty minutes, sufficient time to give enough information to serve as a basis for further study.

8. Discussion

Discussion is one of the most popular e-learning strategies due the possibility of an interactive contact and participation in learning process. Online students are frequently isolated therefore discussion facilitates the development a feeling of belonging to a group, which is critical to success in education (Herring & Dargan, 2002). Several authors find benefits in this learning strategy: is an important tool for increasing interactivity in both online and face-to-face courses (Bannan-Ritland, 2002; Brown, 2001; Healey, 1998; Klemm, 1997), support the creation of a learning community over time (Brown, 2001), enhances the learning process by enabling more opportunities for active learning and collaboration (Klemm, 1997; Land & Dornisch, 2002; Landsberger, 2001), provides opportunities to write and reflect on course content and previous postings (MacKnight, 2000; O'Sullivan, 2001; Rothermel, 2001), allows a constructivist view of a learner-centered classroom, whether physical or virtual (Campos, et al, 2001).

Professor and tutor as an important role in this process and assume the roles of e-moderator, facilitator, and role model (Landsberger, 2001).

Table 3. Conceptions of teaching in virtual environments

- Information transfer, which had the subcategories:
  Providing information: emphasizes the use of information created to be used off-line first as a medium to support face-to-face activities;
  Extending information: the focus is on provision of further information by means of links to websites or other relevant online material;
  Clarifying information: clarifying small points in the content being taught by using, for example, bulletin boards.
- Understanding concepts, which has two subcategories:
  Understanding the topic: emphasizes the understanding of content by explaining content through eLearning tools and monitoring progress through online tests or quizzes;
  Rethinking the topic: students' reflection on the topic encouraged through participation in online tasks.
  Developing the concept, which has one subcategory:
  Developing the topic: eLearning is used to contribute and share ideas. Participation in online discussions is encouraged.

Source: Lameras et al, 2008

Lameras et al. (2008) showed outcomes of a study about conceptions of teaching using a virtual learning environment, held by a group of five university teachers from the area of computer science. Three categories and six subcategories emerged, see Table 3.

VIRTUAL UNIVERSITIES: ADVANTAGES AND CHALLENGES ON THE GLOBAL EDUCATION MARKET IN XXI CENTURY

Virtual universities front some problems and challenges on the global education market. In the fact, we are in the age of the knowledge and the key resource is knowledge that implies to have more educated people. Nowadays intellectual capital and brainpower are strategic resources. The economic structure in western countries, shift from a productive model based on labour intensive products and services to a model based on knowledge intensive products and services. This new reality is linking also with fast changes in technology that reflects new models of social, economic and cultural organization in the world. Information and communication technologies allow rapid communication, creation of networks and generate new ways of collaboration and learning challenges. Additionally, improve the creation of new forms of knowledge accumulation, such as, dynamic images, voices and new sensorial environments.

These global changes bring some advantages to virtual universities:

- Expanding student catchment far beyond their traditional geography limited boundaries. This possibility allows improve productivity of university and achieve a cost structure more flexible and light. During the improvement of cost effectiveness in educational courses;
- Technology able the interaction between students and teachers, i.e., learn and teach in different places;
- Providing open access to learning and training as a mater of equity. Including handicapped and disabled students that can also have access to same courses;
- Granting opportunities for updating skills of the work force;
- Improving the quality of existing educational structures;
- Enhancing the capacity of the educational system;
- Balancing inequalities between age groups;
- Delivering educational campaigns to specific targets audiences;
- Providing emergency training to key target groups;
- Expanding the capacity for education with work and family life;
- Adding an international dimension to educational experience;

- The quality tends to increase indeed virtual universities are open to public scrutiny (Moore & Kearsley, 2012).

Nevertheless, this global and competitive context implies challenges to higher education in general, and also to virtual universities:

- Students have to learn how to study using technology, how communicate for learning, which is not always the same as what they do socially.
- Virtual learning expands the population of the students and subsequently increases their heterogeneity. Consequently, students could present different profiles and styles of learning with effects on learning results and limiting the use of methodologies tailored to each profile;
- Different technology, different teaching techniques and different types of students involves achieve the best ways to manage and administer the programs provided;
- Virtual universities include the concept of distance learning. Distance learning is a multidimensional concept that implies special pedagogy different from the traditional pedagogy used in a classroom. Teachers and facilitators of e-learning must be aligned with this pedagogical virtual model;
- Guarantee a active rather than a passive learning environment;
- Develop global courses adapted to different students profiles and from different geographic origins;
- Develop online collaboration and assessment criteria's fair for all students, attending to the culture and geographical heritages;
- Design courses that able experiences and environments based upon interactive and collaborative learning and also reduce the students drop out.

- With the purpose of giving students more opportunities to contribute, some teachers' applied Web 2.0 tools (blogs, wikis) and services (Flickr, YouTube) within the institution, however some problems occur because of the difficulty to manage external people and services within the institution (Yang, 2006). In this case students don't have the notion of classroom or groups of students where learning services can be delivered and executed. To the services, it is complex for learners to discover and access different web services, and it is not obvious for the teacher to track all the services students have used to assess their learning outcomes (Oskar et al, 2010).

Related with the last challenge presented above, virtual universities in general reveal high dropout rates, some reasons are point out to justify this problem: students don't have enough time and believe that e-learning is less time consuming; students have some expectative about difficulty of e-learning and expect easy level comparing with traditional learning; students reveal problems in time management; some students have a lack of motivation and give up before the first problem; some students reveal problems in adaptation to the technology; lack of student support; poorly and inadequate designed courses and substandard/inexperienced instructors. Subsequently several factors could affect negatively learning process in virtual universities. The social factor is one of each factors, studying in cyberspace can be lonely and isolating and it's also important that student have realistic expectations about e-learning.

Additionally, new challenges for virtual universities include bringing together all of the aspects of e-learning in a holistic framework, and perceiving these concepts in a global context (Ehlers & Schneckenberg, 2010; NAHE, 2008; Soinila & Stalter, 2010). Bates (2009) referred a need for experimentation, innovation and vision where there are challenges, to consider together three competing factors: increasing access; increasing quality or improving outcomes, and reducing costs.

QUALITY CHALLENGES

Nowadays, quality is a challenge and a key factor fronted by virtual universities. The accountability pressure in higher education and a number of less successful e-learning projects has amplified concerns about quality in e-learning (Connolly et al, 2005; Oliver 2005). Improving and assuring quality is crucial to the success of higher education institutions involved in e-learning (Inglis, 2005; Ehlers & Pawlowski 2006). McGorry (2003) solicits more attention to the quality of e-learning in higher education and Zhao (2003) suggests that universities implement a quality assurance plan aimed specifically at e-learning programs. In last years a huge number of models, frameworks, and guidelines have been developed for enhancing and assuring quality in e-learning (Phipps & Merisotis, 2000; Watty, 2003). Some of these principles are common with the quality principles applied in face-to-face teaching (Oliver 2003).

Nevertheless, globalization and the predominance cross-cultural enterprises, require that e-quality models should specifically consider cultural and cultural–pedagogical constructs (Ehlers, 2009).

According with Masoumi & Lindström (2012) any framework or model for assuring and enhancing quality of education explicitly or implicitly should be build on a set of theoretical premises. Otherwise, the aim of the model (what is good teaching/learning, how to improve student learning, and how and when it should be undertaken) cannot be articulated (Biggs 2001; Harvey & Newton 2004). Nonetheless, in various contemporary e-quality models reveal that the theoretical foundation is not articulated. Masoumi & Lindström (2012) argue that some of the models are a composed of an assemblage of the benchmarks,

not structuring on a comprehensive theoretical approach.

Frequently e-quality models have mechanistically approached quality in e-learning, due the dissemination of education. This approach reveals a technocratic top-down approach concerning quality control, with roots in industrial mass production (Ehlers 2009; Masoumi & Lindström 2009). E-learning is nowadays a holistic concept, so it is essential to develop models that also recognize the holistic character of educational processes. Masoumi & Lindström (2012) refer that many of the e-quality models disclose a tendency to focus on single aspects, thus failing to capture the holistic nature of problems and their solutions in virtual institutions.

It's possible finding several approaches to manage e-learning quality. Nevertheless, due the different stakeholders are involved in the use of e-learning products, different attributes of quality are emphasized (Sung et al, 2011). According with the user is possible to identify different attributes. Learners generally emphasize attributes of accessibility, usability and effects; faculty/teachers emphasize the ease of use and efficiency of implementation, while providers/suppliers may emphasize market-boosting and benefit/cost issues (Kidney, et al, 2007). E-learning products follow a life cycle: planning, implementation, use, and evaluation. Different quality attributes and quality management strategies are emphasized in different phases of life cycle (Barker, 2007; Lodzinski & Pawlowski, 2006; Wirth, 2006).

Several universities developed a quality certification. The e-learning Courseware Certification (ECC), allows certify online platforms, multimedia courseware, as well as asynchronous courseware. According Sung et al (2011) ECC comprises four evaluation dimensions: interface, compatibility, production quality and instructional design; under which are 19 evaluation standards, each includes both non-substitutable and substitutable criteria. Inside this topic aspects related with reliability and validity and the impact of implementing the certification, remain ambiguous.

Messick (1989) and Moss (1992) argues that the concept of social consequences of assessment involves actual and potential consequences of the test use, has been included into the concept of validity for assessment.

OPEN UNIVERSITY - PORTUGAL

The University History

Established in 1988, Universidade Aberta (UAb) is the only institution of public higher education in Portugal of Distance Learning. Due to its purpose, UAb uses all the time, in its teaching activities, the most advanced technologies and methods of Distance Learning, saving no geographical borders or physical barriers, and giving special emphasis to the expansion of Portuguese language and culture within the Lusophony space (migrant communities and Portuguese speaking countries). In this context, UAb offers higher education anywhere in the world (Undergraduate, Master and Doctorate degrees) and Lifelong Learning courses. All pedagogical offers are integrated into the Bologna Process and are taught under e-learning since 2008, the year that UAb became a reference European institution in the area of advanced e-learning and online learning through the recognition of its Virtual Teaching Model, unprecedented in Portugal and developed by this institution.

In 2010, Distance Learning practiced at UAb was awarded with the Prize of EFQUEL - European Foundation for Quality in E-learning and certification of The UNIQUe Quality Label for the use of ICT in Higher Education (Universities and Institutes). At the same year, UAb was qualified for an international panel of independent experts as the reference institution for teaching in e-learning system in Portugal. In 2011, UAb was awarded with the 1st Level of Excellency of the European Foundation for Quality Management (EFQM).

Some Facts and Figures

The Open University is a Portuguese virtual university located in Lisbon – Portugal was created in 1988 and has also two regional study centers in Oporto and Coimbra.

Open University has about 12000 students, which about 8000 are in graduate and postgraduate programs and about 4000 are inside Long Life Learning programs. Table 4 present the enrolled students per study cycle and in Long Life Learning (LLL).

Table 5 present students considering the place in world where they are.

This virtual university develop their one pedagogical model of e-learning whose is considering a reference in virtual learning domain and produce also, teaching materials, nowadays mainly in digital format.

Table 6 presents a summary of publications per department.

DCeT: Department of Science and Technology

DCSG: Department of Social Sciences and Management

DEED: Department of Distance Education and Elearning

DH: Department of Humanities

In 2010 the virtual learning developed by Open University received a Prize from EFQUEL – European Foundation for Quality in E-learning and the certification of UNIQUE – The Quality Label for the use of ICT in Higher Education (Universities and Institutes). Also in 2010, Open University was qualified for an International panel of independent expertises as the e-learning reference university in Portugal. In 2011, receive the 1st level of excellence from European Foundation for Quality Management (EFQM).

This University have also an important role in promotes Portuguese language and culture, especially in Portuguese speaking countries.

Concerning with students profile in 2011-2012 (Universidade Aberta, 2012) they are mainly worker-students, Portuguese and residence in

Table 4. Enrolled students per study cycle in academic year 2011/12 and LLL programs in 2012

	1st Cycle	2nd Cycle	3rd Cycle	LLL Programs	Total
No. of enrolled students	7271	564	108	4382	12325

Source: Activity Report of Universidade Aberta 2012, available on http://www.uab.pt/web/guest/english/key-figures/students

Table 5. Students living 'anywhere in the world' per study cycle in academic year 2011/12

Geographical Distribution by Continent Countries are listed in descending order of no. of students	1st Cycle	2nd Cycle	3rd Cycle	Total	% Distribution
Africa Angola, Mozambique, Cape Verde, Sao Tome and Principe, Egypt, Guinea, Israel, Lybia, Malawi, United Republic of Tanzania	442	38	5	485	70,50%
America Brazil, USA, Canada, Argentina, Chile	9	18	10	37	5,40%
Asia & Oceania Macau, Japan, East Timor	11	1		12	1,70%
Europe (not including Portugal) Switzerland, Luxembourg, Germany, France, Spain, Belgium, Netherlands, United Kingdom, Austria, Italy, Croatia, Hungary, Sweden, Andorra, Cyprus, Iceland, Lithuania, Poland, Romania	125	27	2	154	22,40%

Source: Activity Report of Universidade Aberta 2012 available on http://www.uab.pt/web/guest/english/key-figures/students

Table 6. Summary of publications per department in 2012

Publications' Typology		DCeT	DCSG	DEED	DH	Total
Indexed scientific publications in international databases	Books	2	1	0	1	4
	Editor of books or journals	8	9	2	3	22
	Books' chapters	31	7	10	9	57
	Articles in journals	52	26	17	12	107
	Proceedings	19	17	6	7	49
Non-indexed scientific publications in international databases	Books	0	12	5	5	22
	Editor of books or journals	4	15	2	6	27
	Books' chapters	6	37	24	20	87
	Articles in journals	12	24	16	15	67
	Proceedings	35	18	34	10	97
Total		**169**	**166**	**116**	**88**	**539**

Source: Activity Report of Universidade Aberta 2012, available on http://www.uab.pt/web/guest/english/key-figures/publications

Table 7. Pedagogical offer

Pedagogical Offer					
Study Program	**2009/10**	**2010/11**	**2011/12**	**2012/13**	**2013/14**
1st Cycle	15	14	15	12	12
Post-Graduation	3	1	2	5	10
2nd Cycle	15	23	22	22	23
3rd Cycle	18 (a)	18 (a) + 4	4	6	6
Lifelong Learning	11	26	53 (b)	211 (b)	(c)

Sources: UAb's Activity Reports (2009, 2009, 2010, and 2011) and online Information Guide.

Portugal, 56% are females and 44% males. In undergraduate studies and masters the ages are about 40 years old in average and 42,5 years old in the case of the PhD programs. In the same period have about 700 students residents in other countries (Universidade Aberta, 2012). Table 7 presents the pedagogical offer.

1. Pre-Bologna doctoral degrees.
2. Study programs may have several editions per year.
3. No available data yet

The virtual learning model bases on the uses of the e-learning moodle platform, where all pedagogical materials are provided. The platform also support the management of the apprenticeship using several tools that able the development of the knowledge, sharing information and receive feedback, promoting communication and support some assessment activities. The communication

with teachers it's preferentially asynchrony to favoured flexibility and autonomy in management of learning process. It's possible to see some facts and figures in Table 8.

E-LEARNING AND THE VIRTUAL PEDAGOGICAL MODE

In 2008 Open University became a reference European institution in the area of advanced e-learning and online learning through the recognition of its Virtual Pedagogical Model, unprecedented in Portugal and developed by this institution around four cornerstones: student-centered learning, flexibility, interaction and digital inclusion. Since then all degrees and lifelong learning courses are available online and make use of those methodologies and tools.

Table 8. Facts and figures

Universidade Aberta...
- Is the single public Portuguese distance education university
- Has Portuguese speaking students 'anywhere in the world'
- Has developed its own virtual pedagogical model
- Offers more than 40 degrees and dozens of lifelong study programs
- Has ca. 150 teachers and researchers
- Has published hundreds of titles (including e-books and multimedia documents)
- Has more than 400 agreements and protocols signed with different national and foreign entities, either higher education institutions

or not has two regional delegations (in Coimbra and Porto) and 16 Local Learning Centers in Portugal and 1 in Mozambique
- Has a network of facilities all over the world in which its students can attend to presence-based examinations
- Has been awarded the 1st level of 'Committed to Excellence' by the European Foundation for Quality Management (EFQM) in

November 2011

Source: Universidade Aberta, available on http://www.uab.pt/web/guest/english/key-figures

"The advances in technology have been driving distance education to find new teaching and learning methodologies, rethinking the technological mediation characteristic of distance education programs in terms of new forms of interaction, particularly the interaction among students ... The new means of communication through the web allows us to set up new virtual learning contexts, where both directional (teacher-student) and multidirectional (student-teacher and student-student) communication is possible (one-to-one, one-to-many and many-to-many communication). We can, therefore, create virtual classes where students and teachers interact at anytime from anywhere.

...This approach, going beyond instructional methods and tasks, requires the adoption of pedagogical strategies that engage students as active participants, leading them to develop meta cognitive skills (learning to learn) and take a constructive attitude regarding their capacity of self-realization towards lifelong learning, becoming more and more autonomous and being able to interact responsibly in group." *In Universidade Aberta's Pedagogical Model for Distance Education, UAb, 2008 (p. 10-11).*

The ECTS Credit System

Open University officially applies the European Credit Transfer and Accumulation System (ECTS) to its pedagogical offer, being this application defined in the Portuguese Republic Official Journal. ECTS is used for all study programs, including lifelong learning courses and it serves both mobile and non-mobile students, making easy to compare study programs both at national and international levels.

ECTS is a student-centered system based on the student workload, i.e., the time a student takes to complete all planned learning activities. A full-time student is expected to accomplish 60 ECTS during one academic year (30 credits per semester). At UAb, 1 ECTS stands for 26 working hours.

CONCLUDING REMARKS AND GOOD PRACTICES

Nowadays virtual environments are included in day life of most of the people in the world. Globalization of economies implies the development of skills that able people to think and work in multicultural and global environments. Preparing an online course require not only content expert but also some design requirements in order to organize the course considering pedagogy adapted to e-learning contexts.

Some good practices applied to virtual universities could be presented:

- It's important develops a culture that students become able to adequate they're initial expectative to the real context of e-learning. Virtual universities must develop, promote and divulge a culture/image that online learning is so seriously and exigent as the traditional learning;
- Create a social dimension of e-learning. Could be important create social interaction during e-learning experience, may be through the development of team projects, providing task involving e-learners and promoting interact with colleagues, promoting workshops or seminars and through coaching activities;
- Improve course design and improve teachers training and recycling;
- Use multimedia technology via internet;
- Provide access to digital libraries and scholarly journals.

Virtual universities front a set of challenges and opportunities in XXI century. At the same time virtual universities allows a democratization of the education and enlarge the target enabling that a set of access to university, option not possible for part of them in traditional universities, have also an important role in capture others audiences to their e-learning programs, such as long life learn-

Table 9. Lessons learned

Lessons learned from establishing and operating a new virtual university may be valuable to those involved in similar initiatives and to those in other higher education settings. The lessons given here will assist state leaders, administrators, faculty members, and others involved in starting a virtual university:

1. **Deliberate planning** is crucial prior to the establishment of a virtual university. It is important to consult with higher education institutions and seek their input. It is necessary to have a sound strategic plan in place to guide the operation of the virtual university, to stay focused and not become "all things to all people."

2. **Make higher education institutions the primary constituency**. A virtual university directly serves higher education institutions, not individual learners. Be less of a provider, more of a facilitator. Develop partnerships with existing colleges and universities, and build on existing infrastructures and services. Bring higher education institutions together to share information, solve policy issues regarding distance education, and collaborate on developing or offering online courses and programs. Be cautious about working directly with students or learners; this will only invite resistance and resentment from higher education institutions if a virtual university acts independently of higher education institutions.

3. **Secure support and funding from the state**. To do so, a virtual university has to demonstrate the value that it adds to the state and to higher education institutions, whether it is increasing enrollments or developing new programs or services. Constantly conduct formal and informal evaluations to measure organizational performance.

4. **Identify needs of the primary constituencies and provide services in multiple forms for students, faculty, and higher education institutions**. Basic services such as course catalog, technical support, call center, and infrastructure (such as a course management system) were generally considered crucial. Grants, annual conferences, and online resources were most valued by higher education institutions. In delivering services, the goal should be to build institutional capacity, not to compete with higher education institutions. It could be dangerous to bypass colleges and universities by providing services directly to students and faculty.

5. **Communication is the key**. Create committees with various groups of campus participants in terms of level and expertise, including grassroots professionals on campus. Reach out to all the constituencies in multiple ways, and seek feedback from higher education institutions. Lead; do not dictate.

Source: Xu & Morris, 2009, p 52-53.

ing, executive programs, etc. Moreover, the virtual model allows a more efficient internationalization of the education and improves the attraction of the students from other countries. All this arguments justify more studies about this innovative model of learning in higher education.

REFERENCES

Arkkelin, D. (2003). *Putting Prometheus feet to the fire: student evaluations of Prometheus in relation to their attitudes towards and experience with computers, computer self-efficacy and preferred learning style*. Retrieved from http://faculty.valpo.edu/darkkeli/papers/syllabus03.htm

Bannan-Ritland, B. (2002). Computer-Mediated Communication, E-learning, and Interactivity: A Review of the Research. *The Quarterly Review of Distance Education*, 3(2), 161–179.

Barker, K. C. (2007). E-learning quality standards for consumer protection and consumer confidence: A Canadian case study in e-learning quality assurance. *Journal of Educational Technology & Society*, *10*, 109–119.

Bates, A. W. (1995). *Technology, Open Learning, and Distance Education*. London: Routledge.

Bates, A. W. (1999). *Managing Technological Change: Strategies for Academic Leaders*. Jossey-Bass.

Bates, T. (2009). *Re: Using technology to improve the cost-effectivenes of the academy*. Retrieved from http://www.tonybates.ca/2009/10/10/using-technology-to-improve-the-cost-effectiveness-of-the-academy-part-1/

Bates, T. (2010). *Re: Strategic thinking about e-learning*. Retrieved from http://www.tonybates.ca/2010/06/11/strategic-thinking-about-e-learning/

Berge, Z. L. (1998). Barriers to Online Teaching in Postsecondary Institutions: Can Policy Changes Fix It? *Online Journal of Distance Learning Administration, 1*(2). Retrieved from http://www.westga.edu/~distance/ojdla/winter64/meyen64.htm

Biggs, J. (2001). The reflective institution: Assuring and enhancing the quality of teaching and learning. *Higher Education, 41*(3), 221–238. doi:10.1023/A:1004181331049

Bonk, C. J. (2009). *The world is open: How web technology is revolutionizing education.* San Francisco, CA: Jossey-Bass, A Wiley Imprint.

Brown, R. E. (2001). The Process of Community-Building in Distance Learning Classes. *The Sloan Consortium, 5* (2). Retrieved from http://www.aln.org/publications/jaln/v5n2/v5n2_brown.asp

Campos, M., Laferriere, T., & Harasim, L. (2001). The Post-Secondary Networked Classroom: Renewal of Teaching Practices and Social Interaction. *Journal of Asynchronous Learning Networks, 5*(2). Retrieved from http://aln.org/alnweb/journal/Vol5_issue2/Campos/Campos.htm

Chia, H., & Chiu, Y. (2011). Assessing e-learning 2.0 system success. *Computers & Education, 57*(2), 1790–1800. doi:10.1016/j.compedu.2011.03.009

Clark, A., & Pitt, T. J. (2001). Creating Powerful Online Courses using Multiple Instructional Strategies. *eModerators*. Retrieved from http://www.emoderators.com/moderators/pitt.html

Connolly, M., Jones, N., & O'Shea, J. (2005). Quality assurance and e-learning: Reflections from the front line. *Quality in Higher Education, 11*(1), 59–67. doi:10.1080/13538320500077660

Conole, G. (2010). Learning design: Making practice explicit. In *Proceedings of Con-nectED Conference*. Retrieved from http://www.slideshare.net/grainne/connect-ed-conole

Davis, D. F., Bagozzi, P. R., & Warshaw, R. P. (1989). User acceptance of computer technology: A comparison of two theoretical models. *Management Science, 35*(8), 982–1003. doi:10.1287/mnsc.35.8.982

Deci, E. L., & Ryan, R. M. (1985). *Intrinsic motivation and self-determination in human behavior.* New York: Plenum. doi:10.1007/978-1-4899-2271-7

Dutton, W. H., & Loader, B. D. (2002). Competition and Collaboration in Online Distance Learning. In W. Dutton (Ed.), *Digital Academe: The New Media and Institutions of Higher Education and Learning.* New York: Routledge.

Ehlers, U. D. (2009). Understanding quality culture. *Quality Assurance in Education, 17*(4), 343–363. doi:10.1108/09684880910992322

Ehlers, U. D., & Pawlowski, J. (2006). Quality in European e-learning: An Introduction. In U. D. Ehlers & J. Pawlowski (Eds.), *Handbook on quality and standardization in e-learning* (pp. 1–13). Berlin: Springer. doi:10.1007/3-540-32788-6_1

Ehlers, U. D., & Schneckenberg, D. (2010). Introduction: Changing cultures in higher education. In U. D. Ehlers & D. Schneckenberg (Eds.), *Changing cultures in higher education* (pp. 1–14). Berlin: Springer-Verlag. doi:10.1007/978-3-642-03582-1_1

Ekwensi, F., Moranski, J., & Townsend-Sweet, M. (2006). Instructional Strategies for E-learning. *E-learning Concepts and Techniques*. Retrieved from http://iit.bloom.edu/Spring2006_eBook_files/chapter5.htm

Epper, R. M., & Garn, M. C. (2003). *Virtual College and University Consortia: A National Study.* Boulder, CO: State Higher Education Executive Officers.

Ertmer, P. A., & Stepich, D. A. (2002). Initiating and Maintaining Meaningful Case Discussions: Maximizing the Potential of Case-Based Instruction. *Journal on Excellence in College Teaching, 13* (2-3). Retrieved from http://celt.muohio.edu/ject/issue.php?v=13&n=2+and+3

Evans, T., & Nation, D. (2000). *Changing University Teaching: Reactions on Creating Educational Technologies*. London: Kogan Page.

Faigley, L. (1990). Subverting the electronic network: teaching writing using networked computers. In D. Daiker & M. Morenberg (Eds.), *The writing teacher as researcher: Essays in the theory and practice of class-based research*. Portsmouth: Boynton/Cook.

Farrell, G. M. (1999). *The Development of Virtual Education: A Global Perspective*. Vancouver, Canada: Commonwealth of Learning.

Feenberg, A. (1987). Computer conferencing and the humanities. *Instructional Science, 16*, 169–186.

Forsyth, H., Pizzica, J., Laxton, R., & Mahony, M. J. (2010). Distance education in an era of eLearning: Challenges and opportunities for campus-focused institution. *Higher Education Research & Development, 29*(1), 15–28. doi:10.1080/07294360903421350

Gellman-Danley, B., & Fetzner, M. J. (1998). Asking the Really Tough Questions: Policy Issues for Distance Learning. *Online Journal of Distance Learning Administration*. Retrieved from http://www.westga.edu/~distance/danley11.html

Govindasamy, T. (2002). Successful implementation of e-learning: Pedagogical considerations. *The Internet and Higher Education, 4*(3-4), 287–299. doi:10.1016/S1096-7516(01)00071-9

Greenagel, F. L. (2002). *The Illusion of E-Learning: Why We're Missing Out on the Promise of Technology*. Retrieved from http://www.guidedlearning.com/illusions.pdf

Gurbuz, F. (2014). Students' views on distance learning in Turkey: An Example Of Anadolu University Open Education Faculty. *Turkish Online Journal of Distance Education, 15*(2), 239–250.

Guri-Rosenblit, S. (1999). The Agendas of Distance Teaching Universities: Moving from the Margins to the Center Stage of Higher Education. *Higher Education, 37*(3), 281–293. doi:10.1023/A:1003644305026

Guri-Rosenblit, S. (2001). Virtual Universities: Current Models and Future Trends. *Higher Education in Europe, 16*(4), 487–499. doi:10.1080/03797720220141807

Hanna, D. E. (2000). *Higher Education in an Era of Digital Competition*. Madison, WI: Atwood.

Hardy, C. (2002). *Incorporating Active/Interactive Learning Strategies into an Online Course*. Retrieved from http://info.nwmissouri.edu/~chardy/COMPS/EDPS854HumanCognition/EDPS854HumanCognitionIntervention.htm

Harvey, L., & Newton, J. (2004). Transforming quality evaluation. *Quality in Higher Education, 10*(2), 149–165. doi:10.1080/1353832042000230635

Haythornthwaite, C., & Kazmer, M. M. (2002). Bringing the Internet Home: Adult Distance Learners and Their Internet, Home, and Work Worlds. In B. Wellman & C. Haythornthwaite (Eds.), *The Internet in Everyday Life* (pp. 431–463). Malden, MA: Blackwell Publishing. doi:10.1002/9780470774298.ch15

Healey, D. (1998). *Conferencing Online with Nicenet*. English Language Institute Technology Tip of the Month: October 1998. Retrieved from http://oregonstate.edu/dept/eli/oct1998.html

Herring, M., & Dargan, C. (2002). *Using Discussion Boards to Integrate Technology into the College Classroom*. Retrieved from http://www.hawkeye.cc.ia.us/faculty/cpost/using_discussion_boards_paper.htm

Hrastinski, S. (2008). Asynchronous and Synchronous E-Learning. *Educause Quarterly Magazine, 31* (4). Retrieved on http://www.educause.edu/node/163445?time=1238691114

Huynh, M. Q., Umesh, U. N., & Valachich, J. (2003). E-Learning as an Emerging Entrepreneurial enterprise in Universities and Firms. *Communications of the AIS, 12*, 48–68.

Inglis, A. (2005). Quality improvement, quality assurance, and benchmarking: comparing two frameworks for managing quality processes in open and distance learning. *The International Review of Research in Open and Distance Learning*. Retrieved from http://www.microsoft.com/isapi/

Johnson, L., Smith, R., Willis, H., & Haywood, K. (2011). *The 2011 horizon report*. Austin, TX: The New Media Consortium.

Jones, N., & O'Shea, J. (2004). Challenging Hierarchies: The Impact of E-Learning. *Higher Education, 48*(3), 379–395. doi:10.1023/B:HIGH.0000035560.32573.d0

Kabassi, K., & Virvou, M. (2004). Personalized Adult e-Training on Computer Use Based on Multiple Attribute Decision Making. *Interacting with Computers, 16*(1), 115–132. doi:10.1016/j.intcom.2003.11.006

Khan, B. H. (1997). *Web-Based Instruction*. Englewood Cliffs, NJ: Prentice Hall.

Kidney, G., Cummings, L., & Boehm, A. (2007). Toward a quality assurance approach to e-learning courses. *International Journal on E-Learning, 6*, 17–30.

Kirp, D. (2007). *The market and the university: The challenge to higher education*. Sydney: Research Institute for Humanities and Social Sciences, The University of Sydney.

Klemm, W. R. (1997). *Benefits of Collaboration Software for On-site Classes*. Retrieved from http://www.cvm.tamu.edu/wklemm/backup/onsite.htm

Krendl, K. A., & Lieberman, D. A. (1988). Computers and learning: A review of recent research. *Journal of Educational Computing Research, 4*(4), 367–389. doi:10.2190/BP7R-8Y2Y-R57C-5JKL

Kum, L. C. (1999). *A study into students_perceptions of web-based learning environment*. Paper presented at the HERDSA Annual International Conference. Melbourne, Australia.

Lameras, P., Paraskakis, I., & Levy, P. (2008). *Conceptions of teaching using virtual learning environments: Preliminary findings from a phenomenographic inquiry*. Paper presented at the 6th International Conference on Networked Learning. Thessaloniki, Greece.

Land, S. M., & Dornisch, M. M. (2001). A Case study of Student use of Asynchronous Bulletin Boards Systems (BBS) to support Reflection and Evaluation. *Journal of Educational Technology Systems, 30*(4), 365–377. doi:10.2190/A9EM-YBPQ-5JWU-2JWT

Landsberger, J. (2001). Integrating a Web-based Bulletin Board into your Class: A guide for Faculty. *TechTrends, 45*(5), 50–53. doi:10.1007/BF03017092

Laurillard, D. (2006). E-learning in higher education. In P. Ashwin (Ed.), *Changing higher education: The development of learning and teaching* (pp. 71–96). London: Routledge.

Lawrence, M. (1999, November 8). Homework for adults. *The Guardian*.

Littleton, K., & Light, P. (1999). *Learning with Computers: Analysing Productive Interaction.* London: Routledge.

Lodzinski, T., & Pawlowski, J. M. (2006). The quality mark e-learning: developing process- and product-oriented quality. In U. D. Ehlers & J. M. Pawlowski (Eds.), *Handbook on quality and standardization in e-learning* (pp. 109–124). Berlin: Springer. doi:10.1007/3-540-32788-6_8

Lovejoy, D. (1993). Adapting to the needs of its users. *The Architects'. Journal, 10*(November), 27–37.

Lowell, R. (2001). *The Pew Learning and Technology Program Newsletter.* Retrieved from http://www.math.hawaii.edu/~dale/pew.html

Lyons, J. F. (2004). Teaching U.S. History Online: Problems and Prospects. The History Teacher. *Society for the History of Education, 37*(4), 447–456.

MacKnight, C. B. (2000). Teaching Critical Thinking through Online Discussions. *EDUCAUSE Quarterly, 4.* Retrieved from http://www.educause.edu/ir/library/pdf/EQM0048.pdf

Marzano, R. J., & Pickering, D. J. (1997). *Dimensions of learning trainer_s manual.* Alexandria VI: Mid-Continent, Research for Education and Learning. Retrieved from http://www.ascd.org/ASCD/pdf/siteASCD/publications/books/Dimensions-of-Learning-Teachers-Manual-2nd-edition.pdf

Masoumi, D., & Lindström, B. (2009). Foundations of cultural design in e-learning. *International Journal of Internet and Enterprise Management, 6*(2), 124–142. doi:10.1504/IJIEM.2009.023926

Masoumi, D., & Lindström, B. (2012). Quality in e-learning: A framework for promoting and assuring quality in virtual institutions. *Journal of Computer Assisted Learning, 28*(1), 27–41. doi:10.1111/j.1365-2729.2011.00440.x

McGorry, S. Y. (2003). Measuring quality in online programs. *The Internet and Higher Education, 6*(2), 159–177. doi:10.1016/S1096-7516(03)00022-8

Messick, S. (1989). Validity. In R. L. Linn (Ed.), *Educational measurement* (3rd ed., pp. 13–103). Washington, DC: American Council on Education and National Council on Measurement in Education.

Moore, M., & Kearsley, G. (2012). *Distance education – A system view of online learning* (3rd ed.). Wadsmorth, MA: Cengage Learning.

Moss, P. A. (1992). Shifting conceptions of validity in educational measurement: Implications for performance assessment. *Review of Educational Research, 62*(3), 229–258. doi:10.3102/00346543062003229

NAHE (The Swedish National Agency for Higher Education). (2008). *E-learning quality: Aspects and criteria.* Solna: Högskoleverket.

O'Leary, J. (2000, February 16). Students may have to pay higher fees. *The Times.*

O'Reilly, T., & Batelle, J. (2009). *Web Squared: Web 2.0 Five Years On.* Retrieved from http://assets.en.oreilly.com/1/event/28/web2009_websqared-whitepaper.pdf

O'Sullivan, M. F. (2001). *Is Anyone There? Communication and Online learning.* Retrieved from http://www.wwtc.edu/voice/class/vtutor/cw2001.htm

Oliver, R. (2001). Strategies for Assuring the Quality of Online Leaning Australian Higher Education. In M. Wallace, A. Ellis & D. Newton (Eds.), *Proceedings of Moving Online II Conference,* (pp. 222-231). Academic Press.

Oliver, R. (2003). *Exploring benchmarks and standards for assuring quality online teaching and learning in higher education.* Paper presented at the Proceedings of 16th Open and Distance Learning. Canberra, Australia. Retrieved from http://elrond.scam.ecu.edu.au/oliver/2003/odlaa.pdf

Oliver, R. (2005). Quality assurance and e-learning: Blue skies and pragmatism. *Research in Learning Technology, 13*(3), 173–187. doi:10.1080/09687760500376389

Omar, A., Kalulu, D., & Alijani, G. (2011). Management of innovative e-learning environments. *Academy of Educational Leadership Journal, 15*(3), 37–64.

Oskar, C., Portillo, J., Ovelar, R., Benito, M., & Romo, J. (2010). iPLE Network: An integrated eLearning 2.0 architecture from a university's perspective. *Interactive Learning Environments, 18*(3), 293–308. doi:10.1080/10494820.2010.500553

Ossiannilsson, E. (2011). Findings from European Benchmarking Exercises on E-Learning: Value and Impact. *Creative Education, 2*(3), 208–219. doi:10.4236/ce.2011.23029

Phipps, R., & Merisotis, J. (2000). *Quality on the Line: Benchmarks for Success in Internet-Based Distance Education.* Washington, DC: The Institute of Higher Education Policy.

Picciano, G. A. (2002). Beyond student perceptions: Issues of interaction, presence and performance in an online course. *Journal of Asynchronous Learning Networks, 6*(1), 21–40.

Rana, K. S. (2005). *E-learning for Small Groups: The Diplo Foundation's Experience.* Retrieved from http://www.digitallearning.in/jan06/ddiplofoundation.asp

Rosenthal, D. W. (2002). The Case Method – A Joint Venture in Learning: A Message from the Editor. *Journal on Excellence in College Teaching, 13*(2-3). Retrieved from http://celt.muohio.edu/ject/issue.php?v=13&n=2+and+3

Rosevear, S. G. (1999). Lessons for Developing a Partnership-Based Virtual University. *Technology Source.* Retrieved from http://ts.mivu.org/default.asp?show_article&id_30

Rothblatt, S. (1997). *The Modern University and its Discontents: The Fate of Newman's Legacies in Britain and America.* Cambridge, UK: Cambridge University Press. doi:10.1017/CBO9780511582943

Rothermel, D. (2001). *Threaded Discussions: A First Step. Tech Learning.* Retrieved from http://www.ac.wwu.edu/~kenr/TCsite/home-frames.html

Rumble, G. (1996). Labour Market Theories and Distance Education. *Open Learning, 11*(2), 47–51. doi:10.1080/0268051960110208

Saadé, R. G., He, X., & Kira, D. (2007). Exploring dimensions to online learning. *Computers in Human Behavior, 23*(4), 1721–1739. doi:10.1016/j.chb.2005.10.002

Selinger, M., & Pearson, J. (1999). *Telematics in Education: Trends and Issues.* Oxford, UK: Pergamon Press.

Shabha, G. (2000). Virtual universities in the third millennium: An assessment of the implications of teleworking on university buildings and space planning. *Facilities, 18*(5/6), 235–244. doi:10.1108/02632770010328108

Smith, B. (1998). Creating Consortia: Exporting the Best, Import the Rest. *Converge Magazine, 1*, 19–98.

Soinila, M., & Stalter, M. (2010). *Quality assurance of e-learning*. Helsinki: ENQA, The European Association for Quality Assurance in Higher Education.

Soong, M. H. B., Chan, H. C., Chua, B. C., & Loh, K. F. (2001). Critical success factors for on- line course resources. *Computers & Education, 36*(2), 101–120. doi:10.1016/S0360-1315(00)00044-0

Sunal, W. D., Sunal, S. C., Odell, R. M., & Sundberg, A. C. (2003). Research-supported best practices for developing online learning. *Journal of Interactive Online Learning, 2*(1), 1–40.

Sung, Y., Chang, K. C., & Yu, W. C. (2011). Evaluating the reliability and impact of a quality assurance system for E-learning courseware. *Computers & Education, 57*(2), 1615–1627. doi:10.1016/j.compedu.2011.01.020

Thomas, J. W. (2000). *A Review of Research on Project-Based Learning*. Retrieved from http://www.bobpearlman.org/BestPractices/PBL_Research.pdf

Triandis, C. H. (1979). Values, attitudes, and interpersonal behavior. In *Proceedings of Nebraska Symposium on motivation, Beliefs, attitudes and values*. Lincoln, NE: University of Nebraska Press.

Trow, M. (1999). Lifelong Learning through the New Information Technologies. *Higher Education Policy, 12*(2), 201–217.

Tunison, S., & Noonan, B. (2001). On-Line Learning: Secondary Students' First Experience. *Canadian Journal of Education, 26*(4), 495–511. doi:10.2307/1602179

Universidade Aberta. (2012). Factos & Números 2011-2012 Gabinete de Desenvolvimento Estratégico e de Relações Internacionais. Author.

Vallerand, R. J. (1997). Toward a hierarchical model of intrinsic and extrinsic motivation. *Advances in Experimental Social Psychology, 29*, 271–374. doi:10.1016/S0065-2601(08)60019-2

Vate-u-lan, P. (2008). *Borderless eLearning: HITS Model for Web 2.0*. Retrieved from http://ejournals.thaicybern.go.thlindex.php/ictl/article/view/59/62

Venkatesh, V., & Davis, F. D. (2000). A theoretical extension of the technology acceptance model: Four longitudinal field studies. *Management Science, 46*(2), 186–204. doi:10.1287/mnsc.46.2.186.11926

Venkatesh, V., Speier, C., & Morris, M. G. (2002). User acceptance enablers in individual decision-making about technology: Toward an integrated model. *Decision Sciences, 33*(2), 297–316. doi:10.1111/j.1540-5915.2002.tb01646.x

Wagner, N., Hassanein, K., & Head, M. (2008). Who is responsible for E-Learning in Higher Education? A stakeholders' Analysis. *Journal of Educational Technology & Society, 11*(3), 26–36.

Wang, H., Zhang, Y., & Cao, J. (2009). Effective Collaboration with Information Sharing in Virtual Universities. *IEEE Transactions on Knowledge and Data Engineering, 21*(6), 840–853. doi:10.1109/TKDE.2008.132

Waterman, M., & Stanley, E. (2005). *Case Format Variations*. Retrieved from http://cstlcsm.semo.edu/waterman/cbl/caseformats.html

Watty, K. (2003). When will academics learn about quality? *Quality in Higher Education, 9*(3), 213–221. doi:10.1080/1353832032000151085

Weller, M. (2004). Models of Large Scale e-Learning. *Journal of Asynchronous Learning Networks, 8*(4), 83–92. Retrieved from http://www.aln.org/publications/jaln/index.asp?op0=OR&filter0%5B%5D=148

Wilson, L. A. (2006). *One-to-One Teaching and Learning Initiatives – Goals and Results*. Retrieved from http://www.techlearning.com/techlearning/events/techforum06/LeslieWilson_ProgramGuide.pdf

Wirth, M. A. (2006). An analysis of international quality management approaches in e-learning: different paths, similar pursuits. In U.-D. Ehlers & J. M. Pawlowski (Eds.), *Handbook on quality and standardisation in e-learning* (pp. 97–108). Heidelberg, Germany: Springer. doi:10.1007/3-540-32788-6_7

Wisker, G., Exley, K., Antoniou, M., & Ridley, P. (2007). *Supervising, Coaching, Mentoring, and Personal Tutoring*. Routledge.

Wolf, D. B., & Johnstone, S. M. (1999). Cleaning up the Language: Establishing a Consistent Vocabulary for Electronically Delivered Academic Programs. *Change*, *31*(4), 34–39. doi:10.1080/00091389909602698

Xu, H., & Morris, L. V. (2009). A Comparative Case Study of State-Level Virtual Universities. *New Directions for Higher Education*, *146*(146), 45–54. doi:10.1002/he.345

Yang, S. J. H. (2006). Context aware ubiquitous learning environments for peer-to-peer collaborative learning. *Journal of Educational Technology & Society*, *9*(1), 188–201.

Zhao, F. (2003). Enhancing the quality of online higher education through measurement. *Quality Assurance in Education*, *11*(4), 214–221. doi:10.1108/09684880310501395

KEY TERMS AND DEFINITIONS

Asynchronous Online Instruction: Also known as *Asynchronous method* and similar to *Asynchronous learning*. It is associated in the manuscript with: a teaching method that uses online learning resources to facilitate information sharing outside the constraints of time and place among a network of people.

Distance Education: Also known as *online learning* and similar to *learning using IT*. It is associated in the manuscript with: refers to a mode of delivering education and instruction on conditions which occur due to the use of ICT and other electronic media.

E-Learning: Also known as *online learning* and similar to *learning using IT*. It is associated in the manuscript with: refers to the use of electronic media and information and communication technologies (ICT) in education.

Remote Learning: Also known as *e-learning* and similar to *Distance education*. It is associated in the manuscript with: Virtual schools and deliver of public education providing adequate e-learning methodologies and technology.

Synchronous Online Instruction: Also known as *Face to face learning* and similar to *Synchronous learning*. It is associated in the manuscript with: refers to a learning environment in which everyone takes part at the same time.

U-Learning: Also known as *Ubiquitous learning* and similar to *Ubiquitous learning*. It is associated in the manuscript with: This perspective focused on the personalisation and in learners' rights and responsibilities.

Virtual Universities: Also known as *e-universities* and similar to open universities. It is associated in the manuscript with: universities that provides higher education programs through electronic media, typically the Internet.

Chapter 7
Promoting Interaction in an Asynchronous E-Learning Environment

Maria Pavlis Korres
University of Alcalá, Spain

ABSTRACT

Interaction is at the heart of the online learning experience. Theorists consider interaction a defining characteristic of education and regard it as vitally important in the design of e-learning courses. Interaction is a significant component in promoting learners' positive attitudes towards online education and affects their educational performance. This chapter examines the various ways an e-learning environment can promote interaction among participants by using the appropriate communication tools. It presents the results of a pilot e-learning course, confirming that different types of interaction can be promoted at a high level in an online environment and will contribute effectively to the achievement of the learning objectives.

INTRODUCTION

Learners in an online environment have to deal with barriers related to many factors, such as difficulties in accessing the course, technology usability, trusting and/or accepting ICTs in communication, feelings of isolation due to the distance from the educator and other learners, as well as lack of social interaction (Waltonen-Moore, Stuart, Newton, Oswald, & Varonis, 2006; Karalis & Koutsonikos, 2003; Gannon-Leary & Fontainha, 2007).

In their survey, Muilenburg and Berge (2005), identified eight factors as being substantial bar-

riers to online learning: administrative issues, social interaction, academic skills, technical skills, learner motivation, time and support for studies, cost and access to Internet, and technical problems. According to their survey, the single most important barrier to students learning online is the lack of social interaction.

Lack of interaction appears to be the greater barrier in asynchronous communication modes and it should be dealt with, as interaction is considered a very important factor in adult education. Consequently, an effective educational environment has to face all of the above mentioned barriers

DOI: 10.4018/978-1-4666-7316-8.ch007

and promote interaction among participants, as this affects the nature and quality of communication and learning (Pavlis Korres, Karalis, Leftheriotou, & Garcia Barriocanal, 2009; Grooms, 2003; Merlose & Bergeron, 2007).

In the first part of this chapter we focus on the notion of interaction in an online environment and we elaborate on the communication tools which could be used in an asynchronous communication mode to help promotion of interaction among participants (educators and learners). In the second part we present the level and the different types of interaction which have occurred during a pilot e-learning course, carried out for the education of educators of Roma in Greece and aiming at the improvement of their compatibility with their Roma learners.

INTERACTION IN ONLINE LEARNING ENVIRONMENT

Interaction is at the heart of the online learning experience. Moore's (1989) transactional distance theory considers interaction a defining characteristic of education and regards it as vitally important in the design of distance education.

Researchers have shown that interaction is a significant component in promoting learners' positive attitudes towards distance education: when learners perceive a high level of interaction they are more satisfied, while, when they perceive low interaction, they are dissatisfied, which affects their academic performance. (Booher & Seiler, 1982; Thompson, 1990; Fulford &Zhang, 1993; Muirhead, 2001).

Moore (1989) identified three kinds of interaction that support learning: learner-content, learner-instructor, and learner-learner interaction.

Learner-content interaction is the process in which students examine, consider, and process the course information presented during the educational experience. According to Moore and Kearsley (1996), "Every learner has to construct

knowledge through a process of personally accommodating information into previously existing cognitive structures. It is interacting with content that results in these changes in the learner's understanding" (p.128).

Learner-instructor interaction is communication between the learner and the instructor within a course. In the case of online learning, such interaction usually occurs via computer-mediated communication; is not strictly limited to instructional communication that occurs during the educational experience, but may include advising, offline communication, and personal dialogue. Interaction with instructors includes the myriad ways by which instructors motivate, enhance and maintain the learners' interest as well as the ways they present information, demonstrate skills, model attitudes and values, or organize, evaluate, counsel, support and encourage learners. According to Rovai (2002) in Asynchronous Learning Networks (ALN) learner-instructor interaction takes the form of intellectual discussion or stimulating exchanges of ideas. He stresses that facilitating productive interaction is probably the most important responsibility of an online educator. Rovai considers interaction one of the four dimensions (spirit, trust, interaction and learning) of the classroom community. A strategy that enhances these four dimensions should result in stronger feelings of community. If our aim is a strong sense of classroom community, we should learn how to enhance these dimensions, in order to promote within the communities a sense of well being, quality of the learning experience, and effective learning.

Finally, learner-learner interaction is communication between two or more learners, alone or in group settings, with or without the real-time presence of an instructor. Such interaction often occurs via asynchronous computer-mediated communication, although it may include other forms of interpersonal and small group communication, either online or offline, that might occur during the duration of a course. Learner-learner interaction among members of a class or other learning groups is an extremely valuable source for learning, especially in the context of adult education.

This threefold interaction construct has been extended and adapted by subsequent researchers in the area of distance and web-based learning. Other types of interaction have been added to the initial model, such as learner-interface interaction, which occurs when learners use various technologies in order to communicate with the content, ideas and information on the course content with the educator and their classmates (Hillman, Willis, & Gunawardena, 1994). According to Hillman et al. (1994) learners need to be fully literate with the interfaces used in communications technologies within an e-learning course or program "The learner must be skilled in using the delivery system in order to interact fully with the content, instructor and other learners" (p.40). Furthermore, Brunham and Walden (1997) have defined learner-environment interaction as "a reciprocal action or mutual influence between a learner and the learner's surroundings that either assists or hinders learning". Anderson and Garrison (1998) have added three more types of interaction: teacher-teacher, teacher-content and content-content.

Anderson in 2003 developed his equivalency theorem on interaction, according to which "Deep and meaningful formal learning is supported as long as one of the three forms of interaction (student–teacher; student-student; student-content) is at a high level. The other two may be offered at minimal levels, or even eliminated, without degrading the educational experience" (p.4). Anderson states that high levels of more than one of these three modes will likely provide a more satisfying educational experience.

Summing up, it is important for instructional designers and educators to promote a variety of types and mixes of interaction in order to provide an effective e-learning environment.

Asynchronous Learning Environment

The asynchronous learning environment seems to be preferable over the synchronous learning environment for online adult education, as it allows learners to follow their own pace overcoming the constrains of time, and to harmonize their personal, vocational and social life with education (Maydas, 1997; Harsh, 2002; Pavlis Korres et al., 2009). Furthermore, asynchronous online education appears as one of the most appealing instructional methods for adult education as it combines flexible access to educational material with time to reflect, self-study techniques and collaborative learning, while involving the use of low-cost technology (Tsiakos, 2002; Kalin, 1994; Khan, 1997; Dillon & Zhu, 1997; Bostock, 1997).

The advocates of asynchronous learning support that this kind of learning environment provides a "high degree of interactivity" between participants who are separated both geographically and temporally (Maydas, 1997). Since learners have an equal opportunity to participate in an asynchronous communication from where and when it suits them, they can express their thoughts without interruption, they have more time to reflect on and respond to class materials and their classmates than in a traditional classroom (Shea, Pickett, & Pelz, 2003). In communication which takes place in synchronous mode, learners who have a language barrier or those lacking enough confidence do not dare to speak up. The same learners are seen vehemently participating in electronic discussions through asynchronous mode (Shankar, 2007).

Many studies have also highlighted that ongoing asynchronous interaction -such as forums- are preferable to synchronous computer-mediated communication groups in that they help participants to build a better context in which learning can take place (Karsenti, 2007).

There has been argumentation against distance learning, as stated by Kochery (1997), who supports that students learning over a distance often feel alone and separated from not only the teacher, but also from the socialization with other students. Other adversaries to asynchronous learning environment support that students experience isolation and social disconnectedness which, correlated with students' difficulties with the course, result in failing grades, no completion, or withdrawal (Waltonen-Moore et al., 2006).

The answer to the above criticism comes from recent technological innovations, which have reduced significantly the barriers in communication and interaction and have allowed new forms of personal and group interaction as well as course delivery (Pantelidis & Auld, 2002). Designers, developers and educators have to structure and implement their courses incorporating interaction throughout the course.

It is broadly accepted that learning technology has changed the teaching and learning process. Multimedia, communication tools and Internet navigation are becoming more widely used in different educational levels, influencing education, motivating students, promoting learning, and changing classroom interaction.

Another advantage of the asynchronous environment is that all materials and all interactions that occur within this environment, such as e-mails, discussions etc. are archived, so that learners and educators can go back and review course materials, assignments, presentations as well as correspondence and discussions between participants (McNamara & Brown, 2008).

In order to benefit from an asynchronous online learning environment, learners have to overcome the barriers related to the learners' access to computers and the Internet. Although personal computers and web access are becoming more and more pervasive every day, this requirement can be a barrier to entry for many learners.

Once the access barrier is overcome, the acquisition of skills needed to participate in the electronic environment by learners and educators in the beginning of each educational course is considered essential as these skills influence directly all forms of interaction taking place in an e-learning environment (Hillman et al., 1994). Today, most institutions provide a computer network infrastructure and the technical support needed to develop and maintain asynchronous learning environments.

Another crucial factor in promoting interaction in an asynchronous e-learning environment is the creation of a course climate based on communication, cooperation and mutual respect. This is an important prerequisite for effective adult learning as interactive bidirectional relations between educators and learners, as well as between learners, can only be based of sincerity, respect and acceptance. A main concern of the educator of adults is to create an atmosphere of openness and trust within which the learners feel free to exchange their experiences and express thoughts, feelings and assumptions. Rogers (2007) argues that it is the educator who, to a large extent, controls the four elements which define the climate in the class - warmth, directness, enthusiasm and organization - and helps to create the climate of the learning groups. As he very accurately quotes "Their concern is both to promote the emotional well-being of the student participants and to ensure learning" (Rogers, 2007, p. 195).

Brown (2001) argues that interaction builds among learners a sense of community which leads to learner satisfaction, retention and increased learning. In an online environment, in order to promote immediacy and interaction between participants (educator and learners), it is very important to give special attention to the stage of the formation of the learning community. It is during this stage that the social bonds are founded between learners, as well as between educator and learners. The social bond formation stage centers on introductions, so that participants become more familiar with one another (Im & Lee, 2003-2004).

As Pavlis Korres points out (2012):

The initial stages of the group development where the members of the group introduce themselves to one another and begin to identify with and relate to one another are very important in order to build a strong and functional learning group. The first few hours and days of any course are often the most challenging for educators and learners alike. Early in the course the constructive norms of the group have to be established and interaction and immediacy between the members of the learning group have to be promoted. A variety of e-learning activities by using the appropriate communication tools must be used in order to engage learners in the educational process establish norms and build relationships among the learners in online courses (p.1361).

The use of the proper ice-breaking activities can positively help towards formation of strong social bonds in the learning group and establishment of the proper climate in the course, especially when educational objectives are addressing both the cognitive and the affective domain.

The Role of Communication Tools in an Asynchronous e-Learning Environment in Reducing Isolation and Promoting Immediacy, Active Participation, Interaction, and Collaboration

In order to promote immediacy, active participation, interaction and collaboration, as well as fight isolation in an asynchronous e-learning environment, communication tools such as e-mail, forums, threaded discussions, discussion boards, drop box, chat, wikis and blogs become of paramount importance. Course management systems such as Blackboard, Moodle, WebCT, Dokeos and Sakai, have been developed to support online interaction

and collaborative learning, providing tools that allow users to organize discussions, post messages and replies, upload or download files and access multimedia, working in smaller or larger groups. Pavlis Korres (2012) supports that,

By using the proper communication tool at the right time, the learner can be engaged to the educational process, interaction and immediacy between educator and learners as well as between learners themselves is promoted and, finally, the development of the learning group is effectively supported (p.1361).

Among the existing communication tools in an asynchronous e-learning environment the forum/threaded discussion has a great importance in overcoming certain barriers or achieving specific requirements for effective adult learning (Pavlis Korres et al., 2009; Kalin, 1994; Khan, 1997; Dillon & Zhu, 1997; Bostock, 1997).

The Importance of Forum/Threaded Discussions Groups in an Asynchronous e-Learning Environment

As Freire (1970) supports, learning is itself a reflective process and it is dialogue that is central to this reflection.

Discussion forums or threaded discussions are the most preferred whole-class asynchronous communication mechanisms, as they provide the time flexibility and opportunity for in-depth reflection. In discussion forums a sense of community is created through peer interaction and feedback and through the educator's feedback, visible to all learners.

According to Cranton (2000) discussions are especially important when we are working with the middle and higher level of the cognitive domain (application, analysis, synthesis and evaluation) as well as with all levels of the affective domain.

Brookfield (1990) also says that discussion supports both cognitive and affective ends, such as problem solving, concept exploration, and attitude change, as well as the kind of active participatory learning that results in engaged learning within the classroom.

By using asynchronous communications tools, learners actively construct their own learning by engaging themselves and others in reflective explorations of ideas, drawing conclusions based on their explorations and synthesizing those conclusions with previous knowledge.

Therefore, forums/ threaded discussions groups seem to have taken the lead among asynchronous communication tools (Karsenti 2007), promoting collaborative learning and reflection and improving the quality and quantity of education in online learning environments (McNamara & Brown, 2008; Clark, 2009; Hiltz, 1998).

Discussions help learners explore different perspectives, recognize their own values and assumptions, develop their ability to defend ideas and learn to respect others' opinions and viewpoints. Discussion topics should be interesting, meaningful and relevant to everyone in the group. This is in line with the principles of adult education as the needs and interests of learners have to be taken into account if we want them to be engaged and participate actively in the discussions (Cross, 1981; Brookfield, 1986; Knowles, Holton III, & Swanson, 1998; Cranton, 2000; Rogers, 2007).

In forums and electronic discussion groups, people work together to form ideas, argue points and solve problems. All learners have a voice and no one can dominate the conversation. The asynchronous nature of the discussion also makes it impossible for even an instructor to control. Accordingly, many educators note that students perceive online discussion as more equitable and more democratic than traditional classroom discussions (Swan, 2005). Whereas in face-to-face meetings learners must make their statements one after the other synchronously within a limited timeframe, in forums they can take their time and write their messages asynchronously when it suits them, or within a larger timeframe. Since learners can express their thoughts without interruption and in a time convenient for them, they have the opportunity to reflect both on their classmates' contributions while creating their own, and on their own writing before posting (Shea et al. 2003; Pincas, 2000). It is possible for learners to "rewind" a conversation and thus they have time to carefully consider their own and other learners' responses leading to deeper discussion (McNamara & Brown, 2008). This tends to create a certain mindfulness among learners and encourages deeper level of thinking, more meaningful discourse and a culture of reflection in an online course (Sawn, 2005; Hiltz, 1994; Rheingold, 1994). Many researchers suggest that asynchronous threaded discussion boards are a viable instructional method for sustained written interaction that promotes critical thinking (Waltonen-Moore et al., 2006).

Despite the fact that forums/threaded discussion groups are text-based and so lacking in visual and verbal cues, most participants find them strangely personal (Gunawardena & Zittle, 1997) and Walter has called them "hyperpersonal" (Swan, 2005).

MacNamara and Brown (2008) support that discussion forums need to be carefully structured and managed, so as to ensure that they result in the deep level of collaborative reflection that is desired. They propose three factors which should be considered in planning an online discussion: organization of the forum, motivation of students to participate and ability of students to participate effectively.

At this point the role of the educator must be stressed. According to the literature, the most appropriate role for the educator using threaded discussions is that of facilitator (Waltonen-Moore et al. 2006). The educator's tasks with regard to the facilitation of discussion boards are: a) setting the scene, b) monitoring participation, c) facilitating critical thinking and d) promoting student collaboration (Youngblood, Trede, & DiCorpo, 2001).

The educator plays an important role in creating an environment which favors and promotes critical thinking. As Preece (2000) points out "When there is trust among people, relationships flourish; without it, they wither" (p. 191).

A good educator can listen and then ask the kind of questions that help an individual critically reflect on his or her habits of mind. Critical questioning can be used to stimulate content, process, and premise reflection (Cranton, 2006). These types of questions can lead people to make their assumptions explicit and to question the sources and consequences of their assumptions. Educators may lead or facilitate discussion by asking for clarification, summarizing major points, and focusing on the issue, or they may participate as a member of the group while learners take on the roles of keeping things on track and summarizing (Cranton, 2000).

Stephen Brookfield (1995) focuses on the adult learner and asserts that there are two central activities involved in reinforcing critical thinking. The first consists of helping people analyze and challenge the assumptions under which they, and others, are thinking and acting. The other is exploring and imagining alternatives to their current ways of thinking and acting. Brookfield also describes the ideal critical thinking environment for adults as one where six conditions are present:

- *Diversity and divergence would be encouraged;*
- *Flexibility of format and direction would be welcomed;*
- *Risk taking and spontaneity would be valued;*
- *Facilitators would model openness and critical analysis;*
- *There would be no presumption of perfection on the part of the facilitator; and*
- *There would be skepticism of final answers.*

Summing up, it is evident that the use of forums/threaded discussion groups in the e-education of adults could play an important role in promoting reflection, critical thinking, collaborative learning and interaction between learners and educator, as well as interaction between learners. The asynchronous mode seems to provide a more equitable and democratic environment and better time management for learners, enhancing the role of the educator as facilitator.

A PILOT E-LEARNING COURSE FOR EDUCATORS OF ROMA IN GREECE

A group of 16 preservice and inservice educators of Roma in Greece (10 undergraduate students in the Department of Nursery Education of the University of Patras and 6 experienced educators) was selected in order to participate in an e-course aiming to the improvement of their compatibility with their Roma learners by fostering the cognitive and the affective domain. The notion of compatibility is defined by Pavlis Korres (2007) as the level of knowledge and acceptance of, and positive attitude towards, the special group on the part of the educator. The type of compatibility between educators of special groups and the respective learners varies depending on the parameters that define the specific special group as such. These parameters can be social, cultural, ethnic, linguistic or physical. The values for each type of compatibility have been set to very low, low, medium, high, and very high. Thus, the educational objectives of the course were acquirement of knowledge on Roma culture and issues, awareness of the participants themselves on their existing attitudes towards the different and more specifically the special group of Roma, as well as transformation/change of these attitudes.

Pilot educational material -in the form of Learning Objects- was designed and developed and pilot implementation was carried out for four months (November 2008 - February 2009) using the web-based e-learning open source environment Dokeos. During the period of Christmas Holidays, in order to overcome a technical problem which prohibited access to the Dokeos platform, a closed learning group was created in the Facebook to provide a substitute environment for the continuation of the course.

The pilot application program followed all the phases of the "ESG Framework" (a Framework for the e-Education of Educators of Special Groups) which are: Analysis, Design, Development, Implementation, Evaluation and Maintenance of the Learning Community (Pavlis Korres, 2010).

A need analysis took place in order to define the needs, the expectations, the interests and the level of compatibility of the learners. In the phases of design and development, the content of the course was formed and adapted according to the needs analysis results. Development of specific educational material, as well as exploitation of existing multimedia material, was used in order to serve the educational objectives of the course. The content of the educational material corresponded to the different types and levels of compatibility, while its presentation corresponded to the different learning profiles of the learners.

In the phase of implementation, the first step was the familiarization of the learners with the Dokeos learning platform and the acquisition of the necessary skills for using it effectively. During the e-course the learners accomplished 7 Learning Paths (LP) and various learning activities (self-presentations, group activities for the promotion of group cohesion, chatting, participation in forum and threaded discussions, uploading files in the course's photo gallery, use of e-mail and drop box). In the early stages of the group development, special attention was paid to the formation of strong social bonds. Towards this goal, two main activities were implemented.

Using the "Instructional Design Model for Educators of Special Groups" (Pavlis Korres, 2010), the instructional cycle of the course began with an initial multimedia stimulus which triggered

reconsidering and revising of prior knowledge and attitudes, and promoted self-reflection and critical thinking. During each educational activity the learners were asked to keep a diary along specific guidelines posed by the educator. After that, discussion and discourse took over the central role in the instructional process in the forum/threaded discussions groups, where the learners shared and exchanged knowledge, experiences, assumptions, values, beliefs and feelings. After discussion and discourse, the educator provided feedback and support to the learners.

The communication tools used in the course were: e-mail, forum, announcement board, drop box, the possibility of chatting when the participants where online simultaneously, SMS and telephone. The participants have used the communication tools offered in the platform for three distinctive purposes: to participate in the threaded discussions that followed each LP or other learning activity, to communicate with the educator and to communicate with each other. Regardless of the purpose, through the use of all the communication tools there was a significant promotion of interaction between learners and the educator, the content and the interface, as well as between the learners themselves.

Figures 1 and 2 depict all the types of interaction which occurred during the educational process in the online course: interaction between educator and learners, among learners themselves, between learners and content, between learners and interface as well as between educator and content.

Interaction between learners and interface runs through the other 3 types of interaction as it occurs when a learner interacts with the content, the educator or with other learners.

By the use of the ESG Framework and its Instructional Design Model for Educators of Special Groups, the type of interaction between educator and content is also apparent, as new technologies enable the educator to interact with the content easily and creatively. Interaction between educator and content occurs as a result of

Figure 1. Types of interaction which occurred in the online environment of the course

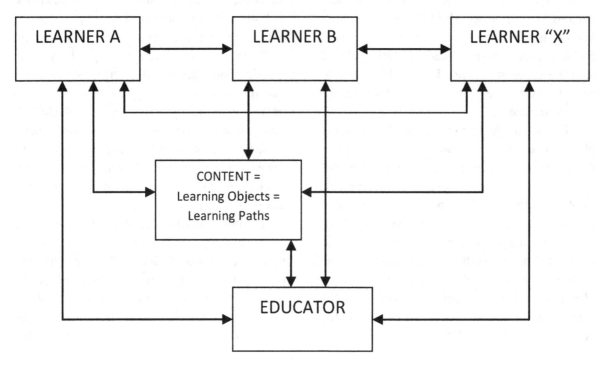

Figure 2. Interaction between learner and interface as well as interaction between educator and interface run through the other types of interaction

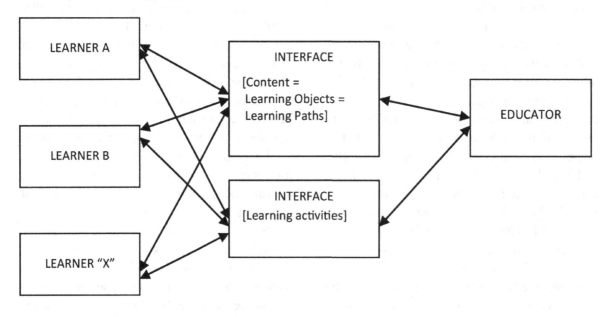

a dynamic educational process, and the educator has the opportunity to update or transform the content and/or the sequence of Learning Objects according to the needs of the learners during the educational period.

Results from the Evaluation of the Course

For the evaluation of the course, formative as well as summative evaluation was implemented. Formative evaluation was conducted in various stages of the course through questionnaires and informal discussions with the educator in the chat room of the course. The results were taken into consideration for making changes in the course structure and the educational material, aiming to the achievement of educational objectives and the improvement of course effectiveness. Summative evaluation was conducted at the end of the course, assessing data from all possible sources, confirming the successful elements of the course or pointing out areas for improvement in future application.

The qualitative analysis of the course through content analysis as well as the formative and summative evaluation provided valuable information concerning the promotion of different types and level of interaction among the participants in the course. All types of interaction, those contained in Moore's (1989) initial model and the fourth type added by Hillman et al. (1994), were sufficiently developed in the course, despite the constrains of its limited duration.

The main results from the evaluation of the course on interaction were:

- All the communication tools offered in the course were proved both sufficient and effective in their use.
- The contribution of each communication tool or learning activity in each type of interaction was identified, according to the extent of their use.

- Educator-learner interaction was promoted mainly through the announcement board, the agenda, the e-mail, the forum and the chat.
- Learner-learner interaction was promoted mainly through the forum/threaded discussions, chat and e-mail.
- Learner-content interaction was promoted mainly through the completion of learning paths, which included postings to the forum/threaded discussions.
- Learner-interface interaction was promoted through all kinds of learners' participation in the course.

The main type of interaction achieved in relation with the communication tool used or learning activity implemented, as found by analysis of the archives of the communication tools and learning activities in the course, is presented in Table 1.

E-MAIL

Exchange of e-mails was extensive from and to all directions between educator and learners. The direction and the distribution of e-mails by frequency and content are presented in Table 2.

The content analysis showed that the vast majority of individual e-mails were relevant to the course. Out of 117 e-mails, 105 provided learners with the ability to ask the educator questions on the content of the course. As very accurately Daley (2007) states,

E-mail offers a sense of privacy that might not be available on a larger class discussion board. If the online discussion board is equivalent to a student asking a question in a live class, then the ability to ask a question or talk via e-mail is equivalent to a student meeting in the instructor's office to talk privately (p. 50).

Table 1. Type of interaction in relation with communication tools and learning activities

Communication tool or learning activity →→→ Type of Interaction ↓↓↓	Announcement board and Agenda	E-Mail	SMS (Short Message Service) Mobile telephones	Forum/ threaded discussions	Chat in Dokeos and FaceBook	FaceBook wall	FaceBook uploaded links (4th LP)	Learning Paths in Dokeos platform
Educator-Learner Interaction	x	x	x	x	x	x	x	
Learner-Learner Interaction		x	x	x	x	x	x	
Learner-Content Interaction				x			x	x
Learner-Interface Interaction	x	x		x	x	x	x	x

The contribution of each one of the communication tools in developing interaction within the course is further elaborated below.

Table 2. Direction and distribution of e-mails during the course

Direction of E-mails	Number of E-Mails	Distribution by Frequency	Distribution by Content
Universal e-mails from the educator to all learners	15		Personal: 1 e-mail Relevant to the course:14 e-mails
Individual e-mails from educator to a single learner	163	3-6 e-mails: 6 learners 7-11 e-mails: 6 learners 12-23 e-mails: 4 learners	Personal: 10 e-mails Relevant to the course: 153 e-mails
Total e-mails from the educator to the learners	178		
E-mails from individual learners to the educator	117	3-6 e-mails: 9 learners 7-11 e-mails: 6 learners 21 e-mails: 1 learner	Personal: 12 e-mails Relevant to the course: 105 e-mails
Total e-mails exchanged between educator and learners	293		

It is evident that through the use of e-mail the interaction between educator and learners is substantially promoted, as e-mail is the main tool for one-on-one communication (Dawley, 2007; DeBard & Guidera, 2000;.Roberson & Klotz, 2002; Huett, 2004).

Table 3. Direction and distribution of SMS during the course

Direction of SMS	Number of SMS	Distribution by Frequency	Distribution by Content
Universal SMS from the educator to all learners	3		Relevant to the course: 3 SMS
Individual SMS from educator to a single learner	15	1 SMS: 10 learners 2-3 SMS: 2 learners	Personal: 3 SMS Relevant to the course: 12 SMS
Total SMS from the educator to the learners	18		
SMS from individual learners to the educator	15	1 SMS: 10 learners 2-3 SMS: 2 learners	Personal: 3 SMS Relevant to the course: 12 SMS
Total SMS exchanged between educator and learners	32		

Similarly, the vast majority of the e-mails from educator to learners -153 out of 178 e-mails- provided enabled the educator to give personalized feedback to her learners. As Pavlis Korres (2012) quotes "By using the e-mail effectively, educators interact with their learners, learners' involvement and motivation is increased and the individual connection is enhanced, as well as the sense of community" (p 1362).

SMS (Short Message Service) through Mobile Telephones

This utility was used by the educator mainly to inform learners about emergency issues such as the date/time of unavailability and re-establishment of the Dokeos platform. A few learners used SMS for wishes on holidays, and some others used this tool to ask about practical information for example, the address of the course-site, or their password in the platform.

The use of the SMS served mainly the needs of immediate communication between educator and learners, such as the announcement of important administrative issues, and the needs of personalized communication, such as the provision of learners' passwords in order to access the platform.

Forum/Threaded Discussions

The forum/threaded discussion was the most important tool in the development of interaction in the course, promoting also immediacy, critical thinking and development of metacognitive skills. The learners' participation in the forum/threaded discussions throughout the course was massive as presented in Table 4.

The participation of learners in threaded discussions is considered impressively high. According to the participants' statements, learners were affected by the comments of the other participants as shown in Table 5.

The effect of interaction in the forum was very important, as it contributed significantly to the development of the learning group as well as to the accomplishment of the educational objectives of the course.

Development of the Learning Group Through Participation in the Forum

The development of the learning group materialized through a series of activities incorporated in the course. Beginning with the "self-presentation" activity, followed by the "commons and differences among the members of the learning group" one, the participants created and established between themselves the desired relations, which were strengthened through exchange of views and experiences during the educational activities of the course.

Once the required social bonds were formed, the participants were more and more interactive with the educator and with each other, gradually opening up in expressing their personal views and experiences and participating actively in the various learning activities, promoting collaborative working.

The "Self-Presentation" Activity

"Self-presentation" of the learners was prompted by the educator who presented herself at the beginning of the course with reference to her studies, expectations of the course, personal data and interests, hobbies and some weak points of her personality such as that she enjoys delicacies and always has to watch her weight. All learners responded positively to the educator's example by incorporating in their self-presentations their personal and social profile, along with their professional profile. Some learners expressed their beliefs, assumptions, dreams and goals in a personal, social and vocational level. Thus, the first activity formed both a very good initial ground in promoting interaction between the participants, and the basis for the second activity.

Table 4. Learners' participation in the Forum/Threaded Discussions throughout the course

Forum "Self-presentation"	Forum of 1st Learning path	Forum "Commons and differences in the learning group"	Forum of 2nd Learning Path		Forum of 3rd Learning Path	Forum of 5h Learning Path	Forum of 6th Learning Path	Forum "cafeteria", "I saw...I heard..."	Forum "Technical issues", "Help"	
16	16	12	15	13	14	14	13	9	9	3

Table 5. Learners' affection by other learners' comments in the forum

How learners were Affected by Other Learners' Comments	Percentage of Learners
Gave them the opportunity to see different views on an issue	87.5%
Gave them the opportunity to see how different people experience the same issue	78.4%
Stimulated critical thinking	68.8%
Helped them to form their opinion on the topic	43.8%
Made them transform their views, attitudes, behaviors	18.8%

The "Commons and Differences Among the Members of the Learning Group" Activity

Having read the participants' self-presentations, each one of them was prompted to find and write commons and differences between himself and the other participants, an exercise through which the educator and the participants began to identify with and relate to one another, a fact which promoted their online socialization.

This first interaction of the learners within the learning group produced some very interesting statements and comments.

Some learners focused on specific commons and differences in participants' daily life:

Like Mrs. "K", "M", and "S", I enjoy cooking and inviting my friends to my house to have fun and drink some wine! (I am also a dainty lover and I can't hide it! I wouldn't say that physical exercise is one of my strong points, but I am trying to make up for this by dancing, which I love). I really like reading and I absolutely agree with "K" and "E" who relax by listening to the music they like

I see that Mrs. "K", "M. P.", Mrs. "P" and "Ili" love cinema, theatre, or both. Although I don't like television, I love films and theatre stuns me! Of course, music is my greatest love, like "M. M", "E" and "Sh", and my love for singing and dancing is even greater, as with "Sof". After finishing my studies, I am planning to attend dancing and singing classes. I am so fond of singing, that I have recorded an old song of "Eli" in an amateur studio. Finally, because as you have realized I am of an artistic nature, I really like painting and I have been painting since I was a child, everything from landscapes to religious paintings of saints, as "M. P" and "S" have. I also love to travel and I grab every opportunity of leaving, as I imagine that "Nik" and "Sof" do. The most pleasant trip for me is a boat trip, because I adore the sea, as I come from an island, beautiful Santorini (another thing in common with "P"). As far as my character is concerned, I think that I am totally optimistic like "Sof", and I am greedy like Mrs. "K". I want to point out that I am the same sign of zodiac as "Ili" and she is only 5 days older than me. With "M.K." we have two things in common, the first is that we both want to obtain our proficiency degree (like "E" also) and we want to learn Spanish, which I personally love to hear. Finally, I must stress the important similarity with my favorite friend "E": as she mentioned herself, our student lives don't differ much and we are intending to take the proficiency exams.

Some participants focused on common interests, anxieties and thoughts about their future:

The things I am interested in are somewhat alike those of the "elders" of our circle. Of course, most of them have professional experience, something that I don't have so far. Some of the participants have previous experience on issues concerning vulnerable social groups and specifically Roma people, while for most students this is their first contact with such issues. Finally, the thing in common for most are the reasons they participated in the program: to overcome our prejudices, learn more about the Roma people and become better human beings.

I would like to say to "Ann", that when we all have our diploma in our hands, we will have the same anxiety for the future. That's something in common! But, contrary to "Ann", I really like computers.... I agree with "Sof" that every obstacle we encounter in our lives turns out well at the end and that if we are well in our health, we can achieve everything... There are many differences between us, like the courses of our careers. My career and those of my fellow students are still beginning. However, despite our differences, there is something common among us. This is the effort for a good cooperation and the exchanges of views which will make us think and become better.

Some others focused on the common interests regarding to the educational objectives of the course and commented in a more philosophical way:

I must point out that all of us who are participating in this program have something in common and this is our interest for a specific social group, the Roma... I have many differences with other members. For example, I don't have the knowledge, the experience and the studies some other members of the program have. I also have different preferences and interests.

Each person is unique and it is marvelous getting to know them! But at the same time, we are all so much alike, that we haven't ever really imagined it. From the presentations, we saw how much alike we are (common wishes and interests), something that we think has created a positive field for co-operation, diminishing natural distances and the distances created between strangers.

We are all of us here, trying to learn from each other by improving ourselves and our relations with others, because we do care after all and I think that this is our basic thing in common. I want to share with you two more phrases, which come from the field of systematic psychology and I think they reflect the whole thing we are experiencing here in our company. The first is that "difference determines the meaning" and the second, that within a group the "promotion of independence can be achieved, even through interdependency."

The success of the initial stages in the development of the learning group contributed significantly to the creation of an excellent collaborative environment, where mutual respect and trust coexisted with openness and friendliness, promoting immediacy and facilitating interaction, as it is clearly shown by the frequency and quality of communication exchanged between all the members of the learning group, confirming the positive outcome of the course in this respect.

Furthermore, all the participants declared that they would like to maintain the communication of the group through Facebook.

Accomplishment of the Educational Objectives of the Course Through Forum/Threaded Discussion

According to the learners' statements they expressed themselves freely and identified their own stereotypes "through the eyes of the others". One learner declared "I felt that my views were important and welcomed by the others, so I expressed them freely..." and another stated "I am now thinking that the way to communicate through a "platform" without having visual contact, not only makes it easier for us express ourselves "freely", but it also makes us pay more attention to the self-presentations and thoughts of the other members of our group."

Concerning awareness of learners' stereotypes and attitudes towards the Roma, content analysis of the forum provided rich information through exchange of experiences, thoughts and opinions among learners, as well as through the achieved interaction between learner and content by the accomplishment of the learning paths. One learner commented "I must confess I am sorry that I have never thought of things in this way", another said that "...the opinions and findings of the other participants were very interesting and made me have new thoughts...", another said "..I liked that we have approached the Roma culture from different points of view...", another stated "I have been aware of my own prejudices and stereotypes and, even though they have not been changed completely I think that I have made the first step forward".

After the first learning path, which was an empathy experience about how the Roma feel when they listen and have to follow instructions in Greek language, the learners have written in the forum:

Is this is how they feel, when they hear us speaking? It was really an experience which made us think and provoked mixed feelings! We still have a long way to go.

I suppose that this is exactly how Roma students feel, when they are required to perform elaborate projects within a narrow framework of support and they are being discouraged from approaching knowledge.

I consider that it was a very clever way to get us into the Roma people's shoes, because all of us can easily say "I understand you". I wonder how easy it is to understand others after all, when we have experienced nothing of the situations they are dealing with. Through this project, I believe that I received a good lesson. That is, I understood the efforts and the bad feelings experienced by those trying to follow some instructions while listening to a language which is relatively unknown to them.

The goal of this exercise was to show that when people from a foreign country hear something unfamiliar to them – like Greek for example-, they feel insecure and uncomfortable, as if all that they hear did not concern them. This is exactly how I felt when I listened to the instructions and it is indeed a very frustrating experience.

I think that the goal of this exercise was exactly the one described in its title: To make us listen with their ears... I felt like being in a world full of Roma people, who speak a language which I have not learned at home. I think that this is how the Roma children around us feel and since they can't understand our language, they feel alien and unprotected...

The goal was perhaps to understand the "fear for the unknown". The differences between something that is very familiar and everyday to us and something that is strange. What would it be like, to be a minority within a society and understand almost nothing of it except our own environment?

After another learning path which contained some interviews of Roma on their school experiences, the interaction between learners and content was very high, as it was expressed in the relative forum:

By listening to these people speaking, one thinks he is dealing with non Roma people. The Roma are in fact more educated and serious than many others. These children are so smart and have such will power, that I wonder if I could find such maturity in a non Roma child. These interviews really changed me!

I must say that I was deeply impressed by the interviews and especially the one of the grandmother, whose speech was so refined although she hadn't been to school, that she made me wonder if she was really "uneducated" compared to others who have the impression that they are "educated". No one has the right to deprive others of knowledge...

I felt lucky listening to these people and their experiences.

Yes, I really feel different now and I think I would also act different, now that I understood even to a small extent the way they see school and they feel when they are treated in this way. Both the texts and the interviews contributed to changing my views.

The best path!!! The teachers and the future teachers participating in the program had a very important opportunity to receive some knowledge about Roma people and school. I always used to believe that Roma people didn't go to school because they didn't have such an institution in their culture. That in their civilization, children were destined to work and make a family at an early stage of their lives, that school was too demanding for them and they preferred to play and walk around. The thing I understood after reading the texts and listening to the interviews is that what I believed is superficial. It's what people who haven't seriously dealt with the issue believe.

A very nice work, very useful information and stimulation for thought.

I believe that I would face Roma children in a different way at school from now on, compared to how I would have faced them before following the educational path, because by doing so, I learned a lot of things about Roma people and, most important of all, it taught me not to be an ostrich.

Furthermore, the comment of a learner after the completion of another learning path focused on stigma is very indicative of the interaction promoted between learners and content:

By walking this path, I managed to express and share with you some personal feelings, experiences and views about stigma. And at the end of the path I realized that everything I mentioned before has made me more tolerant, open, and respectful for others, to think out and understand behaviors (even aggressive ones) and to reform my attitudes and views as a result of that.

The above statements of the learners confirm, that by using the appropriate educational material, interaction between learners and content could be very effective and furthermore enhance the views of those who support that the asynchronous threaded discussions are a viable instructional method for sustained written interaction promoting critical thinking (Waltonen-Moore et al., 2006). As has been mentioned by Kaye (1992), computer conferencing systems provide more reflective and thoughtful analysis and review of earlier contributions than in traditional courses, where an important contribution may be missed forever.

Chatting

For the communication between themselves, the participants mainly used the forum and the chat, but their involvement was not consistent. In the informal forum titled "Cafeteria - I saw…and I

Table 6. Learners' participation in chat

Learners who Participated in the Chat Room of Dokeos	Learners who Chatted in Facebook	Learners who Participated in Dokeos Chat Room in the Last Week (with Fixed Hours)	Maximum Number of Learners Using the Dokeos Chat Room at the Same Time	Learners who Chatted Only Once or Twice in Dokeos Chat Room	Learners who Chatted More than 6 Times in Dokeos Chat Room
14	14	6	5	7	7

heard ..." 19 posts from 9 learners were posted on two issues, while on the "Heeeelp" forum on technical issues only 4 posts from 3 learners were posted.

In the chat room of the Dokeos platform only half of the participants had a consistent presence, as shown in Table 6.

During the period of Christmas Holidays, when the learning group *"Lacio Drom"* in Facebook substituted for the Dokeos platform, 15 out of the 16 learners signed in. In this period the learners posted 59 messages on the wall board of the learning group. Direct chatting in the Facebook further promoted interaction between learners as well as between learners and the educator.

The inconsistency of learners' participation in the chat room of Dokeos is understandable, since the course ran in asynchronous mode and the participants were accessing the platform at different hours of the day. Besides, there was lack of a system displaying the names of persons logged in the chat room and announcing when a new person logs in.

Despite the fact that, following the requests made during formative evaluation, fixed days and times for chatting were defined, the response of the learners was much lower than expected.

According to the archives of the course, the learners who had consistent presence in the chat room of Dokeos platform were those who had adequate skills at using technology and were familiarized with social media (Facebook etc.). This supports Hillman's et al. (1994) views that learners must be skilled at using the delivery system in order to interact fully with other participants.

The Role of the Educator

All participants valued the role of the educator in the e-learning environment very highly. It should be noted that the educator had also the role of administrator in this course. Effective communication with the educator proved extremely important, as it offered the possibility of handling various technical and educational issues in very short time and promoted immediacy and interaction. A vast 93, 8% of the participants considered that communication with the educator played an important role in solving administrative issues, 87, 5% in providing educational guidelines, 81, 3% in solving technical problems, 75% in providing support and feedback and 75% in creating an environment of mutual trust and respect.

The rate of use by the participants of each communication tool offered in the course for the communication with the educator is depicted in Table 7:

Table 7. Use of communication tools by the learners for their communication with the educator

Communication Tool	Percentage of Use by the Learners
E-Mail	93.8%
Announcement Board	75%
Forum	68.8%
Chat	62.5%
Telephone	50%
SMS	43.8%

As it is clearly presented in Table 7, all of the communication tools were used for the communication between educator and learners at high levels. E-mail was the most commonly used tool, mainly for personalized communication, while the announcement board served the purpose of communicating universal administrative and educational guidelines to all learners. In the formative evaluation of the course which took place at the middle of the course, the learners, by a vast majority (81.3%), considered that the "announcements" by the educator contributed positively to the course.

The role of the educator in the threaded discussions, following the instructional design model of the ESG Framework, was that of the facilitator, as she was setting the scene, promoting critical thinking, monitoring participation and providing both personalized and collective feedback to the learners.

CONCLUSION

Interaction is considered by theorists a defining characteristic of education, and its integration in the design of e-learning programs is regarded vitally important. E-learning courses need to promote as many types of interaction as possible for maximum effectiveness, taking into consideration the various teaching tasks of different subject areas and the different stages of development of the learners. High levels of more than one types of interaction provide a more satisfying educational experience and affect the quality and nature of education.

In our days, learning technology is offering a vast variety of communication tools, allowing the promotion of all kinds of interaction by selecting the appropriate media. The selection of communication tools such as e-mail with the instructor and between learners, chat rooms for all the participants, forum/threaded discussion groups, agenda, drop box, wikis and blogs, provides the means

through which different types of interaction could be developed in an online environment. However, it is the educational framework within which these communication tools are used, and the role which these tools play in the educational process, along with the effectiveness of the educator in creating an environment of mutual trust and respect, which dictate the quality and level of interaction developed within the educational course.

The implementation and evaluation of a pilot e-course for the education of educators of Roma in Greece has confirmed that the use of the appropriate communication tools at the right time in an online environment, together with the adoption of the "ESG Framework" and "Instructional Design Model for the Educators of Special Groups", as well as the effectiveness of the educator, can result in the development of all types of interaction contained in Moore's (1989) initial model, plus the fourth type added by Hillman et. al. (1994), to a surprisingly high level.

According to Moore's (1989) categorization of interaction, interaction between learner and content was achieved through Learning Objects in the form of Learning Paths, in which posting in threaded discussions was included. The interaction, immediacy, critical thinking and collaboration between educator and learners as well as between learners were achieved by the use of communication tools existing in the platform (mail, forum, threaded discussions, chat). The fourth type of interaction added by Hillman et. al. (1994), interaction between learner and interface, occurred both in Learning Paths and communication tools as learners used technologies to interact with content and communicate ideas, experiences and information about course content with the educator and other learners.

The promotion of interaction within the guidelines of the "ESG Framework" was not the primary goal of the course, but it was the mean for accomplishing the main educational objective, which was the improvement of compatibility between educators and their Roma learners. As a learner stated about the course "it was a very important experience both on its e-learning and its educational subject. It helped me to be aware of my thinking and how to face Roma students".

Rovai (2001) states that interaction is an important factor supporting both the community-building process and the learning process in the classroom. Educators who perceive the value and the dynamic of the learning group in the learning process should pay special attention on how the sense of community can be stimulated in virtual classrooms through the use of the communication tools and the promotion of interaction.

Finally, as the use of technology is not an end, but a means for the facilitation of learning, the most appropriate communication tools which Learning Technology offers today have to be matched with the respective educational or training goals in each case.

REFERENCES

Anderson, T. (2003). Getting the Mix Right Again: An updated and theoretical rationale for interaction. *International Review of Research in Open and Distance Learning*, 4(2). Available at http://www.irrodl.org/index.php/irrodl/article/view/149/230

Anderson, T., & Garrison, D. R. (1998). Learning in a networked world: New roles and responsibilities. In C. Gibson (Ed.), *Distance Learners in Higher Education* (pp. 97–112). Madison, WI: Atwood Publishing.

Booher, R. K., & Seiler, W. J. (1982). Speech communication anxiety: An impediment to academic achievement in the university classroom. *Journal of Classroom Interaction*, 18(1), 23–27.

Bostock, S. J. (1997). Designing Web-based instruction for active learning. In B. H. Khan (Ed.), *Web-based instruction* (pp. 225–230). Educational Technology Publications.

Brookfield, S. (1986). *Understanding and Facilitating Adult Learning*. Open University Press.

Brookfield, S. D. (1990). Discussion. In M. W. Galbraith (Ed.), *Adult learning methods: A guide to effective instruction* (pp. 187–204). Malabar, FL: Robert E. Krieger.

Brookfield, S. D. (1995). *Becoming a Critically Reflective Teacher*. San Francisco: Jossey-Bass Publishers.

Brown, R. E. (2001, September). The process of community-building in distance learning courses. *Journal of Asynchronous Learning Networks*, 5(2).

Burnham, B. R., & Walden, B. (1997). *Interactions in Distance Education: A report from the other side*. Paper presented at the 1997 Adult Education Research Conference. Stillwater, OK. Retrieved May 30, 2005, from http://www.edst.educ.ubc.ca/aerc/1997/97burnham.html

Clark, J. (2009). *Collaboration tools in online environments*. Retrieved in February 12 2009 from http://www.aln.org/publications/magazine/v4n1/clark.asp

Cranton, P. (2000). *Planning Instruction for Adult Learners* (2nd ed.). Toronto: Wall & Emerson, Inc.

Cross, K. P. (1981). *Adults as Learners*. San Francisco: Jossey-Bass.

Dawley, L. (2007). *The Tools for Successful Online Teaching*. Information Science Publishing. doi:10.4018/978-1-59140-956-4

DeBard, R., & Guidera, S. (2000). Adapting asynchronous communication to meet the seven principles of effective teaching. *Journal of Educational Technology Systems*, 28(3), 219–239. doi:10.2190/W1U9-CB67-59W0-74LH

Dillon, A., & Zhu, E. (1997). Design Web -based instruction: A human-computer interaction perspective. In B. H. Khan (Ed.), *Web-Based Instruction* (pp. 221–224). Educational Technology Publications.

Freire, P. (1970). *Pedagogy of the Oppressed.* New York: Herder and Herder.

Fulford, C., & Zhang, S. (1993). Perception of interaction: The critical predictor in distance learning. *American Journal of Distance Education, 7*(3), 8–12. doi:10.1080/08923649309526830

Galusha, J. M. (2009). *Barriers to Learning in Distance Education.* University of Southern Mississippi. Retrieved in May 2009 from http://www.infrastruction.com/barriers.htm

Gannon-Leary, P., & Fontainha, E. (2007). Communities of practice and virtual learning communities: Benefits, barriers and success factors. *Elearning Papers, 5,* 20-29. Retrieved from http://nrl.northumbria.ac.uk/2147/

Grooms, L. (2003). Computer-Mediated Communication: A vehicle for learning. *International Review of Research in Open and Distance Learning, 4*(2).

Gunawardena, C., & Zittle, F. (1997). Social presence as a predictor of satisfaction within a computer mediated conferencing environment. *American Journal of Distance Education, 11*(3), 8–26. doi:10.1080/08923649709526970

Harsh, O., K. (2002). World Wide Web (WWW) and Global Learning Environment for adults. *Learning Technology Newsletter, 4*(1).

Hillman, D., Willis, D., & Gunawardena, C. (1994). Learner-Interface Interaction in Distance Education: An Extension of Contemporary Models and Strategies for Practitioners. *American Journal of Distance Education, 8*(2), 30–42. doi:10.1080/08923649409526853

Hiltz, S. (1998). Collaborative Learning in Asynchronous Learning Networks: Building Learning Communities. In *Proceedings of Web 98 Symposium.* Orlando, FL: Academic Press. http://eies.njit.edu/~hiltz/collaborative_learning_in_asynch.htm

Hiltz, S. R. (1994). The Virtual Classroom: Learning without Limits via Computer Networks. Academic Press.

Huett, J. (2004). E-mail as an educational feedback tool: Relative advantages and implementation guidelines. *International Journal of Educational Technology Systems, 28*(3), 219–239.

Im, Y., & Lee, O. (2003-2004, Winter). Pedagogical implications of online discussion for preservice teacher training. *Journal of Research on Technology in Education, 36*(2), 155–170. doi:10.1080/15391523.2003.10782410

Kalin, S. (1994). Collaboration: A key to Internet training. *American Society for Information Science, 20*(3), 20–21.

Karalis, T., & Koutsonikos, G. (2003). Issues and Challenges in Organising and Evaluating Web-based Courses for Adults. *Themes in Education, 4* (2), 177-188.

Karsenti, T. (2007). Teacher Education and Technology: Strengths and Weaknesses of Two Communication Tools. In *Proceedings of the 2007 Computer Science and IT Education Conference.* Retrieved in January 2009 from http://csited.org/2007/83KarsCSITEd.pdf

Kaye, A. R. (1992). Learning Together Apart. In A. R. Kaye (Ed.), *Collaborative Learning Through Computer Conferencing* (pp. 1–24). London: Springer-Verlag. doi:10.1007/978-3-642-77684-7_1

Khan, B. H. (1997). *Web-based instruction.* Englewood Cliffs, NJ: Educational Technology Publications.

Knowles, M., Holton, E. III, & Swanson, R. (1998). *The Adult Learner*. Houston, TX: Gulf Publishing Company.

Kochery, T. S. (1997). Distance education: A delivery system in need of cooperative learning. In *Proceedings of Selected Research and Development Presentations at the 1997 National Convention of the Association for Educational Communications and Technology*. Albuquerque, NM: ERIC (ERIC Document Reproduction Service No. ED 409 847).

Mayadas, F. (1997). Asynchronous learning networks: A Sloan foundation perspective. *Journal of Asynchronous Learning Networks, 1*(1).

McNamara, J., & Brown, C. (2008). Assessment of collaborative learning in online discussions. In *Proceedings ATN Assessment Conference 2008, Engaging Students in Assessment*. Adelaide, Australia: University of South Australia.

Merlose, Sh., & Bergeron, K. (2007). Instructor immediacy strategies to facilitate group work in online graduate study. *Australasian Journal of Educational Technology, 23*(1), 132–148.

Moore, M. G. (1989). Three types of interaction. *American Journal of Distance Education, 3*(2), 1–6. doi:10.1080/08923648909526659

Moore, M. G., & Kearsley, G. (1996). *Distance Education: A systems view*. Belmont, CA: Wadsworth.

Muilenburg, L., & Berge, Z. (2005). Student Barriers to Online Learning: A factor analytic study. *Distance Education, 26*(1), 29–48. doi:10.1080/01587910500081269

Muirhead, B. (2001). Interactivity research studies. *Journal of Educational Technology & Society, 4*(3).

Pantelidis, V., & Auld, L. (2002). Teaching virtual reality using distance education. *Themes in Education., 3*(1), 15–38.

Pavlis-Korres, M. (2007). On the requirements of Learning Object Metadata for adults' educators of special groups. In *Proceedings of the 2nd International Conference on Metadata and Semantics Research (MSTR 2007)*. Corfu, Greece: MSTR.

Pavlis Korres, M., Karalis, T., Leftheriotou, P., & Garcia Barriocanal, E. (2009). Integrating Adults' Characteristics and the Requirements for their Effective Learning in an e-Learning Environment. In Best Practices for the Knowledge Society, WSKS, (pp. 570-584). Springer.

Pavlis Korres, M. (2010). *Development of a framework for the e-education of educators of special groups aiming to improve their compatibility with their learners*. (PhD Thesis). University of Alcalá.

Pavlis Korres, M. (2012). The Role of the Communication Tools in the Development of the Learning Group in an Online Environment. *International Journal of Engineering Education, 28*(6), 1360–1365.

Pincas, A. (2000). Features of online discourse for education. *Learning Technology Newsletter, 2*(1).

Preece, J. (2000). *Online communities: Designing usability, supporting sociability*. New York: Wiley & Sons.

Rheingold, H. (1994). *The virtual community*. London: Minerva.

Roberson, T., & Klotz, J. (2002). How can instructors and administrators fill the missing link in online instruction?. *Online Journal of Distance Learning Administration, 5*(4).

Rogers, A. (2007). *Teaching Adults*. Open University Press.

Rovai, A. (2001). Building classroom community at a distance: A case study. *Educational Technology Research and Development, 49*(4), 33–48. doi:10.1007/BF02504946

Rovai, A. (2002). A preliminary look at the structural differences of higher education classroom communities in traditional and ALN courses. *Journal of Asynchronous Learning Networks, 6*(1).

Shankar, V. (2007). *A Discourse on Synchronous and Asynchronous E-Learning.* Retrieved in 11 February 2009 from http://www.articlealley.com/article_142663_22.html

Shea, P. J., Pickett, A. M., & Pelz, W. E. (2003). A follow-up investigation of "teaching presence" in the SUNY Learning Network. *Journal of Asynchronous Learning Networks, 7,* 61–80.

Swan, K. (2005). *Threaded Discussion.* Retrieved in February 2009 from http://www.oln.org/conferences/ODCE2006/papers/Swan_Threaded_Discussion.pdf

Thompson, G. (1990). How can correspondence-based distance education be improved? A survey of attitudes of students who are not well disposed toward correspondence study. *Journal of Distance Education, 5*(1), 53–65.

Tsinakos, A. (2002). Distance Teaching using SYIM educational environment. *Learning Technology Newsletter, 4*(4), 2–5.

Waltonen-Moore, S., Stuart, D., Newton, E., Oswald, R., & Varonis, E. (2006). From Virtual Strangers to a Cohesive Online Learning Community: The Evolution of Online Group Development in a Professional Development Course. *Journal of Technology and Teacher Education, 14*(2), 287–311.

Youngblood, P., Trede, F., & DiCorpo, S. (2001). Facilitating online learning: A descriptive study. *Distance Education, 22*(2), 264–284. doi:10.1080/0158791010220206

KEY TERMS AND DEFINITIONS

Adult Education: Includes the entire body of educational processes, whatever the content, level or method, whether formal, non-formal or informal, whereby persons regarded as adult by the society to which they belong develop their abilities, enrich their knowledge, improve their technical or professional qualifications, or turn them to a new direction and bring about changes in their attitudes or behavior in the twofold perspective of full personal development and participation in balanced and independent social, economic and cultural development.

Asynchronous and Synchronous Communication Mode: Asynchronous refers to electronic bulletin boards, discussion boards, threaded discussions, forum, or electronic mail that participants can access at any time. Synchronous communication mode refers to "real time" interactions, in which participants communicate or "chat" at the same time.

Asynchronous: In online education, the term refers to educator-learner interaction and communication that does not take place at the same time and thus permits learners and educators to respond to each other at a convenient time.

Communication Tool: Any tool which allows and promotes communication between participants in an online educational environment, e.g. e-mail, forum, bulletin board, chat, blog, wiki, video conference.

Educator: A teacher for adults. The term is used in order to define the different approach of the teacher, focused on the dimensions of facilitation, co-learning, guiding and counseling.

Interaction: A dynamic process of communication in a learning environment between participants who modify their actions, behaviors and reactions due to the actions, behaviors and reactions by the interaction partners.

Roma: A group with ethnic, cultural, linguistic and social characteristics which cause social exclusion, discrimination and stigmatization to its members. They are also known as Gypsies.

Chapter 8

M–Learning in the Middle East:
The Case of Bahrain

Evangelia Marinakou
Royal University for Women, Bahrain

Charalampos Giousmpasoglou
Bahrain Polytechnic, Bahrain

ABSTRACT

The introduction of e-learning in higher education has brought radical changes in the way undergraduate and postgraduate programmes are designed and delivered. University students now have access to their courses anytime, anywhere, which makes e-learning and m-learning popular and fashionable among university students globally. Nevertheless, instructors are now challenged, as they have to adopt new pedagogies in learning and teaching. This chapter explores the adoption of m-learning at universities in the Kingdom of Bahrain, as well as the relevant current developments and challenges related to the major stakeholders (educators and students) in higher education. It mainly investigates the educators' views and perceptions of m-learning, as well as its future potential in higher education. Most of the educators use m-learning tools to some limited extent, and there is still opportunity to reach full integration with curriculum and the blended learning approach. Further, it is proposed that professional development should be provided to instructors to enable them to use the available new technologies in an appropriate and effective way.

INTRODUCTION

The rapid technological advancements in the context of globalization have changed our everyday lives at individual and societal level. Universities worldwide are among the first to embrace these changes and prepare their students with the appropriate tools to enter the 'real' world of work. Two decades ago the technological advancements

infiltrated the traditional classrooms with the introduction of e-learning. The extensive use of Information and Communication Technologies (ICTs) – especially the use of the Internet – revolutionized and changed for good the design and delivery of curricula in universities around the world. During the last decade, an unseen 'revolution' emerged from the introduction of e-learning and even more recently of m-learning tools in the

DOI: 10.4018/978-1-4666-7316-8.ch008

classroom. The magnitude of these information technology developments is still not very well understood, simply because practice has run well ahead theory. In addition, many argue that the m-learning community is still fragmented among the various stakeholders, with different national perspectives, differences between academia and industry, and between the school, higher education and lifelong learning sectors (Al Saadat, 2009). Whether one looks at this phenomenon of e-learning and m-learning as a fad, threat, or a solution to educators' problems in delivering mainstream learning in higher education (Peters, 2009), it is currently a hot issue that needs our attention.

The emergence of the World Wide Web supported the development and the popularity of e-learning (Peng, Su, Chou, & Tsai, 2009). In addition, mobile devices such as mobile phones, laptops have increased drastically and are widely used in e-learning (Iqbal & Qureshi, 2012; Koszalka & Ntloedibe-Kuswani, 2010). The use of e-learning in higher education has grown in the past two decades, transforming the nature of higher education, as the technologies are supplementing the course delivery (Bharuthram & Kies, 2013). There are ongoing debate and criticisms on using e-learning, nevertheless most of the literature has shown a positive impact of e-learning in educational contexts, as the drastic developments in technologies have produced a new revolution in education.

Nevertheless, most studies in e-learning and m-learning focus on its acceptance by students in developing countries (i.e. Rhema & Sztendur, 2013; Wang, 2011), on the challenges and opportunities from the adoption of e and m-learning, but very few focus on its acceptance by instructors or on their perceptions of m-learning and its future potential. Therefore, this chapter discusses the origins of m-learning, its pedagogical value and the current developments and challenges in higher education context; in addition, it presents the instructors' perceptions of m-learning in general

in the Middle East and more specifically in the Kingdom of Bahrain. The chapter is organized as follows: the first part provides a summary of the origins and concepts of e-learning and m-learning. The following section explores the opportunities and challenges from the use of m-learning in higher education, as well the instructors' perception and use of m-learning via the survey results. The final part discusses the current and future status of m-learning followed by the conclusions.

THE ORIGINS AND CONCEPTS OF E-LEARNING AND M-LEARNING

E-Learning in Higher Education

Despite the relative recent appearance in literature, the concept of e-learning has fueled a number of debates regarding its usefulness in higher education and more particular, in the development of learning and teaching strategies. The few theoretical models describing this concept are still not adequate to capture the dynamics of the e-learning and m-learning proliferation in universities globally. The growing body of literature is still too narrow and short-sighted to capture the changes that currently take place in higher education. Nevertheless, the future is here, at least from a technological perspective.

In fact, practice has understandably run well ahead of theory, and in some issues and approaches away from theory, for example, the use of virtual learning environments (VLEs) and the use of applications to support them in mobile devices. A VLE is a set of teaching and learning tools designed to enhance a student's learning experience by including computers and the Internet in the learning process (Demian & Morrice, 2012). The principal components of a VLE package include curriculum mapping (breaking curriculum into sections that can be assigned and assessed), student tracking, online support for both teacher and student, electronic communication (e-mail, threaded discussions, chat, Web publishing), and Internet links to outside curriculum resources. There are a number of commercial and customized VLE software packages available, including Blackboard, Moodle and WebCT. A quick search on the Internet reveals that commercial and customized VLEs have introduced e-learning and m-learning applications to allow ubiquitous access for users (i.e. http://www.blackboard.com/platforms/mobile/products/ mobile-learn. aspx). Big search engines for academic content also adopt and follow this trend (i.e. EBSCO, Science Direct, Emerald) as well as international publishers (i.e. Prentice Hall, McGraw Hill, Springer).

Another recent important development is the use of tablet PCs and e-books as integral parts of the m-learning pedagogy. The optimization of mobile devices such as smart phones, e-book readers and tablet PCs, in conjunction with the digitalization of university libraries currently based mainly on e-books in PDF format, has changed for good the way we perceive study in a university environment. The classic view of a university student spending valuable time in a campus library struggling to borrow the last short-loan copies of the books s/he needs, tends to be an image of the past: virtual or e-libraries allow university students access content and borrow e-books for literary anywhere, anytime they wish for. A recent study undertaken as part of the project of the Open University's Building Mobile Capacity initiative, provides strong indications that e-learning is here for good. Despite the various issues reported in this project, it was found that when combined synergistically, the functionality, portability and comprehensiveness of resources offered by e-books, Internet access and mobile group learning, together facilitate rich learning experiences for students (Smith & Kukulska-Hulme, 2012).

As it has been previously discussed, the availability of mobile and wireless devices enables different ways of course contents delivery in higher education. It has also changed the communication between the teacher and the learner, as teachers nowadays are confronted with digitally literate students. In addition, these devices have created learning opportunities different to those provided by e-learning (Peters, 2009). E-learning is also changing by providing instructors and students with a different educational environment that is enabled with the use of mobile devices such as PDAs, mobile phones and other. According to Sarrab, Al-Shihi, and Rehman (2013) e-learning offers two main facilities to improve the educational system. E-learning happens anywhere anytime where learning and educational activities are offered the individuals and groups the opportunity to work online or offline, synchronously and asynchronously via networked or standalone computers and other mobile devices. The main drawback of e-learning according to Sarrab et al. (2013) is that it is bound to the location of personal computers or laptops, hence there is an issue with usability. Therefore, m-learning has been integrated to help make learning more interesting, widely available, more interactive and flexible.

The Emerging Concept of m-Learning

M-learning or mobile learning is an evolving phase of e-learning (Peng et al., 2009), as e-learning is dependent on desktop computers, whereas m-learning is dependent on mobile devices (Orr, 2010). There are a variety of definitions of m-learning, partly because m-learning is a new concept. Most studies define m-learning as an extension of e-learning which is performed using mobile devices such as PDA, mobile phones, laptops etc. (Sad & Goktas, 2013; Motiwalla, 2007). Others highlight certain characteristics of m-learning including portability through mobile devices, wireless Internet connection and ubiquity. For example Hoppe et al. (2003 in Iqbal & Qureshi, 2012), define m-learning as "using mobile devices and wireless transmission" (p.148). Kukulska-Hulme and Traxler (2007, p.35) suggest that "m-learning emphasizes the ability to facilitate the

Table 1. *Difference between normal learning and m-learning*

Normal Learning Style	Mobile Learning
Individual assessment, group projects, group discussions and project presentations will be done through quizzes and tutorials.	The use of multimedia elements in conveying information and receive online feedback.
Students will go to a class or lecture hall to attend the lecture.	The learning process can be done anywhere and at any time.
Students will interact face to face to allow them to communicate effectively.	Able to organize meetings and schedules of all team members at the same time.
Using chalk and talk method in delivering information.	Students can get the lecture notes quickly without copying from the board.

Source: Devinder & Zaitun (2006)

learning process without being tied to a physical location". In the higher education context, the term mobile learning (m-learning) refers to the use of mobile and handheld devices, such as smart phones, laptops and tablet PCs, in the delivery of teaching and learning. Simply put, m-learning is defined as "the process of learning mediated by a mobile device" (Kearney, Schuck, Burden, & Aubusson, 2012). M-learning can be thought of as a subset of e-learning, which is the "the use of computer network technology, primarily through the Internet, to deliver information and instruction to individuals" (Welsh, Wanberg, Brown, & Simmering, 2003).

Brink (2011) divided m-learning in three main types, formal, informal and well-directed or self-directed. Forma learning includes normal learning, which is triggered by notifications and reminders such as short messages. Informal learning encompasses two-way message exchange, hence an interactive relationship, such as Facebook, blogs, Twitter etc. Finally well-directed or self-directed learning uses reference and media-based materials such as videos and podcasts. For example, Table 1 shows the differences between normal and m-learning.

Although, in higher education, students are regarded as pioneers in forcing the faculty to change and adapt m-learning, the literature suggests that there are significant positive outcomes (Sad & Goktas, 2013). The literature suggests that there are several factors that influence readiness for m-learning. For example, demographic influences on users' readiness for m-learning such as gender, age and educational level. Others refer to technology acceptance, ease of use, perceived usefulness, quality of services and cultural factors.

A prerequisite for the delivery of e-learning programmes is the use of fixed locations i.e. in a classroom or where a desktop PC and an Internet connection are available. The remedy to this significant e-learning limitation appeared in the mid-2000s with the advent of m-learning applications for a wide variety of uses such as workplace learning, teaching and social networking. Quinn (2001) argues that m-learning intersects mobile computing with e-learning. The unique features of the new mobile technologies and the unlimited potential they offer in terms of flexibility and customization to individual needs, place it also in the framework of flexible learning (Peters, 2009; Sarrab et al., 2013). In this context, students expect training that is "just in time, just enough and just for me" (Rosenberg, 2001), and that can be delivered and supported beyond the boundaries of traditional classroom settings (Kearney et al., 2012). M-learning emphasizes the *mobility* of learning, whereas others place emphasis on the mobility of learners, and the experiences of learners as they learn by means of mobile devices (El-Hussein & Cronje, 2010, p.14). Similarly, Traxler (2007) claims that m-learning is not about 'mobile' or about 'learning' but is part of a new mobile conception of society. Hence, the

Figure 1. Mobile learning
Source: El-Hussein and Cronje (2010, p. 17)

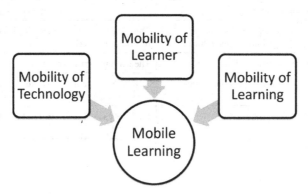

definition of m-learning depends on how each member of the society understands and explains mobile learning. For example, other definitions refer to the physical way in which technology is used and others emphasize on what learners experience when they use mobile technologies in education, whereas others refer to how it can be used to make unique contribution to education and e-learning (El-Hussein & Cronje, 2010, p. 14). Figure 1 illustrates the above view.

The mobility of technology refers to the mobile cellular devices that link to the internet and deliver content and instruction and can enable learning to learn at anytime and anywhere in a form that is culturally prestigious among people in the same group (King, 2006; El-Hussein & Cronje, 2010). The mobility of learners is linked to the mobility of the devices and the fact that the learner is connected to the internet, hence learning can occur at any time and any place (Traxler, 2009). Finally, the mobility of learning is unique as it is "received and processed withing the context in which the learner is situated" (El-Hussein & Cronje, 2010, p. 19).

While the technical advancements in m-learning progress rapidly by satisfying a consumer driven demand, there are still many barriers in the development of an appropriate pedagogical framework for its application in teaching and learning. The aging instructor population is ap-

parently one of the primary barriers in the smooth transition to the new era in higher education. The well-established learning theories of the past are based on teaching by the textbook and memorizing information. Educating and persuading older instructors to use m-learning as part of their learning and teaching approach poses as one of the most difficult challenges. Another issue in the use of m-learning in higher education programmes is that learning practices are changing while learning theories that support them are not (El-Hussein & Cronje, 2010). In addition, Wang (2011) found that e-learning (including m-learning) development tends to focus on technical issues of design and ignores organizational, social, and pedagogical aspects that are necessary for effective e-learning programmes in the workplace. Most applications are lacking of pedagogical underpins on the use of m-learning, and fail to understand learning behavior that takes place in the organizational and social context. It is also suggested that locating distinctive features of learning with mobile devices is an evolving process interwoven with the maturation of the relevant technologies (Kearney et al., 2012). The design of m-learning content for higher education is a complex and difficult task. Account still needs to be taken of learner's and instructors' specific needs as well as the environment which learning takes place. What also needs to be done is to include appraisal and evaluation for each programme, tailored to the different cultural and organisational needs (El-Hussein & Cronje, 2010). The way that people and organisations perceive this new era in teaching and learning is the key to shape the new curricula in higher education. Sharples, Taylor, and Vavoula (2007) identify two layers of m-learning, the semiotic (socio-cultural) and technological; they argue that these two layers will eventually converge. This convergence requires though a total rethink and redesign of formal learning as we know it: a more open and collaborative model which places educators as facilitators of learning in a connected and mobile world, where students participate actively in the learning creation process. On the other hand, others believe that m-learning will never fully replace classroom or other electronic learning approaches (Liaw, Hatala, & Huang, 2010). However, if leveraged properly, mobile devices can complement and add value to the existing learning models and frameworks.

M-learning and e-learning also differentiate from a pedagogical perspective in the learning approach. While e-learning is based primarily on the objectivist learning model (Wang, 2011), m-learning is building on a *constructivist* approach. The objectivist approach is based on the transfer of knowledge from the instructor to the learner; on the other hand the constructivist approach views learning as a process in which learners actively construct or build new ideas or concepts based upon current and past knowledge. In this interactive environment, instructors should let learners participate in meaningful activities so that they can generate their own knowledge (Brown & Campione, 1996). M-learning is also linked with the theory of *connectivism* which states that learners are actively attempting to create meaning through engagement in networks; learning is the process of creating connections and developing a network (Siemens, 2005). King (2006) proposes that the use of m-learning in higher education, reduces the physical walls of the classroom and replaces them with virtual, as the content of the education it delivered by means of a radical new technology, and he adds that "by breaking down the assumptions and process behind writing and speaking, we can go beyond them and find new ways of thinking about the world" (King, 2006, p. 171). Herrington, Herrington, Mantei, Olney, and Ferry (2009) placed m-learning in the context of the *authentic learning* approach. Authentic learning situates students in learning contexts where they encounter activities that involve problems and investigations reflective of those they are likely to face in their real world professional contexts.

Researchers have also explored m-learning perspectives from a wider socio-cultural view. Traxler (2009) described m-learning as noisy and problematic, featuring three essential elements: the personal, contextual and situated. Klopfer, Squire, and Jenkins (2002) propose that mobile devices (handheld computers) "produce unique educational affordances," which are: portability, social interactivity, context sensitivity, connectivity and individuality. Based on the activity theory approach Liaw et al. (2010) investigated the acceptance toward to m-learning as a means to enhance individual knowledge management. They found that factors such as enhancing learners' satisfaction, encouraging learners' autonomy, empowering system functions and enriching interaction and communication activities, have a significant positive influence on the acceptance of m-learning systems. More recently Kearney et al. (2012) presented a framework, which highlights three central features of m-learning: authenticity, collaboration and personalization, embedded in the unique time-space contexts of mobile learning. Sharples et al. (2007, p.4) provide more details on the convergence between learning and technology as shown in the Table 2.

M-learning has attracted attention due to the increasing number of available mobile devices, which are affordable and their costs are increasingly decreasing making them more accessible to people. At the same time these devices have multiple features and capabilities, such as making

Table 2. Convergence between learning and technology

New Learning	New Technology
Personalised	Personal
Learner-centered	User-centered
Situated	Mobile
Collaborative	Networked
Ubiquitous	Ubiquitous
Lifelong	Durable

Source: Sharples, Taylor, and Vavoula (2007, p.4)

phone calls, taking pictures and making videos, storing data and of course accessing the internet (Sarrab, Al-Shihi, & Rehman, 2013). Maccallum and Jeffery (2009) propose that all these capabilities may be used in teaching and learning, for example for classroom activities (Dawabi., 2003). These mobile devices can be used for learning purposes via interactive games, for brainstorming, quizzing and are widely used to support and develop students' own learning and collaborative learning (Iqbal & Qureshi, 2012). Moreover, they are available to users at any time and all time (Giousmpasoglou & Marinakou, 2013). Kukulska-Hulme and Traxler (2007) present several case studies that report and support the experience of educators with mobile technologies in universities. Zawacki-Richter, Brown, and Delport (2009) claim that e-learning and m-learning provide a wide range of opportunities for learners and teachers. However, as it has been previously discussed, Herrington, Mantei, Olney, and Ferry (2009, p.1) claim that it is not still clear whether "m-learning is used in pedagogically appropriate ways".

M-learning is widely used in distance learning as it supports the access to the teaching material for a large number of students, independent of time and space, at low costs. Moura and Carvalho (2009, p.90) suggest that "the development of m-learning as a new strategy for education has implications on the way students learn, on the role of the teachers as well as in the educational

institution". Hence, for the purpose of this chapter m-learning is studied as an element of e-learning and blended learning in general not necessarily as a tool for distance learning, as it also helps in constructing problem-based learning as well as any related assignments and projects that meets the students' interest (Kukulska-Hulme & Traxler, 2007). M-learning allows student-centered learning in which students are able to modify the access and transfer of information to strengthen the knowledge and skills of students to meet their educational goals (Giousmpasoglou & Marinakou, 2013; Sharples et al., 2007). In addition, it can support ubiquitous learning and can make the educational process more comfortable and flexible (Sarrab et al., 2013, p. 828).

Higher education may be presented in a more interactive ways as m-learning provides the support for learning and training. Although, technological developments have made mobile devices strategic tools to the delivery of higher education instruction, these fundamental changes pose new problems, challenges as well as opportunities to the instructors and students as they are discussed in the following.

Opportunities and Challenges from the Use of m-Learning in Higher Education

The introduction of m-learning in universities change radically the way we perceive, design and deliver higher education programmes. In this mobile and always connected world, a number of benefits and challenges arise for both educators and students. Literature indicates that three features are most cited by researchers, practitioners and users: mobility/ ubiquity (anytime, anywhere), personalization, and collaboration. Current technology allows learners to disseminate information and complete coursework even when they are away from their desktop PCs and hard-wired Internet connections. A wireless device has the potential to give instant gratification to students by allowing them to interact with the instructors, other students in the course, and access course related content from anywhere wireless connectivity is available. BenMoussa (2003) identifies three key benefits of mobile connectivity for the users. Firstly, mobile devices offer personalized and/or individualized connectivity. Liaw et al. (2010) also suggest that the relationship between the owner and the mobile/handheld device provides a 'one-to-one' interaction in a personalized manner. Secondly, mobile connectivity improves collaboration via real-time or instant interactivity that may lead to better decision-making. And third, mobile connectivity enhances users' orientation or direction. Kearney et al. (2012) argue that m-learners can enjoy a high degree of collaboration by making rich connections to other people and resources mediated by a mobile device. This often-reported high level of networking creates shared, socially interactive environments so m-learners can readily communicate multi-modally with peers, educators and other experts, and exchange information. Learners consume, produce and exchange an array of "content", sharing information and artefacts across time and place. In addition, Motiwalla (2007) suggests that access to information at the point of relevance may make it possible for m-learners to minimize their unproductive time, which may enhance their work-life-education balance.

The challenges generated from the advent of m-learning in higher education programmes affect mostly those responsible for the design and delivery and evaluation of teaching and learning. Wang (2011) argues that the emergence of Web 2.0. related technologies, brought a radical transformation in e-learning (and thus m-learning) environment: the largely central controlled education system turned to an interactive and conversational learning network. As a direct consequence we observe that learning practices are changing very fast (i.e introduction of e-books instead of traditional textbooks), while the learning theories that support educational practices are not (El-Hussein & Cronje, 2010). Educators are currently unable

to follow the needs of the younger generations of learners described as digital natives (Corbeil & Valdes-Corbeil, 2007). These learners do not see technology as something foreign: they readily accept it and consider it as part of their everyday lives; they are totally immersed and addicted to mobile technologies. Young learners also created and use their own language and signs when communicating either via Short Message Service (SMS), e-mail or live chat through a mobile Internet or Wi-Fi connection (El-Hussein & Cronje, 2010); this is how they were called the text generation. Overall, the traditional teacher-centered, classroom situated learning environment, is now challenged by the digitally literate students who view learning as an open collaborate process without boundaries (Peters, 2009).

M-learning provides flexibility in higher education programmes that may result in some challenges that learners may not have imagined (Motiwalla, 2007). For example, a serious implication from the continuous exposure to information and interaction in a connected world can be the creation of confusion and disorientation to m-learners. Then various security issues regarding the information privacy of the users are raised as in any other commercial application. Mobile devices are currently appear to be more vulnerable than PCs, thus personal data are easily traceable for mobile users (Okazaki, 2011). Finally, there are ethical issues reading the use of m-learning in student assessment, where cheating cannot be easily prevented or traced based on the current technologies and learning philosophies (Banyard, Underwood, & Twiner, 2006).

The challenges of the use of m-learning are many for all stakeholders as it may have many technological restrictions. For instructors, m-learning is a challenge as they should be familiar with technology, not only to use it for teaching and learning but also to support developers who are challenged by the limited memory, the lack of keyboard, the small displays especially when compared to computers and laptops (Iqbal &

Qureshi, 2012; Wang et al., 2009). Instructors should adapt the design of the courses to integrate ICT; this design should be dynamic, easily scalable and should be applied at all times and places (Marwan, Madar, & Fuad, 2013). Moreover, Marwan et al. (2013) suggest that instructors face the lack of time to prepare for class. There is also concern on the educators' ability to understand and respond to digital learning opportunities, as in many cases they are challenged by the need "to collaborate with a wide range of people such as web developers and programmers to deliver successful web-based education" (Peters, 2007). It is a fact that m-learning enables learning to occur at a less formal setting that is teacher-mediated, hence technical skills are required (Kearney et al., 2012). In addition, m-learning experiences can be customized for the learner to meet different learning styles and approaches, they may provide a high degree of collaboration and making connections to other people, creating further challenges to educators whose roles are changing (Mohammad & Job, 2013; Kearney et al., 2012). Thus, educators should be able to understand and analyze the unique challenges in emerging m-learning environments and facilitate insights to support their design and use of m-learning resources.

Students usually have access to the Internet and other applications via their mobile devices such as Facebook, YouTube, MySpace and other. They are also familiar with its use, hence being well introduced to m-learning may lead to its wide use in their own learning. Nowadays students are active and innovative in terms of their learning, they expect a quick response from the tutor and want an interactive learning, student-centered, authentic, collaborative and effective learning with the use of ICT (Marwan et al., 2013). According to Mirza and Al-Abdulkareem (2011, p. 88) "the learner's attitude and lack of prior knowledge of IT use are major factors that affect the acceptance of e-learning by students".

Previous research suggests that there are various factors that contribute to the adoption of m-learning by instructors and students. Ju, Sriprapaipong, and Minh (2007) claim that the perceived usefulness influences the intention to adopt m-learning. On top of usefulness, Wang et al. (2009) and Sarrab et al. (2013) identified other factors such as the self-managed pace of learning, the social influence, the performance and the effort expectancy. Venkatesh, Morris, Davis, and Davis (2003) added the available infrastructure to support the use of any m-learning system, and Liu and Li (2010) add the playfulness. The interface makes the use of mobile devices more interesting for students, as the learning is personalized, more fun, spontaneous, and engaging users to contribute and share (Sarrab et al., 2013). Marwan et al. (2013) add the interactive learning process, the integrated learning information and the high learning needs. Thornton and Houser (2002 in Moura & Carvalho, 2009) propose that recordings, communication and access to information in the local set, sending reminders or relevant information for students are good options of the use of m-learning. Attewell (2011) propose that m-learning assists in the development of the learners' literacy and numerical skills. In addition, m-learning students are able to experience a dynamic class via interaction. To understand the factors that contribute to the adoption of m-learning will help stakeholders (educators, software developers and technicians) to incorporate these factors into the design of the m-learning systems.

Challenges and restrictions of the use of m-learning include the lack of standardization, the low bandwidth, the limited processor speed and small screen size, low storage, short battery life, lack of data input capability (Sarrab et al., 2013; Maniar & Bennett, 2002), low display resolution, limited memory and less computational power (Shiau, Lim, & Shen, 2001). Marwan et al. (2013) claim that classes are difficult to be rescheduled with m-learning. All of the above benefits and challenges of m-learning could be summarized in Table 3.

If students are provided with the educational context in an appropriate and challenging manner, which is exciting and novel, they will be more inclined to use all these mobile devices and m-learning. M-learning has been considered to be a promising approach to complement student learning. At the same time, instructors cannot just be provided with the technology and left on their own; they should be provided with a vision and the necessary resources and support to use e-learning and m-learning.

E-Learning and M-Learning in the Middle East (ME) and Bahrain

Although e-learning has been growing rapidly in the Middle East (ME), North Africa (MENA) region and the Gulf Co-operation Council (GCC) countries, m-learning has been considered as an alternative learning style and a new fashion. In these countries, according to Hamou, Anwar and Benhadria (2012) several initiatives have been introduced such as proliferation of e-books and e-learning devices, as well as flexible access to distance learning. In fact, the Arab region witnesses an increasing penetration of mobile phones and much faster Internet (Muttoo, 2011). However, these initiatives do not show a clear shift towards e-learning and m-learning in the region.

Nevertheless, there are some good examples and initiatives of educational institutions that have contributed to the development of e-learning and m-learning. For example, Hamdan Bin Mohammed e-University (HBMeU) in the UAE has introduced an effective architecture for e-learning, and also contributed to the development of standards for e-learning programme accreditation (Hadj-Hamou, Anwar, & Benhadria, 2012). The *e-learning Declaration* was drafted at the 2008 e-learning Forum in Dubai, providing a new educational model, which is based on research on active research changing teaching and learning from the traditional approach to the student-oriented approach. In addition, they have launched an e-book and e-reader device to help learners use their iPad/iPhone for their learning. They support the blended learning approach, where they integrate the face-to-face learning with online collaborative learning and self-paced learning, as they make effective use of ICT to support delivery of the courses. They use Moodle, which enables the online collaborative learning, and asynchronous study is enabled by interactions with the professors via virtual classrooms (with the use of Wimba) and access to electronic teaching material.

Moreover, in Saudi Arabia, the rapid advancement in mobile technologies, wireless networks and the acceptance of new smart devices have increased the interest in m-learning. In fact, the Ministry of Higher Education (MOHE) has launched a national project "AAFQ" to develop a long-term plan for HE in order to address future challenges including m-learning (Garg, 2013). They have also established other projects such as the National Centre for E-learning and Distance Education (NCELDE) with its own learning portal, the Saudi Digital Library and the Saudi Centre for Support and Counseling to all beneficiaries of e-learning among others. The aim of the center is to become "an international leader in research, development and implementation of an e-learning architecture and infrastructure using open standards" (Mirza & Al-Abdulkareem, 2011, p. 91). Many universities in Saudi Arabia are utilizing distance-learning technologies. For example, King Saud University has recently initiated a new service that offers users with the ability to send text messages directly from a PC to a mobile phone (Altameem, 2011, p. 22). There is also the Knowledge International University (http://www.kiu.com.sa/website/index.php) established in Saudi Arabia in 2007, which specializes in online degrees programmes in Islamic studies (Mirza & Al-Abdulkareem, 2011).

Table 3. Benefits and challenges of m-learning

Benefits of M-Learning	Challenges of M-Learning
Great for people on the go.	May make it easier to cheat.
Anytime, anywhere access to content.	Could give tech-savvy students an advantage over non-technical students.
Can enhance interaction between and among students and instructors.	Can create a feeling of isolation or of being out-of-the-loop for non-techies.
Great for just-in-time training or review of content.	May require media to be reformatted or offered in multiple formats.
Can enhance student-centered learning.	Might render some content outdated because of rapid upgrades – here today, outdated tomorrow.
Can appeal to tech-savvy students because of the media-rich environment.	Could require additional learning curve for non-technical students and faculty.
Support differentiation of student learning needs and personalized learning.	Many be used by a new high-tech package for the same old dull and boring content.
Reduce cultural and communication barriers between faculty and students by using communication channels that students like.	There are different mobile platforms such as iOS, Android etc.
Facilitate collaboration through synchronous and asynchronous communication.	The wireless network trust ability.
Supports distance learning.	

Source: Corbeil and Valdes-Corbeil (2007, p. 54); Sarrab et al. (2013, p. 835-836)

In Oman, the Ministry of Education has established ongoing relations with Edutech Middle East to integrate 590 schools around the country with e-learning solutions (Mirza & Al-Abdulkareem, 2011). They also state that the Syrian Virtual University offers various degrees including diplomas, bachelor's and master's in business, technology and quality management.

As the GCC countries are endowed with oil and gas reserves they have turned their attention to education and to the improvement of the quality of education (World Economic Forum, 2010). Although education is a high priority in the GCC countries, considerable ground has to be covered to make progress in terms of enrolment and quality enhancement (Hadj-Hamou et al., 2012, p. 57). Education has strategic significance in the Arab world, but still there are great variations among the Arab states in their literacy rates. In addition, there is limited financial support for education in a large number of Arab countries. According to the World Bank (2007) the rate of total expenditure in education relative to GDP in all Arab countries is nearly 1.3%.

Table 4 shows the education rank of GCC countries among 134 countries.

The same study reports that there is low quality of research, and low number of publications in the GCC countries in comparison to those from fast developing countries. Most universities are teaching-oriented, rather than research-oriented; the rate of researchers in Arab universities as compared with employees is 2.7 per 10.000. Moreover, the report suggests that there is lack of planning and strategies for education at all levels, lack of information and communications technology (ICT) integration into education, there is centralization of education, intellectual migration and weaker linkages between education and labour markets. Hence, decision-makers can respond to these challenges by exploring the potential of electronic communication for spreading education in the countries (Hadj-Hamou et al., 2012, p.60).

Bahrain is one of the countries in the Arab world that have recently considered the potential

Table 4. Education rank of GCC countries

Country	Quality of Primary Education	Secondary Enrolment	Tertiary Enrolment	Quality of Educational System
Bahrain	41	36	74	38
Kuwait	79	62	92	88
Oman	48	70	81	43
Qatar	5	49	106	4
Saudi Arabia	54	43	75	41
UAE	29	46	84	27

Source: World Economic Forum (2010)

of distance education with the use of e-learning. A study in the Middle East reveals that only 49% of society members are aware of e-learning (CITC, 2007) and the main reason for the limited use of e-learning and m-learning in the region is the low public and teachers' esteem for online learning (Mirza & Al-Abdulkareem, 2011). The first e-learning project in Bahrain was the Future Project at His Majesty King Hamad's Schools, which was established on January 2005 to serve the public secondary education and at a later level to include the private schools as well. There is also the e-learning center at the University of Bahrain, opened in March 2007 under the patronage of the King's wife, Her Majesty Shaikha Sabeeka Bint Ibrahim Al Khalifa, who is also the President of the Supreme Council for Women. The e-learning center plays a significant role in Bahrain's development as the government of Bahrain takes a regional lead in the launch of a range of egovernment services. The center focuses on promoting the adoption of wireless technology to support teaching and learning programmes across eight university departments. It can be accessed by 8000 students, and both staff and students are benefiting with 145 teaching modules already tailored for delivery on the university's network. The center's facilities include a range of e-learning tools including email, and online university chat and discussion rooms, which enable 24-hour interactivity and access to information for academic staff and

students. It ultimately aims to support all University of Bahrain students to become proficient in the use of modern technology in their learning and to develop valuable employment skills. The center has a broader remit to cascade and share the knowledge and expertise acquired through the e-learning and e-teaching with other academic institutes and professionals throughout Bahrain (Albardooli, Alobaidli, & Alyousha, 2006, p. 15).

Moreover, universities in the oil-rich GCC have shown particular interest in m-learning, which currently is treated as fashion (Mohammad & Job, 2013), but at the same time is considered by corporations and educational institutions to be very promising (Sharrab et al., 2013; Unesco, 2012). Nevertheless, there are many challenges identified in the adoption of e-learning and m-learning in the region. Weber (2011) suggests that there are some cultural concerns in the use of the Internet in the region. More specifically, he proposes that cultural taboos prevent or restrict the social interaction of unmarried men and women; hence some of the collaborative tools in the use of e-learning and m-learning "may be at variance with Islamic customs" (Weber, 2011, p. 1). He continues that there might be cultural bias such as language, as in many universities nowadays the communication and teaching and learning language is English. Even the fact that people in this culture are used to communicate mainly orally creates some challenges for the use of m-learning. In his study, Weber (2011) identified women and the issue of literacy as another challenge. He suggests that women's illiteracy in the Arab world is a major concern for women's education and development. Traditional, social and religious affiliations are impacting on women, as they cannot physically attend classes in traditional universities. However, the use of m-learning could be a potential solution to this issue as proposed by Tubaishat (2008) in his study of Zayed University, an all girl university in the UAE.

Finally, Weber (2011) claims that the issue of privacy is also a challenge. Censorship in most ME countries is common practice. There is the fear of misuse of student information similar to this of the use of Facebook. He adds that "Arabian Gulf traditions emphasize the privacy and sanctity of the home and the potential for misuse of online information used in an educational setting is immense" (2011, p. 2). Weber (2011) supports that in the MENA region instructors are concerned about the security of the educational data, and parents are concerned about the use of chats and the safety of the online environment. Mirza and Al-Abdulkareem (2011, p.84) add that exposure to material from the internet "could be considered dangerous to youths and to the religious moral values of those nations".

Moreover, Mirza and Al-Abdulkareem (2011) provide another barrier to e-learning adoption in the ME. They include the passive attitude that some governments took in response to e-learning and the low Internet penetration rate by the general public. They also comment on the conservative religious clerics who were warning of the dangers of the Internet, nevertheless, many adhered to the warning. The low public esteem for online learning was among the reasons for hesitation of many academics to resort to e-learning. This barrier impacted on the lack of online repositories that contain educational material in the Arabic language (Al-Khalifa, 2008).

Although, there is increased interest in m-learning adoption in teaching and learning in the region, there is limited research conducted (Iqbal & Qureshi, 2012; Mirza & Al-Abdulkareem, 2011). Most studies focus on the learners' perceptions and use of m-learning with very little research conducted in the instructors' views (Mirza & Al-Abdulkareem, 2011). Hence, the authors decided to investigate the adoption of m-learning at universities in the Kingdom of Bahrain, and explore the educators' views and perception of m-learning, their intention to use it, as well as its future potential in higher education. This chapter aims to provide an overview of the challenges that instructors face with the use of m-learning and of insights and recommendations on strategies for the use of mobile learning to change and enhance the pedagogies in HE.

SURVEY IN M-LEARNING

This chapter presents the findings of the pilot study of the questionnaire conducted in four out of eight universities in Bahrain; both private and public universities were included in the survey. In order to address the aim and the research questions of the study, Zawachi-Richter, Brown, and Delport (2009) questionnaire titled 'Mobile Learning: From single project status into the mainstream?' was used after having acquired the authors' permission for its use. Instructors were asked to rate the mobile learning and teaching experience of distance educators, the development and growth of mobile learning, the impact of mobile technologies on teaching and learning, mobile learning applications and mobile learning activities, mobile learning and access to (higher) education, and the future development of mobile learning with a 5 Likert scale from (1) strongly disagree to (5) strongly agree.

For the pilot study, a total of 45 questionnaires were collected between April and June 2013, in which educators were asked to provide their attitudes regarding m-learning as a tool in their teaching. The participants in the study were from different faculties such as Business, ICT, Humanities, Art and Design, and from different academic rankings, with the majority being PhD holders (53.3%). 35.6% were female and 64.4% were male.

In order to identify the instructors' perceptions of m-learning frequencies, means and standard deviations were calculated. Moreover to identify the main ideas about the future of m-learning the frequencies of responses were calculated.

M-Learning Survey Results in Bahrain

The current status of the use of m-learning at the institutional level was identified and the results are shown in Table 5. For the purpose of this paper the authors present the most frequent answers or the majority of answers.

It is evident from the above that the majority of the institutions in the study were face-to-face with limited use of e-learning. M-learning was non-existent and most did not have any plans in

developing m-learning. In addition, there was no technical support or in the cases that there was, it was limited. However, 31.1% claimed that a new unit within the organisation has been created for the purpose of m-learning. In reference to the current status on m-learning the participants expressed their opinions on their knowledge on m-learning and on the use of mobile devices. The results are shown in Table 6.

Interestingly, most respondents are aware of m-learning, but only 15.6% are currently doing research and only 4.4% are involved in projects relevant to m-learning. Similarly, 15.6% of the respondents have not heard about mobile learning. The use of mobile devices is shown in Figure 2.

Most of the respondents (43.52%) used a laptop for connecting to the internet, and then their smartphone (22.27%), 16.20% use a tablet PC and only 1.1% use PDAs. Moreover the participants were asked to evaluate their experience in m-learning. The results are shown in Figure 3.

The majority of the responses to this question were towards the strongly disagree (1) area. 28% of

Table 5. M-learning status at institution level

	Response (N=45)	Frequency (%)
C1	A traditional face-to-face or contact-based teaching institution	34 (75.6)
C2	Non-existent	27 (60)
C3	No, there are no institutional plans for developing course materials for use on mobile devices	27 (60)
C4.1	No, there is no institutional support.	14 (31.1)
C4.2	Yes, a new unit at the organisation/institution has been created for this purpose.	14 (31.1)

Table 6. Current personal status

	Response (N=45)	Frequency (%)
B1.1	Yes, I am personally doing research on mobile learning	7 (15.6)
B1.2	Yes, but I am not personally doing research on mobile learning	11 (24.4)
B1.3	Yes, I am involved in mobile learning projects	2 (4.4)
B1.4	I have read a number of articles and papers on mobile learning.	4 (8.9)
B1.5	No, but other persons in my institution are knowledgeable.	14 (31.1)
B1.6	No, I have not heard about mobile learning.	7 (15.6)

Figure 2. Mobile devices

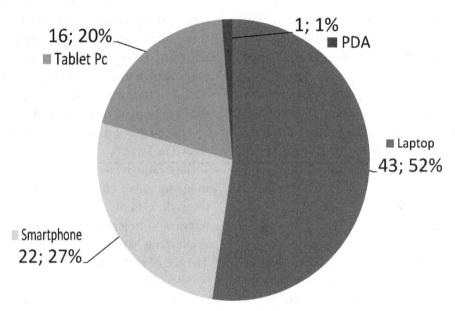

the participants have been involved in m-learning projects, however, 22% of them state that these projects are not within their universities. 14% of the participants were not involved in projects on m-learning but were aware of others who were, and still 20% were not exposed to m-learning at all.

Further, respondents were asked to rate the importance of learning tools for students, the learning activities that are appropriate for mobile devices and the importance of applications. The findings are shown in Table 7. The results suggest that the respondents found very important 'being connected anywhere, anytime' (B4.5), and 'sharing texts, notes and documents' (B4.4), hence they did not find the text messaging or voice calls and e-mails as highly important tools for students. Moreover, they identified as appropriate learning activities for mobile devices 'coursework' (B5.1), 'collaborative learning' (B5.3) and 'information retrieval' (B5.5). The applications found to be more important were all those included in the questionnaire such as mobile office (B6.1), diary and scheduling (B6.2), audio and video applications (B6.3), imaging (B6.4), other accessories

(B6.5) and online data services (B6.6). Finally, the most useful tools were accessing information such as notes, documents etc (B7.2) and again 'being connected anywhere, anytime' (B7.5).

The respondents were asked to rate the new strategies and methodologies that are facilitated by m-learning. The results are shown in Table 8.

Except the 'assessment' (B8.2, Mean=2.69), the rest of the variables were rated close to agree and strongly agree responses. It was evident that they would use m-learning mainly to assess students' knowledge short time before a lecture or a discussion. Interaction (B8.4, Mean=4.02) was the most important of all the strategies that are facilitated by m-learning. Hence, the respondents suggested that m-learning provides more support for collaboration, more support for bottom-up content creation and could be used to consult peers. Next important strategy for m-learning was the resources for m-learning (B8.3, M=3.84). The participants use it for generating information, sharing resources, navigation and other. The major weaknesses of mobile devices that might hinder m-learning were also rated by the respondents as shown in Figure 4.

Figure 3. Experience in m-learning

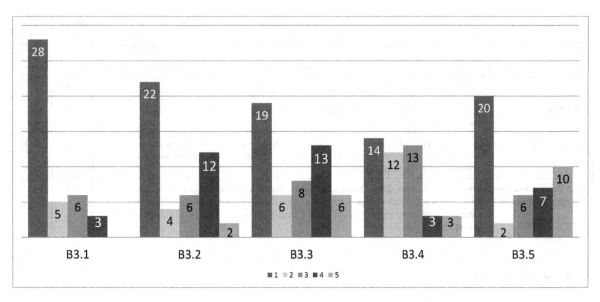

Table 7. Importance rating of importance for tools (B4), learning activities (B5), applications (B6) and learning tools (B7)

Item (N=45)	1 (Freq)	2 (Freq)	3 (Freq)	4 (Freq)	5 (Freq)
B4.1	7 (15.6)	7 (15.6)	10 (22.2)	10 (22.2)	11 (24.4)
B4.2	7 (15.6)	8 (17.8)	13 (28.9)	10 (22.2)	7 (15.6)
B4.3		5 (11.1)	12 (26.7)	18 (40.0)	10 (22.2)
B4.4	3 (6.7)	1 (2.2)	5 (11.1)	18 (40.0)	18 (40.0)
B4.5	3 (6.7)	1 (2.2)	3 (6.7)	14 (31.1)	24 (53.3)
B5.1	6 (13.3)	7 (15.6)	10 (22.2)	6 (13.3)	16 (35.6)
B5.2	3 (6.7)	12 (26.7)	5 (11.1)	12 (26.7)	13 (28.9)
B5.3	2 (4.4)	3 (6.7)	7 (15.6)	19 (42.2)	14 (31.1)
B5.4		5 (11.1)	12 (26.7)	18 (40.0)	10 (22.2)
B5.5		4 (8.9)	10 (22.2)	10 (22.2)	21 (46.7)
B6.1	5 (11.1)	5 (11.1)	7 (15.6)	9 (20.0)	19 (42.2)
B6.2	2 (4.4)	6 (13.3)	8 (17.8)	10 (22.2)	19 (42.2)
B6.3	2 (4.4)	4 (8.9)	15 (33.3)	7 (15.6)	17 (37.8)
B6.4	2 (4.4)	7 (15.6)	10 (22.2)	12 (26.7)	14 (31.1)
B6.5	2 (4.4)	1 (2.2)	11 (24.4)	15 (33.3)	16 (35.6)
B6.6	2 (4.4)		2 (4.4)	7 (15.6)	34 (75.6)
B7.1	1 (2.2)	7 (15.6)	12 (26.7)	11 (24.4)	14 (31.1)
B7.2	2 (4.4)	3 (6.7)	11 (24.4)	15 (33.3)	14 (31.3)
B7.3	1 (2.2)	9 (20.0)	10 (22.2)	12 (26.7)	13 (28.9)
B7.4	1 (2.2)	8 (17.8)	8 (17.8)	15 (33.3)	13 (28.9)
B7.5	1 (2.2)	1 (2.2)	5 (11.1)	10 (22.2)	28 (62.2)

Table 8. Strategies and methodologies

Category	Typical Examples	Mean	SD
B8.1 Learning Activities	(Inter)active learning, authentic learning, explorative learning, project orientated learning, situated and informal learning, Qs & As.	3.60	1.286
B8.2 Assessment	Security for testing and evaluation procedures, assessment to determine students' knowledge a day or two before a lecture/discussion to determine which topics need more attention.	2.69	1.411
B8.3 Resources	Generation of information, sharing resources, data sourcing, access to information, navigation, m-library.	3.84	1.127
B8.4 Interaction	More support for collaboration, more support for bottom-up content creation, enhanced social support, consulting peers & experts. Distance Educators will teach again instead of providing teaching material only.	4.02	1.033
B8.5 Personalisation & Individualisation	New strategies might emerge from better knowledge of learner behaviours and study patterns with technology, which were never examined that closely before, just-in-time learning, addressing learner styles or needs, keeping it simple, focus on small 'chunks' of learning, just-in-time support/job aids.	3.76	.957

Figure 4. Major weaknesses

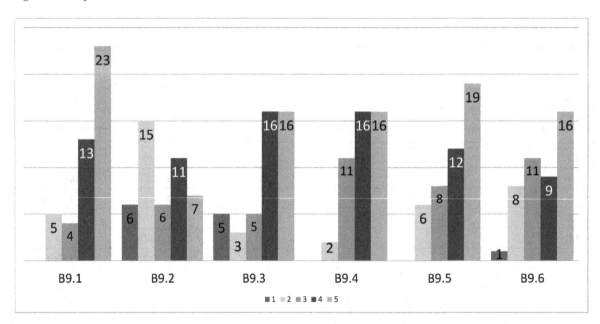

Most of the respondents agreed or strongly agreed with all the variables except the screen size (B9.2). This showed that the size of the screen of mobile devices was not considered to be a hindering factor for m-learning. On the contrary, the small size of the displays was found to be a challenge for m-learning activities. Similarly, the costs of network, the memory size, the device capabilities and the limited battery time were among the most important challenges for applying m-learning.

When respondents were asked their views on the latest trends and developments in teaching and learning as well as on when m-learning will be an integral part of mainstream in HE, this is reflected in Table 9.

Table 9. Respondents' views on trends and developments in m-learning (and in years)

Responses	Technology changes should not have an impact on our teaching & learning strategies and methodologies.	Technology changes should have an impact on our teaching & learning strategies and methodologies, but this is currently not the case at present.	Teaching and learning strategies and methodologies adapt continuously due to new affordances that technology provides.	Technology changes bring about radical changes to our teaching & learning strategies and methodologies.
Frequency	2	23	12	8
(Percent)	(4.4)	(51.1)	(26.7)	(17.8)

Table 10. Future trends of m-learning

Statement	Frequency N=45	Percent
Teaching and learning theories in 20 years...		
In essence remain the same, but new learning paradigms and learning strategies will emerge because of technological developments.	25	55.6
Change completely with new learning theories replacing behaviourism and constructivism due to the radical impact of future technologies.	15	33.3
The attributes and opportunities that mobile technologies afford will...		
Be very helpful in enhancing teaching and learning independent of time and space.	33	73.3
Mobile devices and applications will in future be...		
Only one of many types of computing devices used.	22	48.9
The preferred access and learning device for any type of learning.	15	33.3
The development of m-learning will have an impact on HE		
It will widen access to (higher) education, because of the proliferation of mobile phones and wireless infrastructure – especially in developing countries.	29	64.4
The ideal mobile devices in the future will be...		
Small but still laptop sized devices because of its all-in-one device nature.	12	26.7

Most of the respondents (51.1%) supported the view that although the technology should impact on the teaching and learning, currently this was not the case. 26.7% agreed that teaching and learning strategies and methodologies adapt to the constant changes in technology. In addition, most of the respondents (75.6%) believed that m-learning will become an integral part of mainstream HE within 5 years.

Finally the participants were asked to present their views on the future trends of m-learning. For the purpose of this paper only the majority of responses are illustrated in Table 10.

The majority of the respondents (55.6%) supported the view that new teaching and learning strategies will emerge due to IT developments. In addition, they proposed that they will enhance the teaching and learning, nevertheless, they proposed that the mobile devices will be the preferred device for learning. They also supported that m-learning will widen access to HE, because of the profileration of mobile phones and wireless infrastructure and the devices are expected to be small in size. Most of the respondents (84.4%) agreed that m-learning will facilitate new strategies and methodologies for learner support.

CONCLUSION

M-learning as a relatively recent phenomenon in higher education, enjoys high popularity among university students globally. In the ME region change has already started and e-learning and m-learning are becoming part of the educational system. Some may still be unfamiliar with the technical advancements in e-learning and m-learning, but plans are in place to make these technologies widely known and usable in the near future.

The key opportunity identified in this chapter is the ability of m-learning to provide learning that is "just in time". Mobile devices have the potential to deliver the kind of learning that is embedded in our daily lives, as the use of these devices is well established. Many instructors in higher education, including Bahrain, recognize the benefits of m-learning, but there is limited adoption for educational use. The main challenge identified in the chapter is the age and ability of instructors to use these mobile devices and technologies.

In order to support a strategic response to the opportunities and demands of mobile learners, the higher education sector needs to be informed about the actual use of mobile devices, and about potential future trends in mobile learning. This requires the re-examination and re-design of the foundational assumptions and presuppositions on which all previous understandings of the term "higher education" are constructed. It is imperative that this process foregrounds pedagogy rather than technology. In addition, these on-going structural changes in higher education, provide the potential to make learning more efficient, personal and culturally acceptable for learners. Training and workshops should be provided to increase faculty perception of e-learning and m-learning. This change and the integration of m-learning requires a change in the pedagogical paradigm in agreement with Moura and Calvalho (2009). The authors propose that this change should include transformation in the design and the development of teaching material.

It is also important to introduce by laws that governs the e-learning and distance learning which encourages students to participate at this type of learning. Regardless criticisms and debates, m-learning is now part of the academic curricula; what remains to see is how smooth the transition from the traditional to the contemporary teaching and learning environment can be.

IMPLICATIONS FOR FUTURE RESEARCH

The purpose of this chapter was to investigate the instructors' views on m-learning and its use in teaching and learning in higher education in Bahrain. It is evident from the above that m-learning plays an important role in teaching and learning strategies. Although, most of the participants work in institutions that do not offer m-learning strategies and they use face-to-face teaching, the instructors are considering its use, and some already conduct research in m-learning. Students and faculty will find ways to integrate m-learning in all aspects of their lives including the tasks of teaching and learning. Nevertheless, educational systems should not assume that instructors are proficient in using new technologies. Similarly to Ferry (2008), this chapter proposes that there is a need to integrate appropriate technologies into existing education systems. Professional development programmes should focus not only on the technology, skills and knowledge required to implement m-learning strategies, but also on the targeted use of technologies that support overall learning goals. Hence, further research is required to identify and determine such professional development programmes for instructors in higher education, especially in the Kingdom of Bahrain and the region.

Moreover, it was interesting that the majority of the respondents have not heard of m-learning.

The findings proposed that m-learning could be considered a continuation of traditional learning methods as well as an alternative to the methods of effective learning. It is mainly used for coursework, information retrieval and collaborative learning. The most important elements of m-learning included the fact that instructors are connected anywhere anytime, and they can share texts with their students, supporting the view of Giousmpasoglou and Marinakou (2013). Hence, instructors should be cautious when including e-learning as part of their assessment as the infrastructure and the support is not available at the institutions in the study. This study agrees with Venkatesh et al. (2003) that the available support and infrastructure are important for the use of e-learning and m-learning. Similarly to Sarrab et al. (2013), the main weaknesses identified include the small size of displays, the cost of network, the memory size and the mobile devices capabilities. However, the participants proposed that the new technologies should have an impact on teaching and learning in HE, and they believed that new may emerge, as they may enhance the learning and the teaching strategies. Macallum and Jeffery (2009) also propose that mobile devices may enhance m-learning, and the teaching and learning pedagogies.

Understanding the factors that contribute to the effective use of m-learning may help stakeholders to incorporate those in the design and implementation of m-learning. It is necessary to identify the practices in terms of instructional design and adapt them to reflect the number of changes that have taken place in education from the use of e-learning and m-learning. A transformation towards m-learning requires not only the use of the devices but also awareness and familiarity with new technologies (Wang, 2011), hence mobile tools should be aligned with the course objectives, and instructors should be aligned with m-learning requirements. M-learning should be used appropriately in order to be effective (Herrington et al., 2009), thus instructors should have the technical know-how as they are an essential part of m-learning.

This study proposes that informative meetings and instructors' training on m-learning can enhance the perception and the use of m-learning in higher education in Bahrain. Nevertheless, more empirical research is required to test the effectiveness of e-learning. Future studies can focus on identifying the factors, challenges and weaknesses in specific disciplines as the use of technology varies depending on the field of study for example it can be limited in liberal arts. It would also be interesting to explore the above findings in terms of gender differences.

REFERENCES

Al-Khalifa, H. (2008). Building an Arabic learning object repository with an ad hoc recommendation engine. In *Proceedings of the iiWAS* (pp. 390-394). Linz: iiWAS. doi:10.1145/1497308.1497378

Albardooli, M., Alobaidli, O., & Alyousha, F. (2016). *E-mobile, the future of e learning*. Thesis submitted at the University of Bahrain. Retrieved from www.albardooli.com/dlobjects/EmobileMAlbardooli.pdf

Alsaadat, K. (2009). Mobile learning and university teaching. In *Proceedings of the International Conference on Education and New Learning Technologies* (vol. 6, pp. 5895-5905). Barcelona: IATED.

Altameem, T. (2011). Contextual mobile learning system for Saudi Arabian universities. *International Journal of Computers and Applications*, *21*(4), 21–26. doi:10.5120/2499-3377

Attewell, J. (2011). *From research and development to mobile learning: tools for education and training providers and their learners*. Retrieved from http://www.mlearn.org.za/CD/papers/Attewell.pdf

Banyard, P., Underwood, J., & Twiner, A. (2006). Do enhanced communication technologies inhibit or facilitate self-regulated learning? *European Journal of Education*, *41*(3/4), 473–489. doi:10.1111/j.1465-3435.2006.00277.x

BenMoussa, C. (2003). *Workers on the move: New opportunities through mobile commerce.* Paper presented at the Stockholm Mobility Roundtable. Stockholm, Sweden.

Bharuthram, S., & Kies, C. (2013). Introducing e-learning in a South African higher education institution: Challenges arising from an intervention and possible responses. *British Journal of Educational Technology*, *44*(3), 410–420. doi:10.1111/j.1467-8535.2012.01307.x

Brink, J. (2011). M-learning: The future of training technology. *Training & Development*, *65*(2), 27.

Brown, A., & Campione, J. (1996). Psychological theory and design of innovative learning environments: on procedures, principles, and systems. In L. Schauble & R. Glaser (Eds.), *Innovations in learning: new environments for education* (pp. 289–325). Mahwah, NJ: Erlbaum.

Corbeil, J. R., & Valdes-Corbeil, M. E. (2007). Are you ready for mobile learning? *EDUCAUSE Quarterly*, *30*(2), 51–58.

Dawabi, P., Wessner, M., & Neuhold, E. (2003). Using mobile devices for the classroom of the future. In *Proceedings of Mlearn 2003 Conference on Learning with Mobile Devices* (pp. 14-15). London: Mlearn.

Demian, P., & Morrice, J. (2012). The use of virtual learning environments and their impact on academic performance. *English Education*, *7*(1), 11–19. doi:10.11120/ened.2012.07010011

Devinder, S., & Zaitun, A. B. (2006). Mobile learning in wireless classrooms. *Malaysian Online Journal of Instructional Technology*, *3*(2), 26–42.

El-Hussein, M. O. O., & Cronje, J. C. (2010). Defining Mobile Learning in the Higher Education Landscape. *Journal of Educational Technology & Society*, *13*(3), 12–21.

Ferry, B. (2008). *Using mobile phones to augment teacher learning in environmental education.* Retrieved from http://www.ascilite.org.au/conferences/melbourne08/procs/ferry.pdf

Garg, V. (2013). *The emergence of mobile learning for higher education in Kingdom of Saudi Arabia.* UPSIDE learning blog. Retrieved from http://upsidelearning.com/blog/index.php

Giousmpasoglou, C., & Marinakou, E. (2013). The future is here: M-learning in higher education. *Computer Technology and Application*, *4*(6), 317–322.

Hadj-Hamou, N., Anwar, S. A., & Benhadria, M. (2012). A new paradigm for e-learing in the Arab Middle East: Reflections on e-books and e-Reader devices. In T. T. Goh, B. C. Seet, & P. C. Sun (Eds.), *E-Books & E-Readers for E-Learning* (pp. 92–123). Wellington, New Zealand: Victoria Business School.

Herrington, J., Mantei, J., Olney, I., & Ferry, B. (2009). Using mobile technologies to develop new ways of teaching and learning. In J. Herrington, A. Herrington, J., Mantei, I., Olney, & B. Ferry (Eds.), New technologies, new pedagogies: Mobile learning in higher education (p. 138). New South Wales, Australia: Faculty of Education, University of Wollongong.

Iqbal, S., & Qureshi, I. A. (2012). M-learning adoption: A perspective from a developing country. *International Review of Research in Open and Distance Learning*, *13*(3), 147–164.

Ju, T. L., Sriprapaipong, W., & Minh, D. N. (2007). *On the success factors of mobile learning*. Paper presented at 5ᵗʰ Conference on ICT and Higher Education. Bangkok, Thailand. Retrieved from http://www.mendeley.com/research/success-factors-mobile-learning/

Kearney, M., Schuck, S., Burden, K., & Aubusson, P. (2012). Viewing mobile learning from a pedagogical perspective. *Research in Learning Technology, 20*(1).

King, J. P. (2006). *One hundred philosophers: A guide to world's greatest thinkers* (2nd ed.). London: Apple Press.

Klopfer, E., Squire, K., & Jenkins, H. (2002). Environmental detectives: PDAs as a window into a virtual simulated world. In *Proceedings for the International Workshop on Wireless and Mobile Technologies in Education* (pp. 95-98). Vaxjo, Sweden: IEEE.

Koszalka, T. A., & Ntloedibe-Kuswani, G. S. (2010). Literature on the safe and disruptive learning potential of mobile technologies. *Distance Education, 31*(2), 139–157. doi:10.1080/01587919.2010.498082

Kukulska-Hulme, A., & Traxler, J. (2007). *Designing for mobile and wireless learning*. London: Routledge.

Liaw, S. S., Hatala, M., & Huang, H. M. (2010). Investigating acceptance toward mobile learning to assist individual knowledge management: Based on activity theory approach. *Computers & Education, 54*(2), 446–454. doi:10.1016/j.compedu.2009.08.029

Liu, Y., & Li, H. (2010). Mobile internet diffusion in China: An empirical study. *Industrial Management & Data Systems, 110*(3), 309–324. doi:10.1108/02635571011030006

MacCallum, K., & Jeffrey, L. (2009). Identifying discriminating variables that determine mobile learning adoption by educators: An initial study. In Proceedings of the conference for Same places, different spaces. Auckland: Ascilite. Retrieved from http://www.ascilite.org.au/conferences/auckland09/procs/maccallum.pdf

Maniar, N., & Bennett, E. (2007). Media influence on m-learning? In S. Iqbal, & I.A. Qureshi. (2012). M-learning adoption: A perspective from a developing country. *International Review of Research in Open and Distance Learning, 13*(3), 147–164.

Marwan, M. E., Madar, A. R., & Fuad, N. (2013). An overview of mobile application in learning for student of Kolejpoly-tech Mara (KPTM) by using mobile phone. *Journal of Asian Scientific Research, 3*(6), 527–537.

Mirza, A. A., & Al-Abdulkareem, M. (2011). Models of e-learning adopted in the Middle East. *Applied Computing and Informatics, 9*(2), 83–93. doi:10.1016/j.aci.2011.05.001

Motiwalla, L. F. (2007). Mobile learning: A framework and evaluation. *Computers & Education, 49*(3), 581–596. doi:10.1016/j.compedu.2005.10.011

Moura, A., & Carvalho, A. (2009). Mobile learning: two experiments on teaching and learning with mobile phones. In R. Hijon-Neira (Ed.), *Advanced Learning* (pp. 89-103). Rijeka, Croatia: InTech. Retrieved from http://www.intechopen.com/download/get/type/pdfs/id/8593

Muttoo, S. (2011). *'Mobile' changes in the Arab world*. Middle East economy and Globalization. Retrieved from http://www.strategicforesight.com/inner-articles.php?id=128£.UiRFZD-BWSo

Okazaki, S. (2011). Teaching students while leaking personal information: m-learing and privacy. In *Proceedings of 4th International Conference of Education, Research and Innovations* (pp. 1659-1664). Madrid: IATED.

Orr, G. (2010). Review of the literature in mobile learning: Affordances and constraints. In *Proceeding of the 6th IEEE International Conference on Wireless, Mobile and Ubiquitous Technologies in Education* (pp. 107-111). Taiwan: IEEE. doi:10.1109/WMUTE.2010.20

Peng, H., Su, Y., Chou, C., & Tsai, C. (2009). Ubiquitous knowledge construction: Mobile learning re-defined and conceptual framework. *Innovations in Education and Teaching International, 46*(2), 171–183. doi:10.1080/14703290902843828

Peters, K. (2009). m-Learning: Positioning educators for a mobile, connected future. In M. Ally (Ed.), Mobile learning: Transforming the delivery of education and training (pp. 113-132). Vancouver: Marquis Book Printing.

Quinn, C. (2001). Get ready for m-learning. *Training & Development, 20*(2), 20–21.

Rosenberg, M. (2001). *E-learning: Strategies for delivering knowledge in the digital age.* New York: MacGraw-Hill.

Sad, S. N., & Goktas, O. (2013). Preservice teachers' perceptions about using mobile phones and laptops in education as mobile learning tools. *British Journal of Educational Technology, 45*(4), 606–618. doi:10.1111/bjet.12064

Sarrab, M., Al-Shihi, H., & Rehman, O. M. H. (2013). Exploring major challenges and benefits of m-learning adoption. *British Journal of Applied Science and Technology, 3*(4), 826–839. doi:10.9734/BJAST/2013/3766

Serin, O. (2012). Mobile learning perceptions of the prospective teachers (Turkish Republic of Northern Cyprus sampling). *TOJET: The Turkish Online Journal of Educational Technology, 11*(3), 222–233.

Sharples, M., Taylor, J., & Vavoula, G. (2007). *A theory of learning for the mobile age.* London: Sage Publications.

Shiau, K., Lim, E. P., & Shen, Z. (2001). Mobile commerce: Promises, challenges, and research agenda. *Journal of Database Management, 12*(3), 4–13. doi:10.4018/jdm.2001070101

Siemens, G. (2005). *A Learning Theory for the Digital Age.* Retrieved from http://www.elearnspace.org/Articles/connectivism.htm

Smith, M., & Kukulska-Hulme, A. (2012). Building Mobile Learning Capacity in Higher Education: E-books and iPads. In M. Specht, J. Multisilta, and M. Sharples, (Eds.), *11th World Conference on Mobile and Contextual Learning Proceedings* (pp. 298-301). Helsinki: CELSTEC & CICERO Learning.

Traxler, J. (2009). Learning in a mobile age. *International Journal of Mobile and Blended Learning, 1*(1), 1–12. doi:10.4018/jmbl.2009010101

Tubaishat, A. (2008). Adoption of learning technologies to alleviate the impact of social and cultural limitations in higher education. In *Proceedings of the 1st E-learning Excellence Forum* (pp. 15-18). Dubai: Academic Press.

Venkatesh, V., Morris, M. G., Davis, G. B., & Davis, F. D. (2003). User acceptance of information technology: Toward a unified view. *Management Information Systems Quarterly, 27*(3), 425–478.

Wang, M. (2011). Integrating organizational, social, and individual perspectives in Web 2.0-based workplace e-learning. *Information Systems Frontiers, 13*(2), 191–205. doi:10.1007/s10796-009-9191-y

Weber, A. S. (2011). *Research programme for next-gen e-learning in MENA region*. Paper presented at the 7th International Scientific Conference eLearning and Software for Education. Bucharest, Romania. Retrieved from https://adlunap.ro/else_publications/papers/2011/1758_2.pdf

Welsh, E. T., Wanberg, C. R., Brown, K. G., & Simmering, M. J. (2003). E-learning: Emerging uses, empirical results, and future directions. *International Journal of Training and Development, 7*(4), 245–258. doi:10.1046/j.1360-3736.2003.00184.x

World Bank. (2007). *World development report*. Washington, DC: Author.

World Economic Forum. (2010). *Global competitiveness report 2010-2011*. Davos: Author.

Zawacki-Richter, O., Brown, T., & Delport, R. (2009). Mobile learning: from single project status into the mainstream? *European Journal of Open, Distance and E-learning*. Retrieved from http://www.eurodl.org/?article=357

KEY TERMS AND DEFINITIONS

Bahrain: The Kingdom of Bahrain is a small island country in the Persian Gulf. Since 2012 was ranked 48th in the world in the Human Development Index, and was recognized by the World Bank as a high income economy. Currently, there are 12 universities.

Blended Learning: A method of learning which uses a combination of different resources, especially a mixture of classroom sessions and online learning materials.

Collaboration (Collaborative Learning): Learners making rich connections and sharing resources to other learners and/or educators; this type of communication is mediated by a mobile device.

E-Learning: Any type of learning conducted via electronic media using specialized software, typically on the Internet.

Higher Education: The education offered after secondary education, usually available through colleges, universities, including vocational training, trade schools and other professional certifications.

Information and Communication Technologies (ICTs): The term stresses the role and importance of unified communications and the integration of telecommunications with computers as well as necessary enterprise software, middleware, storage, and audio-visual systems, which enable users to access, store, transmit, and manipulate information.

M-Learning (Mobile Learning): Any activity that allows learners to be more productive when interacting with, or creating information, mediated through a mobile device that the learner carries on a regular basis, has reliable connectivity, and fits in a pocket, a purse or a handbag.

Teaching and Learning: Teaching is undertaking certain ethical tasks or activities the intention of which is to induce learning, to impact knowledge of or skill of. Learning is the act or process of acquiring knowledge or skill.

Ubiquity: The ability of users to access content "anytime – anywhere" though the use of mobile devices.

Virtual Learning Environments (VLEs): A set of teaching and learning tools designed to enhance a student's learning experience by including computers and the Internet in the learning process.

Chapter 9
Mobile Education Mitigating the Heavy Magnitude of Illiteracy in India

Kshama Pandey
Dayalbagh Educational Institute, India

ABSTRACT

This chapter introduces the concept of mobile learning as a means of portable learning. Through the use of mobile technology, citizens of the world will be able to access learning materials and information from anywhere and at any time. Learners will not have to wait for a certain time to learn or go to a certain place to learn. It presents the evolution of classroom learning to mobile learning. There has been made an effort to explore current perspectives of mobile learning. Approaches of m-learning suggest implication of mobile devices in the classroom. Pedagogical methods and instructional approaches of m-learning have also been explored in this chapter. Further, the authors make an attempt to give rational of mobile learning through various theories of m-learning. It suggests opportunities of mobile learning in the Indian scenario. Mobile learning can effectively support a wide range of activities for learners of all ages.

INTRODUCTION

Mobile technology, because of its personal nature, lends itself to a unique integration into the user's life. Advances in technology during the past decade have created a worldwide boom in the sale of this kind of technology, permitting private individuals to enjoy personal, mobile wireless connectivity. The widespread ownership of mobile technology in the form of mobile phones, especially among young people, has created opportunities and challenges for educators.

All humans have the right to access learning materials and information to improve their quality of life regardless of where they live, their status, and their culture. Mobile learning, through the use of mobile technology, will allow citizens of the world to access learning materials and information from anywhere and at any time. Learners will not have to wait for a certain time to learn or go to a certain place to learn. With mobile learning,

DOI: 10.4018/978-1-4666-7316-8.ch009

learners will be empowered since they can learn whenever and wherever they want. Also, learners do not have to learn what is prescribed to them. They can use the wireless mobile technology for formal and informal learning where they can access additional and personalized learning materials from the Internet or from the host organization. Peoples all over the world will want to access learning materials on their existing mobile devices

These opportunities are facilitated by the development of relevant technology platforms and tools, and their effective use to reach a desired outcome. An essential feature relevant to education is that mobile technology removes the limitations of time, space and connectivity that characterize the conventional classroom and other forms of teaching and learning. Because of this it offers the individual user the capacity and freedom to connect to remote information and other resources; enriching, personalizing and extending the learning environment.

Historical Perspective of Mobile Learning

The idea of using computerized mobile devices to support learning was formally conceptualized a surprisingly long time ago. In his paper "Disruptive Devices: Mobile Technology for Conversational Learning," Sharples, 2002 identifies Alan Kay's Dynabook, conceived in the early 1970s, as the first serious attempt to design a computer-mediated mobile learning platform. Although the Dynabook was a concept, the ripples of the project – and Alan Kay's (non-portable, "interim") Dynabook prototypes –can still be felt today, and will probably be felt for decades to come.

Just as groundbreaking as the technology it was Alan Kay's vision for how the technology would be used to support learning. His vision for the Dynabook was based in the then-nascent philosophies of (Social) Constructivism: the theories and models of learning being developed by his contemporaries Lev Vygotsky, Jerome

Bruner and Seymour Papert, (who had studied with developmental psychologist Jean Piaget). Sharples (2002) distills the features of effective learning in constructivist terms via the essential elements of construction, conversation and control. Sharples' m-Learn, 2007 presentation on the history of mobile learning summarizes how the Dynabook concept would have accomplished these requirements, technically and pedagogically. It was to be an interactive machine that would be small and light enough to be carried everywhere by learners. It would have "book-like" qualities in terms of display, yet its interface would be dynamic, with the ability to create, edit and store visual, textual, and audio content. It would have high-bandwidth communication, both locally and globally, and it would cost under \$500. It would be personal, interactive, and would support learning through play, collaborative learning, informal learning, dynamic simulations, and "anytime, anywhere" learning.

It was amazing thinking for 1972. Many of Kay's original ideas for the Dynabook simply weren't possible at the time he conceived them, but have recently come to fruition – such as the Squeak Smalltalk environment which enables children to create and learn using computers (implemented on the OLPC, but boasting cross-platform capabilities). Here's a real example of Squeak being used as a learning tool.

Although small, pocket-sized "electronic organizers" were available in the 1990s; these had, at best, a three line text-only display. Palm Pilot PDAs, introduced in 1996, were the first multi-purpose, customizable handhelds suitable for a range of creative learning activities; and in 2001, SRI International awarded over 100 "Palm Education Pioneer" grants to US teachers who had a vision of how Palm handhelds could be used to improve teaching and learning. Many of the findings of the PEP grants have been confirmed by later "handheld learning" studies. Examples of pertinent findings include the strengths and weaknesses of various models for allocating handheld computers to students, to the degree of success with which various learning activities (e.g. inquiry-based learning or extended writing) can be accomplished using handheld devices.

Today's handheld mobile devices have specifications and capabilities that resemble those of desktop personal computers built just ten years ago. The current crops of PDAs and smartphones have high resolution displays, processor speeds in excess of 600MHz, and memory capabilities exceeding those of premium hard drives from the mid-1990s. Instead of requiring an add-on webcam, current mobile devices often have built-in cameras, as well as the ability to create and edit documents and media: they have become powerful tools for enabling learners to create, collect, and share content.

The other new market that has reduced the demand for PDAs is in ultra-mobile and ultra-portable computers: UMPCs, tablet PCs, and small form-factor laptops. Of particular note in terms of education are the One Laptop per Child project and similar commercial models (such as the Intel Classmate and the Asus EEE) generated by the initial ovation that greeted Nicholas Negroponte's vision for cheap, rugged laptops for learning.

The current generations of mobile devices have brought us closer to realizing Alan Kay's vision of cheap, integrated, connected, computers supporting constructivist learning activities. They can provide a digital, connected learning environment, offering compactness and convenience of information, remote and instant access to a range of people and resources, and data capabilities that were never previously possible.

The current trend in mobile phone penetration makes it virtually certain that not too far in the future all of the world's student community will possess a mobile phone. Moreover the feature of being able to connect any time anywhere makes the mobile phone to be a viable and feasible personal technology for distance learners. This is a sufficient reason and motivation to explore the possibility of making the mobile phone is an important tool in the educational systems of developed and developing countries. If educational technology theory, research, and pedagogy are reconceptualized to include the tools and knowledge that students already possess, then it is imperative to have a clear understanding not only of the technology but also of the students who are using or would use mobile phones in their daily life.

Concept of Mobile Learning

Many communities have defined the concept of mobile learning based on their own particular experiences, uses and backgrounds. This has led to a fertile proliferation of views and perspectives. However, the downside is that the unique nature of mobile learning is becoming very difficult to characterize. Worst still, mobile learning, as a concept, is currently is not well defined; it seems to be all things to all people. Formal definitions from European and Government agencies espouse its relationship to e-learning. Technologists place a high emphasis on novelty and the functionality of the devices (i.e. phones, PDAs, iPods, PSPs etc.) themselves. Some researchers focus on the mobility of the learner. Yet others focus on learning in informal settings, leading to juxtaposition between mobile learning and formal education.

Mobile learning refers to the use of mobile or wireless devices for the purpose of learning while on the move. Typical examples of the devices used for mobile learning include cell phones, smartphones, palmtops, and handheld computers; tablet PCs, laptops, and personal media players can also fall within this scope (K., Hulme & Traxler, 2005). The first generation of truly portable information has been integrated with many functions in small, portable electronic devices (Peters, 2007). Recent innovations in program applications and social software using Web 2.0 technologies for example; blogs, wikis, Twitter, YouTube or social networking sites such as Facebook and MySpace etc. have made mobile devices more dynamic and pervasive and also promise more educational potential.

Table 1. When learning is mobile

Technology / Location	Fixed	Mobile
At Usual Environment (Home, Office, Classroom)	Non-mobile learning	Mobile learning
Away from usual environment	Mobile learning	Mobile learning

(Adopted from MOBllearn by Malley,C. and et al.)

However, it has been widely recognized that mobile learning is not just about the use of portable devices but also about learning across contexts (Walker, 2006). Winter (2006) re-conceptualized the nature of mobile learning and addressed "mediated learning through mobile technology". Pea and Maldonado (2006) used the term wireless interactive learning devices or WILD, an acronym created at SRI International's Center for Technology in Learning, to define technology that made it possible for learners to work at unique activities in ways that were previously impossible.

Peters (2007) viewed mobile learning as a useful component of the flexible learning model. In 2003, Brown summarized several definitions and terms and identified mobile learning as "an extension of e-learning" (Brown, 2005). Peters (2007) also stated that it was a subset of e-learning, a step toward making the educational process "just in time, just enough and just for me" Finally, Pea and Maldonado (2006) stated that mobile learning incorporates "transformative innovations for learning futures".

Meaning of Mobile Learning

Mobile learning or m-learning has been defined as learning that takes place via such wireless devices as mobile phones, personal digital assistants (PDAs), or laptop computers. Some example definitions encountered in the literature include:

It's e-learning through mobile computational devices: Palms, Windows CE machines, even your digital cell phone(Quinn, 2000).

The term mobile learning (m-learning) refers to use of mobile and handheld IT devices, such as PDAs, mobile phones, laptops and tablet PCs, in teaching and learning (Wood, C.2003).

According to software vendors, it's the point at which mobile computing and e-learning intersect to produce an anytime, anywhere learning experience. Transition: it's ability to enjoy an educational moment from a cell phone or personal digital assistant (PDA) (Harris, 2001).

A definition of mobile learning that happens when the learner is not at a fixed, predetermined location or learning that happens when the learner takes advantage of the learning opportunities offered by mobile technologies.

According to UNESCO Policy Guidelines for mobile learning, Mobile learning involves the use of mobile technology, either alone or in combination with other information and communication technology (ICT), to enable learning anytime and anywhere. Learning can unfold in a variety of ways: people can use mobile devices to access educational resources, connect with others, or create content, both inside and outside classrooms. Mobile learning also encompasses efforts to support broad educational goals such as the effective administration of school systems and improved communication between schools and families.

Mobile technologies are constantly evolving: the diversity of devices on the market today is immense and includes, in broad strokes, mobile phones, tablet computers, e-readers, portable audio players and hand-held gaming consoles.

Figure 1. Mobile learning

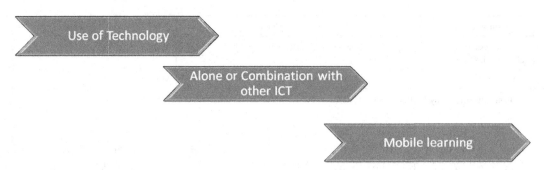

Tomorrow the list will be different. To avoid the quicksand of semantic precision, UNESCO chooses to embrace a broad definition of mobile devices, recognizing simply that they are digital, easily portable, usually owned and controlled by an individual rather than an institution, can access the internet, have multimedia capabilities, and can facilitate a large number of tasks, particularly those related to communication (UNESCO Policy Guidelines for Mobile Learning, 2013).

Current Perspectives of Mobile Learning

Current perspectives on mobile learning generally fall into the following four broad categories:

Technocentric

This perspective dominates the literature. Here mobile learning is viewed as learning using a mobile device, such as a PDA, mobile phone, iPod, PlayStation Portable etc.

Relationship to E-Learning

This perspective characterizes mobile learning as an extension of e-learning. These definitions are often are all-inclusive and do not help in characterizing the unique nature of mobile learning. What is needed is clarity: in agreement with Traxler (2005), the techno centric /e-learning based definitions

only seek to place *"mobile learning somewhere one learning's spectrum of portability"*.

Augmenting Formal Education

Formal education is often characterized as face-to-face teaching, or more specifically, as a stereotypical lecture. However, it is not at all clear that this perspective is wholly correct. Forms of distance education have existed for over 100 years (Peters, 1998), leading to the questions regarding the place of mobile learning in relation to all forms of "traditional" learning, not only the classroom.

Learner-Centred

A strong linkage of research into conceptualizing mobile learning is traceable by reviewing the combined works of Sharples, Taylor, O'Malley and their colleagues. In their early research, the concept of mobile learning was strongly linked to the device (Sharples et al., 2002) and the potential for enabling lifelong learning (Sharples, 2000). However, it soon became clear that rather than the device, the focus should be on the mobility of the learner. This led to considering mobile learning from the learner's perspective, and to the definition that:

Any sort of learning that happens when the learner is not at a fixed, predetermined location, or learning that happens when the learner takes

Figure 2. Current perspectives on mobile learning

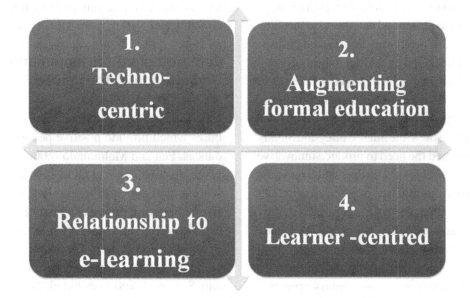

advantage of learning opportunities offered by mobile technologies (O'Malley et al., 2003).

Current work (Sharples, 2005; Taylor et al., 2006) is exploring the notion of learning in the mobile age, to develop a theory of mobile learning that builds on Engeström's conceptualization of Activity Theory and Laurillard's (2002) Conversational Framework. The focus of their work is on mobile learning as communication in context (Sharples, 2005) as shown in Figure 2.

Approaches to Implication of Mobile Devices in Classroom

There are two approaches for mobile device which may be implemented in classroom as follows:

- **Supportive Tool:** As a tool to support educators' mobile devices allow the recording and maintenance of the lessons take place, the instructional procedures, the type of mentoring and the pedagogical approach, the role of the teacher and students. Additionally, they facilitate communication between faculty members and students through file sharing capabilities, built-in networking and a friendly interface with on-line discussion, e-mail options, blogging and interaction through social networking.

- **Instructional Tool:** Mobile devices can also be used as instructional tools to constructive learning. Mobile devices can be treated as tools that help students execute their tasks and promote the balanced development of their mental abilities by functioning as intellectual partners to the instructor and the learner. Educators can provide students with electronic books, school specific context, internet reference sites, graphing calculator, dictionary, and thesaurus etc. Finally, electronic quizzes and tests can be taken through mobile devices.

Curriculum and Learning Materials

The new mobile learning arena imposes significant new design requirements of the curriculum. These requirements are not limited to the ways in which it is delivered and received but moreover in the ways the curriculum is structured and the ways in which it is maintained. Curriculum units can be project-oriented and designed by adding a technological angle in well-defined educational tasks. Furthermore, the social and the developmental value of each project task should be explicitly defined for each unit. Along the same lines, Colley and Steady in 2003 addressed the need to produce innovative material that maintains a clear perspective on the learning goal. Activities within the curriculum can be designed to take place in classroom or mainly outside the classroom as fieldwork. It is unrealistic to support that mobile devices could be used for all classroom activities. As Carboni and et al. (2005) mentioned that it is a complementary approach to the classic classroom lessons. It might not be able to deliver three hour course on a PDA but is it feasible to deliver small learning activities and a number of documents and exercises.

To produce materials and design the content to be appropriate to stimulate and support the learner, knowledge of the technological constraints should exist. Consequently, to produce acceptable learning materials for mobile devices there is a need for educators, engineers, and computer scientists to collaborate and coordinate their actions and activities.

Contents for Mobile Learning

The contents which mobile devices can be applied vary. Research so far shows that the experiments took place in various fields such as: Business and specifically MBA classes, Accounting, English, Social Studies, Mathematics, Science and Geography classes etc. Other activities include innovative games, exploring museums and exhibitions. Additionally, mobile learning devices can be used in order to evaluate students learning as well as assess attitudes to learning. Indian education system offers a diversity of fields of study where mobile devices could be incorporated. Educators are advised to insert and implement mobile devices in the context of teaching and learning in various contents and through various activities.

Technological Attributes and Pedagogical Affordances

Mobile learning has unique technological attributes which provide positive pedagogical affordances. Pea and Maldonado (2006) summarized seven features of handheld device use within schools and beyond: "portability, small screen size, computing power (immediate starting-up), diverse communication networks, a broad range of applications, data synchronization across computers, and stylus input device". As Klopfer and Squire (2008) concluded, "portability, social interactivity, context, and individuality" are frequently cited affordances of mobile learning. Specifically, *portability* is the most distinctive feature which distinguishes handheld devices from other emerging technologies, and this factor makes other technological attributes such as individuality and interactivity possible.

Above all, this mobility enables ubiquitous learning in formal and informal settings by decreasing "the dependence on fixed locations for work and study, and consequently change the way we work and learn" (Peters, 2007). Gay, Rieger, and Bennington (2002) developed the "mobility hierarchy," including four levels of objectives that encourage the use of mobile computers in education settings. This hierarchy presents the contrasting attributes of mobile devices (see table-2). The focus of "productivity" (level 1) is content-intensive, whereas the focus of collaboration and communication (level 4) is communication-intensive. Level 1 aims at individual learning, and level 4 aims at collaborative learning by multiple users. We can see that levels 2 and 3 fall into the "middle-range applications, such as personal tour guides, computer-aided instruction, database activity, mobile libraries, and electronic mail".

As this hierarchy indicates, mobile technology has two comparable attributes. Scheduling and calendar applications are useful to increase an individual's organizational skills and self-regulative or self-directed learning ability; whereas, real-time chat and data sharing applications support communication, collaboration, and knowledge construction. This shows that students can consume and create information both "collectively and individually" (Koole, 2009) and is reflected in Table 2.

Framework for Mobile Learning

In order to move from academic theorizing about mobile learning to operational and successful use frameworks are necessary. There are a variety of such frameworks and, before introducing several which educational institutions may find useful, it is worth recapping a Future lab overview from 2004 outlining six broad theory-based categories of activity shown in Table 3.

Blending Several Approaches of M-Learning

Whilst some initiatives may see mobile learning as a way to foster collaborative interactions, others may foreground more behaviorist approaches. It is possible, of course, to blend several categories of activity.

Laurillard (2002): A Conversational framework for the effective use of learning technologies

For categories of activity that can be described as Constructivist, Situated, Collaborative and/or Informal, Laurillard's Conversational Framework may be appropriate.

The main roles of mobile technology in supporting the 'conversational learning' promoted by Laurillard are therefore:

- Providing an environment to enable conversation
- Enabling learners to build models in order to solve problems

Park (2011): Pedagogical Framework for Mobile Learning

For those institutions looking for an alternative focus, Park's (2011) pedagogical framework for mobile learning is a way of understanding how 'transactional distance' and the 'social' nature of an activity can be mapped against one another. The former is defined as the 'cognitive space' between individuals whereas the latter is to what extent an activity involves interaction with others in order to be completed successfully, this is shown in Figure 4.

Koole: A Model for Framing Mobile Learning (2009)

A more holistic framework for mobile learning comes with Koole's FRAME model. This consists of a three-circle Venn diagram comprising the Learner aspect (L), the Social aspect (S) and the Device aspect (D). Taking two or more of these together at the point at which the circles overlap in the Venn diagram in Figure 5.

Koole provides criteria for each of the sections:

Mobile learning is therefore a combination of the interactions between learners, their devices, and other people, this is shown in Figure 6. Mobile learning provides enhanced collaboration among learners, access to information, and a deeper contextualization of learning. Hypothetically, effective mobile learning can empower learners by enabling them to better assess and select relevant information, redefine their goals, and reconsider their understanding of concepts within a shifting and growing frame of reference the information context (KOOLE 2009).

Table 2. Technological attributes and pedagogical affordances

Levels	Mobility Hierarchy	Sample Applications	Technological Affordances
Level 4	Communication & Collaboration	• Real- time chat • Annotation • SMS(Simple message System) • Wireless e-mail	Communication Intensive Group Work Synchronous
Level 3	Capturing & Integrating Data	• Network data base • Data collection/synthesis • Mobile library	↑ Mobility
Level 2	Flexible Physical Access	• Local Data base • Interactive Prompting • Just-in-time Instruction	↓
Level 1	Productivity	• Calendars • Schedule • Contact Information • Grading	Asynchronous Individual Work Content Incentive

Mobility hierarchy, sample application and technological affordances (Adopted from Gay,Rieger and Bennington,2002)

Table 3. Theory based categories of activity

S.No.	Theory	Activity
1	**Behaviourist**	Activities that promote learning as a change in learners' observable actions
2	**Constructivist**	Activities in which learners actively construct new ideas or concepts based on both their previous and current knowledge
3	**Situated**	Activities that promote learning within an authentic context and culture
4	**Collaborative**	Activities that promote learning through social interaction
5	**Informal and lifelong**	Activities that support learning outside a dedicated learning environment and formal curriculum
6	**Learning and teaching support**	Activities that assist in the coordination of learners and resources for learning activities.

Learning Theories and Their Influences on Learning Technologies

Although the current interest in 'e-learning' and 'm-learning' is relatively emerging phenomenon, especially fuelled by developments in the internet since the WWW was created in 1992, in fact the history of learning with technology goes back much further. In 1996 Koschmann suggests that a reasonable starting point is the development in 1960 0f IBM's first courseware authoring system of CAL, the Kuhnian term which Koschman borrows implies radical shifts in ways of think-ing about learning. However, this may be, on the one hand, an idealized view- much of the world of ICT in education still operates on primitive CAL models of the 1960s, even if the technology is new (i.e. the World Wide Web). However some of those theories have proved the most successful in developing tutoring system with a huge amount of empirical evidence for their effectiveness-this is particularly so of John Anderson's work with the ACT family of tutorial system. Similarly, whilst the predominant in CSCL is based on socio-cultural theory of one form or another (suited learning, activity theory, distributed cognition, and so on),

Figure 3. A Conversational framework for the effective use of learning technologies
Laurillard (2002)

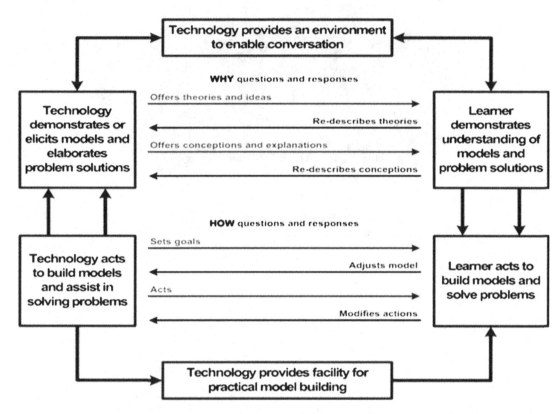

Figure 4. Pedagogical framework for mobile learning, Park (2011)

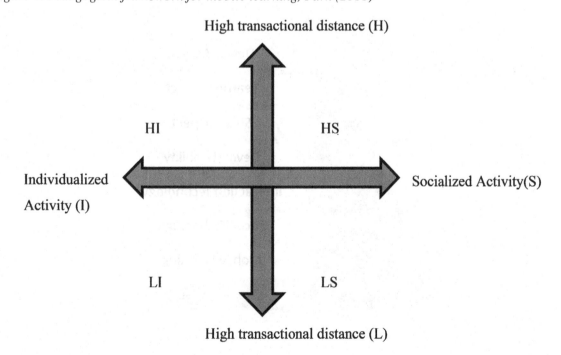

Figure 5. A model for framing mobile learning, Koole: (2009)

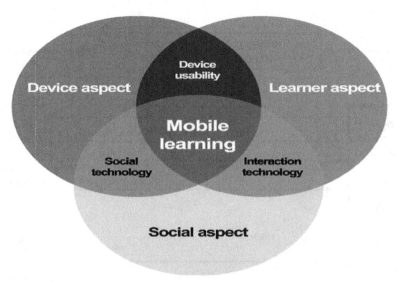

Figure 6. Criteria for framing mobile learning

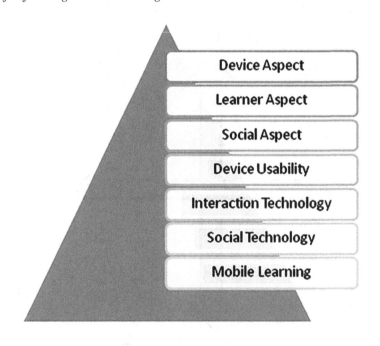

few would want to deny that learning also involves changes occurring at the level of the individual learners. In fact activity theory was developed as a means of analyzing how individual representations could be changed and mediated by social and cultural artifacts, tools and signs.

In the light of these theories, there has been made an effort to examine in what extent, these are useful in thinking about mobile learning contexts, both in formal and informal setting.

Associationism and CAL

The early developments in learning technology during the 1960s were framed by the possibilities offered by the then technology and influenced by the predominant theories of learning of the time-associationism and behaviourism.

The technology of the time involved initially the use of teleprinters, of line printers, and then the development of CRT monitors capable of displaying alphanumeric character of 24 lines and 80 characters per line. The software technologies of the time involved the development and use of high level programming languages such as FORTRAN and PASCAL. Later developments, particularly in high level courseware tools i.e., Course writer, enabled non-programmers to develop courseware.

The learning theories of the time involved the application of Skinner's brand of behaviourism, which held that learning involved the application between a stimulus and a response, enabled by re-inforcement. The method of operant conditioning was used to shape responses to particular stimuli. In terms of application to learning technology, the approach has been characterized as "drill and practice" and then they are given feedback on their response. It was very much a transmission model of teaching, with the tutor seen as driving the learning process.

In terms of its legacy today, CAL remains as a widely used approach, even if the technology is now the World Wide Web and more recently the PDA in some applications of mobile learning.

Information Processing Theory and ITS'

The 1970s was the time of origin of the cognitive revolution and a focus on mental representations and the content of learning and problem solving, absent in the behaviourist paradigm. With respect to general theories of learning under the information processing paradigm, two strands of research have been, debatably, outstanding. The first derives from the work on the General Problem Solver (GPS) by Alan Newell (1969) and Herb Simon (1972). In this approach, learning is seen as a matter of problem solving and proceeds as a function of memory operations, control processes and rules. The methodology for testing the theory involved developing a computational model (GPS) and then comparing the result of the simulation with behaviour in a given task.

GPS was intended to provide a core set of process that could be used to solve a variety of different types of problems. The critical step in solving a problem with GPS is the different types of the problem space in terms of the goal to be achieved and the transformation rules.

While GPS was intended to be a general problem-solver, it could only be applied to well-defined problems such as proving theorems in logic or geometry, word puzzles and chess. However GPS was the basis for other theoretical work by Newell et al. such as SOAR.

SOAR is an architecture for human cognition expressed in the form of a production system (Laird,N. and Rosenbloom,1987)the principal element in SOAR is the idea of a problem space; all cognitive acts are some form of search task. Memory is unitary and procedural; there is no distinction between procedural and declarative memory. Newell in 1990, proposed SOAR as the basis for unified theory of cognition and attempt to show how it explains a wide range of past results and phenomena. For example, he provided interpretations for response time data, verbal learning tasks, reasoning tasks, mental models and skill acquisition. In addition, versions of SOAR have been developed that perform as intelligent systems for configuring computer system and formulating algorithms.

Constructivism: Interactive learning environments

The 1980s was the arrival of the era of the individual computer, with the capability for presenting not only just text, but graphics, video and sound, and input via many different devices such as apps, mice, joysticks and so on with android features, rather than just key boards. These direct manipulation interfaces presented many more possibilities for interactive learning activities. This period saw the two paradigm shifts- to human – centered computing and learner centered education were ripe for exploitation. The chief designer of this was Seymour Papert's approach, summed up famously in his seminal book Mindstorms (1980) was inspired by, if not derived from, Piagetian theory. Aspects of Piaget's developmental theory which Papert took up comprised a view of the learner as actively constructing knowledge, rather than more passively responding to a tutorial action, and a serious endeavor to take up Piaget's arguments about the importance of the physical activity of the learner, particularly his theory of sensory motor intelligence and the internationalization of physical action. With the right tools, Papert argued, the child could learn to gradually abstract principles from reflecting upon the relation between action and perception. The tool he developed for this progressive construction of rule was LOGO.

Case Based Learning

Case based learning propounded by Kolodner and Guzdial in 2000 is one of a number of pedagogical approaches that use concrete situations, i.e. problems or scenarios as a starting point for learning by analogy and abstraction through reflection. A similar view can be perceived in anchored instruc-

tion. In many ways these approaches could come under the section on socio-culture theory, since they represent some of the characteristics of the situated learning approach. However, they vary from situated learning in that the cases, examples or problems are not necessarily selected by learners; neither do they necessarily involve learner's own problem situations.

Problem- Based Learning

Problem – based learning advocated by Koschmann, T.in1996 is a similar approach. It is fairly broadly used in medical education (Albanees & Mitchell, 1993), business administration (Merchant, 1995; Stinson&Milter, 1995) and nursing(Higgins,1994), amongst others. As Koschmann,T.,Kelson, Feltovich and Barrows in 1996 explain it. PBL starts from the observation of Koschmann,T. et al. in1996 that "existing educational systems are producing individuals who fail to develop a valid, robust knowledge- base; who have difficulty reasoning and applying knowledge; and who lack the ability to reflect upon their performance and continue the process of learning"

Generally, PBL is an example of a collaborative, case – centered and learner – directed method of instruction. In its ideal implementation, a small group of students having five or six, together with a PBL tutor or coach, learn in the procedure of working through a collection of clinical teaching cases. Through- out the process of construction a case students create learning issues-areas of knowledge in which members of the group feel they are not sufficiently prepared for understanding the problem they are studying.

In this approach, there is considerable potential in adapting some of the PBL approach in mobile learning. It has been developed and refined especially for context involving life- long learning and professional development. It has had some proven success as a pedagogical strategy in domains of relevance to mobile learning, especially medicine and business administration.

Mobile Device: Development and Learning Possibilities in India

India has a significant base of mobile telecom subscriptions, about 950 million in the third quarter of 2012, according to the Telecom Regulatory Authority of India (TRAI, 2013). Besides this very large number, the speed of range of mobile telephony in India is a vital factor to reminder, with tele-density (number of telephone lines per 100 population) moving from under 4.38 in 2001 (Minges & Simkhada, 2002) to 67.67 in 2011 (ITU, 2011). The urban tele-density is thought be over 100. The spread in rural areas is lower than in urban areas and the TRAI estimates that the number of rural subscriptions as of June 2012 is between 150 million and 160 million. The rural population accounts for 68% of the total population, according to the Census of India, 2011. A typical handset with a rural user is likely to be a basic instrument with voice and texting capabilities. Most such handsets cannot display characters in Indian languages, thus making voice the principal medium of use.

Scenario of Mobile Learning in India with Special Reference to Rural Areas

India has 791 million mobile subscribers according to regulatory body TRAI with a significant share in villages. That is the target group several start-ups and educational institutions are looking at. Krishna Durbha, head of value added services, mobile data and content at Reliance Communications, said, "Mobile is a viable medium for basic education. The mobile learning space is completely new and is waiting to grow. There is a lot of opportunity but there is a need to find the right content. Touch screen and large screen formats will do wonders and they need to be available at cheaper rates. With good network and connectivity we can do lots. We are promoting mobile learning with some

large foreign organizations in social sector with roots in India".

"Mobiles can penetrate better as they have things in favour like better battery life and people do not need any training to operate it. This gives it an upper hand over computers," Sunil Abraham, ED, Center for Internet and Society, said. According to Vikram Nagaich, director and founder, Innovate Edu, on one side, with mobile phones the reach of the content could be very wide. However, the efficacy would have to be delivered through extremely innovative and sophisticated content. For those institutions looking for an alternative focus, Park's (2011) pedagogical framework for mobile learning is a way of understanding how 'transactional distance' and the 'social' nature of an activity can be mapped against one another. Launched in 2009, Nokia Life has brought information and educational opportunities to over 90 million people in India, China, Indonesia and Nigeria (UNESCO policy guidelines for mobile learning, 2013).Towards the promotion of education remotely, SNDT Women's University, Tata Tele Services Ltd., Atom Tech, Mumbai, & Indian PCO Tele-services Ltd have entered into a strategic alliance to develop and disseminate mobile education, an additional vehicle in distance learning, to reach the masses for remote teaching and learning in rural communities and physically challenged.(India's First M-Education Service, 2013).Indian telco-Bharti-Airtel has launched a range of affordable mobile education services, dubbed m-Education, allowing customers access to services such as English lessons, exam preparation and career advice over their handsets (Yap, J.2013).Mobile learning space is rapidly evolving in India and thus is playing a significant role in imparting education. The significance of this medium is slowly and steadily being realized by players in various industries, who are constantly developing the necessary applications to work towards mobile education. The key drivers behind growth of this sector include high portability, small size, low price, adaptable technology of mobile devices and most importantly, its increasing penetration in the country. Anticipating the future potential, several telecoms have started offering m-education services, such as English lessons, dial-in tutorials, school syllabi, question sets, vocabulary general knowledge tutorials, exam tips, exam result alerts and education for the physically challenged. Operators usually partner with software companies to develop these applications. As per our estimation, penetration of m-learning in MVAS is around 7-12% in India, which is expected to grow significantly in the coming years.

Enable M Technologies currently provides multiple m-learning solutions to five operators, including BSNL. Amit Zaveri, chief operating officer, Enable M, says, "We manage the entire learning portfolio for Nokia and also power some of the content. We are also planning to go to Bangladesh. We see a lot of opportunity in the emerging markets as there is low bandwidth and dissemination of content is not standardized. We have already seen a lot of traction. We have a two-pronged strategy - we work with telcos and Nokia, as well as with closed user groups such as corporates, publishers and government."

Overview of Telecom Services in India

In today's cutting age of information and technology, the telecommunication industry has a vigorous role to play. Considered as the pillar of industrial and economic development, the industry has been aiding delivery of voice and data services at rapidly increasing speeds, and thus, has been reforming human communication.

Although the Indian telecom industry is one of the fastest-growing industries in the world, the current tele-density or telecom penetration is extremely low when compared with global standards. India's tele-density of 36.98% in FY09 is amongst the lowest in the world. Further, the urban tele-density is over 80%, while rural tele-density is less than 20%, and this gap is increasing. As majority of the population resides in rural areas, it is important that the government takes steps to improve rural tele-density. No doubt the government has taken certain policy initiatives, which include the creation of the Universal Service Obligation Fund, for improving rural telephony. These measures are expected to improve the rural tele-density and bridge the rural-urban gap in tele-density

The changing demographic profile of India has also played an important role in subscriber growth. The changed profile is characterized by a large young population, a burgeoning middle class with growing disposable income, urbanization, increasing literacy levels and higher adaptability to technology. These new features have multiplied the need to be connected always and to own a wireless phone and therefore, in present times mobiles are perceived as a utility rather than a luxury.

The telecom industry in India has experienced greater growth over the past few years and has been an important contributor to economic growth as well as educational growth; however, the cut-throat competition and strong tariff wars have had a negative impact on the revenue of players. Despite the challenges, the Indian telecom industry will flourish because of the vast potential in terms of new users. The government is keen on developing rural telecom infrastructure and is also set to roll out next generation or 3G services in the country. Operators are on an expansion mode and are investing heavily on telecom infrastructure. Foreign telecom companies are acquiring considerable stakes in Indian companies. Mushrooming middle class and growing spending power, the government's thrust on increasing rural telecom coverage, favorable investment climate and positive reforms will ensure that India's high potential is indeed realized.

Mobile Evolution in India: Market Realities

According the report of Telecom Regulatory Authority of India's Indicator, June, 2012 the number of telephone subscribers in India increased from 951.34 million at the end of March 2012 to 965.52 million at the end of June, 2012, registering a growth of 1.49% over the previous quarter as against 2.68% during the Quarter Ending March, 2012. This reflects year-on-year growth of 8.98% over the same quarter of last year. The overall Tele density in India has reached 79.58 as on 30th June, 2012. Subscription in urban areas grew from 620.53 million at the end of March, 2012 to 621.76 million at the end of June 2012; however Urban Tele-density slightly declined from 169.55 to 169.03. Rural subscription increased from 330.82 million to 343.76 million, and Rural Tele-density increased from 39.22 to 40.66. Share of subscription in rural areas out of total subscription increased from 34.77% at the end of March, 2012 to 35.60% at the end of June 2012. About 91.30% of the total net additions have been in rural areas as compared to 62.39% in the previous quarter. Rural subscription growth rate decreased from 4.91% in Quarter Ending March 2012 to 3.91% in Quarter Ending June 2012, and urban subscription growth rate declined from 1.53% in Quarter Ending March 2012 to 0.20% in Quarter Ending June 2012.

With 14.92 million net additions during the quarter, total wireless (GSM+CDMA) subscriber base registered a growth of 1.62% over the previous quarter and increased from 919.17 million at the end of March 2012 to 934.09 million at the end of June 2012. The year-on-year (Y-O-Y) growth rate of Wireless subscribers for June 2012 is 9.67%. Wireless Teledensity increased from 76.00 at the end of March 2012 to 76.99 at the end of June 2012.

Monthly Average Revenue per User (ARPU) for GSM service declined by 1.94%, from Rs. 97 in QE (Quarter Ending) March 2012 to Rs. 95 in QE (Quarter Ending) June 2012, with Y-O-Y decrease of 2.11%.MOU per subscriber per month for GSM service remained almost at the same level as in the previous quarter i.e. 346. The Outgoing MOUs (167) increased by 0.04% whereas Incoming MOUs (178) declined by 0.19%. Monthly ARPU for CDMA – full mobility service slightly declined by 0.50%, from 75.3 in QE(Quarter Ending) March 2012 to 74.9 in QE June 2012. ARPU for CDMA has increased by 16.31% on Y-O-Y basis.

The total MOU for CDMA per subscriber per month declined by 0.31%, from 229.3 in QE March 2012 to 228.6 QE June 2012. The Outgoing MOUs (115) declined by 1.57% whereas Incoming MOUs (114) increased by 1%.Gross Revenue (GR) and Adjusted Gross Revenue (AGR) of Telecom Service Sector for the QE June 2012 has been Rs. 52512.10 crores and Rs. 35499.01 crores respectively. There has been an increase of 6.64% in GR and an increase of 3.02% in AGR as compared to previous quarter.

Mobile Learning Network in India

Mobile phones can play a significant role in imparting education in India. The importance of this medium is slowly but steadily being realized by players in the telecom industry, who are now developing the necessary applications to work towards mobile education (m-education or m-learning). Several tele-companies have in progress offering m-education services such as English lessons, dial-in tutorials, school syllabi, question sets, vocabulary general knowledge tutorials, exam tips, exam result alerts and education for the physically challenged. These operators usually partner with VAS companies to develop the applications. In present many service operators provides various educational assistance as listed within Figure 7.

At current, many prominent operators are providing m-education services and applications to their subscribers. Aircel, the fifth largest

Figure 7. Telecom services in India

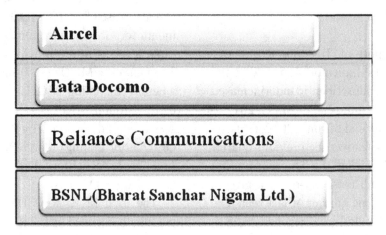

GSM player in the country by subscribers, offers education related services through its m-Gurujee application. The app allows users access to content in areas of engineering, management, civil services and medicine; school syllabi of CBSE and ICSE boards as well as skill development, vocabulary and general knowledge tutorials. A user can subscribe to m-Gurujee and get access to learning content in practice, quiz, timed or tutorial mode. When the user finalizes a question set or the time is over, the results are displayed promptly. The operator charges Rs 5 per question set and Rs 30 per month for subscription to a question set.

Another GSM operator, Tata Docomo, provides an English Seekho service through its mobile portal, Tata Zone. It allows users to take conversational English language lessons on their mobiles through an interactive voice response (IVR) application that guides the user through audio clips. It offers short lessons followed by interactive lessons which enable users to practice what they have learnt through the mobile's keys or through speech recognition. The subscription fee for this service is Rs 20 per month and call charges are 60 paise per minute. It is available in 24 cities.

Reliance Communications too has been doing some work on this front through its mobile portal, R-World. The company first launched an

m-education service in 2003 called m-school, where teachers and parents could access data bases of schools and register queries and complaints. R-Com provides exam results, career counseling, etiquette and grooming sessions. It also provides English learning based on translations in rural areas through its Grameen VAS initiative

State-owned telco BSNL has also started offering an English learning service for its subscribers. It has launched a spoken English program, Learn English, which has been designed by Mumbai-based mobile content provider Enable M Technologies in association with Bangalore-based On Mobile Global. The program teaches spoken English through simple stories and everyday situations that a common man can relate to. Subscribers have the option of selecting their level of learning, based on their proficiency in the language. Daily SMS and practice tests are a part of the package, which is available in nine Indian languages. It also allows subscribers to receive a new word daily through SMS. The subscription cost for this is Rs 20 per month and call browsing charges are 30 paise per minute.

Table 4. Possible learning features of mobile learning

Category	Possible Learning Features
News and Information	Twitter, Reddit: Real-time, citizen reporting, global reach
Note Taking	Evernote: Always synced, multi-device, searchable digital files
Files and Folders	Dropbox, Google Drive, SugarSync: Always synced always accessible, multi- device searchable digital files
Magazines	Flipboard and Currents: More content, always up to date,personalized, access everywhere, share
Education	Khan Academy, Coursera: Interactive, online and accessible by anyone anywhere anytime
Digital Goods	eBay, Amazon: Show-rooming, shopping on the go

Features and Attributes of Mobile as a Learning Tool

The use of mobile phones is attracting considerable interest in the fields of teaching and learning. In India, Every person is access mobile for various uses but still it is surprisingly, there is relatively little systematic knowledge about how mobile devices can be used effectively for learning. Mobile learning is an exciting opportunity for educators, but in many ways we are just scratching the surface of all that can be achieved with it. With appropriate training, and time to explore these high-tech gadgets, teachers will soon be able make rapid strides with them, and be able to support and instruct the use of such devices in the classroom on a regular basis. Now is the time to act. Our digital natives are counting on us. Before the implication of this gadget, we should know the potentialities and attributes of mobile learning. Some possible and major features of m-learning are enlisted within Table 4 and Table 5.

Table 5. Major features of mobile learning

Associating Creation and Sharing of Content
Bridging Learning for with Learning at Work
↓
Bridging Individual and Social Learning
Bridging Informal and Formal Learning Contexts
Bridging (Socio-) Cognitive, Cultural, and Constructivist Perspectives

Pedagogical Methods and Instructional Approaches for Mobile Learning

Some might suggest that m-learning technologies support individualism others might say that it facilitates the application of constructivist techniques where collaboration and team work is enhanced and promoted. We can support that there is a need for a shared, progressive pedagogy for mobile learning that will provide the scientific basis for networked and collaborative learning in both a virtual and a virtual-augmented environment. It must accommodate different teacher- and learner perspectives, promote learner-centered environments and collaboration among learners and between learners and educators.

In mobile learning curriculum should be techno-centric and learner oriented. So that it is a basic need to explore the learners need and analyze it at micro-level. In second phase objective should be decided very carefully. On the basis of need and developed objectives, instructional methods should be implemented thereafter need to examine out-put. Out-put should be evaluated because this out-put is obligatory for feedback. Feed-back works as instrument by which objectives are revised and need are again review. This process enrich curriculum. Curriculum is foundations of content delivery. In mobile learning, content delivery associated with three components i.e. administration, management and marketing. Systematic evaluation process enhanced the quality of all these components which make sure the quality of the content delivery by mobile learning shown in Figure 8.

Mobile technologies, with their reduced size and ease of use, provide the potential to support such activities. With regard to accidental learning, learning episodes are impossible to predict. The personal and portable nature of mobile technologies makes them very strong candidates for recording, reflecting on and sharing this type of informal learning. For the generating pedagogy of mobile learning we should follow the essentials of traditional learning. In traditional learning, first of all we have to develop the curriculum according to need and requirements of learner and then we design instructional method and implement the same. Thereafter we evaluate the achievement of learner. On the basis of learners achievement we gets feedback for the improvement of curriculum. In mobile learning, we need to develop content and convert it into digital format. Administration, management and marketing is involved as a primarily attributes of mobile learning. Pedagogy of mobile learning is simply based on innovative technology and follows needs and requirements of learner.

Concept of Mobile Internet

Mobile Internet denotes to any form of Internet access on a mobile device – feature phones, smartphones and tablets. This sorting is not based on the mode of access. Therefore all forms of access comprising 2.5G (GPRS), 3G, 4G, Wi-Fi connections from fixed Internet and even dongles can be classified as mobile Internet access only if the access device is a mobile device. In some places, due to data availability issues and their relative significance levels, 2.5G and/or 3G metrics may be taken as proxies for mobile Internet users.

Association between Internet and Mobile Learning

Mobile learning combines E-learning and mobile computing. Mobile learning is sometimes considered simply an extension of E-learning, but excellence M-learning can only be delivered with an awareness of the special limitations and benefits of mobile devices. Mobile learning has the benefits of flexibility and its supporting platform. M-learning is a means to enhance the broader learning experience. M-learning is a influential method for engaging learners on their own terms.

Figure 8. Pedagogical perspective of mobile learning

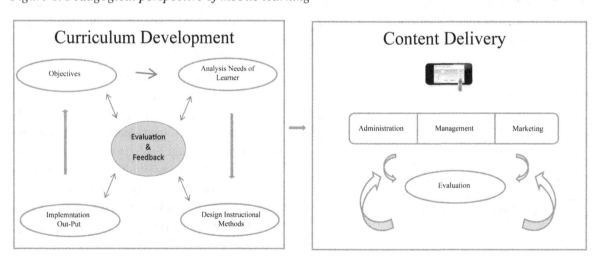

Table 6. E-learning and m-learning associationism

Functionality and Novelty		Mobility		
Computer	Laptop	PDA's handhelds palmtop	Smart Phones	Mobile Phones
E-Learning		Mobile Learning		

Figure 9. Relationship between m-learning & e-learning

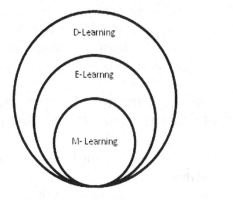 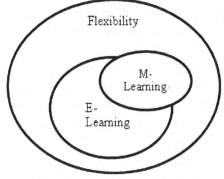

Perspective of learning paradigms
(Georgiev et al., 2004)

Relationship of E-learning, M-learning
& Flexible Learning (Low and O'Connell, 2006)

(Cited in Behera, S. K. International Journal on New Trends in Education and Their Implications, July 2013 Volume: 4 Issue: 3)

E-learning and M-learning diagrammatically mentioned below:

Though there are some differences lies between E-learning and M-learning, they are closely related. M-learning is a sub-set of E-learning. Their relationships are diagrammatically given in Figure 9.

Mobile technology is allowed to open several ways for new educational technologies intended at achieving the country's scholastic needs. There are numerous means to use mobile phones for augmenting learning. Mobile phones ensure an important role in our day-to-day lives in many purposes. One of the important purposes is learning. Mobile learning, as a novel educational approach, encourages flexibility; students do not need to be a specific age, gender, or member of a specific group or geography, to participate in learning opportunities. Restrictions of time, space and place have been lifted. These lucrative features explore association among e-learning, m-learning and d-learning. With special reference to India the following association may be observed:

- The ground-breaking success of India's mobile industry is well known. What is not as well expressed is how the mobile ecosystem is driving Internet penetration in India. The following facts present a preview of that phenomenon:

- India has more than 160 million Internet users, of which 86 million accesses Internet using their mobile devices.
- In the last 3-4 years, the numbers of users who access the Internet through a 3G connection has grown to round 22 million, To put things in perspective, compare this with the 15 million fixed line broadband connections accrued over the last 17 years.
- There are over 36 million smartphone users as against c. 60 million PC users9% of overall Internet page-views in India come from mobile devices.
- Over 40% of searches on Google originate from mobile device 30% of Facebook users in India are mobile-only Internet users and 30% of new registrations are coming through mobile.
- LinkedIn ranks India among its top 4 growth markets for mobile usage Is mobile connectivity infrastructure falling in place?

With all above mentioned realities, we can associate internet services with mobile learning for effective out-put in following way:

- Actual usage of mobile Internet.
- Adequate content, getting created to keep the user engaged.
- Content players should be able to tackle piracy issues, and get users to pay.
- Payment infrastructure should be affordable.
- Advertising opportunities will be appropriate.

Activities Related to Internet

All these internet related activities may be assigned into four basic categories (Gnanasambandam, 2012):

- Uses of Web for support, for example e-commerce, content creation and distribution, and online advertising.
- Telecommunications on Internet protocol (IP) or linked to IP communication (mainly Internet service providers).
- Software and services activities linked to the Internet, such as IT consulting and software development.
- Hardware manufacturers or maintenance providers of Web-specific tools, for example, computers, smartphones, network equipment, and servers.

Mobile Learning: The Prospect of Distance Education in India

Mobile learning space is rapidly evolving in India and thus is playing a significant role in imparting education. The significance of this medium is slowly and steadily being realized by players in various industries, who are constantly developing the necessary applications to work towards mobile education. The key drivers behind growth of this sector include high portability, small size, low price, adaptable technology of mobile devices and most importantly, its increasing penetration in the country. Again, the government support in distributing low-cost tablets (Akash) to students is also propelling the market.

Anticipating the future potential, several telecoms have started offering m-education services, such as English lessons, dial-in tutorials, school syllabi, question sets, vocabulary general knowledge tutorials, exam tips, exam result alerts and education for the physically challenged. Operators usually partner with software companies to develop these applications. As per estimation, penetration of m-learning in MVAS is around 7-12% in India, which is expected to grow significantly in the coming years.

A report, "Indian Distance Learning Market Analysis"(2012), spread in across 45 pages provides an in-depth research and rational analysis of the current status and expected position of the distance education system in India. It also presents an overview of the various government initiatives in India to promote distance learning along with the regulatory norms required to enter into this market.

Additionally, it provides coherent analysis of the demand of higher education in the country during the next few years and based on it determines how distance education market will move in future. Apart from telcos, institutions such as the Indira Gandhi National Open University (IGNOU) have initiated basic mobile services for students spread across the country. IGNOU is using an SMS model for exam alerts, which is available in five regional sectors in India and has a network of 30,000 to 50,000 students.

Nokia Mobile and Learning Solutions started a project in 2008 entitled *Mobile Learning for Mathematics* in collaboration with the South African government. The service, which delivers study packages to students' phones, was highly successful. Two hundred and eighty students in six schools participated in the program's first phase, and 4,000 students and 72 teachers in 30 schools participated in its second phase.

The Juxt (2013) study reveals that India already has more mobile users in its villages as compared to its cities and towns. More than 298 million (54 percent) of the 554.8 million mobile users are in rural areas as compared to 256 million users in urban areas. Despite this, rural India provides ample scope for growth as the dispersion is just 36 percent. In contrast, in urban India, the diffusion has reached 70 percent. While the overall penetration in urban areas looks fairly high, it does not necessarily mean that the market is fully saturated. In fact, there are individual demographic segments both within rural and urban India that operators can target.

With more than 700 million people in rural India, mobile education is an innovative concept with the potential to impact a large scale of the population. However, the basic content delivered

via mobile technology seems better suited for students already attending school.

India must focus on tackling some of its more pressing issues concerning rural education—such as teacher quality and accountability, socioeconomic hurdles, limited resources and student retention—prior to shifting its focus to mobile learning. Only once these issues are addressed can mobile learning serve as an effective supplement to—though not replacement for—an education.

Although many efforts has been done by Indian Government but it is required to link all these efforts with pedagogical paradigms. There is a need to develop content according to relevant models which must be based on appropriate theory. Now mobile is easy access to majority of persons therefore we have to trained our educators to assist their students with mobile learning and also develop awareness to access education through this device. As a result, educators and trainers must design learning materials for delivery on different types of mobile devices. The design of learning materials for mobile devices must follow good learning theories and proper instructional design for the learning to be excellent.

The Design Model of Mobile Learning for Distance Learner

During the last decade, the methodologies used within the distance learning programmes for instructing and course-content production, have been enhanced to incorporate a blend of printed, electronic and where possible face-to-face methods. This has enabled the programme to innovate with distance learning pedagogy and encourage constructivist approaches situated in the learner context that support collaborative and interactive learning activities.

The basic premise of distance learning is that it is not feasible to equip learners at school, college or university with all the knowledge and skills they need to prosper throughout their lifetimes. Therefore, people will need continually to

Table 7. The convergence of distance learning and mobile learning

Distance Learning	Mobile Learning
Individualised	Personal
Learner centred	User centred
Situated	Mobile
Collaborative	Networked
Omnipresent	Omnipresent
Lifelong	Durable

enhance their knowledge and skills, in order to address immediate problems and to participate in a process of continuing vocational and professional development.

M-learning offers the potential to look at a design model for distance learning that starts with what 'Communication for Development' pioneer Don Snowden referred to as 'the first mile'. As connectivity improves the mobile learner becomes empowered to:

- Take their own responsibility for learning anywhere and anytime,
- Interact with and learn from fellow students globally,
- Access formal and informal learning environments and social software,
- Involve in the process of generating learning resources.

These attributes and potentialities of mobile device offer a suggestive model for distance learner. Prerequisite of this model is to generate an open learning environment, relevant mobile assisted content and also facilitate mobile device to learners, so that learner avail required apps and update their knowledge. Demographic variables do not matter to communicate learner from one end to another. Mobile learning makes them able to explore global knowledge. It is well known that in present scenario, social networking is playing a pivotal role to develop awareness and

consciousness among human being. Now people are being aware their surroundings. By providing digital learning opportunities we can eradicate illiteracy and improve the quality of mankind. All the features of mobile learning indicate the hope of ray for learners particularly who are deprived from formal education and facing various kind of disparities. There has been making a humble effort to suggest a design model of mobile learning for distance learner is given in Figure 10.

CONCLUSION

The new mobile learning arena imposes significant new requirements not only for the technological support and implementation but also for the educational perspective. Talking about technological challenge we mean that we must find ways to create and set up highly supportive environments which could provide support to contribute to different kind of learning settings. A technological opportunity is the fundamental transformation from the existing online learning using the advantages of 3G mobile phones and wireless communication networking. Along the same lines, the pedagogical challenge related to m-learning is to find ways on how mobile devices can be integrated into classroom activities as well as successfully address all the parameters related to and influence mobile devices integration in education. A pedagogical opportunity is that the m-learning widens the educational horizons of students as well as enhances the educational options for educators.

Mobile technologies provide for each student to have a personal interaction with the technology in an authentic and appropriate context of use help today's. This does not mean, however that the use of mobile devices is a panacea. Significant technological and administrative challenges are encountered along with more ill-defined challenges: how cans the use of mobile technologies help today's educators to embrace a truly learner

Figure 10. Model of M-Learning for distance learner

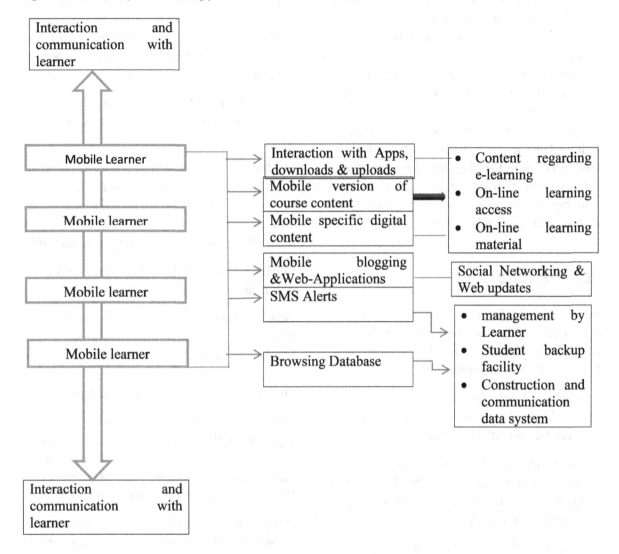

–centered approach to learning. At present, most companies offering m-learning directly or indirectly consider the industry to be very small but see a lot of opportunity in this space with newer applications coming in. Mobile technologies encourage students to be able to study in new ways when they travel and move between technologically diverse locations. Laptop computers provide an example of this, and transform work and study, particularly when wireless connectivity supports connection to the Internet. Mobile phones take this a stage further, and particularly for students based in developing countries where Internet diffusion is limited, this can make a major difference. Mobile learning can effectively support a wide range of activities for learners of all ages.

Talking about the possibilities of m-learning, Sangeet Chowla, (Executive Vice-President of Comviva) states "The learning experience on mobile phones can change dramatically if interactivity comes in. With a higher Band-width, m-learning has the opportunity to get much more interactive. Use of video clips to explain a procedure such as how to change a car tyre, training of employees and vocational stuff will be a big opportunity area. Companies will make use of mobiles for employee training. Enterprise learning is a huge opportunity".

Distance learning is really approaching of age, and offering vast opportunity for innovative resolutions. Most significantly, when m-learning approaches become embedded and entirely accessible, distance learning also has the potential to be used purposefully to address the access constraints to higher education in developed and developing countries, and support organizational training and professional development in new ways.

REFERENCES

Behera, S. K. (2013). E- and m-learning: A comparative study. *International Journal on New Trends in Education and Their Implications, 4*(3). Retrieved from www.ijonte.org

Bereiter, C. (1999). *Education and Mind for the Knowledge Age*. Retrieved from http://csile.oise.utoronto.ca/edmind/edmind.html

Bhattacharjee, S. (2010). *Mobile learning seeks growth curve in India*. Retrieved from http://www.mahindracomviva.com/media/Mobilelearning-seeksgrowthcurveinIndia.pdf

Bhinde, A., et al. (2013). *India's mobile internet: The revolution has begun: An overview of how mobile internet is touching the lives of millions*. Retrieved from http://www.avendus.com/Files/Fund%20Performance%20PDF/Avendus_Report-India's_Mobile_Internet-2013.pdf

Bonk, C. J., & King, K. S. (Eds.). (1998). *Electronic collaborators: Learner-centered technologies for literacy, apprenticeship, and discourse*. Mahwah, NJ: Erlbaum.

Brown, M., & Bewsell, D. (2009). Is elearning a viable option to face-to-face workshops for generating and sharing information within the New Zealand sheep and beef industry?. *Extension Farming Systems Journal, 5* (2)

Brown, T. H. (2005). Towards a model for m-learning in Africa. *International Journal on E-Learning, 4*(3).

Doubler, S., Laferriere, T., Lamon, M., & Rose, R. (2000). *The Next Generation of Online Teacher Learning: A White Paper for the Innovative Learning and Technology Center*. Retrieved from http://www.cilt.org/seedgrant/ online_Learning.html

EduTech. (2012). A World Bank Blog on ICT use in Education. *Education year in Review*.

Gnanasambandam, C., Madgavkar, A., Kaka, N., Manyika, J., Malcolm, G., & Bughin, J. (2012). *Online and upcoming: The Internet's impact on India*. Retrieved from www.Online_and_Upcoming_The_internets_impact_on_India.pdf

Heinecke, W. F., Blasi, L., Milman, N., & Washington, L. (1999). *New directions in the evaluation of the effectiveness of educational technology*. Paper presented at the Secretary's Conference on Educational Technology. Washington, DC.

Herrington, A. (2009). *Design principles for mobile learning, Research on line*. University of Wollongong.

India's First M-Education Service. (2013). Retrieved From http://itvoir.com/portal/

Jordaan, D., & Smith, P. (2012). *Going Mobile with Distance Learners*. Retrieved from http://wikieducator.org/images/8/88/PID_631.pdf

Juxt. (2013). *India Has 143 Mn Internet Users*. Retrieved from http://www.lightreading.in/lightreadingindia/news-wire-feed/271931/india-143-mn-internet-usersjuxt?utm_source=referrence_article

Kay, A. C. (1972). A Personal Computer for Children of All Ages. In *Proceedings of the ACM National Conference*. Retrieved from http://www.mprove.de/diplom/gui/kay72.html

Khanna, N. (2011). *Mobile learning: Worth the effort?* Retrieved from http://beyondprofit.com/mobile-learning-worth-the-effort/

Kukulska-Hulme, A., & Traxler, J. (2005). *Mobile learning: A handbook for educators and trainers*. London: Routledge.

Lamon, M., Scardamalia, M., Shaw, P., & Fullan, M. (2001). *School Improvement through Learning Communities: Virtual and Real*. Toronto: Final Report for the Ontario Ministry of Education and Training.

Lincoln, Y. S. (2000). *Data matrices vs. case studies: Strengths, weaknesses and benefits compared*. Unpublished report prepared for the Second Information Technology in Education Study (SITES-M2) Project.

Martinovic, D., Pugh, T., & Magliaro, J. (2010). Pedagogy for Mobile Learning Using Videoconferencing Technology. *Interdisciplinary Journal of Information, Knowledge, and Management, 5*, 375–393.

Mobile Edu'n Services Proposed By 'Bharati Airtel'. (n.d.). Retrieved from http://education.oneindia.in/news/2013/01/03/mobile-education-services-proposed-by-bharti-airtel-003626.html

Mobile learning: the future of distance education in India. (2012). Retrieved from http://www.rncos.com/press_releases/mobile-learning-the-future-of-distance-education-in-india.htmshare

Neale, D. C., & Carroll, J. C. (1999, December). *Multi-faceted evaluation for complex, distributed activities*. Paper presented at the Computer Supported Collaborative Learning Conference. Stanford University.

Owston, R. D. (1997). The World Wide Web: A technology to enhance teaching and learning? *Educational Researcher, 26*(2), 27–33.

Owston, R. D. (2000). Evaluating Web-based learning environments: Strategies and insights. *Cyberpsychology & Behavior, 3*(1), 79–87. doi:10.1089/109493100316256

Owston, R. D. (2001, February). *Final Report: Case Studies of GrassRoots Implementations* (Centre for the Study of Computers in Education Technical Report No. 2001-1). Toronto: York University, Faculty of Education. Retrieved from http://www.edu.yorku.ca/csce

Park, Y. (2011). A Pedagogical Framework for Mobile Learning: Categorizing Educational Applications of Mobile Technologies into Four Types. *International Review of Research in Open and Distance Learning, 12*(2).

Parsons, D. (2013). *The Future of Mobile Learning and Implications for Education and Training*. Retrieved from http://www.christoph.pimmer.info/wp-content/uploads/2008/08/Pimmer-Pachler-Mobile-Learning-in-the-Workplace1.pdf

Pea, R., & Maldonado, H. (2006). WILD for learning: Interacting through new computing devices anytime, anywhere. In R. K. Sawyer (Ed.), *The Cambridge Handbook of the Learning Sciences* (pp. 427–441). Cambridge, UK: Cambridge University Press.

Peters, K. (2007). *M-learning: Positioning educators for a mobile, connected future. International Journal of Research in Open and Distance Learning, 8*, 2.

Pritamkabe. (2011). *Mobile Technology for Improving Quality of Education in India*. Retrieved from http://pritamkabe.wordpress.com/2011/11/04/mobile-technology-for-improving-quality-of-education-in-india/

Rao, R. (2012). *Digital learning: Education goes mobile worldwide*. Retrieved from http://www.dnaindia.com/academy/1673515/report-digital-learning-education-goes-mobile-worldwide

Scardamalia, M., Bereiter, C., & Lamon, M. (1994). Bringing the classroom into World III. In K. McGilly (Ed.), *Classroom Lessons: Integrating cognitive theory and classroom practice*. Cambridge, MA: MIT Press.

School Net. (2001). Retrieved from http://www.schoolnet.ca/grassroots/e/index.asp

Sharples, M. (2000). The design of personal mobile technologies for lifelong learning. *Computers & Education*. Retrieved from http://citeseerx.ist.psu.edu/viewdoc/summary;jsessionid=295FE8DACA811B98DE70E240A1521030?doi=10.1.1.359.8991

Sharples, M. (2002). Disruptive devices: Mobile technology for conversational learning. *International Journal of Continuing Engineering Education and Lifelong Learning*. Retrieved from http://citeseerx.ist.psu.edu/viewdoc/summary?doi=10.1.1.123.7924

Sherry, L., Lawyer-Brook, D., & Black, L. (1997). Evaluation of the Boulder Valley Internet Project: A Theory-Based Approach to Evaluation Design. *Journal of Interactive Learning Research*, *8*(2), 199–234.

Sundaram, P. (Ed.). (2009). *Overview of Telicom Industry, Bharat Sanchar Nigam Ltd*. Retrieved from https://www.dnb.co.in/IndianTelecomIndustry/OverviewTI.asp

Venkataraman, B., & Prabhakar, T. V. (2013). *Changing the Tunes from Bollywood's to Rural Livelihoods—Mobile Telephone Advisory Services to Small and Marginal Farmers in India: A Case Study*. Retrieved from http://www.christoph.pimmer.info/wpcontent/uploads/2008/08/Pimmer-Pachler-Mobile-Learning-in-the-Workplace1.pdf

Wideman, H. H., & Owston, R. D. (2000). *An evaluation of TVOntario's video-on-demand pilot project* (Centre for the Study of Computers in Education Technical Report No. 2000-1). York University, Faculty of Education.

Windschitl, M. (1998). The WWW and classroom research: What path should it take? *Educational Researcher*, *27*(1), 28–33.

Yap, J. (2013). *Bharti Airtel launches mobile education services*. Retrieved from http://www.zdnet.com/in/bharti-airtel-launches-mobile-education-services-7000009315/

KEY TERMS AND DEFINITIONS

Associationism: It is the attempt to reduce ideas or other mental elements to basic simple/elementary ideas (sometimes just simple, unstructured sensations) that are associated together in the mind, usually through experience.

Behaviorism: Behaviourism is mainly concerned with observable and assessable features of human behaviour. In defining behaviour, behaviourist learning theories focus changes in behaviour that consequence from stimulus-response associations made by the learner. Behaviour is directed by stimuli.

Constructvist: The term refers to the idea that learners construct knowledge for themselves---each learner individually (and socially) constructs meaning---as he or she learns.

Instructional Tool: A tool that helps students executes their tasks and promotes the balanced development of their mental abilities by functioning as intellectual partners to the instructor and the learner.

Mobile Internet: Mobile Internet denotes to any form of Internet access on a mobile device. All forms of access comprising 2.5G (GPRS), 3G, 4G, Wi-Fi connections from fixed Internet and even dongles can be classified as mobile Internet access only if the access device is a mobile device.

Mobile Learning: Mobile learning has been defined as learning that takes place via such wireless devices as mobile phones, personal digital assistants (PDAs), or laptop computers.

Pedagogical Method for M-Learning: There is a need for a shared, progressive pedagogy for mobile learning that will provide the scientific basis for networked and collaborative learning in both a virtual and a virtual-augmented environment.

Prospect of Distance Education in India: Anticipating the future potential, several telecoms have started offering m-education services. Operators usually partner with software companies to develop these applications.

Supportive Tool: As a tool to support educators' mobile devices allow the recording and maintenance of the lessons take place, the instructional procedures, the type of mentoring and the pedagogical approach, the role of the teacher and students.

Technology Attribute: Is quality inherent in or ascribed to someone or something. For example Portability is the most distinctive feature which distinguishes handheld devices from other emerging technologies, and this factor makes other technological attributes such as individuality and interactivity possible.

Chapter 10
The Role of Internet Technology in Higher Education:
A Complex Responsive Systems Paradigm

Robert J. Blomme
Nyenrode Business Universiteit, The Netherlands

ABSTRACT

This chapter introduces the perspective of complex responsive systems for organizational and individual learning. It also discusses how these systems may profit from the use of Internet Technology. Using Herbert Mead's perspective on interactions and learning, the authors discuss the theory of complex responsive systems as learning systems. They also elaborate on the implications of this perspective for the use of Internet Technology as a driver for individual and organizational learning.

INTRODUCTION

For the past forty years, the topic of organizational learning has been well discussed (cf. Pawlowksy, 2000) and this discussion might be of importance to understanding how professionals including teachers and lecturers, develop, maintain and disseminate knowledge in organizations for higher education (cf. Simons, 1999). Cyert and March (1963) and Argyris and Schön (1978) can be ranked among the most important early thinkers on the concept of organizational learning; since the nineteen-nineties, organizational learning has become an increasingly important concept in individual learning and knowledge development (Senge, 1990). In individual learning, the role of the organizational context has been regarded as increasingly relevant to formal ways of learning, for instance in education programmes, training courses and coaching outside the organization (Blomme, 2003; Revans, 1982; Wenger, 1998) but also to informal ways of learning which is important for knowledge sharing and dissemination (Simons, 1999; Blomme, 2003). The latter is especially important in organizations for higher education in which knowledge is an important resource for its primary processes and therefore should be developed, disseminated and maintained (Blomme, 2003).

Within the organizational context, individuals develop activities and practices in which they can ensure the transfer of existing knowledge and contribute to new knowledge by responding to and reflecting upon other organizational members

DOI: 10.4018/978-1-4666-7316-8.ch010

(cf. Wenger, 1998). While many perspectives on organizational learning adopt a cognitive perspective defining the learning individual as a key factor in organizational learning, we introduce a different perspective and one that is not often used: an emergent perspective on organizational learning which emphasizes the responsiveness of the individuals as a condition for organizational learning (cf. Edmondson & Moingeon, 1998; Stacey, 2001; Blomme, 2003). Founded in chaos theory, the theory of complex responsive systems emphasizes the relationships between people and how the quality of relations and interactions may contribute to individual as well as organizational learning (cf. Stacey, 2001). This perspective on organizational learning is rooted in the work of George Herbert Mead who developed his ideas in the twenties of the last century and the work of Ralph Stacey and colleagues who used Mead's ideas for the development of a framework for learning, knowledge creation and change within organizations.

In this chapter, we shall develop the above-mentioned perspective on organizational learning. First, we shall discuss George Herbert Mead's work on interactions and how these can contribute to individual learning. Secondly, we shall consider the work on complex responsive systems published by Ralph Stacey and his colleagues and based on the work of Mead. The subsequent and remaining issue, seen from the perspective of complex responsive systems on organizational learning, concerns the question how Internet Technology can be used in attempts to support organizational learning. The application of Internet Technology in formal training and development situations has been studied extensively (cf. Salmon, 2005; Barczyk, Buckenmeyer & Feldman, 2010; Sangra, Vlachopoulos & Cabrera, 2012; Li, Lau & Dharmendran, 2008). Here, we shall discuss the potential learning contributions of Internet Technology as a distance learning tool for complex responsive systems.

The Social Act

Together with James Hayden Tufts and John Dewey, George Herbert Mead has become known as an important advocate of pragmatism, a philosophical school of thought arguing that something is true when it is confirmed in practice. In his seminal work *Mind, Self and Society*, Mead introduces the concepts of Self and Mind: Self refers to the elements of our personality that comprise self-awareness and self-image, and Mind refers to an individual's knowledge and cognitive skills (Mead, 1967). In his work, Mead states that Self can only evolve and develop through social interaction and experience; individuals can only grow and flourish if they interact with other individuals.

The development of various forms of meaning related to self-image and the environment (the rise of Self and Mind) takes place during the communicative process. In this process, Mead distinguishes two stages: 1) the exchange of expressions (gestures) and 2) the development of a common language, or as Mead puts it: the exchange of relevant expressions (significant gestures). The communication process is a sub-conscious one, and forms of meaning can only arise after the exchange of gestures and acts. A common language in which mutual expressions can be interpreted and new forms of meaning can be developed is born from the initial steps of exchanging gestures and acts, verbal as well as non-verbal. Meaningful communication entails the appropriate understanding by individuals of the meaning and significance of expressions. As this type of communication requires the presence of at least two people, Mead calls it a Social Act. The social act, or interaction, is the process during which forms of meaning evolve. The creation of meaning takes place in three steps: 1) an individual introduces an expression into the process, 2) the other party replies through a certain type of response, and 3) the initial expression acquires meaning. Thus, meaning and different forms of meaning are the result of this interaction process.

Accordingly, a social system may be seen as an extensive and dynamic network of social interactions where the situations in which actors operate constantly have to be defined and redefined.

Social reality is no fixed phenomenon or fact, but rather a product generated by all participants in the interaction process. The meaning of social reality and the meaning of actions are based on an individual's possibilities to anticipate actions carried out by others. Here, it must be borne in mind that the availability of room for anticipation presupposes the presence of certain rules or a particular hierarchy. According to Mead, these social rules influence the extent to which expressions may become meaningful; they are based on meaning created during earlier experiences. The rigour imposed by social rules and roles is based on the fact that people, in the execution of their actions, have to follow these rules and roles to a certain extent in order to be understood and accepted. Nevertheless, this does not mean that individuals become trapped in these rules; their rigour does not result in any form of imprisonment. During the interaction process, people confirm various rules, as a result of which these rules may be altered and subsequently re-confirmed. Mead regards the potential for change as a form of creativity and an inseparable part of self-awareness. He terms this part 'I', as distinct from 'Me', in which people are able to appreciate the roles played by other actors and in which they can adopt the other party's perspective towards their own role. 'Me' is the result of our subconscious allowing us to respond to expectations experienced in the outside world; 'I' represents our self-awareness allowing us to get around our subconscious or to escape from it. Still, if new gestures or interpretations are to be fully and completely understood, then these will have to be in line with what is commonly accepted. Here, Mead indicates that the process of altering action and behaviour patterns (or escaping from them) is an emergent one; fast changes in a social system are unlikely to be accepted and adopted quickly.

The ability to interact is what Mead calls 'role-taking'. Role taking requires an ability on the part of an individual to relate to others and to appreciate their individual experience frameworks. Through the ability to understand oneself as seen through the eyes of others, an individual can predict and assess the expectations set by others. In this way, he can align his own behaviour to behaviour demonstrated by the other party. Should an individual be unable to relate to others or to their frameworks, Mead argues, we may speak of the Act-as-Such. The Act-as-Such concerns the act initiated by an individual on the basis of his preconceived environment. This environment becomes real on the basis of the selective perception that characterizes the relationship between the individual and the outside world. Acts-as-Such, therefore, are no social acts in which new forms of meaning are constructed, but reactions and responses to events taking place in the outside world. In contrast to the Social Act, where people are seen as social objects, the Act-as-Such implies that people are regarded as objectifiable objects.

If expressions are deliberate and intentional, then an expression is a gesture that is meant to trigger a response. The response then becomes the meaning of an expression. Thus, in Mead's approach, the focus lies on the interactional process as a vehicle of communication for the creation of meaning, but this also implies that communication problems are translated from the sender and the channel of transmission to the way in which the *receiver* creates meaning. It therefore means that the focus of attention moves towards information processing and interpretation on the part of the receiver. This shift also highlights another feature of communication. Communication entails *being granted by others* to share meaning or a form of sense, together with these others. Should this fail to come about, individual expressions will remain in limbo and devoid of sense or meaning. Forms of meaning are always subject to continuous change and reconstruction through additions. They are always temporary and preliminary in character;

they are open to ongoing additions and changes via complementary forms of meaning. What may be certain at one point may become ambiguous the next, or it may even become invalid. Seen in this light, forms of meaning never cease to be subject to an ongoing process of construction and deconstruction.

In his approach, George Herbert Mead elaborates on the connection between the creation of meaning and social acting. This is precisely why the insights listed in *Mind, Self and Society* are often typified as *social behaviourism*, a school of thought which counters the ideas promoted at the time by hard-core behaviourists and followers of Freud. Social acting is related to the development of the self and cognition, and these are inextricably linked. Although Mead, in his work, does not explicitly mention learning and learning processes, it must be pointed out here that he does in fact describe an acting theory framework in which the development of meaning - and thus the development of learning - is one of the outcomes of social interaction. Besides this acting theory, Mead also mentions the *emergent* process and the unpredictable character of meaning creation as an outcome of the interaction process. Here, he identifies an important condition for this type of organizational learning. An individual's willingness to act socially and to engage with others determines not only the creation of new forms of meaning but also whether learning actually takes place. What is important to note in this case is that patterns of behaviour can only be altered if individuals are willing to relate to and engage with others. Learning takes place via the introduction of new expressions or new acts. In turn, these will be re-interpreted by others, who will then respond by means of new expressions. This process of interaction is iterative and circular; it will continue to lead to new repertoires in terms of new acts and interpretations. The question is how these patterns of meaning and learning develop in an organizational system. Here, the theory of complex responsive systems can help to have a

further understanding how patterns develop. In the following sections we will build up the theory on complex responsives systems with the notions from the Chaos theory and the theory of Complex Adaptive systems.

Complexity Theory

In his book *Chaos: Making a new Science*, published in 1987, James Gleick introduced complexity as a new perspective to qualify human behaviour. On the basis of insights developed in other science disciplines (physics, for example), he designed a concept to help us understand and predict human behaviour as demonstrated in various systems. Gleick's book triggered a series of highly varied publications in which his concepts were discussed and elaborated (cf. Lorentz, 1993; Marion, 1999). The ideas behind Gleick's complexity theory are founded on three basic principles: 1) actors form a social unit (system) that is determined and limited by its environment, 2) behaviour demonstrated by these actors is largely determined by the way in which the actors respond to each other, and 3) actor behaviour is usually non-linear and tends to be unpredictable. In later discussions reported in the literature, the spontaneous rise of new behaviour patterns is termed 'emergence' or 'self-organization' (e.g. Kaufman, 1995; Bich, 2004; Blomme, 2003). The theory of complex systems is rooted in system dynamics and Chaos theory which will elaborated in the following sections. In this elaboration we will use the work of Stacey (2001) who did ground breaking work on complexity theory and the theory of complex responsive systems.

Chaos Theory and Dissipative Structures

In the field of system dynamics, an important role is played by non-linear equations. This type of equation denotes a mathematical model of relationships in which individual causes may yield disproportionate results or in which more than one result follows from a single cause. In learning organization theory, non-linearity is particularly found in the addition of positive feedback loops. This is in sharp contrast with negative feedback, which lay at the heart of cybernetic systems. Non-linear relationships are deterministic, which means that these relationships themselves do not change or evolve. In other words: they form systems that do not learn. It thus follows naturally that such systems cannot be applied to human relationships, since people do in fact change and evolve. However, non-linear relationships certainly have a certain value as metaphors. In the section below, we shall investigate systems that do evolve, namely complex adaptive systems, but before we get to that point, we first need to consider a number of theories on non-linear deterministic systems.

To gain an impression of the nature of a chaotic system, we need to consider an equation describing the dynamics of population growth and decline. After all, organizations, too, demonstrate growing and declining population numbers (Stewart, 1989). The equation concerned states the following:

$$P_t = cP_{t-1}(1-P_{t-1}).$$

A population at time point P_t is a multiple or fraction c of the population at an earlier time point P_{t-1}, multiplied by a damping factor $1-P_{t-1}$ which hinders population growth. Size is affected by two factors: an amplifying and a damping factor. P may also represent other issues, such as a company's profits, which depend in time t on the level of advertising. In our example, we assume that a simple non-linear relationship exists between advertising and profit. It therefore follows from our equation that profits will increase at some point (due to fraction c) and show a lack of increase at other moments (due to damping factor $1-P_{t-1}$).

At low values of c (varying between 0 and 3), profit will settle in a stable balance or it will develop in regular, repetitive loops (at values of c lying between 3 and 3.5). At values higher than 4, developments become unstable and chaotic. It is especially interesting to see what happens in the area between 3.5 and 4, in between a state of equilibrium and chaos. To determine this, and thus the line between stability and chaos, we need thousands of computer calculations.

At low values of c, the system will demonstrate a certain type of behaviour which chaos theorists term 'point attractor'. An attractor denotes a behavioural state towards which a system is oriented or attracted. In other words, it is the ultimate behavioural state in which the system will establish itself. The point attractor is a steady state of equilibrium. If parameter c increases, attractors will gradually develop into increasingly complex, cyclical attractors. All of these remain highly predictable equilibria, as found in open systems and cybernetics. However, if c increases even further (at values exceeding 3.8), the system becomes highly irregular (unstable) while developing within certain fixed limits (stable). At this point, no regular loops can be distinguished; values seem to be random (within certain limits) and do not resemble any of their earlier forms. This will remain the case, irrespective of the number of repeated calculations.

We may continue to zoom in on the figure of a diagram, but we shall always see identical forms: the structure has infinite depth, we see images contained within images and these are always identical. Such structures are called 'fractals'. From this, it follows that a simple non-linear relationship, a perfectly deterministic relationship, ultimately produces highly complex behavioural patterns. It means that the line of separation between stability and instability is complex and in fact holds both states at the same time (Steward, 1989).

The word 'chaos' as it is used here does *not* refer to a state of disorder, its everyday meaning. Instead, it refers to *mathematical* chaos. Mathematical chaos reveals patterns in phenomena we formerly described as completely random. Paradoxically, these patterns are both regular and irregular, stable and unstable at the same time

(Gleick, 1988). This type of 'chaos' can be found anywhere around us, and one of its best-known examples is the weather. It follows what we call a 'attractor', another name for a chaotic pattern. It means that the weather follows certain recognizable and more or less similar patterns. These patterns, however, are never completely identical; weather systems are highly vulnerable to minute alterations which may develop into massive changes (Stacey, 2001). The chaotic dynamics that typify the weather explain why the current limit for accurate weather forecasts, theoretically speaking, lies at two weeks. In practice, however, detailed predictions can only be made for two or three days.

Although it is impossible to predict specific behavioural trajectories in a state of chaos, we can nevertheless distinguish 'hidden' patterns of behaviour. There is a certain regularity in the weather's irregularity, due to the effects exerted by damping factors: the weather cannot do whatever it pleases. Weather developments stay within certain global limits: in the winter season, for instance, temperatures will not suddenly jump to 30 degrees Centigrade, nor will they suddenly drop to minus 15 in the summer season. In sum, it means that we cannot identify *specific* causes leading to *specific* consequences, but rather that we can only know the boundaries that limit a system's area of movement and that we can only determine the quality of patterns witnessed.

The application of chaos theory principles has not remained exclusively limited to the field of hard science. Economists and social scientists, too, have attempted to use these principles in their specific disciplines (cf. Baumol & Benhabib, 1989; Kelsey, 1988; Anderson, Arrow & Pines, 1988; Wheatley, 1999). Chaos enhances relatively minor changes to create the necessary instability and to disrupt current behavioural patterns, thus facilitating the formation of new patterns. Systems evolve through various stages characterized by instability until they reach a critical point at which they start organizing themselves spontaneously. From these situations of spontaneous self-organization, new structures and behaviours emerge which cannot be predicted on the basis of earlier stages.

The new and more complex structure mentioned above is termed 'dissipative', because it scatters (dissipates) energy in order to maintain the system in its new mode (Priogogine & Stenders, 1984; Nicolis & Prigogine, 1989). Self-organization is a process that develops spontaneously when certain critical values are reached: a completely new pattern is born. In addition, a system should demonstrate sufficient diversity, otherwise it cannot make a spontaneous move towards a new attractor. Stacey (2001) claims that the newly developed pattern forms a dissipative structure that will quickly dissolve if the system moves too far away from the critical values it has generated itself. In contrast to a state of equilibrium, a state which requires very little energy to be maintained and a great deal of energy to be altered, a dissipative structure requires much energy to maintain its status quo and very little energy to alter it (Stacey, 2001). This means that the balance seen in non-linear systems must become significantly disrupted before these systems can develop into dissipative systems. Dissipative systems obtain their energy and information from their environments, after which both energy and information are scattered throughout the system. Initially, this happens in such a way that the system would seem to disintegrate, but with the further absorption of energy or information, a structure evolves which is characterized by irregularity and which breeds renewal through self-organization.

In essence, a dissipative system presents a paradox: although symmetry and uniformity are lost, some form of structure remains. Wasteful and dissipative activities form a necessary part of the process that creates new structures. A dissipative structure is not only a form of result, but also a process that uses disorder to change itself. In addition, it is a self-developing interactive process that temporarily manifests itself in globally stable structures (Stacey, 2001).

The difference between chaotic and dissipative processes is that the former, by definition, do not involve a spontaneous change of attractor, because change is initiated by something *outside* the system. In dissipative processes, on the other hand, spontaneous change is a possibility, because systems like these are sensitive to fluctuations occurring in their interactions with the environment. The internal process within which symmetry is disrupted creates microdiversity in the system as a whole. It would seem as if such a creative system is prevented from reaching a state of equilibrium, and we can immediately see the implications this has for organizations and their management: most management theories view success in terms of finding the right balance and eliminating differences between elements that make up the organization.

Ever since the days of Newton, Bacon and Descartes, scientists all over the globe have defined the world in terms of mechanistic regularity, in which fixed laws define and determine what can and cannot occur (Stacey, 2001). In the perspective discussed above, the world is still understood and determined by laws, but these laws do not express simple linear causalities. Instead, they form non-linear relationships in which the system refers back to itself, making causality reciprocal, or circular. More specifically, theories state that when a deterministic non-linear system transgresses from a state of equilibrium towards a state of explosive instability, it will move through a phase of *bound instability* where it will demonstrate highly complex behaviour (Stacey, 2001). This is the border area between equilibrium and instability, where both forces are infinitely re-arranged into different yet similar patterns. These patterns develop via self-organization, as a characteristic feature of the system itself, and they are not the result of external positive and negative feedback.

The long-term future of a system in a state of bound instability cannot be predicted, because it is the internal structure of the system itself, rather than external changes, that exerts its influence.

There is nothing that may resolve this unknowability or unpredictability. Translated to organizations in similar states of bound instability, it means that each decision process concerning the future is ineffective, by definition.

In the global system as a whole, infinite individual variety can be discerned within broadly defined categories. If we apply this to organizations, it means that decision making processes concerning the future will consist of small steps. We should attempt to discover qualitative patterns via *analogy* and *intuition*. Whoever wishes to operate successfully in the border area between stability and instability needs to see patterns where others search for specific connections between causes and effects. Chaos theory suggests that such connections will disappear altogether if a system operates in a state of bound instability. In such situations, it is impossible for us to trace either past or present; these systems have so many parameters, which also happen to change very rapidly, that it is impossible for us to trace and record every change.

From the above, it follows that nobody can monitor or manage an unbalanced system, in that nobody is able to predict the specific future of a system operating in a state of bound instability. It also means that no other option remains but to take a chance, implement the change and simply wait to see what happens. Here, it must be borne in mind that although we may feel that some sort of prediction could be made, albeit with great effort, it is in fact impossible to do this. The history of systems like these cannot be unravelled.

Compared with system dynamics and chaos theory, the theory of dissipative structures follows a course that is radically different. The 'noise' or 'fluctuations' in the form of variations around any average are incorporated into the model (Stacey, 2001). These fluctuations grant a non-linear and unbalanced system the capacity to move spontaneously from one attractor to another. Prigogine and Stenders (1984) call this 'order through fluctuations' and demonstrate that this takes place through a process of spontaneous self-organization. This order takes the form of a dissipative structure. It is important to note how the nature of self-organization and emergence is conceived in these theoretical developments. Self-organization and emergence are thought of as the collective response of whole populations. The process is described in terms of correlations and communication at a distance.

These new theories have major consequences for organizational theory and learning; they challenge the assumed feasibility and manageability of organizations, and they state that organizational learning stems from dissipative structures and chaos.

Complexe Adaptive Systems

The theory of complex adaptive systems develops and studies models of interaction between large groups of agents operating within a system (Reynolds, 1987). These studies generally start their lives as computer simulations deciphering the logical structure of algorithmic interaction based on digital codes. These digital codes are subsequently used as analogies for other types of interaction, types that resemble 'real life' more closely. To illustrate the point: digital codes can, for instance, be used as an analogy for the genetic code of biological organisms. The properties of these codes can then be applied to the true biological code, an act which requires a certain mode of interpretation.

Ray (1992, in Stacey, 2001) investigated the behaviour of adaptive systems with the help of a computer simulation programme named 'Tierra'. With this programme, he attempted to simulate organic life. Organic life uses energy to organize matter and evolves when organisms cooperate and compete for light and nourishment. During this form of evolution, organic life never ceases to develop new forms in order to become increasingly better equipped for cooperation and competition. Tierra reflects attempts to simulate the behaviour

demonstrated by these 'adaptive' systems. The results thus generated have led us to conclude the following (Blomme, 2012):

- A complex adaptive system produces a type of order that is changeable and diverse, and which emerges spontaneously. This order has not been pre-programmed and it does not have a specific underlying design or plan. This form of spontaneous and self-organizing activity is of key importance to secure the continued evolution of the system itself and its potential to create new things. However, new forms cannot be predicted, so in that sense the system is chaotic.
- The system spontaneously discovers the importance of competition, particularly the type of competition that is associated with cooperation. Via an internal process of self-organization, the system produces what may be termed parasites and phenomena that resemble the dynamics seen between a predator and its prey.
- The system has discovered symbiotic reproduction.

Each of these three insights presents a paradox and is characterized by the simultaneous presence of stability and instability, of order and disorder. In addition, a fourth insight follows from the study of complex systems: life can survive on the edge of disintegration because of its massive built-in redundancy (Blomme, 2012). This redundancy is the source of permanence and order. The human brain, for instance, is highly redundant: certain areas can execute tasks that are usually carried out by other areas. This explains why people are able to survive the loss of relatively large parts of the brain. Weak sources and loose connections put systems in a better position to deal with the pressure exerted by creativity at the edge of system disintegration.

Concerning the nature of complex adaptive systems, Stacey mentions two different perspectives: the orthodox and the radical. An *orthodox* perspective views complex systems in mechanistic and reductionist terms. A complex system is shaped by and objective observer with the aim of predicting its behaviour. Self-organization is not seen as a new ordering principle, and evolution occurs through random mutations and competitive selection. Hardly any attention is paid to radical unpredictability. The system is regarded as a network of cybernetic and cognitive agents: these represent regularities in the form of schemes, as equivalents to mental models. They store these representations in the form of rules which they subsequently use as the basis of their actions. The *radical* perspective, on the other hand, places a main focus on self-organization, which plays a key role in the emergence of new forms that occur spontaneously and remain utterly unpredictable. Effects do not operate at the level of the individual agent, but rather at the level of the agent *and* the morphogenetic field.

Seen from a radical perspective, the following insights are important:

- *Dynamics at the edge of chaos.* These dynamics are paradoxical, for they involve the co-existence of stability and instability. They are a prerequisite for the emergence of new forms and new matter, which develop at critical levels of the parameters concerned. These parameters refer to information or energy streams, to the relationship between agents and to the level of diversity seen among various different types of agents. If information or energy streams are fast, but not too fast, if the number of connections between agents is large, but not too large, and if agents exhibit diversity that is rich, but not too rich, then – and only then – the system will display dynamics at the edge of chaos.

- *The rise of the new followed by decline.* The dynamics discussed above may create new forms and new matter, but these do not guarantee a system's survival. Innumerable minor forms of dissolution will occur as well as some grand ones. Only when a system is sufficiently diverse in terms of its agents will it be able to develop the internal capacity for spontaneous change. Complete long-term unpredictability combined with a large number of details hinders top-down control, showing us that in evolving systems uncertainty is inevitable.

- *Self-organization and the spontaneous emergence of novelty.* These phenomena occur without any definable prior programme or design, in a context that may perhaps be characterized best as a series of random events. External influences cannot be determined: the system is cyclical and causally 'mute'. As creativity is a collective phenomenon, the collective, i.e. the group, plays a primary role.

While the stability-instability paradox makes it possible to formulate certain predictions concerning *specific* time periods, it also makes this *im*possible for the system involved when *other* time periods and details are concerned. Redundant, non-essential activities are, to a certain extent, discoveries and preparations for new opportunities. In this process, self-organization, unstable and redundant activities form a source of renewal. Systems and contexts are engaged in a process of mutual creation.

The differences between the orthodox perspective and the radical perspective as illustrated above are clearly reflected in the many and varied ideas formulated by organization theorists. The orthodox perspective shares certain similarities with perspectives from cognitive psychology, resulting in an organization theory that uses terminology associated with complex systems while following the lines of orthodox discourse. This bifurcation is made possible through the selection of certain time periods and specific levels of detail, which are in fact predictable, and by speaking about self-organization as if managers were able to control these periods and details themselves. The radical perspective shares certain similarities with social constructionism, where an important role is played specifically by the relationships between individuals, and not by individuals operating as agents.

Complex Adaptive Systems and Self-Organization

Blomme (2012) claims that chaos theory, the theory of dissipative structures and the theory of complex adaptive systems as described in earlier sections are characterized by self-reference and self-organization. This means that the agents in a complex system interact *locally* on the basis of an identity that has evolved over time; interactions take place without the agents knowing how the system as a whole will continue to develop, and even without these agents understanding the current state of the system as a whole. A main focus lies on the relationships between entities rather than on individual constituents themselves; this denies knowing individuals the central position they were given in earlier system theories. Furthermore, whatever has been newly created is essentially unpredictable.

Also does Blomme (2012) argue that the position of an external objective observer is a problematic one, because the new complex theories argue that new forms develop *spontaneously* through a process of self-organization. The agents in a system are always participants in this system, and none of them is able to step outside the system to obtain an overview of the system as a whole, let alone have any idea about its evolution. The essential point of self-organization is precisely that none of its agents – either as individuals or as parts of the group – can plan or shape the evolution of the system in any other way than by their local interaction. Through mutual interaction, they contribute

to the development of a system, but none of them organizes interaction, the self-organization across the system as a whole. No single agent determines the rules for others to 'allow' them to organize themselves. If this were to happen, such a system could no longer be regarded as self-organizing. Stacey (2001) mentions two interpretations for the above-mentioned complexity theory:

- The interpretation of agent-based systems consisting of homogeneous agents;
- The interpretation of agent-based systems consisting of heterogeneous agents.

In the first model, self-organization reaches no further than the continued repetition of identical patterns. No new attractor emerges. Interaction patterns are self-directed loops and recreate themselves in forms that are identical to the initial pattern. Some organization theories use this model to demonstrate that managers have the ability to control processes by introducing elementary rules which are assumed to operate more or less automatically. Thus, the manager is equated with the computer programmer, the objective outsider who selects *beforehand* the attractor towards which the organization should move. Still, even if the manager were able to complete this task successfully, then all that happens is *no more* than the emergence of a new attractor. Spontaneous moves towards new attractors are impossible, unless the manager implements new rules. Any organization that is modelled along these lines will demonstrate a complete lack of creativity.

In the *second* model, new patterns do in fact emerge, as indicated by various computer simulations, leading the process of self-organization towards *new* attractors. A central issue here is that the programmer has *not* programmed these new attractors previously, but rather that these attractors emerge spontaneously. They evolve because the system organizes itself within the limits imposed upon it by the programmer; still, the programmer cannot predict which attractors will emerge until they have presented themselves. Here, 'organization' and the interaction pattern itself are one and the same, occuring simultaneously at the level of the individual agents and at the level of the group as a whole. The organization's interpretation of this model implies first and foremost that the equation of manager and programmer is abandoned. We must reject the notion of the objective investigator: the spontaneous development of novelty occurs without any prior plan or design. In organizations, this second interpretation has certain consequences. It means that:

- Conditions are present that both hamper and promote developments;
- Through available resources, all managers are hindered but also assisted in their tasks;
- Whatever organizes itself cannot concern separate individuals, but rather the general pattern of relationships. Consequently, this alters the nature of the agents: they form the general pattern while being shaped by it at the same time.

Self-organization means that agents operating in a system are engaged in mutual interactions according to their own local interaction principles. They react with their own unique ability to respond. There is no reason to assume that some agents do not have better abilities than others and thus do not have better abilities to respond than others. In organizational terms, we may state that some group members have better understanding, more knowledge and more power than others. Additionally, there is no law stipulating the number of agents, large or small, with which a certain agent will interact. Managers have to deal with many individuals, but their numbers are not absolute.

An organization's resources are generally controlled by small groups of powerful individuals who operate at the top of an organization and who thus both limit and promote the options available to other members of the organization. These individuals sometimes justify their actions, and

sometimes they do not. They make decisions that will have major consequences for many people. What they cannot do, however, is programme other people's reactions, which means that they will have to reply to responses that others demonstrate or trigger. What we see here is self-organization in human terms. It concerns an everlasting and omnipresent process of interaction, one which would only cease to continue if people were to respond as (preprogrammed) automatons.

Computer simulations of complex adaptive systems show a number of possibilities (Langton, 1996, in Stacey, 2001):

- Random populations of interacting digital symbols are able to self-organize and form ordered patterns;
- Interaction between patterns formed by a number of homogeneous digital symbols may lead to the spontaneous emergence of collective patterns or attractors. Since these attractors are interaction patterns themselves, it means that interaction promotes the spontaneous emergence of new internal patterns within themselves;
- Since interaction between patterns formed by digital symbols may lead to the spontaneous emergence of patterns and attractors, these new patterns of collective interaction also involve the re-arrangement of individual patterns. Here, too, interaction creates new patterns within itself through a process of self-organization.

The human analogy for the above processes is clearly found in the fundamental ideas of social constructionism, a school of thought which states that human experience is organized through themes, narratives and discussions (cf. Blomme, 2012, Blomme, 2003; Stacey, 2001). According to Stern (1985), relational childhood experiences trigger the formation of themes concerning the *quality* of these experiences. Adults display the same type of behaviour throughout their lives, and this allows us to state that the development of an individual is in fact a process in which social relationships are internalized in the form of patterns centred around interacting themes. Relationships between people operating in a group may be viewed as recurring patterns of intersubjective themes that organize the experience of being together and forming a community. These themes develop naturally, in various different forms, through interactions among group members who organize these interactions themselves. The actions concerned, however, are not incorporeal; although they occur between people and although they are not individually localized, their experience is nevertheless always physical, which means that experiences are always accompanied by all kinds of emotions, gestures and other physical sensations.

The order shaping the way in which behaviour is aligned is termed an *attractor*. An attractor is defined as a behavioural state towards which specific behaviour is drawn. In this way, an attractor ensures stability in a social system; it is responsible for behavioural patterns and routines witnessed within the system. Escaping from behavioural pattern presupposes the introduction of new attractors and the deconstruction or disintegration of existing attractors in the system. Although considerable attention is paid in the literature to the various ways in which attractors function, little research has so far been carried out to determine their precise nature (Blomme, 2012). Stacey and his colleagues (Stacey, 2001; Fonseca, 2002) have tried to address this issue with their approach on complex responsive systems. The basic idea underlying such systems argues that human experience is organized on the basis of themes, narratives and interactions. It is precisely these themes, narratives and interactions that form the attractor facilitating the alignment of behaviour. In the following section we will proceed with an elaboration of complex responsive systems and how the ideas of Mead would be integrated in this theory.

Complex Responsive Systems

Analogous to the complex adaptive system as a whole is the process of human interaction itself. Still, one key difference should be noted here. Human interaction may certainly be termed complex, but to qualify it as adaptive would fail to do sufficient justice to its true intricacy. Humans do not simply and merely adapt. This is why Stacey argues that we should talk about human action and interaction as a *responsive* process showing reactions and answers to acts and gestures; in this perspective, forms of behaviour may or may not be adaptive. To refer to human behaviour, Stacey and colleagues use the term *complex responsive processes*, in line with the concept of complex adaptive systems. Experiences, i.e. communication among groups of people and between individuals, can thus be called complex responsive processes resembling complex adaptive systems. Seen in this light, human interaction concerns the way in which certain themes, in essence, organize experiences as well as themselves. In fact, what these themes concern is human experience, and this is why we may state that themes which organize experience have *the same* meaning as themes that organize themselves. The prime medium for this type of self-organization is interaction. Its most important element is the form of interaction in which meaning is constructed in its most specific form: discourse and discussions. In Stacey's view, discussions are complex responsive processes. During these communicative exchanges, themes and topics are introduced around which the discourse evolves until the moment that additional or completely new developments - a remark, for instance - trigger the introduction of new themes and topics. In this process, we can witness the formation of new attractors and thematic patterns, fuelled by certain self-organizing associations. These processes organize the experiences developed by groups of individuals engaged in discourse, during which individual as well as shared experiences arise simultaneously. Changes only occur when conversation patterns shift to other areas. Individual behaviour only changes when the discussion between individuals is changed, and this can only happen when individual experience in the social relationships concerned becomes altered. In a sense, changes within groups and changes within individuals are identical phenomena; they co-occur.

Rather than embrace a cognitivist, humanistic or psycho-analytical perspective, all of which lead to the definition of organizations as complex adaptive systems in which individuals adopt the role of agents, Stacey and his colleagues distinctly refer to the ideas expressed by George Herbert Mead. Relationships between individuals within groups may be seen as repeated and continuously repeating patterns of intersubjective themes that organize the experience of *being together*. Such themes are born spontaneously, in various different forms, from the interactions between group members, who organize these interactions themselves. Experiences are not exclusively limited to the cognitive domain; they are accompanied by a range of different emotions, gestures and other sensory perceptions. As a consequence, an organization is not viewed as an adaptive *thing* or as an inanimate system or network, but rather as a set of responsive *processes*. Here, self-organizing agents are not the individuals, but symbols that are ordered to form prepositional and narrative themes through which these individuals become related. *Themes* organize an individual's responsive experiences. In other words: it is the themes that interact, not the individuals. Narrative and prepositional themes organize themselves in private as well as in public discourse, and they may be expressed in various different forms, such as fantasies, myths, rituals and ideologies.

Organizational themes that have an ideological character are fundamental to human relationships, because they make power structures seem natural. Relationships always impose constraints on actions, words, and even thoughts. This type of limitation involves power. The narrative and prepositional themes not only form the power structures witnessed among people operating in an organization but, in turn, are also *formed by* these structures. This means that *power* is not localized within a single manipulating or dominant individual, but rather within human relationships. These relationships bind us all, and the patterns of their limitations, as reflected in our relationships, determine the configuration of power structures. Here, Stacey indicates that the power structures of a social configuration are expressed through language. Language involves orientations on the world: language is knowledge and power, and its themes organize experience. Self-awareness concerns the internalization of social relationships and is thus organized by power structures in exactly the same way as social reality.

To support their ideas, Stacey and his colleagues specifically fall back on the work published by Elias (1978), who argues that symbols are no mere representations of the world but rather act as a medium for social orientation and reflection upon ourselves and the world at large. With the help of symbols, humans interact and form social configurations, i.e. patterns that reflect mutual dependence. These configurations are shaped by competitive and cooperative relationships between people and reflect power differences between individuals as well as groups of individuals. Relationships impose restrictions on people, and limitations have immediate effect on power. Power is localized in relationships and not in individuals who impose their will on others; power structures are co-creations. Social relationships impose restrictions on members of a group and create power imbalances. These imbalances lie deeply embedded in the structure of our language and even in our ways of thinking. According to Stacey and his colleagues, the deep structure of language follows binary logic: elements are categorized either as 'A' or as 'non-A'. It would seem that humans are strongly inclined to subject all of their experiences to this form of logic, and thus to polarize them. In groups, for instance, this phenomenon is reflected in the ancient distinction made between 'us' and 'them'. Competition between groups, often based on minor differences, arises as a spontaneously evolving self-organizing process, as is the case with complex systems. Ideologies, too, develop in much the same way: spontaneously and unawares. They are characterized by a binary polarity stemming from our binary (subconscious) thoughts. In Stacey's approach, this means that an ideology is a form of discourse through which the current order is maintained and made to appear natural and self-evident. Like any other form of discourse, an ideology organizes and shapes our experience. As a form of discourse and as a feature of the power structure within a group, ideology is also internalized in private (and silent) discourse. Seen in this light, an ideology is no inanimate 'thing' outside ourselves, but a mutually constructed and continuously repeated form of discourse. According to Stacey, ideology exclusively resides in our language.

We may distinguish legitimate themes and shadow themes. The former can be freely discussed, but the latter cannot. In addition, we may distinguish formal and informal organizations. A formal organization is described in terms of goals, tasks and the roles formally designated to its members; an informal organization consists of all the relationships that have not been formally identified, either on the basis of roles or tasks. The difference between 'formal' and 'informal' is completely distinct from the difference between legitimate and shadow themes; the former refers to the level of formality and the latter to the degree of legitimacy. Most of the themes that organize experience are *subconscious*. One particularly illustrative example of such a theme concerns the urge to rely on certain established power structures in discussions about differences that fuel hatred and in ensuing acts. This concerns the dynamics witnessed when individuals are considered to be 'in' or 'out'. People are generally aware of this distinction, but at the same time unaware of the purpose to be served with it, namely the ultimate

categorization of experience in binary extremes which are subsequently translated into ideologies that make their behaviour seem self-evident and natural.

In an organization, the three extremes mentioned above, *formal-informal, legitimate-shadow* and *conscious-subconscious*, always operate simultaneously. In addition, various different types of interaction can be seen between these extremes. Shadow themes, for instance, are often informal and partly conscious. Formal themes are legitimate and conscious: they serve to manage an organization and may be expressed publicly. Legitimate themes are legitimate because they follow official ideology. Shadow themes, however, lead to discourse and power structures that manifest themselves in the grey area found between the legitimate and the illegitimate, or the illegal. Shadow themes are both at the same time. The term 'shadow' refers to the *way* in which discourse and discussions take place, namely informally, among small groups of individuals and outside official ideology.

Variation and diversity, both of which are necessary in an organization, are maintained by the *imperfection* of human communication. Often, people grasp only partially what other people say, especially during the initial stages of discussion, or they even completely fail to understand each other. We may even state that most discussions only serve to make further sense of its initial utterances and exchanges. Seen from this perspective, the initial failure to understand literally becomes the 'discussion leader': in a sense, it triggers the creation of new attractors towards which the discussion is geared. Having *free* informal discussions is of vital importance for an organization's opportunities to evolve and develop. In truly free discourse, we see a potential for creativity, as a result of which new discourse pattern may arise. In this respect and in line with Mead, Stacey refers to the Social Act. This is where we find the alliance of legitimate themes and shadow themes; these discussions offer the opportunity to express emotions and to test the boundaries of what is considered acceptable. They deal with the unexpected and the ambiguous. Discussions are breeding grounds for new opportunities and new potential for change: organizational chances for creativity lie in these shadow discussions and the field of tension they create with respect to what is legitimate. Free discourse held in the shadow can be creative as well as destructive, but the basis for both directions is formed by trust. Only if people trust each other will they be willing to engage in shadow discussions and will they feel strong enough to explore the limits, to talk about possibilities and impossibilities, and to question established authorities.

A system or an organization can only move from one attractor to the next if sufficient diversity is available. Diversity and creative behaviour can only exist when internal capacity is available to respond to variety. Variety is born from processes involving organizational white noise, for instance, or heterogeneity on the part of individuals. This type of heterogeneity may be determined by differences in experience, personality, origin or knowledge. In terms of human organizations, it means that these can only go through a creative process of change and renewal if they are sufficiently diverse. This, in turn, is related to the very character of the complex responsive processes that form the organization. Changes occur when themes start to organize themselves and thus initiate new changes within themselves. Creative change always materializes in the tension fields between shadow themes and legitimate themes that organize relational experiences.

Complex Responsive Systems as Learning Systems

The ideas expressed by George Herbert Mead offer a number of wise lessons for practitioners and researchers investigating the processes of organizational learning and organizational change. Mead's thoughts were further elaborated by Ralph

Stacey and his colleagues in their theory of complex responsive systems. With this preconception of organizational learning, we may ask ourselves how Internet Technology can contribute to organizational learning and the development, dissemination and maintenance of knowledge. Before we can discuss the various insights, we should state that the framework of interactions seen during a certain period in a fixed and clearly defined social system such as an organization is complex, dynamic and to a certain extent unpredictable. This is precisely what makes an organization a complex system. On the basis of Mead's philosophy, Stacey postulates that although interactions are unpredictable and intricate, they are nevertheless determined and limited by the very themes that arise within an organizational system. Stacey indicates that these themes form the attractors towards which behaviour is aligned and ordered. Themes arrange and order interactions, and at the same time interactions are the medium through which these themes evolve. Power and ideology are the outcomes of learning; they are confirmed by themes in the form of themes. Learning presupposes reflection on themes and topics that arise in organizational interactions. For knowledge-intensive organizations such as institutions for higher education, these are important realizations in attempts to define the potential benefits that Internet Technology has to offer such organizations. The basic question that should be addressed is what Internet Technology can mean for learning and the development of knowledge.

First, according to Singh and Hardaker (2014), the effectiveness of Internet Technology depends on the way in which learning and knowledge development are supported by means of Internet Technology. Its acceptance and use depends on the extent to which management is able to create a positive and stimulating climate in demonstrating collaboration, creativity and trust (Marshall, 2004). If we relate this to the assumption that learning takes place in interactions between individuals in complex responsive systems, we can conclude the following: interactions are the process in which forms of meaning concerning social reality and mutual expectations concerning acts and gestures are constructed and deconstructed. This process of construction and deconstruction can be typified as 'learning' and 'unlearning'. People may have certain intentions and learning goals, but the outcomes of ensuing interactions are unpredictable, which in a sense makes what is learned unpredictable, too. Hence, an important condition for learning in complex responsive systems is that management creates an atmosphere in which it is possible to experiment with new behaviour and in which social acts are made possible. Furthermore, emphasizing the benefits of Internet Technology as an effective means for driving social acts, reflection and learning can be seen as an important symbolic gesture on the part of management made to promote and utilize its potential. In addition, an organization's most important asset and main condition for learning, namely trust, should be brought about and spread throughout the organization by management itself. However, too strong a focus on learning goals and formal learning trajectories will impede the social act and possibilities to experiment. Furthermore, in the design of Internet Technology as a distance learning tool, the element of diversity should be taken into account, for instance in terms of age, gender and generation (cf. Lub, Blomme & Bal, 2011). There are, for example, differences among generations at the level of experience concerning the use of technology and the Internet (Cooper, 2006). This brings us to an important conclusion: Internet Technology should be flexible and adaptive to the needs and learning processes of the individuals concerned. Therefore, to make the social act possible, Internet Technology should be flexible and used by individuals according to the context concerned and their personal needs. This leads us to define our first insight.

Insight 1: Management in organizations for higher education plays an important role in supporting the Social Act amongst individuals, and thus in learning and knowledge development, by creating a trusting atmosphere and by offering Internet Technology which could be used flexibly according to individual needs and learning processes.

Second, another condition for learning and knowledge development is an effective and well-organized technological infrastructure with appropriate administrative support (cf. Benson & Palskas, 2006). High reliability will motivate individuals to make the best possible use of Internet Technology. This brings us to formulate our second insight:

Insight 2: A well-organized and effective technological infrastructure in combination with appropriate administrative support will support learning and knowledge development in organizations for higher education.

In addition, the acceptance of Internet technology is an important condition for its effective application (Singh & Hardaker, 2014). The more convinced inviduals become that Internet Technology can help them in the process of learning and the creation of knowledge, the more they will be inclined to make use of it (cf. Birch & Burnett, 2009). The earlier sections on complex responsive systems indicate that the intentions and attitudes with which group members participate in the interaction process stimulate or limit learning and unlearning. This also holds for the utilization of Internet Technology. What Mead postulates in his Social Act implies that if individuals wish to learn, they should be willing to engage with others and consider their perspectives in order to understand and appreciate their motives, emotions and interests. This means engaging in mutual dialogue; the dialogue is the instrument for the promotion of organizational learning. It also suggests that the Social Act can only take place in a context of trust, and more particularly trust that the mutual exchange of motives, emotions and interests does not carry any negative consequences. Shared trust is a vital condition for learning. This has a number of important consequences for the use of Internet Technology. The quality of the way in which social interaction and direct responses become possible by means of Internet Technology determines the quality of interaction and learning. Research has indicated that overall interaction established with the help of distance learning tools tends to be less intensive than interaction established during face-to-face contact (Hiltz, Johnson, & Turoff, 1986; Hollingshead, 1996). Additionally, in virtual contacts and in a virtual environment, conflict is more likely to arise (cf. Mortensen & Hinds, 2001), and insulting behaviours are more likely to occur in distance communication compared with face-to-face interactions (Siegel, Dubrovsky, Kiesler and Mcguire, 1986). Hence, although Internet Technology offers participants a range of possibilities to engage in actions, they should nevertheless take its limitations and dangers into account. This brings us to the third insight:

Insight 3: When using Internet Technology for interactions and for learning and knowledge development, one must take into account that the use of this type of technology can be less successful in comparison to face-to-face contact.

Above, we discussed the idea that verbal exchanges are an important component of the interaction process and that non-verbal acts may support or destroy verbal communication, or rather that non-verbal acts exert a major influence on the way in which the other party interprets them and on the subsequent attribution of meaning. Still, during the verbal exchange process, a redefinition takes place of social reality and rules - and thus of mutual expectations with respect to acts

and gestures. Therefore, face-to-face interactions and exchanges are the most important process in which learning and knowledge development take place. For organizations and their management, this view on learning and change has significant implications. In a nutshell, it means that organizations are solely able to learn if (and only if) their members engage in different types of discussion. The processes of learning and change require the facilitation of different forms of discourse. This means that face-to-face exchange remains important in learning and knowledge development. Hence, interactions facilitated by means of Internet technology can only *partly* replace face-to-face contact and interactions. This brings us to our fourth insight:

Insight 4: Internet Technology can only partly replace face-to-face interactions and exchanges in the process of learning and knowledge development.

Using the discussion on complex responsive systems, we may conclude that an organization exhibits many different themes. Stacey states that these themes are dichotomies, and he mentions three themes: 1) formal-informal, 2) legitimate-shadow, and 3) conscious-subconscious. The ambiguity and tension evoked by the extremes contained within these three themes ensure the introduction of diversity in the interaction process. A reduction in terms of ambiguity and tension will lead to Mead's Act-as-Such, in which learning and unlearning will be hindered. Thus, true learning in effect presupposes the promotion of ambiguity and tension, as a result of which new forms of discourse will arise. To facilitate this type of interaction, it is therefore essential that organizations and their management create sufficient free space. In this free space, new themes and repertoires will be born which will contribute to current organizational knowledge and which can be put to excellent use in lectures and tutorials offered to students and participants. Hence, instead of perceiving Internet

Technology only as a structured formal means for learning and knowledge development, we suggest that this type of technology should in fact support the ambiguities and tensions evoked by the extremes of organizational themes. Ambiguity and tension can be supported when, despite its limitations, Internet Technology creates room for open (verbal) exchanges. Social media, portals and Voice and Video over IP are examples of technology with which these (verbal) exchanges and related gestures may be realized. This brings us to our final insight:

Insight 5: Internet Technology should not only be used as a formal means for learning and knowledge development, but also as a platform through which (verbal) exchanges and Social Acts are made possible.

CONCLUSION

Modern thinkers, including Karl Weick, Kenneth Gergen and Pierre Bourdieu, have incorporated much of Mead's thoughts and ideas into their own work. In their 1966 publication entitled *The Social Construction of Reality*, the first work describing the principles of social constructionism, sociologists Peter Berger and Thomas Luckmann clearly demonstrate the inspiration they found in George Herbert Mead's philosophy. For Ralph Stacey and his fellow researchers, Mead's insights have aided the development of important new knowledge in their attempts to flesh out their complexity theory, a new family member in the field of organizational research and learning. In sum, we may conclude that the influence of George Herbert Mead remains clearly visible today. His seminal ideas offer highly topical and important contributions to practitioners and researchers alike in their attempts to understand organizational learning. The work published by Mead and Stacey have provided us with valuable new knowledge.

Our newly acquired insights enable us to examine how modern Internet Technology can be applied as a means to increase individual and organizational learning for institutions offering higher education. Using the work of Herbert Mead and that of Ralph Stacey and his colleagues, we have developed a perspective on organizational learning which was addressed above as the complex responsive systems approach. This approach provides new insights not only into organizational learning but also into the ways in which Internet Technology can be used to facilitate learning processes.

We conclude that learning can be facilitated when Internet Technology is used to increase the quality of interaction between organizational members, leading to the Social Act. As is widely agreed upon, modern Internet Technology can be used to set up information portals, e-learning possibilities and social media tools. In view of the perspective on organizational learning reported in this chapter, the added value of Internet Technology likely lies in the use of social media and interactive portals which promote responses and interactions and which facilitate the speedy delivery of feedback (Piotrowski & Vodanovich, 2000). In addition, these portals can be used to connect large audiences, something which may contribute to greater dynamics and more deep-learning experiences (Shrivasta & Schneider, 1984). Furthermore, Internet Technology can be used for the development of virtual communities. Such communities are cost reducing (Robbins, & Judge, 2007), help to increase an organization's competitiveness (Bell, & Kozlowski, 2002; Driskell, Radtke, & Salas, 2003) and provide an effective reply to increased globalization (Hertel, Konradt, & Vos, 2006). Finally, we conclude that Internet Technology may particularly contribute to learning when organizations are viewed as complex responsive systems. With the help of the insights developed through Mead's and Stacey's approaches, learning processes can be stimulated even better when people interact directly and when social acts are possible. Since the social act remains the major condition for learning and knowledge development, a final word of caution is needed here: effective face-to-face interaction can only partly be replaced by Internet Technology.

REFERENCES

Anderson, P. W., Arrow, K. J., & Pines, D. (1988). *The economy as an evolving complex system.* Menlo Park, CA: Addison-Wesley.

Argyris, C., & Schön, D. A. (1978). *Organizational Learning.* Reading, MA: Addison-Wesley.

Barczyk, C., Buckenmeyer, J., & Feldman, L. (2010). Mentoring Professors: A Model for Developing Quality Online Instructors and Courses in Higher Education. *International Journal on E-Learning, 9*(1), 7-26. Retrieved February 23, 2014 from http://www.editlib.org/p/29273

Barsade, S. G. (2002). The rimple effect: Emotional contagion and its influence on group behavior. *Administrative Science Quarterly, 47*(4), 644–675. doi:10.2307/3094912

Baumol, W. J., & Benhabib, J. (1989). Chaos: Significance, mechanism and economic applications. *The Journal of Economic Perspectives, 3*(1), 77–105. doi:10.1257/jep.3.1.77

Bell, B. S., & Kozlowski, S. W. J. (2002). A typology of virtual teams: Implications for effective leadership. *Group & Organization Management, 27*(1), 14–49. doi:10.1177/1059601102027001003

Benson, R., & Palaskas, T. (2006). Introducing a new learning management system: An Institutional Case Study. *Australasian Journal of Educational Technology, 22*(4), 548–567.

Berger, P. L., & Luckman, T. (1966). *The social construction of reality.* New York: Doubleday.

Bich, L. (2006). Autopoiesis and Emergence. In G. Minati, E. Pessa, & M. Abram (Eds.), *Systems of emergence: research and development* (pp. 284–292). New York: Springer. doi:10.1007/0-387-28898-8_20

Birch, D., & Burnett, B. (2009). Bringing academics on board: Encouraging Institution-wide Diffusion of eLearning Environments. *Australasian Journal of Educational Technology, 25*(1), 117–134.

Blomme, R. J. (2003). *Alignement: Een studie naar organiseerprocessen en alignement tussen individuele en organisatiecompetenties.* Groningen: Gopher.

Blomme, R. J. (2012). Leadership, complex adaptive systems, and equivocality: The role of managers in emergent change. *Organizational Management Journal, 9*(1), 4–19. doi:10.1080/15416518.2012.666946

Cooper, J. (2006). The digital divide: The special case of gender. *Journal of Computer Assisted Learning, 22*(5), 320–334. doi:10.1111/j.1365-2729.2006.00185.x

Cyert, R. M., & March, J. G. (1963). *A Behavioral Theory of the Firm.* Englewood Cliffs, NJ: Prentice Hall.

Driskell, J. E., Radtke, P. H., & Salas, E. (2003). Virtual teams: Effects of technological mediation on team performance. *Group Dynamics, 7*(4), 297–323. doi:10.1037/1089-2699.7.4.297

Edmonson, A., & Moingeon, B. (1998). From organizational learning to the learning organization. *Management Learning, 29*(1), 5–20. doi:10.1177/1350507698291001

Elias, N. (1984). *What is Sociology?* New York: Colombia University.

Fonseca, J. (2002). *Complexity and innovations in organizations.* London, UK: Routledge.

Gleick, J. (1988). *Chaos: The making of the new science*. London, UK: William Heineman.

Hertel, G., Konradt, U., & Voss, K. (2006). Competencies for virtual teamwork: Development and validation of a web-based selection tool for members of distributed teams. *European Journal of Work and Organizational Psychology*, *15*(4), 477–504. doi:10.1080/13594320600908187

Hiltz, S. R., Johnson, K., & Turoff, M. (1986). Experiments in group decision making: Communication process and outcome in face-to-face versus computerized conferences. *Human Communication Research*, *13*(2), 225–252. doi:10.1111/j.1468-2958.1986.tb00104.x

Hollingshead, A. B. (1996). Information Suppression and Status Persistence in Group Decision making. *Human Communication Research*, *23*(2), 193–219. doi:10.1111/j.1468-2958.1996.tb00392.x

Kauffman, S. (1995). *At home of the universe: the search for the laws of self-organization and complexity*. New York: Oxford University press.

Kelsey, D. (1988). The economics of chaos or the chaos of economies. *Oxford Economic Papers*, *40*, 1–31.

Langton, C. G. (1996). Artificial life. In M. A. Boden (Ed.), *The philosophy of artificial life*. Oxford, UK: Oxford University.

Li, F., Lau, R., & Dharmendran, P. (2009), A three-tier profiling framework for adaptive e- learning. In *Proceedings of the 8th International Conference on Advances in Web Based Learning*. Aachen. doi:10.1007/978-3-642-03426-8_30

Lorentz, E. (1993). *The essence of chaos*. Seattle, WA: University of Washington. doi:10.4324/9780203214589

Lub, X., Blomme, R. J., & Bal, P. M. (2011). Psychological contract and organizational citizenship behavior: A new deal for new generations? *Advances in Hospitality and Leisure*, *7*, 107–129.

Marion, R. (1999). *The edge of organization: Chaos and complexity theories of formal social systems*. London: Sage.

Marshall, S. (2004). Leading and managing the development of e-learning environments: An issue of comfort or discomfort? In *Proceedings Ascilite*. Retrieved January 1, 2005 from: www.ascilite.org.au/conferences/perth04/.../marshallkeynote.html

Mead, G. H. (1967). *Mind, Self, and Society from the Standpoint of a Social Behaviorist*. Chicago: University of Chicago. doi:10.7208/chicago/9780226516608.001.0001

Mortensen, M., & Hinds, P. J. (2001). Conflict and Shared Identity in Geographically Distributed Teams. *The International Journal of Conflict Management*, *12*(3), 212–238. doi:10.1108/eb022856

Nicolis, G., & Prigogine, I. (1989). *Exploring complexity: An introduction*. New York: W.H. Freeman.

Pawlowsky, P. (2007). The treatment of organizational learning in management science. In A. B. Antal, M. Dierkes, J. Child, & I. Nonaka (Eds.), *Handbook of Organizational Learning & Knowledge* (pp. 61–89). Oxford, UK: Oxford University.

Piotrowski, C., & Vodanovisch, S. J. (2000). Are the reported barriers to internet-based instruction warranted? A synthesis of recent research. *Education*, *21*(1), 48–53.

Prigogine, I., & Stengers, I. (1984). *Order out of chaos: Man's new dialogue with nature*. New York: Bantam Books.

Ray, T. S. (1992). An approach to the synthesis of life. In C. G. Langton, C. Taylor, J. Doyne Farmer, & S. Rasmussen (Eds.), *Artificial life II, Santa Fe Institute, Studies in the sciences of complexity* (p. 10). Reading, MA: Addison-Wesley.

Revans, R. (1982). *Action Learning*. Bromley: Chartwell-Bratt.

Reynolds, C. W. (1987). Flocks, herds and schools: A distributed behaviour model. Proceedings of SIGGRAPH '87. *Computer Graphics*, *21*(4), 25–34. doi:10.1145/37402.37406

Robbins, S. P., & Judge, T. A. (2007). *Organizational Behavior*. Upper Saddle River, NJ: Prentice Hall.

Salmon, G. (2005). Flying not flapping: A strategic framework for e-learning and pedagogical innovation in higher education institutions *ALT-J. Research in Learning Technology*, *13*(3), 201–218. doi:10.1080/09687760500376439

Sangrà, A., Vlachopoulos, D., & Cabrera, N. (2012). Building an Inclusive Definition of E- Learning: An Approach to the Conceptual Framework. *The International Review of Open and Distance Learning, 13*(2). Retrieved February 23, 2014 from http://www.irrodl.org/index.php/irrodl/article/view/1161/2146

Shrivasta, P., & Schneider, S. (1984). Organizational frames of reference. *Journal of Management Studies*, *20*, 7–28.

Siegel, J., Dubrovsky, V., Kiesler, S., & McGuire, T. (1986). Group Processes in Computer-Mediated Communication. *Organizational Behavior and Human Decision Processes*, *37*(2), 157–187. doi:10.1016/0749-5978(86)90050-6

Simons, P. R. J. (1999). Competentieontwikkeling: Van behaviorisme en cognitivisme naar sociaal-constructionisme. *Opleiding & Ontwikkeling*, *1/2*, 41–45.

Singh, G., & Hardaker, G. (2014). Barriers and Enablers to Adoption and Diffusion of eLearning: A Systematic Review of the Literature - A Need for an Integrative Approach. *Education + Training, 56*(2/3). Retrieved February 23, 2014 from http://www.emeraldinsight.com/journals.htm?issn=0040-0912&volume=56&issue=2&

Stacey, R. D. (2001). *Complex Responsive Processes in Organizations: Learning and knowledge creation*. London, UK: Routledge.

Stern, D. N. (1985). *The interpersonal world of the infant*. New York: Basic Books.

Steward, I. (1989). *Does god play dice? The mathematics of chaos*. Oxford, UK: Blackwell.

Wenger, E. (1998). *Communities of Practice: Learning, Meaning, and Identity*. Cambridge, UK: Cambridge University. doi:10.1017/CBO9780511803932

Wheatley, M.J. (1999). *Leadership and the new science: Discovering order in a chaotic world*. San Francisco: Berett-Koehler Publishers Inc.

KEY TERMS AND DEFINITIONS

Act-as-Such: The act initiated by an individual on the basis of his preconceived environment.

Attractor: A behavioural state towards which specific behaviour is drawn.

Complex Responsive System: A perspective on organizations in which human action and interaction are considered as a *responsive* process showing reactions and answers to acts and gestures.

Internet Technology: Technology using Internet for distance learning including E-learning, portals and social media.

Organizational Learning: Is the process by which individuals in an organization collectively learn.

Social Act: Meaningful communication which entails the appropriate understanding by individuals of the meaning and significance of expressions.

Chapter 11

Internet Technology and its Application in Competence Development of Highly Educated Staff:
The Role of Transfer

Robert J. Blomme
Nyenrode Business Universiteit, The Netherlands

ABSTRACT

This chapter discusses how Internet technology can be used as a distant learning means for individual competence development of highly educated staff. By formulating clear perspectives on competencies, competence development, and transfer, it is argued that Internet technology can only partly be used as a means for competence development. Furthermore, hopes are expressed that by understanding the assumptions underlying competencies, competence development, and transfer, researchers and practitioners find themselves invited to develop varied and effective ways to apply Internet technology in highly educated staff learning processes.

INTRODUCTION

Individual competencies of highly-educated staff play a major role in the development of organizational competence: within strategic management approaches, HRM policies (employability, selection and flexibilization) and HRD measures (training programmes, learning and development, on-the-job training) (Blomme, 2003). We define highly educated staff as employees who have followed a higher education programme at a bachelor's or master's level successfully (Blomme, van Rheede & Tromp, 2010). Individual competence development takes place in formal training situations as well as in informal practice settings in which learners have to deal with practical issues. Simons (1999) coined the term *powerful leaning environment* as a prerequisite for learning and education. The concept of powerful learning environments is specifically related to those circumstances and conditions in

DOI: 10.4018/978-1-4666-7316-8.ch011

which learning and competence development can be enhanced, such as learning environments in which learners are challenged and invited to engage in a cooperative and active process of learning. In this way, learners are enabled to learn on the basis of intrinsic motivation, and they become encouraged to take active and independent control of their individual learning processes. Here, trainers have to adopt various different roles. Sometimes they act as coaches; sometimes they facilitate the transfer of information.

One important issue examined in this chapter concerns the question how Internet technology could be applied in a powerful learning environment in which highly-educated staff members may develop their competencies. In other words, how can distance learning through Internet technology lead to competence development within organizations? The options presented by modern Internet technology are varied, as illustrated by the availability of information portals, e-learning possibilities and social media, to mention but a few examples. Education literature has clearly shown that Internet technology may not only aid the transfer of knowledge and information, but also that it may promote group work and facilitate the speedy delivery of feedback (Piotrowski & Vodanovich, 2000). In addition, Internet technology is ideally suited to reach large audiences at relatively low costs (Alavi & Gallupe, 2003) Its application in formal training and development situations has been studied extensively, and its effectiveness has become the topic of many lively debates (cf. Salmon, 2005; Barczyk, Buckenmeyer & Feldman, 2010; Sangra, Vlachopoulos & Cabrera, 2012; Li, Lau & Dharmendran, 2008). Still, the question remains how exactly Internet technology can be used via distance learning in attempts to support the development of highly-educated staff competencies in daily practice.

To explore the role of Internet technology in competence development, we shall first consider the concept of competence. Next, we shall explore the ways in which competencies are developed by defining various different learning trajectories. Subsequently, we shall discuss the concept of transfer. Following our exploration of competencies, competence development and transfer, we shall elaborate on the conditions needed for the effective application of Internet technology in staff learning processes.

COMPETENCE

We speak of competence when we consider working skills from the perspective of individual practitioners (Brater, 1990). Baits and Frei (1980) view competence as the total combination of plans and action programmes that are available to individual workers for the successful execution of their job tasks. Here, problem solving skills form a central element. Competence denotes a theoretical construct and concerns the specific and interrelated aggregate of available knowledge and skills (Frei, Duell & Baitsch, 1984). Competence is not a mere 'catalogue' of knowledge, ethics and skills, but rather a more *holistic* concept which provides the opportunity to regulate actions and which refers to the ability to use a set of skills in combination with knowledge and ethical considerations in order to carry out concrete activities in an appropriate manner (planning, executing, checking and steering). Additionally, we may describe competence as a practitioner's ability to deal effectively with contradictions and transformations encountered in the employment process (Engeström, 1992). In this sense, competence consists of a complex and multi-faceted cluster of skills. Competence is the hallmark of acting individuals operating within organizations; in principle, it is not limited to the actual set of tasks for which it is used. From an organizational perspective, the essence of competence concerns the potential deployment of employees in a series of tasks that may arise and that need not be pre-defined.

Frei and colleagues (1984) indicate that a competency has three dimensions: one referring to its content scope, one denoting sense-making and one concerning reflection (what, why and how). A competency's *scope* is determined by the competent individual himself and is expressed in the form of what is perceived as a set of homogeneous tasks. This dimension can be further elaborated as the aggregate of occupational skills that shape the competency. On the one hand, a concrete skill (or competency) can be viewed as an element of competence; on the other hand, when applied, it can be seen as the expression of an individual's competence. The scope of competence (as a construct) is wider than that demonstrated by the individual: it is also partly shaped by participation in a knowledge system, also termed *collective expertise* (Engeström, 1992) or *distributed cognition* (Salomon, 1993) within an organization. *Sense-making* concerns the involvement and commitment expressed by a competent individual towards the motives and goals underlying work activities. Competent practitioners familiarize themselves with these motives and internalize them. Meaningfulness, commitment and sense-making skills are part of all competencies. *Reflection* first and foremost concerns the body of knowledge embedded within the various available tools and work methods. Two examples are listed below:

- **Reflection-in-Action:** In their analyses, Argyris and Schön (1978) and Argyris (1992) discuss what they term 'reflective practice', in which the practitioner focuses on the theory that is actually applied ('theory-in-use') and on the differences this theory demonstrates when compared with official theory ('espoused theory').
- **Regulation Level:** What is generally known as action regulation theory is aimed at the determination of psychological regulation levels that are needed for the adequate and appropriate execution of tasks. (Mickler et al., 1976).

This particular competence dimension (awareness and reflection) may lead to the development of independent procedural and managerial competencies: in other words, the ability to act and to initiate administrative, organizational and regulatory activities. The three recognized dimensions of competence can be considered to be dimensions of *development* (Frei et al, 1984). Here, we may speak of expansion (content scope), enrichment (intention and sense-making) or deepening (level of reflection or level of competence). Content scope will gradually widen, a process in which comparisons with earlier experiences play an important role. In the development of competencies, the development of intentions and sense-making form a key factor. We recognize expertise through the level of an individual's commitment to the activity concerned and his familiarity with typical or similar situations, as a result of which certain events acquire meaning as 'quick guides' to be consulted in determining the essence of the problem in hand (Benner, 1984). Deepening, awareness raising and competence improvement first and foremost take place through a process of reflection concerning available tools, methods, technologies and other work products.

A distinction can be made between competence development on an *individual* level and competence development on a *collective* level. In the expansion of expertise and innovative competence, this may involve changing and renewing what has come to be seen as standard (standard problems). In this way, the dynamics and the trajectories of learning activities become connected with the dynamics and the organization of job activities. The development of competencies is dependent on the degree to which employees are faced with (core) problems, changes in the various components of the system and their mutual relationships (Engeström, 1992). Additionally, an important focus could be personal growth and competence development on the part of the practitioner himself (Laur-Ernst,1989; Hoff, Lappe & Lempert, 1990).

From an organizational perspective, it is important not only to secure employees' continued participation in the change process, but also to create a reservoir of competencies in view of future and as yet unknown demands on professional skills. (Zarifian, 1995).

In the above analysis of the concept of competence, a main focus lies on *conscious* aims and motives as characteristics of the acts carried out by individuals in organizations. In the *tacit knowledge* approach, however, the *sub*conscious presence of knowledge and skills has a much more prominent position. Holistic, intuitive forms of knowledge and knowledge based on pattern recognition are regarded as the essence of expertise. In tacit abilities, 'skill' precedes 'knowing'. According to the 'tacit skills' approach, which is specifically based on the work published by Polanyi (1958; 1966), the ability to act is characterized by an implicit, subconscious dimension, an awareness of which is very difficult or even impossible to raise but which is essential for the speedy and natural application of a particular skill. Learning to use certain tools in situations that one tries to master implies a *raised awareness* of activities, as a result of which one may reach certain achievements. Tacit *expertise* is particularly important in situations and activities characterized by uncertainty and in which individuals cannot fall back on fixed rules and procedures. The perspective on expertise as demonstrated in 'tacit knowledge' displays a number of different features, namely cognitive, complex and often professionally relevant skills, such as playing chess, making medical diagnoses or taking management decisions. Expertise is based on intuitive action and pattern recognition.

Dreyfus and Dreyfus (1986) describe the above as 'know-how' (as opposed to 'know-that'). Know-how does not take the form of consciously accessible facts or rules. From the analyses enclosed in the 'tacit' dimension, we may consider it likely that the expert can be distinguished from the inexperienced practitioner through broader and more highly motivated and conscious competencies as well as through a more 'holistic' expertise based on pattern recognition and 'intuition'. The development of expertise is no automatic process, but one that has its own demands, concerning work and the professional practice in which expertise can evolve as well as concerning the expert himself, or rather his expert behaviour (Bereiter & Scardamalia, 1993). When new developments and changes occur, the expert will also fall back on the development of new content, sense-making and reflection. This means that in the light of innovation, too, this ability to come up with new and improved competence and expertise may prove to be more important than existing expertise.

In brief, competence refers to the structured and integrated ability needed for the effective and appropriate engagement in work activities and for solving labour problems. Competence has a structure of its own and cannot be characterized as a list of tasks or a summation of necessary skills. Here, what is important are the *connections* and the *relationships* between the composing parts based on the combination of knowledge and skills. Competence concerns an employee's *individuality* rather than the required qualifications that have been defined from an occupational or professional perspective. This makes competence a 'situationally determined' concept; it is not static, but develops along the dimensions mentioned earlier – scope (task content), level of control (command) and sense-making (identity, community). Additionally, competence has a 'tacit' dimension, i.e. the subconscious acquisition of a structured and integrated ability to act by initiating successful and goal-oriented activities. Furthermore, competencies become operational through action processes that are *complete*: preparation, execution and evaluation (reflection) are included.

THE RELATIONSHIP BETWEEN COMPETENCE DEVELOPMENT AND ORGANIZATIONAL DEVELOPMENT

A distinction is generally made between the development of competence at an individual level and at a collective level. In building expertise and expanding innovative competence, this may involve the alteration or redefinition of standards or standard issues. In this process, the evolution and dynamics of learning activities are closely connected with the organization of professional activities and their associated dynamics. Here, competence development depends on the extent to which an employee has to deal with (core) problems, with changes taking place in different parts of the system and with their mutual relationships (cf. Engeström, 1986; Van der Dool, Moerkamp & Onstenk, 1987).

A second important goal concerns the development of competencies and personal growth on the part of individual professionals themselves (Hoff, Lappe & Lempert, 1990). From an organizational perspective, it is important not only to include employees in change processes while obtaining their cooperation and support, but also to create a certain competence surplus in view of possible – and as yet unknown – future demands concerning particular professional skills (Zarifian, 1995).

For educational institutions, a main focus lies on *explicit* and *conscious* goals and motives that are typical of their professional activities. In the *'tacit knowledge'* approach, however, a much more prominent role is attributed to the subconscious and implicit presence of knowledge and skills. Holistic or intuitive knowledge and forms of knowledge based on pattern recognition are considered to be the very essence of expertise. In tacit skills, 'ability' precedes 'knowing'. In the tacit skills approach, based in particular on the work done by Polyani (1958; 1966), the ability to act is typified by its implicit, subconscious nature. This dimension is one that is very hard or almost impossible to make *explicit* but also one that is essential in the fast and natural execution of a certain skill, for instance riding a bicycle, driving a car or typing a text. To illustrate the point: if a person were to think *consciously* about every single stroke on the keyboard, about the way to direct his hands and position his fingers or about the force with which the keys should be hit, it would be impossible to get anything on paper – or rather on the screen. Learning to use certain tools in terms of trying to master a particular situation implies the 'de-implicitization', if one may use this term, of the actions needed to achieve the desired result.

Tacit expertise is particularly important when it comes to the ability to act in uncertain situations and when it is impossible to fall back on earlier defined rules. The approach towards expertise as seen in 'tacit knowledge' has a number of different focus points and accents. These include cognitive, complex and often professionally relevant skills, such as playing chess, formulating medical diagnoses or making management decisions. Expertise is based on intuitive actions and pattern recognition. Dreyfus and Dreyfus (1986) describe this phenomenon as 'know-how' (as opposed to 'know-that'). Know-how cannot be accessed by the conscious mind through rules or facts. Through the analysis of the tacit dimension, it can be argued that experts distinguish themselves from junior professionals thanks not only to more broadly developed, more motivated and more conscious competencies, but also to a more holistic expertise based on pattern recognition and 'gut feeling'.

The development of expertise is certainly no automatic process. It places high demands on the work itself and the area of practice in which expertise is developed as well as on the expert himself – or rather: on expert behaviour (Bereiter & Scardamalia, 1993). When new developments and changes occur, the expert, too, falls back on the development of new content, sense making and reflection. From an innovation perspective, this means that the ability to develop new competence and expertise is in fact more important than using existing expertise.

TOWARDS AN ANALYSIS OF COMPETENCIES

Following our description of the various *dimensions* of competence, we now need to design a *framework* for the analysis of competencies. Here, it does not suffice simply to formulate a detailed task analysis coupled with a matching set of 'necessary qualifications'. We must consider which concrete operation and learning strategies employees need in order to perform their tasks as efficiently and effectively as possible (Scribner, 1984; Nieuwenhuis, 1991).

Based on the various types of problems at which competence is primarily aimed, the following distinctions are made:

- Professsional competence → production problems;
- Methodical competence → regulation problems;
- Managerial and organizational competence → organizational problems;
- Strategic competence → inclusion problems;
- Socio-communicative competence → co-operation problems;
- Normative and cultural competence → community problems.

The above framework could be termed a 'synchronous analysis' of competencies. What also needs to be considered is the dimension of time reflected in the individual careers of the employees themselves. People should be able to grow in line with developments and changes related to their job tasks, and their careers usually reflect a series of positions that are more or less well matched. Considering this perspective, we may identify a final important category: learning and development competencies, aimed at resolving learning and development problems.

In the definition of the various types of competence, a main focus lies on work problems and professional issues, but this by no means excludes the relevance of certain competencies and skills for the stimulation of personal growth or for their application in life situations outside the professional environment. The competencies identified above may be regarded as the ingredients of broad and comprehensive professional expertise, but the list is not intended to be exhaustive. Instead, it presents an analytical framework combined with a list of illustrative examples referring to clusters of skills that may form part of the framework. Dimensions need to be defined and made concrete for each individual profession or position. This means that clusters are not meant to form strictly isolated categories; particularly procedural knowledge, tacit knowledge and expertise share professional as well as methodical elements. Socio-communicative as well as managerial and organizational skills are almost inextricably linked with operation strategies and learning skills.

Bontius, Boogert and Huisman summarize the seven dimensions listed above and distinguish three types of competence:

- **Methodical-Instrumental Competencies:** These are aimed at the resolution of content problems concerning the product to be manufactured or the service to be rendered;
- **Organizational-Strategic Competencies:** These are aimed not only at managing and steering activities in organizational contexts but also at ensuing tasks;
- **Socio-Communicative Competencies:** These are focused on personal attitude and cooperation in interactions with others.

The above competence types can be viewed as a group of dimensions within which one dimension may dominate another, depending on the type of task to be completed. In addition to these three types, the authors distinguish a fourth: *learning and development competencies* (Blomme, 2003). This dimension concerns the ability to learn via self-steering and thus to become increasingly expert and more competent as the process evolves. Compared with the other types, this dimension is of a different order, and this is why it needs a separate mention. We cannot rank it among the others.

In brief, we distinguish two types of learning processes:

- Acquiring competencies, or learning to operate competently (methodical-instrumental, organizational-strategic, socio-communicative);
- Steering the development process, via self-learning, towards increasingly higher levels of competence (learning and development competence).

In their approach towards competence, Bontius et al. place a major emphasis on the process of growth and development rather than an individual's static characteristics. As a result of dynamics and developments witnessed in the realm of professional practice (Den Boer & Hövels, 1999), operating competently knows no final goal; it only calls for the continuation of learning and development.

PROFESSIONAL EXPERTISE AND CORE PROBLEMS

Onstenk used the typology of competence mentioned in the previous section to develop a definition of broad occupational expertise. The ability to operate competently or skillfully requires an ability to deal adequately with demands, expectations and problems that may become apparent within and among various different professional situations. It first and foremost concerns an ability to deal effectively with *core problems* related to operating in a professional environment: problems and dilemmas which are central to the professional tasks involved and with which an employee is confronted frequently – and which thus form the distinguishing features of the profession itself. Core problems indicate the structure and connectedness of areas in which professionals encounter issues related to production, management and socio-communicative or cultural phenomena. In essence, these problems structure the actual tasks faced by professionals, and they highlight the dilemmas, choices and decision moments associated with their professional activities. The well-considered application of knowledge and skills, the deployment of the correct repertoire of action and the speed with which this is done determine an individual's level of professional competence and skills. By definition, labour cannot be predicted or planned completely and unequivocally, since it is characterized by unexpected events, developments and contradictions with which professionals must be able to deal. In fact, what lies at the heart of professional expertise is the ability to handle the *combination* of routine activities and non-routine problems (Stinchcombe, 1990). In addressing disruptions, this form of expertise and the use of tacit knowledge play a vital role, because they offer the framework of reference for determining the characteristics and peculiarities of specific situations.

Still, individual professionals may not always have the necessary expertise readily available themselves. To be able to apply the necessary resources and to join the realm of collective expertise in the best possible way, they at least need to have sufficient methodical, managerial and organizational competencies as well as the necessary socio-communicative skills.

COMPETENCE ACCORDING TO KESSELS

A different view on competence is the knowledge-oriented approach formulated by Kessels (1999). His interest has always been fuelled by the question what precisely employees should learn to make useful and effective contributions to their professional work. On the basis of this question, we investigate the need for learning and education: can present or future issues be resolved in the best and most inexpensive way through learning processes?

Kessels prefers using the term 'expertise' rather than 'competence'. Thus, he seeks to reduce the ambiguity and inconsistency frequently associated with the latter term (Kessels, 1999). Expertise and knowledge have become increasingly intertwined. It can even be argued that knowledge is the most important form of expertise in a knowledge economy. On the other hand, one could also argue that expertise constitutes the most important element of knowledge.

Still, it remains to be seen whether the sobering conclusion that competence is a broad skill can be of any use in our search for satisfactory answers to the question asking what competencies are actually relevant (Mulder, 1998). A tremendously increased interest in topics such as knowledge management and competence has a certain downside: nobody seems to be willing or able to adhere to a uniform framework of concepts and definitions. At the moment, the concept of competence would seem to be used first and foremost as a *searchlight* assisting us in determining our priorities and the best ways to realize these.

Little help is to be found either in broadly defined or highly detailed descriptions of the concept of competence. Although general descriptions allow us to apply this concept widely, they are nevertheless of insufficient use if we wish to answer questions asking how competencies may be developed or how proof may be obtained showing that someone has actually acquired conscious expertise. Conversely, we have seen that highly detailed descriptions hardly lend themselves for the design of competence tests or for the design of training programmes (Kessels, 1999). Today's discussions and debates on the topic echo the thought that competencies have a *strategic function*. This could lead to what is known as

competence management: acquiring (recruiting) and developing (training) competencies.

A second line of thought emphasizes *personal* interests, i.e. motivation and curiosity, which likely play an even more prominent role than that played by an organization's formal strategy. For the development of personal expertise, it is important for employees to participate in networks which acknowledge and respect such expertise and which invite employees to broaden and deepen their skills even further. If these networks also assist their members in developing their self-steering abilities, very little management effort is required. In this sense, competence development could very well form the foundation for a new wave of emancipation, namely the emancipation of the knowledge worker, and signal the end of our current belief in strategic approaches and of our firm conviction that we can manage everything that is important to us.

If we consider knowledge to mean personal expertise, its definition (encoding knowledge and making it explicit) will only yield information about a person's expertise, or about our own: no more and no less. Here, it must be borne in mind sharply that this type of information is *not* the same as the expertise itself. A skill cannot be shared, transferred, bought or sold. Much of our so-called 'knowledge', as stored in various knowledge systems, is merely second hand: it concerns information about somebody else's expertise. This has a number of highly relevant implications for the design of training programmes; concepts such as 'knowledge transfer' and 'curriculum' become void. Expertise needs to be *acquired* – and therefore trained and improved.

Competency-based learning and education centres on the idea that skills and expertise form the basis of knowledge and understanding. This calls for learning situations in which employees investigate which skills are important to them and which are not. They will subsequently acquire and further develop the desired skills, either independently or with specific support from experienced colleagues or expert educators. The final aptitude test will then be a powerful means with which an employee can demonstrate proof of competency. The best place to develop the necessary skills is an employee's daily work environment. If competency cannot be developed there, a training programme offered elsewhere will be unsuccessful, too.

Kessels's perspective is a highly interesting one, because of his focus on the concept of knowledge rather than the concept of competence. Knowledge is tied to the individual; knowledge and expertise are best acquired and developed in the work environment. Here, Kessels implicitly introduces learning in organizational processes, in which individuals construct their roles as the learning process unfolds and in which, on the basis of these roles, employees educate each other in acquiring knowledge associated with their roles. The development of competence takes place via the transfer of knowledge and skills that belong to the roles constructed through interaction.

INPUT AND OUTCOMES MODELS

We may now ask ourselves how competencies can be determined. The literature mentions two important approaches (Blomme, 2003): input models and output models.

Input models are aimed at determining specific and individually distinguishable characteristics. According to this model, candidates displaying certain characteristics will be able to function naturally and adequately when tasks or jobs are concerned that require precisely such characteristics. Output models assume that competencies consist of personal attributes or features, and they sometimes refer to concepts such as personal effectiveness, perseverance and commitment, to name but a few. With these types of models, we aim to expand the concept of competence; a central role is taken by the search for general characteristics and identifying attributes rather

than context. However, the process following input (a professional's personal characteristics) and preceding output (the outcome of acts) is *not* analyzed, rendering this process a 'black box'.

Outcomes models are based on the presupposition that *learning* constitutes a personal experience. Their basic principle states that individuals steer their own learning processes in ways that match their own learning styles, preferred forms of learning, learning opportunities and the time available for learning (Jessup, 1995). Outcomes approaches are dynamic in that they take into account the changes that may occur within the organization itself or in available technologies. These approaches have a broad basis: they not only imply forms of interaction between technical and organizational environments, but they are also aimed at routine activities and concepts such as adaptability, predictability and unpredictability, change and innovation.

Next to specific individual knowledge and expertise, outcomes models address other issues, too, including process, context and action outcomes. In his work on outcomes models, Mansfield (1990) distinguishes the following characteristics:

- Models are based on descriptions of the *aim, process and results* of professional activities.
- Models are *not* exclusively limited to descriptions of knowledge, expertise or other individual features.
- Models also contain an analysis of the *interaction* between technical job *roles* and the organizational *context*.
- Models are *dynamic*. Changes concerning the organization of work as well as technological developments are taken into account.
- Models refer to general, more *abstract* competencies (versatility, creativity, the ability to innovate) as well as *routine* activities.

Table 1. Input-based and outcomes-based approaches (Klarus, 1998)

	Input Models	Outcomes Models
Labour	Analysis of professional activities, resulting in: • Descriptions of personal characteristics: knowledge, skills, attitudes; • One-dimensional or static frameworks.	Analysis of professional activities, work contexts and work outcomes, resulting in: • Descriptions of (core) competencies; • Transfer skills; • Contextualized skills; • Iterative or dynamic frameworks.
Learning	• Learning mainly concerns transfer and instruction; • Knowledge, skills and attitude concern individual entities to be taught and developed separately.	• Multi-faceted situational and problem-based learning; • Integration of cognitive and operational skills.
Standards	• Criterion-oriented; • (Personal) characteristics.	• Criterion-validated; • Cognitive operational skills and results.

Table 1 summarizes, in key words, the main differences between input models and outcomes models.

Advocates of outcomes models mention the following advantages (cf. Mansfield, 1999):

- Consecutive job analysis steps are continuously and directly related to the aims associated with the professional activities to be executed. This approach will enhance the definition of desired competencies.
- A standard based on outcomes is not exclusively limited to one specific form of education or training; it is independent of teaching methods. Acquired competence can be acknowledged, as a result of which career moves are more easily made.
- Describing learning targets and learning process outcomes prevents the over-regulation of learning trajectories. Since competence can be achieved via many different routes, assessing the learning trajectory itself is ineffective. Attention for learning processes therefore mainly concerns the alignment with individual needs and individual potential.
- Outcomes models are mainly aimed at what people can achieve in their professional practice. Practical knowledge and

tacit knowledge are included in the assessment of acquired competencies.

- Outcomes models demonstrate a comprehensive vision, particularly with respect to the development of human potential. These models reveal hidden talent and maximize the potential for individual growth. By acknowledging people's individually unique ways of developing expertise, more employees are enabled to meet the necessary competence criteria.

COMPETENCIES

Competencies are related or integrated cognitive and practical professional skills with which

- A particular professional aim is realized; or
- A particular product or result is generated.

What matters in the assessment of competence is the confrontation of general qualification standards and individual expertise. This involves a confrontation on two levels: the level of individual abilities and the level of supra-individual requirements to be met in professional practice situations. In brief, in the concept of *competence,* it is *process* dimensions and the individual that are given centre stage. The concept of qualification uses a perspective of systems and structures. A qualification system aimed to operate independently and irrespective of teaching methods will have to take both perspectives and both realities into account.

Widely developed or broad expertise may be defined as a *specific set of competencies,* at the level of specific professional positions, in terms of its applicability in various different functions and situations, and finally with respect to its contribution to the development of the labour system itself (Onstenk, 1997). What is concerned here is not simply a set of isolated elements; seen from the system of professional activities concerned, structure and connectedness are determined by the core problems associated with a profession or a particular function.

The issues discussed above lead us to formulate our first insight with respect to competencies:

Insight 1: Competence can de defined as a multi-dimensional, structured and connected set of professional, methodical, managerial, strategic, socio-communicative, normative, cultural and learning competencies aimed at the adequate resolution of core problems related to the profession.

Expertise can in fact be broadened when an ability is developed to act innovatively and in the best possible way, something which in addition to the expansion of content also requires a larger degree of commitment and reflection. This conclusion combined with the analysis presented in this chapter allows us to formulate a second insight, one about broad expertise:

Insight 2: Requirements concerning broad expertise become even broader in the following situations:

- When an increasing number of problems needs to be solved in the shop floor production process, as a result of which issues concerning regulation, cooperation and commitment become more important for daily professional practice;

- When employees are expected to contribute to organizational changes or to the optimization of the production process – a current and increasingly frequent phenomenon.

If and when such developments arise, employees need to have broad professional qualifications enabling them to deal with professional challenges and conflict effectively and independently (Dedering & Schimming, 1984; Hövels & Römkens, 1993).

In actual practice, however, various different production and organization models co-exist. This very fact points to contradictory developments in the current system of professional activities, a phenomenon which warrants the *active* pursuit of training and vocational education. In this way, active and stimulating attempts can be made to develop new production concepts and to promote qualified labour. We can now formulate a third insight.

Insight 3: Competencies in combination with broad expertise should be used as a form of guidance in the design of learning goals involved in function and profession-oriented learning and education. Vocational training programmes need to be aimed at a broad area of related functions and should, additionally, prepare students for a professional career; thus, they should be aimed at the future. Next to addressing strictly professional qualifications, education profiles and qualification analyses should also focus on the acquisition of broad expertise. In this process, a main starting point should be formed by the competence and skills structures that result from altered characteristics of production, management and cultural systems.

By distinguishing between competencies and qualifications, we create room for the explicit definition of *informally* acquired competencies. Individuals are granted a qualification (formal proof), an acknowledgement of their accomplishments, when they demonstrate abilities that meet the requirements set by certain qualification standards. These requirements (listed in the set of qualification standards) are termed qualification *criteria* and are used to assess acquired competencies. This should be done in a manner that is independent of education profiles, i.e. independent of the way in which these competencies have been acquired.

In the determination of qualification criteria, we employ a system of analysis that is aimed at the outcomes of professional activities. Competencies can be distinguished when they emerge in the form of actions and action outcomes, in the form of products or in the form of activities. Thus, outcomes concern not only technical skills, but also more general abilities such as social, communicative and problem solving skills. In this approach, the outcomes of professional labour form the foundation of qualification standards and qualification structures.

With the above, we have presented an approach towards the definition and positioning of broad expertise and competencies. The construction process evolving in professional practice and fuelled by acts and interaction can also be described as 'learning'. This chapter has offered a brief discussion of the learning and development process associated with competencies. The next chapter will elaborate on the learning and development processes demonstrated by individuals.

COMPETENCE DEVELOPMENT

Competencies are developed interactively in a context within which employees carry out their activities. In an interactive view of the concept of competence, a central role is played by learning in relation to *acting within a certain context* (Hager, Gonczi & Athanasou, 1994). Not only behaviour, but also the applied frameworks of thought, sense-making and a practitioner's learning potential are important factors (Hodkinson, 1992). In the interactive competence model, the following elements play a central role (Blomme, 2013):

- **Context and Culture:** Learning is never separated from the context in which it takes place;
- **Cognition:** Cognition is related not only to factual knowledge, but also to the processing of information and frameworks of thought. Cognition has its own context and is situationally determined;
- **Behaviour:** The ways in which individuals perceive themselves, their roles and their environments partly determines how they behave. Changes in behaviour imply changes in the applied frameworks of thought and interpretation;
- **Frameworks of Thought and Interpretation:** These frameworks are mental representations including interconnected categories that are used, among other things, to attribute meaning to new experiences;
- **Intellectual Processes:** Changes in frameworks and behaviour presuppose the application of complex and interrelated intellectual processes.

Another central element in the interactive approach is formed by the relationship between thought and *context*. Various theories of acting specifically point towards the determined and consciously operating individual as the starting point for competence development (cf. Hodkinson, 1992). Firstly, competencies are subject to a dynamic process of permanent change of which learning is an intrinsic part. Secondly, learning is a context-dependent and social process. Individuals internalize knowledge and manipulate it, in order to externalize it in situations that require action. In other words: by acting, individuals generate knowledge. Moreover, learning only becomes true learning when we can speak of a 'cognitive framework for acting'. This framework is shaped by the conscious ability to harness and demonstrate skills. Finally, competence development can take place through what is known as immanent learning, a process we speak of in the absence of external agents such as managers, instructors or trainers who may interfere with this it or steer it.

Knowledge and knowledge acquisition in combination with the development of cognitive frameworks for acting and learning how to use these are always integrated in an *activity* (Van Parreren, 1971). Cognition consists of more than the sole combination of knowledge and understanding. It also concerns the ability to handle and apply cognitive skills when concrete problems arise that require action. 'Acting' yields knowledge, particularly *procedural* knowledge (knowing 'how'). In each act, we may distinguish three forms of knowledge (Pieters, 1992): declarative knowledge (knowing 'that'), procedural knowledge (knowing 'how') and conditional knowledge (knowing 'where' and 'when'). This knowledge may then manifest itself as 'conscious' knowledge, but also as 'tacit' knowledge (cf. Giddens, 1985).

A second essential point in the development of mental processes is the vital role played by language, signs and symbols (cf. Vygotski, 1985). It almost goes without saying that these factors are crucial in assessment processes, too. In the selection of assessment forms, it is therefore important to pay explicit attention to the question whether, in our attempts, we actually assess those forms of knowledge and awareness that we aim to assess. The answer to this question is of particular interest when we wish to determine the value of tacit knowledge and select methods that include the assessment of this specific competence feature. If we consider tacit knowledge to involve intuitive, cognitive activity, this will be discernible – thus allowing us to assess its results or outcomes. Still,

not *all* aspects of competence can be assessed exclusively on the basis of cognitive representations. It is the actions themselves and their results that form the starting point for the assessment of all competence elements (cf. Blum, Hensgen, Kloft, & Maichle, 1995).

Blomme (2003) distinguishes three ways in which learning takes place in organizations: deduction, induction and abduction. The difference between deduction and induction is closely linked to the distinction made by Van Onna (1985) between theorization and concretization. Concretization is aimed at the direct application of learning content in the execution of tasks. Theorization concerns learning content as the combination of general knowledge principles and knowledge laws. On the basis of these general laws, conclusions are drawn for the execution of professional activities. Both concretization and theorization always occur in specific contexts. In addition to inductive and deductive strategies, we distinguish a third: one in which thoughts and acts are more closely integrated. It is a strategy which Chong-Ho (19914) terms *abductive*. In abductive learning, we speak of learning that takes place in special situations, for instance when a problematic issue or a crisis arises. In subsequent stages, a specific potential resolution is selected from a variety of available options: one that may guide the approach needed to tackle the problem or the effectuation of the solution. This approach is then applied and evaluated. If required, the same abductive procedure is used again to seek different or additional explanations and solutions.

In addition, Marsick and Watkins (1990) use the terms *action* and *reflection* as the extremes of a continuum in which three learning situations are distinguished: formal, informal and incidental learning. The extreme termed 'action' is definitely not intentional; 'reflection', on the other hand, is mostly intentional. Between these poles, the range of incidental learning is evenly spread - via informal learning - towards formal learning. Here, 'incidental' is situated close to the pole defined by 'action', and 'formal' is positioned close to the pole that is termed 'reflection'.

Action and reflection are poles; they are not each other's opposites. Action without reflection is equally inconceivable as reflection without action. A learner's concrete activities determine whether we may truly speak of learning. Learning, according to Marsick and Watkins, is an ongoing, dialectic process of action and reflection. The latter, reflection, implies that individuals are aware of the fact that they are learning, which presupposes a certain degree of intentionality. However, intentionality, the very awareness of the fact *that* learning takes place in combination with an awareness of *what* is learned, is not necessarily related to a certain situation. Of course, learning situations may differ in terms of the degree to which certain explicit learning goals are strived for.

In sum, competence development may occur in many different ways, and it may follow many different routes. So far, we have not discussed the extent to which learning effects in one situation may also lead to improved professional behaviour or improved (i.e. more effective) learning in other, new situations. This is precisely where transferability and transferable skills play an important role (Blomme, 2013).

THE TRANSFER OF COMPETENCIES

Transfer concerns the relevance and application of skills as well as an individual's capabilities. In the first situation, we speak of *transferable* skills, and the second refers to *transfer* skills (*transition* skills).

Transferable skills are 'skills known or expected to be applicable in various different (professional) situations' (Moerkamp, 1991:5). Examples include widely applicable work skills involving professional cognitions (information processing, logical and analytical thought, problem solving), organizing competencies (planning and logistics), socio-communicative competencies (cooperation,

discussions and the exchange of information), and finally (preferred) ways of acting (responsibility, identification and reliability).

With the help of *transfer skills* or *transitional skills*, individuals become able not only to translate acquired or existing knowledge and skills to new or changing situations, but also to apply them in such situations. Moerkamp (1991) distinguishes four types of competencies that contribute to transferability: integrated *personal knowledge*, the availability of *meta-cognitive and self-regulating strategies* (also known as 'situational skills'), the availability of strategies aimed at *determining a context's general principles*, and finally *attitudes* such as transfer motivation, confidence in the outcomes of transfer and an open and conscious approach towards one's own knowledge and skills. Extending this line of thought, Onstenk (1992) defines transfer skills as follows: learning to learn, decontextualization, re-contextualization, and the combination of transfer skills and transferable skills.

In addition, Perkins and Salomon (1989) mention two learning trajectories: the 'low road' and the 'high road'. The first concerns the process of intense learning and practice that individuals engage in for as long as it takes to internalize and automate a particular skill, a process that makes the skill transferable. The second road involves the conscious and deliberate explicitation and abstraction of knowledge elements or cognitive skills from a particular situational perspective.

The terms 'high road' and 'low road' refer to the process in which transfer skills are developed. The outcomes of a trajectory aimed at transfer can be divided into *near* and *distant* transfer. We speak of distant transfer when major differences exist between the original task and the newly required task (Resnick, 1987). In near (or analogous) transfer, practice situations closely resemble actual work situations. What is involved here mostly concerns the execution of routine tasks. Distant transfer presupposes the decontextualization of domain-specific information, i.e. it presupposes meta-cognitive skills. These skills can be related to a large number of specific domains through learning activities or professional endeavours; they form, among other things, the basis of planned (professional) activities and reflections. These skills are often implicit (tacit knowledge), and as such not immediately discernible (Samarapungavan & Milikowski, 1992). This means that the assessment of implicit meta-cognitive skills can only take place in an *indirect* manner, for instance via outcome assessments. Both Ceci and Liker (1986) and Perkins and Salomon (1989) doubt the existence of a general competency for 'far transfer' to all imaginable practice domains. This is demonstrated, among other things, by the fact that most people are generally unable to transfer competencies from their professional environments to their everyday private lives.

Simons (1990) distinguishes nine personally determined conditions which may improve the chances of transfer and which can be influenced during the learning process with the help of certain interventions. The first two conditions concern the existence of a *memory trail* and the quality of the integration of *memory representations*. These are the two conditions that Simons mentions first. After all, if knowledge has not been acquired or memorized, transfer will not be possible. Whether experiences will ultimately lead to memory representations depends on the extent to which concepts are clarified and on whether links are established with other experiences and concepts. This is explained by the fact that the process of learning becomes more effective when deliberate attempts are made to establish relationships between formal and informal knowledge. Here, one of the most important elements is the integration of newly acquired knowledge into an individual's own knowledge framework.

The third condition mentioned by Simons is the degree of *compilation*, denoting the transition from 'knowing that' to 'knowing how'. What is concerned here is the degree to which we are capable of combining simple 'if-then-else relationships'

and our ability to determine new relationships on the basis of our existing knowledge. To this end, procedural knowledge is needed that transcends single and specific business situations (Bartram, 1992). Combining simple relationships and distinguishing new ones through practice can be done in formal as well as informal learning trajectories. Offering sufficient room for manoeuvre is an added advantage; limiting this room reduces the number of options available for reformulation.

Simons' fourth condition involves the availability of effective and appropriate strategies: strategies for *problem solving, self-regulation* and *transfer*. These strategies include:

- The ability to dissect a problem and determine its composing parts;
- The ability to monitor the problem solving process;
- The formulation of interim goals;
- The planning and evaluation of outcomes;
- The conscious and deliberate search for knowledge, skills and solutions that have proven to be effective in earlier situations.

What is of particular importance here is that learners become aware of the fact that many different strategies exist to aid them in the problem solving process. It is especially the individual learners' own specific experiences that may facilitate (or hinder) the acquisition and application of meta-cognitive knowledge and cognitive strategies through incidental learning. If these strategies are available, they may also be enhanced without external support.

Simons' fifth condition refers to knowledge about one's own individual knowledge: *meta-cognitive knowledge*. One of the most important techniques to acquire this form of knowledge involves the explicit definition, formulation and exchange not only of knowledge and ideas but also of ways in which individuals gather, interpret and use knowledge. Here, too, external support can play an important role. In incidental learning, for example, this may be realized by setting examples or providing feedback (positive or negative).

The sixth condition concerns our *awareness of the importance of knowledge*. It partly determines whether or not we actually deploy the knowledge and skills that we have at our disposal. In informal learning, (learning) activities take place in such a way that their outcomes are also immediately and directly experienced. It implies the increased presence of intrinsic motivation that is related to the situation concerned. This means that learning in incidental and spontaneous trajectories is first and foremost based on the subjective needs and requirements felt by learners; after all, there is no external body which orders them to learn. The position of formal learning, however, is a different one. In determining the benefits of formal learning activities, it is not always possible to refer to practical applications. This is why, in this type of learning, we speak of 'graded benefits' (Simons, 1990).

Simons' seventh condition mentions the *context* within which transfer should occur. The ability to apply knowledge and skills and to retrieve knowledge from memory depends on the (subjectively) perceived similarities between old and new activities and old and new learning situations. Learning in real or simulated contexts leads to improved chances of transfer (Blomme, 2013). However, learning via incidental paths holds the risk of negative transfer, something which occurs when knowledge and skills acquired within a certain context are transferred to a new context automatically and without any further thought, as a result of which new task performance is negatively affected (Simons & Verschaffel, 1992). We can only truly speak of transfer when we manage to separate acquired knowledge and skills from the context in which they were developed and subsequently manage to apply them in different or completely new situations. The effectiveness of this process of decontextualization determines the success of the transfer process. In addition, decontextualization is a necessary prerequisite for

the successful introduction of independent learning assessments. To formulate valid and reliable judgements, all candidates must be assessed on the basis of identical criteria and assignments, irrespective of their learning histories. During the assessment process, and depending on the extent to which acquisition and assessment situations prove to be dissimilar, a candidate's transfer abilities will be addressed to a smaller or larger degree.

The eighth and pre-final condition that Simons lists is the ability to *decontextualize*. This ability can be developed when a *variety* of experiences and types of problems can be discerned. Decontextualization, however, is no automatic process. Only when an individual has already shown to meet certain transfer conditions (particularly meta-cognitive knowledge and cognitive strategies) can we also speak of decontextualization in the process of informal learning-on-the-job. In all other cases, an external source (coach, supervisor, manager, co-worker) is needed to meet these transfer conditions.

The final transfer condition concerns factors such as *motivation* and *attitude*. By assessing whether transfer has been realized, the motivation to engage in the process of transfer may increase. Here, Simons points out that in situations where factual knowledge is tested through multiple choice questions, candidates are not assessed on their ability to establish a successful transfer, but rather on their ability to score good grades. This phenomenon is likely to occur more frequently in formally organized learning environments.

DISCUSSION

In the above sections, we argued that learning – and thus the development of competence – is a socially and contextually determined process. The type of organization and a learner's personal characteristics affect the speed with which competencies can be developed as well as the level at which this is done. In addition, it is important to acknowledge the fact that, in some learning situations, learners may withdraw from any form of external interference or external manipulation. Tacit knowledge – mentioned earlier as an important element of organizational competence – is often constructed without external influence or steering and is greatly determined by context. We have seen that transfer plays a key role in the possible application of individual competencies in work situations and activities. What is important in the learning process is an individual's intention or motivation to learn. Here, the learning process is not exclusively limited to the construction of new competencies, but also includes the application of these competencies in daily practice and within organizations. Individuals need to be motivated to learn and to use their competencies for the benefit of the organization through various different contexts .

In the perspective drawn by Simons (1999) applied to highly-educated people, we can formulate the organizational context, provided that it has a positive influence on individual learning behaviour and individual competence development, as a *powerful learning environment*. The way in which we consider this powerful learning environment to be a motivator for competence development is also meaningful in itself – and therefore a learning process, too. Whether individuals operating within an organizational context actually interpret variables such as a powerful learning environment depends on their pre-existing constructs and experiences. In their literature review of e-learning, Singh and Hardaker (2014) indicate two levels at which an organizational context may be established: the macro level and the micro level.

Macro Level

The macro level indicates the extent to which an organization supports the development of competence through Internet technology. Here, the role played by management is an important factor in demonstrating trust, creativity and cooperation in

attempts to create a positive and stimulating learning environment (cf. Marshall, 2004). Another key factor in supporting the learning process of employees is the availability of sufficient funds and time for these learners, in combination with management efforts to set the right example (Singh & Hardaker, 2014). Still, a significant pitfall remains if management places too strong a focus on learning goals and formal learning trajectories when informal learning plays an important role in individual competence development. The use of Internet technology in the formalization of learning processes in prescribed routines may lead to tunnel vision and the loss of problem solving abilities (Blomme, 2012). This brings us to our first newly gained insight:

Insight 1: Management's exemplary role and the acknowledgement of formal as well as informal learning are important contributors to the effective application of Internet technology in the development of individual competence.

In addition to the role played by management, a well-organized and effective technological infrastructure is needed in combination with appropriate administrative support to enable learners to learn (cf. Benson & Palskas, 2006). A reliable infrastructure and a successful support framework will also enhance employees' motivation to make the best possible use of Internet technology. If employees are forced to go to great lengths in order to embrace technology and experience its advantages, they may well give up their learning efforts. This means that whatever is offered with the help of technology should be carefully and specifically aligned to a learner's learning process. A simple "one-way" approach will likely be less effective (Singh & Hardaker, 2014); effective instruction and training may be of much greater assistance (Pallof & Pratt, 2001). This brings us to our second new insight:

Insight 2: A well-organized and effective technological infrastructure in combination with appropriate administrative support will aid the enhancement of individual competence development.

Micro Level

Singh and Hardaker (2014) argue that the acceptance of Internet technology is an important condition for its effective application. Individuals are more readily inclined to use Internet technology when they experience the advantages it offers compared to traditional learning interventions, when they become convinced that this type of technology offers them a better connection with their professional practice, and finally when they see its user-friendliness (cf. Birch & Burnett, 2009). In addition, Singh and Hardaker indicate that a perceived sense of *in*competence concerning the use of Internet technology may lead to feelings of unease and subsequently to its rejection. In this respect, each individual employee will demonstrate a different attitude, which is why it is vital to make sure that each individual receives sufficient attention, so that employees may be able to deal with these feelings of unease and incompetence in an appropriate manner. In the approaches adopted towards individuals, the element of diversity should be taken into account, for instance in terms of age, gender and generation (cf. Lub, Blomme & Bal, 2011). Considerable differences exist, particularly among generations, in terms of the level of experience concerning the use of technology, the Internet and educational concepts such as e-learning (Cooper, 2006). This means that an important role is set aside for support staff, trainers and managers, and it brings us to formulate our third new insight:

Insight 3: A determined and tailor-made approach will lead to higher levels of acceptance and a better use of Internet technology as a means of learning.

Another topic addressed by Singh and Hardaker (2014) concerns the amount of time available to employees to engage in learning with the help of Internet technology and the amount of time that is needed to develop actual learning content. Here, an added requirement for the acceptance and the use of Internet technology as a means of learning is the amount of time made available to trainers to formulate and deliver active feedback on employee assignments or communications. Information, and course materials in the case of e-learning, need to be promptly developed and distributed. Here, it almost goes without saying that expiry dates can be extended when more general knowledge is concerned. Still, when knowledge is more closely related to a learner's professional practice, it needs to be updated or upgraded more quickly (Boettscher & Conrad, 2010). Another important consideration concerns the fact that employees tend to underestimate the amount of time needed for the effective use of Internet technology. When insufficient time is granted for the application of Internet technology, the integration of learning into professional practice will become an endangered process. In fact, it may even prove impossible to realize this integration. In this case, learning with the help of Internet technology will be perceived as less valuable, as a result of which less and less use will be made of it (cf, Eynon, 2005). This allows us to formulate our fourth new insight:

Insight 4: The amount of time available for content development and learning is an important condition for the use of Internet technology as a means of learning.

As their final point, Singh and Hardaker (2014) mention the ownership of content. An important condition for interactive activities is the idea held by learners that they are able to indicate their learning requirements. Blomme (2003) defines the role played by learners as follows:

- Learners learn best when they can play an active role in the learning process;
- Learners' subjective and personal experiences need to be encouraged;
- Learners gradually develop their own perspectives;
- Learners' knowledge and understanding are developed gradually;
- Through dialogue and cooperation, learners work on the construction of meaning.

Forcing learning content onto learners may prove counterproductive (Boettschers & Conrad, 2010). This means that responsibility and ownership concerning the learning process lie with the learner himself. Still, for the effective alignment of *individual* competence development and *organizational* competence development, responsibility also lies with the organization itself, i.e. its trainers and managers, and this brings us to our final insight.

Insight 5: Responsibility and ownership concerning the development of learning content lie with learners as well as trainers and managers.

CONCLUSION

In the preceding Discussion section, we formulated five new insights to aid us in the effective application of Internet technology as a means of learning in the process of individual competence development of highly-educated staff. We shall now list a number of conclusions related to the topics dealt with in the sections above.

First, the use of Internet technology may be of assistance in distance learning processes, but only as part of a large number of other conditions that will lead to competence development and transfer. As such, and from the perspective of competence elaborated earlier, it is not enough to use the Internet merely to test employees on

their knowledge and skills. Learners should be assessed precisely on the knowledge and skills associated with the desired learning processes and on the ways in which learners can integrate these in their professional practice. Here, learning involves the creation of new perspectives through interactions with others, including trainers and managers. In the assessment of new knowledge and skills, direct supervisors and managers play an increasingly important role.

Second, the vision presented in this chapter sees learning as a social process in which networks and engaging in networking activities together with others form a key element. This means that in the compilation of training programmes, designers need to adopt a learner perspective, and that forms of learning such as discovery learning, problem-based learning, action learning, case-based learning and learning projects, to name but a few, need to be given a much more prominent position. This allows learners to create and share their own perspectives, resulting in better commitment and bottom-up alignment. In this process, Internet technology could offer support through the use of social media, although research into the effectiveness of this type of use is scarce.

In addition, the development of individual competence does not concern *training* policy, but rather *learning* policy. In this respect, a careful balance needs to be sought in terms of training programmes, action learning and experiential learning in combination with the application of Internet technology. In the perspective presented here, another central role in learning and job environments is taken up by the development (spontaneous as well as stimulated) of competencies by providing effective opportunities that stimulate and facilitate this process, professionally as well as in other environments.

In conclusion, we can state that the use of Internet technology may serve as a means of learning in individual competence development of highly-educated staff. The same holds for the acquisition of transferable skills. However, the social context in which learning and competence assessment take place is not easily replaced by Internet technology. Transfer skills are determined by context and mostly developed through action and reflection. Still, communities of practices defined by means of Internet technology may offer important contributions to reflection practices aimed to assess individual performance – and thus learning performance. What may be of particular assistance here is the use of specific experiments that take into account the five newly gained insights formulated above.

REFERENCES

Alavi, M., & Gallupe, B. (2003). Using Information Technology in Learning: Case Studies in Business and Management Education Programs. *Academy of Management Learning & Education*, *2*(2), 139–153. doi:10.5465/AMLE.2003.9901667

Argyris, C., & Schön, D. A. (1978). *Organizational Learning*. Reading, MA: Addison-Wesley.

Argyris, C. A. (1992). On organizational learning. Oxford, UK: Blackwell Publishers.

Baitsch, C., & Frei, F. (1980). *Qualifizierung in der arbeidstätigkeit*. Bern: Verlag Hans Huber.

Barczyk, C., Buckenmeyer, J., & Feldman, L. (2010). Mentoring Professors: A Model for Developing Quality Online Instructors and Courses in Higher Education. *International Journal on E-Learning*, *9*(1), 7-26. Chesapeake, VA: AACE. Retrieved February 23, 2014 from http://www.editlib.org/p/29273

Benner, P. (1984). *From novice till expert: Excellence and power in clinical nurse practice*. Menlo Park, CA: Addison-Wesley.

Benson, R., & Palaskas, T. (2006). Introducing a new learning management system: An Institutional Case Study. *Australasian Journal of Educational Technology*, *22*(4), 548–567.

Bereiter, C., & Scardamalia, M. (1993). *Surpassing ourselves: An inquiry into the nature and implications of expertise*. Chicago: Open Court.

Birch, D., & Burnett, B. (2009). Bringing academics on board: Encouraging Institution-wide Diffusion of eLearning Environments. *Australasian Journal of Educational Technology*, *25*(1), 117–134.

Blomme, R. J. (2003). *Alignement: Een studie naar organiseerprocessen en alignement tussen individuele en organisatiecompetenties*. Groningen: Gopher.

Blomme, R. J. (2012). Leadership, complex adaptive systems, and equivocality: The role of managers in emergent change. *Organizational Management Journal*, *9*(1), 4–19. doi:10.1080/15416518.2012.666946

Blomme, R.J., Van Rheede, A., & Tromp, D.M. (2010). The use of the psychological contract to explain turnover intentions in the hospitality industry: A research study on the impact of gender on the turnover intentions of highly-educated employees. *The International Journal of Human Resource Management, 21*(1-3), 144-163.

Blum, F., Hensgen, A., Kloft, C., & Maichle, U. M. (1995). Erfassung von handlungskompetenz in den prüfungen der industrie- und handelskammern. Bonn: Institut für Bildungsforschung (IBF).

Boettcher, J., & Conrad, R. (2010). *The online teaching survival guide: Simple and practical pedagogical tips*. San Francisco, CA: Jossey-Bass.

Bontius, I., Boogert, K. & Huisman, J. (2001). *Het leren van competenties: Drie ideaaltypische opleidingsontwerpen*. S´Hertogenbosch: CINOP.

Brater, M. (1990). Ende des Taylorismus: Paradigmenwechsel in der berufspädagogik? In U. Lauer-Ernst (Ed.), Neue fabriksstructuren und veränderte qualifikationen (pp. 83-91). Berlijn: BIBB.

Ceci, S. J., & Liker, J. (1986). Academic and non academic intelligence: An experimental separation. In J. Sternberg & R. K. Wagner (Eds.), *Practical intelligence: Nature and origins of competence in the everyday world* (pp. 119–142). Cambridge, UK: University Press.

Chong-Ho, Y. (1994*). Abduction? Deduction? Induction? Is there a logic of exploratory data analysis?* New Orleans: American Educational Research Association.

Cooper, J. (2006). The digital divide: The special case of gender. *Journal of Computer Assisted Learning, 22*(5), 320–334. doi:10.1111/j.1365-2729.2006.00185.x

Dedering, H., & Schimming, P. (1984). Qualifikationsforschung und arbeitsorientierte bildung: Eine analyse von konzepte zur arbeitsqualifikation aus pädagogischer sicht. Opladen, Duistland: Westdeutscher verlag. doi:10.1007/978-3-322-88526-5

den Boer, P., & Hövels, B. (1999). *Contextontwikkelingen en competenties*. Nijmegen: ITS.

Dreyfus, H. L., & Dreyfus, S. E. (1986). *Mind over machine: The power of human intuition and expertise in the era of the computer*. New York: Free press.

Engeström, Y. (1992). *Interactive expertise: Studies in distributed working intelligence. Research Bulletin 83*. Helsinki: Department of Education, Universiteit Helsinki.

Engeström, Y., & Engeström, R. (1986). Seeking the zone of proximal development in physicians' work activity. In *Proceedings of the 1ˢᵗ international congress in activity theory*, (vol. 3, pp. 471-496). Berlijn: System Druck.

Eynon, R. (2005). The use of the Internet in higher education: Academics experiences of using ICTs for teaching and learning. *Aslib Proceedings, 57*(2), 168–180. doi:10.1108/00012530510589137

Frei, F., Duell, E., & Baitsch, C. (1984). *Arbeit und kompetenzuntwikkelung: Theoretischer konzepte zur psychologie arbeitsimmanenter qualifizierung*. Bern: Verlag Hans Huber.

Giddens, A. (1985). Structuratietheorie en empirisch onderzoek. In Q.J. Munters, E. Meijer, H. Mommaas, H. Van de Poel, R. Rosendal, & G. Spaargazen (Eds.), Anthony Giddens: Een kennismaking met de structuratietheorie (pp. 27-56). Wageningen: Universiteit Wageningen.

Hager, P., Gonczi, A., & Athanasou, J. (1994). General issues about assessment competence. *Assessment & Evaluation in Higher Education, 19*(1), 3–16. doi:10.1080/0260293940190101

Hodkinson, P. (1992). Alternative models of competence in vocational education and. *Journal of Further and Higher Education and Training, 16*(2), 30–39. doi:10.1080/0309877920160204

Hoff, E., Lappe, L., & Lempert, W. (1985). *Arbeitsbiographie und persönlichkeitsentwikkelung. Schriften zur Arbeitspsychologie, 40*. Bern: Verlag Hans Huber.

Hövels, B. (1993). Terug naar de inhoud op het snijvlak tussen onderwijs en arbeid. In B. Hövels & L. Römkens (Eds.). Notities over kwalificaties (pp. 4-67). ´s-Hertogenbosch: CIBB.

Jessup, G. (1995). *Outcomes. NVQ's and the emerging model of education and training*. London: Farmer.

Kessels, J. W. M. (1999). Het verwerven van competenties: Kennis als bekwaamheid. *Opleiding & Ontwikkeling, 1/2*, 7–11.

Kessels, J. W. M. (2001). *Verleiden tot Kennisproductiviteit*. Oratie Universiteit Twente.

Klarus, R. (1998). *Competenties erkennen: Een studie naar modellen en procedures voor leerwegonafhankelijke beoordeling van beroepscompetenties*. SHertogenbosch: CINOP.

Lauer-Ernst, U. (1989). *Schlüsselqualifikationen: Innovativer ansätze in den neugeordenten berufen und ihre konsequenzen für lernen*. Berlin: BIBB.

Li, F., Lau, R., & Dharmendran, P. (2009), A three-tier profiling framework for adaptive e-learning. In *Proceedings of the 8th International Conference on Advances in Web Based Learning*. Aachen: Academic Press. doi:10.1007/978-3-642-03426-8_30

Lub, X., Blomme, R. J., & Bal, P. M. (2011). Psychological contract and organizational citizenship behavior: A new deal for new generations? *Advances in Hospitality and Leisure, 7*, 107–129.

Mansfield, B. (1990). Competence and standards. In J. Burke (Ed.), *Competency based education and training* (pp. 26–53). Barcom Lewes, UK: The Falmer Press.

Marshall, S. (2004). Leading and managing the development of e-learning environments: An issue of comfort or discomfort? *Proceedings Ascilite*. Retrieved January 1, 2005 from: www.ascilite.org.au/conferences/perth04/.../marshallkeynote.html

Marsick, V., & Watkins, K. E. (1990). *Informal and incidental learning in the workplace*. London: Routledge.

Mickler, O., Dittrich, E., & Neumann, U. (1976). *Technik, arbeitsorganisation und arbeit*. Frankfurt: Aspekte Verlag.

Moerkamp, T. (1991). Leren voor een loopbaan: Het verwerven van transitievaardigheden in HAVO en MBO. Amsterdam: SCO (OSA-werkdocument W 92).

Mulder, M. (1998). Het begrip competenties. Enkele achtergronden en invullingen. *Opleiding & Ontwikkeling, 10/11*, 5–9.

Onstenk, J. (1997). *Lerend, leren werken: Brede vakbekwaamheid en de integratie van leren, werken en innoveren*. Delft: Eburon.

Palloff, R., & Pratt, K. (2001). *Lessons from the cyberspace classroom: The realities of online teaching*. San Francisco: Jossey-Bass.

Perkins, D.N. & Salomon, G. (1989, January-February). Are cognitive skills context-bound? *Educational Researcher,* 16-25.

Pieters, J. M. (1992). *Het ongekende talent: Over het ontwerpen van artefacten in de instructietechnologie*. Enschede: Universiteit Twente.

Piotrowski, C., & Vodanovisch, S. J. (2000). Are the reported barriers to internet-based instruction warranteed? A synthesis of recent research. *Education, 21*(1), 48–53.

Polyani, M. (1958). Skills. In M. Polyani (Ed.), *Personal knowledge: towards a post critical philosophy* (pp. 49–65). London: Routledge & Kegan Paul.

Polyani, M. (1967). *The tacit dimension*. Garden City, NY: Anchor.

Salmon, G. (2005). Flying not flapping: A strategic framework for e-learning and pedagogical innovation in higher education institutions *ALT-J. Research in Learning Technology, 13*(3), 201–218. doi:10.1080/09687760500376439

Salomon, G. (1993). *Distributed cognitions: Psychological and educational considerations*. Cambridge, UK: Cambridge University.

Samarapungavan, A., & Milikowski, M. (1992). The relation between metacognitive and domain specifik knowledge. *Tijdschrift voor Onderwijsresearch, 17*(5), 303–312.

Sangrà, A., Vlachopoulos, D., & Cabrera, N. (2012). Building an Inclusive Definition of E- Learning: An Approach to the Conceptual Framework. *The International review of Open and Distance Learning, 13*(2). Retrieved February 23, 2014 from http://www.irrodl.org/index.php/irrodl/article/view/1161/2146

Scribner, S. (1986). Thinking in action: Some characteristics of parallel thought. In R. J. Sternberg & R. K. Wagner (Eds.), *Practical intelligence: Nature and origins of competence in the everyday world* (pp. 13–30). Cambridge, UK: Cambridge University.

Simons, P. R. J. (1990). *Transfervermogen*. Nijmegen: Quick Print.

Simons, P. R. J. (1999). Competentieontwikkeling: Van behaviorisme en cognitivisme naar sociaal-constructionisme. *Opleiding & Ontwikkeling*, *1/2*, 41–45.

Simons, P.R.J. & Verschaffel, L. (1992). Transfer: Onderzoek en onderwijs. *Tijdschrift voor Onderwijsresearch*, *17*(3), 3-16.

Singh, G., & Hardaker, G. (2014). Barriers and Enablers to Adoption and Diffusion of eLearning: A Systematic Review of the Literature - A Need for an Integrative Approach. *Education + Training*, *56*(2/3). Retrieved February 23, 2014 from http://www.emeraldinsight.com/journals. htm?issn=0040-0912&volume=56&issue=2&

Stinchcombe, A. L. (1990). *Information and organizations*. Berkeley, CA: University of California Press.

van den Dool, P. C., Moerkamp, T., & Onstenk, J. (1987). *Wissels tussen werk en leren*. Amsterdam: SCO.

Van Onna, B. (1985). Arbeid als leersituatie. In G. Kraayvanger & B. Van Onna (Eds.), Arbeid en leren: Bijdragen tot volwasseneneducatie (pp.49-69). Baarn: Nelissen.

Van Parreren, C. F. (1971). *Psychologie van het leren I*. Deventer: Van Loghum Slaterus.

Vygotski, L. S. (1978). *Mind in society: The development of higher psychological process*. Cambridge, MA: Harvard University.

Zarifian, P. (1995). Kwalificerende organisatie en competentiemodel: Waarom en met wat voor leerprocessen? *Beroepsopleiding*, *1995*(2), 5–10.

KEY TERMS AND DEFINITIONS

Competence: The holistic perspective on the total combination of plans and action programmes that are available to individual workers for the successful execution of their job tasks.

Competency: The specific three dimensions of a competence including one referring to its content scope, one denoting sense-making and one concerning reflection (what, why and how).

Internet Technology: Technology using Internet for distance learning including E-learning, portals and social media.

Powerful Learning Environment: Those organizational circumstances and conditions in which learning and competence development can be enhanced.

Transfer Skills: Ability not only to translate acquired or existing knowledge and skills to new or changing situations, but also to apply them in such situations.

Transferrable Skills: Skills known or expected to be applicable in various different (professional) situations.

Chapter 12

Google Educational Apps as a Collaborative Learning Tool among Computer Science Learners

Vasileios Paliktzoglou
University of Eastern Finland, Finland

Tasos Stylianou
Technological Educational Institute of Central Macedonia, Greece

Jarkko Suhonen
University of Eastern Finland

ABSTRACT

The purpose of this chapter is to investigate students' engagement using Google Educational Applications as educational social media tools to support teamwork. The participants of the study were a cohort of Computer Science students enrolled in the State-of-Art Technologies in Education (SOAT) online course at the University of Eastern Finland. The data was collected through pre- and post-Google Educational Collaborative Applications experience questionnaires and an interview. Based on the findings, it is evident that social media, and more specifically Google Educational Applications, can support social-constructivist models of pedagogy and that Google Educational Applications (as social media tools) have the potential to play an important role in the future of learning environments. The chapter provides experimental evidence that the use of Google Educational Applications can increase student engagement, and thus, Google Educational Applications can be used as an educational tool to support teamwork.

INTRODUCTION

Social media have evolved into mainstream technologies used by many institutions for educational purposes in numerous, innovative ways (Conole & Alevizou, 2010), even to the extent of such tools being utilized in traditional face-to-face classroom situations (Redecker, Ala-Mutka, Bacigalupo,

DOI: 10.4018/978-1-4666-7316-8.ch012

Ferrari, & Punie, 2009). Bruns (2008) proposes that "the World Wide Web has been radically transformed, shifting from an information repository to a more social environment where users are not only passive receivers or active harvesters of information, but also creators of content" (p. 22). Furthermore, Suter, Alexander and Kaplan (2005) state that Web-based technologies are encompassing the socializing features of the virtual spaces that emerged as zones for information sharing, community formation, collaboration and extension. It is noteworthy that a revised version of Bloom's taxonomy of educational objectives (Anderson, Krathwohl, & Bloom, 2005) has been extended to include the relevant terminology needed to describe the learning process through the use of social media tools (Churches, 2007) indicating the drift of adoption of such tools into modern education.

The motivation for this study stems from the researchers opinion that there is a lack of empirical studies on the specific use of Google Educational Applications as an instructional tool, particularly in Higher Education. There is still much to be investigated concerning the use of Google Educational Applications, which is often viewed as a much marginalised educational tool. Therefore, the aim of this study is to investigate the experience of using Google Educational Applications as an educational social media tool. A cohort of Computer Science students, enrolled in State-of-Art Technologies in Education (SOAT) online course at the University of Eastern Finland, participated in the study. The students used Google Educational Applications in their group work when dealing with the course topic, Social Media. They had to create a plan (scenario) for deploying state of the art technologies in education (SOAT) in real learning settings. In their scenario they had to identify a specific learning situation where the SOAT technology would be applied to support the learning process of the learners. We collected data regarding students' views and experiences *before* and *after* they had

used Google Educational Applications to complete their coursework. The project aimed to answer the following research questions:

1. How familiar are the Computer Science students with the specific social media tool, Google Educational Applications?
2. What is the students' level of acceptance and how do they perceive the use of Google Educational Applications as an educational tool?

The experiences and feedback relating to the use of Google Educational Applications were gathered by means of pre- and post-course questionnaires, as well as by interviewing some of the participants. This paper will also discuss the experiences and challenges faced by the researcher in designing a teaching and learning project which integrated the use of Google Educational Applications. Finally, potential implications and recommendations for future implementations will be discussed.

BACKGROUND

Web 2.0 and Social Media in Education

In the 21st century modern education is becoming increasingly complex due to the technological environment within which it operates. This new environment offers exciting new possibilities but also raises challenges. Low cost, ubiquity, accessibility and ease of use are all potential affordances, which are making social media technologies an attractive option for transforming teaching and learning environments.

During the last years different authors (Alexander, 2006; Zimmer, 2008; O'Reilly, 2008) have tried to define Web 2.0 from many different view points. Despite the fact that almost all the definitions are debatable, none of them exclude one another. In a recent work (Junco, Heiberger & Loken, 2011), it was stated that social media are a collection of Internet websites, services and practices that support collaboration, communication, participation and sharing. On the other hand, Web 2.0 has been defined as "an ambiguous concept - a conglomeration of folksonomies and syndication, wikis and mashups, social networks and reputation, ubiquitous content and perhaps even kitchen sinks" (Lindstrom, 2007, p. 6). Bryer and Zavatarro (2011) define social media as new technologies that aid social interaction and collaboration whilst also enabling deliberation amongst stakeholders. These technologies include blogs, wikis, media (audio, photo, video, text) sharing tools, networking platforms (Facebook and Twitter) and virtual worlds.

Some Web 2.0 technologies and services that are contributing to the Higher Education domain are blogs, microblogs, wikis, multimedia sharing services and content syndication through RSS, podcasting and content tagging services, social networking sites and other social software. Many of these applications are relatively mature and they have been used for many years. On the other hand, new features and capabilities are being added regularly. In the next section we will discuss the features of main Web 2.0 services.

Blogs

Jorn Barger was the first person who introduced the term *blog* in 1997. He was referring to a simple webpage which consisted of a few brief paragraphs (containing personal opinions), information and personal diary entries which were called *posts*. All these posts were arranged chronologically, with the most recent placed first (Doctorow et al., 2002). Most of the blogs allow visitors to add comments below the posts.

But what is the importance of blogs in education? First of all we can use blogs to capture real-world writing experiences. Secondly, we can organize class blogs together into one area to bet-

ter facilitate easy tracking. Educators can provide quick feedback to students and the students can also comment on each other's work, thus building peer networks which, in turn, develop their own knowledge. Educators can also update new information, meant for the students, relating to homework and assignments. Finally, we can use comments in blogs to encourage students to help each other with their writing, and we can illicit responses to questions without receiving the same answer twenty times (Grosseck, 2009).

Wikis

According to Ebersbach, Glaser and Heigle (2006) a *wiki* is a webpage or a set of web pages which anyone, who has been allowed access, can easily edit. Wikipedia became very popular because the concept of the wiki as a collaborative tool that facilitates the production of group work, is widely understood and upheld.

With wikis we can share ideas, receive updates to and live coverage of events and we can build and trust a community. They can also be used for student projects, collaborating on ideas and organizing documents and resources from individuals and groups of students. Wikis can further be used as a presentation tool, such as e-portfolios and as a group research project for a specific idea. They can manage school and classroom documents and we can use them as a collaborative handout for students.

Tagging and Social Bookmarking

A *tag* is a keyword that refers to a digital object (e.g. a website, picture or video clip) which it helps to describe, but it cannot actually be used as part of a formal classification system.

Social *bookmarking* systems help to share a number of common features (Millen, Feinberg, & Kerr, 2005). The users are allowed to create lists of 'bookmarks' or 'favorites' and to store these on a remote service (rather than within the client browser) which can later be shared with other users of the system. These bookmarks can also be tagged with keywords. Social bookmarking can further be used to create a set of resources which can be accessed from any computer connected to the internet. With bookmarking we can conduct research and share it with peers. We can also rate and review bookmarks to help students decide on the usefulness of resources.

Social Networking

Social Networks are professional and social networking sites which can be used for meeting people, finding like minds and sharing content (Cobb 2010). The examples of social networking sites that can be used in education are too numerous to list but the most popular include Facebook, Twitter, Ning, Flickr, Tumblr, Utterz, NPR, WW-WEDU (Moran, Seaman, & Tinti-Kane, 2011).

RSS and Syndication

RSS is a group of formats that allows users to access content updates from RSS-enabled websites and blogs without the need to visit the related sites. The information from the different websites is collected within a feed (usually using the RSS format) and it is then shown to the user in a process known as syndication.

RSS is very helpful in professional development as it saves time in updating information in a teaching area. With RSS feeds we can replace email lists and reduce emailing. Finally, we can keep the course specific WebPages relevant and current.

Google Educational Apps

Google Apps can be characterized as one of the most powerful communication and collaboration tools. It can be accessed via the web, so everyone can connect with everyone else, no matter where they are. It is very flexible, easy to use and web-based so there is no need for hardware maintenance or software installation. As shown in Table 1 it is a suite of applications that includes Gmail, Google Calendar (shared calendaring), Google Drive (store and share), Google Talk (instant messaging and voice over IP), Google Docs, Spreadsheets and Slides (online document hosting and collaboration), Google Sites (team site creation and publishing), Google Vault (Add Archiving and e-discovery to Google Apps for Education), Start Page (a single customizable access point for all applications), Google Video and Google Security and Compliance. Google Apps are causing quite a stir in the academic environment.

Some other useful Apps from Google include Google Moderator (for creating a series about a discussion topic to which students can submit questions, ideas and suggestions), YouTube (for sharing and accessing videos with educational content), Google Maps, Picasa (for sharing and exploring photos), Scholar (for searching academic literature across many sources) and Blogger.

Related Research on Experiences of Using Social Media in Higher Education

The benefits of Web 2.0 technologies for Higher Education are multiple and have been identified by several researchers (Alexander, 2006; Elgort, Smith, & Toland, 2008; Lamb, 2004). Many of these studies focus on one particular tool, for example, blogs. In their work (Ellison & Wu, 2008; Farmer, Yue, & Brooks, 2008; Hall & Davison, 2007; Williams & Jacobs, 2004; Xie, Ke, & Sharma, 2008) they report that blogs encourage students to read whilst providing them with peer feedback. They also found that blogs enhance reflection and higher-order learning skills. As regards wikis, the majority of studies have found that not only do they improve students' writing skills, but they also engage students and facilitate collaborative learning in various disciplines (Luce-Kapler, 2007; Parker & Chao, 2007).

Table 1.

Google Apps	Characteristics
Gmail	Google Apps offer 25GB of storage per user. It also offers powerful spam filtering and a 99.9% uptime SLA. All these are hosted by Google and there is no cost and no advertisements for students, faculty or staff.
Google Calendar	Helps teachers and faculties to organize their time. Anyone can easily schedule lessons and meetings. Multiple calendars can be overlaid to see when people are available - a great way to manage staff schedules (can send invitations and manage RSVPs).
Drive	Provides a storage place for up-to-date versions of files from anywhere. Educators can share individual files or whole folders with specific people or an entire team. Can facilitate the creation of and reply to comments on files in order to get feedback or add ideas.
Docs	With Google Docs anyone can create rich documents with images, tables, equations, drawings, links and more. Gather input and manage feedback with social commenting.
Sheets	Google Sheets can keep and share lists, track projects, analyze data and track results with the spreadsheet editor. There are some very useful tools like advanced formulas, embedded charts, filters and pivot tables to help get new perspectives on data.
Slides	Helps in the creation of slides with presentation editor, which supports features like embedded videos, animations and dynamic slide transitions. The presentations can be published on the web so anyone can view them, or they can be shared privately.
Sites	Sites are shared workspaces for classes and faculties. The students can build their own project sites without the need to write in code. It is as easy as writing a document. There are many pre-designed templates. In addition, Google Site provides a system and site-level security controls.
Vault	Google vault is an added archiving and e-discovery feature to Google Apps for Education. It is optional and adds archiving, e-discovery and information governance capabilities. With vault anyone can define retention policies, place legal holds on users as needed, and can run reports on user activity and actions in the archive.

In a study by Sandars and Schroter (2007) with main focus Web 2.0 technologies, they surveyed students' familiarity with the use of Web 2.0 technologies. They ascertained that there is a very high level of familiarity with Web 2.0 technologies but a low level of use as regards most of them (with the exception of social networking tools). Although there was a high level of interest in the use of Web 2.0 tools for educational purposes, there was a perceived lack in user experience in the areas of learning and/or teaching.

Brill and Park (2008) examined all new technologies and their abilities to improve students' learning through increasing their engagement. They state that all the students show great interest, make an effort, are motivated and spend time on task: these all having been identified as well established learning constructs which support engaged learning. They also identify three themes. The *first theme* relates to students' responsibility to

take ownership of their learning; the *second theme* deals with the flexible collaboration of working in groups, and the *third*, and final theme, is the use of different and relevant human and non-human resources to support learning.

The adoption of Web 2.0 technologies by faculty members was examined by Ajjan and Hartshorne (2008). They tried to examine the process of adoption by inquiring into the faculty members' knowledge and understanding of the tools. Their results have indicated that the majority of the faculty members were aware of the multitude of benefits that these tools could offer them, but that there was a disconnection when it came to the actual adoption or future plans to incorporate them into their teaching. Finally they suggested that more efforts should be invested in boosting the educators' overall confidence and level of comfort with the new technologies (Ajjan & Hartshorne, 2008). Hemmi, Bayne and Land

(2009) have conducted some case studies on three different classroom use occurrences in which they have tried to explore, from a pedagogical point of view, how Higher Education has been implementing Web 2.0 technologies. Their results have shown that both students and faculty are approaching these new tools and methods with caution. They attributed this result to the unwillingness of the academia to stray from the traditional models. However, the authors were very encouraged to see that Higher Education institutions have begun to recognize social media's immense possibilities (Hemmi et al., 2009).

Related Research on Social Media

Research on social media in education suggests that integrating social media in learning and teaching environments may yield new forms of inquiry, communication, collaboration, identity work, knowledge development and also effect positive (or negative) cognitive, social and emotional impacts (Ranieri, Manca, & Fini, 2012).

Previous researches have documented the relationship between the use of the Social Networking Service (SNS) Facebook and increased levels of *social capital* (Burke, Kraut, & Marlow, 2011; Ellison, Steinfield, & Lampe, 2007; Valenzuela, Park, & Kee, 2009), a form of capital that describes resources embedded in social relationships and interactions within a network. Facebook may be especially well suited for accruing bridging social capital, which speaks to the benefits associated with weaker more heterogeneous social ties such as novel information and broadened world-views (Ellison et al., 2007), in part because the site enables users to create "social supernets" made up of hundreds of social connections (Donath, 2007).

Many aspiring and practicing educators have faced unfortunate consequences because of the way in which others perceive the use of SNS tools such as MySpace and Facebook (Carter, Foulger, & Ewbank, 2008). Although anecdotal examples of in-service educator use of SNS to enhance instruction and generate interest in school clubs and programs have been reported upon (Carter et al., 2008), studies of larger samples of pre-service teachers' use of Social Networks are only recently emerging (Steinbrecher & Hart, 2012).

In his study Bosch (2009) reports that students use Facebook instinctively to support both their academic and social goals. His evidence also seems to suggest that students' main motive for using Facebook is social connectivity but that they are receptive to the possibilities of integrating Facebook into university courses. There is a potential for gaining learning benefits associated with increased communication among students, greater access to course materials and improved logistical management of courses.

A qualitative study which was conducted by Selwyn (2009) amongst United Kingdom university students using Facebook, reported that they used Facebook to criticize learning, exchange information, extend moral support and, paradoxically, promote themselves as being academically disengaged or incompetent. His final conclusions were that rather than attempting to *either* appropriate Facebook for educationally "appropriate" and "valid" uses, *or* else to regulate students' use through coercion or surveillance, university authorities and educators are best advised to allow these practices to continue unabated and firmly "backstage". Also, while Facebook deserves no particular merit as an educational application, it should neither be feared nor dismissed. According to Selwyn (2009) Facebook it does serve a "vital contribution to the successful provision of offline university education" (p.173).

Kamarul, Norlida and Zainol (2010) investigated the role of Facebook as one of the most popular SNSs among many English Second Language (ESL) speakers as well as English First Language (EFL) learners at university level as it provides them with opportunities to create and join groups within the online community.

Although the potential of SNSs in general, and Facebook in particular, in providing language learners with the opportunities to be involved in online learning communities to practice English and writing skill is evident, several previous researchers have identified challenges faced by learners in using Facebook as part of classroom learning. These challenges include issues pertaining to learners' privacy (Rosenblum, 2007), tricky relationships between students and teachers (Simon, 2008), learners' diminished completion rates and the inability to control their learning (Grandzol & Grandzol, 2010), waste of time, the development of negative habits and attitudes and time management (Kamarul et al., 2010).

In a recent paper Promnitz-Hayashi (2011) found that following the incorporation of Facebook activity, many of the more introverted students became increasingly motivated in class and were also communicating more readily with their classmates. He also noticed that students began to express more opinions and gave extended reasoning in not only their face-to-face interactions but also in their written class work. According to his findings, it is possible that social networking may have played a role as it appears to gift students with choices and opportunities to take control of their own learning. These kinds of opportunities and environments may thus create conditions for the facilitation and development of learner autonomy.

Chou (2012) found that most students exhibit a positive attitude towards the adoption of the Facebook group tool as their class website. Students can employ functions embedded in the Facebook class website to engage in exchange and information communication. Since current literature lacks knowledge relating to the Facebook class website, this study only reports on preliminary findings.

Eren (2012) suggests that Facebook can be very useful as an educational tool and that students' attitudes towards it are mostly positive. The students welcome the use of the social networking sites as supplementary to the curriculum and most of them have shown that they love spending time

on Facebook. Videos and other sharing activities in groups are useful in improving their language skills. Teachers, who consider applying such an activity in their classrooms, need to be sensitive to some points. In addition, the learning goals must be defined clearly so that the group members can understand what they must do and share the relevant activity.

There are various factors which play a part in student engagement, including investment in the academic experience at a college, involvement in co-curricular activities and interaction with teachers and peers (Junco, 2012). When engaging, students use physical and psychological energy, both of which are important to the students' success. Students who spend time and effort in in-class and out of class engagements are more likely to attain their desired academic outcome.

The relationship between Facebook usage and group engagement has been limited by the focus on measuring *individual student engagement* rather than *group engagement*. Junco (2012) focuses on the relationship between frequency of Facebook use, participation in Facebook activities and student engagement.

Connection to Previous Research on the Topic

The present work is part of the first author's doctoral studies. The aim of the studies is to investigate the potential of social media in Higher Education. The doctoral research work consisted of a series of studies related to the use of social media in Higher Education. Furthermore, we experimented with the following social media tools: Edmodo, Wiki and Facebook in difference learning settings. The concepts of microblogging, social networks and wikis were investigated in order to explore the potential use of these social media technologies as educational tools in Higher Education. Moreover the studies were performed in different learning settings in online learning, blended learning and Problem Based Learning settings. It is worth mentioning that these studies were performed in different cultural but also socio-economical environments with groups of students from multinational and inter-disciplinary environments. The students were also at different academic levels; enrolled in Bachelor, Masters or PhD studies. In all the presented series of studies, the student groups had to work in teams and collaborate using the suggested social media tool. The social aspect of the introduced tools was highlighted since we believe that, in order for social media to be successfully introduced in Higher Education as an educational tool, it needs to be used collaboratively and more specifically in a collaboration to solve a common problem or project.

One of our first studies was an investigation into the potential of microblogging in Higher Education: the Edmodo case study among Computer Science learners in Finland (Paliktzoglou & Suhonen, 2014b). Microblogging is one of the social media technologies with the greatest potential. The features of a microblogging platform vary from sending and receiving messages via the web, SMS, instant messaging by clients and third party applications. Even though social media networking sites are commonly used in Higher Education, very little empirical evidence is available concerning the impact of social media use on students' learning and engagement, albeit some studies on the use of Twitter as a microblogging tool in educational settings have been done by Gao, Luo and Zhang (2012). In this study, we analyzed the level of familiarity, engagement and frequency of use of social media technologies amongst university-level Computer Science students in Finland. Additionally, we analyzed the experience of using a specific microblogging social media, Edmodo, as a learning aid to support group work. The specific focus of the study was to examine the reception of the students towards the Edmodo platform. The data was collected through a social media familiarity questionnaire, Edmodo experience questionnaire and interviews. The main findings were that the cohort was not very familiar with social media at the beginning of the course. However, the use of the Edmodo (a microblogging social media networking site) as a learning tool had a positive impact on the students. This study provided experimental evidence that microblogging social networking sites, and more specifically Edmodo, can be used as an educational tool to help better engage students in the use of other social media networking sites.

In our second study we investigated microblogging as an assisted learning tool in Problem Based Learning (PBL) in Bahrain (Paliktzoglou & Suhonen, 2014c). We investigated the students' level of familiarity, engagement and their frequency of use of social media technologies. We further analyzed the experiences of using the Edmodo tool to support *PBL*, and we related participants' opinions regarding the use of the tool. The data was collected using two questionnaires and a focus group interview at the end of the course. The main findings of this study are comparable and somehow familiar to our previous study (Paliktzoglou & Suhonen, 2014c). Moreover, with regards to the adoption of Edmodo as a learning tool to support *PBL*, although literature argues that cultural differences play an important role in the acceptance of learning tools (Cheung, Chiu, & Lee, 2011), our results indicate that Edmodo had a positive reception as learning tool in blended learning to support *PBL*.

In our third study we investigated social networks, and more specifically Facebook, which is one of the Web 2.0 technologies with applications in many domains, including that of education. This study described the students' engagement with Facebook as an assisted learning tool in Problem-based Learning (PBL) in Bahrain (Paliktzoglou & Suhonen, 2014a). Additionally, we analyzed the reception of the students towards Facebook as a learning aid tool. A range of mixed method data collection techniques and triangulation was performed to reveal the complexity of the topic under investigation. The data collection was through pre- and post-questionnaires and an interview. The empirical data showed that the use of Facebook, as a learning tool, had a positive impact on students. The study provides experimental evidence that social networks, and more specifically Facebook, can be used as an educational tool in a PBL context to help engage students in the use of social media (Web 2.0).

In our fourth study the investigation was based on the current level of familiarity, engagement and frequency of use of educational technology (including Web 2.0) tools in Higher Education student cohorts in Cyprus. Additionally it focused on a specific Web 2.0 tool (Wiki) which was prescribed to the students as a learning aid. Its reception by the student cohort was examined, and the data was collected mainly through questionnaires (pre and post) and a post-module focus group. The main findings were that the cohorts were not very familiar with Web 2.0 tools at the beginning of the course. The use of the Wiki for part of the semester had a positive impact on the students, even those who had been negative towards it at the beginning of the study (Alexakis, Paliktzoglou, & Suhonen, 2012).

In the above mentioned series of studies the instructor's role was also examined and, in most cases, it was clear that working with social media tools was interactive and enjoyable though a significant amount of time and effort is required to moderate these tools, especially when there are more than three groups working on diverse subjects. Certain reservations were expressed regarding the effort the instructors would need to put into facilitating bigger cohorts/groups than the ones in the studies. A final observation is that as students and instructors become more experienced in the use of these social media tools, less instructor input is anticipated, and thus the above mentioned issues could become less pertinent.

RESEARCH DESIGN

The Role of Google Educational Applications in the Study

In our experiment, the Google Educational Applications tools were introduced as a collaborative platform to support group work in one of the course modules during the State-of-Art Technologies in an Education online course at the School of Computing, University of Eastern Finland. The students, after completing the first questionnaire, received a general introduction as to the use of Google Educational Applications. Detailed instructions were provided to the students on how to use the tools via a set of practical tasks and video tutorials.

The next step was to launch the group work. The topics given to the groups were related to the content of the State-of-the-Art Technologies in Education course. The following teams were formed: Team 1 (Wilostar3D-Virtual worlds); Team 2 (Web 2.0 technologies and social software); Team 3 (Aplusix - software for learning arithmetic and algebra calculations); Team 4 (Interactive whiteboard); Team 5 (Sura Ya Ukimwi - a story based e-learning environment to learn about HIV/AIDS) and Team 6 (Greenfoot - environment for creating visual exercises to support learning about programming). The aim of the group work was to design a concrete scenario using the team's state-of-the-art technology in real life learning settings.

After selecting the teams, the groups started their work, which was supported by Google Educational Applications. A team leader was nominated by each team and his/her task was to ensure that all the outlined tasks and milestones were met timeously. We expected that each group and individual group members would use Google Educational Applications during the group work in the following manner: *Gmail* to stay in touch with other members; *Google Groups* to discuss possible strategies/issues regarding the project; *Google Docs* to collaboratively write their assignment; *Google Calendar* to set up milestones and deadlines for their project; *Google Notebook* to record important notes and bookmarks about their assignment; *GTalk* to facilitate the opportunity for synchronous contact/collaboration/meeting and lastly *Google Sites* in order to present and reflect on the work done for their project. It is worth mentioning that the instructor was constantly supporting, stimulating and facilitating collaboration on a day to day basis. Part of the learning strategy was to motivate students to collaborate, share resources and discuss their work using Google Educational Applications. For example, each of the students had to post at least 3 post per week related to the topic of their group work as part of the collaboration process and then reply to the posts of the other group members. In this way students became active participants in Google Applications and participation was rewarded as part of the course marks. For the duration of the course the instructor was responsible for constantly presenting the student groups with relevant literature in the form of posts including videos, links to books, articles etc.

Research Methodology

The participants of the study were multi-ethnic (n=24, 3 female, 13% and 21 male, 88%) consisted of 5 under-graduate (Bachelor), 15 post-graduate (Master) and 4 PhD students studying at School of Computing, University of Eastern Finland. The majority of the students were aged 20 to 30 (16 participants, 66.7%), 7 over 30 (29.2%) and only one under 20 (4.2%).

The research data were collected via two questionnaires and an interview. The first questionnaire activity formed part of the first week's *tasks to do* list (the students were given a list of tasks that needed to be completed by the

end of each week). The students were not given any information regarding Google Educational Applications, since we sought to discover if they had any prior knowledge. The survey was split into four parts: the *first part* covered demographic information of the participants (name, age, level of studies) the *second part* covered student familiarity, the *third part* the context of use and the *fourth part* the frequency with which Google Educational Applications were used. The questions were prepared with the Likert scale where the students could rate each item on a 1 to 5 response scale. The students' *familiarity questions* on the Likert scale varied from "very familiar (frequent user)" to "not known", in the *context of use* the questions on the Likert scale varied from "personal learning/studying (as tool for studying/learning)" to "other" and in the *frequency of use* on the Likert scale they varied from "daily" to "never". It was compulsory to answer all the questions.

The second (post-module) questionnaire activity also formed part of the last week's *tasks to do* list. The survey was designed in two parts: the first part covered the participants' demographic information (name, age, level of studies) and the second part focused on their engagement during the course with the Google Educational Application tools. The questions were formulated using a Likert 1 to 5 response scale. At the end of the survey one open ended question was included where students were able to add comments or make suggestions regarding possible future improvements to the use of Google Educational Application tools. At the end of the questionnaire there was a clear explanation regarding the nature of the research. The participants were also asked for their official approval to proceed with the study and they were given the assurance that all data would be treated as confidential.

The data analysis of the interviews was performed in two stages. Analysis of the data from transcripts requires an open mind and immersion in the text (Morrison, Haley, Sheehan, & Taylor, 2011). Stage one consisted of the preparation of transcripts, the identification of themes, concepts and events and the coding of these in order to retrieve information relating to specific ideas (Polonsky & Waller, 2010). The process of coding the themes required the researcher to engage with the data in order to fully understand the meanings and insights related to the data. The second phase used the data to formulate a description of the setting (Polonsky & Waller, 2010) and interpret how these themes and insights relate to the research questions (Polonsky & Waller, 2010). Each informant's interview was audio recorded and then transcribed to cross reference for key themes of identity creation and consumer influence.

RESULTS

Pre-Questionnaire: Familiarity and Use of Google Educational Applications

The aim of the study was to investigate the students' engagement with and perceptions to the use of Google Educational Applications.

Familiarity

In the first questionnaire the following questions were posed to the participants: *How familiar are you with the following Google Educational Applications: Gmail, Google Groups, Google Docs, Google Calendar, Google Notebook, GTalk, Google Sites?* The participants could choose from

Figure 1. Familiarity with Google educational applications

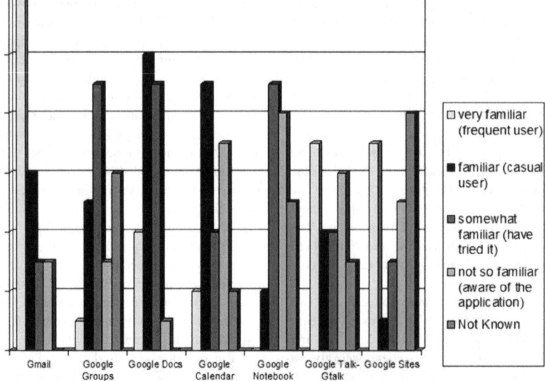

five options: very familiar (frequent user), familiar (casual user), somewhat familiar (have tried it), not so familiar (aware of the application) and unknown. The results are presented in Figure 1.

Students indicated that from all the listed Google Educational Applications they were most familiar with Gmail. In addition most of the participants were frequent or casual users of the Google Docs and Google Calendar. The participants have tried Google Groups and Google Notebook, but they were less familiar with these applications than with Gmail and Google Docs. Some of the respondents stated that they had used Google Talk and Google Sites, but these two applications were least known to respondents.

Frequency of Use

In the second part of the questionnaire, we asked the participants to evaluate the frequency with which they use Google Educational Applications. The participants were asked: *How often do you use the following Google Educational Applications: Gmail, Google Group, Google Docs, Google Calendar, Google Notebook, GTalk, Google Sites?* The answer options were: daily, weekly, monthly, occasionally and never. The results are presented in Figure 2.

The participants revealed that (from the Google Educational Applications) they most frequently used Gmail (Google email) and Google Docs. Moderate use of Google Calendar and Google Groups was reported by the participants in addi-

Figure 2. Frequency of use of Google educational applications

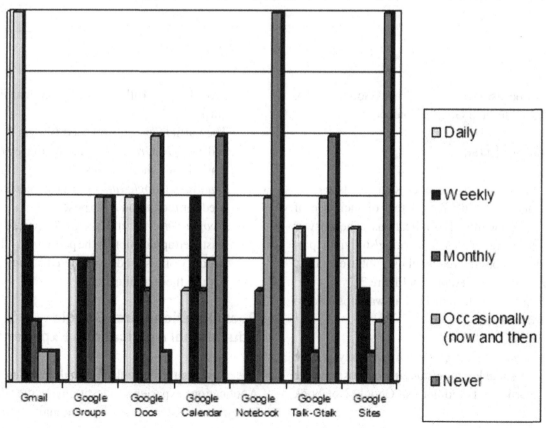

Figure 3. Context of use of Google educational applications

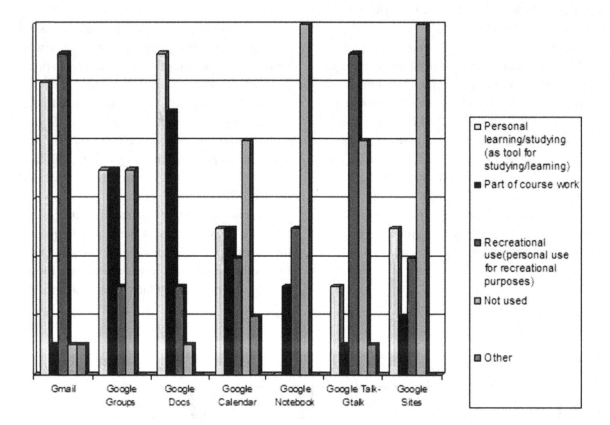

tion to occasional use of GTalk (Google Talk), Google Sites and Google Notebook.

Context of Use

The third part of the questionnaire asked the students to identify the context of their use of Google Educational Applications. The answer options were: personal learning/studying, part of course work, recreational use, not used, other. The results are presented in Figure 3.

From the data collected it was possible to ascertain that:

1. *Gmail* and *Google Docs* were mostly used for personal learning/studying purposes, while participants did not use Google Notebook

and Google Talk for personal learning purposes.

2. The participants mostly used *Google Docs* and *Google Groups* as part of the course work during their studies.

3. *Gmail* and *Google Talk* were most frequently used for recreational purposes.

4. *Google Notebook* and *Google Sites* were the least used application by the participants. The majority of respondents stated that they did not use these applications.

Post Questionnaire: Google Educational Applications Experience

The participants filled out the Google Educational Applications experience questionnaire after they had worked with Google Educational Applica-

Figure 4. Impact of Google educational applications (frequency)

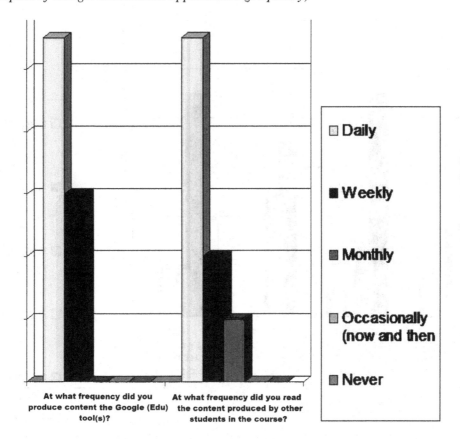

tions during the course. The students were given a questionnaire that included a set of statements related to their user experience of Google Educational Applications during the course. The students were asked to give their opinion in response to the statements using the five point Likert Scale: completely agree, agree, neither agree nor disagree (neutral), disagree and completely disagree.

Use, Participation and Added Value

In the first part of the questionnaire, we wanted to know how often students produced content and read the content produced by others during the course. Figure 4 shows the students' estimation of their participation during the course.

The results show the positive impact of Google Educational Applications as learning tool. The

students were producing and reading content in Google Educational Applications "daily" with the highest frequency (65%).

Secondly we wanted to enquire as to the influence of instructor's participation in the use of the Google Educational Applications during the course. We also wanted to know about how the learning activity structure influenced the use of the Google Educational Applications. As seen in Figure 5 the students stated that the instructor did influence their use of the tools with higher frequency ("agree", 41%). It was indicated that the structure of the learning activities in the course motivated the participants to use Google Educational Applications with the highest frequency ("agree", 53%).

Most of the students were of the opinion that the use of Google Educational Tools added value to

Figure 5. Participation and collaboration

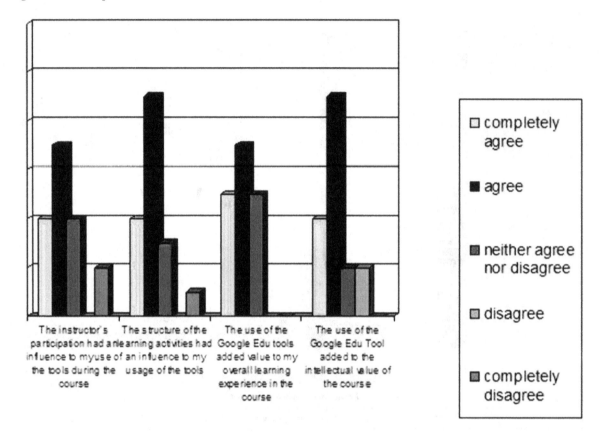

the overall learning experience during the course. Finally, we wanted to know whether the use of Google Educational Tools, in the students' opinion, had added value to their learning experience and also to the intellectual value of the course. Most of the participants agreed that Google Educational Applications had added value to their learning experience and most of the participants were of the opinion that Google Educational Applications had increased the intellectual value of the course.

Reflection and Processing of Course Content

In the second part of the questionnaire we wanted to know the students' opinions regarding the role of Google Tools during the module, as shown below in Figures 6 and 7.

The students agreed (with the higher frequency) that the tools had facilitated and captured their thoughts. As such it was recorded that the participants agreed (with the higher frequency) that the tools had facilitated their personal reflection and had further supported them in connecting concepts with cases and examples during the teamwork. The participants reported that the Google Educational Applications had supported collaboration and helped to build on ideas or resources presented in the course. Furthermore, it was reported that Google Educational Applications supported students to discuss course concepts and created a sense of comfort and community. Finally, from the data gathered, students mentioned that they were able to get more information or support from the instructor using the tools.

Figure 6. Reflection and processing of content

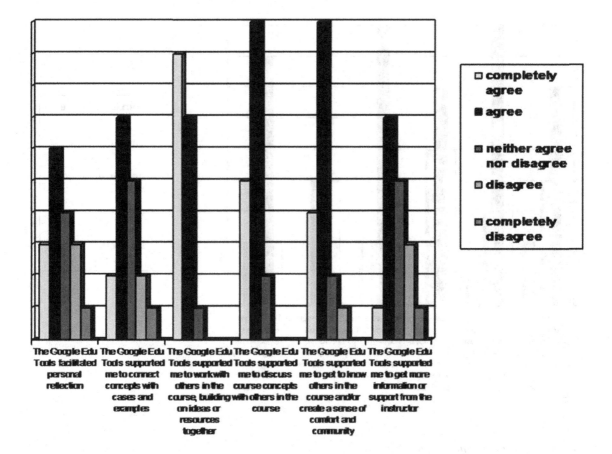

Further Use of Google Educational Applications

As shown in Figure 8, students reported that they would recommend the use of this approach in other courses with ("I recommend", 41%) a higher frequency. Finally most of the students, when asked to comment or suggest improvements to Google Educational Applications, mentioned that this is a great learning tool and that they definitely would suggest that it be used in other courses as well.

Interview

The interview was held at the end of the course. The respondents were randomly selected to take part in the interview in which they were afforded

the opportunity to speak freely regarding central factors relating to the topics and the use of Google Educational Apps. The interview focused on two major questions but the informal interactions resulted in further probing and questioning by the researcher. Questions ranged from those probing *mere surface level information* (such as asking how the participants liked using Google Educational Applications) to *more intuitive questions* (such as what is the participant's perception regarding the use of Google Educational Applications for educational purposes). The two preliminary interview questions are detailed below:

1. Do you have other comments or suggestions to help improve the use of the introduced

Figure 7. Reflection and processing of content

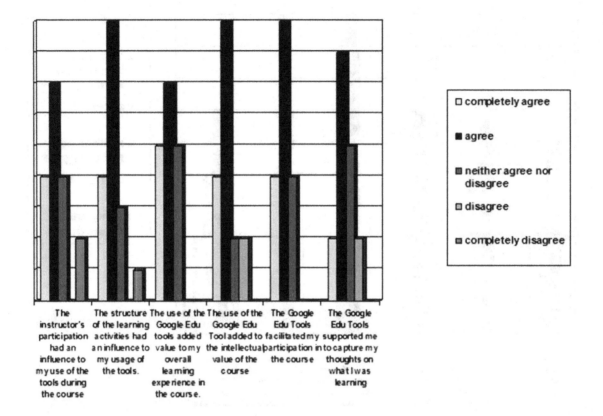

Figure 8. Expectation and recommendation

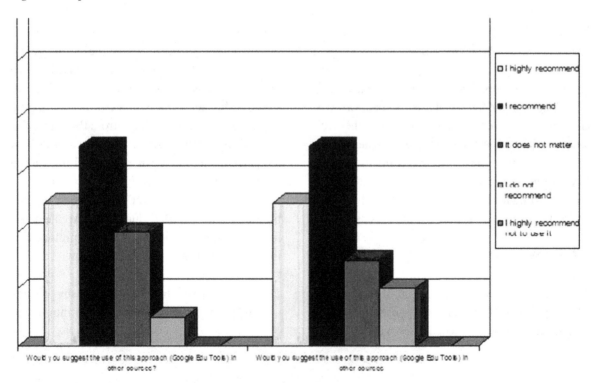

Google Edu App Tools environment in courses?

2. How would you compare features of Google Apps Tools with the standard proprietary (Microsoft Office) or open source (Open Office) products?

As mentioned above the informal interactions resulted in further probing and questioning by the researcher and the following five questions emerged:

1. What did you like in Google Apps Tools?
2. What was working well? What needs to be improved? Please list three good aspects (or features/ functionalities) of Google Apps Tools and three aspects (or features/ functionalities) that need improvement.
3. How would you compare Google Apps Tools to Moodle?
4. Please describe any problems that you may have experienced whilst using Google Apps Tools.

The interviews provided an understanding of the participants' experiences in using the Google Educational Applications during the SOAT course. Analysis of data gained from the interviews "entails classifying, comparing, weighing, and combining material from interviews to extract the meaning and implications, to reveal patterns, or to stitch together descriptions of events into coherent narratives" (Rubin & Rubin, 2005, p. 201).

Collaboration and Feedback

Collaboration among students was easy in most cases however some did report that: "...disjointed and not very intuitive to use, especially when using several different apps tools together. For example, Google docs in itself is fantastic, but to use it with other apps together is just painfully stiff...." On the other hand, students felt confident to work collaboratively stating: "...as a net collaboration

Google Apps are very good..."; "Main 'bonus' of Google tools is immediate sharing and ability to simultaneously edit documents by multiple people...." Furthermore, emphasizing the positive collaborative learning opportunities, a student commented that: "...with the help of Google tools communication is faster, sharing of documents is easier and more comfortable. To build a group work Google Tools are the best choice."

Motivation and Familiarization

Some of participants stated that they needed time to get use to Google Apps. Although, the exact time span needed for students to become comfortable with its use varied. Students commented that: "...A separate individual module on how to use the tools to ensure that everyone is on the same level when you start group work. For example, two of my team members had used Google tools before whereas the third student didn't even have a Gmail account and consequently fell well behind as the learning curve was steep...." Some of them felt that the material provided by Google should be more detailed stating: "They would need better tutorials...." Nevertheless, the students remained motivated to use the tool effectively to address their learning needs in the course. It is noteworthy that one student mentioned: "Collaborative feature of Google Apps Tools is much better than others."

Comparison with the Standard Proprietary (Microsoft Office) or Open Source (Open Office) Products

Students had several different views on the matter. One of them mentioned that: "It's not as nice as Office...." Another could not find any difference: "...they look to me almost the same...." On the other hand, some students were more critical mentioning that: "The features in Microsoft office and open office are more organised though they cannot allow you to work on the same document at the same time in real time environment like

Google application tools...." Moreover, students mentioned that Google Apps are easier to use because of its simplicity which makes it easier to understand: "Google Apps are simpler to use. Most of the requirements are embedded there. It can expand as well..." and "...it is better to share and update it online. You don't need to install any application onto your computer. Besides, every group members can see updates in the same time...." There were some students that reported that: "Google Apps didn't have all the tools which for example we had used in MS word."

Examples of Positive and Negative Receptions

Some students mentioned: "Not very intuitive, and not very interconnected. For example, the movement from one tool to another is not intuitive and not very well linked. I should be able to create a calendar where adding a group is a one-click process. Sometimes the calendar didn't work, the tools are still flaky." Another student commented: "It is more advanced platform and it facilitates our learning and interacting with other people." Overall, students commented that they had enjoyed using online tools for study or personal recreation.

Views on Educational Impact

Students used Google Apps because the tools allowed them to feel connected to their tutors and other students in the class. One interview participant said: "It's a very interesting tool in education especially in SOAT based on cloud computing, the work is shared online with a different team members edited, modified and updated online. I suggest that Google tools should be used in education for both instructors and students from low to high level of education."

On the other hand one respondent mentioned that using a few of the Google Apps could be more beneficial to bigger groups: "Maybe for bigger teams these could be a fine addition, now they weren't needed and Calendar just seemed like a hindrance that had to be used with something as it was required."

Furthermore, another student highlighted the fact that both educators and students are able to contribute and build upon one another's contribution: "Google Apps give users more flexibilities working in collaborative environments. Google Apps are advanced."

DISCUSSION

Google Apps have had positive impact on modern education. The effective use of the features and the opportunities afforded by these applications support and empower instructors towards infusing the educational process with active learning, creativity, problem solving, cooperation and multifaceted interactions. Student also benefit by using these apps as they improve their academic performance, stimulate their enquiring minds and foster alternative thinking skills. In this study we set out to investigate the experience of using the specific social media tools, Google Educational Applications, as a learning aid to support group work. The specific focus of the study is to examine the students' reception of Google Educational Applications.

Many of the past studies focus on one particular tool, for example, blogs. In contrast this study (and its related surveys) focuses on all the Google Education Applications as used by Computer Science students. Another differentiating element of our study is that it focuses on students' acceptance and perception of the use of Google Educational Applications as an educational tool. Furthermore, according to the literature review, although there was a high interest in using Web 2.0 tools for educational purposes, a lack in the experience to use them for learning or teaching was perceived. Our study results indicate that students are very familiar with Google Educational Applications.

Moreover the results of many studies have shown that both students and faculty are approaching these new tools and methods with caution. Our results have shown that students are very familiar with Google Educational Applications and they are using them almost daily.

Given this background, the main strength of this study is its contribution to the literature on the use of Google Educational Applications. As previously noted there is a lack of empirical studies on the specific use of Google Educational Applications as an instructional tool, particularly in Higher Education. Furthermore this study investigates the experience of using Google Educational Applications as educational social media tools. Our results have shown that the students are very familiar with Google Educational Applications, in particular Google Docs and Gmail. It also revealed that students use these applications almost every day. The students use Gmail mainly for personal learning/studying and/or for recreational use. Google Groups and Google Docs are used mainly for personal learning/studying as well as part of coursework. The other Google Apps (such as Google Calendar, Google Notebook, GTalk and Google Sites) are not commonly used by the students.

It is noteworthy to mention the instructor's observation that the students tend to use Google Docs for the collaborative writing of their assignment and Gmail for keeping in touch.

This finding indicated towards the positive impact of Google Educational Applications as a learning tool. The students were using Google Educational Applications "daily" to produce and read content. They also stated that the instructor influenced them to use the tools with higher frequency. From these results we can deduce that Google Educational Applications added value to the learning experience of the students in the course.

Students mentioned that the "module structure" motivated them to use Google Educational Applications. The Google Educational Applications also supported the students to work with others in the course, building on ideas or resources together. Google Apps support the students to discuss course concepts with one another in the course and it also created and fostered a sense of comfort and community. The students were also able to receive more information and support from their instructor. As regards the module, the students reported that it met their expectations and they suggested that this approach be used in other courses as well. The interviews provided an understanding of the participants' experiences in using Google Educational Applications during the course. In many cases the collaboration was easy and the students felt confident in their work, however, some students reported that they found it challenging to use different apps together.

As for motivation and familiarization, some participants stated that they needed time to become accustomed to Google Apps. Although, the exact time span needed for students to become comfortable with its use varied. Nevertheless, the students remained motivated to become proficient in the use of the tool to effectively master the learning needed in the course. Regarding the comparison to the standard proprietary or open source products, the students had different views on the matter. Some of them found it to be similar whilst others did not experience it as user friendly as Office. There were many different opinions among the students but overall they commented that they had enjoyed using online tools for study and/or recreation.

Finally the students added that they used Google Apps because the tools allow them to feel connected to their tutors and other students in the class. On the other hand some respondents mentioned that using only a few of the Google Apps could be more beneficial in bigger groups.

Our results provide strong evidence to support the claim that the researchers have to infuse student ideas, to integrate their energy and talent into the "new university" which is using the technologies of Web 2.0 and more specific the Google Educational Applications. These results are consistent with the majority of the research work in the field of Web 2.0 technologies (Alexander & Levine, 2008; Cobb, 2010; Lindstrom, 2007). Web 2.0 and Google Applications will enable students, faculty and administrators to communicate, collaborate and share their ideas. The results from the survey seem to confirm the hypothesis that students are very positive towards the use of Google Educational Applications and this is also a reflection of students' positive experiences with Applications.

This educational experience proved to be beneficial for students in as far as the sharing of ideas, raising of diverse learning issues and, most importantly, collaborating successfully with their peers and lecturers in a different environment. Uniquely equipped Google Apps provided more resources which the lecturer could use to monitor students' online communication, provide feedback to shared lecture presentations and to discuss course concepts.

CONCLUSION

The study provides experimental evidence that the use of Google Educational Applications can increase student engagement, and thus, Google Educational Applications can be used as an educational tool. Moreover we provided evidence to suggest that students and the instructor were both highly engaged in the learning process through communication and collaboration. The participants positively suggested the use of Google Educational Applications in other courses. It is worth mentioning that one specific limitation of our experiment was that the participants were restricted to the specific group of Computer Science students from University of Eastern Finland.

It would be advisable to conduct similar studies with a broader set of participants in order to compare them to these settings. Nevertheless, from our findings it is evident that social media (and more specifically the Google Educational Applica-

tions) can support social-constructivist models of pedagogy and that Google Educational Applications, as social media tools, have the potential to play an important role in the future of learning environments. Finally, in the light of the growing trend towards using social media in Higher Education, it is hoped that this study will motivate further controlled studies of Google Educational Applications in order to evaluate how emerging technologies can be more efficiently utilized and adopted into the Higher Education domain.

REFERENCES

Ajjan, H., & Hartshorne, R. (2008). Investigating faculty decisions to adopt Web 2.0 technologies: Theory and empirical tests. *The Internet and Higher Education*, *11*(2), 71–80. doi:10.1016/j.iheduc.2008.05.002

Alexakis, C., Paliktzoglou, V., & Suhonen, J. (2012). Assessment of the familiarity, adoption and use of educational technology by higher education students in Cyprus. In C. Vrasidas & P. Panaou (Eds.), *Design Thinking in Education, Media + Society* (pp. 154–163). Nicosia: Cuprus.

Alexander, B. (2006). Web 2.0: A new wave of innovation for teaching and learning? *EDUCAUSE Review*, *41*(2), 32.

Alexander, B., & Levine, A. (2008). Web 2.0 storytelling: Emergence of a new genre. *EDUCAUSE Review*, *43*(6), 40–56.

Anderson, L. W., Krathwohl, D. R., & Bloom, B. S. (2005). *A taxonomy for learning, teaching, and assessing*. New York: Longman.

Bosch, T. E. (2009). Using online social networking for teaching and learning: Facebook use at the University of Cape Town. *Communicatio*, *35*(2), 185–200. doi:10.1080/02500160903250648

Brill, J. M., & Park, Y. (2008). Facilitating engaged learning in the interaction age taking a pedagogically-disciplined approach to innovation with emergent technologies. *International Journal of Teaching and Learning in Higher Education, 20*(1), 70–78.

Bruns, A. (2008). *Blogs, Wikipedia, Second Life, and beyond: From production to prod usage.* New York, NY: Lang.

Bryer, T. A., & Zavattaro, S. M. (2011). Social media and public administration. *Administrative Theory & Praxis, 33*(3), 325–340. doi:10.2753/ATP1084-1806330301

Burke, M., Kraut, R., & Marlow, C. (2011). Social capital on Facebook: Differentiating uses and users. In *Proceedings of the 2011 Annual Conference on Human Factors in Computing Systems* (pp. 571-580). New York: ACM. doi:10.1145/1978942.1979023

Carter, H. L., Foulger, T. S., & Ewbank, A. D. (2008). Have you googled your teacher lately? Teachers' use of social networking sites. *Phi Delta Kappan, 89*(9), 681–685. doi:10.1177/003172170808900916

Cheung, C. M. K., Chiu, P. Y., & Lee, M. K. O. (2011). Online social networks: Why do students use facebook? *Computers in Human Behavior, 27*(4), 1337–1343. doi:10.1016/j.chb.2010.07.028

Chou, P. (2012). The integration of Facebook into class management: An exploratory study. *Educational Research, 3*(7), 572–575.

Churches, A. (2007). *Educational Origami: Bloom's and ICT Tools.* Retrieved from: http://edorigami.wikispaces.com/file/view/bloom%27s+Digital+taxonomy+v3.01.pdf

Cobb, J. (2010). *Learning 2.0 for Associations.* Retrieved from http://www.tagoras.com/docs/Learning-20-Associations-2ed.pdf

Conole, G., & Alevizou, P. (2010). *A literature review of the use of Web 2.0 tools in Higher Education.* A Report Commissioned by the Higher Education Academy. Retrieved from http://www.jisctechdis.ac.uk/assets/EvidenceNet/Conole_Alevizou_2010.pdf

Doctorow, C., Dornfest, R., Johnson, S., Powers, S., Trott, B., & Trott, M. (2002). *Essential Blogging: Selecting and Using Weblog Tools.* Sebastopol, CA: O'Reilly.

Donath, J. S. (2007). Signals in social supernets. *Journal of Computer-Mediated Communication, 13*(1), 231–251. doi:10.1111/j.1083-6101.2007.00394.x

Ebersbach, A., Glaser, M., & Heigl, R. (2006). *Wiki: Web collaboration.* Springer-Verlag Berlin Heidelberg.

Elgort, I., Smith, A. G., & Toland, J. (2008). Is wiki an effective platform for group course work? *Australasian Journal of Educational Technology, 24*(2), 195–210.

Ellison, N., Steinfield, C., & Lampe, C. (2007). The benefits of Facebook "friends": Social capital and college students' use of online social networking sites. *Journal of Computer-Mediated Communication, 12*(4), 1143–1168. doi:10.1111/j.1083-6101.2007.00367.x

Ellison, N., & Wu, Y. (2008). Blogging in the classroom: A preliminary exploration of student attitudes and impact on comprehension. *Journal of Educational Multimedia and Hypermedia, 17*(1), 99–122.

Eren, O. (2012). Students' attitudes towards using social networking in foreign language classes: A Facebook example. *International Journal of Business and Social Science, 3*(20), 288–294.

Farmer, B., Yue, A., & Brooks, C. (2008). Using blogging for higher order learning in large cohort university teaching: A case study. *Australasian Journal of Educational Technology, 24*(2), 123–136.

Gao, F., Luo, T., & Zhang, K. (2012). Tweeting for learning: A critical analysis of research on microblogging in education published in 2008-2011. *British Journal of Educational Technology, 43*(5), 783–801. doi:10.1111/j.1467-8535.2012.01357.x

Grandzol, C. J., & Grandzol, J. R. (2010). Interaction in online courses: More is not always better. *Online Journal of Distance Learning Administration, 13*(2).

Grosseck, G. (2009). To use or not to use web 2.0 in higher education? *Procedia: Social and Behavioral Sciences, 1*(1), 478–482. doi:10.1016/j.sbspro.2009.01.087

Hall, H., & Davison, B. (2007). Social software as support in hybrid learning environments: The value of the blog as a tool for reflective learning and peer support. *Library & Information Science Research, 29*(2), 163–187. doi:10.1016/j.lisr.2007.04.007

Hemmi, A., Bayne, S., & Land, R. (2009). The appropriation and repurposing of social technologies in higher education. *Journal of Computer Assisted Learning, 25*(1), 19–30. doi:10.1111/j.1365-2729.2008.00306.x

Junco, R. (2012). The relationship between frequency of Facebook use, participation in Facebook activities, and student engagement. *Computers & Education, 58*(1), 162–171. doi:10.1016/j.compedu.2011.08.004

Junco, R., Heiberger, G., & Loken, E. (2011). The effect of Twitter on college student engagement and grades. *Journal of Computer Assisted Learning, 27*(2), 119–132. doi:10.1111/j.1365-2729.2010.00387.x

Kamarul, M. K., Norlida, A., & Zainol, A. M. J. Z. (2010). Facebook: An online environments for learning English in institutions of higher education. *The Internet and Higher Education, 75*(4), 179–187.

Lamb, B. (2004). Wide open spaces: Wikis, ready or not. *EDUCAUSE Review, 39*, 36–49.

Lindstrom, P. (2007). *Securing "Web 2.0" technologies*. Midvale, UT: Burton Group EDUCAUSE Center for Applied Research.

Luce-Kapler, R. (2007). Radical change and wikis: Teaching new literacies. *Journal of Adolescent & Adult Literacy, 51*(3), 214–223. doi:10.1598/JAAL.51.3.2

Millen, D., Feinberg, J., & Kerr, B. (2005). Social bookmarking in the enterprise. *Queue, 3*(9), 28–35. doi:10.1145/1105664.1105676

Moran, M., Seaman, J., & Tinti-Kane, H. (2011). *Teaching, Learning, and Sharing: How Today's Higher Education Faculty Use Social Media*. Retrieved from http://www.pearsonlearningsolutions.com/educators/pearson-social-media-survey-2011-bw.pdf

Morrison, M. A., Haley, E., Sheehan, K. B., & Taylor, R. E. (2011). *Using qualitative research in advertising: strategies, techniques, and applications*. Thousand Oaks, CA: SAGE Publications, Inc.

O'Reilly, T. (2008). *Why Dell.com (was) more Enterprise 2.0 than Dell IdeaStorm*. Retrieved from: http://radar.oreilly.com/2008/09/why-dell-dot-com-is-more-enterprise.html

Paliktzoglou, V., & Suhonen, J. (2014a). Facebook as an assisted learning tool in problem-based learning: The Bahrain case. *International Journal of Social Media and Interactive Learning Environments, 2*(1), 85–100. doi:10.1504/IJSMILE.2014.059694

Paliktzoglou, V., & Suhonen, J. (2014b). Microblogging in higher education: The Edmodo case study among Computer Science learners in Finland. *Journal of Cases on Information Technology, 16*(2), 39–57.

Paliktzoglou, V., & Suhonen, J. (2014c). Microblogging as an assisted learning tool in Problem Based Learning (PBL) in Bahrain: The Edmodo case. In F. V. Cipolla-Ficarra (Ed.), *Handbook of Research on Interactive Information Quality in Expanding Social Network Communications.* Hershey, PA: IGI Global.

Parker, K. R., & Chao, J. T. (2007). Wiki as a teaching tool. *Interdisciplinary Journal of Knowledge and Learning Objects, 3*(1), 57–72.

Polonsky, M. J., & Waller, D. S. (2010). *Designing and managing a research project: A business student's guide.* London: SAGE Publications.

Promnitz-Hayashi, L. (2011). A learning success story using Facebook. *SiSAL Journal, 2*(4), 309–316.

Ranieri, M., Manca, S., & Fini, A. (2012). Why (and how) do teachers engage in social networks? An exploratory study of professional use of Facebook and its implications for lifelong learning. *British Journal of Educational Technology, 43*(5), 754–769. doi:10.1111/j.1467-8535.2012.01356.x

Redecker, C., Ala-Mutka, K., Bacigalupo, M., Ferrari, A., & Punie, Y. (2009). *Learning 2.0: The impact of Web 2.0 innovations on education and training in Europe.* Final Report. European Commission-Joint Research Center-Institute for Porspective Technological Studies, Seville. Retrieved from ftp://ftp.jrc.es/pub/EURdoc/EURdoc/JRC55629.pdf

Rosenblum, D. (2007). What anyone can know: The privacy risks of social networking sites. *IEEE Security and Privacy, 5*(3), 40–49. doi:10.1109/MSP.2007.75

Rubin, H. J., & Rubin, I. S. (2005). *Qualitative interviewing: The art of hearing data.* Thousand Oaks, CA: Sage Publications.

Sandars, J., & Schroter, S. (2007). Web 2.0 technologies for undergraduate and postgraduate medical education: An online survey. *Postgraduate Medical Journal, 83*(986), 759–762. doi:10.1136/pgmj.2007.063123 PMID:18057175

Selwyn, N. (2009). Faceworking: Exploring students' education-related use of Facebook. *Learning, Media and Technology, 34*(2), 154–174. doi:10.1080/17439880902923622

Simon, M. (2008). *Online student-teacher friendships can be tricky.* Retrieved from http://articles.cnn.com/2008-08-12/tech/studentsteachers.online_1_facebook-users-myspace-social-networking-sites?_s=PM:TECH

Steinbrecher, T., & Hart, J. (2012). Examining teachers' personal and professional use of Facebook: Recommendations for teacher education programming. *Journal of Technology and Teacher Education, 20*(1), 71–88.

Suter, V., Alexander, B., & Kaplan, P. (2005). Social Software and The Future of Conferences Right Now. *EDUCAUSE Review, 40*(1), 47–59.

Valenzuela, S., Park, N., & Kee, K. F. (2009). Is there social capital in a social network site: Facebook use and college students' life satisfaction, trust, and participation. *Journal of Computer-Mediated Communication, 14*(4), 875–901. doi:10.1111/j.1083-6101.2009.01474.x

Williams, J. B., & Jacobs, J. (2004). Exploring the use of blogs as learning spaces in the higher education sector. *Australasian Journal of Educational Technology, 20*(2), 232–247.

Xie, Y., Ke, F., & Sharma, P. (2008). The effect of peer feedback for blogging on college students' reflective learning processes. *The Internet and Higher Education, 11*(1), 18–25. doi:10.1016/j.iheduc.2007.11.001

Zimmer, M. (2008). Preface: Critical Perspectives on Web 2.0. *First Monday*, *13*(3). doi:10.5210/fm.v13i3.2137

KEY TERMS AND DEFINITIONS

Blended Learning: A hybrid approach to teaching and learning, where the traditional face to face approach is mixed with web based one.

Edmodo: Educational microblogging tool.

Engagement: Understands concepts and incorporate then in our daily life.

Familiarity: Knowledge of something.

Microblogging: Posting short and frequent microblogs.

Social Media: Web 2.0 web sites and applications.

Chapter 13
Factors Influencing Behavior of Selecting Touch Screen Mobile Phones

Muhammad Khalique
Universiti Malaysia Sarawak, Malaysia

Senorita Lokie Tunggau
Universiti Malaysia Sarawak, Malaysia

ABSTRACT

The main aim of this chapter is to examine the influence of factors affecting the behavioural intention of customers. In this chapter, perceived ease of use, perceived usefulness, and social influence are considered as predictors while behavioral intention is employed as dependent variable. A total of 260 participants were involved in this study. The participants were selected through non-probability sampling technique, namely Snow Ball. In order to achieve the objective of this study, three research hypotheses were constructed. The proposed hypotheses were tested by using multiple regression analysis. The findings demonstrate that three hypotheses are supported. The findings show that three factors are playing a significant role in developing the behavioral intention. This study will be a millstone for the potential researchers.

INTRODUCTION

Mobile phones act as tools of instant communication that provide a platform to support distant collaborative work (Hakilla & Mantyjarvi, 2005). In 2009 the penetration of mobile phones was expand very sharply (Karim, Alias, Mokhtar & Rahim, 2009). A few years ago, touch screen mobile phones were introduced into the market, and now the uses of touch screen technology

gradually replaced traditional keypads with the emergence of smart phones such as Apple iPhone (Park & Han, 2010). Lipsman (2009) argued that the number of touch screen mobile phones users in the U.S. had grown at a rate of 159 percent in August compared to the previous year with 23.8 million users. Besides that, Petty and Tudor (2010) also reported that 58 percent of touch screen mobile devices are expected to contribute to the worldwide mobile devices sales by 2013 and touch

DOI: 10.4018/978-1-4666-7316-8.ch013

screen technologies are now being integrated into many midrange phones.

There is no doubt that the touch screen interfaces have attracted attention in recent years because their flexibility, functionality and usability have become more widely known and acceptable. It can be used in public-use terminals such as automated teller machines, ticket machines and information kiosks. Recently, they are used for small device interfaces such as Apple's iPhone and iPod Touch. Many touch screen systems are targeted at the public-market. For that reason, users' skills and experiences are expected to vary widely. Users would refuse to use a touch screen device if the text entry method was perceived as having low usability.

Consumers, are known as influencers, and mostly influenced by family members when generally purchasing technological devices, as well as by friends when specifically purchasing mobile phones. This could suggest that customers rely on the opinion of their friends when looking for a new phone because friends are more likely use their phones in the same way and frequency as they do, whereas family may include older adults who use their phones differently. These family members, however, are likely to be more experienced or knowledgeable in other technology fields such as televisions, computers, cameras, home printers, appliances and various other items (Tucker, 2011).

Behavior is one of the keys that influence the decision when purchasing mobile phones. It plays a major role in the market success. Mobile communication technology has been intersecting with long standing patterns of behavior. The increasing variety of mobile communication devices is affecting people's lives dramatically, directly and on a vast scale that no technology has ever adopted so quickly and by so many people' (Goggin, 2009).

We live in a world where fast communication is many times more essential. Phones and cell phones continue to develop. Many people embrace cellular-phone technology as the device that can fit in a pocket and be carried everywhere, helping people keep in contact with each other. The constant development over the years allows producers to include many features into cell phones.

Certain researchers claimed that touch screen is not a good model for technology adoption study. For instance, Sun and Zhang (2006) criticized that touch screen explanatory power is limited. Nevertheless, there are some researchers who found that touch screen is a significant topic in technology adoption study. For example, there are past studies concentrating on ordinary mobile phones versus touch screen (Lu & Zhang, 2008; Karim et al., 2009; Biljon & Kotze, 2007), mobile internet (Shin, 2007), mobile marketing (Bauer, Barnes, Reichard &, 2005), m-commerce (Yang, 2005), and so forth. These studies are similar to users' adoption and acceptance of mobile phones. Mobile related study on touch screen is very limited and considerably less pronounced. Due to the lacking of past studies on users' adoption and acceptance of touch screen, particularly in Malaysia, the factors affecting their satisfaction to adopt touch screen are somehow uncertain at this point of time.

Today, the growth of service marketing in Malaysia, especially mobile phones industry, is still in its infancy stage as compared to the industrially advanced countries. There are various mobile phones' service providers in our country and they are playing an essential role in fulfilling the needs of the customers. Nowadays, the customers are more dynamic and volatile. Their tastes, needs, wants, as well as preferences can change with current scenarios very spontaneously. Hence, the development of cellular industry mainly depends on the level of customer satisfaction.

For touch screen devices, their sizes can be categorized into these groups; small, medium and large. Small touch screen devices include mobile and smart phones, Personal Digital Assistants (PDA's) and hand held computers. Their effective touch screen area is small; hence, on screen objects become small. Therefore, users typically use a stylus to manipulate the small effective area. Devices with small effective touch screen area can also be used with just fingers instead of a stylus. This type of device has become more popular in the research community since Apple's iPhone and iPod touch screen were released. Medium size touch screen devices include standard PCs and Tablet PCs. Large touch screen devices come with table-top displays, wall-sized display and projectors.

The touch screen feature on mobile phones is created in such a way that enables it to be displayed on screen with software. For that reason, flexibility in the design and functionality are important in every touch screen mobile phone. A phone's menu can be created and displayed easily on a touch screen function. It is also easy to record a sequence of typed characters, predict subsequent character based on dictionary function, and show a list of candidate words. A customized function can be realized when designing touch screen mobile phones. For example, the layout, the size, shape, color, font and borderline can be set. Consequently, this study is aimed to investigate the overview of the factors influencing the decision making factor in choosing touch screen mobile phones amongst students in Universiti Malaysia Sarawak (UNIMAS).

Consumers Behavior

Generally it is believed that the consumer behavior is affected by many factors that are beyond ones control. In the others words, consumer buying process is a complex process, affected by many internal and external factors. Since the study at hand is emphasizing on the influence behavior of selecting touch screen phone, it is necessary to define the meaning of selecting touch screen mobile phones in terms of their influence on consumer behavior intentions.

Kotler and Keller (2006) argued that the consumer behavior as the study of how individuals, groups and organizations select, buy, use, and dispose of goods, services, ideas or experiences

to satisfy their needs and wants. Kotler and Keller (2006) provided clues for improving or introducing products or services, setting prices, devising channels, crafting messages and developing other marketing activities. Thus, understanding consumer choice and usage in the mobile markets will have both theoretical and management implications for marketing planning and make industry players market-oriented rather than product or service-oriented.

The mobile phone is a type of information good whose value is depend on the information embedded in it or facilitated by it and depends on a network to realize it full value. It shares some characteristics of an experience good in that some its features may be sampled ahead of time, but the device's value becomes clear once the consumer begun uncertainty. Lanchance and Bernier (2004), asserted that the young people seem to show many deficiencies in term of consumer competence in the mobile services and that very little know about information sources would help to develop their competence in this area. Youth is a time for many new and important consumer experiences and for learning consumer preference, attitudes and behaviors, many of which will persist the rest of their adult life. Wilska (2003), further argues that the younger the consumer, the more hedonistic features he or she tends to value in mobile phones. Mobile phone choice and use, he concludes was related to prior consumption styles.

Touch Screen Mobile Phone Information

Touch screen is a display that is sensitive to touch of a finger of stylus. Widely used on ATM machines, retail point-of-sale terminals, car navigation systems, medical monitors and industrial control panels, the touch screen became wildly popular on handhelds after Apple introduced the iPhone in 2007 (Touch screen, 2008). In "Touch screen Screens Redefine the market" the handsets are crammed with hardware such as digital photograph and video cameras, music players and the dandy screens (Mark, 2009). The devices may soon evolve into small computers about size of a clutch purse. Hewlett-Packard and others have begun offering such "net-books" with 3G Internet capabilities; cell phone service is expected soon (Mark, 2009). Smart phones pack an incredible array of telecommunications capabilities, including e-mail messengers, Web browsers, GP navigators and the actual cell phone.

Perceived Ease of Use

Perceived ease of use is defined as "an individual believes that the degree of effort needed to use a particular new technology or system will be easy or effortless" (Rouibah & Abbas, 2006). Ramayah and Ignatius (2005) carried out a research pertaining to the intention to shop online. The population of this research was those who have been exposed to the concept of internet shopping; whereas the sample included staff of public institution of higher learning. As a result, they had concluded that perceived ease of use of the technology is positively related with the e-shopper's behavior intension. In addition, Sung and Yun (2010) conducted a research about adoption of mobile multimedia service. Population in this research comprised college students and the sample size consisted of undergraduate students in a large mid-western university. This research concludes that there is a positive relationship between perceived ease of use and behavior intension. Suki (2011) reported that there is a positive relationship between perceived ease of use and behavior intention in the research of 3G mobile services adoption factors. Subscribers of 3G mobile services made up the population and data was collected from subscribers of 3G mobile services.

Perceived Usefulness

Perceived use means the prospective user's subjective probability that using a specific application system or new technology will enhance his job expression within an organizational context (Suki, 2011). In the study of the intention to use world-wide-web (Moon & Kim, 2001), it has been claimed that the perceived use has a positive relationship with behavior intension. The population consisted of individual who has use WWW in their tasks and the sample included graduate students who were majoring in school of management. Li, Chau and Lou (2005), conducted a study on the selecting of instant messaging, perceived use is positively associated with behavior intention. The population was made up of undergraduate students taking business courses in the universities and the sample consisted of students from two mid-western public universities. Conci, Pianesi and Zancanaro (2009) concluded the selection of phone by older people perceived use has a positive relationship with behavior intention to use. Elders were the population in this journal and the elders who joined the activities of third Age University of Trento were the sample.

Social Influence

Social influence refers the influences one's behaviors. It is defined as a kind of belief, which is significant enough to influence a person to participate in an activity (Chong, Darmawan, Ooi & Lee, 2010). They further stated that social influence is distinguished into mass media and interpersonal influence. Wei et al. (2009) claimed that mass media comprises of newspapers, magazines, radio, television, internet and so forth; whereas interpersonal influence is derived from social network such as friends and peers.

Additionally, Hsu et al. (2004) found that users' behavior intention to play an online game is positively affected by social influence. The population of the research consisted of online game users in Taiwan and the sample was self-selected online game users who saw the massage placed on over 50 heavily trafficked online message boards on popular game related web sites. Kim et al (2009) conducted a research on the selecting factors of mobile phone entertainment service and they had found out that social influence has a positive relationship with the behavior intention to adopt mobile entertainment service. Their study was based on the college students. Kulviwat, Bruner II and Al-Shuridah (2009) also conducted study on the role of social influence in the adoption of high tech innovations. Students in Midwestern U.S. University made up the population of this study. The sample was drawn from students enrolled in a large class with a wide variety of majors. A positive relationship between social influence and the behavior intention to adopt an innovation was concluded in this study. Sani, Yusof, Kasim and Omar (2009) stated that the Malaysia has a strong family based society and community cohesiveness has been powerfully prioritized over the individual rights in Malaysia. Jung and Kau (2004) found that family decision does play an important role in influencing consumers purchasing behavior. Thus, in Malaysia social influence would be a crucial factor in affecting the behavior intention to selection touch screen mobile phones.

Conceptual Framework

Perceived ease of use has been studied extensively in the context of IT adoption and diffusion; it is an important factor contributing to increased user satisfaction (Roshanak, 2009). Atkinson et al. (1997) stated that the perceived usefulness is the important factors, which influence the acceptance of applications. The reason why perceived usefulness is considered because it is an extremely decades that perceived usefulness is a factor which affects the intention to use. Venkatesh et al. (2003)

defined social influence as the degree to which an individual perceives that important others believe consumers should use the new system. Social influence as a construct stem from a conception that the individual's behavior is influenced by they believe others will view them as a result of having used the technology. Since the study at hand is emphasizing on the influence behavior of selecting touch screen mobile phones, it is necessary to define the meaning of behavior in term their influence on consumer behavioral intention.

Research Hypotheses

The past studies have stated that perceived ease of use, perceive usefulness and social influence affect the behavior of purchasing mobile phones. Others talk about the hardly different concept of usability of perceived ease of use towards touch screen mobile phones. The concept of usability refers to the effort required to use a technical system. "Nowadays it is usually associated to ease-of-use of device and is considered a critical factor on the development of electronic commerce" (Casalo, Flavian & Guinaliu, 2007, p.326). This determinant has been widely studied to have a positive influence on the behavior intention towards a technology (Davis, 1989; Dong, 2007; Lee, Cheung & Chen, 2007). Therefore, the behavioral intention serves as the main dependent variable in most of the analysis. Other authors also integrated several concepts like perceived usefulness and intrinsic and extrinsic motivations into this construct (Kijsanayotina et al., 2009, p.405). There have been several previous studies on the positive influence of perceived usefulness on behavior of mobile phone selection (Davis et al., 1992; Heijden, 2004; Lee et al, 2007). The effect of social influence on behavior to use technology has been shown to be significant in several previous acceptance studies although some studies exhibited a non-significant effect (Kijsanayotina et al., 2009, p. 405). Therefore, the following hypothesis is tested:

Hypothesis 1: Perceived ease of use has a positive influence on the behavior of touch screen mobile phones.

Hypothesis 2: Perceived usefulness has a positive influence on the behavior of touch screen mobile phones.

Hypothesis 3: Social influence has a positive influence on the behavior of touch screen mobile phones.

Methodology

In this study, perceived ease of use, perceived usefulness, social influence are employed as independent variables and behavior intention of generation Y to Adopt touch screen phones was used as a dependent variable. This research is employed a causal research design. Causal research design is used mostly to gain information on cause-and-effect of one or more variables. The three independent variables was measured and tested by using appropriate tools to indentify which factor have influence on the behavior of selecting touch screen mobile phones in Universiti Malaysia Sarawak, Malaysia.

Population

Population can be described as the group of people that will be concentrated in a research with the necessary attributes. The population of this study was based on 7980, undergraduates from Universiti Malaysia Sarawak (UNIMAS). Students are used as respondents because they can represent homogeneity and are able to reduce the potential for random error compared if the respondents are taken from the general public (Bakewell & Mitchell, 2003).

However, the students who participated in this research include particular those who have experience in using smart mobile phones. For example, studies have reported that behavior of mobile phone as fashion is especially high among young people (Green, 2003), including adolescents

as well as young. With this, the researchers were able to identify which factor is the most critical based on the students. The researchers try to find out whether they put more emphasize on perceived usefulness, perceived ease of use and social influence.

Sampling

Sample is part of the individuals selected from the population as respondents in the research. Sampling is key stage of choosing a suitable number of elements from the population. This research study is concentrating on the factor that is affecting the factor behavior of selecting touch screen mobile phones among students in Universiti Malaysia Sarawak. A total of 260 undergraduate were involved in this study. The sample was derived by using Luck, Taylor and Robin, (1987) formula. The respondents were chosen on a non-probability sampling techniques namely Snowball sampling technique. Snowball sampling technique, the initial respondents were asked to name others belongs to the target populace of interest (Malhotra, 2004). Therefore, the following respondents were selected through the recommendations of the initial respondents.

Research Instrument and Data Collection

The data were gathered through the distribution of survey questionnaires. The structured questionnaires were measured through scaling techniques. A total of 260 questionnaires printed in English languages were distributed. The questionnaires were consisting of two sections. Questionnaire was used in this study because not only it was less expensive, but it is also stable, consistent and could help to avoid bias and errors caused by the attitudes of the interviewer (Sarantakos, 1993). The first section was regarding the demographic questions such as gender, years in university and others related questions. The second section was

Table 1. Construct of perceived ease of use (PEOU)

No	Questions	Strongly Disagree	Disagree	Neutral	Agree	Strongly Agree
PEOU1	It is easy to learn how to use touch screen phone	1	2	3	4	5
PEOU2	Touch screen phone is understandable and clear	1	2	3	4	5
PEOU3	Touch screen is easy-to-use	1	2	3	4	5

addressed to four constructs namely perceive ease of use; perceive usefulness social influence and behavioral intention on young adults selecting touch screen mobile phones. A five point Likert Scale was used to measure the perception about the each item ranged from (Strongly Disagree = 1 and Strongly Agree = 5). Likert scale has been generally employed in a questionnaire and it is the most broadly used a scale in survey research.

Measurement of Variables

Perceive ease of use is a defined as the degree to which an individual believes that using a particular system would be free of physical and mental efforts. Ease of use and familiarity will improve over time as a person gets experienced with the product while perceive enjoyment will possibly decrease when a person gets bored over time with the product. Three items from Wei et al., (2009) were adopted to measure this construct. The items are shown in Table 1.

Perceive usefulness is a defined as the degree to which a person believes that using mobile phones will enhance to reach one's general goal in life (Davis, 1989). Four items from Menget et al. (2010) and Sung et al. (2010) were borrowed to capture this employed construct. The items of construct are given in Table 2.

Social influence is a defined as the degree to which an individual perceives that important others believe he or she should use a new technology. Especially, from a professional perspective social influence can be high. People often imitate others in a public social context because it seems the easiest way to adopt to others interactions (Shin, 2009). To measure the construct five items from Wei et al. (2009) were used in this study. The items are given in Table 3.

A behavior would be indentify of a problem involves selecting specific problem behaviors, describing them precisely and then using these description to formulate hypotheses, predictions and referral questions that need to be answered in order to plan an intervention (Ajzen & Fishbein,

Table 2. Construct of perceive usefulness (PU)

No	Questions	Strongly Disagree	Disagree	Neutral	Agree	Strongly Agree
PU1	Using touch screen mobile phone brings me many benefits	1	2	3	4	5
PU2	Using touch screen mobile phone improves the performance of my tasks	1	2	3	4	5
PU3	Using touch screen mobile phone enables me to accomplish tasks more quickly	1	2	3	4	5
PU4	Using touch screen mobile phone increase my task productivity	1	2	3	4	5

Table 3. Construct of social influence

No	Questions	Strongly Disagree	Disagree	Neutral	Agree	Strongly Agree
SI1	Friend's suggestion and recommendation will affect my decision to use touch screen mobile phone	1	2	3	4	5
SI2	Family members/relatives have influence on my decision to use touch screen mobile phone	1	2	3	4	5
SI3	I will use touch screen mobile phone if my colleagues/friend/relatives use it	1	2	3	4	5
SI4	Mass media (e.g. TV, newspaper, articles, radio) will influence me to use touch screen mobile phone	1	2	3	4	5
SI5	I will use touch screen mobile phone if it is widely used by people in my community	1	2	3	4	5

Table 4. Construct of behavioral intention

No	Questions	Strongly Disagree	Disagree	Neutral	Agree	Strongly Agree
BI1	I believe my interest towards touch screen mobile phone will increase in the future.	1	2	3	4	5
BI2	I believe I will use touch screen mobile phone in the future.	1	2	3	4	5
BI3	I will strongly recommend others to use touch screen mobile phone.	1	2	3	4	5

1980). In this study behavior intention was measured by using three items that were adopted from Moon et al. (2001). The items are given in Table 4.

Reliability o f the Instrument

The measurement scale was assessed by using Cronbach's alpha. Reliability test is used to determine the stability and consistency of measuring instrument (Choy, Ng & Ch'ng, 2011). The alpha value for the factors influence scales were ranging 0.7 as suggested by previous research (Lai et al. 2011), any value higher than 0.7 would deem to have high reliability. Khalique (2012) argued that 0.5 is acceptable for the exploratory study having sound theoretical background. Cronbach's alpha was used in this study and found that all items of construct meet the requirement and it assumed that the items are reliable.

Data Analysis

Scientific Package for social science (SPSS), a computer software package was used to test the selected research hypotheses.

Demographic Profile of Respondents

A total of 260 individual were involved in this study to analyze the data. The detail about the characteristics of respondents is given in Table 5.

Hypotheses Testing

Multiple regression analysis was used to test the proposed research hypotheses. Regression is a robust technique to examine the relationship of independent variables with dependent variable. The coefficient of determination (R^2) is mostly

Table 5. Respondents' demographics

Demographics		Frequency	Percentage
Gender	Male	119	45.8
	Female	141	54.2
Year	1	129	49.6
	2	57	21.9
	3	74	28.5
Faculty	Social Science	16	6.2
	Applied and Creative Art	33	2.7
	Computer Science and Information Technology	44	16.9
	Economic and Business	33	2.7
	Engineering	43	16.5
	Cognitive Science and Human Development	31	11.9
	Resource Science and Technology	60	23.1
Age	18-22	129	49.6
	23-27	120	46.2
	28-32	11	4.2
State of origin	Perlis	6	2.3
	Kedah	15	5.8
	Penang	12	4.6
	Perak	11	4.2
	Kuala Lumpur	22	8.5
	Selangor	16	6.2
	Johor	18	6.9
	Pahang	10	3.8
	Kelantan	16	6.2
	Terengganu	25	9.6
	Sarawak	74	28.5
	Sabah	16	6.2

used to examine the goodness of the regression model. The result reported (R^2) 0.262% (R square = 0.262) is jointly explained by the independent variables ($F = 30.260$; Sig. = 0.000). This indicated that 26.2% of the variance in behavior intention was explained by the contributions of perceived ease of use, perceived usefulness, and social influence.

In Table 6, the results showed that all the three variables namely, easy ($t = 9.09$, $\beta = 0.151$, $p = 0.000$), usefulness ($t = 3.45$, $\beta = 0.178$, $p = 0.001$) and influence ($t = 4.387$, $\beta = 0.199$, $p = 0.000$) are significant. The results demonstrated that all three predictors as a combined and individually play significant contribution to the predicted variable. Therefore, on the basis of the findings we conclude that the proposed three hypotheses are supported.

Table 6. Regression results

Independent Variables	Dependent Variable (Organizational Performance)		Significant Level
	Unstandardized Coefficients	*t*-values	
Constant (β)	2.10		0.000
Easy	0.151	9.09	0.000
Usefulness	0.178	3.45	0.001
Influence	0.199	4.387	0.000
R 0.512			
R Square 0.262			
F Value 30.26			0.00

CONCLUSION AND DISCUSSION

The main aim of this study is to examine the relationship between consumers, represented by the students of Universiti Malaysia Sarawak (UNI-MAS), and their behaviour as well as intention to purchase touch screen mobile phones. The findings of this study reported that there is indeed a positive relationship. Therefore, perceived ease of use is appeared to be significant contributor in explaining the behavior of students. Prior researches such as the ones by Suki (2011) and Ramayah (2005) suggested that perceived ease of use has a positive influence as well as a positive and significant effect on the behavioral intention. Nevertheless, the results yielded are the same as the results of studies on m-commerce adoption (Cho, Kwon & Lee, 2007; Yan, K. E. & Sutanonpaiboon, 2009), which have affirmed that perceived ease of use is significant in explaining the behavior.

Perceived usefulness is also one of the significant predictors of behaviour intention because there is an existence of positive relationship among them. This result is supported by some past researches relating to m-commerce (Jayasigh & Eze, 2009; Faziharudean & Tan, 2011) and e-commerce (Yanghoubi & Bahmani, 2010). The result shows that students would only adopt touch screen mobile phones if they find their usefulness, thus the adoption rate of touch screen mobile phones will increase if the young generation finds that there are more practical benefits, compared to using traditional phones. The rational is possibly because of the fact that touch screen mobile phone are based on a new technology, contributing to the unique characteristic of touch screen mobile phones. Finally, social influence has a significant relationship with behaviour intention. This validate the past researches on m-commerce (Shin, 2007; Kim et al., 2009; Wei et al., 2009), which also report that social influence has a positive and significant association with behavior intention. For further studies we recommended to the potential researchers to conduct their studies on this topic with larger sample size and diverse population.

REFERENCES

Ajzen, I., & Fishbein, M. (1980). *Understanding attitudes and predicting social behavior*. Prentice Hall, Inc.

Atkinson, M., & Kydd, C. (1997). Individual Characteristics Associated with World Web Use: An Empirical Study of Playfulness and Motivation. *The Data Base for Advances in Information Systems*, *28*(2), 53–61. doi:10.1145/264701.264705

Bakewell, C., & Mitchell, V. (2003). Generation Y female consumer decision making styles. *International Journal of Retail & Distribution Management, 31*(2), 95–106. doi:10.1108/09590550310461994

Bauer, H. H., Barnes, S. J., Reichardt, T., & Neumann, M. M. (2005). Driving consumer acceptance of mobile marketing: A theoretical framework and empirical study. *Journal of Electronic Commerce Research, 6*(3), 181–192.

Biljon, J. V., & Kotze, P. (2007). Modeling the factors that influence mobile phone adoption. In *Proceedings of the 2007 annual research conference of the South African institute of computer scientists and information technologists on IT research in developing contries*, (pp. 152-161). Academic Press.

Casalo, J., Flavian, C., & Guinaliu, M. (2007). The role of perceived usability, reputation, satisfaction and consumer familiarity on the website loyalty formation process. *Computers in Human Behavior, 24* (2008), 325–345.

Cho, D. Y., Kwon, H. J., & Lee, H. Y. (2007). Analysis of trust in internet and mobile commerce adoption. In *Proceedings of the 40th Hawaii International Conference on System Sciences*, (pp. 1-10). IEEE. doi:10.1109/HICSS.2007.76

Chong, A. Y., Darmawan, N., Ooi, K. B., & Lee, V. H. (2010). Determinants of 3G adoption in Malaysia: A structural analysis. *Journal of Computer Information.*

Choy, J. Y., Ng, C. S., & Ch'ng, H. K. (2011). Consumers' perceived quality, perceived value and perceived risk towards purchase decision on automobile. *American Journal of Economics and Business Administration, 3*(1), 47–57. doi:10.3844/ajebasp.2011.47.57

Conci, M., Pianesi, F., & Zancanaro, M. (2009). Useful, social and enjoyable: Mobile phone adoption by older people. *Lecture Notes in Computer Science, 5726*, 63–76. doi:10.1007/978-3-642-03655-2_7

Davis, F., Bagozzi, R., & Warshaw, R. (1992). Extrinsic and intrinsic motivation to use computers in the workplace. *Journal of Applied Social Psychology, 22*(14), 1111–1132. doi:10.1111/j.1559-1816.1992.tb00945.x

Davis, F. D. (1989). Perceived usefulness, perceived ease of use, and user acceptance of information technology. *Management Information Systems Quarterly, 13*(3), 319–340. doi:10.2307/249008

Dong, S. H. (2007). User acceptance of mobile Internet: Implication for convergence technologies. *Interacting with Computers, 19*(4), 472–483. doi:10.1016/j.intcom.2007.04.001

Goggin, G. (2009). Mobile technologies: From telecommunications to media. *Routledge Research in Cultural and Media Studies*, (6), 297.

Greene, N. (2003). Outwardly mobile: Young people and mobile technologies. In J. Katz (Ed.), *Machines That Become Us: The social context of communication technology*. New Brunswick, NJ: Transaction Publishers.

Hakkila, J., & Mantyjarvi, J. (2005). Collaborative in context-aware mobile phone applications. In *Proceedings of the 38th Hawaii International Conference onSystem Sciences*. IEEE. doi:10.1109/HICSS.2005.145

Heijden, H. V. (2004). User acceptance of hedonic information system. *MIS Quartely, 28*(4), 695–704.

Hsu, C. L., & Lu, H. P. (2004). Why do people play on- line games? An extended TAM with social influences and flow experience. *Information & Management, 41*(7), 853–868. doi:10.1016/j.im.2003.08.014

Jayasingh, S., & Eze, U. C. (2009). An empirical analysis of consumer behavioural intention toward mobile coupons in Malaysia. *International Journal of Business and Information, 4*(2), 221–241.

Jung, K., & Kau, A. (2004). Culture's influence on consumer behaviours: Differences among ethnic groups in a multiracial Asian country. *Advances in Consumer Research. Association for Consumer Research (U. S.), 31,* 366–372.

Karim, N. S., Alias, R. A., Mokhtar, S. A., & Rahim, N. Z. (2009). Mobile phone adoption and appropriation in Malaysia and the contribution of age and gender. In *Proceedings of International Conference on Information and Multimedia Technology,* (pp. 485-490). Academic Press.

Khalique, M. (2012). *Impact of Intellectual Capital on the Organizational Performance of Selected Small and Medium Enterprises in Malaysia and Pakistan.* (PhD Thesis). Universiti Malaysia Sarawak.

Kijsanayotin, B., Pannarunothai, S., & Speedie, S. M. (2009). Factors influencing health information technology adoption in Thailand's community health centers: Applying the UTAUT model. *International Journal of Medical Informatics, 78*(6), 404–416. doi:10.1016/j.ijmedinf.2008.12.005 PMID:19196548

Kim, K., Kim, G. M., & Eun, S. K. (2009). Measuring the compability factors in mobile entertainment service adoption. *Journal of Computer Information Systems, 50*(1), 141–148.

Kotler, P., & Keller, K. L. (2006). Marketing Management (12th ed.). Upper Saddle River, NJ: Pearson.

Kulviwat, S., Bruner, G. C. II, & Al-Shuridah, O. (2009). The role of social influence on adoption of high tech innovations: The moderating effect of public/private consumption. *Journal of Business Research, 62*(7), 706–712. doi:10.1016/j.jbusres.2007.04.014

Lachance, M. J., & Bernier, N. C. (2004). College students' consumer competence: A qualitative exploration. *International Journal of Consumer Studies, 28*(5), 433–442. doi:10.1111/j.1470-6431.2004.00390.x

Lai, H. M., & Chen, C. P. (2011). Factors influencing secondary school teachers' adoption of teaching blogs. *Computers & Education, 56*(4), 948–960. doi:10.1016/j.compedu.2010.11.010

Lee, E. L. (2007). The Chinese Malaysians' selfish mentality and behaviours rationalizing from the native perspectives. *Chinese Media Research, 3*(4), 91–119.

Lee, M. K. O., Cheung, C. M. K., & Chen, Z. (2007). Understanding User Acceptance of Multimedia Messaging Services: An Empirical Study. *Journal of the American Society for Information Science and Technology, 58*(13), 2066–2077. doi:10.1002/asi.20670

Li, D., Chau, P. Y., & Lou, H. (2005). Understanding individual adoption of instant messaging: An empirical investigation. *Journal of the Association for Information Systems, 6*(4), 102–129.

Lipsman, A. (2009). *Touchscreen Mobile Phone Adoption Grows at Blistering Pace in U.S. During Past Year.* Retrieved March 2, 2011, from comScore,Inc.: http://comscore.org/Press_Events/Press_Releases/2009/11/Touchsceen_Mobile_phone_adoptiongrowsatBlistering_PaceinU.S_During_Past_Year

Lu, W., & Zhang, M. (2008). The adoption and use of mobile phone in rural China: A case study of Hubei, China. *Telematics and Informatics, 25*(3), 169–186. doi:10.1016/j.tele.2006.10.001

Luck, D. J., Taylor, W. G., & Robin. (1987). *Marketing Research.* Prentice Hall.

Malhotra, N. K. (2004). *Marketing Research: An Applied Orientation.* London: Prentice Hall International.

Mark, F. (2009). *Touch screen redefine the market* (International Editions). Scientific American.

Moon, J. W., & Kim, Y. G. (2001). Extending the TAM for a World-Wide-Web context. *Information & Management*, *38*(4), 217–230. doi:10.1016/S0378-7206(00)00061-6

Petty, C., & Tudor, B. (2010). *Gartner says touch screen mobile device sales will grow 97 percent in 2010*. Retrieved May 3, 2013, from Gartner: http://gartner.com/it/pages.jsp?id=1313415

Ramayah, T., & Ignatius, J. (2005). Impact of perceived usefulness, perceived ease of use and perceived enjoyment on intention to shop online. *Journal of Systems Management*, *3*(3), 36–51.

Roshanak, S. (2009). Human/Social Factors Influencing Usability of E commerce Websites and Systems. *Application of Information and Communication Technologies*, 1-5.

Rouibah, K., & Abbas, H. (2006). A modified technology acceptance model for camera mobile phone adoption: Development and validation. In *Proceedings of 17th Australasian Conference on Information Systems*, 1-1

Sani, M., Yusof, N., Kasim, A., & Omar, R. (2009). Malaysia in transition: A comparative analysis of Asian values, Islam Hadhari and 1 Malaysia. *Journal of Politics and Law*, *2*(3), 110–118. doi:10.5539/jpl.v2n3p110

Sarantakos, S. (1993). *Social research*. Macmillan Education Australia Pty Ltd.

Shin, D. H. (2007). User acceptance of mobile Internet: Implication for convergence technologies. *Interacting with Computers*, *19*(4), 472–483. doi:10.1016/j.intcom.2007.04.001

Shin, D. H. (2009). An empirical investigation of a modified technology acceptance model of IPTV. *Behaviour & Information Technology*, *28*(4), 361–372. doi:10.1080/01449290701814232

Suki, N. M. (2011). Subscribers' intention towards using 3G mobile services. *Journal Of Economics and Behavioral Studies*, *2*(2), 67–75.

Sun, H., & Zhang, P. (2006). The role of modelling factors in user technology acceptance. *International Journal of Human-Computer*, *64*(2), 53–78. doi:10.1016/j.ijhcs.2005.04.013

Sung, J., & Yun, Y. (2010). Toward a more robust usability concept with perceived enjoyment in the context of mobile multimedia services. *International Journal of Human Computer Interaction*, *1*(2), 12-32.

Touch Screen. (2008). *Touch screen hardware*. Retrieved 10 December 2012, from, http://www.reghardware.com/2008/12/13/koy_touch-screen_phones/

Tucker, T. (2011). *What influences young adults' decision to adopt new technology. Communication science*. Elon University.

Venkatesh, V., Morris, M., Davis, G., & Davis, F. (2003). User Acceptance of Information Technology: Toward a Unified View. *Management Information Systems Quarterly*, *27*(3), 425–478.

Wei, T. T., Marthan, G., Chong, A. Y. L., Ooi, K. B., & Arumugam, S. (2009). What drives Malaysian m-commerce adoption? an empirical analysis. *Industrial Management & Data Systems*, *109*(3), 370–388. doi:10.1108/02635570910939399

Wilska, T. (2003). Mobile phone use as part of young people's comsumtion styles. *Journal of Consumer Policy*, *26*(4), 441–663. doi:10.1023/A:1026331016172

Yaghoubi, N. M., & Bahmani, E. (2010). Factors affecting the adoption of online banking: An integration of technology acceptance model and theory of planned behavior. *Pakistan Journal of Social Sciences*, *7*(3), 231–236. doi:10.3923/pjssci.2010.231.236

Yan, A. W., Khalil, M. N., Emad, A. S., & Sutanonpaiboon, J. (2009). Factors that affect mobile telephone users to use mobile payment solution. *International Journal of Economics and Management*, *3*(1), 37–49.

Yang, K. C. (2005). Exploring factors affecting the adoption of mobile commerce in Singapore. *Journal of Telematics and Informatics*, *22*(3), 257–277. doi:10.1016/j.tele.2004.11.003

KEY TERMS AND DEFINITIONS

Behavioral Intention: Behavioral intention is defined as a person's perceived probability that he or she will employ in a given behavior.

Perceived Ease of Use: The perception of individual about the effort required to use a particular new technology or system will be easy or effortless.

Perceived Usefulness: The perception of individual about the uses of particular system would enhance his or her performance.

Social Influence: Social influence is an impact on the mind of individual to adopt and utilize of new information systems and technology.

Chapter 14
Mobile Wireless Technologies Application in Education

Maryam Haghshenas
MAGFA Company, Iran

Roghayeh Shahbazi
Alzahra University, Tehran–Iran

Abouzar Sadeghzadeh
University of Bradford, UK

Mojtaba Nassiriyar
University of Tehran–Iran

ABSTRACT

This chapter brings the reader's attention to understanding how technologies are aiding education with a focus on mobile technologies. In the early sections of this chapter, mobile technologies are explained briefly along with their significance to education. Implications for all involved in the education process using these technologies are then discussed. A pedagogical framework for mobile learning is then introduced along with standard theories commonly used, such as the transactional distance theory. Technological limitations and considerations are discussed to highlight future measures when designing these technologies specifically for educational purposes. Examples of mobile technology implementations in current education stages are then presented, such as mobile technology uses in higher education along with technologies used for early learners. Finally, the main objective of this chapter is presented to discuss the future of mobile technologies thoroughly, including assumptions of how these technologies will be part of everyday life for future learners.

INTRODUCTION

Mobile technologies have been a part of most people's lives for a number of years now especially in western countries. It has become normal for people to be able to talk to others anytime from anywhere, take pictures, record data and obtain information from all over the world. As time passes, mobile technologies develop at consid-erable speed to offer even richer experiences for their growing number of users.

In order to utilize mobile technologies for learning purposes, educators' main task is to recognize best practices to use these resources to support education. Currently, even though applications are being developed for many purposes on a daily basis, the ones with learning objectives are lacking.

DOI: 10.4018/978-1-4666-7316-8.ch014

MOBILE WIRELESS TECHNOLOGIES

Mobile or wireless technologies are often mistaken as being the same as mobile wireless technologies. Mobile wireless technologies are different from mobile or wireless technologies simply because not all mobile technologies are wireless nor are all wireless technologies mobile. Mobile technologies consist of two aspects: mobility and computing. Mobile computing generally represents continuous access to network resources without limitation of time and location. Wireless generally represents the transmission of any kind of data such as text, voice, video or image which are conducted through radio waves, infrared waves or microwaves instead of wires. Therefore, mobile wireless technologies is defined as any wireless technology that uses radio frequency spectrum in any band to aid transmission of text data, voice, video or multimedia services to mobile devices freedom of time and location limitation.

MOBILE TECHNOLOGIES ACCESS TO NETWORK RESOURCES

Due to technical complexities, understanding how teachers and students access network resources using mobile wireless devices are not easy. However, understanding how mobile wireless devices work may provide clearer insights to the use of this technology in all aspects of our society specifically education.

Wireless computers operate in a similar way to regular computers without the wires. A wireless network interface card is installed in laptop computers and uses a very low frequency instead of a wired connection to connect to a network, then sends a very low power signal to a wireless access point which is installed in buildings and classrooms. The wireless access points are connected to a wired network such as a local area network. Therefore, the wireless access points

serve as the bridge between the wireless network interface card and the wire network. The wireless access points support transmission for many users simultaneously and far more than wired networks. However, using wireless access points to connect to a network limits the speed of transmission compared to wired computers.

In the case of PDAs and mobile wireless phones, users need to subscribe to wireless services which are provided by operators such as AT&T, Vodafone, and T-mobile etc. With wireless services subscription, teachers and students simply press some buttons on their mobile wireless devices to access the network. Different infrastructure is required for different mobile wireless devices in order to access network resources.

HOW CAN MOBILE TECHNOLOGIES BE SIGNIFICANT TO EDUCATION?

Most technologies for personal use are mobile devices that can fit in our pockets and enable worldwide communication. This universal appeal creates an interest in utilizing these resources for learning purposes. There are many examples of learning using mobile devices such as personal digital assistants and mobile phones but are part of a larger space of possible mobile technologies which are mostly classified into the two dimensions of personal vs. shared and portable vs. static.

Education using mobile technologies is starting to reach institution wide implementations. Educators and developers should take into account the following factors for successful implementations:

- **Context:** Utilization of contextual information which may go against learner's privacy rights.
- **Mobility:** Being able to learn outside the classroom may cause learners to participate in activities what clash with the educators program or curriculum.

- **Learning over Time:** Useful tools are required for recording, organizing and obtaining learning experiences.
- **Informality:** Certain technologies may be abandoned if learners feel their social network is being compromised.
- **Ownership:** Learners wish to control personal technology which presents a dilemma when brought to the classroom.

MOBILE LEARNING WITH AN ACTIVITY-BASED APPROACH

A lot of the research concerning mobile technologies focuses on new devices features which is expected considering the speed at which mobile computing is developing. These features inspire new practices but applications specifically for learning are still lacking. Klopfer (2002) defines five properties for mobile devices which have unique educational affordances:

- **Portability:** The size of mobile devices enables them to be taken to different locations or be moved around within a location.
- **Social Interactivity:** Data exchange can happen between learners.
- **Context Sensitivity:** Mobile devices can be used to gather and respond to real or simulated data specific to current locations and time.
- **Connectivity:** A shared network may be created by the connection of a mobile device to other data collection devices or to a common network.
- **Individuality:** Complex activities can be customized for individual learners

Classification of Activities

The classification of activities concerning mobile technologies has been structured into six themes:

- **Behaviorist:** Changes in observable actions caused by these activities.
- **Constructivist:** Learners come up with innovations based on current and previous knowledge.
- **Situated:** Using an authentic context and culture to promote learning.
- **Collaborative:** Social interaction to promote learning.
- **Informal and Lifelong:** Learning outside a formal curriculum.
- **Learning and Teaching Support:** Coordination of learners and resources for learning.

Behaviorist Learning

Utilizing mobile technologies to gain responses from learners and provide feedback goes well within the paradigm of behaviorist paradigm. According to this paradigm, learning is best done when both a stimulus and response are generated. Taking this paradigm into the context of learning technologies, computer-aided learning can take the role of the stimulus while contribution from users could be the response. This type of learning adopts a transmission model since information is transmitted from the tutor to the learner.

In the field of mobile delivery, similar problems to the ones related to computer-assisted learning systems occur. In comparison to desktop computers, mobile devices have limited displays and input methods along with low connectivity rates. Despite these problems, there are advantages of stimulus and response activities such as tailored content and feedback to support particular curriculum fields and gathered data about learner's progress. Classroom response systems enable whole class drill and feedback activities by helping tutors to:

- Provide content-specific questions. Possible solutions are provided in the form of multiple choice options displayed on the students devices.

- Collect student responses quickly and anonymously.
- Maintain individual anonymity.

Constructivist Learning

Constructivist learning theories were formed in the 60s and 70s. It was theorized that learning was an active process where learners constructed new concepts based on previous and current knowledge.

The personal home computer that was available in the 80s provided advantages in terms of display features and was no longer an interface for displaying information but was a means of information manipulation. Therefore, the computer became the tutee and the learner programmed the computer to perform required tasks and solve problems. This way, learners were actively forming their own knowledge and were educated by building interactive models.

A constructivist learning framework would cause students to discover principles on their own. An appropriate environment along with necessary tools must be provided for learners to transform them from passive recipients of information to active constructors of knowledge. Mobile devices give learners an exclusive opportunity to access supporting tools as well as being embedded in a realistic context.

Situated Learning

This paradigm was formed by (Lave & Wenger, 1991) which states that learning is not only acquired by individuals but is a social participation process. The situation where learning takes place has critical affect on the learning process. Cognitive apprenticeship was also mentioned where teachers and students collaborate to create appropriate situations to aid students to solve problems. There are three relevant strands when it comes to mobile devices and situated learning:

- **Problem-Based Learning:** Aims to enhance students critical thinking skills by presenting potential problems that practicing professionals may encounter. The problem is used as a basis for "learning by analogy and abstraction via reflection" O'Malley (2003).
- **Case-Based Learning:** Is similar to problem-based learning but presents clearer problems that students may or may not come across when practicing as a professional. It is more flexible than problem-based learning in that it can be used in small or large classes as an assessment or topic of discussion in class lectures.
- **Context-Aware Learning:** This is a relatively new field of research. Context awareness is gathering environmental information to give the learner an idea of their surroundings. Activities taking place around the learner and device can be made available. Mobile devices are suitable for context aware applications since they are suited appropriately to different contexts and can use these contexts to improve learning activities. Context-aware mobile devices can aid users to maintain their attention to the real world and offer necessary help when needed. Examples on the use of context-aware mobile devices are the museum and gallery sector where information about exhibitions is displayed based on visitors location.
- **Collaborative Learning:** The wide context of use for mobile devices along with their various capabilities provides a collaborative environment. Communication using mobile devices enables learners to share data, files and messages while also being connected to a data network which enhances further communication. Learning is more effective when learners exchange information and share their understandings thus it is by this mutual conversation

that a shared understanding is formed. The most effective learning takes place when learners control their activities, perform experiments, ask questions and finally collaborate with other people to obtain new information and knowledge to plan new ideas.

Informal and Lifelong Learning

Learning is influenced by both the environment and the situations learners come across. Informal learning may be informal via deliberate learning projects or accidental through media, observations and conversations. Research in this field shows that most adults learning experiences take place outside formal education and are a reality in people's lives. They may not however, recognize these experiences as learning. Technology used to support learning should merge seamlessly with everyday life. Therefore, mobile technologies with their size and ease of use can support such activities appropriately.

In the case of accidental learning, these cannot be predicted. The portable nature of mobile technologies makes them the most efficient way of sharing such accidental learning experiences.

Learning and Teaching Support

Using mobile technologies for learning purposes is not limited to learning activities. Learning relies greatly on the coordination of learners and resources. Mobile devices can be utilized by tutors to control attendance, student marks, schedule management, and can provide course material for students to inform them about assignment deadlines and timetable changes. Due to the informal nature of these devices, teachers may inform parents about student's progress or problems.

IMPLICATIONS FOR LEARNERS, TEACHERS AND DEVELOPERS

Teaching and learning using mobile technologies is becoming popular from small scale pilots to large scale departmental and institutional implementations. There are significant challenges concerning mobile technology in comparison with desktop technology:

- **Context:** Gathering personal information about the user and their environment enables learning to be personalized. Personal information must be gathered with user's permission and there are also security concerns to prevent third parties from gaining access to this information. This problem is also relevant to coupling the information layer from devices and existing communication layers of the classroom or similar environments.
- **Mobility:** Since mobile devices have the 'anytime', 'anywhere' capability, students are encouraged to learn outside a classroom managed by teachers. However, students may also link activities from to the outside world from the classroom which presents clear challenges to traditional teaching.
- **Learning over Time:** Lifelong learners require appropriate tools to organize and reflect on their mobile learning experiences.
- **Informality:** The informality advantages of mobile devices may be under threat if students feel their social networks may be compromised.
- **Ownership:** The ownership of mobile devices is a key consideration since personal and group learning are more effective when each user owns a device. Tangible and intangible advantages exist by using mobile devices. Intangible advantages include personal commitment and comfort from the sense of personal belonging. Although,

personal ownership brings a challenge to institutional control of mobile technology.

THE EVOLUTION TO UBIQUITOUS LEARNING

As Weiser (1991), stated, "The most profound technologies are those that disappear." He was one the first scholars to believe ubiquitous computing was an environment where the computer is merged into everyday life. In the education field, ubiquitous learning happens where all students have access to various digital devices preferably connected to the internet whenever and wherever necessary. In the education field "ubiquitous computing allows us to envision a classroom in which the teacher remains focused on his or her field of expertise while still utilizing technology to enhance student learning" (Crowe, 2007).

TECHNOLOGICAL ATTRIBUTES AND PEDAGOGICAL AFFORDANCES

Due to the unique technological attributes of mobile learning, pedagogical affordances are provided. Pea and Maldonado (2006) summarized seven attributes of handheld devices for use in schools and beyond: "small screen size, portability, computing power, diverse communications networks, a broad range of applications, data synchronization across computers, stylus input device".

Mobility enables ubiquitous learning in formal and informal formats by eliminating dependence on fixed locations and in turn, changing the way users work and learn. Mobile technology has two comparable features. Scheduling and calendar applications are required to aid user's organizational skills and learning ability whereas real-time chat and data sharing aid collaboration and knowledge construction. Therefore, users can consume and create information collectively and individually.

Another unique attribute of mobile technology is the capability to provide face to face communication when students are using their devices in the classroom since students do not need to crowd around a desktop computer when using their mobile devices.

LIMITATIONS AND CONSIDERATIONS

Mobile devices have limitations as with all types of technology. They have shown usability limitations and as Kulkulksa and Hulme (2007) summarized:" physical attributes of mobile devices such as small screen, size, inadequate memory, short battery life. Content and software application limitations including lack of built in functions, the difficulty of adding applications, challenges in learning how to work with a mobile device and difference between applications and circumstances of use. Network speed and reliability, and physical environment issues such as problems with using the device outdoors, excessive screen brightness, concerns about personal security, possible radiation exposure from devices using radio frequencies, the need for rain covers in rainy or humid and so on."

These issues must be taken into account when designing the learning environment. Traxler (2007) stated that " looking at how rapidly new mobile products are improving, with advanced functions and numerous applications and accessories available these days, the technical limitations of mobile devices may be a temporary concern. Also, the use of mobile technologies in education is moving from small-scale and short-term trials or pilots into sustained and blended development projects."

The most prominent problem with mobile learning is the lack of a reliable theoretical framework which can offer clear guidance for instructional design and be able to evaluate the quality of programs that depend considerably on mobile technologies. Many attempted to conceptualize mobile learning since mobile technologies were introduced. (Traxler,2007) provided six categories by reviewing previous trials and pilot case studies in the public domain: 1) technology-driven mobile learning, 2) miniature but portable e-learning, 3) connected classroom learning, 4) informal, personalized, situated mobile learning, 5) mobile training/performance support, and 6) remote, rural, development mobile learning.

(Koole, 2009) designed a framework for the rational analysis of mobile education model that highlights three aspects of mobile learning: the device, the learner, and the social environment. The intersection of each aspect is also presented. This model is useful since it provides required criteria and examples for each aspect and interaction along with the checklist that aids educators develop mobile learning environments.

Definitions, existing frameworks and technological attributes relevant to mobile learning will help readers understand mobile learning and the way in which this technology will be an integral part of teaching in the future. Previous researches lack a clear pedagogical framework. A few mobile technology applications related to learning show a few links to established pedagogical theories. Various directions and unique applications must be logically categorized within the context of distant education. Educational applications must be categorized with mobile technologies and they must be placed in a logical framework in order to develop a set of comprehensive design guidelines to use in the future.

TRANSACTIONAL DISTANCE THEORY

This is an educational theory that defines the critical concepts of distance learning. This implies that teachers and learners are separated. Since its early publications in the 70s, this theory has affected many researchers and practices. Transactional distance theory is defined not only in terms of geographical separation but more importantly in terms of a pedagogical concept. Both types of education are included in this theory such that it states a program in which the sole or principal form of communication is by technology and where technology mediated communication is ancillary to the classroom. This is specifically critical for mobile learning since mobile devices often enter the school setting as an ancillary factor but are mostly used outside the classroom in non-traditional, informal, and non-institutional environments. Because of the inclusive nature of the transactional distance theory and its applicability and flexibility, it offers a vital contribution to the mobile learning framework.

This theory was defined using the concept of trans-action which in many researchers opinion is the most evolved level of inquiry in comparison to self-action and inter-action. Therefore, transactional distance is defined as "interplay of teachers and learners in environments that have the special characteristics of their being spatially separate from one another" Moore (2007). In other words, transactional distance is the extent of psychological separation between learners and teachers.

The transactional distance is controlled and managed by three interrelated factors: the program's structure, the dialogue exchanged between teachers and learners, and the learner's autonomy. (Moore,2007) explained that these factors were derived from the analysis of curricula of the distance learning program, communication between teachers and learners, and the role of learners in deciding what, how, and how much to learn. The most interesting part of Moore's transactional distance theory is the inverse relationship between dialogue and structure. As structure increases, transactional distance increases. However, as dialogue increases, transactional distance decreases. Another interesting aspect is the effect of communication media on transactional distance. For example, a television or radio program is thought to have clear structure because the program would not adjust itself to individual learners requirements which results in relatively high transactional distance as opposed to an audio or video teleconference between a teacher and student where there is high degree of dialogue since the teacher can change the structure according to the students needs which results in low transactional distance.

A PEDAGOGICAL FRAMEWORK OF MOBILE LEARNING

Garrison (2000) pointed out that "understanding transactional distance very much depends upon whether we are discussing a two-by-two matrix, a single continuum, or distinct clusters". Three variables (structure, dialogue, and autonomy) control transactional distance but the interrelationships are inverse or orthogonal between structure and dialogue and overlapping or hierarchical between structure and autonomy.

Transactional distance is defined as a psychological gap between teacher and learner but also contradicts definitions of structure and dialogue. Because of recent developments in communications technologies, learning structures are not only designed by instructional designers but also by collective learners. Also, dialogue is not formed between teachers and students but also between students. In terms of dialogue types, inter-learner dialogue can enable distance learners to create knowledge. Structure and dialogue have always been controlled by the teacher but have recently evolved so that learners can also affect their

formation. Due to this realization, all definitions relevant to transactional distance should include interaction among learners which contradicts the previous definition of transactional distance as a communications gap between teacher and learner. In order to solve this problem, dialogue and structure that influence transactional distance should only be defined as interaction between teacher and learner and interactions between learners must be excluded. Dialogue and structure formed solely by learners must be considered in a different dimension.

This dimension connotes "individual versus collective or social" activities by considering the importance of social aspects of learning as well as newer forms of social technologies. This idea was formed by the influence of cultural-historical activity theory that (Kang & Gyorke, 2008) compared with transactional distance theory.

Some researchers recognize activity theory as a powerful framework for designing constructivist learning environments and student-centered learning environments (Jonassen, Rohrer, &Murphy, 1999). However, certain limitations and unsolved problems in activity theory have been raised. Barab, Evans and Baek (1996) pointed out that "life tends not to compartmentalize itself of act in ways that are always wholly consistent with our theoretical assumptions."

MOBILE LEARNING EFFECTIVE IMPLEMENTATION

The following guidelines for effective implementation are based on theory and practice of learning with traditional tools or results from the available studies of mobile learning. These guidelines are most effective for mobile learning direct users but may also be effective for defining policy initiatives.

1. Cost model for infrastructure, technology and services.

When structuring a cost model, there are additional costs that must be taken into account apart from the initial capital required for devices and network costs such as technical support and other hidden charges. Various options for infrastructure and related services exist and institutions must make the most of their facilities to keep costs to a minimum. Mobile devices are the cheapest way in which students can keep connected to the internet even when taken home or elsewhere. As the education market becomes more competitive, mobile learning opportunities have advantages especially in filling training niches such as in medical training where considerable costs incur for students who fail or drop out. Existing technologies may also experience leverage such as SMS for mobile phones.

2. Assessing requirements for all involved in technology use to ensure usability.

Usability must account for users who will be creating mobile content and those who will use mobile applications to learn or to teach.

3. Study whether the technology is suitable for the learning task and assess advantages and disadvantages of each technology before deciding on which to use.

In order to make mobile learning implementation effective, a clear pedagogical approach is required to highlight learning objectives and to enable teachers to be involved directly in planning and defining the curriculum.

4. Define required roles for initiating and supporting mobile learning.
   a. A technical promoter to clarify system capabilities.
   b. A promoter to ensure the technical promoter's views are presented to those in charge.
   c. Technical experts to deal with devices failures and ensure equipment enhancements.
5. Define strategies for equipment management for institutions.

These include strategies to assign equipment to students, synchronizing hand held devices to desktop computers, reviewing student's tasks, implementing parental agreements in the case of loss and theft and hardware management.

6. Training and technical support for teachers to enhance current activities and establish new instructional activities.

Relevant training and good practice propagation are required for staff to familiarize themselves with the complete range of mobile computing. Educators and learners must have enough time to learn new devices functions.

EDUCATIONAL APPLICATIONS OF MOBILE TECHNOLOGIES

There are four types of mobile learning generated in the context of distance education. These include high transactional distance socialized mobile learning, high transactional distance individualized mobile learning, low transactional distance socialized mobile learning and low transactional distance individualized mobile learning. Each type will be explained further.

1. High transactional distance and socialized mobile learning activity (HS).

A mobile learning activity is classified as this type when:

• The learners have more psychological and communication space with their instructor or institutional support

- The learners are involved in group learning or projects where they communicate, negotiate and collaborate with each other
- Learning materials or the rules of activity are delivered from the predetermined program through mobile devices
- Transactions mainly occur among learners, and the instructor or teacher has minimal involvement in facilitating the group activity. This type might replace the traditional technology-mediated classroom group activity where students in a group or pair conduct given tasks of assignments.

2. High transactional distance and individualized mobile learning activity (HI).

Mobile learning activities are classified under this type when:

- The individual learners have more psychological and communication space with the instructor or instructional support.
- The individual learners receive tightly structured and well organized content and resources (e.g. recorded lectures, readings) through mobile devices.
- The individual learners receive the content and control their learning process in order to maser it.
- The interactions mainly occur between the individual learner and content. This type demonstrates an extension of e-learning which allows greater flexibility and portability. Individual learners fit this flexible learning into their mobile lifestyle. This type is mostly influenced by the context regarding when and where to learn. It also includes mobile learning that makes access to the educational system possible for students in rural areas.

3. Low transactional distance and socialized mobile learning activity (LS).

In this type, individual learners interact both with the instructor and other learners as they use mobile devices. They have the following circumstance:

- Less psychological and communication space with the instructor.
- Loosely structured instruction.
- Work together in a group as they solve the given problem and try to achieve a common goal.
- Engage in social interaction, negotiation and frequent communication naturally. This type demonstrates the most advanced forms in terms of the versatility of mobile devices and learners social interactions.

4. Low transactional distance and individualized mobile learning activity (LI).

This last type of mobile activity refers to:

- Less psychological and communication space between instructor and learners.
- Loosely structured and undefined learning content.
- Individual learners interact directly with the instructor.
- The instructor leads and controls the learning in an effort to meet individual learners' needs while maintaining their independence. This type shows characteristics unique to mobile learning that support blended or hybrid learning.

A range of different mobile wireless devices are used in higher education. These include web-enabled wireless phones such as smart phones; web enabled wireless handheld computers such as palmtops and tablets, wireless laptop computers and personal digital assistants. In learning environments, mobile wireless computers, PDAs and handheld devices are the most popular devices used. Mobile phones make up a small portion of current usage of mobile wireless devices. However, researchers on this subject claim that in the not so distant future more institutions of higher education will require mobile phones for students and faculty members for education purposes.

Mobile wireless computers normally called wireless laptops are most popular form of mobile wireless technologies used in higher education. Wireless laptops have a wireless card that enables short range wireless voice and data communications. There are many schools and higher education courses that make it mandatory for students to use wireless laptops in class.

In the year 2000, PDAs became the newest emerging technology for educational purposes. Similar to other forms of technology, PDAs were first used for business purposes. These hand-held devices combine functions of computing, telephoning, internet and network. They have features such as cellular phone, face, organizer and web browser. In some universities in the US, undergraduate students were required to purchase PDAs especially students taking law and medical courses.

Mobile phones are the most popular mobile wireless technology used mainly as personal communication tool. Types of mobile wireless technology phones include:

- **Web-Enables Cellular:** These devices have the capability of accessing the web. The internet can be accessed through wireless application protocol (WAP). Often they are called WAP phones.
- **Wireless Handset:** A type of cellular phone providing a communications system with extended features such as voice-activated dialing, WAP browser, and two-way text messaging.
- **Smartphone:** A combination of mobile phones and computers.

In comparison to wireless enabled computers of PDAs, mobile phones are still in their early stages for educational purposes. PDAs are often used with mobile wireless services, such as SMS and MMS. Some higher education institutes have integrated mobile phones into their teaching and learning environments.

SMS or text messaging is the transmission of short text messages to and from mobile phones, fax machines and/or IP addresses. SMS may be one of the most common wireless applications that are used with mobile phones to support teaching and learning. By using SMS, lecturers and students can send and receive text messages to and from most mobile phone devices.

MMS is a more recent messaging application in comparison to SMS therefore fewer institutions utilize this application as a teaching and learning method. MMS also enables automatic and prompt delivery of personal messages. MMS has more benefits compared to MMS in that it can deliver all types of information such as sound, images and video messages. In the not so distant future, the use of SMS and MMS will increase in the education field as technology advances.

The number of universities and higher education institutes using mobile wireless technologies as teaching and learning tools is increasing. In the US, over 90% of public universities and 80% of private universities adopt some sort of mobile wireless technologies such as mobile wireless devices and networks. Some universities even require students to have mobile wireless devices for their assignments. In the near future, mobile wireless devices and wireless networks may be mandatory for all students and universities. Also, it will be possible for faculty members and students to use mobile wireless devices virtually at all locations on college and university campuses since more buildings and places are being retrofitted for wireless technologies. Many main buildings and places such as libraries, lecture theatres, cafeterias, and research centers on college and university campuses are already equipped for wireless access.

BENEFITS OF MOBILE TECHNOLOGY IN HIGHER EDUCATION

The development of mobile wireless technology has generated a considerable amount of excitement among practitioners and academics due to its results in changing the academic environment from traditional settings to mobile learning. Increasing numbers of institutions of higher education offer courses using mobile technologies as alternative teaching and learning tools. Regardless of these interests in mobile technologies in higher education, there is lack of academic research on the use of mobile technologies in higher education. For the past decades, wired technologies have been used by educators, administrators, students and others in higher education to aid them in teaching and learning. In this century institutions of higher education are moving towards mobile technologies. Mobile technologies were first used in industry settings such as business. The movement of mobile technologies to the education field is a recent occurrence and is now becoming the most popular technology in higher education. For the past few years educators and learners in higher education have enjoyed the many advantages of wired technologies. Wired technologies have their limitations in that they cannot provide anytime, anywhere functionality which is offered by mobile technologies. With the benefits of mobility, mobile wireless technologies aid in the effectiveness and efficiency in teaching and learning.

Wireless PCs have the same features as wired PCs, therefore students and teachers can benefit from the same capabilities and functionalities with their wireless computers as they with their wired PCs. Wireless computers have additional benefits such as ease of movement, relaxed fit, strategic deployment, low profile, flexibility, cleanliness, convenience, simplicity, and speed. The smaller size is also an added bonus for both teachers and students. In addition to these benefits, there are also economic benefits. The cost of mobile wireless computers and services has decreased substantially in recent years. Currently, the price of wireless computers is similar to that of wired computers simply due to the fact that hardware and software prices for wireless computers have decreased. The primary difference between wireless computers and wired computers is that wireless computers use wireless network interface cards. Thus, maintenance, set-up, and integration with other technologies is made easier compared to PCs. Installing a wireless network can be more affordable since wireless networks can reduce the cost to deploy and operate. Wireless networks are easier to setup and manage therefore are more productive since they enable mobility. Without wires, teaching and learning increase in terms of efficiency and effectiveness. The greatest advantage derived from wireless computing was communication, followed by student learning, faculty teaching, and collaboration between learners and faculty. Communications play a vital role since a good communication channel between teachers and teachers, students and students, and students and teachers results in enhanced teaching and learning processes.

Advantages of mobile wireless phones have been recognized recently since a few higher education institutions use them for teaching and learning. Some of these advantages include providing students with freedom of location and time, increasing speed in teaching and learning, enabling one to one learning based on individual educational histories or test results and allowing teachers to keep up the new educational subjects for future education. Mobile wireless phones provide teachers and students with much better communications opportunities than other mobile wireless devices. In terms of communication, wireless computers and PDAs are mostly used for text message communication, but mobile wireless phones can be used for voice communication. Improved communication between teachers and students improve teaching and learning. Another bonus of utilizing mobile wireless phones is their use in seminars and group discussions. Students improve their learning processes by using wireless handsets in a group discussion or teamwork. Common problems in a seminar class include a lack of participation by students, tendency for some students to dominate group discussions, and the difficulty in ensuring discussion focus. In such cases, wireless handsets could be useful to enable collaboration in group discussions easily and more efficiently. For example, students may use a numeric keypad on wireless handsets, and then a handset sends a signal to a receiver that is linked to a wireless computer loaded with global positioning system software used to communicate with other software simultaneously. Therefore, wireless handsets provide a discussion environment where all responses and opinions are anonymous so students may express their thoughts with more freedom without worrying about offending other students. The use of wireless handsets in seminars also provides greater participation and the increases the number of ideas generated. Students feel mobile wireless technologies are easy to use and would be useful for further sessions. For example, nowadays people use mobile phones to study on the way to school or work as often as someone reading a book on public transport. With current web based e-learning courses, students are able to take courses, pick up and turn in their homework assignments from their own computers and communicate with other students and lecturers online. Students are able to do all that and more through their mobile phones. Such mobile learning will provide no limits on location and time efficiency for students who want to take some courses from long distance. Although mobile learning is still under development but in the near future m-learning will be a common method in teaching and learning.

Mobile technologies are a relatively recent addition to learning. Their power to change the way of educating people is astonishing. Mobile technologies are the frontier for education institutions. Currently and in the future many educational opportunities are made possible because of mobile technologies unique characteristics and positive impacts identified in education. Mobile technologies use in education will continue to grow and will become the learning environment of choice. Not much academic research has been carried out to give clear understanding of mobile technologies advantages in education therefore making it difficult for research in the use and adoption of these technologies. Many issues must be taken into account before adopting mobile technologies with security issues being the most crucial one. Doubts about security issues from users have lead to the slow adoption of these technologies specifically in the business sector where financial transactions take place. Regardless of these issues, more and more higher education institutions are adopting the use of mobile technologies to present m-learning environments to both teachers and learners.

Mobile wireless technologies are still distant from use in everyday life for educational purposes compared to computers or calculators. In order to use these technologies effectively, administrators, educators, and students must cooperate to determine efficient methods for using these technologies to achieve their educational goals instead of greeting them reluctantly.

IMPLEMENTING EDUCATIONAL TECHNOLOGY FOR EARLY LEARNERS

Educators and parents are observing how today's children are exposed to advanced technology from an early age with tablets, e-readers, and smart phones being more popular choices. Technological experiences make way for unique learning opportunities. However, without an educational component, these experiences cannot reach full potential for supporting children's learning and advancements. Utilizing an educational component for children of an early age means that adult supervision is necessary to interact with children and provide peer to peer learning methods to enhance children's skills to succeed in school. In order to use educational technology for children of an earlier age they need to be developmentally appropriate for children, include tools to aid teachers implement these technologies successfully and be able to integrate them into the classroom and curriculum.

Teachers have been utilizing various technologies for teaching children for decades but the development of new technologies and their presence in classrooms in becoming more and more common. Interactive single-touch and multi-touch screens in various dimensions have changed the way children use technology. Major improvements have been made in terms of providing learning content specifically for mobile devices. Educational technology plays a vital role in children's learning when aligned with curriculum goals.

Many researches indicate the fact that computers support and increase children's skills in the social, cognitive, language, literacy, writing and mathematical fields. Children of an early age interact with peers when using educational technology. They help each other and cooperate to solve problems. Adult supervision for children using technology is proportional with increases in abstract reasoning, planning behavior, visual-motor coordination and visual memory (Primavera, Wiederlight & DiGiacamo 2001). For example, teachers can enable children to focus better by asking them to carefully pay attention to the actions on a screen or by asking them how they would react when a particular situation comes up while using particular software. When teachers help children and rich learning content is integrated in the curriculum via various technologies, technology experiences enable improved language and literacy results such as improved recognition, sequencing, listening and comprehension, vocabulary, and understanding stories concepts. For example, children who had daily access to educational software and were supervised made improvements but those who

had a weekly session with a mentor who enabled technology use made better improvements. When children use technology along with adult supervision their mathematics skills improve in terms of number recognition, counting, shape recognition and composition. Usability studies with newer technologies such as tablets and mobile phones found that preschool children learn to use these devices easily, independently and confidently. Another study consisting of utilizing mobile devices indicated that children between the ages of 3 to 7 made gains in vocabulary and phonological awareness with these gains being more substantial with children ages 3 to 5.

Based on research carried out in 2012, it was concluded that for technology to be developmentally appropriate, it should be responsive to the ages and developmental levels of children, to their individual interests, and to their social and cultural contexts. Another finding was that it is critical to support early childhood practitioners in gaining knowledge and skills to choose and utilize technology in appropriate ways. There can be negative effects on learning and development when educators fail to attain the knowledge required to aid children in using educational technologies appropriately.

A primary step is to establish learning goals for the children. These goals may include fostering children's literacy and mathematics or social emotional development. Some technologies promise useful attention and the integration of all aspects of learning but it is unlikely that instructional excellence will be achieved. Learning goals must be prioritized even though technologies do not require in meeting every single goal. The next step is to identify the technology available or useful for classroom. For example, software designed as applications on tablets and mobile phones can not generally be transferred to the whiteboard. Finally, the content of these software programs must be considered. Generally, the areas which have potential to strongly affect children's learning experiences include the educational value of the program, its ability to engage a child in learning, its child friendliness, the interactivity between child and program, and the software program's capability to assess children's learning progress. However, these areas are not comprehensive since other areas such as durability and costs are not taken into account since they do not focus entirely on the educational areas. So in summary the key steps to successfully evaluate educational technologies include:

- Establish learning goals for the children.
- Identify the hardware or devices required.
- Analyze features and software content in reaching learning goals.
- Plan how the educational technology will be integrated into the curriculum.

Hatch Early Learning Institute defined an Early Childhood Educational Technology Evaluation Kit as a conclusion to reviewing the elements considered when evaluating educational technology for early learners. The toolkit addresses aspects of recent methods and features that newer technologies can support such as progress monitoring. Also, it considers the context in which the educational technology will be used such as children's ages, type of learners for example children with disabilities or are dual language learners, type of device and elements that affect integration such as professional development to support educators technology skills.

If an educational curriculum includes educational technology such as software packages and wants to evaluate this choice with the mentioned toolkit, educators can share the ratings with families to help them understand the reasons for their choices. By utilizing this toolkit, the following areas are considered:

- Educational Value:
  ○ Is the content based on research/ standards?

  ○ Does the software follow the correct developmental course and effective teaching paths?
- Engagement to enhance learning:
  ○ Are the activities presented in a playful manner?
  ○ Are the rewards used appropriately?
- Child-friendly:
  ○ Are there multiple opportunities for success?
  ○ Can the children use the software independently?
- Interactivity:
  ○ Does the program respond to and/or can it be customized to the child?
  ○ Does the program allow new activities to be created?
- Progress monitoring:
  ○ Is there a progress monitoring feature?
  ○ How are the results presented and are they easily used?

When children use technology, teachers often think about demonstrating, trouble-shooting or monitoring. Less attention is paid towards interacting with children to improve positive learning approaches. However, doing so depicts education in educational technology. By putting this into practice with technology means active engagement, group participation, interactivity and feedback, and connecting technology to real-world contexts. One method is scaffolding the use of technology by children. By utilizing this method children reach defined goals more often, work more effectively, and use higher thinking levels when solving problems.

- **Cognitive Scaffolding:** Educators use cognitive scaffolding to enhance children's understanding of concepts. This method resembles traditional scaffolding between adult/teacher and child. Activities used include questioning, modeling, and collaboration with peers.

- **Technical Scaffolding:** Technology features are used to support learning which means the technology itself which is used to facilitate problem solving. For example using computer programs based on children's responses so the child learns at an appropriate level.
- **Affective Scaffolding:** By using this method children are encouraged to think at higher levels. For example, a character may appear on the screen to indicate what should be done next to affirm or encourage the child to carry on.

When a software program is being considered, features that support teachers in a technical sense such as tutorials and help functions, guide content use such as lesson samples, extension activities and options to create new activities, enhance teacher's ability to present instructional support effectively such as results and reports relevant to children's learning progressions are necessary.

Learning communities are also useful in uniting people in achieving a common goal. A recent report from the Joan Ganz Cooney Center titled "Take a Giant Step: A Blueprint for Teaching Children in a Digital Age" Barron (2011), explains national goals and immediate measures, acknowledging the fact that leaders in education must restructure their time to enable teachers to cooperate together and with students to utilize technology. The easiest way to start a learning community is for teachers to gather regularly in groups to discuss their goals. They can also discuss developing lessons by using technology. Another learning community includes using the experiences of technology coaches and mentors which will enable teachers to make substantial progress alongside children.

To support early learner's positive development, identifying education in educational technology is vital. The main areas talked about to reach this goal are developmental appropriateness, supported implementation, classroom and curriculum integration. When taken into account together, these aspects enhance the technological potential to support meaningful learning for young children.

THE FUTURE OF MOBILE TECHNOLOGIES IN EDUCATION

A high percentage of people in western society have mobile phones that have both voice calls and textual functions. Newer phones can also connect wirelessly to the internet. PDAs have been distributed by employers to keep their personnel active while on the move. Laptops, which are considered as already established technologies, can now be synchronized with mobile phones to connect to the internet (tethering).

There is an abundance of interest from educators to discover newer methods of engaging mobile technologies for teaching. These technologies provide opportunities for major change in education away from computer labs to more embedded use beyond classrooms. (Vavoula & Sharples, 2002) suggest there are three ways of learning mobile: "Learning is mobile in terms of space, i.e. it happens at the workplace, at home, and at places of leisure; it is mobile between different areas of life, i.e. it may relate to work demands, self-improvement, or leisure; and it is mobile with respect to time, i.e. it happens at different times during the day, on working days or no weekends".

Knowledge is widely regarded as information in context and due to the fact that mobile devices enable context-specific information delivery, they are well coordinated to enable learning and knowledge construction.

Mobile technologies provide experiences to engage and educate learners which are mostly different from conventional desktop computers. They are used dynamically with different settings and give access to vast activities. Due to their personal nature, learners can individualize their experiences and have responsibility over their work.

Classification of Mobile Devices

Mobile to most gives the meaning of portable and movable. It is also considered personal as opposed to shared in terms of context. The terms 'mobile' and 'personal' are often interchangeable but devices may be one without necessarily being the other. Figure 1 shows categorization of mobile technologies by two orthogonal dimensions of personal vs. shared and portable vs. static.

Quadrant one shows devices that can be categorized as both portable and personal. These are common devices such as PDAs, mobile phones, tablets, laptops, portable video games consoles. Due to the single-user nature of these products, they are normally considered very personal though the information they contain may easily be shared.

Quadrant two consists of devices that are less portable but are used to respond anonymously to multiple choice questions set by teachers on a central server. These devices are considered static due to their usage in one location but are still personal because of their single-user nature which is why they are called personal static technologies.

Quadrant three shows technologies where the devices are not mobile but offer services to users on the move. In these examples such as street kiosks, interactive displays, and various kinds of installed devices enable users to access information and offer learning services. Since these devices are used by many, they are not considered personal. These are shared portable technologies.

Other interactions are shared more between users and must therefore be larger and are less portable. Quadrant four shows examples such as whiteboards and video conferencing devices thus are not counted as mobile technologies. Quadrants one to three are generally thought of as mobile technologies but quadrant four is classified as at the extreme end of static dimension.

Mobile computing devices are reaching a stage where they are mostly embedded, ubiquitous and networked. Mobile phones, PDA's, consoles, cameras features will all merge to provide a single portable hand held device. These integrated features will enable users to capture time, location, weather etc details. Therefore, such technologies will have great affect on learning. Apart from referring to portable internet-based resources, users will be able to manage their learning resources by consulting personal diaries and virtual learning environments. This will in turn cause them to become investigators since they can publish their observations as digital media. Applications will enable users to record their findings in which they can refer to later when needed. Distributed collaborations and teamwork will also become more popular using mobile devices.

Educators and technology developers have the task of ensuring learning is highly situated, personal, collaborative and long term. Educators will have to adopt the role of learning resources guiders and technology developers will need to take into account security and privacy issues when developing devices and services.

Mobile devices have found their way into classrooms whether they are welcome or not therefore productive ways must be established in terms of educational practice. The success of learning and teaching by utilizing mobile technologies depends on how easily they are accepted into everyday lives with the best case scenario being at a point where it is not recognized as learning at all.

The way in which mobile technology is introduced into the learning space is important. Finding out how users are using their devices is important for developers to understand the starting point and enables them scope to structuralize existing applications or develop newer ones. Initially, making learning resources mobile-friendly is necessary. This will open the scope for learners to access their required content. Another step may be to present an information service application to close the gap between life in and out of school enabling students' access to search tools and information that are similar to those available more generally which is especially useful when

Figure 1. Categorization of mobile technologies by two orthogonal dimensions of personal vs. shared and portable vs. static

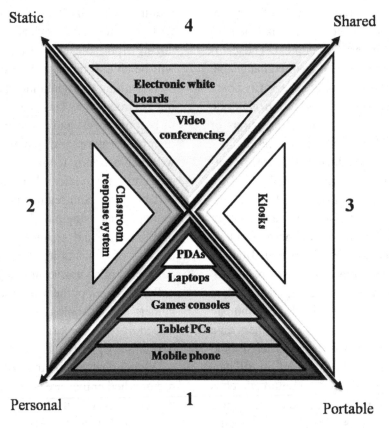

resources are presented in various formats such as written, audio and video.

An initial challenge an introducing mobile technology for learning has always been convincing participants, faculty members and staff to trust a different approach. There will always be a resistance to change since existing teaching methods are tried and accepted. Both teachers and learners may be reluctant if they are not familiar with the technology or fear it will require extra workload. This technology can potentially adjust the role of educators from knowledge deliverers to facilitators of learning resources. Also, by introducing new technology to the classroom, tech-savvy students may have an advantage over non-technical students which may result in isolation for non-technical students.

Choosing the appropriate technology may seem difficult since there are so many things to consider. No single device is better than the other and each device has its advantages. Phones are good for audio files and capturing data but a tablet is better for consuming information. The first consideration is whether to provide a device at the outset or ask participants to use their own devices. There are advantages and disadvantages to both. By providing a device to students, developers are able to install native applications specific to the needs of students. They are also able to provide resources in a way that is controlled by the institution. The disadvantage is that it is less likely for this device to merge into students lifestyles since they may already have their own phone of choice. It becomes an extra device to carry and be left at home. Preferably, the learning device is the one that is with them anytime and anywhere.

There is more consideration around technology and ownership. Who owns the learning and on which device does it belong. This is a question for participants with a business phone and personal phone which may have various operating systems. Who owns the learning resources? Is it the user or the cooperation paying for the user to attend the course? Privacy issues are also of importance as well as personal time versus work time. These issues are worth mentioning for future policy making decisions.

Another issue regarding choosing the right technology for learning purposes is the related costs. If providing students with devices there is considerable initial capital expenditure as well as ongoing cost of infrastructure and technical support. Further consideration should be given to design costs where third party developers may be brought in to design products such as applications. An investigation of a cost model for structure, technology and services that includes the cost of providing IP addresses and bandwidth should be carried out. Whilst institutions may consider mobile learning as a cost saving measure, pedagogy has to remain a priority and as such can incur costs. Designing and implementing new concepts can be costly in terms of time. Although, the combination of appropriately planned medium to long term strategies together with students bringing their own devices could save money in the long run. Institutions making use of their existing facilities and services should try to lower costs. Also, some of the more ad hoc ideas which structuralize learning can cost very little and only require imagination and experiments.

It is vital to know the needs of those involved in a new mobile learning offer. This includes faculty, content creators, other staff and the learners themselves. Meeting these needs should influence levels of engagement. It is also important to gather background information about student preferences, habits, and attitudes towards their phone usage and well as learning. For example, what devices do they own and when do they use them, when do they access the internet and what, if any, are the distinctions between home and work devices. This way, it should be possible to identify how, when and where the learning experience can be enhanced by mobility. The visitor-resident distinction may be useful when considering which technologies to provide for mobile learners. For example if your learners are mainly visitors, they are less likely to take advantage of any feed based system for aggregated information you may put in place. They may also require extra encouragement to blog or comment as part of a course. The resident will expect to have the opportunity to offer opinions on topics and to socialize around a program for study. Beyond those using mobile applications to learn from or teach with, account needs to be taken of those users creating mobile content. In fact they are likely to find ways of doing this even if they are not officially provided. It is important to stress that visitor-resident categorization cannot be assumed; measures that reliably distinguish learners and their preferences, as well as identifying where learners fall on the visitor-resident scale need to be established.

It is important to think about content and what is suitable for transmission to mobile devices. Indeed, the case studies provide many examples of content being made available for mobile users. These can be applications, podcasts, web pages, codes, learning resources and messaging which are all in no way exhaustive. This is also not a one way transmission but is feasible that learners will create content for collaboration, evaluation, evidencing or just for fun. As mentioned before, residents will likely expect the opportunity to share and will find ways of doing this even if they are not officially provided. Therefore there has to be choice whether to provide a forum for a collaboration of content created by participants. Educators and developers can assist participants by making content more readily available and in formats that are easily accessible from mobile devices. How can the quality of the instructional content be improved, enhanced or downgraded by transferring to a mobile compatible format, can the content be read on a mobile phone screen, it is advised to test assumptions regarding these factors.

Support is also an issue concerning mobile learning for both teachers and students. Without support and direction, mobile learning may well be a solitary unsupported effort. This in itself is not necessarily a disadvantage but top down support creates a paradigm shift which captures the full potential of mobile learning. Further support includes a promoter of mobile learning who can demonstrate the capabilities of a system and can exploit the whole range of capabilities that mobile devices offer. There also needs to be a pedagogical support for teachers. This may involve introducing and developing new and innovative methods of could simply involve going back to traditional ways and working on how to enhance them. On a practical level, support services need to be available for the management of equipment and online services. Technical support is especially required if the institution is providing devices or installations to deal with equipment failures and ongoing system improvements. Support needs to be ongoing and must be provided to both staff and students. They must have sufficient time to familiarize themselves with new devices or installations. This is especially true for those who may not want to or are not sure about using unfamiliar technologies.

One of these issues is that previous learning assessment methods was based on traditional learning offers. Mobile technology breaks with tradition and disrupts what has been used before. Indeed, as a new concept it might be difficult to know what to assess although measures of reactions, learning, behavior and outcomes related to mobile use are possible. Stakeholders may be keen to see evidence of the effectiveness of learning that comes from using mobile devices. A properly designed assessment could provide confirmation to support business cases for further use.

Future steps for those interested in implementing a learning strategy are to consider making content and information available in formats that are easily accessible on participants' mobile devices. Having a mobile learning resource available in this way allows learners to access information that is reliable and convenient. They will look for information on their mobile phones anyway so it is best to have resources that are approved by educators. This is counted as a limited initial step and there are many more steps to be taken that can and will enhance the experience of mobile learners and education providers alike. These will be different depending on levels of support, innovation and experimentation and will gradually merge.

Questions to ask in order to develop a mobile learning strategy:

- What are your beliefs, hopes and fears concerning mobile learning in executive education?
- What bearing could participants' physical locations and movements have on teaching and learning?
- In what ways can a mobile strategy be used to its advantage in an executive education learning offer?
- In what ways can mobile learning support and even increase student engagement and motivation?
- What does a mobile learning strategy mean in terms of professional development, hands on experience, technical and pedagogical support, software development and testing, support or evaluation?
- What implications are there for all those involved such as participants, course teams, program teams, faculty, and lecturers?

The uses of mobile learning have potential effect on all education, including executive education. As mobile learning capabilities continue to expand new methods of learning will continue to evolve and the next few years will see a period of rapid growth for mobile learning, with evolutionary rather than evolutionary changes.

REFERENCES

Albanese, M., & Mitchell, S. (1993). Problem-based learning: A review of the literature on its outcomes and implementation issues. Journal of the Association of American Medical Colleges, 68(1), 14-16.

Barron, B., Cayton-Hodges, G., Bofferding, L., Copple, C., Darling-Hammond, L., & Levine, M. (2011). *Take a Giant Step: A Blueprint for Teaching Children in a Digital Age*. New York: The Joan Ganz Cooney Center at Sesame Workshop.

Bascsich, P., Ash, C., Boniwell, K., & Kaplan, L. (1999). *The Cost of Networked Learning. In Networked Learning: Perspectives and Issues* (pp. 27–48). Springer London.

Bruner, J. (1966). *Toward a Theory of Instruction.* Cambridge, MA: Harvard University Press.

Colella, J., & Stead, G. (2003). Take a bite: Producing accessible learning materials for mobile devices. In *Proceeding of the Second European Conference on Learning with Mobile Devices - MLEARN 2003* (pp. 23-27). London: MLEARN.

Cortez, C., Nussbaum, M., Santelices, R., Rodriguez, P., Zurita, G., Correa, M., & Cautivo, R. (2004). Teaching science with mobile computer supported collaborative learning (MCSCL). In *Proceedings of the 2nd IEEE International Workshop* (pp. 67-74). Taiwan: IEEE Computer Society.

Garrison, R. (2000). Theoretical challenges for distance education in the 21ˢᵗ century: A shift from structural to transactional issues. *The International Review of Research in Open and Distance Learning, 1*(1), 12-24.

Hennessy, S. (1999). The potential of portable technologies for supporting graphing investigations. *British Journal of Educational Technology, 30*(1), 57–60. doi:10.1111/1467-8535.00090

Holme, O., & Sharples, M. (2002). Implementing a student learning organizer on the pocket PC platform. In *Proceedings of MLEARN 2002: European Workshop on Mobile and Contextual Learning* (pp. 14-17). Birmingham, UK: MLEARN.

Jonassen, D., & Rohrer-Murphy, L. (1999). Activity theory as a framework for designing constructivist learning environments. *Educational Technology Research and Development, 47*(1), 61–79. doi:10.1007/BF02299477

Kang, H., & Gyorke, A. S. (2008). Rethinking distance learning activities: A comparison of transactional distance theory and activity theory. *The Journal of Open, Distance and e-Learning, 23*(3), 203-214.

Klopfer, E., & Squire, K. (2007). Environmental Detectives: The development of an augmented reality platform for environmental simulations. Education research technology and development. *Journal of Educational Technology Research and Development, 56*(2), 203–228. doi:10.1007/s11423-007-9037-6

Kukulska-Hulme, A. (2007). Mobile usability in educational context: What have we learnt? *The International Review of Research in Open and Distance Learning, 8*(2), 10-12.

Lave, J., & Wenger, E. (1991). Situated Learning: Legitimate Peripheral Participation. Cambridge, UK: Academic Press. doi:10.1017/CBO9780511815355

Lonsdale, P., Baber, C., Sharples, M., & Arvantis, T. N. (2003). Context-awareness architecture for facilitating mobile learning. In *Proceedings of MLEARN 2002: Mobile Learning anytime anywhere* (pp. 17-19) Birmingham, UK: MLEARN.

O'Malley, C., Vavoula, G., Glew, J. P., Taylor, J., Sharples, M., & Lefrere, P. (2003). Guidelines for Learning/Teaching/Tutoring in a Mobile Environment. *Journal of MOBlearn.*, *8*(12), 14–26.

Pea, R., & Maldonado, H. (2006). WILD for learning: Interacting through new computing devices anytime, anywhere. In The Cambridge handbook of the learning science (pp. 24-28). Cambridge University Press.

Piaget, J. (1929). *The Child's Conception of the World*. New York: Harcourt, Brace, Jovanovich.

Primavera, J., Wiederlight, P. P., & Digiacamo, T. M. (2001). Technology Access for Low-Income Preschoolers: Bridging the Digital Divide. In *Technology Access for Preschoolers* (pp. 1-26). Academic Press.

Traxler, J. (2007). Defining, discussing, and evaluating mobile learning: The moving finger writes and having writes. *The International Review of Research in Open and Distance Learning*, *8*(2), 11-18.

Vavoula, G. N., & Sharples, M. (2002). KLeOS: A personal, mobile, knowledge and learning organization system. In *Proceedings of IEEE International Workshop on Wireless and Mobile Technologies* (pp. 152-156). IEEE. doi:10.1109/WMTE.2002.1039239

Wang, M., Shen, R., Novak, D., & Pan, X. (2009). The impact of mobile learning on students' learning behaviours and performance. *British Journal of Educational Technology*, *40*(4), 673–695. doi:10.1111/j.1467-8535.2008.00846.x

Weiser, M. (1991). The computer for the 21st century. *Scientific American*, *265*(3), 94–104. doi:10.1038/scientificamerican0991-94

Zurita, G., & Nussbaum, M. (2007). A conceptual framework based on activity theory for mobile CSCL. *British Journal of Educational Technology*, *38*(2), 211–235. doi:10.1111/j.1467-8535.2006.00580.x

KEY TERMS AND DEFINITIONS

Mobile Technologies: Mobile technologies consist of being both mobile and being able to carry out computing tasks. These technologies are continuously connected to network resources without limitations of time and location.

Wireless: The transmission of any sort of data conducted over radio waves, infrared waves or microwaves instead of wires. The radio frequency spectrum is used to transmit data such as text data, voice, video or multimedia without limitations in terms of time and location.

Educational: Activities that serve the purpose of educating including technologies utilized for this purpose.

Pedagogical: Instructional activities normally used by educators to educate learners.

Ubiquitous: Present, appearing and found everywhere. Referring to universal learning methods where technology is utilized to remove obstacles to achieve ubiquitous learning.

Compilation of References

Activeworlds offers a comprehensive platform. (n.d.). Retrieved July 13, 2012 from http://www.activeworld.com

Ahrens, A., & Zaščerinska, J. (2010). Social Dimension of Web 2.0 in Student Teacher Professional Development. In *Proceedings of Association for Teacher Education in Europe Spring Conference 2010: Teacher of the 21st Century: Quality Education for Quality Teaching,* (pp. 179-186). Riga, Latvia: University of Latvia.

Ahrens, A., Zaščerinska, J., & Andreeva, N. (2013). Engineering Students' Blended Learning in Higher Education. In *Proceedings of International Scientifical Conference Society, Integration, Education of Rezekne Higher Education Institution Faculty of Education and Design Personality Socialization Research Institute in collaboration with Department of Civil Engineering and Architecture,* (vol. 1, pp. 34-44). Rēzekne, Latvia: Rēzeknes Augstskolas Izdevniecība 2013.

Ahrens, A., Bassus, O., & Zaščerinska, J. (2013). Engineering Students' Direct Experience in Entrepreneurship. In *Proceedings of 6th ICEBE International Conference on Engineeirng and Business Education Innovation, Entrepreneurship and Sustainability,* (pp. 93-100). Wismar, Germany: University of Wismar.

Ajjan, H., & Hartshorne, R. (2008). Investigating faculty decisions to adopt Web 2.0 technologies: Theory and empirical tests. *The Internet and Higher Education, 11*(2), 71–80. doi:10.1016/j.iheduc.2008.05.002

Ajzen, I., & Fishbein, M. (1980). *Understanding attitudes and predicting social behavior.* Prentice Hall, Inc.

Alavi, M., & Gallupe, B. (2003). Using Information Technology in Learning: Case Studies in Business and Management Education Programs. *Academy of Management Learning & Education, 2*(2), 139–153. doi:10.5465/AMLE.2003.9901667

Albanese, M., & Mitchell, S. (1993). Problem-based learning: A review of the literature on its outcomes and implementation issues. Journal of the Association of American Medical Colleges, 68(1), 14-16.

Albardooli, M., Alobaidli, O., & Alyousha, F. (2016). *E-mobile, the future of e learning.* Thesis submitted at the University of Bahrain. Retrieved from www.albardooli.com/dlobjects/EmobileMAlbardooli.pdf

Alexakis, C., Paliktzoglou, V., & Suhonen, J. (2012). Assessment of the familiarity, adoption and use of educational technology by higher education students in Cyprus. In C. Vrasidas & P. Panaou (Eds.), *Design Thinking in Education, Media + Society* (pp. 154–163). Nicosia: Cuprus.

Alexander, B. (2006). Web 2.0: A new wave of innovation for teaching and learning? *EDUCAUSE Review, 41*(2), 32.

Alexander, B., & Levine, A. (2008). Web 2.0 storytelling: Emergence of a new genre. *EDUCAUSE Review, 43*(6), 40–56.

Alexander, P. A., & Murphy, P. K. (1998). The research base for APA's learner-centered psychological principles. In N. M. Lambert & B. L. McCombs (Eds.), *Issues in school reform: A sampler of psychological perspectives on learner-centered schools* (pp. 33–60). Washington, DC: American Psychological Association. doi:10.1037/10258-001

Alkan, F., & Bala Alkan, H. (1998). Asynchronous learning in planning and architecture education. In *Proceedings of Forum II, Architectural Education for the 3RD Millennium*, (pp. 555-560). Gazimagusa, North Cyprus: Academic Press.

Al-Khalifa, H. (2008). Building an Arabic learning object repository with an ad hoc recommendation engine. In *Proceedings of the iiWAS* (pp. 390-394). Linz: iiWAS. doi:10.1145/1497308.1497378

Ally, M. (2013). Mobile learning: From research to practice to Impact Education. *Learning and Teaching in Higher Education: Gulf Perspectives, 10*(2), 9–22.

Al-Musawi, N., Al-Bustan, A. A., & Al-Mezel, S. M. (2013). Developing a Scale to Measure Attitudes of University Students towards E-learning. In *Proceedings of Association for Teacher Education in Europe (ATEE) Winter Conference "Learning & Teaching with Media & Technology"* (pp. 13-20). Brussels: Association for Teacher Education in Europe (ATEE).

Alsaadat, K. (2009). Mobile learning and university teaching. In *Proceedings of the International Conference on Education and New Learning Technologies* (vol. 6, pp. 5895-5905). Barcelona: IATED.

Altameem, T. (2011). Contextual mobile learning system for Saudi Arabian universities. *International Journal of Computers and Applications, 21*(4), 21–26. doi:10.5120/2499-3377

Alyahya, S., & Gall, J. E. (2012). iPads in Education: A Qualitative Study of Students' Attitudes and Experiences. In AmielT.WilsonB. (Eds.), *Proceedings of World Conference on Educational Multimedia, Hypermedia and Telecommunications 2012* (pp. 1266-1271). Chesapeake, VA: AACE.

Anderson, L. W., Krathwohl, D. R., & Bloom, B. S. (2005). *A taxonomy for learning, teaching, and assessing*. New York: Longman.

Anderson, P. W., Arrow, K. J., & Pines, D. (1988). *The economy as an evolving complex system*. Menlo Park, CA: Addison-Wesley.

Anderson, T. (2003). Getting the Mix Right Again: An updated and theoretical rationale for interaction. *International Review of Research in Open and Distance Learning, 4*(2). Available at http://www.irrodl.org/index.php/irrodl/article/view/149/230

Anderson, T., & Garrison, D. R. (1998). Learning in a networked world: New roles and responsibilities. In C. Gibson (Ed.), *Distance Learners in Higher Education* (pp. 97–112). Madison, WI: Atwood Publishing.

Argyris, C. A. (1992). On organizational learning. Oxford, UK: Blackwell Publishers.

Argyris, C., & Schön, D. A. (1978). *Organizational Learning*. Reading, MA: Addison-Wesley.

Arkkelin, D. (2003). *Putting Prometheus feet to the fire: student evaluations of Prometheus in relation to their attitudes towards and experience with computers, computer self-efficacy and preferred learning style*. Retrieved from http://faculty.valpo.edu/darkkeli/papers/syllabus03.htm

Association of Mathematics Teacher Educators (AMTE). (2013). *Standards for elementary mathematics specialists: A reference for teacher credentialing and degree programs*. Retrieved from: http://amte.net/sites/all/themes/amte/resources/EMS_Standards_AMTE2013.pdf

Association to Advance Collegiate Schools of Business (AACSB) International. (2007). *Quality Issues in Distance Learning*. Tampa, FL: The Association to Advance Collegiate Schools of Business. Retrieved from http://www.aacsb.edu/publications/whitepapers/quality-issues-distance-learning.pdf

Atkinson, M., & Kydd, C. (1997). Individual Characteristics Associated with World Web Use: An Empirical Study of Playfulness and Motivation. *The Data Base for Advances in Information Systems, 28*(2), 53–61. doi:10.1145/264701.264705

Attard, C., & Northcote, M. (2011). Teaching with technology: mathematics on the move: Using mobile technologies to support student learning (Part 1). *Australian Primary Mathematics Classroom, 16*(4), 29–31.

Attewell, J. (2011). *From research and development to mobile learning: tools for education and training providers and their learners.* Retrieved from http://www.mlearn.org.za/CD/papers/Attewell.pdf

Averill, J. R. (1980). A constructivist view of emotion. *Emotion: Theory, Research and Experience, 1*, 305-339.

Baitsch, C., & Frei, F. (1980). *Qualifizierung in der arbeidstätigkeit.* Bern: Verlag Hans Huber.

Bakewell, C., & Mitchell, V. (2003). Generation Y female consumer decision making styles. *International Journal of Retail & Distribution Management, 31*(2), 95–106. doi:10.1108/09590550310461994

Bala Alkan, H., & Arat, Y. (2013). Digital pedagogy using social network tools in architectural education. *AWERProcedia Information Technology & Computer Science, 3*, 160–166.

Bala Alkan, H., & Bussiere, M. (2012). Pedagogical implication for international cooperation in architectural design studio. *AE-Lusafona Architectural & Education Journal, 6*(7), 9–27.

Balaban, M. E. (2012). Dünyada ve Türkiye'de uzaktan eğitim ve bir proje önerisi. *Bilgiye Erişim ve Paylaşım Projesi: Uzaktan Eğitim.*

Bannan-Ritland, B. (2002). Computer-Mediated Communication, E-learning, and Interactivity: A Review of the Research. *The Quarterly Review of Distance Education, 3*(2), 161–179.

Bannon, S., Martin, G., & Nunes-Bufford, K. (2012). Integrating iPads Into Mathematics Education. In P. Resta (Ed.), *Proceedings of Society for Information Technology & Teacher Education International Conference 2012* (pp. 3519-3522). Chesapeake, VA: AACE.

Banyard, P., Underwood, J., & Twiner, A. (2006). Do enhanced communication technologies inhibit or facilitate self-regulated learning? *European Journal of Education, 41*(3/4), 473–489. doi:10.1111/j.1465-3435.2006.00277.x

Barczyk, C., Buckenmeyer, J., & Feldman, L. (2010). Mentoring Professors: A Model for Developing Quality Online Instructors and Courses in Higher Education. *International Journal on E-Learning, 9*(1), 7-26. Retrieved February 23, 2014 from http://www.editlib.org/p/29273

Barker., et al. (1989). Interactive distance learning technologies for rural and small schools: A resource guide. ERIC Mini-Review. New Mexico State University, ERIC Clearinghouse for Rural Education and Small Schools.

Barker, K. C. (2007). E-learning quality standards for consumer protection and consumer confidence: A Canadian case study in e-learning quality assurance. *Journal of Educational Technology & Society, 10*, 109–119.

Barnett, W., & Jardines, J. (2012). *Technology now: Research Networking.* Washington, DC: The Clinical and Translational Science Award (CTSA) Research Networking Affinity Group. Retrieved from https://www.aamc.org/download/278098/data/technologynow-researchnetworking.pdf

Barron, B., Cayton-Hodges, G., Bofferding, L., Copple, C., Darling-Hammond, L., & Levine, M. (2011). *Take a Giant Step: A Blueprint for Teaching Children in a Digital Age.* New York: The Joan Ganz Cooney Center at Sesame Workshop.

Barr, R., & Tagg, J. (1995). From Teaching to Learning: A New Paradigm for Under Graduate Education. *Change, 27*(6), 12–26. doi:10.1080/00091383.1995.10544672

Barsade, S. G. (2002). The rimple effect: Emotional contagion and its influence on group behavior. *Administrative Science Quarterly, 47*(4), 644–675. doi:10.2307/3094912

Barth, K., Jones, V., Le Joly, K. & Alsaleh, K. (2013). *iPads in the Classroom: Teaching and learning innovations at Education City.* Paper presented at the Technology in Higher Education 2013 conference (THE2013). Doha, Qatar.

Başaran, S., & Tulu, B. (1999). Bilişim çağında asenkron eğitim ağlarının konumu. In Proceedings of 5nci. Ankara: İnternet Konferansı Tebliğleri. Retrieved from inet-tr.org.tr/inetconf5/oneri/asekron.doc

Bascsich, P., Ash, C., Boniwell, K., & Kaplan, L. (1999). *The Cost of Networked Learning. In Networked Learning: Perspectives and Issues* (pp. 27–48). Springer London.

Bassus, O., & Zaščerinska, J. (2012). *Innovation and Higher Education.* Berlin: Mensch & Buch.

Bates, T. (2009). *Re: Using technology to improve the cost-effectivenes of the academy.* Retrieved from http://www.tonybates.ca/2009/10/10/using-technology-to-improve-the-cost-effectiveness-of-the-academy-part-1/

Bates, T. (2010). *Re: Strategic thinking about e-learning.* Retrieved from http://www.tonybates.ca/2010/06/11/strategic-thinking-about-e-learning/

Bates, A. W. (1995). *Technology, Open Learning, and Distance Education.* London: Routledge.

Bates, A. W. (1999). *Managing Technological Change: Strategies for Academic Leaders.* Jossey-Bass.

Bauer, H. H., Barnes, S. J., Reichardt, T., & Neumann, M. M. (2005). Driving consumer acceptance of mobile marketing: A theoretical framework and empirical study. *Journal of Electronic Commerce Research, 6*(3), 181–192.

Baumol, W. J., & Benhabib, J. (1989). Chaos: Significance, mechanism and economic applications. *The Journal of Economic Perspectives, 3*(1), 77–105. doi:10.1257/jep.3.1.77

Bay-Williams, J. M., McGatha, M., Kobett, B. M., & Wray, J. A. (2013). *Mathematics coaching: Resources and tools for coaches and leaders, K-12.* Upper Saddle River, NJ: Pearson.

Behera, S. K. (2013). E- and m-learning: A comparative study. *International Journal on New Trends in Education and Their Implications, 4*(3). Retrieved from www.ijonte.org

Bell, B. S., & Kozlowski, S. W. J. (2002). A typology of virtual teams: Implications for effective leadership. *Group & Organization Management, 27*(1), 14–49. doi:10.1177/1059601102027001003

BenMoussa, C. (2003). *Workers on the move: New opportunities through mobile commerce.* Paper presented at the Stockholm Mobility Roundtable. Stockholm, Sweden.

Benner, P. (1984). *From novice till expert: Excellence and power in clinical nurse practice.* Menlo Park, CA: Addison-Wesley.

Bennett, R., & Broadfoot, O. (2003). Design studios: Online? In *Proceedings of Apple University Consortium Academic and Developers Conference,* (pp. 9-21). Wollongong: Apple University Consortium Academic and Developers. Retrieved from http://auc.uow.edu.au/conf/conf03/papers/AUC_DV2003_Broadfoot.pdf

Benson, R., & Palaskas, T. (2006). Introducing a new learning management system: An Institutional Case Study. *Australasian Journal of Educational Technology, 22*(4), 548–567.

Bereiter, C. (1999). *Education and Mind for the Knowledge Age.* Retrieved from http://csile.oise.utoronto.ca/edmind/edmind.html

Bereiter, C., & Scardamalia, M. (1993). *Surpassing ourselves: An inquiry into the nature and implications of expertise.* Chicago: Open Court.

Berg, A. (2005). Factors related to observed attitude change toward learning chemistry among university students. *Chemistry Education Research and Practice, 6*(1), 1–18. doi:10.1039/b4rp90001d

Berger, P. L., & Luckman, T. (1966). *The social construction of reality.* New York: Doubleday.

Berge, Z. L. (1998). Barriers to Online Teaching in Postsecondary Institutions: Can Policy Changes Fix It? *Online Journal of Distance Learning Administration, 1*(2). Retrieved from http://www.westga.edu/~distance/ojdla/winter64/meyen64.htm

Bester, G., & Brand, L. (2013). The effect of technology on learner attention and achievement in the classroom. *South African Journal of Education, 33*(2), 1–15.

Bharuthram, S., & Kies, C. (2013). Introducing e-learning in a South African higher education institution: Challenges arising from an intervention and possible responses. *British Journal of Educational Technology, 44*(3), 410–420. doi:10.1111/j.1467-8535.2012.01307.x

Bhattacharjee, S. (2010). *Mobile learning seeks growth curve in India.* Retrieved from http://www.mahindracomviva.com/media/MobilelearningseeksgrowthcurveinIndia.pdf

Bhinde, A., et al. (2013). *India's mobile internet: The revolution has begun: An overview of how mobile internet is touching the lives of millions.* Retrieved from http://www.avendus.com/Files/Fund%20Performance%20PDF/Avendus_Report-India's_Mobile_Internet-2013.pdf

Bich, L. (2006). Autopoiesis and Emergence. In G. Minati, E. Pessa, & M. Abram (Eds.), *Systems of emergence: research and development* (pp. 284–292). New York: Springer. doi:10.1007/0-387-28898-8_20

Biggs, J. (2001). The reflective institution: Assuring and enhancing the quality of teaching and learning. *Higher Education, 41*(3), 221–238. doi:10.1023/A:1004181331049

Biljon, J. V., & Kotze, P. (2007). Modeling the factors that influence mobile phone adoption. In *Proceedings of the 2007 annual research conference of the South African institute of computer scientists and information technologists on IT research in developing contries*, (pp. 152-161). Academic Press.

Birch, D., & Burnett, B. (2009). Bringing academics on board: Encouraging Institution-wide Diffusion of eLearning Environments. *Australasian Journal of Educational Technology, 25*(1), 117–134.

Blomme, R.J., Van Rheede, A., & Tromp, D.M. (2010). The use of the psychological contract to explain turnover intentions in the hospitality industry: A research study on the impact of gender on the turnover intentions of highly-educated employees. *The International Journal of Human Resource Management, 21*(1-3), 144-163.

Blomme, R. J. (2003). *Alignement: Een studie naar organiseerprocessen en alignement tussen individuele en organisatiecompetenties*. Groningen: Gopher.

Blomme, R. J. (2012). Leadership, complex adaptive systems, and equivocality: The role of managers in emergent change. *Organizational Management Journal, 9*(1), 4–19. doi:10.1080/15416518.2012.666946

Blum, F., Hensgen, A., Kloft, C., & Maichle, U. M. (1995). Erfassung von handlungskompetenz in den prüfungen der industrie- und handelskammern. Bonn: Institut für Bildungsforschung (IBF).

Boettcher, J., & Conrad, R. (2010). *The online teaching survival guide: Simple and practical pedagogical tips*. San Francisco, CA: Jossey-Bass.

Bonk, C. J. (2009). *The world is open: How web technology is revolutionizing education*. San Francisco, CA: Jossey-Bass, A Wiley Imprint.

Bonk, C. J., & King, K. S. (Eds.). (1998). *Electronic collaborators: Learner-centered technologies for literacy, apprenticeship, and discourse*. Mahwah, NJ: Erlbaum.

Bontius, I., Boogert, K. & Huisman, J. (2001). *Het leren van competenties: Drie ideaaltypische opleidingsontwerpen*. S´Hertogenbosch: CINOP.

Booher, R. K., & Seiler, W. J. (1982). Speech communication anxiety: An impediment to academic achievement in the university classroom. *Journal of Classroom Interaction, 18*(1), 23–27.

Bosch, T. E. (2009). Using online social networking for teaching and learning: Facebook use at the University of Cape Town. *Communicatio, 35*(2), 185–200. doi:10.1080/02500160903250648

Bostock, S. J. (1997). Designing Web-based instruction for active learning. In B. H. Khan (Ed.), *Web-based instruction* (pp. 225–230). Educational Technology Publications.

Boyer, E. L., & Mitgang, L. D. (1996). *Building community: A new future for architecture education and practice*. Princeton, NJ: The Carnegie Foundation for the Advancement of Teaching.

Brater, M. (1990). Ende des Taylorismus: Paradigmenwechsel in der berufspädagogik? In U. Lauer-Ernst (Ed.), Neue fabriksstrukturen und veränderte qualifikationen (pp. 83-91). Berlijn: BIBB.

Brill, J. M., & Park, Y. (2008). Facilitating engaged learning in the interaction age taking a pedagogically-disciplined approach to innovation with emergent technologies. *International Journal of Teaching and Learning in Higher Education, 20*(1), 70–78.

Brink, J. (2011). M-learning: The future of training technology. *Training & Development, 65*(2), 27.

Broad, M., Matthews, M., & McDonald, A. (2004). Accounting education through an onlinesupported virtual learning environment. *Active Learning in Higher Education, 5*(2), 135–151. doi:10.1177/1469787404043810

Brookfield, S. (1986). *Understanding and Facilitating Adult Learning*. Open University Press.

Brookfield, S. D. (1990). Discussion. In M. W. Galbraith (Ed.), *Adult learning methods: A guide to effective instruction* (pp. 187–204). Malabar, FL: Robert E. Krieger.

Brookfield, S. D. (1995). *Becoming a Critically Reflective Teacher*. San Francisco: Jossey-Bass Publishers.

Brophy, S. P., Norris, P., Nichols, M., & Jansen, E. D. (2003). Development and Initial Experience with a Laptop-based Student Assessment System to Enhance Classroom Instruction. In *Proceedings of the 2003 American Society for Engineering Education*. ASEE. Retrieved from http://www.asee.org/

Brown, M., & Bewsell, D. (2009). Is elearning a viable option to face-to-face workshops for generating and sharing information within the New Zealand sheep and beef industry?. *Extension Farming Systems Journal, 5*(2)

Brown, M., Castellano, J., Hughes, E., & Worth, A. (2012). Integration of iPads into a Japenese university English language curriculum. *The Jalt Call Journal, 8*(3), 197-209.

Brown, A., & Campione, J. (1996). Psychological theory and design of innovative learning environments: on procedures, principles, and systems. In L. Schauble & R. Glaser (Eds.), *Innovations in learning: new environments for education* (pp. 289–325). Mahwah, NJ: Erlbaum.

Brown, R. E. (2001, September). The process of community-building in distance learning courses. *Journal of Asynchronous Learning Networks, 5*(2).

Brown, T. H. (2005). Towards a model for m-learning in Africa. *International Journal on E-Learning, 4*(3).

Bruner, J. (1966). *Toward a Theory of Instruction*. Cambridge, MA: Harvard University Press.

Bruns, A. (2008). *Blogs, Wikipedia, Second Life, and beyond: From production to prod usage*. New York, NY: Lang.

Bryer, T. A., & Zavattaro, S. M. (2011). Social media and public administration. *Administrative Theory & Praxis, 33*(3), 325–340. doi:10.2753/ATP1084-1806330301

Burke, M., Kraut, R., & Marlow, C. (2011). Social capital on Facebook: Differentiating uses and users. In *Proceedings of the 2011 Annual Conference on Human Factors in Computing Systems* (pp. 571-580). New York: ACM. doi:10.1145/1978942.1979023

Burma, Z.A. (2008). AB'ye geçiş sürecinde meslek elemanlarının uzaktan öğretim ile eğitimi. *Bilişim Teknolojileri Dergisi, 1*(2).

Burnham, B. R., & Walden, B. (1997). *Interactions in Distance Education: A report from the other side*. Paper presented at the 1997 Adult Education Research Conference. Stillwater, OK. Retrieved May 30, 2005, from http://www.edst.educ.ubc.ca/aerc/1997/97burnham.html

Buselic, M. (2012). *Distance Learning-concepts and contributions*. Oeconomica Jadertina.

Çağdaş, G. (2005). Enformasyon teknolojilerindeki evrimsel sürecin mimari tasarım eğitimine Yansımaları. *Stüdyo Tasarım Kuram Elestiri Dergisi, 2*(4-5). Retrieved from http://www.studyomim.itu.edu.tr/sayi2/enformasyon_tek_evrimsel_sur_2-6.pdf

Çağdaş, G., & Tong, H. (2005). Global bir tasarım stüdyosuna doğru. *Stüdyo Tasarım Kuram Elestiri Dergisi, 3*(4-5). Retrieved from http://www.studyomim.itu.edu.tr/sayi3/global_bir_tasarim_studyosuna_dogru.pdf

Çağdaş, G., Kavaklı Thorne, M., Özsoy, A., Altaş, N. E. & Tong, H. (2000). Virtual design studio VDS 2000 as a virtual construction site: Digital media is design media, not a drawing tool. *International Journal of Design Computing*.

Campos, M., Laferriere, T., & Harasim, L. (2001). The Post-Secondary Networked Classroom: Renewal of Teaching Practices and Social Interaction. *Journal of Asynchronous Learning Networks, 5*(2). Retrieved from http://aln.org/alnweb/journal/Vol5_issue2/Campos/Campos.htm

Carey, J. (2011). Faculty of 1000 and VIVO: Invisible colleges and team science. *Issues in Science and Technology Librarianship, 65*.

Carter, H. L., Foulger, T. S., & Ewbank, A. D. (2008). Have you googled your teacher lately? Teachers' use of social networking sites. *Phi Delta Kappan, 89*(9), 681–685. doi:10.1177/003172170808900916

Casalo, J., Flavian, C., & Guinaliu, M. (2007). The role of perceived usability, reputation, satisfaction and consumer familiarity on the website loyalty formation process. *Computers in Human Behavior, 24* (2008), 325–345.

Çavaş, B., & Huyugüzel, P. (2001). *Web destekli eğitim: Teletop yaklaşımı.* Retrieved February 18, 2003, from http://www.bilisimsurasi.org.tr/cg/egitim/kutuphane/WebDestekliEgitim.doc

Ceci, S. J., & Liker, J. (1986). Academic and non academic intelligence: An experimental separation. In J. Sternberg & R. K. Wagner (Eds.), *Practical intelligence: Nature and origins of competence in the everyday world* (pp. 119–142). Cambridge, UK: University Press.

Çetiner, M., Gencel, Ç., & Erten, M. (2009). *İnternete dayalı uzaktan eğitim ve çoklu ortam uygulamaları.* Retrieved from http://inet-tr.org.tr

Charnigo, L., & Barnett-Ellis, P. (2007). Checking out facebook.com: The impact of a digital trend on academic libraries. *Information Technology and Libraries, 26,* 23–34.

Chen, W., & You, M. (2003). A framework for the development of online design learning environment. In *Proceedings of 6th Asian Design Conference.* Retrieved from http://www.idemployee.id.tue.nl/g.w.m.rauterberg/conferences/CD_doNotOpen/ADC/final_paper/584.pdf

Cheung, C. M. K., Chiu, P. Y., & Lee, M. K. O. (2011). Online social networks: Why do students use facebook? *Computers in Human Behavior, 27*(4), 1337–1343. doi:10.1016/j.chb.2010.07.028

Chia, H., & Chiu, Y. (2011). Assessing e-learning 2.0 system success. *Computers & Education, 57*(2), 1790–1800. doi:10.1016/j.compedu.2011.03.009

Cho, D. Y., Kwon, H. J., & Lee, H. Y. (2007). Analysis of trust in internet and mobile commerce adoption. In *Proceedings of the 40th Hawaii International Conference on System Sciences,* (pp. 1-10). IEEE. doi:10.1109/HICSS.2007.76

Chong, A. Y., Darmawan, N., Ooi, K. B., & Lee, V. H. (2010). Determinants of 3G adoption in Malaysia: A structural analysis. *Journal of Computer Information.*

Chong-Ho, Y. (1994). *Abduction? Deduction? Induction? Is there a logic of exploratory data analysis?* New Orleans: American Educational Research Association.

Chou, P. (2012). The integration of Facebook into class management: An exploratory study. *Educational Research, 3*(7), 572–575.

Choy, J. Y., Ng, C. S., & Ch'ng, H. K. (2011). Consumers' perceived quality, perceived value and perceived risk towards purchase decision on automobile. *American Journal of Economics and Business Administration, 3*(1), 47–57. doi:10.3844/ajebasp.2011.47.57

Churches, A. (2007). *Educational Origami: Bloom's and ICT Tools.* Retrieved from: http://edorigami.wikispaces.com/file/view/bloom%27s+Digital+taxonomy+v3.01.pdf

Clark, A., & Pitt, T. J. (2001). Creating Powerful Online Courses using Multiple Instructional Strategies. *eModerators.* Retrieved from http://www.emoderators.com/moderators/pitt.html

Clark, J. (2009). *Collaboration tools in online environments.* Retrieved in February 12 2009 from http://www.aln.org/publications/magazine/v4n1/clark.asp

Clark, W., & Luckin, R. (2013). *What the research says iPads in the classroom.* London Knowledge lab & The Institute of Education at the University of London. Retrieved from https://www.lkldev.ioe.ac.uk/lklinnovation/wp-content/uploads/2013/01/2013-iPads-in-the-Classroom-v2.pdf

Clinical and Translational Science Award (CTSA) Research Networking Affinity Group. (2012). *Clinical and Translational Science Award (CTSA) Research Networking Evaluation Guide.* Retrieved from https://www.ctsacentral.org/documents/CTSA-RN-Guide.pdf

Cobb, J. (2010). *Learning 2.0 for Associations.* Retrieved from http://www.tagoras.com/docs/Learning-20-Associations-2ed.pdf

Cohen, L., Manion, L., & Morrsion, K. (2003). *Research Methods in Education.* London: Routledge/Falmer Taylor & Francis Group.

Cohen, S. (2005). *Teachers' professional development and the elementary mathematics classroom: Bringing understandings to light.* Mahwaw, NJ: Lawrence Erlbaum Associates, Inc.

Colella, J., & Stead, G. (2003). Take a bite: Producing accessible learning materials for mobile devices. In *Proceeding of the Second European Conference on Learning with Mobile Devices - MLEARN 2003* (pp. 23-27). London: MLEARN.

Common Core State Standards Initiative. (2011). *Common Core State Standards in Mathematics*. Retrieved from: http://www.corestandards.org/Math

Conci, M., Pianesi, F., & Zancanaro, M. (2009). Useful, social and enjoyable: Mobile phone adoption by older people. *Lecture Notes in Computer Science, 5726,* 63–76. doi:10.1007/978-3-642-03655-2_7

Connelly, J., & Gregory, P. (2012). Instructor use of Tablet PCs in a college pre-calculus course: Implementation & assessment. *Mathematics Faculty Publications* (Paper 9). Sacred Heart University. Retrieved from http://digitalcommons.sacredheart.edu/math_fac/9?utm_source=digitalcommons.sacredheart.edu%2Fmath_fac%2F9&utm_medium=PDF&utm_campaign=PDFCoverPages

Connolly, M., Jones, N., & O'Shea, J. (2005). Quality assurance and e-learning: Reflections from the front line. *Quality in Higher Education, 11*(1), 59–67. doi:10.1080/13538320500077660

Conole, G. (2010). Learning design: Making practice explicit. In *Proceedings of Con-nectED Conference*. Retrieved from http://www.slideshare.net/grainne/connect-ed-conole

Conole, G., & Alevizou, P. (2010). *A literature review of the use of Web 2.0 tools in Higher Education.* A Report Commissioned by the Higher Education Academy. Retrieved from http://www.jisctechdis.ac.uk/assets/EvidenceNet/Conole_Alevizou_2010.pdf

Contractor, N. S., & Monge, P. R. (2002, November). Managing knowledge networks. *Management Communication Quarterly, 16*(2), 249–258. doi:10.1177/089331802237238

Cooper, J. (2006). The digital divide: The special case of gender. *Journal of Computer Assisted Learning, 22*(5), 320–334. doi:10.1111/j.1365-2729.2006.00185.x

Corbeil, J. R., & Valdes-Corbeil, M. E. (2007). Are you ready for mobile learning? *EDUCAUSE Quarterly, 30*(2), 51–58.

Cornelius, R. R. (1996). *The science of emotion: Research and tradition in the psychology of emotion.* New York: Prentice Hall.

Cortez, C., Nussbaum, M., Santelices, R., Rodriguez, P., Zurita, G., Correa, M., & Cautivo, R. (2004). Teaching science with mobile computer supported collaborative learning (MCSCL). In *Proceedings of the 2nd IEEE International Workshop* (pp. 67-74). Taiwan: IEEE Computer Society.

Cranton, P. (2000). *Planning Instruction for Adult Learners* (2nd ed.). Toronto: Wall &Emerson, Inc.

Crites, S., Fabrigar, L. R., & Petty, R. E. (1994). Measuring the affective and cognitive properties of attitudes: Conceptual and methodological issues. *Personality and Social Psychology Bulletin, 20*(6), 619–634. doi:10.1177/0146167294206001

Crook, C., & Harrison, C. (2008). *Web 2.0 technologies for learning at key stages 3 and 4: Summary report.* Retrieved from http://schools.becta.org.uk/upload-dir/downloads/page_documents/research/ web2_ks34_summary.pdf

Cross, K. (2010, September 11). iPad replaces uni textbooks at University of Adelaide science faculty. *The Advertiser*. Retrieved from http://www.adelaidenow.com.au/technology/ipad-replaces-uni-textbooks-at-university-of-adelaide-science-faculty/story-fn5jh-v6y-1225918213032)

Cross, K. P. (1981). *Adults as Learners.* San Francisco: Jossey-Bass.

Cyert, R. M., & March, J. G. (1963). *A Behavioral Theory of the Firm.* Englewood Cliffs, NJ: Prentice Hall.

Davis, D. F., Bagozzi, P. R., & Warshaw, R. P. (1989). User acceptance of computer technology: A comparison of two theoretical models. *Management Science, 35*(8), 982–1003. doi:10.1287/mnsc.35.8.982

Davis, F. D. (1989). Perceived usefulness, perceived ease of use, and user acceptance of information technology. *Management Information Systems Quarterly, 13*(3), 319–340. doi:10.2307/249008

Davis, F., Bagozzi, R., & Warshaw, R. (1992). Extrinsic and intrinsic motivation to use computers in the workplace. *Journal of Applied Social Psychology, 22*(14), 1111–1132. doi:10.1111/j.1559-1816.1992.tb00945.x

Dawabi, P., Wessner, M., & Neuhold, E. (2003). Using mobile devices for the classroom of the future. In *Proceedings of Mlearn 2003 Conference on Learning with Mobile Devices* (pp. 14-15). London: Mlearn.

Dawley, L. (2007). *The Tools for Successful Online Teaching*. Information Science Publishing. doi:10.4018/978-1-59140-956-4

De Vierville, J. P. (1999). Emotion. *Electronic library of Waikato University*. Retrieved from http://72.14.253.104/search?q=cache:lqr5mSpe6MQJ:ww.accd.edu/spc/mitchell/powerpoint3d/emotion.ppt+definition+of+emotion&hl=zh-CN&ct=clnk&cd=6

DeBard, R., & Guidera, S. (2000). Adapting asynchronous communication to meet the seven principles of effective teaching. *Journal of Educational Technology Systems*, *28*(3), 219–239. doi:10.2190/W1U9-CB67-59W0-74LH

Deci, E. L., & Ryan, R. M. (1985). *Intrinsic motivation and self-determination in human behavior*. New York: Plenum. doi:10.1007/978-1-4899-2271-7

Dede, C., Ketelhut, D. J., Whitehouse, P., Breit, L., & McCloskey, R. M. (2009). A research agenda for online teacher professional development. *Journal of Teacher Education*, *60*(1), 8–19. doi:10.1177/0022487108327554

Dedering, H., & Schimming, P. (1984). Qualifikationsforschung und arbeitsorientierte bildung: Eine analyse von konzepte zur arbeitsqualifikation aus pädagogischer sicht. Opladen, Duistland: Westdeutscher verlag. doi:10.1007/978-3-322-88526-5

Delfino, M., & Persico, D. (2007). Online or face-to-face? Experimenting with different techniques in teacher training. *Journal of Computer Assisted Learning*, *23*(5), 351–365. doi:10.1111/j.1365-2729.2007.00220.x

Demian, P., & Morrice, J. (2012). The use of virtual learning environments and their impact on academic performance. *English Education*, *7*(1), 11–19. doi:10.11120/ened.2012.07010011

Demirkıran, V., & Silahtaroğlu, G. (2010). *Uzaktan eğitim; Ne zaman, nasıl?* Retrieved from http://uzaktanegitim.istanbul.edu.tr/index.php/component/content/article/187.html

den Boer, P., & Hövels, B. (1999). *Contextontwikkelingen en competenties*. Nijmegen: ITS.

Dennen, V. P. (2007). Presence and positioning of online instructor persona. *Journal of Research on Technology in Education*, *40*(1), 95–108. doi:10.1080/15391523.2007.10782499

Devinder, S., & Zaitun, A. B. (2006). Mobile learning in wireless classrooms. *Malaysian Online Journal of Instructional Technology*, *3*(2), 26–42.

Dillon, A., & Zhu, E. (1997). Design Web-based instruction: A human-computer interaction perspective. In B. H. Khan (Ed.), *Web-Based Instruction* (pp. 221–224). Educational Technology Publications.

Doctorow, C., Dornfest, R., Johnson, S., Powers, S., Trott, B., & Trott, M. (2002). *Essential Blogging: Selecting and Using Weblog Tools*. Sebastopol, CA: O'Reilly.

Doiron, G. (2012). The digital divide and single-gender undergraduate education in the UAE. *Learning and Teaching in Higher Education: Gulf Perspectives*, *9*(2), 1–10.

Dolan, K. A. How Ijad Madisch Aims To Disrupt Science Research With A Social Network. *Forbes*. Retrieved from http://www.forbes.com/sites/kerryadolan/2012/07/19/how-ijad-madisch-aims-to-disrupt-science-research-with-a-social-network/

Donath, J. S. (2007). Signals in social supernets. *Journal of Computer-Mediated Communication*, *13*(1), 231–251. doi:10.1111/j.1083-6101.2007.00394.x

Dong, S. H. (2007). User acceptance of mobile Internet: Implication for convergence technologies. *Interacting with Computers*, *19*(4), 472–483. doi:10.1016/j.intcom.2007.04.001

Doubler, S., Laferriere, T., Lamon, M., & Rose, R. (2000). *The Next Generation of Online Teacher Learning: A White Paper for the Innovative Learning and Technology Center*. Retrieved from http://www.cilt.org/seedgrant/online_Learning.html

Douglas, D. (2011, May 3). *iPad study released by Oklahoma State University*. Retrieved from https://news.okstate.edu/press-releases/929-ipad-study-released-by-oklahoma-state-university

Downing, J. J., & Dyment, J. E. (2013). Teacher educators' readiness, preparation, and perceptions of preparing preservice teachers in a fully online environment: An exploratory study. *Teacher Educator, 48*(2), 96–109. doi:10.1080/08878730.2012.760023

Dreyfus, H. L., & Dreyfus, S. E. (1986). *Mind over machine: The power of human intuition and expertise in the era of the computer*. New York: Free press.

Driskell, J. E., Radtke, P. H., & Salas, E. (2003). Virtual teams: Effects of technological mediation on team performance. *Group Dynamics, 7*(4), 297–323. doi:10.1037/1089-2699.7.4.297

Duru, S. (2006). *Sanal mimari tasarım stüdyosunda pedagojik yaklaşımlar*. İstanbul: İstanbul Teknik Üniversitesi, Fen Bilimleri Enstitüsü, Yüksek Lisans Tezi.

Dutton, W. H., & Loader, B. D. (2002). Competition and Collaboration in Online Distance Learning. In W. Dutton (Ed.), *Digital Academe: The New Media and Institutions of Higher Education and Learning*. New York: Routledge.

Dyment, J. E., Downing, J. J., & Budd, Y. (2013). Framing teacher education engagement in an online environment. *Australian Journal of Teacher Education, 38*(1), 134–149. doi:10.14221/ajte.2013v38n1.6

East Village. (n.d.). Retrieved March 12, 2011 from http://www.evexperience.com/

Ebersbach, A., Glaser, M., & Heigl, R. (2006). *Wiki: Web collaboration*. Springer-Verlag Berlin Heidelberg.

Edmonson, A., & Moingeon, B. (1998). From organizational learning to the learning organization. *Management Learning, 29*(1), 5–20. doi:10.1177/1350507698291001

EduTech. (2012). A World Bank Blog on ICT use in Education. *Education year in Review*.

Ehlers, U. D. (2009). Understanding quality culture. *Quality Assurance in Education, 17*(4), 343–363. doi:10.1108/09684880910992322

Ehlers, U. D., & Pawlowski, J. (2006). Quality in European e-learning: An Introduction. In U. D. Ehlers & J. Pawlowski (Eds.), *Handbook on quality and standardization in e-learning* (pp. 1–13). Berlin: Springer. doi:10.1007/3-540-32788-6_1

Ehlers, U. D., & Schneckenberg, D. (2010). Introduction: Changing cultures in higher education. In U. D. Ehlers & D. Schneckenberg (Eds.), *Changing cultures in higher education* (pp. 1–14). Berlin: Springer-Verlag. doi:10.1007/978-3-642-03582-1_1

Ekwensi, F., Moranski, J., & Townsend-Sweet, M. (2006). Instructional Strategies for E-learning. *E-learning Concepts and Techniques*. Retrieved from http://iit.bloom.edu/Spring2006_eBook_files/chapter5.htm

Elgort, I., Smith, A. G., & Toland, J. (2008). Is wiki an effective platform for group course work? *Australasian Journal of Educational Technology, 24*(2), 195–210.

El-Hussein, M. O. O., & Cronje, J. C. (2010). Defining Mobile Learning in the Higher Education Landscape. *Journal of Educational Technology & Society, 13*(3), 12–21.

Elias, N. (1984). *What is Sociology?* New York: Colombia University.

Ellison, N., Steinfield, C., & Lampe, C. (2007). The benefits of Facebook "friends": Social capital and college students' use of online social networking sites. *Journal of Computer-Mediated Communication, 12*(4), 1143–1168. doi:10.1111/j.1083-6101.2007.00367.x

Ellison, N., & Wu, Y. (2008). Blogging in the classroom: A preliminary exploration of student attitudes and impact on comprehension. *Journal of Educational Multimedia and Hypermedia, 17*(1), 99–122.

Engeström, Y., & Engeström, R. (1986). Seeking the zone of proximal development in physicians' work activity. In *Proceedings of the 1st international congress in activity theory*, (vol. 3, pp. 471-496). Berlijn: System Druck.

Engeström, Y. (1992). *Interactive expertise: Studies in distributed working intelligence. Research Bulletin 83*. Helsinki: Department of Education, Universiteit Helsinki.

Epper, R. M., & Garn, M. C. (2003). *Virtual College and University Consortia: A National Study*. Boulder, CO: State Higher Education Executive Officers.

Eren, O. (2012). Students' attitudes towards using social networking in foreign language classes: A Facebook example. *International Journal of Business and Social Science, 3*(20), 288–294.

Ertmer, P. A., & Stepich, D. A. (2002). Initiating and Maintaining Meaningful Case Discussions: Maximizing the Potential of Case-Based Instruction. *Journal on Excellence in College Teaching, 13* (2-3). Retrieved from http://celt.muohio.edu/ject/issue.php?v=13&n=2+and+3

Etkina, E., & Mestre, J. P. (2004). *Implications of Learning Research for Teaching Science to Non-Science Majors.* Washington, DC: SENCER. Retrieved from http://www.sencer.net/Resources/pdfs/Backgrounders/Implicationsof LearningResearchforTeachingScience.pdf

European Commission Directorate-General for Education and Culture. (2004). *Implementation of "Education and Training 2010" Work Programme: Working Group B "Key Competences" Key Competences for Lifelong Learning.* a European Reference Framework. Retrieved from http://europa.eu/legislation_summaries/education_training_youth/lifelong_learning/c11090_en.htm

Evans, T., & Nation, D. (2000). *Changing University Teaching: Reactions on Creating Educational Technologies.* London: Kogan Page.

Eynon, R. (2005). The use of the Internet in higher education: Academics experiences of using ICTs for teaching and learning. *Aslib Proceedings, 57*(2), 168–180. doi:10.1108/00012530510589137

Fabian, K., & MacLean, D. (2014). Keep taking the tablets? Assessing the use of tablet devices in learning and teaching activities in the Further Education sector. *Research in Learning Technology, 22*(0). doi:10.3402/rlt.v22.22648

Faigley, L. (1990). Subverting the electronic network: teaching writing using networked computers. In D. Daiker & M. Morenberg (Eds.), *The writing teacher as researcher: Essays in the theory and practice of class-based research.* Portsmouth: Boynton/Cook.

Farmer, B., Yue, A., & Brooks, C. (2008). Using blogging for higher order learning in large cohort university teaching: A case study. *Australasian Journal of Educational Technology, 24*(2), 123–136.

Farrell, G. M. (1999). *The Development of Virtual Education: A Global Perspective.* Vancouver, Canada: Commonwealth of Learning.

Fazel-Zarandi, M., Devlin, H. J., Huang, Y., & Contractor, N. (2011). Expert recommendation based on social drivers, social network analysis, and semantic data representation. In *Proceedings of 2nd International Workshop on Information Heterogeneity and Fusion in Recommender Systems* (pp. 41-48). New York: Association for Computing Machinery. doi:10.1145/2039320.2039326

Feather, J., & Sturges, P. (Eds.). (2003). *International Encyclopedia of Information and Library Science* (2nd ed.). London: Routledge.

Fee, K. (2009). *Delivering e-learning.* London: Kogan Page Limited.

Feenberg, A. (1987). Computer conferencing and the humanities. *Instructional Science, 16,* 169–186.

Felder, R. (1992). How About a Quick One? *Chem. Engr. Education, 26*(1), 18–19.

Ferreira, J. B., Klein, A. Z., Freitas, A., & Schlemmer, E. (2013). Mobile Learning: Definition, Uses and Challenges. In L. A. Wankel & P. Blessinger (Ed.), Increasing Student Engagement and Retention Using Mobile Applications: Smartphones, Skype and Texting Technologies (Cutting-edge Technologies in Higher Education, Volume 6) (pp. 47-82). Bingley, UK: Emerald Group Publishing Limited.

Ferry, B. (2008). *Using mobile phones to augment teacher learning in environmental education.* Retrieved from http://www.ascilite.org.au/conferences/melbourne08/procs/ferry.pdf

Fishman, B. J., Marx, R. W., Best, S., & Tal, R. T. (2003). Linking teachers and student learning to improve professional development in systemic reform. *Teaching and Teacher Education, 19*(6), 643–658. doi:10.1016/S0742-051X(03)00059-3

Fister, K. R., & McCarthy, M. L. (2008). Mathematics instruction and the tablet PC. *International Journal of Mathematical Education in Science and Technology, 39*(3), 285–292. doi:10.1080/00207390701690303

Fonseca, J. (2002). *Complexity and innovations in organizations.* London, UK: Routledge.

Forsyth, H., Pizzica, J., Laxton, R., & Mahony, M. J. (2010). Distance education in an era of eLearning: Challenges and opportunities for campus-focused institution. *Higher Education Research & Development, 29*(1), 15–28. doi:10.1080/07294360903421350

Frei, F., Duell, E., & Baitsch, C. (1984). *Arbeit und kompetenzuntwikkelung: Theoretischer konzepte zur psychologie arbeitsimmanenter qualifizierung.* Bern: Verlag Hans Huber.

Freire, P. (1970). *Pedagogy of the Oppressed.* New York: Herder and Herder.

Fulford, C., & Zhang, S. (1993). Perception of interaction: The critical predictor in distance learning. *American Journal of Distance Education, 7*(3), 8–12. doi:10.1080/08923649309526830

Galligan, L., Loch, B., McDonald, C., & Taylor, J. (2010). The use of tablet and related technologies in mathematics teaching. *Australian Senior Mathematics Journal, 24*(1), 38–51.

Galusha, J. M. (2009). *Barriers to Learning in Distance Education.* University of Southern Mississippi. Retrieved in May 2009 from http://www.infrastruction.com/barriers.htm

Gannon-Leary, P., & Fontainha, E. (2007). Communities of practice and virtual learning communities: Benefits, barriers and success factors. *Elearning Papers, 5,* 20-29. Retrieved from http://nrl.northumbria.ac.uk/2147/

Gao, F., Luo, T., & Zhang, K. (2012). Tweeting for learning: A critical analysis of research on microblogging in education published in 2008-2011. *British Journal of Educational Technology, 43*(5), 783–801. doi:10.1111/j.1467-8535.2012.01357.x

Garet, M., Porter, A., Desimone, L., Briman, B., & Yoon, K. (2001). What makes professional development effective? Analysis of a national sample of teachers. *American Educational Research Journal, 38*(4), 915–945. doi:10.3102/00028312038004915

Garg, V. (2013). *The emergence of mobile learning for higher education in Kingdom of Saudi Arabia.* UPSIDE learning blog. Retrieved from http://upsidelearning.com/blog/index.php

Garrison, R. (2000). Theoretical challenges for distance education in the 21st century: A shift from structural to transactional issues. *The International Review of Research in Open and Distance Learning, 1*(1), 12-24.

Gawelek, M. A., Spataro, M., & Komarny, P. (2011). *Mobile perspectives: On iPads. Why mobile?* Retrieved from EDUCAUSE Learning Initiative website: http://www.educause.edu

Gecer, A., & Dag, F. (2012). A Blended Learning Experience. *Educational Sciences: Theory and Practice, 12*(1), 438–442.

Geist, E. (2011). The game changer: Using iPads in college teacher education classes. *College Student Journal, 45*(4), 758–768.

Gellman-Danley, B., & Fetzner, M. J. (1998). Asking the Really Tough Questions: Policy Issues for Distance Learning. *Online Journal of Distance Learning Administration.* Retrieved from http://www.westga.edu/~distance/danley11.html

George, P., Dumenco, L., Doyle, R., & Dollase, R. (2013). Incorporating iPads into a preclinical curriculum: A pilot study. *Medical Teacher, 35*(3), 226–230. doi:10.3109/0142159X.2012.735384 PMID:23425119

Gewin, V. (2010, December 15). Collaboration: Social networking seeks critical mass. *Nature, 468*(7326), 993–994. doi:10.1038/nj7326-993a

Giddens, A. (1985). Structuratietheorie en empirisch onderzoek. In Q.J. Munters, E. Meijer, H. Mommaas, H. Van de Poel, R. Rosendal, & G. Spaargazen (Eds.), Anthony Giddens: Een kennismaking met de structuratietheorie (pp. 27-56). Wageningen: Universiteit Wageningen.

Giousmpasoglou, C., & Marinakou, E. (2013). The future is here: M-learning in higher education. *Computer Technology and Application, 4*(6), 317–322.

Gitsaki, C., Robby, M., Priest, T., Hamdan, K., & Ben-Chabane, Y. (2013). A research agenda for the UAE iPad initiative. *Learning and Teaching in Higher Education: Gulf Perspectives, 10*(2), 23–41.

Glazer, E. M., & Hannafin, M. J. (2006). The collaborative apprenticeship model: Situated professional development within school settings. *Teaching and Teacher Education, 22*(2), 179–193. doi:10.1016/j.tate.2005.09.004

Gleick, J. (1988). *Chaos: The making of the new science.* London, UK: William Heineman.

Gnanasambandam, C., Madgavkar, A., Kaka, N., Manyika, J., Malcolm, G., & Bughin, J. (2012). *Online and upcoming: The Internet's impact on India.* Retrieved from www. Online_and_Upcoming_The_internets_impact_on_India. pdf

Goggin, G. (2009). Mobile technologies: From telecommunications to media. *Routledge Research in Cultural and Media Studies,* (6), 297.

Gorgievski, N., Stroud, R., Truxaw, M., & DeFranco, T. (2005). Tablet PC: A preliminary report on a tool for teaching calculus. *The International Journal for Technology in Mathematics Education, 12*(3), 95–102.

Govindasamy, T. (2002). Successful implementation of e-learning: Pedagogical considerations. *The Internet and Higher Education, 4*(3-4), 287–299. doi:10.1016/S1096-7516(01)00071-9

Grandzol, C. J., & Grandzol, J. R. (2010). Interaction in online courses: More is not always better. *Online Journal of Distance Learning Administration, 13*(2).

Greenagel, F. L. (2002). *The Illusion of E-Learning: Why We're Missing Out on the Promise of Technology.* Retrieved from http://www.guidedlearning.com/illusions.pdf

Greene, N. (2003). Outwardly mobile: Young people and mobile technologies. In J. Katz (Ed.), *Machines That Become Us: The social context of communication technology.* New Brunswick, NJ: Transaction Publishers.

Grgurovic, M. (2011). Blended Learning in an ESL Class: A Case Study. *CALICO Journal, 29*(1), 100–117. doi:10.11139/cj.29.1.100-117

Groeben, N. (1986). *Handeln, Tun, Verhalten als Einheiten einer verstehend-erklärenden Psychologie.* Tübingen: Francke.

Grooms, L. (2003). Computer-Mediated Communication: A vehicle for learning. *International Review of Research in Open and Distance Learning, 4*(2).

Grosseck, G. (2009). To use or not to use web 2.0 in higher education? *Procedia: Social and Behavioral Sciences, 1*(1), 478–482. doi:10.1016/j.sbspro.2009.01.087

Gunawardena, C., & Zittle, F. (1997). Social presence as a predictor of satisfaction within a computer mediated conferencing environment. *American Journal of Distance Education, 11*(3), 8–26. doi:10.1080/08923649709526970

Gupta, M. L. (2009). Using emerging technologies to promote student engagement and learning in agricultural mathematics. *The International Journal of Learning, 16*(10), 497–508.

Gurbuz, F. (2014). Students' views on distance learning in Turkey: An Example Of Anadolu University Open Education Faculty. *Turkish Online Journal of Distance Education, 15*(2), 239–250.

Guri-Rosenblit, S. (1999). The Agendas of Distance Teaching Universities: Moving from the Margins to the Center Stage of Higher Education. *Higher Education, 37*(3), 281–293. doi:10.1023/A:1003644305026

Guri-Rosenblit, S. (2001). Virtual Universities: Current Models and Future Trends. *Higher Education in Europe, 16*(4), 487–499. doi:10.1080/03797720220141807

Guskey, T. R. (2000). *Evaluating professional development.* Thousand Oaks, CA: Corwin Press.

Hadj-Hamou, N., Anwar, S. A., & Benhadria, M. (2012). A new paradigm for e-learing in the Arab Middle East: Reflections on e-books and e-Reader devices. In T. T. Goh, B. C. Seet, & P. C. Sun (Eds.), *E-Books & E-Readers for E-Learning* (pp. 92–123). Wellington, New Zealand: Victoria Business School.

Hager, P., Gonczi, A., & Athanasou, J. (1994). General issues about assessment competence. *Assessment & Evaluation in Higher Education, 19*(1), 3–16. doi:10.1080/0260293940190101

Hakkila, J., & Mantyjarvi, J. (2005). Collaborative in context-aware mobile phone applications. In *Proceedings of the 38th Hawaii International Conference onSystem Sciences*. IEEE. doi:10.1109/HICSS.2005.145

Hall, H., & Davison, B. (2007). Social software as support in hybrid learning environments: The value of the blog as a tool for reflective learning and peer support. *Library & Information Science Research, 29*(2), 163–187. doi:10.1016/j.lisr.2007.04.007

Hamann, K., & Wilson, B. M. (2003). Beyond search engines: Enhancing active learning using the internet. *Politics & Policy, 31*(3), 533–553. doi:10.1111/j.1747-1346.2003. tb00161.x

Handal, B., Campbell, C., Cavanagh, M., Petocz, P., & Kelly, N. (2012). Integrating Technology, Pedagogy and Content in Mathematics Education. *Journal of Computers in Mathematics and Science Teaching, 31*(4), 387–413.

Hanna, D. E. (2000). *Higher Education in an Era of Digital Competition*. Madison, WI: Atwood.

Hanson, D., Maushak, N., Schlosser, C., Anderson, M., & Sorensen, M. (1997). *Distance education:Review of the literature* (2nd ed.). Washington, DC: Association for Educational Communications and Technology.

Hardy, C. (2002). *Incorporating Active/Interactive Learning Strategies into an Online Course*. Retrieved from http://info.nwmissouri.edu/~chardy/COMPS/EDPS854Human-Cognition/EDPS854HumanCognitionIntervention.htm

Hargreaves, A. (1998). The emotional practice of teaching. *Teaching and Teacher Education, 14*(8), 835–854. doi:10.1016/S0742-051X(98)00025-0

Harmer, J. (2001). *The Practice of English Language Teaching*. London: Longman.

Harré, R. (1986). *The social construction of emotion*. New York: Basil Blackwell.

Harsh, O., K. (2002). World Wide Web (WWW) and Global Learning Environment for adults. *Learning Technology Newsletter, 4*(1).

Harvey, L., & Newton, J. (2004). Transforming quality evaluation. *Quality in Higher Education, 10*(2), 149–165. doi:10.1080/1353832042000230635

Haythornthwaite, C., & Kazmer, M. M. (2002). Bringing the Internet Home: Adult Distance Learners and Their Internet, Home, and Work Worlds. In B. Wellman & C. Haythornthwaite (Eds.), *The Internet in Everyday Life* (pp. 431–463). Malden, MA: Blackwell Publishing. doi:10.1002/9780470774298.ch15

Healey, D. (1998). *Conferencing Online with Nicenet*. English Language Institute Technology Tip of the Month: October 1998. Retrieved from http://oregonstate.edu/dept/eli/oct1998.html

Heck, D. J., Banilower, E. R., Weiss, I. R., & Rosenberg, S. L. (2008). Studying the effects of professional development: The case of the NSF's local systemic change through teacher enhancement initiative. *Journal for Research in Mathematics Education, 39*(2), 113–152.

HEFCE. (2011). *Collaborate to compete: Seizing the opportunity of online learning for UK higher education*. Report to the Higher Education Funding Council for England (HEFCE) by the Online Learning Task Force. Retrieved from: http://www.hefce.ac.uk/pubs/year/2011/201101/

Heijden, H. V. (2004). User acceptance of hedonic information system. *MIS Quarterly, 28*(4), 695–704.

Heinecke, W. F., Blasi, L., Milman, N., & Washington, L. (1999). *New directions in the evaluation of the effectiveness of educational technology*. Paper presented at the Secretary's Conference on Educational Technology. Washington, DC.

Hemmi, A., Bayne, S., & Land, R. (2009). The appropriation and repurposing of social technologies in higher education. *Journal of Computer Assisted Learning, 25*(1), 19–30. doi:10.1111/j.1365-2729.2008.00306.x

Hennessy, S. (1999). The potential of portable technologies for supporting graphing investigations. *British Journal of Educational Technology, 30*(1), 57–60. doi:10.1111/1467-8535.00090

Henningsen, M., & Stein, M. K. (1997). Mathematical tasks, and student cognition: Classroom-based factors that support and inhibit high-level mathematical thinking and reasoning. *Journal for Research in Mathematics Education, 28*(5), 534–549. doi:10.2307/749690

Herring, M., & Dargan, C. (2002). *Using Discussion Boards to Integrate Technology into the College Classroom*. Retrieved from http://www.hawkeye.cc.ia.us/faculty/cpost/using_discussion_boards_paper.htm

Herrington, J., Mantei, J., Olney, I., & Ferry, B. (2009). Using mobile technologies to develop new ways of teaching and learning. In J. Herrington, A. Herrington, J., Mantei, I., Olney, & B. Ferry (Eds.), New technologies, new pedagogies: Mobile learning in higher education (p. 138). New South Wales, Australia: Faculty of Education, University of Wollongong.

Herrington, A. (2009). *Design principles for mobile learning, Research on line*. University of Wollongong.

Hertel, G., Konradt, U., & Voss, K. (2006). Competencies for virtual teamwork: Development and validation of a web-based selection tool for members of distributed teams. *European Journal of Work and Organizational Psychology*, *15*(4), 477–504. doi:10.1080/13594320600908187

Hetebry, J., & Caporn, N. (2007). *Tablet PC's a tool for teaching-learning at Penrhos College*. Paper presented at IADIS. New York, NY.

Hewitt, A., & Forte, A. (2006). Crossing boundaries: Identity management and student/faculty relationships on the facebook. In *Proceedings ofComputer Supported Cooperative Work Conference*. Banff, Canada: IEEE.

Hill, J., Reeves, T., & Heidemeier, H. (2000). *Ubitquitous Computing for Teaching, Learning and Communicating: Trends, Issues and Recommendations, White Paper*. Department of Instructional Technology, College of Education, University of Georgia. Retrieved from http://lpsl.coe.uga.edu/Projects/AAlaptop/pdf/UbiquitousComputing.pdf

Hillman, D., Willis, D., & Gunawardena, C. (1994). Learner-Interface Interaction in Distance Education: An Extension of Contemporary Models and Strategies for Practitioners. *American Journal of Distance Education*, *8*(2), 30–42. doi:10.1080/08923649409526853

Hiltz, S. (1998). Collaborative Learning in Asynchronous Learning Networks: Building Learning Communities. In *Proceedings of Web 98 Symposium*. Orlando, FL: Academic Press. http://eies.njit.edu/~hiltz/collaborative_learning_in_asynch.htm

Hiltz, S. R. (1994). The Virtual Classroom: Learning without Limits via Computer Networks. Academic Press.

Hiltz, S. R., Johnson, K., & Turoff, M. (1986). Experiments in group decision making: Communication process and outcome in face-to-face versus computerized conferences. *Human Communication Research*, *13*(2), 225–252. doi:10.1111/j.1468-2958.1986.tb00104.x

Hodges, C. B., & Cowan, S. F. (2012). Preservice teachers' views of instructor presence in online courses. *Journal of Digital Learning in Teacher Education*, *28*(4), 139–145. doi:10.1080/21532974.2012.10784694

Hodkinson, P. (1992). Alternative models of competence in vocational education and. *Journal of Further and Higher Education and Training*, *16*(2), 30–39. doi:10.1080/0309877920160204

Hoff, E., Lappe, L., & Lempert, W. (1985). *Arbeitsbiographie und persönlichkeitsentwikkelung. Schriften zur Arbeitspsychologie, 40*. Bern: Verlag Hans Huber.

Hollingshead, A. B. (1996). Information Suppression and Status Persistence in Group Decision making. *Human Communication Research*, *23*(2), 193–219. doi:10.1111/j.1468-2958.1996.tb00392.x

Holme, O., & Sharples, M. (2002). Implementing a student learning organizer on the pocket PC platform. In *Proceedings of MLEARN 2002: European Workshop on Mobile and Contextual Learning* (pp. 14-17). Birmingham, UK: MLEARN.

Hövels, B. (1993). Terug naar de inhoud op het snijvlak tussen onderwijs en arbeid. In B. Hövels & L. Römkens (Eds.). Notities over kwalificaties (pp. 4-67). 's-Hertogenbosch: CIBB.

Hrastinski, S. (2008). Asynchronous and Synchronous E-Learning. *Educause Quarterly Magazine*, *31* (4). Retrieved on http://www.educause.edu/node/163445?time=1238691114

Hsu, C. L., & Lu, H. P. (2004). Why do people play online games? An extended TAM with social influences and flow experience. *Information & Management*, *41*(7), 853–868. doi:10.1016/j.im.2003.08.014

Huber, G. (2004). *Cooperative learning*. Riga, Latvia: RaKa.

Huett, J. (2004). E-mail as an educational feedback tool: Relative advantages and implementation guidelines. *International Journal of Educational Technology Systems, 28*(3), 219–239.

Huynh, M. Q., Umesh, U. N., & Valachich, J. (2003). E-Learning as an Emerging Entrepreneurial enterprise in Universities and Firms. *Communications of the AIS, 12*, 48–68.

Illinois Institute of Technology. (2011, April 14). *Illinois Institute of Technology confirms iPads for undergraduates each year.* Retrieved from http://www.iit.edu/departments/pr/mediaroom/article_viewer_db.php?articleID=434

Im, Y., & Lee, O. (2003-2004, Winter). Pedagogical implications of online discussion for preservice teacher training. *Journal of Research on Technology in Education, 36*(2), 155–170. doi:10.1080/15391523.2003.10782410

İnceoğlu, M. (2002). Mobil öğretime hazır mıyız? In *Proceedings of Anadolu Üniversitesi.* Eskişehir: Açık ve Uzaktan Eğitim Sempozyumu.

India's First M-Education Service . (2013). Retrieved From http://itvoir.com/portal/

Inglis, A. (2005). Quality improvement, quality assurance, and benchmarking: comparing two frameworks for managing quality processes in open and distance learning. *The International Review of Research in Open and Distance Learning.* Retrieved from http://www.microsoft.com/isapi/

Iqbal, S., & Qureshi, I. A. (2012). M-learning adoption: A perspective from a developing country. *International Review of Research in Open and Distance Learning, 13*(3), 147–164.

Jayasingh, S., & Eze, U. C. (2009). An empirical analysis of consumer behavioural intention toward mobile coupons in Malaysia. *International Journal of Business and Information, 4*(2), 221–241.

Jelemenská, K., Cicák, P., & Dúcky, V. (2011). Interactive presentation towards students' engagement. International Conference on Education and Educational Psychology (ICEEPSY 2011). *Procedia: Social and Behavioral Sciences, 29*, 1645–1653. doi:10.1016/j.sbspro.2011.11.407

Jessup, G. (1995). *Outcomes. NVQ's and the emerging model of education and training.* London: Farmer.

Johnson, L., Smith, R., Willis, H., & Haywood, K. (2011). *The 2011 horizon report.* Austin, TX: The New Media Consortium.

Jonassen, D., & Rohrer-Murphy, L. (1999). Activity theory as a framework for designing constructivist learning environments. *Educational Technology Research and Development, 47*(1), 61–79. doi:10.1007/BF02299477

Jones, N., & O'Shea, J. (2004). Challenging Hierarchies: The Impact of E-Learning. *Higher Education, 48*(3), 379–395. doi:10.1023/B:HIGH.0000035560.32573.d0

Jordaan, D., & Smith, P. (2012). *Going Mobile with Distance Learners.* Retrieved from http://wikieducator.org/images/8/88/PID_631.pdf

Ju, T. L., Sriprapaipong, W., & Minh, D. N. (2007). *On the success factors of mobile learning.* Paper presented at 5th Conference on ICT and Higher Education. Bangkok, Thailand. Retrieved from http://www.mendeley.com/research/success-factors-mobile-learning/

Junco, R. (2012). The relationship between frequency of Facebook use, participation in Facebook activities, and student engagement. *Computers & Education, 58*(1), 162–171. doi:10.1016/j.compedu.2011.08.004

Junco, R., Heiberger, G., & Loken, E. (2011). The effect of Twitter on college student engagement and grades. *Journal of Computer Assisted Learning, 27*(2), 119–132. doi:10.1111/j.1365-2729.2010.00387.x

Jung, K., & Kau, A. (2004). Culture's influence on consumer behaviours: Differences among ethnic groups in a multiracial Asian country. *Advances in Consumer Research. Association for Consumer Research (U. S.), 31*, 366–372.

Juxt. (2013). *India Has 143 Mn Internet Users.* Retrieved from http://www.lightreading.in/lightreadingindia/newswire-feed/271931/india-143-mn-internet-usersjuxt?utm_source=referrence_article

Kabassi, K., & Virvou, M. (2004). Personalized Adult e-Training on Computer Use Based on Multiple Attribute Decision Making. *Interacting with Computers, 16*(1), 115–132. doi:10.1016/j.intcom.2003.11.006

Kalin, S. (1994). Collaboration: A key to Internet training. *American Society for Information Science, 20*(3), 20–21.

Kamarul, M. K., Norlida, A., & Zainol, A. M. J. Z. (2010). Facebook: An online environments for learning English in institutions of higher education. *The Internet and Higher Education, 75*(4), 179–187.

Kang, H., & Gyorke, A. S. (2008). Rethinking distance learning activities: A comparison of transactional distance theory and activity theory. *The Journal of Open, Distance and e-Learning, 23*(3), 203-214.

Karakaya, M. (2005). *Uzaktan eğitim.* Ankara: Ankara Üniversitesi, Eğitim Bilimleri Enstitüsü, Eğitim Bilimleri Anabilim Dalı, Eğitim Yönetimi ve Teftişi Yüksek Lisans Programı, Eğitim Reformu Dersi.

Karalis, T., & Koutsonikos, G. (2003). Issues and Challenges in Organising and Evaluating Web-based Courses for Adults. *Themes in Education, 4* (2), 177-188.

Karim, N. S., Alias, R. A., Mokhtar, S. A., & Rahim, N. Z. (2009). Mobile phone adoption and appropriation in Malaysia and the contribution of age and gender. In *Proceedings of International Conference on Information and Multimedia Technology,* (pp. 485-490). Academic Press.

Karsenti, T. (2007). Teacher Education and Technology: Strengths and Weaknesses of Two Communication Tools. In *Proceedings of the 2007 Computer Science and IT Education Conference.* Retrieved in January 2009 from http://csited.org/2007/83KarsCSITEd.pdf

Kauffman, S. (1995). *At home of the universe: the search for the laws of self-organization and complexity.* New York: Oxford University press.

Kay, A. C. (1972). A Personal Computer for Children of All Ages. In *Proceedings of the ACM National Conference.* Retrieved from http://www.mprove.de/diplom/gui/kay72.html

Kaye, A. R. (1992). Learning Together Apart. In A. R. Kaye (Ed.), *Collaborative Learning Through Computer Conferencing* (pp. 1–24). London: Springer-Verlag. doi:10.1007/978-3-642-77684-7_1

Kearney, M., Schuck, S., Burden, K., & Aubusson, P. (2012). Viewing mobile learning from a pedagogical perspective. *Research in Learning Technology, 20*(1).

Keegan, D. (1986). *The foundations of distance education.* London: Croom Helm.

Kelsey, D. (1988). The economics of chaos or the chaos of economies. *Oxford Economic Papers, 40,* 1–31.

Kessels, J. W. M. (1999). Het verwerven van competenties: Kennis als bekwaamheid. *Opleiding & Ontwikkeling, 1/2,* 7–11.

Kessels, J. W. M. (2001). *Verleiden tot Kennisproductiviteit.* Oratie Universiteit Twente.

Khaddage, F., Lattemann, C., & Bray, E. (2011). Mobile apps integration for teaching and learning: Are teachers ready to re-blend? In M. Koehler & P. Mishra (Eds.), *Proceedings of Society for Information Technology & Teacher Education International Conference 2011* (pp. 2545-2552). Chesapeake, VA: AACE.

Khalique, M. (2012). *Impact of Intellectual Capital on the Organizational Performance of Selected Small and Medium Enterprises in Malaysia and Pakistan.* (PhD Thesis). Universiti Malaysia Sarawak.

Khan, B. H. (1997). *Web-based instruction.* Englewood Cliffs, NJ: Educational Technology Publications.

Khanna, N. (2011). *Mobile learning: Worth the effort?* Retrieved from http://beyondprofit.com/mobile-learning-worth-the-effort/

Kidney, G., Cummings, L., & Boehm, A. (2007). Toward a quality assurance approach to e-learning courses. *International Journal on E-Learning, 6,* 17–30.

Kijsanayotin, B., Pannarunothai, S., & Speedie, S. M. (2009). Factors influencing health information technology adoption in Thailand's community health centers: Applying the UTAUT model. *International Journal of Medical Informatics, 78*(6), 404–416. doi:10.1016/j.ijmedinf.2008.12.005 PMID:19196548

Kim, K., Kim, G. M., & Eun, S. K. (2009). Measuring the compability factors in mobile entertainment service adoption. *Journal of Computer Information Systems, 50*(1), 141–148.

King, J. P. (2006). *One hundred philosophers: A guide to world's greatest thinkers* (2nd ed.). London: Apple Press.

Kirp, D. (2007). *The market and the university: The challenge to higher education.* Sydney: Research Institute for Humanities and Social Sciences, The University of Sydney.

Klarus, R. (1998). *Competenties erkennen: Een studie naar modellen en procedures voor leerwegonafhankelijke beoordeling van beroepscompetenties.* SHertogenbosch: CINOP.

Klemm, W. R. (1997). *Benefits of Collaboration Software for On-site Classes.* Retrieved from http://www.cvm.tamu.edu/wklemm/backup/onsite.htm

Klopfer, E., Squire, K., & Jenkins, H. (2002). Environmental detectives: PDAs as a window into a virtual simulated world. In *Proceedings for the International Workshop on Wireless and Mobile Technologies in Education* (pp. 95-98). Vaxjo, Sweden: IEEE.

Klopfer, E., & Squire, K. (2007). Environmental Detectives: The development of an augmented reality platform for environmental simulations. Education research technology and development. *Journal of Educational Technology Research and Development, 56*(2), 203–228. doi:10.1007/s11423-007-9037-6

Knowles, M., Holton, E. III, & Swanson, R. (1998). *The Adult Learner.* Houston, TX: Gulf Publishing Company.

Kochery, T. S. (1997). Distance education: A delivery system in need of cooperative learning. In *Proceedings of Selected Research and Development Presentations at the 1997 National Convention of the Association for Educational Communications and Technology.* Albuquerque, NM: ERIC (ERIC Document Reproduction Service No. ED 409 847).

Komarraju, M., Musulkin, S., & Bhattacharya, G. (2010). Role of Student-Faculty Interactions in Developing College Students' Academic Self-Concept, Motivation, and Achievement. *Journal of College Student Development, 51*(3), 332–342. doi:10.1353/csd.0.0137

Ko, S., & Rosen, T. (2010). *Teaching online: A practical guide.* New York: Routledge.

Koszalka, T. A., & Ntloedibe-Kuswani, G. S. (2010). Literature on the safe and disruptive learning potential of mobile technologies. *Distance Education, 31*(2), 139–157. doi:10.1080/01587919.2010.498082

Kotler, P., & Keller, K. L. (2006). Marketing Management (12th ed.). Upper Saddle River, NJ: Pearson.

Krendl, K. A., & Lieberman, D. A. (1988). Computers and learning: A review of recent research. *Journal of Educational Computing Research, 4*(4), 367–389. doi:10.2190/BP7R-8Y2Y-R57C-5JKL

Kriumane, L. (2013). *Mūzikas skolotāja emocionālās kompetences pilnveide augstskolas studiju procesā.* (Unpublished doctoral dissertation). University of Latvia, Riga, Latvia.

Kukulska-Hulme, A. (2007). Mobile usability in educational context: What have we learnt? *The International Review of Research in Open and Distance Learning, 8*(2), 10-12.

Kukulska-Hulme, A., & Traxler, J. (2005). *Mobile learning: A handbook for educators and trainers.* London: Routledge.

Kukulska-Hulme, A., & Traxler, J. (2007). *Designing for mobile and wireless learning.* London: Routledge.

Kulviwat, S., Bruner, G. C. II, & Al-Shuridah, O. (2009). The role of social influence on adoption of high tech innovations: The moderating effect of public/private consumption. *Journal of Business Research, 62*(7), 706–712. doi:10.1016/j.jbusres.2007.04.014

Kum, L. C. (1999). *A study into students_ perceptions of web-based learning environment.* Paper presented at the HERDSA Annual International Conference. Melbourne, Australia.

Lachance, M. J., & Bernier, N. C. (2004). College students' consumer competence: A qualitative exploration. *International Journal of Consumer Studies, 28*(5), 433–442. doi:10.1111/j.1470-6431.2004.00390.x

Lai, H. M., & Chen, C. P. (2011). Factors influencing secondary school teachers' adoption of teaching blogs. *Computers & Education, 56*(4), 948–960. doi:10.1016/j.compedu.2010.11.010

Lamb, B. (2004). Wide open spaces: Wikis, ready or not. *EDUCAUSE Review, 39*, 36–49.

Lameras, P., Paraskakis, I., & Levy, P. (2008). *Conceptions of teaching using virtual learning environments: Preliminary findings from a phenomenographic inquiry.* Paper presented at the 6th International Conference on Networked Learning. Thessaloniki, Greece.

Lamon, M., Scardamalia, M., Shaw, P., & Fullan, M. (2001). *School Improvement through Learning Communities: Virtual and Real.* Toronto: Final Report for the Ontario Ministry of Education and Training.

Land, S. M., & Dornisch, M. M. (2001). A Case study of Student use of Asynchronous Bulletin Boards Systems (BBS) to support Reflection and Evaluation. *Journal of Educational Technology Systems, 30*(4), 365–377. doi:10.2190/A9EM-YBPQ-5JWU-2JWT

Landsberger, J. (2001). Integrating a Web-based Bulletin Board into your Class: A guide for Faculty. *TechTrends, 45*(5), 50–53. doi:10.1007/BF03017092

Langton, C. G. (1996). Artificial life. In M. A. Boden (Ed.), *The philosophy of artificial life.* Oxford, UK: Oxford University.

Lasmanis, A. (2003). *Māksla apstrādāt datus: pirmie soļi.* Riga, Latvia: "P&K". (in Latvian).

Lauer-Ernst, U. (1989). *Schlüsselqualifikationen: Innovativer ansätze in den neugeordenten berufen und ihre konsequenzen für lernen.* Berlin: BIBB.

Laurillard, D. (2006). E-learning in higher education. In P. Ashwin (Ed.), *Changing higher education: The development of learning and teaching* (pp. 71–96). London: Routledge.

Lave, J., & Wenger, E. (1991). Situated Learning: Legitimate Peripheral Participation. Cambridge, UK: Academic Press. doi:10.1017/CBO9780511815355

Lawrence, M. (1999, November 8). Homework for adults. *The Guardian.*

Lee, E. L. (2007). The Chinese Malaysians' selfish mentality and behaviours rationalizing from the native perspectives. *Chinese Media Research, 3*(4), 91–119.

Lee, M. K. O., Cheung, C. M. K., & Chen, Z. (2007). Understanding User Acceptance of Multimedia Messaging Services: An Empirical Study. *Journal of the American Society for Information Science and Technology, 58*(13), 2066–2077. doi:10.1002/asi.20670

Leont'ev, A. N. (1978). *Activity, Consciousness, and Personality.* Prentice-Hall.

Levy, A. (2013). Bill Gates Joins $35 Million Funding in Startup ResearchGate. *Bloomberg.* Retrieved from http://www.bloomberg.com/news/2013-06-04/bill-gates-joins-35-million-investment-in-startup-researchgate.html

Liaw, S. S., Hatala, M., & Huang, H. M. (2010). Investigating acceptance toward mobile learning to assist individual knowledge management: Based on activity theory approach. *Computers & Education, 54*(2), 446–454. doi:10.1016/j.compedu.2009.08.029

Li, D., Chau, P. Y., & Lou, H. (2005). Understanding individual adoption of instant messaging: An empirical investigation. *Journal of the Association for Information Systems, 6*(4), 102–129.

Li, F., Lau, R., & Dharmendran, P. (2009), A three-tier profiling framework for adaptive e- learning. In *Proceedings of the 8th International Conference on Advances in Web Based Learning.* Aachen. doi:10.1007/978-3-642-03426-8_30

Lin, T. (2012). Cracking Open the Scientific Process. *The New York Times.* Retrieved from http://www.nytimes.com/2012/01/17/science/open-science-challenges-journal-tradition-with-web-collaboration.html?ref=thomaslin&_r=0

Lincoln, Y. S. (2000). *Data matrices vs. case studies: Strengths, weaknesses and benefits compared.* Unpublished report prepared for the Second Information Technology in Education Study (SITES-M2) Project.

Lindstrom, P. (2007). *Securing "Web 2.0" technologies.* Midvale, UT: Burton Group EDUCAUSE Center for Applied Research.

Lipsman, A. (2009). *Touchscreen Mobile Phone Adoption Grows at Blistering Pace in U.S. During Past Year.* Retrieved March 2, 2011, from comScore,Inc.: http://comscore.org/Press_Events/Press_Releases/2009/11/Touchsceen_Mobile_phone_adoptiongrowsatBlistering_PaceinU.S_During_Past_Year

Littleton, K., & Light, P. (1999). *Learning with Computers: Analysing Productive Interaction.* London: Routledge.

Liu, Y., & Li, H. (2010). Mobile internet diffusion in China: An empirical study. *Industrial Management & Data Systems, 110*(3), 309–324. doi:10.1108/02635571011030006

Lodzinski, T., & Pawlowski, J. M. (2006). The quality mark e-learning: developing process- and product-oriented quality. In U. D. Ehlers & J. M. Pawlowski (Eds.), *Handbook on quality and standardization in e-learning* (pp. 109–124). Berlin: Springer. doi:10.1007/3-540-32788-6_8

Lonsdale, P., Baber, C., Sharples, M., & Arvantis, T. N. (2003). Context-awareness architecture for facilitating mobile learning. In *Proceedings of MLEARN 2002: Mobile Learning anytime anywhere* (pp. 17-19) Birmingham, UK: MLEARN.

Looi, C., Seow, P., Zhang, B., So, H., Chen, W., & Wong, L. (2009). Leveraging mobile technology for sustainable seamless learning: A research agenda. *British Journal of Educational Technology, 41*(2), 154–169. doi:10.1111/j.1467-8535.2008.00912.x

Lorentz, E. (1993). *The essence of chaos.* Seattle, WA: University of Washington. doi:10.4324/9780203214589

Loucks-Horsley, S., Love, N., Stiles, K. E., Mundry, S., & Hewson, P. W. (2009). *Designing professional development for teachers of science and mathematics* (3rd ed.). Thousand Oaks, CA: Corwin Press.

Lovejoy, D. (1993). Adapting to the needs of its users. *The Architects'. Journal, 10*(November), 27–37.

Lowell, R. (2001). *The Pew Learning and Technology Program Newsletter.* Retrieved from http://www.math.hawaii.edu/~dale/pew.html

Lub, X., Blomme, R. J., & Bal, P. M. (2011). Psychological contract and organizational citizenship behavior: A new deal for new generations? *Advances in Hospitality and Leisure, 7*, 107–129.

Luce-Kapler, R. (2007). Radical change and wikis: Teaching new literacies. *Journal of Adolescent & Adult Literacy, 51*(3), 214–223. doi:10.1598/JAAL.51.3.2

Luck, D. J., Taylor, W. G., & Robin. (1987). *Marketing Research.* Prentice Hall.

Luhmann, N. (1988). *Erkenntnis als Konstruktion.* Bern: Benteli.

Lūka, I. (2008). Development of Students' ESP Competence and Educator's Professional Activity in Tertiary Level Tourism Studies. In *Proceedings of ATEE Spring University Conference Teacher of the 21st Century: Quality Education for Quality Teaching* (pp. 689-697). Riga, Latvia: University of Latvia.

Lu, W., & Zhang, M. (2008). The adoption and use of mobile phone in rural China: A case study of Hubei, China. *Telematics and Informatics, 25*(3), 169–186. doi:10.1016/j.tele.2006.10.001

Lyons, J. F. (2004). Teaching U.S. History Online: Problems and Prospects. The History Teacher. *Society for the History of Education, 37*(4), 447–456.

MacCallum, K., & Jeffrey, L. (2009). Identifying discriminating variables that determine mobile learning adoption by educators: An initial study. In Proceedings of the conference for Same places, different spaces. Auckland: Ascilite. Retrieved from http://www.ascilite.org.au/conferences/auckland09/procs/maccallum.pdf

MacKnight, C. B. (2000). Teaching Critical Thinking through Online Discussions. *EDUCAUSE Quarterly, 4.* Retrieved from http://www.educause.edu/ir/library/pdf/EQM0048.pdf

Maher, M. L., & Simoff, S. J. (2000). Collaboratively designing within the design. Collaborative design. In *Proceedings of Codesigning,* (pp. 391-400). London: Springer-Verlag. Retrieved from http://www.acmc.uq.edu.au/pdfs/Collaborative_designing_within_the_Design.pdf

Maisie, E, (2012). *Blueprint for Change in an Era of Rapid Reinvention.* Paper presented at Educause. Denver, CO.

Malhotra, N. K. (2004). *Marketing Research: An Applied Orientation.* London: Prentice Hall International.

Malins, J., Gray, C., Pirie, I., Cordiner, S., & Mckillop, C. (2003). The virtual design studio: Developing new tools for learning, practice and research in design. In Proceedings of Techne. Barcelona, Spain: Design Wisdom European Academy of Design. Retrieved from http://www.ub.es/5ead/PDF/10/Malins.pdf

Maniar, N., & Bennett, E. (2007). Media influence on m-learning? In S. Iqbal, & I.A. Qureshi. (2012). M-learning adoption: A perspective from a developing country. *International Review of Research in Open and Distance Learning, 13*(3), 147–164.

Mansfield, B. (1990). Competence and standards. In J. Burke (Ed.), *Competency based education and training* (pp. 26–53). Barcom Lewes, UK: The Falmer Press.

Marion, R. (1999). *The edge of organization: Chaos and complexity theories of formal social systems.* London: Sage.

Mark, F. (2009). *Touch screen redefine the market* (International Editions). Scientific American.

Marshall, S. (2004). Leading and managing the development of e-learning environments: An issue of comfort or discomfort? In *Proceedings Ascilite*. Retrieved January 1, 2005 from: www.ascilite.org.au/conferences/perth04/.../marshallkeynote.html

Marsick, V., & Watkins, K. E. (1990). *Informal and incidental learning in the workplace.* London: Routledge.

Martinovic, D., Pugh, T., & Magliaro, J. (2010). Pedagogy for Mobile Learning Using Videoconferencing Technology. *Interdisciplinary Journal of Information, Knowledge, and Management, 5,* 375–393.

Marwan, M. E., Madar, A. R., & Fuad, N. (2013). An overview of mobile application in learning for student of Kolejpoly-tech Mara (KPTM) by using mobile phone. *Journal of Asian Scientific Research, 3*(6), 527–537.

Marzano, R. J., & Pickering, D. J. (1997). *Dimensions of learning trainer_s manual.* Alexandria VI: Mid-Continent, Research for Education and Learning. Retrieved from http://www.ascd.org/ASCD/pdf/siteASCD/publications/books/Dimensions-of-Learning-Teachers-Manual-2nd-edition.pdf

Maslo, E. (2007). Transformative Learning Space for Life-Long Foreign Languages Learning. In *Proceedings of International Nordic-Baltic Region Conference of FIPLV Innovations in Language Teaching and Learning in the Multicultural Context* (pp. 38-46). Rīga: SIA "Izglītības soļi".

Maslo, I. (2006). Kompetences jēdziena izpratnes daudzveidība un ar to saistītas problēmas Latvijas izglītības organizācijas sistēmas izveidē. In I. Maslo (Ed), No zināšanām uz kompetentu darbību, (pp. 46.-56). Riga, Latvia: Latvijas Universitātes Akadēmiskais apgāds. (in Latvian).

Masoumi, D., & Lindström, B. (2009). Foundations of cultural design in e-learning. *International Journal of Internet and Enterprise Management, 6*(2), 124–142. doi:10.1504/IJIEM.2009.023926

Masoumi, D., & Lindström, B. (2012). Quality in e-learning: A framework for promoting and assuring quality in virtual institutions. *Journal of Computer Assisted Learning, 28*(1), 27–41. doi:10.1111/j.1365-2729.2011.00440.x

Mathews, B. S. (2006). Do you facebook? Networking with students online. *College & Research Libraries News, 37,* 306–307.

Matias, A., & Wolf, D. F. (2013), Engaging Students in Online Courses Through the Use of Mobile Technology. In L. A. Wankel & P. Blessinger (Eds.), Increasing Student Engagement and Retention Using Mobile Applications: Smartphones, Skype and Texting Technologies (Cutting-edge Technologies in Higher Education, Volume 6) (pp. 115-142). Emerald Group Publishing Limited.

Matthew, A. (2012). Managing distraction and attention in diverse cohorts: 21st century challenges to law student engagement. *QUT Law & Justice Journal, 12*(1), 45–65.

Mayadas, F. (1997). Asynchronous learning networks: A Sloan foundation perspective. *Journal of Asynchronous Learning Networks, 1*(1).

Mayisela, T. (2013). The potential use of mobile technology: Enhancing accessibility and communication in a blended learning course. *South African Journal of Education, 33*(1), 1–18.

Mayring, P. (2004). Qualitative Content Analysis. In U. Flick, E. Von Kardoff, & I. Steinke (Eds.), *A Companion to Qualitative Research* (pp. 266–269). Glasgow, UK: SAGE.

Mayring, P. (2007). On Generalization in Qualitatively Oriented Research. *Forum Qualitative Sozialforschung / Forum: Qualitative. Social Research, 8*(3), 1–8.

Mazer, J. P., Murphy, R. E., & Simonds, C. J. (2007). I'll see you on 'Facebook': The effects of computer-mediated teacher self-disclosure on student motivation, affective learning, and classroom climate. *Communication Education, 56*(1), 1–17. doi:10.1080/03634520601009710

McCrory, R., Putnam, R., & Jansen, A. (2008). Interaction in Online Courses for Teacher Education: Subject Matter and Pedagogy.[Chesapeake, VA: SITE.]. *Journal of Technology and Teacher Education, 16*(2), 155–180.

McGhee, R., & Kozma, R. (2001). *New teacher and student roles in the technology-supported classroom.* Paper presented at the Annual Meeting of the American Educational Research Association. Seattle, WA. Retrieved from http://www.cehd.umn.edu/carei/publications/documents/newrolestechnology.pdf

McGinley, S. (2012). UAE colleges switch to iPad-only classrooms. *ITP.net.* Retrieved from http://www.itp.net/590333-uae-colleges-switch-to-ipad-only-classrooms#.Uim3wCIoH1w

McGlynn, A. P. (2008). Millenials in College: How do we motivate them? *Education Digest*, 20–22.

McGorry, S. Y. (2003). Measuring quality in online programs. *The Internet and Higher Education, 6*(2), 159–177. doi:10.1016/S1096-7516(03)00022-8

McKenzie, J. (2001). The Unwired Classroom: Wireless Computers Come of Age. *From Now On-The Educational Technology Journal, 10*(4).

McNamara, J., & Brown, C. (2008). Assessment of collaborative learning in online discussions. In *Proceedings ATN Assessment Conference 2008, Engaging Students in Assessment*. Adelaide, Australia: University of South Australia.

McRae, K., Ochsner, K. N., Mauss, I. B., Gabrieli, J. J. D., & Gross, J. J. (2008). Gender Differences in Emotion Regulation: An fMRI Study of Cognitive Reappraisal. *Group Processes & Intergroup Relations, 11*(2), 143–162. doi:10.1177/1368430207088035

Mead, G. H. (1973). *Geist, Identitat, und Gesselschaft*. Frankfurt: A. M.

Mead, G. H. (1967). *Mind, Self, and Society from the Standpoint of a Social Behaviorist*. Chicago: University of Chicago. doi:10.7208/chicago/9780226516608.001.0001

Mentz, E., & Goosen, L. (2007). Are groups working in the information technology class? *South African Journal of Education, 27*(2), 329–343.

Merlose, Sh., & Bergeron, K. (2007). Instructor immediacy strategies to facilitate group work in online graduate study. *Australasian Journal of Educational Technology, 23*(1), 132–148.

Messick, S. (1989). Validity. In R. L. Linn (Ed.), *Educational measurement* (3rd ed., pp. 13–103). Washington, DC: American Council on Education and National Council on Measurement in Education.

Mickler, O., Dittrich, E., & Neumann, U. (1976). *Technik, arbeitsorganisation und arbeit*. Frankfurt: Aspekte Verlag.

Millen, D., Feinberg, J., & Kerr, B. (2005). Social bookmarking in the enterprise. *Queue, 3*(9), 28–35. doi:10.1145/1105664.1105676

Mirza, A. A., & Al-Abdulkareem, M. (2011). Models of e-learning adopted in the Middle East. *Applied Computing and Informatics, 9*(2), 83–93. doi:10.1016/j.aci.2011.05.001

Mizban, N., & Roberts, A. (2008). A Review of experiences of the implementation of e-learning in architectural design education. *CEBE Working Papers*.

Moallem, M. (2003). An interactive online course: A collaborative design model. *Educational Technology Research and Development, 51*(4), 85–103. doi:10.1007/BF02504545

Mobile Edu'n Services Proposed By ' Bharati Airtel'. (n.d.). Retrieved from http://education.oneindia.in/news/2013/01/03/mobile-education-services-proposed-by-bharti-airtel-003626.html

Mobile learning: the future of distance education in India. (2012). Retrieved from http://www.rncos.com/press_releases/mobile-learning-the-future-of-distance-education-in-india.htmshare

Moerkamp, T. (1991). Leren voor een loopbaan: Het verwerven van transitievaardigheden in HAVO en MBO. Amsterdam: SCO (OSA-werkdocument W 92).

Moody, L., & Schmidt, G. (2004). Going wireless: The emergence of wireless networks in education. *Journal of Computing Sciences in Colleges*, *19*(4), 151–158.

Moon, J. W., & Kim, Y. G. (2001). Extending the TAM for a World-Wide-Web context. *Information & Management*, *38*(4), 217–230. doi:10.1016/S0378-7206(00)00061-6

Moore, M. G. (1989). Three types of interaction. *American Journal of Distance Education*, *3*(2), 1–6. doi:10.1080/08923648909526659

Moore, M. G., & Kearsley, G. (1996). *Distance Education: A systems view*. Belmont, CA: Wadsworth.

Moore, M., & Kearsley, G. (2012). *Distance education – A system view of online learning* (3rd ed.). Wadsmorth, MA: Cengage Learning.

Moran, M., Seaman, J., & Tinti-Kane, H. (2011). *Teaching, Learning, and Sharing: How Today's Higher Education Faculty Use Social Media*. Retrieved from http://www.pearsonlearningsolutions.com/educators/pearson-social-media-survey-2011-bw.pdf

Morrison, M. A., Haley, E., Sheehan, K. B., & Taylor, R. E. (2011). *Using qualitative research in advertising: strategies, techniques, and applications*. Thousand Oaks, CA: SAGE Publications, Inc.

Mortensen, M., & Hinds, P. J. (2001). Conflict and Shared Identity in Geographically Distributed Teams. *The International Journal of Conflict Management*, *12*(3), 212–238. doi:10.1108/eb022856

Moss, P. A. (1992). Shifting conceptions of validity in educational measurement: Implications for performance assessment. *Review of Educational Research*, *62*(3), 229–258. doi:10.3102/00346543062003229

Motiwalla, L. (2007). Mobile learning: A framework and evaluation. *Computers & Education*, *49*(3), 581–596. doi:10.1016/j.compedu.2005.10.011

Moura, A., & Carvalho, A. (2009). Mobile learning: two experiments on teaching and learning with mobile phones. In R. Hijon-Neira (Ed.), *Advanced Learning* (pp. 89-103). Rijeka, Croatia: InTech. Retrieved from http://www.intechopen.com/download/get/type/pdfs/id/8593

Movahedzadeh, F. (2011). Improving Students' Attitude Toward Science Through Blended Learning. *International Journal Science Education and Civic Engagement*, *3*(2).

Muilenburg, L., & Berge, Z. (2005). Student Barriers to Online Learning: A factor analytic study. *Distance Education*, *26*(1), 29–48. doi:10.1080/01587910500081269

Muirhead, B. (2001). Interactivity research studies. *Journal of Educational Technology & Society*, *4*(3).

Mulder, M. (1998). Het begrip competenties. Enkele achtergronden en invullingen. *Opleiding & Ontwikkeling*, *10/11*, 5–9.

Munoz, C. L., & Towner, T. (2009). Opening facebook: How to use facebook in the college classroom. In *Proceedings of Society for Information Technology and Teacher Education Conference*. Charleston, SC: Academic Press.

Murray, O. T., & Olcese, N. R. (2011). Teaching and learning with iPads, ready or not? *TechTrends*, *55*(6), 42–48. doi:10.1007/s11528-011-0540-6

Muttoo, S. (2011). *'Mobile' changes in the Arab world.* Middle East economy and Globalization. Retrieved from http://www.strategicforesight.com/inner-articles.php?id=128£.UiRFZD-BWSo

NAHE (The Swedish National Agency for Higher Education). (2008). *E-learning quality: Aspects and criteria*. Solna: Högskoleverket.

National Partnership for Excellence and Accountability in Teaching (NPEAT). (2000). *Revisioning professional development: What learner-centered professional development looks like*. Oxford, OH: Author. Retrieved September 10, 2003, from http://www.nsdc.org/library/policy/npeat213.pdf

Neale, D. C., & Carroll, J. C. (1999, December). *Multi-faceted evaluation for complex, distributed activities*. Paper presented at the Computer Supported Collaborative Learning Conference. Stanford University.

Nicolis, G., & Prigogine, I. (1989). *Exploring complexity: An introduction*. New York: W.H. Freeman.

Nilsson, A., & Pareto, L. (2010). The Complexity of integrating technology enhanced learning in special math education–A case study. Sustaining TEL: From Innovation to Learning and Practice. *Lecture Notes in Computer Science, 6383*, 638–643. doi:10.1007/978-3-642-16020-2_67

NMC Horizon Report. (2013). Higher Education Edition. New Media Consortium.

North Carolina Elementary Mathematics Add-on Licensure Team. (2009). *Elementary Mathematics Add-on. License*. Proposal to the UNC General Administration for Proposed Program of Study and Licensure Recognition.

O'Connor, E. A. (2011). The effect on learning, communication, and assessment when student-centered Youtubes of microteaching were used in an online teacher-education course. *Journal of Educational Technology Systems, 39*(2), 135–154. doi:10.2190/ET.39.2.d

O'Reilly, T. (2008). *Why Dell.com (was) more Enterprise 2.0 than Dell IdeaStorm*. Retrieved from: http://radar.oreilly.com/2008/09/why-dell-dot-com-is-more-enterprise.html

O'Reilly, T., & Batelle, J. (2009). *Web Squared: Web 2.0 Five Years On*. Retrieved from http://assets.en.oreilly.com/1/event/28/web2009_websqared-whitepaper.pdf

O'Sullivan, M. F. (2001). *Is Anyone There? Communication and Online learning*. Retrieved from http://www.wwtc.edu/voice/class/vtutor/cw2001.htm

O'Donnell, E., & Sharp, M. (2012). Students' views of E-Learning: The impact of technology on learning in higher education in Ireland. In K. Moyle & G. Wijngaards (Eds.), *Student Reactions to Learning with Technologies: Perceptions and Outcomes*. Hershey, PA: Information Science Reference (an imprint of IGI Global). doi:10.4018/978-1-61350-177-1.ch010

Okazaki, S. (2011). Teaching students while leaking personal information: m-learing and privacy. In *Proceedings of 4th International Conference of Education, Research and Innovations* (pp. 1659-1664). Madrid: IATED.

O'Leary, J. (2000, February 16). Students may have to pay higher fees. *The Times*.

Oliver, R. (2001). Strategies for Assuring the Quality of Online Leaning Australian Higher Education. In M. Wallace, A. Ellis & D. Newton (Eds.), *Proceedings of Moving Online II Conference*, (pp. 222-231). Academic Press.

Oliver, R. (2003). *Exploring benchmarks and standards for assuring quality online teaching and learning in higher education*. Paper presented at the Proceedings of 16th Open and Distance Learning. Canberra, Australia. Retrieved from http://elrond.scam.ecu.edu.au/oliver/2003/odlaa.pdf

Oliver, B., & Gorke, V. (2007). Australian undergraduates' use and ownership of emerging technologies: Implications and opportunities for creating engaging learning experiences for the Net Generation. *Australasian Journal of Educational Technology, 23*(2), 171–186.

Oliver, R. (2005). Quality assurance and e-learning: Blue skies and pragmatism. *Research in Learning Technology, 13*(3), 173–187. doi:10.1080/09687760500376389

O'Malley, C., Vavoula, G., Glew, J. P., Taylor, J., Sharples, M., & Lefrere, P. (2003). Guidelines for Learning/Teaching/Tutoring in a Mobile Environment. *Journal of MOBlearn., 8*(12), 14–26.

Omar, A., Kalulu, D., & Alijani, G. (2011). Management of innovative e-learning environments. *Academy of Educational Leadership Journal, 15*(3), 37–64.

Omar, M. (1992). Attitudes of college students towards computers: A comparative study in the United States and the Middle East. *Computers in Human Behavior, 8*(2-3), 249–257. doi:10.1016/0747-5632(92)90009-4

Ong, C. H., & Lai, J. Y. (2006). Gender differences in perceptions and relationships among dominants of elearning acceptance. *Computers in Human Behavior, 22*(5), 816–829. doi:10.1016/j.chb.2004.03.006

Onstenk, J. (1997). *Lerend, leren werken: Brede vakbekwaamheid en de integratie van leren, werken en innoveren.* Delft: Eburon.

Orr, G. (2010). Review of the literature in mobile learning: Affordances and constraints. In *Proceeding of the 6th IEEE International Conference on Wireless, Mobile and Ubiquitous Technologies in Education* (pp. 107-111). Taiwan: IEEE. doi:10.1109/WMUTE.2010.20

Orrill, C. H. (2001). Building learner-centered classrooms: A professional development framework for supporting critical thinking. *Educational Technology Research and Development, 49*(1), 15–34. doi:10.1007/BF02504504

Oskar, C., Portillo, J., Ovelar, R., Benito, M., & Romo, J. (2010). iPLE Network: An integrated eLearning 2.0 architecture from a university's perspective. *Interactive Learning Environments, 18*(3), 293–308. doi:10.1080/10494820.2010.500553

Ossiannilsson, E. (2011). Findings from European Benchmarking Exercises on E-Learning: Value and Impact. *Creative Education, 2*(3), 208–219. doi:10.4236/ce.2011.23029

Owston, R. D. (2001, February). *Final Report: Case Studies of GrassRoots Implementations* (Centre for the Study of Computers in Education Technical Report No. 2001-1). Toronto: York University, Faculty of Education. Retrieved from http://www.edu.yorku.ca/csce

Owston, R. D. (1997). The World Wide Web: A technology to enhance teaching and learning? *Educational Researcher, 26*(2), 27–33.

Owston, R. D. (2000). Evaluating Web-based learning environments: Strategies and insights. *Cyberpsychology & Behavior, 3*(1), 79–87. doi:10.1089/109493100316256

Özer, B. (1989). *Türkiye'de uzaktan eğitim: Anadolu Üniversitesi Açıköğretim Fakültesi'nin uygulamaları.* Retrieved from www.emu.edu.tr/.../1989.Türkiye'de%20uzaktan.pdf

Pai, D. D., & Borba, G. S. (2012). The role of digital technologies for the innovation of the learning experience in the university classroom. *Strategic Design Research Journal, 5*(2), 59–69.

Paliktzoglou, V., & Suhonen, J. (2014). *Microblogging in Higher Education: The Edmodo case study among computer science students in Finland.* Manuscript submitted for publication.

Paliktzoglou, V., & Suhonen, J. (2014). *Microblogging as an assisted learning tool in Problem Based Learning (PBL) in Bahrain: The Edmodo case.* Manuscript submitted for publication.

Paliktzoglou, V., & Suhonen, J. (2014). Facebook as an assisted learning tool in problem-based learning: The Bahrain case. *International Journal of Social Media and Interactive Learning Environments, 2*(1), 85–100. doi:10.1504/IJSMILE.2014.059694

Palloff, R., & Pratt, K. (2001). *Lessons from the cyberspace classroom: The realities of online teaching.* San Francisco: Jossey-Bass.

Palmer, S. A., & Holt, D. M. (2009). Students' perceptions of the value of the elements of an online learning environment: Looking back in moving forward. *Interactive Learning Environments, 18*(2), 135–151. doi:10.1080/09539960802364592

Pantelidis, V., & Auld, L. (2002). Teaching virtual reality using distance education. *Themes in Education., 3*(1), 15–38.

Parker, K. R., & Chao, J. T. (2007). Wiki as a teaching tool. *Interdisciplinary Journal of Knowledge and Learning Objects, 3*(1), 57–72.

Park, Y. (2011). A Pedagogical Framework for Mobile Learning: Categorizing Educational Applications of Mobile Technologies into Four Types. *International Review of Research in Open and Distance Learning, 12*(2).

Parsons, D. (2013). *The Future of Mobile Learning and Implications for Education and Training*. Retrieved from http://www.christoph.pimmer.info/wp-content/uploads/2008/08/Pimmer-Pachler-Mobile-Learning-in-the-Workplace1.pdf

Parsons, T. (1976). *Theorie sozialer Systeme*. Opladen: Westdeutscher Verlag. doi:10.1007/978-3-322-83798-1

Pavlis Korres, M. (2010). *Development of a framework for the e-education of educators of special groups aiming to improve their compatibility with their learners*. (PhD Thesis). University of Alcalá.

Pavlis Korres, M., Karalis, T., Leftheriotou, P., & Garcia Barriocanal, E. (2009). Integrating Adults' Characteristics and the Requirements for their Effective Learning in an e-Learning Environment. In Best Practices for the Knowledge Society, WSKS, (pp. 570-584). Springer.

Pavlis Korres, M. (2012). The Role of the Communication Tools in the Development of the Learning Group in an Online Environment. *International Journal of Engineering Education*, 28(6), 1360–1365.

Pavlis-Korres, M. (2007). On the requirements of Learning Object Metadata for adults' educators of special groups. In *Proceedings of the 2nd International Conference on Metadata and Semantics Research (MSTR 2007)*. Corfu, Greece: MSTR.

Pawlowsky, P. (2007). The treatment of organizational learning in management science. In A. B. Antal, M. Dierkes, J. Child, & I. Nonaka (Eds.), *Handbook of Organizational Learning & Knowledge* (pp. 61–89). Oxford, UK: Oxford University.

Pea, R., & Maldonado, H. (2006). WILD for learning: Interacting through new computing devices anytime, anywhere. In The Cambridge handbook of the learning science (pp. 24-28). Cambridge University Press.

Pea, R., & Maldonado, H. (2006). WILD for learning: Interacting through new computing devices anytime, anywhere. In R. K. Sawyer (Ed.), *The Cambridge Handbook of the Learning Sciences* (pp. 427–441). Cambridge, UK: Cambridge University Press.

Pelton, T., & Pelton, F. L. (2013). 1:1 iPad Adoption – Preparing Middle School Teachers to Teach Math. In R. McBride & M. Searson (Eds.), *Proceedings of Society for Information Technology & Teacher Education International Conference 2013* (pp. 4837-4842). Chesapeake, VA: AACE.

Peng, H., Su, Y., Chou, C., & Tsai, C. (2009). Ubiquitous knowledge construction: Mobile learning redefined and conceptual framework. *Innovations in Education and Teaching International*, 46(2), 171–183. doi:10.1080/14703290902843828

Perkins, D.N. & Salomon, G. (1989, January-February). Are cognitive skills context-bound? *Educational Researcher*, 16-25.

Peters, K. (2009). m-Learning: Positioning educators for a mobile, connected future. In M. Ally (Ed.), Mobile learning: Transforming the delivery of education and training (pp. 113-132). Vancouver: Marquis Book Printing.

Peters, K. (2007). *M-learning: Positioning educators for a mobile, connected future. International Journal of Research in Open and Distance Learning, 8*, 2.

Petty, C., & Tudor, B. (2010). *Gartner says touch screen mobile device sales will grow 97 percent in 2010*. Retrieved May 3, 2013, from Gartner: http://gartner.com/it/pages.jsp?id=1313415

Phipps, R., & Merisotis, J. (2000). *Quality on the Line: Benchmarks for Success in Internet-Based Distance Education*. Washington, DC: The Institute of Higher Education Policy.

Piaget, J. (1929). *The Child's Conception of the World*. New York: Harcourt, Brace, Jovanovich.

Picciano, G. A. (2002). Beyond student perceptions: Issues of interaction, presence and performance in an online course. *Journal of Asynchronous Learning Networks*, 6(1), 21–40.

Pieters, J. M. (1992). *Het ongekende talent: Over het ontwerpen van artefacten in de instructietechnologie*. Enschede: Universiteit Twente.

Pincas, A. (2000). Features of online discourse for education. *Learning Technology Newsletter, 2*(1).

Pintrich, P. R. (1994). Student motivation in the college classroom. In K. W. Prichard & R. M. Sawyer (Eds.), *Handbook of college teaching theory and applications* (pp. 23–43). Westport, CT: Greenwood.

Piotrowski, C., & Vodanovisch, S. J. (2000). Are the reported barriers to internet-based instruction warranteed? A synthesis of recent research. *Education, 21*(1), 48–53.

Pletka, B. (2007). *Educating the net generation: How to engage students in the 21st century.* Santa Monica, CA: Santa Monica Press.

Polly, D. (2012). Designing and teaching in an online elementary mathematics methods course: Promises, barriers, and implications. In R. Hartshorne, T. Heafner, & T. Petty (Eds.), *Teacher education programs and online tools: Innovations in teacher preparation* (pp. 335–356). Hershey, PA: IGI Global; doi:10.4018/978-1-4666-1906-7.ch018

Polly, D. (2013). The influence of an online elementary mathematics pedagogy course on teacher candidates' performance. *Journal of Distance Education, 27*(2). Retrieved from http://www.jofde.ca/index.php/jde/article/view/854

Polly, D. (2014). Deepening pre-service teachers' knowledge of technology, pedagogy, and content (TPACK) in an elementary school mathematics methods course. *Journal of Computers in Mathematics and Science Teaching, 33*(2), 233–250.

Polly, D., & Hannafin, M. J. (2010). Reexamining technology's role in learner-centered professional development. *Educational Technology Research and Development, 58*(5), 71. doi:10.1007/s11423-009-9146-5

Polly, D., & Hannafin, M. J. (2011). Examining how learner-centered professional development influences teachers' espoused and enacted practices. *The Journal of Educational Research, 104*(2), 120–130. doi:10.1080/00220671003636737

Polly, D., McGee, J. R., & Martin, C. S. (2010). Employing technology-rich mathematical tasks to develop teachers' technological, pedagogical, and content knowledge (TPACK). *Journal of Computers in Mathematics and Science Teaching, 29*(4), 455–472.

Polonsky, M. J., & Waller, D. S. (2010). *Designing and managing a research project: A business student's guide.* London: SAGE Publications.

Polyani, M. (1958). Skills. In M. Polyani (Ed.), *Personal knowledge: towards a post critical philosophy* (pp. 49–65). London: Routledge & Kegan Paul.

Polyani, M. (1967). *The tacit dimension.* Garden City, NY: Anchor.

Porumb, S., Orza, B., Vlaicu, A., Porumb, C., & Hoza, I. (2011). Cloud Computing and its Application to Blended Learning in Engineering. In *Proceedings of Cloud Computing 2011: The Second International Conference on Cloud Computing, GRIDs, and Virtualization.* Red Hook, NJ: Curran Associates.

Preece, J. (2000). *Online communities: Designing usability, supporting sociability.* New York: Wiley & Sons.

Prigogine, I., & Stengers, I. (1984). *Order out of chaos: Man's new dialogue with nature.* New York: Bantam Books.

Primavera, J., Wiederlight, P. P., & Digiacamo, T. M. (2001). Technology Access for Low-Income Preschoolers: Bridging the Digital Divide. In *Technology Access for Preschoolers* (pp. 1-26). Academic Press.

Pritamkabe. (2011). *Mobile Technology for Improving Quality of Education in India.* Retrieved from http://pritamkabe.wordpress.com/2011/11/04/mobile-technology-for-improving-quality-of-education-in-india/

Promnitz-Hayashi, L. (2011). A learning success story using Facebook. *SiSAL Journal, 2*(4), 309–316.

Qiu, M., & Chen, L. (2011). A Problem-based Learning Approach to Teaching an Advanced Software Engineering Course. In *Proceedings of 2nd International Workshop on Education Technology and Computer Science* (pp. 252-255). Los Alamitos, CA: The Printing House.

Quality Matters. (n.d). *Higher Education Program: Rubric.* Retrieved from: https://www.qualitymatters.org/rubric

Quinn, C. (2001). Get ready for m-learning. *Training & Development, 20*(2), 20–21.

Rahal, T. (2010). Learning styles: Learning that empowers students? *Learning and Teaching in Higher Education, 7*(2), 33–51.

Ramayah, T., & Ignatius, J. (2005). Impact of perceived usefulness, perceived ease of use and perceived enjoyment on intention to shop online. *Journal of Systems Management, 3*(3), 36–51.

Rana, K. S. (2005). *E-learning for Small Groups: The Diplo Foundation's Experience*. Retrieved from http://www.digitallearning.in/jan06/ddiplofoundation.asp

Ranieri, M., Manca, S., & Fini, A. (2012). Why (and how) do teachers engage in social networks? An exploratory study of professional use of Facebook and its implications for lifelong learning. *British Journal of Educational Technology, 43*(5), 754–769. doi:10.1111/j.1467-8535.2012.01356.x

Rao, R. (2012). *Digital learning: Education goes mobile worldwide*. Retrieved from http://www.dnaindia.com/academy/1673515/report-digital-learning-education-goes-mobile-worldwide

Ray, T. S. (1992). An approach to the synthesis of life. In C. G. Langton, C. Taylor, J. Doyne Farmer, & S. Rasmussen (Eds.), *Artificial life II, Santa Fe Institute, Studies in the sciences of complexity* (p. 10). Reading, MA: Addison-Wesley.

Redecker, C., Ala-Mutka, K., Bacigalupo, M., Ferrari, A., & Punie, Y. (2009). *Learning 2.0: The impact of Web 2.0 innovations on education and training in Europe*. Final Report. European Commission-Joint Research Center-Institute for Porspective Technological Studies, Seville. Retrieved from ftp://ftp.jrc.es/pub/EURdoc/EURdoc/JRC55629.pdf

Reich, K. (2005). *Systemisch-konstruktivistische Pädagogik*. Beltz: Weinheim u.a.

Reitz, J. M. (2004). Bibliographic database. In *Dictionary for Library and Information Science*. Westport, CT: Libraries Unlimited.

Revans, R. (1982). *Action Learning*. Bromley: Chartwell-Bratt.

Reynolds, C. W. (1987). Flocks, herds and schools: A distributed behaviour model. Proceedings of SIGGRAPH '87. *Computer Graphics, 21*(4), 25–34. doi:10.1145/37402.37406

Rheingold, H. (1994). *The virtual community*. London: Minerva.

Robbins, S. P., & Judge, T. A. (2007). *Organizational Behavior*. Upper Saddle River, NJ: Prentice Hall.

Roberson, T., & Klotz, J. (2002). How can instructors and administrators fill the missing link in online instruction?. *Online Journal of Distance Learning Administration, 5*(4).

Rogers, A. (2007). *Teaching Adults*. Open University Press.

Romney, C. (2010). Tablet PCs in undergraduate mathematics. In *Proceedings of ASEE/IEEE Frontiers in Education Conference*. IEEE.

Romney, C. (2011). Tablet PC use in freshman mathematics promotes stem retention. In *Proceedings of ASEE/IEEE Frontiers in Education Conference*. IEEE.

Rosenberg, M. (2001). *E-learning: Strategies for delivering knowledge in the digital age*. New York: MacGraw-Hill.

Rosenblum, D. (2007). What anyone can know: The privacy risks of social networking sites. *IEEE Security and Privacy, 5*(3), 40–49. doi:10.1109/MSP.2007.75

Rosenthal, D. W. (2002). The Case Method – A Joint Venture in Learning: A Message from the Editor. *Journal on Excellence in College Teaching, 13*(2-3). Retrieved from http://celt.muohio.edu/ject/issue.php?v=13&n=2+and+3

Rosevear, S. G. (1999). Lessons for Developing a Partnership-Based Virtual University. *Technology Source*. Retrieved from http://ts.mivu.org/default.asp?show_article&id_30

Roshanak, S. (2009). Human/Social Factors Influencing Usability of E commerce Websites and Systems. *Application of Information and Communication Technologies*, 1-5.

Rothblatt, S. (1997). *The Modern University and its Discontents: The Fate of Newman's Legacies in Britain and America*. Cambridge, UK: Cambridge University Press. doi:10.1017/CBO9780511582943

Rothermel, D. (2001). *Threaded Discussions: A First Step. Tech Learning.* Retrieved from http://www.ac.wwu.edu/~kenr/TCsite/home-frames.html

Rouibah, K., & Abbas, H. (2006). A modified technology acceptance model for camera mobile phone adoption: Development and validation. In *Proceedings of 17ᵗʰ Australasian Conference on Information Systems,* 1-1

Rovai, A. (2001). Building classroom community at a distance: A case study. *Educational Technology Research and Development, 49*(4), 33–48. doi:10.1007/BF02504946

Rovai, A. (2002). A preliminary look at the structural differences of higher education classroom communities in traditional and ALN courses. *Journal of Asynchronous Learning Networks, 6*(1).

Rubin, H. J., & Rubin, I. S. (2005). *Qualitative interviewing: The art of hearing data.* Thousand Oaks, CA: Sage Publications.

Rudzinska, I. (2008). The Quality of Aim Setting and Achieved Results in English for Specific Purposes-Study Course in Lecturers and Students' Opinion. In *Proceedings of the ATEE Spring University Conference Teacher of the 21st Century: Quality Education for Quality Teaching* (pp. 366-373). Riga, Latvia: University of Latvia.

Rumble, G. (1996). Labour Market Theories and Distance Education. *Open Learning, 11*(2), 47–51. doi:10.1080/0268051960110208

Russell, M., Bebell, D., O'Dwyer, L., & O'Connor, K. (2003). Examining teaching technology use: Implications for preservice and inservice teacher preparation. *Journal of Teacher Education, 54*(4), 297–310. doi:10.1177/0022487103255985

Saadé, R. G., He, X., & Kira, D. (2007). Exploring dimensions to online learning. *Computers in Human Behavior, 23*(4), 1721–1739. doi:10.1016/j.chb.2005.10.002

Sad, S. N., & Goktas, O. (2013). Preservice teachers' perceptions about using mobile phones and laptops in education as mobile learning tools. *British Journal of Educational Technology, 45*(4), 606–618. doi:10.1111/bjet.12064

Salmon, G. (2005). Flying not flapping: A strategic framework for e-learning and pedagogical innovation in higher education institutions *ALT-J. Research in Learning Technology, 13*(3), 201–218. doi:10.1080/09687760500376439

Salomon, G. (1993). *Distributed cognitions: Psychological and educational considerations.* Cambridge, UK: Cambridge University.

Samarapungavan, A., & Milikowski, M. (1992). The relation between metacognitive and domain specifik knowledge. *Tijdschrift voor Onderwijsresearch, 17*(5), 303–312.

Sandars, J., & Schroter, S. (2007). Web 2.0 technologies for undergraduate and postgraduate medical education: An online survey. *Postgraduate Medical Journal, 83*(986), 759–762. doi:10.1136/pgmj.2007.063123 PMID:18057175

Sangrà, A., Vlachopoulos, D., & Cabrera, N. (2012). Building an Inclusive Definition of E- Learning: An Approach to the Conceptual Framework. *The International Review of Open and Distance Learning, 13*(2). Retrieved February 23, 2014 from http://www.irrodl.org/index.php/irrodl/article/view/1161/2146

Sani, M., Yusof, N., Kasim, A., & Omar, R. (2009). Malaysia in transition: A comparative analysis of Asian values, Islam Hadhari and 1 Malaysia. *Journal of Politics and Law, 2*(3), 110–118. doi:10.5539/jpl.v2n3p110

Sarantakos, S. (1993). *Social research.* Macmillan Education Australia Pty Ltd.

Sarrab, M., Al-Shihi, H., & Rehman, O. M. H. (2013). Exploring major challenges and benefits of m-learning adoption. *British Journal of Applied Science and Technology, 3*(4), 826–839. doi:10.9734/BJAST/2013/3766

Scardamalia, M., Bereiter, C., & Lamon, M. (1994). Bringing the classroom into World III. In K. McGilly (Ed.), *Classroom Lessons: Integrating cognitive theory and classroom practice.* Cambridge, MA: MIT Press.

Schön, D. A. (1987). *Educating the reflective practitioner.* San Francisco: Jossey-Bass Inc.

School Net. (2001). Retrieved from http://www.schoolnet.ca/grassroots/e/index.asp

Scribner, S. (1986). Thinking in action: Some characteristics of parallel thought. In R. J. Sternberg & R. K. Wagner (Eds.), *Practical intelligence: Nature and origins of competence in the everyday world* (pp. 13–30). Cambridge, UK: Cambridge University.

Self Evaluation Report. (2005). *Self evaluation report.* European University Association Institutional Review Program, Selcuk University Accreditation Committee, Konya.

Selinger, M., & Pearson, J. (1999). *Telematics in Education: Trends and Issues.* Oxford, UK: Pergamon Press.

Selwyn, N. (2007). "Screw blackboard…do it on Facebook!": An investigation of students' educational use of Facebook. In *Proceedings of Poke 1.0-Facebook Social Research Symposium.* University of London.

Selwyn, N. (2009). Faceworking: Exploring students' education-related use of Facebook. *Learning, Media and Technology, 34*(2), 154–174. doi:10.1080/17439880902923622

Serin, O. (2012). Mobile learning perceptions of the prospective teachers (Turkish Republic of Northern Cyprus sampling). *TOJET: The Turkish Online Journal of Educational Technology, 11*(3), 222–233.

Shabha, G. (2000). Virtual universities in the third millennium: An assessment of the implications of teleworking on university buildings and space planning. *Facilities, 18*(5/6), 235–244. doi:10.1108/02632770010328108

Shankar, V. (2007). *A Discourse on Synchronous and Asynchronous E-Learning.* Retrieved in 11 February 2009 from http://www.articlealley.com/article_142663_22.html

Sharples, M. (2000). The design of personal mobile technologies for lifelong learning. *Computers & Education.* Retrieved from http://citeseerx.ist.psu.edu/viewdoc/summary;jsessionid=295FE8DACA811B98DE70E240A1521030?doi=10.1.1.359.8991

Sharples, M. (2002). Disruptive devices: Mobile technology for conversational learning. *International Journal of Continuing Engineering Education and Lifelong Learning.* Retrieved from http://citeseerx.ist.psu.edu/viewdoc/summary?doi=10.1.1.123.7924

Sharples, M., Corlett, D., & Westmancott, O. (2002). The design and implementation of a mobile learning resource. *Journal of Personal and Ubiquitous Computing, 6*(3), 220–234. doi:10.1007/s007790200021

Sharples, M., Taylor, J., & Vavoula, G. (2007). *A theory of learning for the mobile age.* London: Sage Publications.

Shea, P. J., Pickett, A. M., & Pelz, W. E. (2003). A follow-up investigation of "teaching presence" in the SUNY Learning Network. *Journal of Asynchronous Learning Networks, 7,* 61–80.

Sheperd, I.J., & Reeves, B. (2011, March 1). *iPad or iFad - The reality of a paperless classroom.* Paper presented at the Abilene Christian University - Mobility Conference.

Sherry, L., Lawyer-Brook, D., & Black, L. (1997). Evaluation of the Boulder Valley Internet Project: A Theory-Based Approach to Evaluation Design. *Journal of Interactive Learning Research, 8*(2), 199–234.

Shiau, K., Lim, E. P., & Shen, Z. (2001). Mobile commerce: Promises, challenges, and research agenda. *Journal of Database Management, 12*(3), 4–13. doi:10.4018/jdm.2001070101

Shin, D. H. (2009). An empirical investigation of a modified technology acceptance model of IPTV. *Behaviour & Information Technology, 28*(4), 361–372. doi:10.1080/01449290701814232

Shrivasta, P., & Schneider, S. (1984). Organizational frames of reference. *Journal of Management Studies, 20,* 7–28.

Shuler, C. (2012). *ILearnII: An analysis of the education category of the iTunes App Store.* New York: The Joan Ganz Cooney Center at Sesame Workshop.

Siegel, J., Dubrovsky, V., Kiesler, S., & McGuire, T. (1986). Group Processes in Computer-Mediated Communication. *Organizational Behavior and Human Decision Processes, 37*(2), 157–187. doi:10.1016/0749-5978(86)90050-6

Siemens, G. (2005). *A Learning Theory for the Digital Age.* Retrieved from http://www.elearnspace.org/Articles/connectivism.htm

Simon, M. (2008). *Online student-teacher friendships can be tricky*. Retrieved from http://articles.cnn.com/2008-08-12/tech/studentsteachers.online_1_facebook-users-myspace-social-networking-sites?_s=PM:TECH

Simons, P.R.J. & Verschaffel, L. (1992). Transfer: Onderzoek en onderwijs. *Tijdschrift voor Onderwijsresearch, 17*(3), 3-16.

Simonson, M., Smaldino, S., Albright, M., & Zvacek, S. (2011). Teaching and learning at distance foundations of distance education (4th ed.). Academic Press.

Simonson, M. (2002). In case you are asked: The effectiveness of distance education. *Quarterly Review of Distance Education, 3*(4).

Simons, P. R. J. (1990). *Transfervermogen*. Nijmegen: Quick Print.

Simons, P. R. J. (1999). Competentieontwikkeling: Van behaviorisme en cognitivisme naar sociaal-constructionisme. *Opleiding & Ontwikkeling, 1/2*, 41–45.

Singh, G., & Hardaker, G. (2014). Barriers and Enablers to Adoption and Diffusion of eLearning: A Systematic Review of the Literature - A Need for an Integrative Approach. *Education + Training, 56*(2/3). Retrieved February 23, 2014 from http://www.emeraldinsight.com/journals.htm?issn=0040-0912&volume=56&issue=2&

Smith, M., & Kukulska-Hulme, A. (2012). Building Mobile Learning Capacity in Higher Education: E-books and iPads. In M. Specht, J. Multisilta, and M. Sharples, (Eds.), *11th World Conference on Mobile and Contextual Learning Proceedings* (pp. 298-301). Helsinki: CELSTEC & CICERO Learning.

Smith, B. (1998). Creating Consortia: Exporting the Best, Import the Rest. *Converge Magazine, 1*, 19–98.

Sneller, J. (2007). The Tablet PC Classroom: Erasing borders, stimulating activity, enhancing communication. In *Proceedings of 37th ASEE/IEEE Frontiers in Education Conference*. IEEE.

Sobel, D. M., Sands, D. I., Dunlap, J. C. (2009). Teaching intricate content online: It can be done and done well. *Action in Teacher Education, 30*(4).

Soinila, M., & Stalter, M. (2010). *Quality assurance of e-learning*. Helsinki: ENQA, The European Association for Quality Assurance in Higher Education.

Solem, M., Chalmers, L., Dibiase, D., Donert, K., & Hardwick, S. (2006). Internationalizing Professional Development in Geography through Distance Education. *Journal of Geography in Higher Education, 30*(1), 147–160. doi:10.1080/03098260500499808

Soong, M. H. B., Chan, H. C., Chua, B. C., & Loh, K. F. (2001). Critical success factors for on- line course resources. *Computers & Education, 36*(2), 101–120. doi:10.1016/S0360-1315(00)00044-0

Špona, A., & Čehlova, Z. (2004). *Pētniecība pedagoģijā*. Riga, Latvia: RaKa. (in Latvian)

Stacey, R. D. (2001). *Complex Responsive Processes in Organizations: Learning and knowledge creation*. London, UK: Routledge.

Stein, A., & Alsaleh, K. (2013). *Lesson learned: Supporting iPads at Education City*. Paper presented at the Technology in Higher Education 2013 conference (THE2013). Doha, Qatar.

Steinbrecher, T., & Hart, J. (2012). Examining teachers' personal and professional use of Facebook: Recommendations for teacher education programming. *Journal of Technology and Teacher Education, 20*(1), 71–88.

Stern, D. N. (1985). *The interpersonal world of the infant*. New York: Basic Books.

Steward, I. (1989). *Does god play dice? The mathematics of chaos*. Oxford, UK: Blackwell.

Stickel, M. (2008). Effective use of Tablet PCs for engineering mathematics education. In *Proceedings of Frontiers in Education Conference*, (pp. S3J-7 – S3J-12). doi:10.1109/FIE.2008.4720564

Stinchcombe, A. L. (1990). *Information and organizations*. Berkeley, CA: University of California Press.

Suki, N. M. (2011). Subscribers' intention towards using 3G mobile services. *Journal Of Economics and Behavioral Studies, 2*(2), 67–75.

Sunal, W. D., Sunal, S. C., Odell, R. M., & Sundberg, A. C. (2003). Research-supported best practices for developing online learning. *Journal of Interactive Online Learning, 2*(1), 1–40.

Sundaram, P. (Ed.). (2009). *Overview of Telicom Industry,Bharat Sanchar Nigam Ltd.* Retrieved from https://www.dnb.co.in/IndianTelecomIndustry/OverviewTI.asp

Sung, J., & Yun, Y. (2010). Toward a more robust usability concept with perceived enjoyment in the context of mobile multimedia services. *International Journal of Human Computer Interaction, 1*(2), 12-32.

Sung, Y., Chang, K. C., & Yu, W. C. (2011). Evaluating the reliability and impact of a quality assurance system for E-learning courseware. *Computers & Education, 57*(2), 1615–1627. doi:10.1016/j.compedu.2011.01.020

Sun, H., & Zhang, P. (2006). The role of modelling factors in user technology acceptance. *International Journal of Human-Computer, 64*(2), 53–78. doi:10.1016/j.ijhcs.2005.04.013

Surikova, S. (2007). *Organisation of Micro-group Activity for the Improvement of Pupils' Social Competence.* (Unpublished Dissertation). University of Latvia, Riga, Latvia.

Suter, V., Alexander, B., & Kaplan, P. (2005). Social Software and The Future of Conferences Right Now. *EDUCAUSE Review, 40*(1), 47–59.

Swan, K. (2005). *Threaded Discussion.* Retrieved in February 2009 from http://www.oln.org/conferences/ODCE2006/papers/Swan_Threaded_Discussion.pdf

Swan, M. (2012, September 24). HCT and UAE University students to learn using iPads. *The National.* Retrieved from http://www.thenational.ae/news/uae-news/education/hct-and-uae-university-students-to-learn-using-ipads

Tallent-Runnels, M. K., Thomas, J. A., Lan, W. Y., Cooper, S., Ahern, T. C., Shaw, S. M., & Liu, X. (2006). Teaching courses online: A review of the research. *Review of Educational Research, 76*(1), 93–135. doi:10.3102/00346543076001093

Tapscott, D. (2009). *Grown up digital: How the Net Generation is changing your world.* New York: McGraw-Hill.

Taylor, P. C., & Medina, M. N. D. (2013). Educational Research Paradigms: From Positivism to Multiparadigmatic. *The Journal of Meaning-Centered Education, 1.*

Thomas, J. W. (2000). *A Review of Research on Project-Based Learning.* Retrieved from http://www.bobpearlman.org/BestPractices/PBL_Research.pdf

Thompson, G. (1990). How can correspondence-based distance education be improved? A survey of attitudes of students who are not well disposed toward correspondence study. *Journal of Distance Education, 5*(1), 53–65.

Thornburg, E., Hung, B., & Jackson, J. (2012). *Learning with iPad: Does this technology help or hinder student understanding.* Paper presented at Joint Mathematics Meeting. Boston, MA.

Thornburg, E. J. (2012). *Using iPads in undergraduate mathematics: Master Teacher Program.* Center for Teaching Excellence.

Toker Gökçe, A. (2008). Küreselleşme Sürecinde Uzaktan Eğitim. *D.Ü. Ziya Gökalp Eğitim Fakültesi Dergisi, 11*, 1–12.

Touch Screen. (2008). *Touch screen hardware.* Retrieved 10 December 2012, from, http://www.reghardware.com/2008/12/13/koy_touchscreen_phones/

Towner, T., & VanHorn, A. (2007). Facebook: Classroom tool for a classroom community? In *Proceedings of the Annual Meeting of the Midwest Political Science Association.* Chicago, IL: Academic Press.

Traxler, J. (2007). Defining, discussing, and evaluating mobile learning: The moving finger writes and having writes. *The International Review of Research in Open and Distance Learning, 8*(2), 11-18.

Traxler, J. (2009). Learning in a mobile age. *International Journal of Mobile and Blended Learning, 1*(1), 1–12. doi:10.4018/jmbl.2009010101

Triandis, C. H. (1979). Values, attitudes, and interpersonal behavior. In *Proceedings of NebraskaSymposium on motivation, Beliefs, attitudes and values.* Lincoln, NE: University of Nebraska Press.

Trow, M. (1999). Lifelong Learning through the New Information Technologies. *Higher Education Policy, 12*(2), 201–217.

Tsinakos, A. (2002). Distance Teaching using SYIM educational environment. *Learning Technology Newsletter, 4*(4), 2–5.

Tubaishat, A. (2008). Adoption of learning technologies to alleviate the impact of social and cultural limitations in higher education. In *Proceedings of the 1st E-learning Excellence Forum* (pp. 15-18). Dubai: Academic Press.

Tucker, T. (2011). *What influences young adults' decision to adopt new technology. Communication science.* Elon University.

Tunison, S., & Noonan, B. (2001). On-Line Learning: Secondary Students' First Experience. *Canadian Journal of Education, 26*(4), 495–511. doi:10.2307/1602179

Türkiye Bilişim Derneği. (2003). Retrieved April 21, 2014, from www.tbd.org.tr

Türkoğlu, R. (2003). İnternet Tabanlı Uzaktan Eğitim Programı Geliştirme Süreçleri. *The Turkish Online Journal of Educational Technology, 2*(3).

U.S. Department of Education (USDE). (2008). *Foundations for Success: The Final Report of the National Mathematics Panel.* Retrieved from: http://www2.ed.gov/about/bdscomm/list/mathpanel/report/final-report.pdf

Universidade Aberta. (2012). Factos & Números 2011-2012 Gabinete de Desenvolvimento Estratégico e de Relações Internacionais. Author.

Ünkap, Ö. (2006). *Sanal mimarlik stüdyosu uygulamalari üzerine bir değerlendirme.* İstanbul: İstanbul Teknik Üniversitesi, Fen Bilimleri Enstitüsü, Yüksek Lisans Tezi.

Uzaktan eğitim. (n.d.). Retrieved April 21, 2014 from http://www.uluslararasiegitim.com/uzak/default.asp

Uzaktan eğitimde eğitimcinin rolü ve sorumlulukları. (n.d.). Retrieved April 21, 2014 from http://www.ceng.metu.edu.tr/~e1448737/ceit321/proje/week1_reading_1.php

Valenzuela, S., Park, N., & Kee, K. F. (2009). Is there social capital in a social network site: Facebook use and college students' life satisfaction, trust, and participation. *Journal of Computer-Mediated Communication, 14*(4), 875–901. doi:10.1111/j.1083-6101.2009.01474.x

Vallerand, R. J. (1997). Toward a hierarchical model of intrinsic and extrinsic motivation. *Advances in Experimental Social Psychology, 29*, 271–374. doi:10.1016/S0065-2601(08)60019-2

van den Dool, P. C., Moerkamp, T., & Onstenk, J. (1987). *Wissels tussen werk en leren.* Amsterdam: SCO.

Van Onna, B. (1985). Arbeid als leersituatie. In G. Kraayvanger & B. Van Onna (Eds.), Arbeid en leren: Bijdragen tot volwasseneneducatie (pp.49-69). Baarn: Nelissen.

Van Parreren, C. F. (1971). *Psychologie van het leren I.* Deventer: Van Loghum Slaterus.

Vate-u-lan, P. (2008). *Borderless eLearning: HITS Model for Web 2.0.* Retrieved from http://ejournals.thaicybern.go.thlindex.php/ictl/article/view/59/62

Vavoula, G. N., & Sharples, M. (2002). KLeOS: A personal, mobile, knowledge and learning organization system. In *Proceedings of IEEE International Workshop on Wireless and Mobile Technologies* (pp. 152-156). IEEE. doi:10.1109/WMTE.2002.1039239

Venkataraman, B., & Prabhakar, T. V. (2013). *Changing the Tunes from Bollywood's to Rural Livelihoods — Mobile Telephone Advisory Services to Small and Marginal Farmers in India: A Case Study.* Retrieved from http://www.christoph.pimmer.info/wpcontent/uploads/2008/08/Pimmer-Pachler-Mobile-Learning-in-the-Workplace1.pdf

Venkatesh, V., & Davis, F. D. (2000). A theoretical extension of the technology acceptance model: Four longitudinal field studies. *Management Science, 46*(2), 186–204. doi:10.1287/mnsc.46.2.186.11926

Venkatesh, V., Morris, M. G., Davis, G. B., & Davis, F. D. (2003). User acceptance of information technology: Toward a unified view. *Management Information Systems Quarterly, 27*(3), 425–478.

Venkatesh, V., Speier, C., & Morris, M. G. (2002). User acceptance enablers in individual decision-making about technology: Toward an integrated model. *Decision Sciences, 33*(2), 297–316. doi:10.1111/j.1540-5915.2002.tb01646.x

Vlăsceanu, L., Grünberg, L., & Pârlea, D. (2004). *Quality Assurance and Accreditation: A Glossary of Basic Terms and Definitions*. Bucharest: UNESCO.

Vygotski, L. S. (1978). *Mind in society: The development of higher psychological process*. Cambridge, MA: Harvard University.

Wagner, N., Hassanein, K., & Head, M. (2008). Who is responsible for E-Learning in Higher Education? A stakeholders' Analysis. *Journal of Educational Technology & Society, 11*(3), 26–36.

Waltonen-Moore, S., Stuart, D., Newton, E., Oswald, R., & Varonis, E. (2006). From Virtual Strangers to a Cohesive Online Learning Community: The Evolution of Online Group Development in a Professional Development Course. *Journal of Technology and Teacher Education, 14*(2), 287–311.

Wang, H., Zhang, Y., & Cao, J. (2009). Effective Collaboration with Information Sharing in Virtual Universities. *IEEE Transactions on Knowledge and Data Engineering, 21*(6), 840–853. doi:10.1109/TKDE.2008.132

Wang, M. (2011). Integrating organizational, social, and individual perspectives in Web 2.0-based workplace e-learning. *Information Systems Frontiers, 13*(2), 191–205. doi:10.1007/s10796-009-9191-y

Wang, M., Shen, R., Novak, D., & Pan, X. (2009). The impact of mobile learning on students' learning behaviours and performance: Report from a large blended classroom. *British Journal of Educational Technology, 40*(4), 673–695. doi:10.1111/j.1467-8535.2008.00846.x

Warschauer, M. (2003). Technological change and the future of CALL. In S. Fotos & C. M. Browne (Eds.), *New perspectives on call for second language classrooms* (pp. 15–26). Mahwah, NJ: Lawrence Erlbaum Associates.

Waterman, M., & Stanley, E. (2005). *Case Format Variations*. Retrieved from http://cstlcsm.semo.edu/waterman/cbl/caseformats.html

Watty, K. (2003). When will academics learn about quality? *Quality in Higher Education, 9*(3), 213–221. doi:10.1080/1353832032000151085

Weber, A. S. (2011). *Research programme for next-gen e-learning in MENA region*. Paper presented at the 7th International Scientific Conference eLearning and Software for Education. Bucharest, Romania. Retrieved from https://adlunap.ro/else_publications/papers/2011/1758_2.pdf

Weiser, M. (1991). The computer for the 21st century. *Scientific American, 265*(3), 94–104. doi:10.1038/scientificamerican0991-94

Wei, T. T., Marthan, G., Chong, A. Y. L., Ooi, K. B., & Arumugam, S. (2009). What drives Malaysian m-commerce adoption? an empirical analysis. *Industrial Management & Data Systems, 109*(3), 370–388. doi:10.1108/02635570910939399

Weller, M. (2004). Models of Large Scale e-Learning. *Journal of Asynchronous Learning Networks, 8*(4), 83–92. Retrieved from http://www.aln.org/publications/jaln/index.asp?op0=OR&filter0%5B%5D=148

Welsh, E. T., Wanberg, C. R., Brown, K. G., & Simmering, M. J. (2003). E-learning: Emerging uses, empirical results, and future directions. *International Journal of Training and Development, 7*(4), 245–258. doi:10.1046/j.1360-3736.2003.00184.x

Wenger, E. (1998). *Communities of Practice: Learning, Meaning, and Identity*. Cambridge, UK: Cambridge University. doi:10.1017/CBO9780511803932

Wheatley, M.J. (1999). *Leadership and the new science: Discovering order in a chaotic world*. San Francisco: Berett-Koehler Publishers Inc.

White, D. S., & Le Cornu, A. (2011). Visitors and residents: A new typology for online engagement. *First Monday, 16*(9), 9–5. doi:10.5210/fm.v16i9.3171

Wideman, H. H., & Owston, R. D. (2000). *An evaluation of TVOntario's video-on-demand pilot project* (Centre for the Study of Computers in Education Technical Report No. 2000-1). York University, Faculty of Education.

Williams, J. B., & Jacobs, J. (2004). Exploring the use of blogs as learning spaces in the higher education sector. *Australasian Journal of Educational Technology, 20*(2), 232–247.

Wilska, T. (2003). Mobile phone use as part of young people's comsumtion styles. *Journal of Consumer Policy*, *26*(4), 441–663. doi:10.1023/A:1026331016172

Wilson, L. A. (2006). *One-to-One Teaching and Learning Initiatives – Goals and Results*. Retrieved from http://www.techlearning.com/techlearning/events/techforum06/LeslieWilson_ProgramGuide.pdf

Windschitl, M. (1998). The WWW and classroom research: What path should it take? *Educational Researcher*, *27*(1), 28–33.

Wirth, M. A. (2006). An analysis of international quality management approaches in e-learning: different paths, similar pursuits. In U.-D. Ehlers & J. M. Pawlowski (Eds.), *Handbook on quality and standardisation in e-learning* (pp. 97–108). Heidelberg, Germany: Springer. doi:10.1007/3-540-32788-6_7

Wise, J., Toto, R., & Lim, K. Y. (2006). Introducing Tablet PCs: Initial results from the classroom. In *Proceedings of the 36th Annual ASEE/IEEE Frontiers in Engineering Conference*, (pp. S3F-17 - S3F-20). IEEE. doi:10.1109/FIE.2006.322657

Wishart, J., & Green, D. (2010). *Identifying Emerging Issues in Mobile Learning in Higher and Further Education: A report to JISC*. University of Bristol.

Wisker, G., Exley, K., Antoniou, M., & Ridley, P. (2007). *Supervising, Coaching, Mentoring, and Personal Tutoring*. Routledge.

Wolf, D. B., & Johnstone, S. M. (1999). Cleaning up the Language: Establishing a Consistent Vocabulary for Electronically Delivered Academic Programs. *Change*, *31*(4), 34–39. doi:10.1080/00091389909602698

Work, A. P. A. Group of the Board of Educational Affairs (1997). Learner-centered psychological principles: A framework for school reform and redesign. Washington, DC: Author.

World Bank. (2007). *World development report*. Washington, DC: Author.

World Economic Forum. (2010). *Global competitiveness report 2010-2011*. Davos: Author.

Wu, W., Wu, Y. J., Chen, C., Kao, H., Lin, C., & Huang, S. (2012). Review of trends from mobile learning studies: A meta-analysis. *Computers & Education*, *59*(2), 817–827. doi:10.1016/j.compedu.2012.03.016

Xie, Y., Ke, F., & Sharma, P. (2008). The effect of peer feedback for blogging on college students' reflective learning processes. *The Internet and Higher Education*, *11*(1), 18–25. doi:10.1016/j.iheduc.2007.11.001

Xu, H., & Morris, L. V. (2009). A Comparative Case Study of State-Level Virtual Universities. *New Directions for Higher Education*, *146*(146), 45–54. doi:10.1002/he.345

Yaghoubi, N. M., & Bahmani, E. (2010). Factors affecting the adoption of online banking: An integration of technology acceptance model and theory of planned behavior. *Pakistan Journal of Social Sciences*, *7*(3), 231–236. doi:10.3923/pjssci.2010.231.236

Yan, A. W., Khalil, M. N., Emad, A. S., & Sutanonpaiboon, J. (2009). Factors that affect mobile telephone users to use mobile payment solution. *International Journal of Economics and Management*, *3*(1), 37–49.

Yang, K. C. (2005). Exploring factors affecting the adoption of mobile commerce in Singapore. *Journal of Telematics and Informatics*, *22*(3), 257–277. doi:10.1016/j.tele.2004.11.003

Yang, S. J. H. (2006). Context aware ubiquitous learning environments for peer-to-peer collaborative learning. *Journal of Educational Technology & Society*, *9*(1), 188–201.

Yap, J. (2013). *Bharti Airtel launches mobile education services*. Retrieved from http://www.zdnet.com/in/bharti-airtel-launches-mobile-education-services-7000009315/

Yıldırım, U., & Öner, Ş. (2005). Bilgi toplumu sürecinde yerel yönetimlerde eğitim-bilişim teknolojisinden yararlanma: Türkiye'de e-belediye uygulamaları. *The Turkish Online Journal of Educational Technology*, *3*(1). Retrieved April 18, from http://www.tojet.net/articles/318.pdf

Youngblood, P., Trede, F., & DiCorpo, S. (2001). Facilitating online learning: A descriptive study. *Distance Education*, *22*(2), 264–284. doi:10.1080/0158791010220206

Zarifian, P. (1995). Kwalificerende organisatie en competentiemodel: Waarom en met wat voor leerprocessen? *Beroepsopleiding*, *1995*(2), 5–10.

Zaščerinska, J., & Ahrens, A. (2013). E-business Applications to Students' Blended Learning in Higher Education. In *Proceedings of the 4th International Conference on Data Communication Networking (DC NET 2013), 10th International Conference on e-Business (ICE-B 2013) and 4th International Conference on Optical Communication Systems (OPTICS 2013)*, (pp. 290-297). Lisboa, Portugal: SciTePress - Science and Technology Publications.

Zaščerinska, J. (2013). *Development of Students' Communicative Competence within English for Academic Purposes Studies*. Berlin: Mensch & Buch.

Zawacki-Richter, O., Brown, T., & Delport, R. (2009). Mobile learning: from single project status into the mainstream? *European Journal of Open, Distance and E-learning*. Retrieved from http://www.eurodl.org/?article=357

Zhao, F. (2003). Enhancing the quality of online higher education through measurement. *Quality Assurance in Education, 11*(4), 214–221. doi:10.1108/09684880310501395

Zimmer, M. (2008). Preface: Critical Perspectives on Web 2.0. *First Monday, 13*(3). doi:10.5210/fm.v13i3.2137

Zurita, G., & Nussbaum, M. (2007). A conceptual framework based on activity theory for mobile CSCL. *British Journal of Educational Technology, 38*(2), 211–235. doi:10.1111/j.1467-8535.2006.00580.x

About the Contributors

Patricia Ordóñez de Pablos is a Professor in the Department of Business Administration in the Faculty of Economics and Business of the University of Oviedo, Spain. Her teaching and research interests focus on the areas of strategic management, knowledge management, intellectual capital measuring and reporting, organizational learning, human resources management, and IT. She serves as Executive Editor of the *International Journal of Learning and Intellectual Capital* and the *International Journal of Strategic Change Management*. She also serves as Associate Editor of *Computers in Human Beaviour*.

Robert D. Tennyson is Professor of Educational Psychology at the University of Minnesota. He is editor of a professional journal, *Computers in Human Behavior*. He also serves on editorial boards for seven other peer reviewed journals. His research and publications include topics on problem solving, concept learning, intelligent systems, testing and measurement, instructional design, and advanced learning technologies. He has directed sponsored workshops and advanced study institutes in Germany, Greece, Norway, Spain, and Taiwan. He has authored over 300 journal articles, books, and book chapters.

Miltiadis D. Lytras is lecturer at the American College of Greece. His research focuses on Semantic Web, knowledge management, and e-learning, with many publications in these areas. He has co-edited 25 special issues in international journals (e.g. *IEEE Transaction on Knowledge and Data Engineering, IEEE Internet Computing, IEEE Transactions on Education, Computers in Human Behavior, Interactive Learning Environments, Journal of Knowledge Management, Journal of Computer Assisted Learning*, etc.).

* * *

Andreas Ahrens received the DiplIng degree in Electrical Engineering from the University of Rostock in 1996. From 1996 to 2008, he was with the Institute of Communications Engineering of the University of Rostock, from which he received the DrIng and DrIng habil degree in 2000 and 2003, respectively. In 2008, he became a Professor for Signal and System theory at the Hochschule Wismar, University of Technology, Business, and Design, Germany. His main field of interest includes error correcting codes, multiple-input multiple-output systems, iterative detection for both wireline and wireless communication, as well as social computing.

Diana Audi is currently a senior instructor in the Mathematics Department at the University of Sharjah (AUS). Before that, she was at the Mathematics Department at the American University of Beirut (AUB). Her research interests include Hausdorff dimensions and its applications in Harmonic analysis. Her current research work focuses on educational methodologies for teaching mathematics to university and college students.

Havva Alkan Bala graduated from the Department of Architecture of Middle East Technical University (1995), completed her MSc in Architecture at Selcuk University (1997), received PhD degree from the Department of Architecture of Selcuk University (2003). Currently, she is associate professor at the Department of Architecture, Faculty of Architecture, Selcuk University, Konya. Her research interests are Architectural Design, Architectural Education, Architecture and Cinema, Urban Interface/Space.

Robert J. Blomme is Full Professor of Management and Organization and Director of the Centre for Leadership and Management Development at Nyenrode Business Universiteit, Breukelen, the Netherlands. His teaching and research cover a wide range of topics in organizational behavior, organizational sociology, and organizational theory. He is also Chair Professor in Human Resource Management (HRM) at International University for Hospitality, *Hotelschool Den Haag*, where his main area of research is the labor market and HRM-related issues in the hospitality industry.

Luísa Carvalho held a PhD in Management in University of Évora – Portugal. Professor of Management on Department of Management and Social Sciences – Open University - Lisbon – Portugal. Guest professor in international universities teaches in courses of master and PhDs programs. Researcher at CEFAGE (Center for Advanced Studies in Management and Economics) University of Evora – Portugal. Author of several publications in national and international journals, books and book chapters.

Charalampos (Babis) Giousmpasoglou has dual background as a practitioner in luxury hospitality industry and as an academic in higher education. His research interests focus in managerial work, hospitality management, culture, human resources management, and mobile learning. Dr. Charalampos is a holder of two first Degrees in Hospitality and Tourism Management from Greece (ASTER & TEI), an MSc in Hospitality Management from BCFTCS, an MA in Personnel Management (CIPD) from Leeds Metropolitan University, a PgD in Research Methodology, and a PhD in Hospitality and HRM from the University of Strathclyde.

Rim Gouia is an Assistant Professor at the Department of Mathematics at American University of Sharjah. She holds a PhD in Applied Mathematics from the University of Texas at Arlington, USA. Before joining AUS, she taught Mathematics at various colleges in the US. She also worked at Bougues-Construction in France and XTO Energy (currently ExxonMobil) in the USA. Dr. Gouia was part of a multidisciplinary research team supported by the US Department of Defense aimed at improving ultrasound imaging for cancer screening. She is specialized in integral geometry, particularly the mathematical problems of radon transform applied to advanced imaging.

Cindy Gunn is the Director of the Faculty Development Center and Professor in the Department of English at American University of Sharjah. As the Director of the Faculty Development Center, she works closely with the Academic Computing Group to offer workshops on effective use of technology in the classroom as well as assisting individual faculty members in their endeavors to utilize technology in the classroom. Her main research paradigm is Exploratory Practice focusing on the contributions teachers and learners make to classroom research. Her main research interests are reflective teaching and learning, materials development, and technology use in education.

Maryam Haghshenas was born in 1985 and earned BSc degree in Computer Hardware Engineering from Islamic Azad University, South Tehran branch, Tehran, Iran, in 2007. She then received a MSc degree in IT management at Islamic Azad University, Science & Research branch, Tehran, Iran, in 2011, and is currently a PhD student of Media management in university of Tehran in Iran. She is IT expert in MAGFA ITDC as an affiliate of the Industrial Development and Renovation Organization of Iran. She has more than 50 papers in the fields of e-learning and knowledge management presented at national and international conferences and has been published in prestigious journals. Ms. Haghshenas is a member of Young Researchers Club at Islamic Azad University, Science & Research Branch in Iran.

Mousa I. Hussein received the MSc and PhD degrees from University of Manitoba, Winnipeg, MB, Canada, in 1992 and 1995, respectively, both in Electrical Engineering. Currently, he is an Associate Prof. at the United Arab Emirates University. Dr. Hussein's research interests are in computational electromagnetics, electromagnetic scattering, antenna analysis, and design. Dr. Hussein is the head of the Electrical Engineering department ABET assessment committee, and acted as the head of curriculum committee.

Muhammad Khalique, PhD, is a Senior Lecturer in the Department of Business Management, Faculty of Economics and Business, Universiti Malaysia Sarawak, Malaysia. He received his PhD degree from the same university in 2012. He has published more than 45 articles in international refereed journals, in conference proceedings, and as book chapters. His research focuses on intellectual capital management, knowledge management, entrepreneurship, innovation, SMEs, and organizational performance.

Maria Pavlis Korres obtained a university degree in Political Sciences in Athens (1981). From 1983 until today, she works on Adult Education in the Greek Ministry of Education. She has participated as an expert in the first research on Roma Education conducted by the European Council (1985-1986), and she has participated in educational and research projects on Roma Education implemented by the EE, the General Secretariat for Lifelong Learning in Greece, the University of Ioannina and the University of Athens, Greece. Since 2005, her research interests are focused on e-learning, and she became a PhD student in the University of Alcalá, Spain. In 2008, she obtained her Advance Studies Degree from the Computer Science Department of the University of Alcalá, and in 2010, she obtained her PhD with honors. The subject of her PhD is "Development of an E-Education Framework for the Education of Educators of Special Groups in Order to improve their Compatibility with their Learners." Since 2012, she is a member of the scientific staff of Hellenic Open University, and she has been assigned to teach Adult Education in postgraduate courses. She has published several articles, chapters, and books on Roma, adult education, and e-learning. Her current interests are focused on design, development, and evaluation of educational projects for adults, face-to-face and e-learning, as well as the group dynamics in an online environment and the appropriate use of communication tools in order to promote interaction in an online environment.

Evangelia (Lia) Marinakou has an extensive teaching and dissertation supervision experience in HE at undergraduate and postgraduate level. She is a Fellow member of the Higher Education Academy (UK). She is active in research with papers presented at international conferences and published in academic journals. Her main research interests are gender issues in management, leadership, hospitality management, and education. She has also acted as project leader to European-funded programmes on vocational education and training in tourism studies. She has extensive experience on curriculum design, academic quality assurance, and training the trainers. Additionally, she has worked in the hospitality and tourism industry for many years.

H. Filiz Alkan Meşhur graduated from the Department of City and Regional Planning of Gazi University (1995), completed her MSc in City Planning at METU (1999), received PhD degree from the Department of Architecture of Selcuk University (2006). Currently, she is associate professor at the Department of City and Regional Planning, Faculty of Architecture, Selcuk University, Konya. Her research interests are Information and Communication Technologies (ICTs), suburbanization and housing areas planning, teleworking, disability, and universal and barrier free design.

Mojtaba Nassiriyar was born in Tehran in 1983. He graduated with a BSc degree in 2006 in Industrial Management from the University of Tehran. His Master's degree was completed in IT Management in 2009. He is IT expert in MAGFA ITDC. He has published three papers in the IT management field and has written a book on IT service oriented and knowledge based projects management. He currently manages data center projects at national level and teaches IT engineering management courses at Payam Noor University, Tehran.

Vasileios Paliktzoglou has several years of experience in universities such as the University of Pisa, the Aegean University, Robert Gordon University, Mediterranean University College, and the University of Wales having an active role as: Researcher, Tutor, Supervisor, Lecturer, and Programme Manager. His research interests are in the fields of social media, Web 2.0, communities of practices, e-learning in which he is actively involved in several international research projects. He is currently a Doctoral researcher at the University of Eastern Finland and faculty member at Bahrain Polytechnic.

Kshama Pandey has been working as an Assistant Professor in the Department of Foundations of Education. She has more than 10 years teaching experience in undergraduate and postgraduate classes. Her Doctoral work relates to the Human Rights Understanding and Consciousness. She has been working in the area of Educational Psychology, Innovative Teaching Pedagogy, and Human Rights Education. She is a creative writer and has a wide range of published papers (25) and book chapters (11) in national/international referred journals. At present, she is working on innovative pedagogy and enriched the field by producing instructional material. She is associated with a number of Academic and Professional Bodies and Apex Bodies like NUEPA, NCERT, AIAER, IRA IJTEL, and HREA, etc. for various assignments.

Drew Polly, PhD, is an Associate Professor in the Department of Reading and Elementary Education at the University of North Carolina at Charlotte in the USA. His research interests include examining the impact of professional development on teachers' instruction and examining how to best support teachers' integration of technologies and reform-based pedagogies into their mathematics classroom.

Abouzar Sadeghzadeh was born in 1985 and graduated with a BSc honors degree in Electronics and Telecommunications Engineering from the University of Bradford, UK, in 2006. He then completed a MSc degree in radio frequency and communications engineering the following year from the same university. His MSc thesis is titled "Mobile Information System," which concerns mobile technology and its uses. Upon completing his studies, he worked for Huawei Technologies as a project manager before joining various other companies in IT fields namely IT consultancy in MAGFA ITDC (Information Technology Development Center).

Roghayeh Shahbazi was born in 1987 and has graduated with a BSc degree in Applied Mathematics from Arak University, Iran, in 2010. She then graduated with a MSc degree in IT management at Alzahra University, Tehran, Iran, in 2014. Her MSc project was about the adoption of cloud computing and relevant investment returns. She is an IT expert in MAGFA ITDC. Activity fields of MAGFA include the implementation of national projects in BI and KM fields. In addition, she has over 3 years experience in IT consultancy.

Tasos Stylianou is an Adjunct Lecturer in the Department of Accounting and Finance at the Technological Educational Institute of Central Macedonia at Serres (TEI of Central Macedonia). Tasos completed his PhD, MSc, MS, and his undergraduate studies at University of Macedonia (Greece-Thessaloniki). His research interests lie in the area of computer science and applied economics. He has collaborated actively with researchers in disciplines of computer science, econometrics, and education. Tasos has served on over 25 conference and workshop program committees. He has over 10 publications in scientific journals and chapters in books. He is currently a reviewer in *Journal of Economics and Management Sciences* (JEMS).

Jarkko Suhonen holds a senior researcher position at the School of Computing, University of Eastern Finland. His main research interests are related to design and development of open and distance learning technologies, as well as smart design methods in educational technology. Jarkko has more than 10 years of experience in design, development, and running of online higher education study programmes. He is currently the manager and coordinator of the IMPDET (http://www.impdet.org) online Doctoral study programme at University of Eastern Finland. Dr. Suhonen has written more than 50 peer-reviewed academic papers.

Senorita Lokie Tunggau was a student in the Department of Business Management, Faculty of Economics and Business, Universiti Malaysia Sarawak.

K. C. Vashishtha completed his research in Education, in significant area of personality make-ups in Long Residing Convents of India under the guidance of Prof. C. L. Kundu, Ex. V. C. Himachal Pradesh University, Shimla. He has about a dozen of PhDs under his credit and completed a number of minor and major research projects of UGC and ICSSR. He is a prolific writer and has written 10 books, highly accredited by research scholars and the teachers in India. Equally, he has a wide range of published papers in national/international referred journals. Currently, he is working on Learning Disability and developed and enriched the field by generating teaching-learning materials and by diagnosing various perspectives helping for making classroom an enjoyable place for them. He is associated with a number of Academic and Professional Bodies, ASCs, and Apex Bodies like UGC, NCERT, ICSSR, NAAC, NCTE for various assignments. He is the teacher of full commitment to the profession and the prime stakeholder the students. At present, he is working as a consultant for UNESCO/UNICEF project on ICT in Tribal Belt of Madhya Pradesh.

Jeļena Zaščerinska received the diploma in Russian Philology in 1994 from the Daugavpils University, Daugavpils, Latvia, Master Degree in English Philology in 2002 and Dr. paed. Degree in 2011 from the University of Latvia, Riga, Latvia. In January 2012, she became a leading researcher at the Centre for Education and Innovation Research, Riga, Latvia. From 2009-2013, Jeļena Zaščerinska was awarded a couple of research grants. In 2012, Jeļena Zaščerinska was bestowed expert rights by the Latvian Council of Science, Riga, Latvia, and in 2013 by Horizon 2020 – the Framework Programme for Research and Innovation, the European Commission, Brussels, Belgium. In June 2013, she was appointed as the Editorial Board Member and Reviewer, *International Journal of Modern Education Forum* (IJMEF).

Index

A

Act-as-Such 230, 244, 248
Add-On License 97
Adult Education 154, 156, 159, 175
alternative media 1-2, 24
Architectural 1-2, 10, 12-14, 16-17, 19, 21, 24, 28, 107
Associationism 211, 226
Asynchronous 1-2, 8-11, 19, 24-25, 28, 78, 80-81, 83, 85-86, 92-94, 97, 134, 136, 141, 153-160, 169-170, 175, 185
Asynchronous and Synchronous Communication Mode 175
Asynchronous Learning 1-2, 8-11, 28, 153, 155-157
Asynchronous Online Instruction 78, 153
Attractors 232-234, 237, 239, 241-242, 248

B

Bahrain 176-177, 185-189, 194-195, 199, 279
Behavioral Intention 297, 301, 303, 306, 310
Behaviorism 226
Blended Learning 16, 29, 31-32, 41-42, 44-46, 114, 176, 182, 185, 199, 279, 296
Blended Teaching 41-43, 59

C

Collaboration 4, 12-13, 16, 18-19, 47, 62, 91-93, 101, 138-139, 158, 160, 171, 181-184, 190, 199, 206-207, 217, 221, 242, 273-277, 279, 281, 286, 289, 291-292, 316, 322-323, 329
Collaboration (Collaborative Learning) 199
Communication tools 28, 154-155, 157-159, 161, 163, 171-172
Complex Responsive System 248
Constructvist 226
Cooperative 137, 240, 250

D

Developers 93, 157, 183-184, 312, 315, 327-329
digital pedagogy 1-2, 14, 16-17

D (continued)

Distance Education 2-8, 10, 19, 24, 131-132, 145, 153, 155, 185, 187, 204, 220-221, 227, 319
Distance Learning 1-8, 28-33, 35, 37-41, 45-46, 49-55, 59, 142, 157, 182, 185, 194, 213, 220-222, 224, 229, 243-244, 248, 250, 267, 271, 317

E

East Village. 2, 17, 20-21
Edmodo 278-279, 296
Educational 1-2, 4-6, 8, 10, 12, 14, 17, 19, 24-25, 30-33, 35, 38-44, 46, 49-51, 53-55, 59-61, 73, 88, 100-102, 132-133, 141, 154-158, 160-161, 163, 165, 167-172, 175, 177-179, 181-183, 185, 187-188, 194, 202-203, 206-207, 212-215, 219, 222, 253, 266, 272-273, 275-287, 289-292, 296, 311, 313, 317, 319, 321-327, 332
Educator 8, 10, 30, 42-43, 59, 154-163, 165-166, 170-171, 175, 277
e-Learning 8, 10, 17, 45, 61, 102, 108-109, 111-112, 115, 131-133, 135-136, 138, 140-142, 144-145, 153-158, 160-161, 170-172, 176-189, 194-195, 199, 202-204, 208, 219, 245, 248, 250, 265-266, 271, 280, 317, 323
Elementary School 78-81, 84-85, 88, 93, 97
Engagement 62, 65, 71, 181, 252, 272, 276, 278-282, 292, 296, 325, 329

F

Familiarity 61, 195, 251, 276, 279-282, 296, 303

G

good practices 131-132, 145
Google Applications 281, 292

H

Higher Education 4, 29-33, 35, 38-41, 45-46, 49-51, 53-55, 59-62, 70, 72, 77, 93, 115, 131-133, 135-136, 140-142, 146, 153, 176-183, 185, 188, 194-195, 199, 221, 224, 228, 242, 245, 249, 273-275, 277-280, 291-292, 311, 320-323

I

Information and Communication Technologies 1-2, 16, 44, 59, 115, 131, 139, 153, 176, 199
information communication 278
Institutionalized Educational Process 41, 59
Instructional Tool 226, 273, 291
international cooperation 17, 24
Internet Technology 7, 228-229, 242-246, 248-250, 265-268, 271
iPads 60, 62-72, 77
iPads in Higher Education 60, 77

L

Laptop Program, Laptop Project 115
Learning Outcomes 3, 64, 80, 87-90, 92, 97-98, 100, 106
Learning Quality & Satisfaction 115

M

Mathematical Tasks 83-91, 93, 97
Mathematics Education 77, 79-80, 97
Microblogging 278-279, 296
M-Learning (Mobile Learning) 60-62, 70, 72, 77, 100, 115, 176-185, 188-195, 199-215, 217-224, 227, 311, 313, 316-320, 322-323, 329-331
Mobile 16, 29-33, 37-40, 42, 45-46, 50-55, 59-62, 70, 72, 77, 100-103, 115, 145, 165, 177-185, 188-190, 192-195, 199-207, 209-212, 214-223, 226-227, 297-303, 306, 311-315, 317-324, 326-329, 331-332
Mobile Devices in Contemporary Mathematics Education 77
Mobile Internet 183, 218, 226-227, 298
Mobile Technologies 29-33, 35, 37-40, 42, 45-46, 49-55, 59, 61, 77, 101, 179-180, 182-183, 185, 188, 203, 205, 218, 222-223, 311-313, 315-317, 319, 322-323, 326-328, 332

O

Online Course 81, 92, 94, 97, 145, 159, 161, 272-273, 280
Organizational Learning 228-229, 231, 235, 242, 244-245, 248

P

Pedagogical 14, 17, 31, 33, 38, 55, 86, 88, 104, 114, 132, 141-142, 144-145, 177, 180-181, 194, 200, 206-207, 209, 212-213, 217-218, 221-222, 227, 277, 311, 316-319, 330, 332
Pedagogical Method for M-Learning 227
Perceived Ease of Use 297, 300-302, 305-306, 310
Perceived Usefulness 179, 184, 297, 300-302, 305-306, 310
Polytechnic Architectural 2, 17
Powerful Learning Environment 250, 265, 271
Prospect of Distance Education in India 220, 227

R

Remote Learning 134, 153
Roma 155, 160, 167-169, 171-172, 175

S

SAIT Polytechnic 2, 17
Selcuk University 1-2, 17, 28
Social Act 229-230, 241, 243-246, 248
Social Influence 184, 297, 300-303, 305-306, 310
Social Media 14, 170, 245, 248, 250, 267, 271-275, 277-280, 290-292, 296
Students' Attitude 29-33, 35, 38, 40, 49, 51-55, 59
Students' Perceptions of Technology Use 77
Supportive Tool 227
Survey 65, 67-68, 89-91, 100, 107-115, 154, 177, 188-189, 281, 292, 302-303
Synchronous Online Instruction 134, 153

T

Teacher-Leaders 78-79, 83-94, 97
Teachers 3, 6, 14, 16-17, 55, 62, 71, 78-81, 84-87, 94, 133, 135-136, 139, 141, 144-145, 169, 178, 182, 187, 201, 216-217, 221, 228, 277-278, 312, 314-315, 317-319, 322-328, 330
Teaching and Learning 1-2, 8, 16, 25, 32, 78-79, 85-86, 88, 97, 101, 106, 110, 114, 145, 157, 177, 179-183, 185, 187-188, 192-195, 199, 201, 203, 206, 213, 217, 273, 296, 315, 321-323
Technology Attribute 227
Technology for Teaching 77
Threaded Discussion 158-160, 165, 168, 171

Transferrable Skills 271
Transfer Skills 262, 268, 271

U

U-Learning 132, 153

V

Virtual Architectural Design Studio 13, 28
Virtual Learning Environments 133, 177, 199, 327

Virtual Learning Environments (VLEs) 177, 199
Virtual Universities 131-134, 139-141, 145, 153

W

Web 2.0 12, 183, 202, 273-277, 279-280, 290-292, 296